GOD VS. THE GAVEL: THE PERILS OF EXTREME RELIGIOUS LIBERTY

Revised Second Edition

Clergy sex abuse, polygamy, children dying from faith-healing, companies that refuse to do business with same-sex couples, and residential neighborhoods forced to host homeless shelters and rehab clinics next door to children. What do these have in common? They are all examples of believers harming others and demanding religious liberty regardless of the harm. This book unmasks those responsible, explains how this new set of rights is not derived from the First Amendment, and argues for a return to common-sense religious liberty.

God vs. the Gavel: The Perils of Extreme Religious Liberty sets the record straight, through facts and documented stories, about the move toward extreme religious liberty in the United States. This thoroughly revised second edition features a new introduction, epilogue, and new examples and stories that revise the previous edition by more than half. All Americans need this book, before they or their friends and family are harmed by believers' newfound capacity to break the law at will.

Marci A. Hamilton is one of the United States' leading church/state scholars and holds the Paul R. Verkuil Chair in Public Law at the Benjamin N. Cardozo School of Law, Yeshiva University. Her blog with Professor Leslie Griffin on religious liberty, women's rights, and children's rights can be found at http://hamilton-griffin.com/. She also hosts www.RFRAperils.com, which tracks free exercise statutes in all 50 states and the federal government.

Professor Hamilton is also an author and lecturer on the protection of children from sex abuse and a national leader and advocate for legislative reform of statutes of limitation through her website, www.sol-reform .com. She is the author of *Justice Denied: What America Must Do to Protect Its Children* (2008) and is a bi-monthly columnist for www.justia.com/ verdict. Hamilton received the National Crime Victim Bar Association's Frank Carrington Champion of Civil Justice Award; the E. Nathaniel Gates Award for outstanding public advocacy and scholarship; and the Lifetime Achievement Award for Pro Bono Legal Service to veterans groups. She also has been honored as one of Pennsylvania's Women of the Year and as a Distinguished Alumnus of Wheaton North High School, Wheaton, IL. She clerked for Supreme Court Justice Sandra Day O'Connor and Judge Edward R. Becker.

GOD vs. THE GAVEL

THE PERILS OF EXTREME RELIGIOUS LIBERTY

Revised Second Edition

MARCI A. HAMILTON
PAUL R. VERKUIL CHAIR IN PUBLIC LAW
BENJAMIN N. CARDOZO SCHOOL OF LAW
YESHIVA UNIVERSITY

CAMBRIDGE
UNIVERSITY PRESS

CAMBRIDGE
UNIVERSITY PRESS

32 Avenue of the Americas, New York, NY 10013-2473, USA

Cambridge University Press is part of the University of Cambridge.

It furthers the University's mission by disseminating knowledge in the pursuit of
education, learning, and research at the highest international levels of excellence.

www.cambridge.org
Information on this title: www.cambridge.org/9781107456556

© Marci A. Hamilton 2005, 2014

First published 2005
Reprinted 2005
First paperback edition 2007
Reprinted 2011
Revised electronic edition 2014
Second revised edition 2014

A catalog record for this publication is available from the British Library.

Library of Congress Cataloging in Publication Data

ISBN 978-1-107-08744-6 Hardback
ISBN 978-1-107-45655-6 Paperback

CONTENTS

ACKNOWLEDGMENTS

This new extensively revised edition would not have been possible without extraordinary work by a number of my students at Benjamin N. Cardozo School of Law and the support of the school itself. Emma Glazer, Courtney Soliday, Rebecca Maller, Tammy Lam, Shane Martins, Alyssa Figueroa, and my graduate Fellow, Jordan Walsh, did tremendous research, put in long hours, and made great suggestions. I thank each and every one of them. I must also thank my intern, Julianne Toia.

In addition, thanks are due to Leslie Griffin, Chip Lupu, Andrea Moore-Emmett, and Rita Swan for reading and commenting on various sections.

I am also indebted to Cambridge University Press, and in particular my editor, John Berger, who has supported my work without fail and given me opportunities to reach a larger audience on issues that were taboo when we published the first edition but are now getting the attention they deserve. I am very grateful to him.

Finally, thanks as always must go to my family. I couldn't and I wouldn't have the courage or fortitude to do the work I do without them. Thank you.

PREFACE TO THE SECOND EDITION

It's a serendipitous story, but I represented Boerne, Texas, before the Supreme Court challenging the Religious Freedom Restoration Act, or RFRA. We won in 1997, and I was led on a journey into the underside of religion, because all the groups that lobby against religion sought me out. They earnestly and generously educated me about the facts of religiously motivated illegal behavior. At first, I was just appalled. Children were *dying* in faith-healing homes? We don't regulate summer camps or day care centers if they are religious? Prisoners demand *what* in prison?! I started a file of "Religion Misbehaving," which turned into multiple files. Then I knew that I had an obligation to share what I had learned with the public, which is why I wrote GOD VS. THE GAVEL: RELIGION AND THE RULE OF LAW a decade ago.

Ten years later, I am no longer shocked at the unacceptable behavior of too many believers, but I am even more determined that Americans learn about the dangers inherent in the religious liberty regime that was initiated in 1993 with the RFRA. The Framers called too much liberty "licentiousness." I simply call it extreme.

INTRODUCTION: THE WAGES OF RFRA

It has taken more than twenty years, but the American public is finally getting a true taste of the perils of extreme religious liberty. Finally, the Religious Freedom Restoration Act, or RFRA, and its progeny have emerged for what they are: a license for believers to assert rights to discriminate against homosexuals, abuse or neglect children, constrain a woman's right to choose, and force huge projects on residential neighborhoods and families. But RFRA is only a part of the extreme religious liberty problem, because lawmakers too often grant religious lobbyists and claimants privileges that let them harm others. Judges also blindly grant religious preferences on the basis of their own religious beliefs or on trial records that are misleading.

RFRA is evidence of an agenda of one-way accommodation, where the religious believer is the center of the universe and the rest of us are supposed to make way. Each one of us is, on this theory, a self-enclosed universe where our only obligations are to ourselves. It is a recipe for intolerance; self-centered practices; harm to children, women, and the vulnerable; and, ultimately, if permitted to fester, religious war. Do you know why we haven't had a religious civil war yet, like the rest of the world? Because we did not countenance extreme religious liberty until now.

To put it plainly, we are in the grip of a push for Me-Me-Me religious liberty, or, just plain narcissism. To be clear from the beginning: this is no indictment of the Supreme Court, whose First Amendment doctrine has established the most successful religious liberty regime in the history of the world – for believers and potential victims of religious conduct. The new statutes like RFRA do not "restore" the First Amendment, but rather go well beyond it.

The RFRA formula, which directs the courts to tailor every law to each believer, promised disaster early on, but only a few of us saw it. And we have been called everything from "hysterical" to "overreacting." What could be wrong with religious liberty, everyone, especially members of Congress, said? A lot when it is extreme.

It took huge for-profit companies with revenues in the billions like Hobby Lobby demanding a "right" not to be "complicit" in their female employees' reproductive health decisions to get the country's attention. The company hoisted RFRA to avoid including emergency contraception in its health care plans, because of its owners' and board members' beliefs. Dozens of businesses followed suit, with an array of objections to women's reproductive health care. The move should violate Title VII, because it discriminates on the basis of gender and religion, but that did not deter Hobby Lobby, which took its claimed right to avoid "complicity" in women's most personal and private decisions to the Supreme Court. In a decision I dreaded but expected, five Catholic, male Justices held that RFRA trumped any rights the women might have and ruled in favor of Hobby Lobby.[1]

Civil rights groups were shocked, as were many women, at the sheer nerve of the claim and the decision. They woke up none too soon.

While Hobby Lobby was reminding women that evangelicals and the Catholic bishops do not respect their legal rights to privacy, the RFRA formula was working its magic in the states, where arch-conservative groups were pushing ever more extreme RFRA-on-steroids bills that would permit businesses to refuse to deal with homosexuals and same-sex couples. *Finally*, civil rights groups, the press, and the public took notice of this insidious law and cried foul. Arizona's Governor Jan Brewer vetoed the Arizona version, and similar bills across the country were withdrawn as Republican sponsors were accused (rightly in my view) of taking us back to the Jim Crow era. Except Mississippi, whose new, "ordinary" RFRA invites businesses to discriminate as part of their extreme free exercise rights, due to the definition of "person"under state law.

Some of the 2014 state bills "just" permitted discrimination on the basis of sexual orientation. Arizona's went further, as it was written so that businesses could invoke religious reasons to discriminate against *anyone*. Businesses, including the National Football League and Major League Baseball, balked, and it was vetoed. If future lawmakers were to pass such a bill, expect the empowerment of Biblical and neo-pagan white supremacists like Frazier Glenn Cross, who recently killed three people in Kansas City for his beliefs.

RFRA introduced an era of extreme religious liberty in the United States that would have been rejected by the Framers, who understood the difference between ordered liberty and licentiousness. We need to return to that distinction, or risk the end of our largely peaceful religiously diverse country.

Who is empowered under this new regime? Employers and believers who sexually abuse, abandon, or medically neglect children, engage in animal cruelty, oppose all family planning, and engage in invidious discrimination based on disability, race, gender, and sexual orientation. Not to mention the religious land developers who find inexpensive parcels in residential zones and then use extreme religious liberty statutes to force their large projects on families and neighborhoods. When neighbors complain about the intensity of the use, and the land use application is appropriately denied, the religious applicant calls everyone anti–their religion and races to federal court, where it can force the city to do its bidding and taxpayers to foot its attorneys' fees, even in weak cases. It is not that believers *win* every case under these new rules. It is bad enough they can burden judges, courts, taxpayers, and everyone else with such claims. The claims alone, which would not have been raised under prior doctrine, increase religious rancor as well.

This pro-believer wave also subverts justice. It has persuaded vote-hungry legislators not only to pass ill-considered statutes, but also to defer to religious demands to block access to justice for child sex abuse victims, to fail to prosecute child predators, and to cooperate in the cover-up of abuse.

Who loses? Employees, children, child sex abuse victims and their families and friends, women, homosexuals, minorities, homeowners, cities, counties, taxpayers, and society itself. What is being demanded is licentiousness, not liberty. It is time to reverse the tide and return to common sense religious liberty.

A brief history of how we got here

I will detail this history further in Chapters 1 and 8, but it is worth providing an overview for the reader first. Before RFRA was adopted, there were three constitutional principles. Belief is absolutely protected. Religiously motivated conduct can be regulated. Religious persecution is forbidden.

Except in rare cases, religious claimants have not had a right to trump the laws that govern everyone else simply because they were religious. Thus, the First Amendment did not grant the Amish a right to avoid Social Security taxes.[2] In an iconic statement that captures where we were and where we should be, the *Lee* court explained how the Hobby Lobby case should be decided:

> ... *Congress and the courts have been sensitive to the needs flowing from the Free Exercise Clause, but every person cannot be shielded from all the burdens incident to exercising every aspect of the right to practice religious beliefs.* When followers of a particular sect enter into commercial activity as a matter of choice, the limits they accept on their own conduct as a matter of conscience and faith are not to be superimposed on the statutory schemes which are binding on others in that activity. Granting an exemption from Social Security taxes to an employer operates to impose the employer's religious faith on the employees.[3]

Likewise, Jimmy Swaggart Ministries lost its bid to avoid sales taxes,[4] Native American believers had no right to direct how the federal government develops federal land,[5] Jewish merchants could not force the weekly day of no retail sales to coincide with their Sabbath,[6] and a Native American family could not refuse to obtain a Social Security number for their 2-year-old daughter as a precondition to getting federal welfare.[7] Here is the Court nicely explaining these principles:

> Certain aspects of religious exercise cannot in any way be restricted or burdened by either federal or state legislation. Compulsion by law of the acceptance of any creed or the practice of any form of worship is strictly forbidden. The freedom to hold religious beliefs and opinions is absolute ...

> However, the freedom to act, even when the action is in accord with one's religious convictions, is not totally free from legislative restrictions.... [L]egislative power over mere opinion is forbidden, but it may reach people's actions when they are found to be in violation of

important social duties or subversive of good order, even when the actions are demanded by one's religion.[8]

The Court then held that the laws that impose indirect burdens on conduct do not violate the First Amendment.

Believers also have a strong right against discrimination, targeting, and persecution. In fact, there have been very few laws that fit this description in the United States, but the Santerians in Hialeah, Florida, who ritually sacrifice animals during worship services, won when the Court held that they could not be driven out of town by an ordinance that outlawed the "sacrifice" of animals, but let stand similar practices by others.[9] Nor can the government favor secular reasons over religious reasons when crafting exceptions to a law. Adell Sherbert, a textile mill operator and Seventh-day Adventist, whose Sabbath was on Saturday, was fired after missing Saturday work to attend church. The Court reasoned that she could not be denied unemployment compensation when an employee who had missed work for a doctor's appointment could receive it.[10]

Religious actors also have the right and power to petition lawmakers for exemptions, like the exemption for the use of Communion wine for Catholics during Prohibition and the many others discussed in this book. If you add up all of this history, Americans enjoy absolute protection of belief, obligations to obey the laws over conduct balanced by generous legislative accommodations for many practices, and a strong rule against persecution.

The one outlier case in this history was *Wisconsin v. Yoder*, where the Court turned on its prior cases to grant a right to the Amish to remove their children from school at age 14, and thereby trump Wisconsin's compulsory education law, which required students to attend school until age 16. The Court focused on the Amish's belief "that salvation requires life in a church community separate and apart from the world and worldly influence." The Amish reject higher education, because of its "influences that alienate man from God." The Court was unwilling to let Wisconsin educate the Amish children fully, because it recognized a right to avoid the "destruction of the old Order Amish church community as it exists in the United States today." As I discuss later, this decision was not well-reasoned, but rather a love letter to the Amish, who, according to the Court had "an excellent record as law-abiding and generally self-sufficient members of society. . . . had never been known to commit crimes, . . . to receive public assistance [or to be] unemployed."[11]

Having sung the religious entity's praises, the Court then discounted the government's and society's interest in an adequately educated citizenry, assumed that no child would ever want to leave the faith, ignored the potential for this decision to deprive children in other faiths, and failed to take into account the needs of children to be educated at least through high school. No group of humans is as perfect as the Court assumed in *Yoder*, and this decision shows just how far Americans will go to assume religious actors are intrinsically good people. Unfortunately, they are all too human.

There is no other decision with the same level of hero worship, but also no other decision where the Court permits a religious entity to overcome a neutral, generally applicable law. There is a lesson in this opinion, and that is the Framers' deeply held conviction that every one of us is fallible, even those who appear to be godly. Since *Yoder*, we have learned that there are indeed problems in the Amish community, like those that range across humankind. There is violence; alcoholic and drug addiction, incest, particularly sibling incest; and it is a religious organization that will support the rapist, while shunning the victim. Moreover, when it shuns the victim, that girl is sent out into the real world unprepared, with an inadequate education, because the Supreme Court discounted the states' interest in requiring a high school education on a one-sided record. (Imagine a world where all religious groups can simply freeze their beliefs and not have to interact with the culture.)

With these cases behind it, in 1990 the Supreme Court took up the case of two drug counselors who used illegal drugs and were fired. Their theory was that they had a right to use drugs, even if they were drug counselors, because the use was religious. They lost, which should have surprised no one, but religious lobbyists made the case a cause célèbre, and RFRA was the unfortunate result.

The Supreme Court's 1990 decision, *Employment Div. v. Smith*, held that the drug counselors could be denied unemployment compensation if they were fired for using peyote.[12] The Court employed the reasoning from the vast majority of its cases, except *Yoder*, which they distinguished in a way that marginalized it. I was clerking for Justice Sandra Day O'Connor that year. None of us thought this was much of a case. In actuality, it triggered the most political fallout of any case that Term.

The majority, with Justice Scalia writing, relied principally on all of the Court's free exercise cases, starting with its first, *Reynolds v. United States*, in which the Court declared that belief is absolutely protected, but conduct is not. Quoting Thomas Jefferson's Letter to the Danbury Baptists, the Court stated that the First Amendment requires "'that the legislative powers of the government reach actions only, and not opinions.'" Thus, "Congress was deprived of all legislative power over mere opinion, but was left free to reach actions which were in violation of social duties or subversive of good order."[13] This belief/conduct distinction would become the framework of ordered liberty.

Religious groups and legal academics had persuaded themselves that *Yoder* should govern every case, because of a misguided, naïve, and ridiculous view that more liberty is always good liberty. (I was one of those schlars at one point.) The Framers had a name for extreme religious liberty: licentiousness.

When *Yoder* did not control *Smith*, they stormed Congress demanding its members reverse the Supreme Court's interpretation of the First Amendment. To their discredit, House members, Senators, and President Clinton could not resist the temptation to pander to this united front of religious and civil rights groups, and so they agreed to take over the Court's free exercise doctrine and to make it even stronger. Voila! RFRA was born.

There is plenty of blame to go around. RFRA was supported initially by a coalition that included religious groups and the American Civil Liberties Union (ACLU), People for the American Way, and Americans United for Separation of Church and State (Americans United). The latter three groups normally fight for the separation of church and state, but like the members of Congress, they fell for the call to "restore" supposedly true religious liberty.

During three years of hearings, religious lobbyists told members of Congress the Court had "abandoned" religious liberty again and again. The solution: supposedly "restore" the Court's doctrine it had purportedly left behind. It was all so simple; here was the problem, and there was the solution. The answer offered, though, was not the Court's prior doctrine, but rather a new extreme religious liberty formula.

Under the RFRA of 1993, a religious believer could ignore every law in the country unless it served a "compelling interest," which is a state interest of surpassing importance, *and* the law served that end in the "least restrictive" way for this one religious believer. In layman's terms, believers could build a moat around their particular religious beliefs that would deny access to the law.

What was missing? Well, how about members of Congress asking why the religious groups were in need of such extreme rights. Which laws did believers need to break? They should have demanded answers before endorsing RFRA. Instead, they treated it like a no-brainer when it should have engaged them. The House didn't even do a roll call vote, which would have recorded each member's vote. It was passed by "unanimous consent," the reprehensible procedure by which leadership puts up a bill for a vote with no one there and no record of where each member stands. Today, supporters of RFRA routinely claim it was passed "unanimously," but that is just not true.

Or, better yet, the ACLU, People for the American Way, and Americans United should have considered that they were sitting at a table with their natural political enemies. How could the ACLU not have understood that fair housing laws were at risk? Or women's reproductive health? What was Americans United thinking?

The problems we now face

Almost a decade has passed since the first edition of *God vs. the Gavel*. As veteran New York Times Supreme Court reporter, Linda Greenhouse, recently said to me, I "saw around the corner" on RFRA before anyone else did, but not because I wanted to. I had to.

The irony is that this book is grounded in my sincerely held religious belief in the inherent fallibility of all humans – whether clergy, legislator, or judge. I am writing this new edition, *God vs. the Gavel: The Perils of Extreme Religious Liberty*, because the U.S. is on the precipice of a permanent shift that threatens to transform the country from a thriving, diverse community of religious believers who share a marketplace and a public square into a collection of separate mini-theocracies, where we are more concerned about the religion of the person sitting next to us than the fact that he or she is a fellow American, where an employee needs to know the religion of a Fortune 500 company's owners to know what the health coverage will be, and where goods are tagged with religious identity. RFRA and its state counterparts and its other spawn, the Religious Land

Use and Institutionalized Persons Act (RLUIPA),[14] have sewn religious discord we don't need.

I must also admit that I am frightened by the sheer narcissism of the recent demands made by male-dominated, religious organizations who wish to have a say in women's reproductive health decisions. I am appalled at the Hollywood representations of polygamy in one reality show after another, which downplay women's inequality and children's suffering for ratings. I will never forget my shock and disgust when I learned Catholic bishops across the country were paying their lobbyists millions to keep victims of child sex abuse from having access to justice. Nor will I accept lightly that officials in New York City have done so little to protect babies from getting potentially life-threatening herpes from ultra-Orthodox Jewish circumcisions or that the Brooklyn District Attorney was cooperating with ultra-Orthodox Jews to cover up child sex abuse or that American Muslim fathers have subjected their daughters to "honor" killings, and parents have shipped daughters overseas for female genital mutilation. Of course, no American can forget that the World Trade Center and Boston Marathon bombings were fomented by religion. It's ugly religion, but it is religion nonetheless.

At some point, I simply came to expect that religious leaders are capable of betraying not only society's values, but their own. Most recently, I was not surprised to learn that the leader of the evangelical Christian movement for the "submissiveness" of women to men and children to adults, and home-schooling, Bill Gothard, was credibly accused by many women and teenage girls of sexual harassment and abuse.[15] Is it any wonder that respect for religious leaders is at an all-time low?[16]

Now is the time for Americans to understand exactly what religious entities are demanding and doing to our beloved country.

PART ONE

RELIGIOUS LIBERTY IS NOT A LICENSE TO HARM OTHERS

1

THE PROBLEM

The United States has suffered from a romantic attitude toward religious believers, as though they can do no wrong. Were religious institutions and individuals always beneficial to the public, I would not have needed to write this book, and there would be little to add nearly a decade later.

In fact, the public needs this book now more than ever. The headlines confirm it daily: the notion that religion is always a positive is naive. The United Nations recently slammed the Vatican for its relentless failure to protect children; two young radical Muslims killed and disabled runners at the 2013 Boston Marathon; large, for-profit businesses are invoking their owners' beliefs to impose the cost of their beliefs about contraception on employees; and in some states, businesses run by believers have demanded a right to avoid doing business with homosexuals or same-sex couples.

When I first wrote *God vs. the Gavel*, the discussion of religious actors breaking the law was taboo. People didn't want to know, the press didn't see the need to cover it, and the victims felt invisible. In the decade since, the tide has changed. The recent United Nations Committee on the Rights of the Child hearings called on the Vatican to account for the Roman Catholic Church's persistent endangerment of children and inadequate response to the sex abuse perpetrated by its priests. That was historic itself. But, for me, it was the worldwide, frank media coverage that underscored how far we have come. The victims of religious organizations are now talking, because we are finally listening.

The purpose of this book when it was first published (and still) is to persuade people to take off the blinders and to come to terms with the necessity of making religious individuals and institutions accountable to the law so that they do not harm others. To be sure, many religious entities provide important benefits to society, but good deeds don't make up for bad acts.

Catholic Charities, the United Jewish Communities, and numerous other mission organizations do wonderfully good works. They feed and house the poor, counsel the addicted, minister to the downtrodden, and educate on a large scale. In 2011, religious organizations received approximately 32 percent of all charitable contributions in the United States, which translates into over $95 billion to spend on their mission here and abroad.[1] For example, in 2013, religious relief organizations were indispensable in helping the victims of Typhoon Haiyan in the Philippines.[2] It is nearly impossible to imagine how the United States or the world could function without the services of these good people. There would be a severe deficit in public welfare if they were to close their doors. This public service, though, is no justification to grant them latitude to break criminal and civil laws and harm others.

Religion is an important and necessary part of every society. Religious belief and ritual also can be a powerful source of inspiration, comfort, and healing, as the hard sciences now acknowledge.[3] It can ease the suffering caused by disease, the death of a loved one, and the other catastrophes of human life. I know this firsthand, as I have turned to prayer many times in my life.

Religious beliefs and speech are also a crucial source of critique of the state, and at their best bring the human drive for power into perspective.

Religion can be a liberating force. For example, believers challenged slavery in the United States as early as the 18th century, built the slave-liberating Underground Railroad in the late 19th century, and then led the civil rights marches in the 1960s. There are religious voices today speaking up for the rights of women, children, and homosexuals. We cannot pretend, though, that religious beliefs have not also provided justifications for slavery, South African apartheid, the oppression of women and homosexuals, and the mistreatment of children worldwide.

No country, of course, can afford to ignore religion's force on the people, as China is learning with its unsuccessful attempts to eliminate Falun Gong, Tibetan Buddhists, Uighur Muslims, Protestants, and Catholics.[4] China has responded to its burgeoning religious pluralism with increasingly repressive policies. There could not be a gentler religion than the Falun Gong; three values – truth, compassion, and tolerance – form the backbone of Falun Gong's philosophy. Yet, its existence has threatened the political monopoly in China. Since July of 1999, communist officials have campaigned to "eradicate" Falun Gong and any support for it among the Chinese people or foreign governments. Hundreds of thousands have suffered relentless oppression in prisons, forced labor camps, and brainwashing facilities.[5] China's relentless persecution of believers has led to sanctions from the United States and other countries and attention from Amnesty International.[6] The 2013 Report of the U.S. Commission on International Religious Freedom documents the Chinese government's persistence as it:

> continues to perpetrate particularly severe violations of the freedom of thought, conscience, and religion or belief. Religious groups and individuals considered to threaten national security or social harmony, or whose practices are deemed beyond the vague legal definition of 'normal religious activities,' are illegal and face severe restrictions, harassment, detention, imprisonment, and other abuses.[7]

Nor can even a powerful country stamp out religion as Russia learned when it tried to suppress the Orthodox Church under communism. Church members escaped to the catacombs, where they created an underground church and developed an elaborately encrypted method of communication. Despite the imprisonment and execution of church leaders in Soviet Gulags and concentration camps, the secret church survived and was shepherded through the Soviet era by priests and believers who continued to perform consecrations and religious services.[8] Religion simply cannot be denied.

Despite its many virtues and its enduring presence, though, a good deal of religious conduct cannot be tolerated by enlightened societies. Herein lies the problem – some religious conduct deserves freedom and some requires limitation. Ridding society of religion is no answer, and therefore we must grapple with religion at its worst and its best. *God vs. the Gavel* argues that the right balance is achieved by subjecting believers to the rule of law that applies to everyone else – unless they can prove that an exemption will not significantly harm others.

The "no-harm" rule

Thomas Jefferson famously said: "The legitimate powers of government extend to such acts only as are injurious to others. But it does me no injury for my neighbor to say there are twenty gods, or no god." In other words, government has no business interfering with our beliefs, but legitimately protects us from each other. This is the belief/conduct distinction I mentioned in the Foreword.

My principle point in this book is that religious liberty is important and valuable, but that it must have a limit: when the religious actor will harm another person. It is an idea embedded in American society, and derived in large degree from John Stuart Mill, as I discuss in Chapter 8. Americans particularly need to be reminded of it in this day and age, because we walk around with blinders when it comes to religion, willing the bad behavior right in front of us to disappear.

I will call this the "no-harm principle," but I do not mean "no" literally. What I mean by "no harm" is that the law needs to keep harm to a minimum. The *goal* is no harm – even if absolutely no harm is impossible. Negligible harm may be tolerated, but not significant harm, and *God vs. the Gavel* is focused on the significant harms rendered by religious actors. How the "no-harm" principle should work out in cases on the margins I will leave to a later book. If we can meet the challenges raised in this book, it will be a relief to worry over the cases involving *de minimis* harm.

My concern about religious conduct today is much closer to the Protestant Reformer John Calvin's than atheist Richard Dawkins' criticisms of religion. I do not seek to eradicate religion, but rather to right the balance between religion and the law. There is nothing in this book that can take away religion's virtues, and I have no intention to do so, because reality is more complicated than any drive to paint religion as either all good or all bad. As much good as it sponsors, religion's force can be just another iteration of Nietzsche's will to power and wreak horrible wrongs against individuals and society.

The examples are legion. Sometimes the fight goes on for centuries, as it did in Ireland between Catholics and Protestants, and in Iraq between Muslim sects, and in Egypt between Muslims and Christians.[9] Christians led the horror-filled years of the Medieval Inquisition and the Spanish Inquisition.[10] Britain's Queen Mary and Queen Elizabeth executed or exiled scores of "infidels" who did not profess the queen's religion.[11] The Hindu majority in India and the Muslim majority in Pakistan have been battling over the Kashmir border region since the British partition in 1947.[12] Israel has been in conflict with Palestinians over the West Bank for over 50 years. In the United States, the Salem witches were hung or, in one man's case, crushed to death, for religious reasons.[13] In this era, Islamic radicals, many of whom are part of a fundamentalist movement that was initiated in 1928,[14] are waging a war of terror worldwide, as New York and Boston know all too well. To this day, there are male fundamentalist polygamists in secret enclaves who enslave women, sexually and physically abuse their girls, and abandon their teen-age boys.[15] Faith-healing parents stand by as children die agonizing deaths from easily treated diseases.[16] Clergy in many denominations have sexually abused thousands upon thousands of children. To the extent that the United States has sublimated the potential risks of religious entities, it has sold out its most vulnerable.

Despite the facts, there has been a strong temptation in the United States to treat religion as an unalloyed good. Yet, this is a belief one can embrace only at one's peril, as too many former altar boys, yeshiva students, and girl brides will attest. There has been an increasingly strident chorus from some religious corners that the United States has been secularized and that religion is on its heels. Ironically, though, as they have complained about the purported secularization of this deeply religious society, their political power has not diminished. Indeed, it seems to have grown.

The path to extreme religious liberty

Religious lobbyists have used the "secularism" and "discrimination" arguments to cover their voracious and seemingly insatiable demands to obtain rights to act however they choose. They "need" legislatures to help them, because they are so weak and so discriminated against, or at least that is their shtick. In 1990, the Supreme Court's decision in *Employment Div. v. Smith*[17] unintentionally gave them a moment of political opportunity like none before. They demanded Congress grant them a new extreme right to religious liberty, and they received it.

The *Smith* Court involved two drug counsellors who used an illegal drug, peyote, as part of a religious service and were fired. They applied for unemployment compensation and, under Oregon law, were denied. The Supreme Court held that under the First Amendment, and the "vast majority" of their cases, the men lost. The Court's reasoning was an accurate summary of the First Amendment, but did not reflect the standard religious claimants would have preferred.

Without thinking clearly, or asking the hard questions, Congress acquiesced, and now we have the insidious federal RFRA persuading for-profit businesses that their owners have a "right" to shape employee benefits according to their owners' religious lights. This move to impose a religious template on others in the marketplace is the latest in a luge-like slope of demands. Americans rightly must wonder where RFRA came from. Lead co-sponsor Senator Hatch (Utah, R.) worked himself into a lather over the purported trivialization of religion that justified RFRA:

> So, the time has come to put an end to the motivations blame game that seems to have become the fashion in this country. All too often, our society dismisses out-of-hand those who admit a religious motivation. The term "religious fanatic" is so overused – and misused – that anyone who seeks to translate religious belief into political action is demonized as a fanatic . . . And that's what the Religious Freedom Restoration Act is all about – allowing people with sincere religious beliefs to act upon those beliefs, to participate in the public debate without having to run the gauntlet of unnecessarily large Government roadblocks.[18]

His statement makes RFRA sound much more reasonable than it is. In fact, RFRA did not merely remove the "unnecessarily large roadblocks" from religious conduct; it removed all legal roadblocks other than those deemed most necessary (as applied to one particular religious believer) by the courts.

RFRA was passed to impose a new super-strict scrutiny framework on neutral and generally applicable laws:

The Religious Freedom Restoration Act of 1993

(a) Findings

The Congress finds that–

(1) the framers of the Constitution, recognizing free exercise of religion as an unalienable right, secured its protection in the First Amendment to the Constitution;

(2) laws "neutral" toward religion may burden religious exercise as surely as laws intended to interfere with religious exercise;

(3) governments should not substantially burden religious exercise without compelling justification;

(4) in *Employment Div. v. Smith*, 494 U.S. 872 (1990) the Supreme Court virtually eliminated the requirement that the government justify burdens on religious exercise imposed by laws neutral toward religion; and

(5) the compelling interest test as set forth in prior Federal court rulings is a workable test for striking sensible balances between religious liberty and competing prior governmental interests.

(b) Purposes

The purposes of this chapter are–

(1) to restore the compelling interest test as set forth in *Sherbert v. Verner*, 374 U.S. 398 (1963) and *Wisconsin v. Yoder*, 406 U.S. 205 (1972) and to guarantee its application in all cases where free exercise of religion is substantially burdened; and

(2) to provide a claim or defense to persons whose religious exercise is substantially burdened by government.

(a) In General. – Government shall not substantially burden a person's exercise of religion even if the burden

---

> results from a rule of general applicability, except as provided in subsection (b) of this section.
>
> (b) Exception. – Government may substantially burden a person's exercise of religion only if it demonstrates that application of the burden to the person -
>
>   (1) is in furtherance of a compelling governmental interest; and
>
>   (2) is the least restrictive means of furthering that compelling governmental interest.
>
> 42 U.S.C. § 2000bb, bb-1 (2012).

This is all legalese, which has permeated RFRA and later RLUIPA[19] and the state RFRAs, and given them breathing room to develop because even most legislators don't know what they mean. Unfortunately, it is legalese we all need to understand.

Six phrases are critical to understand free exercise law, whether it is part of the First Amendment's interpretation of it, or legislative language: "neutral and generally applicable," "rationality review," "strict scrutiny," "compelling interest," "narrow tailoring," and "least restrictive means."

First, a "neutral and generally applicable law" is one that is nondiscriminatory and that applies the same law to everyone who engages in the same act. In other words, it's a fair law that regulates conduct, regardless of who does it.

Second, the Court employs "rationality review" of the vast majority of statutes, which means that it defers to legislative judgment. Unless the law is irrational, the law is constitutional.

Third, "strict scrutiny" is what the Supreme Court applies to laws that are likely unconstitutional. If there is reason to suspect a law is unconstitutional, the courts drop their normal deference to the legislature and look closely at the law. Under strict scrutiny, the courts require the government to prove that a law serves a compelling interest and is narrowly tailored to the ends it serves.

Fourth, a "compelling interest" is a state interest of the highest order. The essence of all that has been said and written on the subject is that only those interests of the highest order and those not otherwise served can overbalance legitimate claims to the free exercise of religion."[20]

Fifth, "narrow tailoring" means that the law is well-tailored to the government interests it is supposed to serve, but it does not mean that the means must be specifically tailored to each individual claimant, which instead would be the "least restrictive means" test described next. For narrow tailoring, the government does not have to prove that it has considered and rejected all less restrictive alternatives.[21]

Sixth, the "least restrictive means" means that the law must be tailored to this particular believer. As Justice Powell stated in 1980, and it still remains true, "this 'means' test has been virtually impossible to satisfy."[22]

In a nutshell, here is what you need to know to understand how extreme the RFRA and its progeny are. First, the Supreme Court has applied rationality review to neutral, generally applicable laws, which is to say, most laws, under the First Amendment's Free Exercise Clause, as it held in *Smith*. Second, the First Amendment has reserved strict scrutiny for laws that are not neutral or generally applicable. Third, the Court has *never* applied the "least restrictive means" test in a First Amendment free exercise case. RFRA and its progeny *do not restore anything*, but rather concoct a new, extreme standard (the burden of showing a compelling interest and the least restrictive means) against the government when it defends neutral, generally applicable laws.

The paradox in the Smith-RFRA dialectic

There was a paradox underlying the *Smith*-RFRA discourse. In *Smith*, the Court said that it expected legislatures would be generous with exemptions and pointed to specific examples of state laws that had exempted the religious use of peyote. In short, the Court pointed to the path of religious liberty for the *Smith* plaintiffs themselves: the legislature. Here is the part of this history that rarely is told by RFRA's supporters – while religious lobbyists and civil rights groups harped against *Smith* at congressional hearings, because it had "abandoned" religious liberty by leaving religious liberty to lawmakers, dozens of legislatures enacted exemptions for the religious use of peyote. That's right – *Smith* was followed by real legislative religious liberty. So all of the rhetoric about the end of religious liberty was just that. The Court was correct: United States' legislatures are religion-friendly. During the push for RFRA and its progeny, lobbyists never pointed to the thousands of religious exemptions in the U.S., including everything from the Amish's exemption from Social Security taxes; faith healers' exemptions from childhood vaccinations; and summer camp and day care exemptions for any religious entity from state regulation for the safety of children.

It is with this political reality in mind that I suggest that religious liberty is adequately protected under the Court's First Amendment doctrine and the legislative process, because the process described in *Smith* works. If a law is constitutional, let the exemption request enter the legislative process, where lawmakers can consider all those affected by a legal rule, including society as a whole before rendering an exemption. Courts are constrained to consider only the two parties in front of them; lawmakers can assess a much broader and deeper record. Permissive legislative accommodation makes sense.

Of course the legislative process is not perfect. Sometimes they go too far on the basis of a very thin record, as they did with RFRA. Its legislative sponsors failed to comprehend the irony of the entire RFRA process. Purportedly, RFRA was needed because the Supreme Court had thrown religious actors to the legislative process (translation, wolves), and one couldn't trust lawmakers to do the right thing by religion.[23] On this reasoning, legislatures could not be trusted to protect religious liberty. But, wait. First, in RFRA, Congress enacted the most far-reaching statute in favor of religious entities in United States history. Second, at the same time, the very religious practice unprotected by the First Amendment in *Smith* was legislatively accommodated across the country. Third, lawmakers knew religious entities have political power and experience, because their lobbyists meet with them *all the time*, whether in legislative offices or the ubiquitous prayer breakfasts and annual Red Masses.

There is something so fundamentally wrong with this picture it is hard to know where to start. Suffice it to say that Congress's willingness to pass a blind accommodation statute for dozens of religious groups – without asking whether disabling every law in the country might be a mistake – negates the theory that the Court had thrown believers off a cliff. It looks like a pretty soft landing.

While I do not question the sincerity or conviction of the members of Congress, I do have to question their common sense for two reasons. First, the scope of RFRA was mind-boggling. RFRA, by its terms, potentially disabled every law in the country, presumably including many that the members had fought to enact. Yet, the members stayed within the religious advocate's bubble, where all that matters is making sure the believer is free, and which shoves discussion of the harm that might accrue to the fringes of the debate. As elected representatives, their job is to think outside the box of every legislative proposal, but it does not appear that it ever occurred to them that there was anything beyond the RFRA box.

Part of the problem lay in the bill's modus operandi: it was constitutional mumbo jumbo. Moreover, the bill's breadth was so enormous that it drove analysis away from specific examples. If one is thinking of every law in the land, it is tough to come down to particular issues. There was no natural starting point to criticize it, so almost all of the analysis (with the exception of concerns about prison security at the end of the bill's trajectory) resided at a lofty and abstract level. None of this is to excuse the members for failing to ask the hard questions, but it is an explanation. And the members were not the only ones who didn't penetrate the surface of RFRA to its inherent problems – neither did plenty of its supporters at the time.

Second, the variety of religious faiths in the United States is boundless, and only some of them were invited to join the Coalition for the Free Exercise of Religion, which lobbied for RFRA. The groups whose practices would have sent up red flags – like Satanists who practice human sacrifice, the Children of God, who believe in sex with young children, the jihadists, and the polygamists – were intentionally invisible.

Members of Congress had to have known that religious groups with dangerous practices exist. In addition to the few just listed, what about the Ku Klux Klan, or the other white supremacists in prisons, who trace their racist beliefs back to the Bible or neo-paganism? What about the religious militia in Montana and Idaho? Or the faith-healing believers whose children happen to die when they do not take them to the doctor? RFRA was before September 11, so the members get a quasi-pass on thinking about terrorists, although the first bombing of the World Trade

Center was nine months before RFRA was signed into law on November 16, 1993.[24]

Religion and Iran were in the news with the ongoing religious wars between Israelis and Palestinians, Hindus and Muslims in Kashmir, and Protestants and Catholics in Ireland. The year RFRA was first passed, the Irish Republican Army bombed a fish shop in Belfast, killing 10.[25] Did the members think that none of that religious fanaticism could reach the United States? The answer is that they simply did not think at all. One can imagine the members going to sleep the night RFRA passed the House by "unanimous consent," secure in the knowledge that they had done the "right thing." Unfortunately they had not.

In the members' defense, there were dozens of religious organizations behind RFRA as well as most of the major civil rights organizations. Even Americans United for Separation of Church and State loved it! The members seemed to believe that the unity of religious and civil rights groups ensured that the law had to be a good idea. This is only a partial list of those who were lobbying for the bill, which appeared in the Congressional Record.

Agudath Israel of America, American Association of Christian Schools, American Civil Liberties Union, American Conference of Religious Movements, American Humanist Association, American Jewish Committee, American Jewish Congress, American Muslim Council, Americans for Democratic Action, Americans for Religious Liberty, Americans United for Separation of Church and State, Anti-Defamation League, Association of Christian Schools International, Association of American Indian Affairs, Baptist Joint Committee, Coalitions for America, Concerned Women For America, Episcopal Church, Christian Legal Society, Church of Jesus Christ of Latter-day Saints, Church of Scientology, Evangelical Lutheran Church, Conference of Seventh-day Adventists, Jesuit Social Ministries, Mennonite Central Committee, National Association of Evangelicals, National Council of Churches, People for the American Way, Presbyterian Church, Southern Baptist Convention, Traditional Values Coalition, Union of American Hebrew Congregations, Union of Orthodox Jewish Congregations, United Methodist Church, United States Catholic Conference.[26]

The group dubbed itself the Coalition for the Free Exercise of Religion, and by the time the coalition filed an amicus brief in favor of RFRA in the *City of Boerne v. Flores* case, the list doubled:

- American Association of Christian Schools
- Agudath Israel of America
- American Baptist Churches USA
- American Civil Liberties Union
- American Conference on Religious Movements
- American Ethical Union, Washington Ethical Action Office
- American Humanist Association
- American Jewish Committee
- American Jewish Congress
- American Muslim Council
- Americans for Democratic Action
- Americans for Religious Liberty
- Americans United for Separation of Church and State
- Anti-Defamation League
- Association of Christian Schools International
- Association on American Indian Affairs
- Baptist Joint Committee on Public Affairs
- B'nai B'rith
- Central Conference of American Rabbis
- Christian Church (Disciples of Christ)
- Christian Legal Society
- Christian Life Commission, Southern Baptist Convention
- Christian Science Committee on Publication
- Church of the Brethren
- Church of Scientology International
- Coalition for Christian Colleges and Universities
- Coalitions for America
- Concerned Women for America
- Council of Jewish Federations
- Council on Religious Freedom
- Council on Spiritual Practices
- Criminal Justice Policy Foundation

- Episcopal Church
- Friends Committee on National Legislation
- General Conference of Seventh-day Adventists
- Guru Gobind Singh Foundation
- Hadassah, the Women's Zionist Organization of America, Inc.
- Home School Legal Defense Association
- International Association of Jewish Lawyers and Jurists
- International Institute for Religious Freedom
- The Jewish Reconstructionist Federation
- Mennonite Central Committee U.S.
- Muslim Prison Foundation
- Mystic Temple of Light, Inc.
- National Association of Evangelicals
- National Campaign for a Peace Tax Fund
- National Committee for Public Education and Religious Liberty
- National Council of Churches of Christ in the USA
- National Council of Jewish Women
- National Council on Islamic Affairs
- National Jewish Commission on Law and Public Affairs
- National Jewish Community Relations Advisory Council
- National Sikh Center
- Native American Church of North America
- Native American Rights Fund
- North American Council for Muslim Women
- People for the American Way Action Fund
- Peyote Way Church of God
- Clifton Kirkpatrick, as Stated Clerk of the General Assembly of the Presbyterian Church (USA)
- Rabbinical Council of America
- Sacred Sites Inter-faith Alliance
- Soka-Gakkai International – USA
- Traditional Values Coalition
- Union of American Hebrew Congregations
- Union of Orthodox Jewish Congregations of America
- Unitarian Universalist Association of Congregations
- United Church of Christ, Office for Church in Society

- The United Methodist Church and The General Board of Church and Society and The General Council on Finance and Administration
- United Synagogue of Conservative Judaism
- Wisconsin Judicare
- Women of Reform Judaism, Federation of Sisterhoods[27]

The dynamics of the group are worth more than one sociologist's or political scientist's career, as religious and civil rights groups that normally go head-to-head in the public sphere suddenly were sitting at the same table.

The contrasts were stark. It is not often that the ACLU and the Traditional Values Coalition are on the same side. The Presbyterians and the Methodists were pro-choice, while the Southern Baptists and the Orthodox Jews (except in cases involving the life of the mother) surely were not. Unitarian ministers had been officiating at religious same-sex marriages since the 1970s while the Church of Jesus Christ of Latter-day Saints deeply disapproved of same-sex marriage, as the country later learned through its pivotal role in getting California's Proposition 8 passed. The Christian Scientists believed that the law should not interfere with their faith-based decision to refuse treatment for ill children, but a plethora of coalition members would require medical treatment in the same circumstances. The ACLU was energetically opposed to housing discrimination against homosexuals and unmarried adults, while the Christian Legal Society was pushing hard to ensure its members could discriminate against such couples. Each group surely knew its public policy enemies, yet the abstract quality of the "right to religious liberty" in the RFRA formulation led them to lay down their usual weapons. It was not politically rational, but they were operating under false information about the Supreme Court's recent rulings on free exercise (as I discuss in Part Two), and drinking deep of the American myth that all religious actors are good.

In fact, each religious organization harbored certain causes that they hoped would be furthered by RFRA. But that was not the topic of discussion at the table (at least that is what I am told). Rather, their attention was trained on making it difficult for the government to enforce the law against religious actors. Until RFRA's invalidation at the Supreme Court in 1997, in *Boerne v. Flores*,[28] the coalition was able to operate relatively smoothly. One of the key issues that would cleave the organization, though, was housing discrimination.

The move for expansive religious liberty statutes did not stop with the *Boerne* decision, though. Incredibly, three political paths led away from the Court's invalidation of RFRA: (1) Congress considered a RFRA clone, the Religious Liberty Protection Act (RLPA), which failed (One cannot fault them for their skill at choosing names that sound a lot like "apple pie, motherhood, and patriotism."); (2) lobbyists fanned out to the states to demand state RFRAs; and (3) Congress in 2000 enacted RLUIPA and amendments to RFRA to make it solely applicable to federal law and intended to make it look as though *Boerne* had not invalidated it in its entirety.

The problem for the coalition with this next iteration was that RFRA, while it was in effect from 1993 to 1997, had awakened the slumbering groups whose interests were harmed by religious conduct: unmarried couples, children's advocates, corrections officials, regulatory agencies, juvenile and family courts, city planners, historical preservationists, and cities, among others.

They had been caught off-guard previously, because a title like "Religious Freedom Restoration Act" yields precious few clues that their objectives were about to be undermined. After all, they were in favor of religious liberty, too, just like every other American. As RFRA had been applied to individual laws over the course of its three-and-a-half year life, however, its power to undermine certain policies became increasingly apparent, and these groups slowly came to the realization that they needed to fight this law, even if it did sound like the ultimate all-American initiative. This realization took years, first because of the abstract quality of the statute and, second, because there were individual members even in these organizations unfamiliar with the full panoply of harm religious entities could cause.

Eventually, various groups lobbied against RLPA. In the beginning, the strategy was to push for wholesale defeat of not only RLPA, but the idea behind it. The more effective tactic, though, turned out to be having each group specifically lobby to have their particular interest exempted from RLPA's reach. This posed a serious problem for the coalition, which was viable only so long as its members operated at an abstract level. With each request to have an area of law stripped from RLPA's reach, for example, children's issues, or land use, or prison administration, or housing discrimination, the dormant issues that normally would have divided the members finally came to the fore.

To keep RLPA (and the state RFRAs) from being riddled with multiple exemptions, and to keep the coalition together, the group devised an interesting strategy: if there was any attempt to peel off a law or a category of law from RFRA, RLPA, or a state RFRA, the entire group would say, "no exemptions." By 1997, though, the strategy did not work at the federal level, because our elected representatives were becoming educated about RFRA's actual and RLPA's likely impacts, and the downside of extreme religious liberty was becoming apparent. The members therefore resisted RLPA's one-size-fits-all formula, which it had inherited from RFRA.

The coalition's strategy succeeded for some of the state RFRAs, like Connecticut, Florida, and Alabama, which have no exceptions. By the time Texas took the matter under consideration in 1999, though, private property advocates and cities were vocal, active, and effective. They succeeded in obtaining a limitation in the Texas RFRA for land use laws.[29] Pennsylvania's Religious Freedom Protection Act of 2002 (RFPA), removed a number of categories from its reach, including criminal offenses; motor vehicles; licensing of health professionals; the health or safety of individuals in facilities operated under the public welfare code; the safe construction and operation of health-care facilities; health and safety in construction; and mandatory reporting of child abuse.[30] To be sure, not every entity that would have opposed the bill was heard; RFPA was passed quickly and without hearings, so by the time local government and land use interests learned of the bill, it was too late for them to be relieved of its burdens.

The burgeoning understanding that this was not such a magical formula led to its defeat in states like Maryland and California in 1998, and North Dakota and Colorado in 2012,[31] but there are nineteen states that have been persuaded to pass such a law.[32] Recently, the pace has been quickening, because, as same-sex marriage becomes a fait accompli, religious lobbyists are seeking creative ways to permit their believers to discriminate against homosexuals and same-sex couples. To this end, the most recent state RFRA iterations are even more extreme than the original counterparts, e.g., religious lobbyists have pushed to decrease the burden of proof on the believer and/or increase the burden on the state. For example, some are triggered not by a believer proving a "substantial burden," but rather any burden. This approach was recently enacted in Kentucky,[33] though it was rejected in Texas.

Civil rights groups did the United States no favors when they failed to comprehend how dangerous the original RFRA was. As most people know, the ACLU has been on the other side of those pressing for religious interests in cases involving challenges to the Ten Commandments, prayer at public school football games, and government-sponsored religious holiday displays.[34] Yet, its president enthusiastically endorsed RFRA at hearings in the House, saying,

> The ACLU strongly supports [RFRA] because it restores religious liberty to its rightful place as a preferred value and a fundamental right within the American constitutional system. The First Amendment's guarantee of the "free exercise of religion" has proven to be the boldest and most successful experiment in religious freedom the world has known.[35]

Frankly, the ACLU was right about the First Amendment but wrong on RFRA. There were conservative Christian and Orthodox groups at the table that were opposed to the ACLU's position on the fair-housing laws; their interests were furthered by RFRA, while the ACLU's were not. It took years for the ACLU to realize that it had made a colossal mistake in supporting RFRA's abstruse formula, and that it had in fact supported a law that was directly opposed to its primary agendas. When RLPA was considered in 1999, the ACLU testified against it, because of its impact on anti-discrimination laws.

> [W]e are no longer part of the coalition supporting RLPA because we could not ignore the potentially severe consequences that RLPA may have on State and local civil rights laws.... We have found that landlords across the country have been using State religious liberty claims to challenge the application of State and local civil rights laws protecting persons against marital status discrimination.[36]

At the time, the religious lobbyists did not stop with RFRA, the failed RLPA, or the state RFRAs. They also pitched RLUIPA, which hands religious landowners a ticket to federal court if they don't get everything they demand in the local land use process and encourages prisoners to challenge prison regulations, which I will discuss in more detail in Chapters 4 and 6, respectively.

Following in the footsteps of the civil liberties groups, it took the American Planning Association (APA) years before it weighed in on an RLUIPA land use case, even though these cases almost always involve arguments that are directly contrary to the APA's core principles.

One of the reasons that RLPA never became law is that the ACLU, People for the American Way, and Americans United ceased to be enthusiastic supporters of extreme religious liberty. This is not to say that the ACLU got out of the business altogether; RLUIPA was drafted by someone in the ACLU, along with assistance from the Department of Justice.

In more recent years, though, state-based ACLUs have awakened to fight alongside gay rights groups to try to halt the latest march of extreme state RFRAs, which are intended in part to permit discrimination against homosexuals. The ACLU and other civil rights groups also have taken a stance against the corporation claimants in the Affordable Care Act contraceptive mandate cases.[37]

The big picture

A test of religious liberty that would fail to take into account this self-serving, voracious side of religion guarantees overreaching and suffering. Religious entities have the capacity for great good and great evil, and society is not duty-bound by any constitutional principle to let them avoid duly enacted laws, especially when their actions harm others. To say that religious liberty must encompass the right to harm others is to radicalize the First Amendment. The Framers did not intend to create extreme religious liberty, to turn the U.S. into a collection of mini-theocracies, or to give believers the power to impose their beliefs on others. They, instead, assumed acts harming safety and public welfare, and licentious acts, would be illegal for everyone.

Part One catalogues examples of believers who have harmed the public good, and documents facts about religion that require sunshine and public debate. It is intended to be an education – one that is sorely needed if true liberty for all is ever to be achieved. It is not intended to be an argument to eradicate religion. To the contrary, the impetus for this book lies in a belief in the depthless good that religious believers can and do supply. But that belief is tempered by my deep disappointment in learning the truth of what some religious entities actually have done and continue to do. My rose-colored glasses broke years ago. The truth about religion is safer than our comfortable presuppositions.

From the ivory tower, it is easy to spin abstract arguments about the high principle of protecting religious conduct. Many law professors are guilty of thoughtless protection of potentially bad behavior. For example:

> Having engaged in my own weighing of the value of religious diversity against the potential for anarchy and having determined that religious diversity is highly valuable while the fear of anarchy is without basis at this time in history, I would push the line to be drawn in these cases to the farthest extreme compatible with the viability of a living democracy, which is to say that the exercise of religion should trump most governmental regulation.[38]

I'm embarrassed to say that I published that the year RFRA passed, so I am not without blame, either. If one's theory of protecting religious conduct is based on hypotheticals, ideals, and Sunday School, as mine was at the time, it is not difficult to construct a theory of religious liberty that permits believers to sail above the law and the people. My views have changed 180 degrees, because I have been educated and now know the severe harm religious entities can cause. With the facts in front of me, I had to conclude that most laws should govern religious conduct, and the only legitimate exceptions occur when the legislature has determined that immunizing religious conduct is consistent with public welfare, health, and safety. Discrimination against religion is never acceptable, but neutral, generally applicable regulation is a necessity.

In recent decades, religious entities have lobbied and litigated to immunize their actions, either by obtaining specific legislative exemptions or blind, omnibus exemptions like RFRA, the state RFRAs, and RLUIPA. They have always waved the banner of "religious liberty," and few Americans, particularly elected officials, have thought to question them. What could be more important in a free society? When the question is left in the abstract, the answer is obvious. But when one knows the facts, the answer to the question is that there are all sorts of interests that must trump religious conduct in a just and free society – such as the interest in deterring terrorism, protecting civil rights, preventing childhood sexual abuse, protecting women's rights, preserving private property rights, or deterring homophobia. Every citizen should have at least as much right to be free from these harms as a believer has to be free from government regulation.

In effect, though never explicitly, religious entities have been lobbying for the right to hurt others without legal consequences. They want to be laws unto themselves. In a representative form of democracy like this one, the laws are supposed to serve the larger public good, and no one should be permitted to significantly harm another person without account. True religious liberty recognizes an absolute right of belief and a right not to be discriminated against, but also recognizes the government's necessary power to regulate religious conduct to serve the public good.

Believers can and do lobby for specific exemptions to neutral, generally applicable laws. After *Smith* was decided, Native American Church members lobbied the state and federal legislatures for exemptions for religious use of peyote and received them. A more troubling example is the Christian Scientists' longstanding campaign to exempt parents from the medical neglect laws so that parents are not legally liable for failing to obtain medical treatment for their children, which I will address in Chapter 2.

At other times, believers lobby for exemptions not just to protect religiously motivated conduct, but also to avoid liability for their misconduct. For example, it is commonplace for the states to impose mandatory reporting requirements on professionals who have regular contact with children and suspect abuse. An obvious category would be clergy. The Catholic Church's bishops, however, invested in lobbying to obtain exemptions for clergy so that they would not have to report child abuse (knowing as it did that many of its priests were in fact abusing children). The bishops sought to avoid reporting obligations even when a report would not violate the confessional; they also routinely argue in the sex abuse cases that every report of abuse is in fact a "confession" and, therefore, privileged and confidential. The Vatican even today, under the popular Pope Francis, continues to prevaricate as it says that bishops should report abuse . . . *if the law requires it.* This year, the Italian bishops disclosed that they will not report clergy abuse to the authorities, because Italy does not require it. The Vatican knows full well that the law often does not require clergy to report, *because its own bishops lobby to ensure it doesn't!*

The free exercise statutes are "blind exemption" laws. Religious lobbyists have persuaded lawmakers to grant believers a presumptive right to trump all laws or an entire category of law, on the theory that the religious deserve "autonomy" from the law. Examples include RFRA, the state-level mini-RFRAs (some of which are worse than the original), and RLUIPA, each of which will be discussed in more detail in Chapter 4. They are the vanguard of extreme religious liberty.

The other form of extreme religious liberty resides in some practice-specific exemptions, e.g., the ones that permit parents to medically neglect their children if motivated by religious beliefs in faith healing. Far too often, specific exemptions have been passed without the general public – and often the legislators – knowing how the exemption will affect others. In a typical scenario, a religious group quietly approaches a legislator (inside or outside the capitol), and the legislator then slips the exemption into some bill on a different subject. There are no hearings, no public debate, and no in-depth reporting to unmask the dangers of freeing religious entities from the targeted law. Everyone who knows about it goes home satisfied – the legislator because he has done a "good deed" that day, and the religious entity, because it will avoid liability for its actions. Yet, the under-the-table system means that neither the future victims nor their advocates know what is coming, and legislators are free to mimic the hear-no-evil, see-no-evil, speak-no-evil monkeys. This has been religious liberty, American-style, in recent years. The results, documented in Part One, are not pretty.

The blind exemption free exercise statutes like the RFRAs and RLUIPA tend to be passed with more fanfare, because they are cast in incomprehensible legalese. On their shiny surfaces, they promise a virtuous religious freedom, but they hide many devils in the details. Thus, these blind exemptions are bandied about for all to see, but their terms are so technical, hardly anyone comprehends how the law will operate in specific cases. RFRA, the grand blind exemption of all time, is as opaque on its surface as they come. The RFRA legislative history is filled with paeans to religious liberty, but precious little analysis of what would happen if religious individuals and institutions had the power to overcome all laws on a routine basis. The Affordable Care Act contraception mandate litigation is just one example, but it is finally the example that has attracted the attention of the public, over twenty years after RFRA was first passed.

Not all freedom from the law occurs as a result of legislation. Sometimes there is religious "liberty" from the law when prosecutors fail to enforce the law and instead pander to religious leaders, ergo, perceived voting blocs. For decades, prosecutors across the United States knew about the abuse in the Catholic dioceses, but hesitated to prosecute for fear of Catholic backlash. To this day, few cities other than Philadelphia have done the deep digging needed to uncover the depth of the depravity and deliberate indifference to the welfare of children.[39] Former Brooklyn District Attorney Charles Hynes cooperated with ultra-Orthodox Jewish rabbis to keep rampant abuse in the community secret. Utah Attorney General Mark Shurtleff, instead of rescuing the women, girls, and boys at risk in fundamentalist polygamist communities, established a "Safety Net" to help them obtain government aid. Since the first edition of God vs. the Gavel, there has been a noticeable shift. Some elected officials are choosing children and public safety over religious groups, and finally that appears to be smart politics, with Hynes losing his long-held position to Ken Thompson, who ran on a platform of protecting children in the Hasidic community and elsewhere.

In addition to seeking legislative exemptions and urging prosecutors not to press charges, religious entities have argued vigorously in the courts (and the legislatures) for a presumptive constitutional right to avoid the law under federal and state constitutions. They have foisted a definition of the First Amendment onto the American people that means, in effect, that they are immune to all but the most necessary laws. They have attempted to use the First Amendment as a shield in prosecutions involving child abuse, statutory rape, underage marriage, and medical neglect. But their efforts have not stopped at the First Amendment. They have also employed due process, ex post facto, and separation of powers theories to argue that the law should not apply to them, often because they are religious. They also have developed a nefarious theory of "church autonomy," which persuades believers that they are unaccountable and privileged and which is far removed from what James Madison intended when he drafted the First Amendment and the Supreme Court's free exercise doctrine.

Part One describes six arenas where religious individuals and institutions have insisted on the right to avoid the law as they have harmed others: children, marriage, schools, land use in neighborhoods, prisons and the military, and the anti-discrimination laws. Sometimes the claimed exemption is consistent with the public good and no harm accrues, but too often, their legal theory means immunity for them but harm to the victim who suddenly has no recourse under the law.

Part Two charts the fall of special privileges for religious conduct in Anglo-American history and the rise of the rule that religious entities have no legal right to harm others. After centuries of development, it is quite clear that harm is harm, and whoever causes it must be held to account. I will endorse the Supreme Court's unfairly maligned opinion in *Employment Div. v. Smith*, and I will argue that there is no constitutional right to harm others simply because the conduct is religiously motivated. The Court's First Amendment doctrine is wise. Legislatures can exempt the religious from some laws, but only where legislators and prosecutors ask the hard questions and where the religious entities have borne the burden of proving that exempting them renders significant harm.

Now is the time for Americans to pay attention. The advent of extreme religious liberty has morphed into a supposed right to impose one's religious beliefs on others. The for-profit company, Hobby Lobby, which is an arts and crafts store, along with a host of other for-profit companies, has demanded the right to impose its owners' religious worldview on its female employees' medical benefits. It cannot hire according to religious belief, and, therefore, this is a request to impose one's religion on those who do not share the owners' beliefs. The Supreme Court held that the First Amendment does not protect such extreme demands, but RFRA does. This brazen move to impose a religious template on others in the marketplace is the latest in a scary new world. With the Supreme Court's ruling, the push to create a zone of autonomy around religious believers that makes them unaccountable to others will not end until voters punish presidents, legislators, and prosecutors who pander while the vulnerable suffer and legislatures repeal the blind, extreme accommodation statutes, RFRA, RLUIPA, and the state RFRAs. It is time to halt the tyranny of religious believers in the U.S.

2

CHILDREN

Warning: If this chapter were a movie, it would have an NC-17 rating, because it describes horrible things that have been done to children beneath the cloak of religion in the United States. Children have been raped, beaten, and permitted to die excruciating deaths – at the hands of their priests, rabbis, pastors, and parents.

Young people are at risk from religious believers and institutions in two main ways: (1) through the misuse of religious power to abuse the child; and (2) through their parents' religiously motivated medical neglect or physical abuse. The suffering is often unimaginable, because the children have been trained to trust and be obedient to their clergy and parents. They lack the ability to protect themselves from those they have been taught are here on earth to love and protect them.

In the first instance, some clergy, day care providers, coaches, and religious schoolteachers use their position to take advantage of children. No person can be trusted to hold power without some check on it, and that is why we have child protection laws. A religious authority figure can be the most outwardly pious individual, but without the law's ability to make the person accountable, he or she can be capable of physical and spiritual murder. The believer is not just a wolf – but a lion – in sheep's clothing. Oftentimes this power-based abuse takes the form of sexual abuse, but it can also be physical, emotional, and/or ritualistic abuse. Many children, especially those who are already in difficult family situations, lack the life skills to fend off the clergy member who seduces them with attention and affection and only then turns into a sexual predator.

In the second scenario, the parents impose sincere religious beliefs on their child that endanger him or her. One example is faith-healing, where the parent's faith precludes medical treatment and the child suffers from easily treatable ailments, such as diabetes, which, left untreated, leads to an agonizing death. More prevalent today is the failure to immunize children and then to send them into the schools. There is also the tragedy of female genital mutilation.

When one person's liberty to act is expansive, it is often at the cost of another, and this is doubly true in the medical-neglect cases. This is a zero-sum game, and too often it is the children who are sacrificed, instead of the religious conduct.[1]

No person who has ever loved a child can keep from asking the question: what kind of society permits children to be hurt like this? The answer is the United States, when it overzealously or thoughtlessly protects the right to religious conduct, and when it treats children as expendable.

Childhood sexual abuse by clergy

The following stories only touch the tip of the iceberg of clergy childhood sexual abuse. Some of these are notorious; others are run-of-the-mill. There are many more reported cases, and even more unreported cases, because the shame of the acts and the threats of the perpetrators often lead the victims to abide in shadow rather than sunlight. The perpetrators are clergy members – the men and women children are taught to trust with their very souls. These pedophiles and ephebophiles (adults who target pre-pubescent children and adolescents for sex) use their position of religious authority to lure vulnerable children into sexual molestation.[2] Although the precise details of the sexual attacks vary, the grievous harm to the victims then and later in life is the same.

Victims of sexual attacks by clergy typically have no idea what has happened to them immediately after the sexual attack occurs. They are confused, ashamed, and afraid. After the clergy member tells them that they (or their parents) will burn in hell if they tell anyone – which happens on a regular basis – the victims are very often silent. The victims are children, after all, and this is usually their very first introduction to sex (unless they were already sexually abused by another adult). Typically, it takes decades of emotional turmoil and multiple missed dreams for them to finally realize that the acts that were done to them as children disabled some essential part of their psyche.[3] They often require intense counseling, family support, and even then may never achieve their full potential. The Roman Catholic canon law expert and hero, Father Thomas Doyle, who has dedicated his life to helping clergy-abuse victims, has accurately labeled what is done to these children as "soul murder." There is no better way to describe it, and it applies across all denominations.

Religious institutions have been havens for pedophiles for three reasons. First, up until now, the U.S. has so trusted clergy that no one questioned the priest or pastor or elder who volunteered to spend extra time with Bobby. As the Penn State and Woody Allen scandals have reinforced, when adults revere a man, he gets latitude that can endanger the children in his sphere.[4] Second, religion is an authoritative structure in a person's life, so that demands by clergy are oftentimes equated with commands from God, and therefore are treated as imperatives. Third, religious institutions, especially those that form tight-knit communities, often succumb to the temptation to shield their reputation by keeping internal sexual abuse secret, which ensures the authorities will not be contacted and permits the pedophiles to continue to operate. The circumstances are tailor-made for the child molester. In the words of a former elder of the Jehovah's Witnesses, the religious organization can be a "pedophile paradise," especially where it features a "closed society, elder authority, [and a] masculine dominated society."[5]

As if it is not bad enough that religious institutions are magnets for pedophiles (partly because of the laws the religious institutions have endorsed), some religious institutions themselves have actively aided and abetted the abuse. For decades (really centuries), the Roman Catholic Church, the Jehovah's Witnesses, and the ultra-Orthodox Jews, among others, have handled reports of clergy abuse as though the public good were not their problem and have insisted on silence as they refused to report the crimes to authorities. At this stage in history, there is no question that they placed the good of the organization above the needs of the child and the legitimate demands of society.[6] Their disregard for the public good is even more sinister when one discovers that they sacrificed the public good to elevate their earthly needs. The silence is an integral part of a twofold strategy: protect the institution's public image and shelter its finances.

Thirty years ago, an internal report was offered to the U.S. Catholic Bishops that cast the phenomenon of clergy abuse in terms of an epidemic of clergy abuse cases waiting to explode.[7] It urged them to adopt a three-part strategy including pastoral outreach to victims, in-depth research, and a crisis intervention team of experts to assist bishops with individual cases.[8] The report was ignored. Instead, the hierarchy pretended it harbored no pedophiles. As we all know now, cardinals, archbishops, and bishops shuffled known pedophiles from parish to parish without notice to anyone, leaving behind a trail of young victims.[9] It was the perfect environment for the crime, which is why it happened over and over again, so that today there are thousands upon thousands of Catholic victims.[10] This is true of the Jehovah's Witnesses, ultra-Orthodox Jews, and many others.[11] The secrecy permitted the religious institutions to maintain a moral high ground in public and at the same time to rob children of the forces of society that otherwise might have protected them – parents, prosecutors, judges, the media, and civil rights groups.

The parents were often kept in the dark, even when a known pedophile was assigned to their parish or children's religious school, and their lack of knowledge yielded two distinct difficulties. First, they had no idea they needed to act to protect their children from their own clergy in the first instance. Second, because of their ignorance, some refused to believe a child who tried to tell them about the abuse. Indeed, in some circumstances, the abused child was beaten by a parent for having the nerve to suggest their beloved clergy would do something so heinous, so abuse piled on top of abuse.

Before 2001, when the *Boston Globe* broke the story of the coverup by Cardinal Bernard Law, prosecutors only learned of a small number of such cases, and therefore extrapolated to the conclusion that there must be only a small number. Since the problem appeared to be a negligible social problem, when the bishop or cardinal would ask them to let the church take care of its dirty laundry internally, prosecutors were all too willing. There was and is also a more insidious problem, because prosecutors are elected officials that pander to religious groups for votes. Utah prosecutors routinely fail to protect women and children from the notorious Fundamentalist Church of Jesus Christ of Latter-day Saints (FLDS) polygamous sect. In New York, for years, Former Brooklyn District Attorney Charles Hynes shielded ultra-Orthodox Jewish men from child sex abuse claims through lax enforcement and cooperation in keeping their stories secret.[12] As it gains steam, the child protection movement is uncovering and fighting their politically convenient arrangements – Hynes lost his last election.[13] In fact, he lost twice. First, he lost the Democratic primary. Then he switched to the Republican ticket for the general election, and lost again.

It is somewhat of a mystery why the press did not break the story of widespread clergy abuse sooner. Perhaps they too were ignorant that there were so many unspeakable crimes being committed in their jurisdictions. In all likelihood – like the prosecutors – they also deferred to the local bishop's pleas to protect the image of the church. Powerful men protect each other in every domain. It is not that the press has let religious entities off the hook for all crimes. The Pulitzer Prize has been awarded many times for stories that uncovered financial misdealings in a religious institution,[14] and at least one reporter, Jason Berry, was focused on the Catholic Church's clergy-abuse problem as early as the 1980s.[15] But until 2003, no newspaper had won an award as a result of covering a national news story about clergy abuse.

1984 was a bellwether year for clergy abuse. Roman Catholic Father Gilbert Gauthe of Lafayette, Louisiana, was indicted for the abuse of 35 children.[16] The question was: "How did Gauthe get away with abusing that many children?" It was quite obvious: Gauthe had used his position in the church to obtain victim after victim.[17] Clear-headed reporting would have driven a good reporter into the internal operations of the Roman Catholic Church and its devotion to secrecy on these issues, and, in fact, there was intense interest by the press at the height of the scandal.[18] That interest was abetted by an increased national focus on the issue of child abuse.[19] In the same year, congressional testimony by FBI supervisory special agent Kenneth Lanning explained that pedophiles gain access to children by choosing occupations with access to children: "teacher, camp counselor, babysitter, school bus driver... physician, minister, photographer, social worker, police officer, etc."[20] A *Newsweek* article about an alleged Methodist minister child abuser quoted an expert as saying, "There should be a presumption that child abusers will gravitate to work with children."[21] Also, child molesters "are among the more respected members of their communities."[22] Thus, the elements were in place for the story to break in the mid-1980s.

Yet, stories detailing a larger Church problem beyond Gauthe did not appear until 2001 in Boston when the *Boston Globe* unmasked the depth of the Boston Archdiocese's turpitude. Eventually winning a Pulitzer Prize, the *Globe* was praised for its courage, but we must ask what took so long? For decades, children were being abused at will by pedophiles who were wearing a collar and grooming their young victims with charm and attention – across the country and the world. To be sure, there is no one answer, but some component must be that at the end of the day, it was hard for even the jaded press both to comprehend the enormity of the evil perpetrated by a single religious institution and to withstand the pressure from bishops to keep the abuse private. Nor can one underestimate the lengths to which the Catholic hierarchy went to keep its ugly secrets to itself. One lay Catholic described it as follows: "Their structure and social chemistry is almost identical to the Mafia. There is a deep secrecy and a fierce loyalty to the organization."[23]

Father Andrew Greeley, sociologist and well-known novelist, hypothesized at least 100,000 victims in 1993.[24] In 2004, the U.S. church's lay review board conducted an internal audit of the dioceses and concluded that there were roughly 10,000 victims.[25] The audit was tainted, however, by the bishops who refused to open their Secret Archives to the investigation.

We can't blame the children for not telling us. They are powerless in every sphere. It was not that long ago when children were cautioned not to speak unless spoken to. To be sure, there are dedicated organizations, like the American Academy of Pediatrics and CHILD, Inc., and individuals who push hard for children's rights,[26] but the U.S. has a history of granting "rights" to adults at the expense of children. Children don't vote, to quote many a child advocate.

Civil rights groups have failed our children as well. They are adult-centered and have not championed the plight of children, unless they were vehicles for larger agendas. State civil liberties organizations often turn down children's advocates who ask for their support. For example, despite protest from children's and women's groups, the Utah Civil Rights and Liberties Foundation spearheaded a lawsuit in Utah to defend polygamy as a constitutionally protected religious practice, even in the face of widely circulated accounts of underage marriage and statutory rape.[27] They lost, but they paved the way for reality TV polygamist Kody Brown and his wives to file a lawsuit that carved back polygamy laws in Utah, which endangers women and children.[28] The decision held that there is no illegal polygamy unless the family tries to obtain two or more marriage licenses, and ignored common law marriage, which occurs when couples hold themselves out as married for a set period of years.

The ACLU supported RFRA, which worked against children's interests from the beginning, but only withdrew support for such extreme religious liberty legislation when its leadership realized it undermined the fair housing laws. The children's issues, despite being pressed by various groups earlier, in the end did not move the ACLU.

The crimes and tortious acts described in this chapter have occurred in every state – and in many countries around the world. Each victim has a unique story, so that it is impossible to generalize to a single paradigm, but pedophiles as a general matter share a modus operandi. Lanning, now retired from the FBI, testified before the Senate Judiciary Committee's Subcommittee on Juvenile Justice and described the pedophile's tactics:

> He typically nonviolently seduces children that he has befriended through the use of attention, affection and gifts. The pedophile is skilled at recognizing and then temporarily filling the emotional and physical needs of children. He is usually willing to spend as much time as it takes to seduce the targeted child.[29]

In most instances, he is a "nice guy," for the obvious reason that it furthers his schemes.[30] They seek children through various means, but the primary avenue is occupation, which permits them "to impose authority and control on the child and thus make the seduction process easier and more secure."[31]

Despite law enforcement's ability to profile pedophiles, individual clergy-abuse stories need to be told for the public to understand what has been done to children and the public good by these religious individuals and institutions who, when confronted by the law, furiously wave the First Amendment and free exercise statutes – in hopes the public will not focus on the evil. For example, after the *Boston Globe* dropped the dime on the Boston Archdiocese's practice of moving pedophile priests around parishes and unveiled two of its most notorious pedophiles – John Geoghan, who abused at least 130 children,[32] and Paul Shanley, who openly advocated the North American Man-Boy Love Association[33] – the Church tried to block discovery by claiming it had free exercise rights not to disclose its files.[34] It is a favored tactic for any religious organization that has known about the pedophiles in its ranks and failed to protect children, which is the vast majority, sadly. Sometimes they even band together to press their demands for "autonomy" from the law, like the Catholic and Mormon bishops in a case before the Nevada Supreme Court.[35]

In this arena, the attempts to fashion the First Amendment into a refuge for harmful behavior have not been widely successful: most state courts have rejected the notion that the First Amendment creates immunity from the tort laws deterring and redressing sexual assault or abuse.[36] They like to argue that the First Amendment and statutory free exercise rights like the state religious liberty statutes (or "mini-RFRAs") grant them "autonomy" from the law. In fact, they have coined their own name for a doctrine that doesn't exist: the "church autonomy doctrine." Their arguments are built on exaggerations and distortions of existing United States Supreme Court doctrine. And they are dangerous.

Whether a religious group avoids the law through the failure of prosecutors, constitutional arguments, or free exercise statutes, the end result is harm to our most vulnerable.

Childhood sex abuse is a plague on our society, and no less in the religious context. The following case studies make three points: abuse happens everywhere; it is non-denominational; and economic status is irrelevant. These cases also establish that believers too often let children suffer as they protect the adults in the organization and its reputation instead.

BROOKLYN, NEW YORK. The Satmar Hasidim Orthodox Jewish community is insular to an extreme and has hidden the truth about child sex
abuse until recently, when survivors started to break free. Under with-
ering and persistent criticism for his failure to prosecute the abusers in
the community, Brooklyn District Attorney Charles Hynes finally took
a Satmar Hasidim case to trial. The victim was an 18-year-old young
woman who a jury found was abused by Nechemya Weberman, a widely
respected member of the community and a student counselor to whom
families sent their "problem children." He groped her and forced her to
perform oral sex on him during counseling sessions from age 12 to 15. As
so often happens within tightly knit religious communities, the victim
was shunned and mistreated for telling the truth to outsiders, like law
enforcement. Until this case, Hynes had let Satmar perpetrators keep
their names out of public records, and had never brought any to trial,
despite many reports of sex abuse in the community. The Satmars also
exhibited a callous disregard for the justice system in their case. The
Jewish Week reported:

> From the moment she reported the abuse, the victim – one of several
> "wayward" girls referred to Weberman for "help" – was subjected to
> intense pressure to withdraw her claim, including intimidation, harass-
> ment, social ostracism of her family and even a reported $500,000
> bribe. Last spring, members of the Satmar community held a lavish
> fundraiser for Weberman's defense. Not long after, four men were
> arrested and charged with witness tampering in connection with the
> case. And on Nov. 29, four chasidic men were arrested for taking the
> young woman's picture – which was then posted online – as she testified
> in the courtroom.[37]

Weberman was convicted and will be in jail until he is 97 years old, and
the man who tried to bribe her boyfriend, Abraham Rubin, was sent to
jail for four months. Justice was done, but she continues to be a pariah,
which sends a loud message to other Satmar victims that they must make
a cruel choice: justice or community. This cruel choice was reinforced
when the Satmars staged a large celebration upon his release and praised
him in print as a hero.[38]

HAYWARD, CALIFORNIA. The following facts are taken from a video made
prior to trial by lawyers for a brave childhood sexual abuse victim to

document her experience so that others could learn about clergy abuse.[39] After grooming her with loving words and attention over several months, Monsignor George Francis took a five-year-old parishioner by the name of Jennifer Chapin into his room in the rectory and digitally penetrated her. He called her his "little princess." Then on weekends, he would take her to a hotel, where he ritualistically and sexually abused her. First, he taught this barely school-age child how to make manhattans, and then he tied her arms above her head and forced her legs apart so that he could fondle and rape her while he commanded her to tell him, "I love you." When he was done, he said she was "Satan's child," because she had tempted a priest. He then turned to ritualistic abuse to "purify" her by sprinkling her with holy water, inserting a scepter into her vagina, and hitting her while she was still tied to the bed.[40] Then he undressed and proceeded to rape her in a "loving style," as opposed to a ritualistic manner. He declared that if she told anyone, one of her family members would be killed by God. This ritualistic and sadistic abuse continued for five years. A neighbor who suspected abuse notified the diocese, but nothing was ever done.

As is usually the case, Chapin was not the only victim. Terrie Light was abused by Francis when she was seven years old,[41] and she claims that she has spoken to five other women, besides Chapin, who were victims of Francis.[42]

When Chapin's attorneys asked the church to release Francis's files to the public, the archdiocese refused and asserted that the First Amendment protected it from discovery in the case and that supposed privacy concerns for other victims prevented disclosure of the files. Both sides decided to forego a trial. On January 24, 2004, the Roman Catholic Church's Oakland diocese agreed to pay $3 million in damages and up to $50,000 in counseling and to add (at her request) her video to its program of educating parishioners, priests, and diocesan employees on the prevention of childhood sexual abuse.[43] Francis's files were not released at that point, but other victims are suing. Francis's files are still private; however, other archdioceses around the country have been forced to publicly release their personnel files by the courts.[44]

MIDDLETON, MASSACHUSETTS. In Massachusetts, Christopher Reardon was hired as a youth worker at the parishes of St. Agnes in Middleton and St. Rose's in Topsfield, Massachusetts. At the same time, he was hired to teach swimming at the YMCA in Danvers. During the 1990s, he abused scores of boys, aged 11 to 13, some of whom later attempted suicide, many of whom saw As and Bs on their report cards turn into failing marks, and virtually all of whom suffered extreme emotional scarring.[45] After being arrested in June 2000, Reardon pleaded guilty of 75 counts of abuse, including rape, of 24 boys, and received up to 50 years in prison for his crimes. The YMCA quickly settled the boys' claims against it; but the church held out for another year.[46] The Boston Archdiocese finally paid $85 million to settle the claims of 552 victims, including Reardon's, in September 2003.[47]

Part of the horror of the Reardon story is that it appears that St. Agnes parish priest Jon C. Martin knew about the abuse well before Reardon was arrested, and therefore could have stopped it. Victims alleged in their lawsuit that when Martin discovered two boys in Reardon's office in 1998, he simply warned Reardon that it might not look right. Even after a retired priest from St. Rose's parish contacted Martin to tell him he had seen a young boy go into Reardon's office, Martin took no action, which made it possible for Reardon to continue to commit crime after crime.[48] This has been a repetitive pattern in the United States, where the Roman Catholic Church, the Jehovah's Witnesses, Orthodox Jews, and other denominations have had evidence that one of their own was a predatory pedophile, yet they responded by ignoring the problem, ultimately endangering thousands of children.

GREENVILLE, SOUTH CAROLINA. Fundamentalist Christian Bob Jones University lost its tax-exempt status when it forbade interracial dating in 1983. Later, its policies changed on interracial dating, but its current sex abuse policies appear to be in line with other religious groups, which have erred on the side of protecting image rather than children. The school has been accused of mishandling sexual assault by employees and reports by students of abuse as children in their fundamentalist homes. Catherine Harris was told in the 1980s that if she reported her abuse to the authorities, she "was damaging the cause of Christ, and ... responsible for the abuser going to hell." A victim of sexual assault in the 1990s by a University employee was asked whether her clothing was "too tight" and that "it wouldn't look good for her" if she told anyone.[49] When stories seeped out, the university hired a Christian group to investigate abuse issues and make recommendations. Just before the report was to be issued, the university pulled the plug on it. Under public pressure, the report was re-started and should appear sometime in 2014.

ST. FRANCISVILLE, ILLINOIS. Gina Trimble Parks was a teenage girl, who in the 1970s assisted with the cleaning at the local rectory. The following are the allegations of abuse that appeared in the court's published decision. One day, while cleaning Father Raymond Kownacki's bedroom, the priest said he would show her a voodoo trick. He had her close her eyes and chant, and then he raped her. She became his sexual slave after he persuaded her parents to let him take her to a "better" school in a different parish. She was set up in the rectory with him and was required to do his sexual bidding. When she tried to break away by dating a boy her own age, and she became pregnant, Kownacki (who claimed to have had a vasectomy) became enraged and abused her physically and verbally. He gave her a dose of quinine, which he believed would cause an abortion, and then while she was unconscious, he manually aborted the fetus.

When the family sued Kownacki for what he had done to their daughter, he successfully defended himself on the ground that they had missed the statute of limitations, which was only two years long.[50] The brevity of the statutes of limitations has been a significant and persistent hurdle to clergy-abuse victims finding justice. If future children are to be protected, these statutes need to be abolished. The sad truth is that religious entities have not jumped on this bandwagon for kids. Instead, they have either been silent or, worse, lobbied to keep the statutes of limitations just as they are in order to protect their purse and their image. They have been especially effective in preventing amendment where the proposal is to make civil claims retroactive so that existing victims have some means of gaining some justice.[51]

Of course, Kownacki did not have only one victim. Other claims against him have been widely reported, and he was barred from active ministry in 1995, though not defrocked until 2013.[52] In 2003, an Illinois man who wanted to remain anonymous filed a suit against Kownacki for abusing him during a three-year period between 1979 and 1982.[53] In 2004, the diocese fought release of Kownacki's files and was fined by an Illinois Court for failure to comply with the court's order. This is typical stonewalling. However, the files were never released, because the appellate courts sided with the diocese.[54] The diocese did settle with the victim in 2011.[55]

PURCELLVILLE, VIRGINIA. Patrick Henry College was founded in 2000 as a refuge for home-schooled evangelical students. Dubbed "God's Harvard," it is rigorous and supportive of the Christian patriarchy movement, which subjugates women to being a submissive "helpmeet" to their husbands. Women are told they must guard their virginity and not tempt men, who are subject to "urges" that are "irresistible forces of nature."[56] Female students who report sexual assaults are reprimanded, shamed, and/or forced to leave. And, like the ultra-Orthodox culture, a woman who has had sex – even if it is rape – is treated as damaged goods.

UTAH, TEXAS, AND CANADA. In the late 19th century in the United States, the Church of Jesus Christ of Latter-day Saints, also known as the Mormons, practiced polygamy, which was a divine mandate. The practice was formally renounced in 1890, roughly 30 years after Congress placed a general ban on all polygamous practices.[57] Today, the mainstream Mormons do not practice polygamy, though it is featured in their views of the afterlife.[58] Various splinter sects have refused to accept the Mormons' reversal on polygamy, however, and still practice it today – despite the fact it is illegal under state and federal law.

One such group, the FLDS, is currently led by Warren Jeffs, who is the prophet and president and who rules the sect with complete authority, even from jail. Despite Jeffs' sentence to life in prison in 2011,[59] he is still believed to be sending spiritual directives to his followers.[60]

His nephew, Brent Jeffs, filed suit against the prophet and the FLDS for compensatory and punitive damages alleging that when Brent was between the ages of four and six, Warren Jeffs and his brothers Leslie and Blaine Jeffs took Brent out of Sunday School, into a lavatory, and sodomized him. They allegedly told him that the abuse was "God's work," done so that he would "become a man," and told him he would suffer "eternal damnation" if he ever told anyone.[61] Brent allegedly was regularly passed around between the men during these sessions.[62] Although the leadership of the church knew about the abuse for years, the complaint alleged the leadership did nothing to stop it.[63] The case was dismissed when Brent withdrew it.[64]

The FLDS was in the news in 2008 when Texas authorities raided their Yearning for Zion Ranch, and discovered girls who appeared to be pregnant, records of underage marriages, and a bed in the sanctuary.[65] The authorities prosecuted and convicted eleven men, including Warren Jeffs.[66] Throughout the proceedings, their lawyers argued that the prosecutions were "anti-religious" and were in violation of their constitutional rights. This is the kind of discourse we, as a culture, have encouraged. It is dangerous when courts listen. While the men were convicted, the Texas Supreme Court, seemingly bowing to their religious character, ordered the children to be returned to their families despite credible allegations of statutory rape and underage marriage and pregnancy.[67]

The local authorities in Bountiful, Canada, entered into a pact with the FLDS in the early 1990s entitled the Child Protection Protocol Agreement.[68] It allegedly provided that any child-abuse allegations would have to be screened by sect leader Rulon Jeffs (Warren's now-deceased father) and his successor, Winston Blackmore, before local authorities would have to be contacted, and the elders held the power to decide whether to report the alleged child abuse. As one might have expected, there have been no reports. As with other sexual misconduct within religious institutions, the rule in Bountiful apparently has been silence. One person testified before the Hansard Legislative Assembly, "[S]ilence is the code word in Bountiful. No one, under fear of harm, is allowed to talk. The kids are taught to keep quiet; the women are taught to keep quiet."[69] They must "keep sweet," which is to say submissive to the men. This is part and parcel of the "patriarchal principle," which the Supreme Court noted when it upheld the anti-polygamy law in *Reynolds v. United States*.

The FLDS was not the only entity to maintain silence on the issue, however. For decades, the government in British Columbia paid little heed to the complaints by women who had escaped from Bountiful. There appears to have been some misguided thinking that the community's violation of the laws was protected by the constitutional right to the free exercise of religion.[70] In 2004, a number of women filed allegations with the British Columbia Human Rights Tribunal, charging the government with permitting "massive contraventions of females' and children's human rights... which reduce women and children to chattel status and oppress their lives, [and which] prevent Bountiful's women and children from participating fully in Canada's economic and social life, as is their right."[71] The complaint describes the fate of one Deborah Palmer, who was in the commune between 1957 and 1988. At 15, she was given to Roy Blackmore, 57, to be his sixth wife, or "concubine," in the terms of the complaint, and later to two more husbands. She eventually escaped with her eight children. Given the alleged inbreeding within Bountiful, she is stepmother, sister-in-law, and niece all to the same man, Winston Blackmore. Women are taught to obey the men, or "their souls will burn for all eternity in Hell," and that their life's purpose is to assist the men in reaching "godhood," which is attained if the man has many concubines. Merrill Palmer, who is the principal of the Bountiful Elementary-Secondary School; James Oler, the current bishop of Bountiful; Winston Blackmore, the former bishop of Bountiful; and the Ministries of the Attorney-General and Education were the named defendants. Seven women who escaped Bountiful are allegedly willing to come forward, but only if they are protected by complete anonymity from the FLDS's practice of "blood atonement," which their complaint alleges is violence against those who dare to challenge the sect.[72] In a turnaround from the government's previous permissive stance toward Bountiful, the tribunal agreed to hear the case and it is pending.[73] In the most recent legal ruling involving the group, in 2011, the British Columbia Supreme Court upheld Canada's law banning polygamy.

COLORADO CITY, ARIZONA, AND HILDALE, UTAH. Another arm of the FLDS organization has established an enclave in the border cities of Colorado City, Arizona, and Hildale, Utah, where the church need not worry about the fact that child abuse and polygamy violate state law, because local law enforcement belong to the church and acquiesce in the violations.[74] The complete disregard for state and federal law and the arrogation of the right to make and enforce its own law is about as anarchical as an organization can get. These groups are discussed in further detail in Chapter 3. The FLDS's attitude, though, is only a more extreme version of the pervasive belief held by some in the United States that religion is above the law. The federal government is taking action, however.

The U.S. Department of Justice filed a complaint against Colorado City and Hildale in June 2012, alleging that by acquiescing to the influence of the FLDS Church in the areas of law enforcement, housing, and access to public facilities, and discriminating against non-FLDS residents, the two areas and agencies under their control violated the First, Fourth, and Fourteenth Amendments to the United States Constitution, as well as the Fair Housing Act and Title III of the Civil Rights Act of 1964.[75] The lawsuit is currently pending.

WOODLAND, CALIFORNIA. For those not familiar with the Jehovah's Witnesses, they are the individuals who are seen handing out the *Watchtower* publication in public places. They are a closely-knit organization. Here is how one member explained the group on national television:

> [A]s a Jehovah's Witness, you associate only with members in good standing. And that leaves you in a position where everybody you know, everybody you trust, everybody you've ever known or trusted, is somebody who's inside that organization. The threat of being thrown out of that and shunned from them is one powerful enough [to keep victims of abuse silent when told to do so by the organization].[76]

The organization has observed a rule that no charge of abuse would be believed unless there were two eyewitness accounts,[77] a standard that is usually impossible to satisfy when the crime is adult-on-child sexual abuse (or any sex assault scenario).

Daniel West and two others alleged that Timothy Silva, a leader of a Jehovah's Witnesses "adolescent book studies," sexually abused them. By the time the three alleged victims were ready to file charges, the criminal and civil statute of limitations had long since expired. Fortunately, they were able to take advantage of California's one-year window during 2003 that repealed the statute of limitations for civil actions involving childhood sexual abuse, no matter when the abuse occurred.[78] According to the complaint, West was 13 years old when the molestation occurred, and while the church knew about it, it did nothing and did not notify the authorities. Indeed, the church appears to have taken the offensive and accused him of "participating in homosexual activity."

Another one of Silva's alleged victims, Shane Pence, claimed to have been sexually attacked for five years, starting at the tender age of seven. When his mother reported the abuse to the church, the family was warned not to contact the authorities and assured that the church would deal with the issue. The church, in a fashion prototypical of other churches in these cases, did not notify the police, according to the complaint.

The same pattern was evident in the abuse cases of Heidi Meyer and Amber Long, who told television reporter Connie Chung that the Witnesses threatened "excommunication," or as they call it, "disfellowship," if they told the police about the abuse they suffered.[79]

When Meyer filed suit, the congregation and Watchtower, the Witnesses' parent organization, raised the First Amendment as a defense, and the court ruled in their favor. Employing reasoning that is indefensible in an ordered society, the court ruled misguidedly that neither the congregation nor Watchtower had a duty to protect the children, because they had "acted within their constitutional right to religious freedom, which includes the authority to 'independently decide matters of faith and doctrine' and 'to believe and speak what it will.'"[80] A church does have a right to speak and believe at will, but it has no right to use those beliefs to justify endangering children. In effect, this reading of the First Amendment immunizes actions that display callous disregard for society's most important norms.

One former Jehovah's Witnesses elder is Bill Bowen, who now runs www.silentlambs.org, a website to assist victims of childhood sexual abuse within the organization. He says there is a pattern in the abuse cases: when victims went to the elders, they were told to keep the abuse secret, and the abusers were permitted to remain in the fold.[81] Sometimes the girls reporting the abuse were banished from their close-knit congregations and denied contact with fellow members thereafter.[82] Those outside the Witnesses' world are considered part of Satan's world, so these girls were thrown into a society they had been taught is evil and debased.[83] Despite the lurid facts involving defenseless children, the Witnesses typically argue that the institution has a First Amendment right to avoid criminal and civil liability. Religious defendants in Maine,[84] Connecticut,[85] and Tennessee have persuaded courts that applying neutral principles of law to their actions would require them to inquire into the defendants' beliefs and, therefore, victims lose. They have also won the right, purportedly under the First Amendment, to shun disfavored members.[86]

I will explain in Part Two how erroneous this reasoning is, but suffice it to say, the courts that have reached these conclusions have felt that they were backed into a corner by the reality of the harm and a misunderstanding of free exercise guarantees. The Supreme Judicial Court of Maine clearly stated that it understood the "enormity" of the harm done to children where sexual abuse is "inflicted in the context of religious activities," and then provided a rote recitation of the principle that judicial examination of a religious organization's conduct is "wholly forbidden by the Free Exercise Clause of the First Amendment."[87] The good news is that an increasing majority of the state courts contemplating the weighty evidence of massive misconduct by religious institutions has figured out that the First Amendment is not a haven for scoundrels, but rather consistent with the rule of law and the rule of no harm.[88]

SPRINGFIELD, MISSOURI. A Roman Catholic Church priest, Rev. Michael Brewer, hosted Michael Gibson and a friend for a sleepover to watch movies in the rectory. Michael alleged that, at some point in the morning, Brewer fondled him sexually. When Michael's parents contacted the diocese to complain, they were allegedly told "this happens to young men all the time." The diocesan authorities added that Michael "would get over it," and suggested the Gibsons work it out with Brewer themselves. When they heard about other boys suffering the same treatment from Brewer, and complained again, the diocese told them that Brewer had done no more than give Michael "an innocent pat on the butt," that they should "forgive and forget," and that they should move on. The Gibsons filed a lawsuit against Brewer and the diocese that cited nine neutral principles of law that would have been invoked and applied to the defendants were they a teacher who fondled a child and a school that knowingly placed children in the reach of a pedophile: "battery, negligent hiring/ordination/retention, negligent failure to supervise, negligent infliction of emotional distress, intentional infliction of emotional distress, breach of fiduciary duty, conspiracy, agency liability, and independent negligence of the Diocese."[89] The defendants denied the allegations and sought the protection of the First Amendment.

In one of the more extreme and unfortunate decisions in the country, the Missouri Supreme Court, en banc, held that the First Amendment immunized the institution from negligent hiring, ordination, retention, and supervision liability. According to the court, the action could not go forward, because the courts were not permitted to "[a]djudicat[e] the reasonableness of a church's supervision of a cleric – [because it] would create an excessive entanglement, inhibit religion, and result in the endorsement of one model of supervision."[90] Thus, a religious institution was relieved of significant civil liability for negligent hiring, retaining and covering for a pedophile on the basis of supposed First Amendment principles. Only the intentional tort claims could be pursued against the institution, which are typically nearly impossible to prove in a clergy sex abuse case.

The unanimous decision was written by Chief Justice William Duane Benton and joined by Judges Stephen N. Limbaugh, Jr. (cousin of conservative radio personality Rush Limbaugh), Edward D. Robertson, Jr., Ann K. Covington, Ronnie L. White, John C. Holstein, and Senior Judge Flanigan. The *Gibson* case still stands and has blocked many victims from achieving justice in Missouri.

POCONO MOUNTAINS, PENNSYLVANIA. David Chaifetz attended the all-boys summer camp, Camp Dora Golding, where a 28-year-old rabbi sexually abused him repeatedly when he was 13 years old. When he told the camp directors, they sent him home, where his parents had no reaction, and his perpetrator was not charged, but rather had a long career in education. When he later disclosed the abuse to his yeshiva high school principal, he was told, "No, Duvid, he could not have been a rabbi. Rabbis never do such things."[91] His experience is a prime example of the tendency among religious institutions to pay more attention to their public reputations, and to hold fast to the belief that clergy do no wrong, while ignoring the needs of children. In David's words, "I listen to the voices in the ultra-Orthodox community citing mesirah – the notion that one Jew cannot hand over another Jew to the non-Jewish authorities – a remnant of medieval fear of hostile gentile governments."[92] For the Catholic Church for centuries, the principle was not "mesirah," but rather a rule against "scandal."[93]

PORTLAND, OREGON. Franklin Richard Curtis was an 87-year-old high priest of the Church of Jesus Christ of Latter-day Saints when he allegedly sexually abused Jeremiah Scott in 1990 and 1991. Scott was 11 years old at the time, which yields a 76-year difference between the two. Scott sued the church in 2001, alleging that the church knew that Curtis had abused a minimum of five other children in one ward but had not warned anyone.[94] Nor were the police notified, according to the complaint. In another ward, the bishop also allegedly knew of Curtis's pedophilic tendencies, but remained silent, because Curtis repented. The worst part of the story is next: the complaint alleges that when Curtis asked to live with a family during his last days, Jeremiah's mother, Sandra Scott, offered her home, and the bishop who knew Curtis's past told her only that it was not a good idea – not that she was bringing a pedophile into her home. Because of a shortage of bed space, Curtis ended up sleeping in Scott's bed with him, and for six months, Curtis allegedly abused Scott on a nightly basis.

The court hearing Scott's case ordered the church to produce any and all records involving childhood sexual abuse in its files. In what reads like a scripted response by a U.S. religious organization to claims of internal childhood sexual abuse, the church declared it had a First Amendment right to keep its records secret. Before it had to produce the records, the church settled the case for $3 million. The church's lawyer, Von G. Keetch, declared that the case "lacked merit" and the settlement reflected only a desire to end costly litigation.[95] One can only wonder at the temerity of religious institutions that have been accused of such specific crimes and torts yet insist they are settling individual *nuisance* suits for millions of dollars.

SALT LAKE CITY, UTAH. Lynette Earl Franco was allegedly abused in 1986 when she was 7 years old by a 14-year-old boy. They were both members of the same local ward of the Church of Jesus Christ of Latter-day Saints. For seven years, she repressed the memory, but when she reached her teens, she needed counseling. She and her parents sought assistance from the local ward, where they were allegedly told to "forgive, forget, and seek Atonement." When they asked for a referral to a mental health professional, the parents claim their local bishop, Dennis Casaday, and president, David Christensen, suggested a "doctor," whose business card included the phrases, "Individual, Marital, and Family Counseling" and "General Psychiatry." The problem with the doctor, according to the Francos, was that he was not a licensed psychiatrist, and his advice to

Lynette and her parents was to forgive the perpetrator, forget the incidents, and avoid going to the police. When they independently found a mental health professional, that person reported the sexual abuse to the police, after which their fellow Mormons "ostracized and denigrated" Lynette. They left the Church, and then sued it, Casaday, Christensen, and Browning (along with the Bountiful Health Center where he "practices") for clerical malpractice, gross negligence, negligent infliction of emotional distress, breach of fiduciary duty, intentional infliction of emotional distress, and fraud.[96]

The church and other defendants won on all theories. The Supreme Court of the State of Utah found that the first three claims were barred by the First Amendment's Establishment Clause, on the theory that it would have required the court to delve into LDS beliefs. The court was right that clerical malpractice is not a legitimate theory, because it invites the courts to determine the standards of care for a clergy member of a particular faith. Courts are not allowed to determine or set beliefs within a religious organization, and clerical malpractice is too close for comfort under the First Amendment. On the other theories, however, the court's reasoning was plain wrong. The court read the various negligence theories as duplications of the clergy malpractice claim, but that is a fundamental misunderstanding of the law. Clerical malpractice claims would force the courts to ask what the religious entity would have its clergy do, but negligence requires a determination of what the "reasonable person" in the circumstances would do. If the person acts unreasonably and has a duty to act reasonably, he or she is liable for damages. The reasonable person here would not have aided in perpetrating a fraud against a vulnerable sex-abuse victim. At least one hopes that is true! The court would not have needed to determine the church's beliefs to reach a negligence holding, but rather would have had to apply neutral principles to factual action, regardless of motivation.

The court also rejected the other claims, because the defendants' actions were not sufficiently "outrageous," and because the complaint failed to allege that Casaday and Christensen knew that Browning was not a licensed psychiatrist. Not every state would have ruled the same way, but the moral of this case is "believer beware." Some courts will bend over backward to make sure the religious are protected from accountability for their bad actions.

NEW YORK, NEW YORK. This is a classic case of pedophilic behavior by a trusted clergy member – where the law worked as it should. Seventh Day Adventist pastor Brian N. Savage was charged with aggravated criminal sodomy, two counts of criminal sodomy, two counts of aggravated indecent solicitation of a child, and aggravated indecent liberties with a child for the sexual crimes he committed against a 13-year-old boy, whom he had groomed to be his victim. At the time of the molestation, Savage was 44, and the victim was one of his parishioners. Savage was friendly with the victim and began to take on a fatherly demeanor with him. They emailed each other, with Savage writing, "You are like a son to me," and signing off, "Love, Dad." In the midst of this love and affection, he sodomized the boy. Some of the sexual abuse occurred in the church. He pled guilty and was sentenced to 200 months, or roughly 16.6 years, in prison.[97] Of course, there were other victims. For those victims, Savage pled guilty and was sentenced to an additional five years.[98]

VIRGINIA, MARYLAND, PENNSYLVANIA. The most dangerous and abundant pedophiles are not the "Stranger Danger" many of today's adults were warned about as children, but rather "nice" guys who know how to operate at a child's level. Religious pedophiles, like all pedophiles, exploit whatever pathways they can to obtain victims, and the Internet is a favored path. In this case, a Seventh-day Adventist pastor, Barry William Katzer, lured a Virginia boy to meet him in person after spending four weeks conversing with him in an Internet chat room. Katzer picked up the boy and took him to a Maryland motel, where he sexually abused the boy amidst pornographic magazines and tapes.[99] Only an anonymous call to the police about suspicious activity at the hotel stopped the abuse. Katzer was sentenced to 11 months in jail after admitting he had sex with the boy.[100] Every abused child should have such a guardian angel.

There has not yet been a religious organization that has defended internal childhood sexual abuse on the ground that it believed in such abuse, though there are some that could, like the cult, the Children of God.[101] Rather, these cases have been about adults misusing their positions of authority to prey on trusting children and religious institutions turning a blind eye to heinous crimes, immoral actions, and the victims' deforming pain. There is no good argument to treat either the perpetrators or their institutional aides and abettors any differently than any other entity harming children. The First Amendment was never intended to foster social irresponsibility by religious institutions. In fact, the framing generation rejected religious liberty for "licentiousness."

Religious organizations will go far to avoid responsibility for
the sexual abuse of children by clergy

The abuses by individual clergy in religious organizations are evil; the persistent cover ups by religious organizations, which empowered clergy pedophiles to get ever more victims, is worse; but the Roman Catholic hierarchy's lobbying against access to justice for all child sex abuse victims is about as cynical as it gets. Religious groups lobby as much or more than corporations in the United States, and the Conference of Catholic Bishops in each state legislature is a part of the lobbying woodwork. They chime in on a wide variety of issues, but in recent years have spent millions lobbying to ensure that the states do not increase or eliminate the statutes of limitations for child sex abuse victims. Their goal is to keep their still well-kept secrets from the public, and to avoid their responsibility for the suffering of these victims. I have written extensively on the issue including *Justice Denied: What America Must Do to Protect Its Children*[102] and so will not belabor it here, but it is one of those facts that proves that religious groups are active lobbyists and have agendas that hurt the vulnerable.

The medical neglect cases discussed next involve defenseless children and parents who choose faith over health. In these cases, children sometimes die of untreated medical ailments, but the parents defend themselves on the ground that their actions were compelled by their belief in prayer over modern medicine. The question is posed whether parents can make martyrs of their children.

Medical issues

Parents have a legal obligation to protect their children's health. Sometimes, however, they decide not to for religious reasons.

VACCINATION EXEMPTIONS. One of the most remarkable advancements in human health in the twentieth century was the near eradication of many serious childhood illnesses through immunization. In order for vaccinations to protect the larger society, it must achieve what is called "herd immunity," which means a large percentage need to have been vaccinated to effectively eliminate the illness. Most states have enacted exemptions from the general vaccination requirement for parents who object on religious grounds.

These religious exemptions have been exploited by misguided parents, leading to a reduction in herd immunity. At one point vaccinations contained mercury, to which some children were allergic and which can be a dangerous chemical. Parents invoked the exemption to avoid the mercury. But then mercury was removed from vaccinations, except for trace amounts. Then some parents claimed that there was a link between vaccinations and autism, a claim firmly rejected by the medical establishment. Again, parents lined up for the exemptions. Whether the exemptions are religious or not, they threaten not only the unvaccinated children, but also the ill or disabled who could not be immunized, and also the general population.

The result has been a new era of childhood illnesses reappearing. According to a December 2013 report from the Center for Disease Control and Prevention (CDC), over 175 cases of measles were documented that year – the highest number in seventeen years.[103] By 2014, there were more measles cases nationwide than the last twenty years.

Exemptions for religious use endanger adults and children. In 2013, twenty-one members of a Texas anti-vaccine megachurch – including children – contracted measles. None of the children had been vaccinated.[104]

School districts trying to cope with such outbreaks have been forced to send unvaccinated students home once outbreaks start for the duration of the risk of contagion, or risk contracting and spreading potentially deadly diseases. Those families have complained, claiming that this type of policy singles out their children, and denies them the right to an education because of religious beliefs.[105]

The vaccination problem highlights how religious exemptions can spur claims for nonreligious exemptions, and a breakdown in the purposes of the law in the first place. Parents who unfortunately bought into the autism hype around vaccinations and saw that religious parents were obtaining exemptions demanded the same for themselves. In free exercise cases, religious believers routinely argue that if a law has any exceptions and no exception for religious reasons, that they should get the benefit of the exception, too. It works the other way, too. If there is a religious exemption, it is hard to argue that exemptions undermine the law, and so how about some other exemptions, e.g., philosophical or moral ones. This reasoning is particularly dangerous when it comes to vaccinations against potentially deadly diseases. In order to have the benefit of herd immunity, which is needed to eliminate the disease, a large percentage of people must receive the vaccine. By granting religious exemptions in the first place, herd immunity was potentially affected. It is definitely affected when it is expanded. In truth, there is no constitutional right to immunization exemptions. If the unvaccinated numbers continue to grow, states will legitimately have to consider whether even the religious exemption is safe public policy.[106]

FEMALE GENITAL MUTILATION, OR FEMALE CIRCUMCISION. While President Clinton is responsible for the misguided RFRA and RLUIPA, which endanger the vulnerable, he did sign a 1996 law that limited a religious practice to the benefit of potential victims. That practice is female genital mutilation (FGM). FGM is observed in and around Muslim communities. Some scholars argue it is not mandated by the Muslim faith, but a number of African and Middle Eastern Muslim communities believe it is. It is also observed by Christian Copts in Egypt and Sudan, and a few other groups. The practice requires the cutting or removal of the woman's external genitalia, labia and/or clitoris, and at its most extreme, the sewing together of the vulva. The purpose is to reduce the pleasure women have during sex and to forestall infidelity.

With its large Muslim population, France has worked assiduously to end the practice, though England has not, which means numerous French girls are taken to Britain for the procedure. While the United States bars FGM within its borders, there is no federal law yet that punishes parents for taking their daughters to their countries of origin for FGM. Bills to deter the transport of girls for FGM have been introduced since 2010, but have not yet passed, which means girls who do not receive an illegal FGM here may still be transported to another country. FGM is usually performed without anesthesia, and often results in infection and persistent and recurring pain.

MEDICAL NEGLECT. Religions like the First Church of Christ, Scientist, commonly known as Christian Science, that rely on faith rather than medicine to cure illness have obtained a number of exemptions in the states from laws that normally protect children. For example, all states except Mississippi and West Virginia permit parents to refuse to vaccinate their children on religious grounds.[107] Many have exemptions from newborn testing.[108] There are also many exemptions from the requirement of providing medical care to a sick child.

The federal government is partly at fault for the many state exemptions permitting the medical neglect of children. From 1974 to 1983, the states were required to enact such exemptions to qualify for federal funding related to children.[109] This federal law was the result of Christian Scientists in positions of power in the Nixon Administration. In other words, the states would not receive federal funding unless they instituted exemptions. It was a classic carrot-and-stick approach, and roughly 30 states plus the District of Columbia now have exemptions for religious parents from the medical neglect laws. In effect, this means that faith-healing parents need not obtain medical care for their children unless the children are near death or permanent disability,[110] and even then, in some states, the parents may be immunized from manslaughter or felonious murder charges. From the children's perspective, the harm is even more imminent than it would be if the parents were acting out of secular motivation, because in too many circumstances, the parents either do not recognize serious illness and imminent death, or they hold the misguided belief that they should not be subject to the law. Whether they see imminent harm or state interference, they may be motivated to hide their extremely ill children from the authorities whose job it is to ensure that children do not die or suffer permanent disability from medical neglect. The result is suffering, unnecessary death, and the martyrdom of children who have not been permitted to reach adulthood when they could make an informed choice to live or die for their religious beliefs.

Some may argue that parents have a right to teach their children any religious belief they choose, and they would be correct. But parents do not have an unfettered right to act in ways that harm their children, even if they are acting on religious beliefs. It is now well settled that religious motivation is no defense to illegal conduct. In addition, the

Supreme Court has explained that children have rights independent of their parents:

> Parents may be free to become martyrs themselves. But it does not follow that they are free, in identical circumstances, to make martyrs of their children before they have reached the age of full legal discretion when they can make that choice for themselves.[111]

Justice Douglas in *Yoder* echoed this concept, pointing out that the Amish children should be allowed to object to their parents' decision to take them out of school before they were 16. For those children that would not choose the agrarian Amish way of life, that decision makes them a martyr to their parents' faith. The preeminent right is the right to live, so the exemptions do raise some interesting constitutional questions whether a child might well have a constitutional (as well as a statutory) right to receive medical treatment despite the parents' beliefs. At the very least, the Constitution does not prohibit the states from mandating medical treatment for seriously ill children of faith-healing parents. The religious entities' capacity to avoid the child-welfare laws is derived from their political power and moxie, not any constitutional right.

Despite the value normally placed on life in this society, and the many laws that deter individuals from causing or permitting others to die, states frequently provide religious exemptions when the victim is a child. While abortion has the attention of the American public, deaths of children arising from religiously motivated conduct have not galvanized the people. The problem is education. Few – other than those who benefit and the legislators that grant the exemption – know about or understand the exemptions or their consequences. Yet, exemptions for medical neglect are pervasive. At this time, thirty-eight states and the District of Columbia have religious exemptions for civil claims of medical neglect, fifteen states for criminal misdemeanors, and seventeen states for felonious medical neglect.[112] To be clear, these exemptions are not benign grants of religious liberty with no victims. They mean that religious parents and caretakers may not be charged with the crimes specified when they withheld readily available medical treatment from their child. The exemptions erase the deterrence function of the criminal laws and enable devout adult believers who would martyr their children to be a serious risk to children. They also send a message that it is acceptable to let one's child die, if the death is for religious reasons, which is to say, the child's life is not all that valuable. These exemptions are particularly ironic in states with strong anti-abortion measures. It is a familiar lament among children's advocates that many in the United States value a fetus's right to live more than a child's.

The Christian Scientists have put significant pressure on state and federal legislatures for the purpose of obtaining the many exemptions from the medical neglect laws,[113] although they are not the only religious entity that benefits.[114] Their most recent coup is an exemption from health insurance in the Affordable Care Act.[115] Christian Science theology teaches that modern medicine is unnecessary, because "[h]ealth is not a condition of matter, but of Mind," and that illness is evidence of sin that needs to be treated by prayer.[116] Yet, Christian Science leaders claim that their theology does not prohibit medical care, which implies that believers have a choice between medical care and prayer alone.[117] Indeed, when challenged, they defend their faith by saying that prayer is not the only option, just the "preferred option." For example, a teenage girl had a broken ankle and was asked by her parents what she "wanted to do – pray or go to a hospital. [She] felt prayer was reliable."[118]

If one follows the logic of this supposed choice, it also seems to imply that deaths by medical neglect are not the responsibility of the church.[119] The Church can and will say the parents had a choice. Yet, the failure to rely on prayer alone is looked upon as a serious spiritual failing, and Christian Science practitioners often chide worried parents not to give into the temptation to obtain medical attention and to pray more fervently, which translates into a message that those who face the most dire medical emergencies are holier if they avoid medical treatment and that those who seek treatment are less devout.[120] An editor of the *Christian Science Sentinel* wrote that the "most impressive and persuasive ways [to show their children God loved them] often had to do with turning to God for *healthcare*. Children remember being healed, thanks to prayer alone, of children's diseases, organic problems, hernia, mononucleosis, serious sports injuries."[121] In Mary Baker Eddy's words, "The habitual struggle to be always good is unceasing prayer,"[122] a sentiment that has been translated by contemporary Christian Scientists to mean that "[d]isease really has mental roots. If you go to the root of the problem in thought – and fear is usually a factor – you'll eliminate it."[123]

Christian Scientists support, train, and provide faith-healing caretakers to offer end-of-life care. These caretakers are deemed "practitioners" and "nurses," although they may have no medical training, and if they do, must renounce it.[124] Christian Science treatment centers are in fact hospices where no medical science is practiced and no pain medication is provided, but minimal bodily needs are tended to as the patient expires.[125] They are supported in no small part through Medicare funding.

Historically, Christian Scientists have put a great deal of effort into seeking exemptions from federal and state laws that would otherwise hold faith-healing parents accountable for harm done to their children.[126] They lobbied and argued in favor of the federal regulation that led states to enact medical neglect exemptions in order to obtain federal aid.[127] They also have been active in state legislatures.[128] At least one of their former members is trying to put a stop to the Christian Scientists' efforts. Rita Swan, a former Christian Scientist whose 16-month-old son, Matthew, died of spinal meningitis as a result of religiously motivated medical neglect, works tirelessly to protect children from faith-healing. She and Seth Asser, M.D. (Dept. of Pediatrics at U.C.S.D. School of Med.), co-wrote an article detailing the deaths of more than 200 children from medical neglect during the years 1975–95.[129]

When a child dies of a treatable medical ailment resulting from faith-healing, practitioners (and churches) often raise a First Amendment defense, even to criminal charges. There are two legal regimes governing medical neglect across the states – those that treat religious parents like other citizens, and hold them accountable, and those that exempt the faith-healing parent or church and therefore make them unaccountable for the harm they inflict on an untreated, ill child. The first illustrates the principles of the rule of law and the no-harm principle I will develop in Part Two. The second showcases overzealous state legislatures that have confused liberty with lawlessness and sacrificed children on the altar of religious anarchy.

The Christian Scientists are the most well-known opponents of medical care, but others also endanger their children.

NEW YORK, NEW YORK. Sometimes medical neglect occurs, because the prosecutors simply look the other way. Orthodox Jews celebrate the birth of a male infant with a bris, a ceremony where a mohel performs a ritual circumcision on the infant. Most Orthodox Jews celebrate the bris in ways that do not endanger the child. Some ultra-Orthodox sects, however, have adopted a practice that has resulted in infant deaths and disability. The practice is to perform the circumcision and then the mohel sucks the blood off of the infant boy's penis with his mouth. Sadly, infants have died or suffered permanent brain damage because the mohel transmitted the herpes simplex virus through the oral-genital contact. Others have contracted the virus and suffer painful lesions on their penises. There is no cure.

This is a practice that is beyond tolerable in a civilized society purportedly protecting the health of children, but for political reasons, the New York City Health Department has failed to take action against it. Under Mayor Michael Bloomberg, the Health Department instituted a requirement that parents must give informed consent before a mohel can perform the circumcision. What should be happening is that these parents and mohels performing this procedure should be subjected to criminal charges, as others would be if they were not engaged in a religious ritual.

WESTON, WISCONSIN. Kara Neumann died in 2008 of untreated diabetes after her parents, who were members of an internet-based faith-healing group, shunned medical treatment in favor of prayer for 3 weeks prior to her death. Kara's initial symptoms included dehydration, weakness, and exhaustion, and gradually worsened to the point that Kara could not eat, drink, stand, or control her bladder. Throughout the time that Kara experienced these symptoms, her parents, Dale and Leilani Neumann, avoided medical treatment for her in reliance on their belief that sickness has spiritual root causes and prayer will remedy any health ailments. After Kara's death, the Neumanns were arrested and charged with second-degree homicide.[130] The emergency doctor at the hospital testified that Kara's condition was treatable even on the day of her death, and the trial court found each of them guilty, sentencing them both to 25 years in prison. The Supreme Court of Wisconsin upheld the convictions, and found that by failing to request medical treatment for Kara in the hours before her death, her parents were responsible for her death.[131] Kara literally died for her parents' faith.

OREGON CITY, OREGON. Oregon, beginning in 1995, exempted faith-healing parents from its criminal laws, which is to say religiously

motivated parents could raise an affirmative defense to criminal liability simply by proving their belief in prayer alone to heal.[132] In 1997
and 1998, the Followers of Christ Church in Oregon City, Oregon,
allowed three children to die of medical neglect. During the subsequent
investigation, authorities discovered a cemetery of 78 children, and the
alarm bells began to ring. Medical authorities estimated that 21 of the
deceased children could have been saved by routine medical care, and
38 died before their first birthday.[133] Prosecutors were determined to convict those responsible for the infant deaths, but were stymied by Oregon
law that allowed individuals who let their children die as a result of their
religious beliefs to use their faith as a defense in homicide and child
abuse prosecutions.[134] "It is an affirmative defense to a charge of [crim-
inal homicide by neglect or maltreatment] that the child or dependent
person was under care or treatment solely by spiritual means pursuant to
the religious beliefs or practices of the child or person or the parent or
guardian of the child or person."[135] Prosecutors, and the public, were outraged. Children were dying for no good reason. As a result of lobbying
efforts from 1999 to 2011, advocates were successfully able to repeal the
Oregon legislation granting the religious exemptions related to medical
care of sick children.[136]

Cases prior to the full repeal of the medical neglect exemptions in 2011
confirmed the need to do more to protect children from their parents'
religious beliefs. In March 2008, a 15-month-old named Ava Worthington
died of bacterial pneumonia in Oregon City[137] after her parents withheld
medical care from her based on their spiritual beliefs, which were The
Followers of Christ Church.[138] Although Ava's father, Carl Worthington,
was convicted of a lesser charge of criminal mistreatment with a jail
sentence of 60 days,[139] both Carl and his wife Raylene were acquitted
of the more serious manslaughter charges against them.[140] The family's
beliefs were on trial for a second time when Ava's grandparents, Jeffrey
and Marci Beagley (who had been present at Ava's death), let their 16-year-
old son Neil's urinary tract obstruction go untreated, causing his death.
After a two-week trial, Neil's parents were found guilty of criminally
negligent homicide, and sentenced to sixteen months in prison.[141] The
Oregon Court of Appeals affirmed the decision in June 2013.[142]

In June 2011, another Oregon couple, Timothy and Rebecca Wyland,
was convicted of first-degree criminal mistreatment of their six-month-old

daughter Alayna. Alayna suffered from a benign tumor called a hemangioma that grew to the size of a baseball on her face, pushing her eyeball out of its socket. Alayna was removed from her parents' care and placed in foster care by the state.[143] And in September 2011, Followers of Christ Church members, Dale and Shannon Hickman, were found guilty of second-degree manslaughter by a jury and sentenced to 6 years and 3 months in prison for the 2009 death of their infant David. David died of staph pneumonia after living for only 9 hours. Expert witnesses testified that had David been taken to the hospital after he turned gray and showed difficulty in breathing, he likely would have survived.[144] Taking these four cases together, three children died needlessly and their parents were sentenced to a grand total of seven years and nine months. That is a travesty.

Despite the end of the criminal liability exemptions in 2011, it would be too much to say that Oregon's children are fully protected from faith-healing parents. Oregon law "still allows religious exemptions for immunizations, metabolic screening (for conditions like PKU), newborn hearing screening, vitamin K and prophylactic eye drops for newborns, and bicycle helmets. Ashland, Oregon has the highest school vaccine exemption rate of any US city; and in one school in Eugene, 76% of students had rejected one or more vaccines for religious reasons."[145]

IDAHO. Even with the history of child deaths in Oregon, and the deaths of several Followers' children in Idaho since 2009, the Idaho state legislature recently could not bring itself to protect its children from death by faith-healing parents. One 15-year-old girl died of food poisoning after her esophagus collapsed following prolonged vomiting. Other children, from babies to teens, died of pneumonia. For obvious reasons, Idaho Rep. John Gannon introduced a bill based on Oregon's, which would have scaled back the religious defenses to the death of a child. Because of other members' concerns that such a bill would restrict the religious liberty of the parents, the bill was shelved.[146] Another travesty.

SACRAMENTO, CALIFORNIA. In contrast, California legislation places religious parents and caretakers on a level playing field with all others who commit manslaughter. Laurie Grouard Walker, a Christian Scientist, treated her four-year-old daughter for bacterial meningitis solely with prayer, and the child died. When the Sacramento District Attorney's Office filed criminal charges against the mother, she argued that she was "absolutely protected" from criminal liability by the religion clauses of the federal and California constitutions. The mother and the church (which was not a defendant, but filed a friend-of-the-court brief in support of the mother) also claimed that the court must consider the least restrictive alternative for punishing her. They argued that criminal liability was too burdensome on religious belief and that civil dependency proceedings would further the government's interest in a way that was less burdensome on the mother's religious beliefs. In other words, the mother argued that she need not be criminally liable for the preventable death of a child, because the death was a result of religiously motivated conduct, and that civil penalties would be sufficient. The sole frame of reference was supposed to be the adult believer's faith, rather than the best interests of the child. The court rejected these arguments, because the interest in deterring the death of children was so high, and held that there is no less restrictive or more effective way to deter parents from letting their children die.[147] Even so, the mother reached an agreement with the district attorney that amounted to no jail time, less than five years' probation, a $300 fine, and community service. In addition, her teenage daughter was to be permitted to choose between her mother's beliefs and modern medical science.[148] Considering she permitted a child to die, the failure to sentence this mother to any jail time is troubling,[149] but at least criminal liability attached to a parent's actions that culminated in the death of her child.

MINNEAPOLIS, MINNESOTA. Similar arguments were raised in a suburban Minneapolis, Minnesota, case where a divorced, Christian Science mother let her son die the agonizing death of an untreated diabetic. Had he been seen by a medical professional during the last weeks of his life, Ian Lundman's symptoms would have been easily diagnosed as diabetes. Insulin, administered as late as a few hours before death, would have saved him. Yet, his mother entrusted him to Christian Science caretakers, who cared for him by "reading hymnals to him." His condition worsened to the point that his mother knew she should seek outside help, but she did not. The boy died after three days of excruciating suffering. The father, who no longer subscribed to the Christian Science faith, had left the family before Ian became ill. When he learned of his son's death, he sued his wife, the church, and the practitioners who treated Ian for wrongful death. Following a seven-week trial, a jury awarded the father $14.2 million – $5.2 million in compensatory damages and $9 million in punitive damages, an award that had tremendous deterrence potential.[150]

Compensatory damages are awarded to redress the actual harm to the victim, while punitive damages are granted for reprehensible behavior that deeply offends U.S. values. The defendants raised a religious defense to the award, arguing that the damages were precluded by their free exercise rights. While the court properly found that the mother and the Christian Science practitioners did not have a free exercise right to avoid damages for their conduct, it absolved the church. The appellate court held that the church had no duty to Ian, because "[t]o rule otherwise would make too much of the consequences of the church's adherence to and promotion of its core tenet." The church that inculcated the dangerous beliefs was held harmless, while the mother and the practitioners did have a duty to the child. In other words, the court ruled that a sect's beliefs can immunize it from responsibility for the natural consequences of its members' actions. Though it would not hold the church accountable for the death in that case, the court found that it was perfectly proper for "disputes involving the consequences of religious-based conduct [to] be brought before the civil courts where, as here, the underlying lawsuit is not a vehicle for attacking religious belief."[151] With respect to the church, this was a pyrrhic victory, at best.

The Minnesota Supreme Court reversed the punitive damage award, but allowed the compensatory damages (then reduced by the trial court to $1.5 million) to stand. The punitive damages were rejected because of the religious character of the neglect: "We do not grant churches and religious bodies a categorical exemption from liability for punitive damages. But under these facts, the risk of intruding – through the mechanism of punitive damages – upon the forbidden field of religious freedom is simply too great."[152] This is indefensible reasoning. In effect, the court ruled that religiously motivated individuals who let children die extremely painful deaths do not need to be deterred. The opposite is in fact true. Religious conduct occupies no "forbidden field," but rather stands shoulder-to-shoulder with all other conduct that engenders the same harm. The question was whether the behavior was so reprehensible as to deserve punitive damages. Obviously, a jury thought so.

SANDY, UTAH. Sometimes the state gives up, even when the child is in plain danger. While the Church of Jesus Christ of Latter-day Saints does not endorse faith-healing alone, some adherents disfavor medical treatment.[153] During the fall of 2003, a drama began in the state of Utah involving Mormon parents, and their 12-year-old son, Parker Jensen, who was diagnosed with Ewing's sarcoma, which is a lethal cancer. Doctors recommended chemotherapy, and gave him a 70 percent chance of surviving with the treatment, and only 20 percent without it.[154] His parents, Daren and Barbara Jensen, refused the treatment, saying he did not have cancer[155] and several days later asserted that the treatment would make him sterile and impede his growth.[156] They fled Utah and were wanted for kidnapping, but when they voluntarily returned, the state announced it would not seek custody of the boy for medical purposes, because the Jensens agreed to abide by the recommendations of an oncologist. When the state backed out of the picture, and the oncologist recommended nearly a year of chemotherapy and a bone marrow test, they once again asserted the cancer did not exist and refused to follow the doctor's recommendation. The Utah legislature has responded to the drama by pursuing a bill that would increase parents' rights to deny medical treatment to their children.[157]

TAUNTON, MASSACHUSETTS. Infants have no chance when their religiously motivated parents do not feed them. There is a recurring belief on the part of a small but significant number of religious parents that a baby should not be defiled by ordinary sustenance. One pregnant mother, Karen Robidoux, who was a member of a cult called "The Body," submitted to her sister-in-law's "vision from God" that required her to take her infant son Samuel (who was the son of the cult's leader, Jacques Robidoux) off of solid food and to revert back to breast milk only. "Dubbed The Body, the isolationist group believes in paddling children as young as one and rejects the authority of the government and doctors."[158] The mother was relegated to the basement and threatened with losing her unborn child if she did not follow the prophecy. When her body stopped producing adequate milk for him, baby Samuel wasted away and eventually died just before his first birthday. The mother was acquitted by a jury of second-degree murder, because she claimed that she had been brainwashed and lacked the requisite intent. Instead, the jury convicted her of assault and battery. Her sister-in-law pled guilty to being an accessory to assault. In contrast, a jury convicted the baby's father of first-degree murder, and he received life in prison for the death of his son.[159] That was precisely the right result for the father. Prosecutors are still shaking their heads, however, over the fact that the mother, who took no action to leave the basement or to save the child, received only assault and battery for letting her son die day-by-day of starvation.[160] Even if the death was unintended, it was manslaughter.

PHILADELPHIA, PENNSYLVANIA. In another case of infant death after a lack of medical treatment, two children in the same suburban Philadelphia family died after their parents refused to obtain medical treatment for them. After 2-year-old Kent Schaible died of bacterial pneumonia in 2009, Herbert and Catherine Schaible, who were members of the fundamentalist congregation First Century Gospel Church,[161] were found guilty of involuntary manslaughter and endangering the welfare of a child, and were only sentenced to 10 years probation, though the court ordered them to seek medical attention for their children when they became sick in the future.[162] While the Schaibles were on probation, their 7-month-old son Brandon died in April 2013, also from bacterial pneumonia and dehydration. This time, however, the couple was charged with third-degree murder and involuntary manslaughter, among other charges. They entered a no-contest plea and were sentenced to 3.5 to 7.5 years in 2014.[163] They are unfit parents, and one can only hope that their many other children are not returned to them after prison. "Their pastor, Nelson Clark, has said the Schaibles lost their sons because of a 'spiritual lack' in their lives and insisted they would not seek medical care even if another child appeared near death."[164]

Abandonment

Sometimes religiously motivated neglect takes the form of abandonment. There is no more disturbing example than the practices of the polygamous FLDS, whose members routinely leave their compounds to take non-conforming teenage boys to large cities, where they are dropped off on a corner with no money and no means of survival. They have been dubbed the "lost boys."[165] This abandonment is one way to deal with rebellious boys and necessary to ensure that the older men can success-fully obtain numerous younger women as their wives. It is pure math: if the young boys stay, they will compete for the available women. If the boys are abandoned, the older men's odds increase dramatically. Some of the boys have sued, and the FLDS's response has been the First Amendment, with one of the church's legal representatives telling one reporter, "There is no exception in the First Amendment for minors."[166] Nor is there an exception in family law for the religious abandonment of children. In fact, there is no First Amendment principle that protects any organization, religious or not, from discarding its children at will. Parents have responsibilities to their underage children, and any interpretation of the First Amendment that says otherwise has hijacked fundamental prin-ciples in an ordered society. Yet, elected officials, including prosecutors, have dragged their feet instead of prosecuting parents for abandonment. In this era, one can never overestimate the likelihood that an elected official will fail to hold religious entities accountable.

Physical abuse

There are times when spiritual care is in fact physical abuse, and children are severely hurt. In the following case, an exorcism led to a child's death.

MILWAUKEE, WISCONSIN. In Milwaukee in 2003, a storefront church of few members in Milwaukee gathered around 8-year-old Terrance Cottrell, Jr., during extended services with the intention of exorcising his autism. The child fought the members' (including his mother's) hands that restrained him, while the pastor, Ray Anthony Hemphill, pressed his knee against the boy's chest. After three weeks of meetings, the child quieted down, but when the 12th ceremony ceased, the boy could not be revived, because he had died of suffocation. Hemphill defended himself on the grounds that he was engaging in a religious practice to no avail, but his religious motivation seems to have softened the prosecutor's will. A jury convicted him of child abuse, and he was sentenced to a mere 30 months in prison and barred from performing exorcisms for 10 years without formal training in the practice.[167] He appealed, but lost.[168] He should have been charged with reckless homicide at the least, but the prosecutor did not have whatever it takes to do what is right: subject him to the same neutral, applicable laws that any non-religious individual would face. This man's deeds killed this boy. That religious beliefs were involved does not alter that fact one iota.

PHILADELPHIA, PENNSYLVANIA. It is tempting to trust one's own clergy with one's child, but clergy can be hazardous – just like any other adult. A pastor at the Third Christian Church in Overbrook (in Philadelphia), the Rev. Javan McBurrows, opened his home to Erika Daye's four-year-old son, Michael, and two siblings at a time when she was having difficulties coping.[169] She was one of his parishioners. Known as a man who believed in strict discipline, McBurrows had certain house rules, including a rule that children had to close their eyes when they entered the bathroom. When Michael did not close his eyes one day and saw another child on the toilet, McBurrows responded with a vicious beating. He swung a metal-edged carpenter's level (which is a straight metal bar hollowed out on the inside like a long, thin rectangle) at Michael six to ten times, and then forced the toddler to walk on his injured legs. He then commanded the boy to walk outside and rubbed snow in his face, according to testimony by his wife. That night, Michael died of multiple traumas. McBurrows immediately packed up his family and drove to Stone Mountain, Georgia, where he was arrested. The initial charge was first-degree murder, which could have led to the death penalty. At a nonjury trial, he was convicted of third-degree murder and then sentenced to 22 to 45 years in prison.[170] Anyone – religious or not – who does that to a child deserves to be in prison at least that long. Life would have been more appropriate.

AUSTIN, TEXAS. Choosing a religious camp rather than a secular camp does not necessarily increase the odds that a child will be safe. Discipline, in particular, can be harsh. A summer Bible camp in Texas put a 12-year-old boy, Louie Guerrero, in the intensive care ward for a week with near kidney failure and in need of a blood transfusion. Camp operators Joshua and Caleb Thompson severely beat the boy with a switch from a tree to "get the devil out of [him]."[171] A jury convicted the men of serious injury to a child and aggravated assault. At the sentencing phase, the two men argued they should receive probation rather than prison time. Properly,

Joshua received 26 years for beating the boy and Caleb received 14 years for holding him down.[172] Whatever their motivation, the boy's injuries justified stiff sentences for the abuse. Of course, abuse at religious camps is not limited to any one denomination.

Orthodox Jewish camps also have had their share of problems, as discussed above in the case of Camp Dora Golding.[173]

KANSAS CITY, KANSAS. Although most of American society has moved away from it, corporal punishment is still a tenet of some religious organizations. Neil E. Edgar and Christy Y. Edgar, the leaders of a small Kansas City church, God's Creation Outreach Ministry, disciplined their nine-year-old son, Brian, by wrapping him in duct tape, only leaving space for his nose. He died by suffocation, as a result of choking on his own vomit.[174] Mother, father, and babysitter all received life sentences.[175] Further investigation into the storefront church led investigators to bring abuse charges against five more women who abused the ministers' children and a family friend. At least two of the women pled guilty and received probation.[176]

ATLANTA, GEORGIA. Preacher Arthur R. Allen, Jr., was convicted of beating children in the early 1990s and then again in 2002.[177] In the latter case, he engaged in the whippings of two boys in a ceremony within the church.[178] At trial, he and other members of his House of Prayer congregation refused legal counsel on the ground that they believed corporal punishment was permissible in Georgia and the Bible, and necessary to shore up struggling families. He served three months in jail and was released on ten years' probation. The terms of his probation "allow[ed] him only to hand spank his own children and forbid him from encouraging others to punish their children."[179] Almost immediately upon his release, Allen made it clear he had no intention to follow the conditions of his probation. Allen declared that he and his fellow believers follow the biblical teaching that "sparing the rod spoils the child." He was rearrested and found guilty of violating his probation, for which he received two additional years in jail.[180] Obviously, the civil authorities had made no impression on him. So long as he demonstrated an intent to abuse children, the state had an obligation to incarcerate and to monitor him.

SCOTTSDALE, ARIZONA. Religious boot camps typically minister to "at-risk" or "troubled" youth, and are often the last resort for parents desperate to correct their wayward children. In Scottsdale, Arizona, Teen Reach, a faith-based evangelical youth facility that charges approximately $35,000 per year for drug and alcohol rehabilitation, was ordered to close for child abuse when a child was seriously bruised from religiously motivated spanking in 2004. In another instance, four or more adults allegedly held a child, while a fifth lay across his back, in order to deliver a spanking, which is a practice grounded in the organization's textual reading of the Bible. The administrator who ordered the closing, David Matthews of the Arizona State Department of Economic Security, quite correctly reasoned that the religious motivation for the child abuse was irrelevant. "There is no agency in the state that is permitted to beat a child."[181] Teen Reach responded aggressively to the closing, and filed a lawsuit against the state for violating its First Amendment right to the freedom of religion, as well as other claims. It also resolutely refused to obtain a license for its operations. A state judge rejected the argument that Teen Reach was not a child welfare agency, which means it will have to be licensed to reopen. Teen Reach is appealing.[182] At roughly the same time it defied the state's licensing requirement, a bill was introduced into the Arizona legislature that would have exempted faith-based agencies from having to be licensed,[183] which would permit religiously motivated abuse of children to go forward without state knowledge or oversight.[184]

MISSOURI. Missouri, which does not require faith-based child-care homes to be licensed,[185] has been home to some disturbing religious boot camps, which physically abused their residents, intentionally deprived them of sleep, and even disciplined a child by tying him to the back of a moving vehicle, an ATV, so that he would have to run behind it, and dragged if he fell.[186] These abuses have not been forestalled by Missouri's system of letting religious entities police themselves. "Any child-care facility maintained or operated under the exclusive control of a religious organization" is exempt from state licensing requirements. Instead, the facilities are required to notify parents in writing, for example, that the facility is in compliance with "fire, health and sanitation requirements," that all employees have been subject to background checks, and about the "disciplinary philosophy and policies of the child-care facility;

and [t]he educational philosophy and policies of the child-care facility."
The facility must undergo annual fire and safety inspections, and submit
copies of its written notice to parents to the state, but that is the extent of
the state's oversight in the interest of children.[187] It is a system wherein
parents either have no helping hand to ensure their children are safe
or are complicit in the religiously motivated abuse. The statute operates
from a parental rights perspective, at the expense of children.

JACKSONVILLE, FLORIDA. A Baker County, Florida, church camp for
troubled youth has been cited more than once by children as a place
where they suffered abuse. Pastor Wilford McCormick sets strict rules
for the campers – little family contact, a minimum year stay, dress codes,
no medical or dental treatment unless there is an emergency or a camp
employee specially requests it, and a five-minute limit on incoming calls
with no outgoing calls permitted. The camp was investigated by the state
of Florida in 1983 after three runaways charged there was abuse. It was
investigated again by a grand jury in 1987, and is now the subject of at
least two civil lawsuits. Kirk Griffin and Jason Berglund filed lawsuits in
2003, each saying that they were subjected to repeated demands for oral
and anal sex and to cruel physical abuse.[188] Berglund alleged that he was
threatened with physical harm if he spoke of the extreme abuse he suffered in 1993 at the age of 12.[189] Griffin alleged he had been abused from
1989 to 1992.[190] Both Berglund and Griffin claimed the alleged abuse
occurred after a Baker County grand jury already had disapproved of
Camp Tracey for its corporal punishment methods involving handcuffs
and ropes. The grand jurors objected to: the use of ropes and handcuffs
to restrain children, the fact that the children were forced labor for a
private farmer, the limited parental contact, and the inclusion of a convicted felon on the staff.[191] No charges were filed, however, because the
existing law was inadequate to hold the camp accountable. McCormick
denigrated the report as "bureaucratic harassment,"[192] as though he was
the relevant victim.

Instead of amending Florida law to make such camps accountable for
the well-being of the children who attend, Florida took the opposite tack.
After the camp complained about having to submit to state licensing,
including health and fire inspections, in a classic case of bending to
religious interests regardless of the effect on children, Florida exempted

religious organizations from those requirements.[193] Children who attend a camp that has been alleged to permit child abuse in the past (and is not even required to undergo routine fire and safety inspections that any fast-food restaurant would have to permit) are being placed at risk. It is really that simple, and the state of Florida should be castigated for elevating the religious entities' convenience above children's welfare. Any legislator who responds by saying that religious institutions are good for children, and therefore should not have to bear the monetary burden and inconvenience of state inspections of their premises, needs to read this chapter carefully, maybe more than once.

Failure to provide a safe environment for children

In the 1970s, states began to require that child-care centers be licensed. Three factors were at work: the growing number of mothers entering the workforce, in-depth studies about the importance of early childhood education, and licensing as a condition of receiving government funds. Areas of coverage included child-to-staff minimum ratios, space requirements (i.e., square footage/child), prohibitions on smoking, certain nutritional guidelines, and minimal health and safety requirements, for example, smoke alarms or sprinklers in large facilities.[194] In recent years, some religious organizations have lobbied to avoid such requirements. Their primary argument – in a nutshell – is that they should not be forced to pay for such requirements, because they are tight on funds and have other priorities for the money. In essence, they are saying that they should be trusted with the health and safety of children, even though they are fighting the laws passed for the intention of protecting children from foreseeable harms.

Three legal regimes make it possible for religious entities to run child-care centers without having to abide by the usual state licensing requirements. First, some states have exempted religious child-care centers from their licensing system altogether. For example, Missouri exempts "[a]ny child-care facility maintained or operated under the exclusive control of a religious organization[,]" so long as the facility receives no state or federal funding.[195] Second, some states require religious child-care centers to register rather than obtain a license. The registration approach typically means that the state is not monitoring the child-care center to ensure the safety and health of children, but rather accepting a registration and taking action only if a complaint is filed. It is passive regulation. The licensing system thus is preventive, while the registration system is reactive at best, which means it may well be too late to protect any particular child.[196] Third, other states require all child-care facilities to meet state standards, religious or not.[197] The first two schemes displace the state's responsibility to ensure the wellbeing of children with blind deference to religious entities.

As I hope *God vs. the Gavel* makes abundantly clear, abject deference to religious believers abdicates the welfare of society. It is not that every religious day care will harm children, but some may, and given the prevalence of religious day care recalcitrance to state safety and health regulation, no parent be certain about child safety. Nor can anyone be certain that any particular denomination or religious leader is safe for children without some licensing requirements. General licensing requirements are neutral and necessary to ensure children's safety is not being sacrificed for budget reasons or other such priorities. When the state acts as a check on abuse or neglect or danger and prescribes reasonable licensing requirements, it is doing precisely what the public good demands.

Other states have enacted state RFRAs, as I discuss in Chapter One and Part Two, that make it impossible for the state to apply its laws to religious entities unless the law was passed for a compelling purpose and it is the least restrictive means of regulating the child-care center.[198] While only the most extreme defender of religious liberty would argue the state does not have a compelling interest in protecting children from physical harm at day-care centers, legal disputes are likely to center on what is the "least restrictive means" of applying the law to the believers. For example, a large center might argue that even though fire safety is a very strong state interest, the requirement that it install sprinklers is far more restrictive than smoke detectors, because of the cost. This is a theme that runs through much of church/state litigation. If the religious entity has to bear the cost of a legally imposed duty (whether it is criminal or tort liability or regulation), it will argue that its religious mission is undermined. Yet, it is the state's obligation to assess what is necessary to ensure children are safe – and that value transcends whether the owner of the operation is religious or secular.

None of the states that have taken this route have preserved the laws that protect children, with the lone exception of Pennsylvania, which exempts day care licensing and the duty to report child abuse. Every other Pennsylvania law affecting children is impaired by the act, which is to say that children's rights to life, liberty, and protection from harm by religious entities are at risk in Pennsylvania and every state with a religious liberty protection act.

The extreme free exercise statutes require the government to prove it has a compelling interest that is served with the least restrictive means. There is no question that the protection of a girl from female genital mutilation serves a compelling interest. The practice is painful and has the potential to harm the girl into adulthood. But what is the "least restrictive means" of punishing the father who inflicts genital mutilation on his daughter for religious reasons? Sending such a father to prison is more restrictive than fining him. Do we seriously want these laws that create opportunities for religious parents to hurt their children, and then argue for the more lenient sentence simply because they acted out of religious motivation?

Why has U.S. law and society failed these children so miserably?

This chapter describes a lot of suffering. To those who would argue that these are just the bad apples, that is simply not the case. These are only a very small number of the many, many instances of religious entities that have betrayed children. But even if these are only the bad apples, these bad apples are precisely whom the law is intended to deter and punish. Even one child's life sacrificed for an adult's religious beliefs is one too many.

Some states have let religious entities off the hook when what is needed is stronger deterrence. At this point, only three states continue to hold that the First Amendment is a defense to child sex abuse.[199] But there are too many medical neglect exemptions and too many legislators that have ignored abuse in religious communities.

Legal doctrine has not been the only cause of harm to these children. There has also been a long era, at least since 1950, during which the people of the United States have believed as a general matter that religion is always moral and that it is as innocuous as apple pie. This view was fostered in the latter 20th century by Stephen Carter's widely read book, *The Culture of Disbelief*. This Pollyanna understanding of religion sold these children short and cannot be sustained in the face of these facts.

It is also a mistake for prosecutors to permit religious institutions to handle their own "dirty laundry," which happened too often. When this is combined with the typical difficulties attendant upon removing molesters out of the way of children, the deficiencies of the law and its enforcement – from a child's perspective – become apparent.[200] With rare exceptions, the media also gave religious entities a pass. That dirty laundry was the public's problem and needed public airing, and if either had fulfilled their appropriate roles, more children might have been saved from such harm. Blind trust in any human, whether religious or not, is misplaced.

It is also a profound fact that power protects power. Then and now: A-list religious leaders, media owners and editors, and politicians trade favors. The Penn State sex abuse scandal was riveting in part because it was the story of clergy abuse without the religious baggage. How many times do we have to hear the story of the men who put each other's reputation above the welfare of children?

Ultimately, society pays when religious entities are allowed to place themselves above the law, and thus all of us are victims. When religious organizations hide the facts about child molesters, they kept these monsters out of prison in the first instance and then permanently when the statute of limitations expired during their prolonged secrecy. When they let a clergy member off the hook, they typically did not alert anyone outside their closed circle that a pedophile would now be on the loose, free to groom and seduce other children at will. That means that former priests can now be found performing karaoke or pumping gas, and living lives with plenty of access to children.[201]

In the midst of all this state law, you may be asking what the federal government is doing to protect children from religious-based abuse. The short answer is: nothing. Despite the daily news stories about sex abuse cover-ups in one religious institution after another, not one President or member of Congress has come to the aid of these victims in word or deed. Unlike Ireland and Australia, each of which launched in-depth government investigations about the abuse of their children, the U.S. has been mute. No hearings, no outcry from our elected representatives.

When the Holy See lost a case against a solitary victim from Oregon in the Ninth Circuit, it petitioned the Supreme Court for review. The case raised only state law interpretation questions – no legal issue on which the Court would normally consider granting consideration. The Justices delayed ruling on the petition to hear from then-Solicitor General Elena Kagan, whose office, along with the Department of State and Secretary of State Hillary Clinton took the side of the Vatican! They knew that the Court could not take the case on the merits, so they just recommended that the Court summarily reverse in favor of the Vatican and send it back to the lower courts. On behalf of the survivor, I persuaded the Court that this was not a case where they would ever weigh in, and they finally denied review. Religious groups have a strange hold on our elected officials even at the highest level, who I hope at least, have the common decency not to be able to sleep at night when they put children at risk and fail to hold perpetrators and the institutions that protect them accountable.

Society is also severely burdened when polygamous sects deprive women of education and at the same time they saddle them with multiple children, and society at large is further hindered when these same sects abandon their boys to keep the ratio of girls-to-men optimal for the older men. Public assistance too often becomes necessary in both instances – which means the average taxpayer is being forced to prop up the illegal polygamous society. Finally, when faith healers permit children to die or to become permanently disabled, or when fundamentalist disciplinarians permanently injure or kill children, they deprive society of the talent and the good those children could have brought into the world. The cost is enormous, and it is the result of an abundance of religious license, as opposed to liberty. It is also proof positive that religious individuals and institutions cannot be permitted to act as though they have no obligations to their children and the rest of us.

3

MARRIAGE

Whether the issue is gay marriage or polygamy, both topics have earned headlines in recent years, and both involve religious entities demanding hegemony over the issue, in the case of gay marriage, or exemptions at the expense of women and children, in the case of polygamy. Polygamists are claiming a constitutional right to have multiple spouses, while fundamentalist Christians and Orthodox Jews are demanding that same-sex couples not be permitted to marry, for religious reasons.

The First Amendment grants all citizens, including religious believers, the right to contribute their viewpoints to public debate and to try to persuade leaders and fellow citizens that their views on social problems have merit; wisdom can be found in many corners. But they do not have a right in the United States to mold public policy solely according to their beliefs, and their beliefs alone. And legislators are not permitted to make public policy solely according to religious belief. These are First Amendment basics.

The hard legislative choices depend on a more broad-ranging inquiry than any one religious worldview encompasses (even when that perspective is shared by a large number of citizens). A complication in the debates over marriage in 21st-century America has been that few of our elected representatives seem to understand or are willing to shoulder their representative role, which demands significantly more than deference to religious entities or the enactment of their religious preferences.

Citizens may speak to them from the heart and soul, but it is up to our elected officials to contextualize the debate by ensuring that it is about the common good, and the larger public, not solely about their most vociferous religious constituents' views on their own.

I am not advocating secularization, as those who would employ religious rhetoric to drown out competing discourse sometimes insist, but rather describing the hallmarks of a successful representative democracy. If government officials do not move conversation off of a solely religious platform, they have shortchanged everyone and abdicated their constitutional obligations. To be sure, it is easier to react to religious voices and to give them what they demand, especially if they are viewed as a voting bloc. They are, after all, typically quite passionate. But that is no excuse for elected representatives to abandon the public good, or to ignore invidious discrimination or harm to the vulnerable. None whatsoever.

SAME-SEX MARRIAGE. Over the past several years, the recognition of same-sex marriage has changed drastically at both the state and federal levels. In 2003, the Supreme Judicial Court of Massachusetts held that same-sex couples had a state constitutional right to get married.[1] In a nutshell, their argument was that their unions were not distinguishable from heterosexual unions. They were monogamous and dedicated, and they nurtured their children. The purposes of Massachusetts's marriage laws were served by their unions, and therefore, Massachusetts's distinction between gay and traditional marriages rested on invidious discrimination on the basis of sexual orientation.[2]

The Massachusetts Senate then asked the court whether the Massachusetts Constitution would permit it to enact Senate No. 2175, which accorded homosexual couples civil union – but not marital – status. The answer was, "No." The court explained that the traditional, historic nature and meaning of civil marriage in Massachusetts is as a wholly secular and dynamic legal institution, the governmental aim of which is to encourage stable adult relationships for the good of the individual and of the community, especially its children. The very nature and purpose of civil marriage, the court concluded, renders unconstitutional any attempt to ban all same-sex couples, as same-sex couples, from entering into civil marriage.[3]

The Iowa Supreme Court reached the same conclusion under the Iowa Constitution.[4] Since Massachusetts and Iowa recognized same-sex marriage under their state constitutions, fifteen other states and the District of Columbia have followed suit.[5] Conservative backlash resulted in 26 states passing laws or constitutional amendments banning gay marriage.[6]

The immediate response from some conservative religious organizations to the Massachusetts decision was swift and fierce.[7] To quote: "This decision is on an order of magnitude that is beyond the capacity of words. The court has tampered with society's DNA, and the consequent mutation will reap unimaginable consequences for Massachusetts and our nation."[8] Part of the opposition arose out of deep-seated disapproval of homosexuality *per se*, not just of homosexual marriage. For example, according to the Christian Coalition of America, the Massachusetts decision was wrong, because "marriage is one of the last obstacles to the complete normalization of homosexuality in America."[9]

Many demanded, from a religious perch, that the federal government take action, which was their right. Unfortunately, some members of Congress followed suit – employing religious perspectives and precious little reasoned argument – by enacting the Defense of Marriage Act (DOMA), which did not permit the federal government to accord benefits to married couples unless they were heterosexual, even if their marriage was legal under state law, and which permitted states to refuse to recognize other states' same-sex marriages.[10]

In 2013, the U.S. Supreme Court struck down the provision of DOMA that barred federal benefits for same-sex couples married under state law.[11] The Court did not hold, as the Massachusetts court had held almost ten years earlier, that same-sex marriage is required by equal protection. Rather, the Court mandated deference by the federal government to the states' definitions of marriage.[12] Thus, couples who are legally married under state law must be treated the same under federal law for purposes of receiving federal benefits. The Court also held that DOMA was unconstitutional because it was not based on reason, but rather animus.[13] The Obama Administration followed that opening by adding same-sex couples to federal benefits even if their resident state did not sanction gay marriages.

The decision made a quick difference. Following *Windsor*, a federal court in Utah held the Utah state constitutional ban on gay marriage violated the United States Constitution.[14] Over 1,000 couples subsequently wed, until the United States Supreme Court issued a stay in January 2014 pending a decision on the merits.[15] Also in January 2014, a federal court in Oklahoma held the state ban on same-sex marriage unconstitutional.[16] Texas, Virginia, and Kentucky federal courts also followed suit.[17]

Congress also kicked around a constitutional amendment in 2004, the Marriage Protection Amendment (MPA) (formerly known as the Federal Marriage Amendment), which would have banned all gay marriages in the United States.[18] It is a classic example of elected representatives using religion and religion only to justify a law. Representative Marilyn Musgrave (R – Colo.) spoke more like a pastor in support of the MPA than an elected official:

> The very foundational document of our nation assumes that our rights exist within the context of God's created order. The self-evident differences and complementary design of men and women are part of that created order. We were created as male and female, and for this reason a man will leave his father and mother and be joined with his wife, and the two shall become one in the mystical spiritual and physical union we call "marriage."[19]

Former Rep. William Dannemeyer of California also supported a court-stripping bill to forestall same-sex marriage in equally religious language: "Decisions of the federal judiciary over the last half century have resulted in the theft of our Judeo-Christian heritage."[20] For these politicians, their interpretation of the Bible, which for them is the only interpretation, blessed only heterosexual marriage. The snag is that they are (or were) elected representatives charged with serving all Americans, not just those who are Christian. Neither Musgrave nor Dannemeyer are currently in office.

Catholic ethicist and Princeton professor Robert P. George, writing in the *Wall Street Journal*, insisted that there was a natural law justification for fighting same-sex marriage, when he justified a ban on same-sex marriage on the basis of the purportedly self-evident "nature of marriage as a 'one-flesh union' of sexually complementary spouses" and the corresponding entitlement of mixed-sex marriages to receive "benefits, privileges, rights or immunities" because the spouses are of the opposite sex.[21] Apparently, the physical characteristics of males and females predetermine the law of marriage. His circular reasoning implied that no legislature should consider the issue other than to reach his religiously-based conclusion, a conclusion once again that is an argument from theocracy. Accordingly, he promoted the idea of a federal constitutional amendment to ban all marriages other than those between a man and a woman, without entering into the debate over what forms of marriage are best for children, the economy, or the public good. His is a revealed legal regime, not a reasoned one.

POLYGAMY. Once Massachusetts legitimated gay marriage, the subject of polygamy leapt into the public square as well. Some have tried to link the two issues by saying that opening the door to one necessarily opens the door to the other, but they have missed the point of the Massachusetts decision, which was that two-partner marriages, whether between heterosexuals or homosexuals, are no different in terms of the goals of the state. They have also missed what a state government needs to take into account in crafting marriage law. When one examines the appropriate neutral principles, same-sex marriage and polygamy are apples and oranges.

In 1878, the Supreme Court upheld the federal law outlawing polygamy in the Utah Territory.[22] Before polygamy was outlawed in Utah, it was illegal in every state in the United States, since the earliest days of the country. Thus, while some argue that the law applied to Utah targeted the Church of Jesus Christ of Latter-Day Saints – which was the only group engaging in polygamy at the time – it was simply conforming the law of the Utah Territory to the rest of the country.

The Court upheld the law against plaintiff George Reynolds' free exercise arguments in part because of the well-known evils of polygamy, including the "patriarchal principle ... which, when applied to large communities, fetters the people in stationary despotism, while that principle cannot long exist in connection with monogamy."[23] The United Nations and many others have documented those same wrongs today, as I will discuss later in this Chapter.

Civil marriage is a legal construct for the ordering of society, the protection of children, and the orderly transfer of property. Under the First Amendment, the government must be neutral on religion, and, therefore, it cannot be just a theological construct that a state endorses. The Establishment Clause forbids a government from a preference for "one religion over another, or religion to irreligion."[24] It also requires legislators to have a secular purpose for a law. Legislators are supposed to determine what marital construct best serves the common good, which means they should take into account how the arrangement best protects and serves children, inheritance, property ownership, and the culture at large, for starters. From that perspective, the two challenges to traditional marriage – gay marriage and polygamy, which are factually quite distinct – are also, for public policy purposes, separate topics for legislative consideration.

The Supreme Court explained in *Reynolds* what is wrong with polygamy, and its historical background as follows:

[T]here never has been a time in any State of the Union when polygamy has not been an offence against society, cognizable by the civil courts and punishable, with more or less severity. In the face of all this evidence, it is impossible to believe that the constitutional guaranty of religious freedom was intended to prohibit legislation in respect to this most important feature of social life. Marriage, while from its very nature a scared obligation, is nevertheless, in most civilized nations, a civil contract, and usually regulated by law. Upon it society may be said to be built, and out of its fruits spring social relations and social obligations and duties, with which government is necessarily required to deal. In fact, according as monogamous or polygamous marriages are allowed, do we find the principles on which the government of the people, to a greater or less extent, rests. Professor[] Lieber says, polygamy leads to the patriarchal principle, and which, when applied to large communities, fetters the people in stationary despotism, while that principle cannot long exist in connection with monogamy. Chancellor Kent observes that this remark is equally striking and profound.

2 Kent, Com. 81 note (*e*). An exceptional colony of polygamists under an exceptional leadership may sometimes exist for a time without appearing to disturb the social condition of the people who surround it; but there cannot be a doubt that, unless restricted by some form of constitution, it is within the legitimate scope of the power of every civil government to determine whether polygamy or monogamy shall be the law of social life under its dominion.[25]

Same-sex marriage is a binary, where two consenting adults enter an equal civil contract. Polygamy, by definition, cannot be an equal contract between two equal parties. It is almost always, in every culture, one man controlling the actions of multiple women. Polygamy assumes that one gender – almost always male – is entitled to the entire quantum of emotional and psychological and sexual and material support from multiples of the opposite sex, but that the female receives only a fraction of those goods from their spouse. It violates deep-seated principles of gender equality.

Some religious polygamists have challenged the laws that ban polygamy.[26] Polygamist Tom Green, who was married to five women and had dozens of children, and was convicted of four counts of bigamy and later of child rape,[27] lost when he raised a constitutional challenge to Utah's anti-bigamy laws. There have been other challenges as well, but all of the arguments were found unpersuasive, until recently.[28] In the Tom Green case, the court reasoned that the first marriage was legal, but that the four additional women in the household were also married to him even without a license, based on common law marriage.[29] (Common law marriage occurs when a couple lives together for a certain number of years and hold themselves out as married. One does not need a ceremony to be married if together long enough.) He served time and was released in 2007.

More recently, Kody Brown and his wives, of the reality show, *Sister Wives*, challenged Utah's anti-polygamy and cohabitation laws and won a partial victory. A federal district court ruled that a polygamous marriage does not occur until the group obtains more than one marriage license.[30] The court failed to consider that the additional women in the home were married in common law marriages (as was argued in the *Green* case). Since the Browns did not obtain more than one marriage license, the court held that they were not in violation of the polygamy laws. Second, the court ruled that Utah's cohabitation laws violated their rights to sexual autonomy and religious freedom. Therefore, their arrangement was protected from state law. The case is being appealed by the state, as it should be.

The *Brown* ruling, if left to stand, is guaranteed to result in confusion. For example, which of his children have a right to inherit from him? According to the court, he has one legal marriage, and then additional mistresses. Therefore, for legal purposes, the children of his first wife have stable rights under state and federal law involving inheritance, and parental obligations. That cannot be said for the rest of the wives and children, whose claims are on un-firm ground.

Their arguments belong in the legislative sphere, where many voices – religious, secular, activist, and traditional – can contribute to finding the optimal public policy. The problem with the *Kody Brown* decision is that the State of Utah did a terrible job. Courts have only the record set forth by the parties before them and Utah did not enter the copious evidence available showing the inherent harms of polygamy to women, children, and society at large. From an economic standpoint alone, the families typically face multiple bankruptcies, like the Browns,[31] or persistent dependence on public welfare, like families within the FLDS.[32] It is also routinely a system where the women are second-class citizens, whose only option in life is to be married and take care of multiple children from a young age; the girls are married off at a young age, and some boys are discarded. Without these facts, the court was constrained to rule on the record.

In contrast, a legislature can do much more than a court to establish the facts. If polygamy's proponents can show a legislature that opening the definition of marriage to include polygamy is consistent with the public good, it can be done. Similarly, if gay rights groups and others persuade state legislatures that same-sex marriage is in the public interest while those opposed express their views, the legislature has the power to expand the definition of marriage. In response to the Massachusetts decision mandating same-sex marriage, the Alliance for Marriage advocated returning the debate "to the democratic process at the state level authority that is currently being usurped by courts at the request of activist organizations."[33] They are right to look to state legislatures, but they will not avoid the actions of "activist" organizations by removal to the legislature. Indeed, one of the advantages of dealing with these issues in the state legislatures rather than the courts is that more voices can be heard.

Although the resolution of each issue is ultimately a matter for the state legislatures, which I will explain in more detail in Part Two, these two social issues represent two paradigmatic ways religion interacts with the culture. In the gay marriage context, some believers have insisted in the public square that their biblical values provide the only answer to the public policy question. They are intent on using what political power they have to ensure the law mirrors their religious worldview. Those trying to forestall gay marriage talk in terms of the "Christian tradition" and the necessity of maintaining social order.

The polygamy debate is quite different. The polygamists are not trying to impose their beliefs on everyone else (other than those born into the group). Rather, they are asking for relief from the law that governs everyone else. It is typical, therefore, to hear polygamists talk in libertarian terms and to dwell on the right to be left alone by the government. Despite the differences, though, in the end, both religious constructs are trying to shape the law to their religious conduct, and it is the government's obligation to persistently reframe the issues in light of public interest, the protection of the vulnerable, and the principle of no harm.

Same-sex marriage bans fall, because they are based on nothing more than religion-fueled hate

After California passed a law permitting gay marriage in 2008, religious advocates, led and financed by the Latter-Day Saints, campaigned for state ballot initiative and state constitutional amendment, Proposition 8, which stated: "Only marriage between a man and a woman is valid or recognized in California."[34] By a vote of 52.3% to 47.7%, in 2008, they won, and same-sex couples were no longer permitted to marry.[35]

The arguments against gay marriage in California were not only funded by a religious organization, but also drew on religious assumptions. Acclaimed pastor Rick Warren came out in support of the ballot initiative stating, "For 5,000 years, every culture and every religion – not just Christianity – has defined marriage as a contract between men and women. There is no reason to change the universal, historical definition of marriage to appease 2% of our population."[36] One evangelical pastor in California, Jim Garlow, went so far as to say, "If Proposition 8 fails, there is an inevitable loss of religious freedom."[37]

There was a concerted attempt by those opposed to gay marriage on religious grounds to set up an us-against-them political scene. The "us" was every true American with the "correct" view: against same-sex marriage. The "them" were the infidels who would introduce same-sex marriage. One of the most active groups against same-sex marriage, the Alliance Defending Freedom, declared, "God has defined marriage as one man married to one woman... [and] radical activist groups in the U.S. are attempting to twist the law to change the definition of the family to include same-sex 'marriage,' polygamy, and other structures."[38] The Alliance for Marriage, one of whose missions is to block gay marriage, claimed to incorporate a broad swath of believers, saying it "cuts across traditional party lines and includes Catholic, Jewish and Muslim leaders as well as ministers in historically black Protestant denominations."[39] In short, the Alliance (note the name) hopes to convey the image that all Americans stand shoulder-to-shoulder with them. Others joining the chorus of disapproval included Catholics and Orthodox Jews,[40] and "the Southern Baptist Convention, Focus on the Family, several Catholic dioceses, and the Traditional Values Coalition."[41] It is a politically strong array, but it does not encompass every Christian or believer in the United States by a long shot.

At the same time, a significant cadre of religious and secular groups supported same-sex marriage, including the Human Rights Campaign,[42] the Leadership Conference on Civil and Human Rights,[43] and the American Sociological Association.[44] Certain Reform and Conservative Jewish groups also support same-sex marriage, as does the American Jewish Committee.[45] Among Protestant churches, the Unitarian Universalist Church has been the leader on gay rights, has many gay ministers, and performs same-sex marriages.[46] For many, the Bible simply does not say what the fundamentalists say it does. In fact, all forms of marriage are "recognized" in the Bible, along with an injunction to men to marry their rape victims:

> If a man meets a virgin who is not betrothed, and seizes her and lies with her, and they are found, then the man who lay with her shall give to the father of the young woman fifty shekels of silver, and she shall be his wife, because he has violated her. He may not divorce her all his days. Deut. 22:28–29.

And if a man abducts a woman, he must make her his bride:

Then they thought of the annual festival of the LORD held in Shiloh, between Lebonah and Bethel, along the east side of the road that goes from Bethel to Shechem. They told the men of Benjamin who still needed wives, "Go and hide in the vineyards. When the women of Shiloh come out for their dances, rush out from the vineyards, and each of you can take one of them home to be your wife! And when their fathers and brothers come to us in protest, we will tell them, 'Please be understanding. Let them have your daughters, for we didn't find enough wives for them when we destroyed Jabesh-gilead. And you are not guilty of breaking the vow since you did not give your daughters in marriage to them.' "So the men of Benjamin did as they were told. They kidnapped the women who took part in the celebration and carried them off to the land of their own inheritance. Judges 21: 10–24.

There is also the regulation of sexual slavery accomplished through child sale:

When a man sells his daughter as a slave, she will not be freed at the end of six years as the men are. If she does not please the man who bought her, he may allow her to be bought back again. But he is not allowed to sell her to foreigners, since he is the one who broke the contract with her. And if the slave girl's owner arranges for her to marry his son, he may no longer treat her as a slave girl, but he must treat her as his daughter. If he himself marries her and then takes another wife, he may not reduce her food or clothing or fail to sleep with her as his wife. If he fails in any of these three ways, she may leave as a free woman without making any payment. Exodus 21:7–11.

At least the proponents of heterosexual marriage have not advocated those positions.

The Episcopal Church, have landed on a compromise position for now where they bless gay marriages even if they do not formally recognize them.[47] Thus, the fight cannot be drawn on "Christian" or "Judeo-Christian" lines. Once the debate could not be framed by one religious tradition, the door opened to a more tempered public debate over the common good, or at least to competing theories of the good.

Same-sex marriage advocates argued from the beginning that it was unfair to ban homosexuals from marriage because there was no evidence they would be bad parents or poor contributors to society. They turned the debate to their merits. Definitive studies in the U.S. and Australia have established that gay couples are as capable of being good parents as heterosexual couples.[48] Opponents tightly embraced their religious arguments, in part because they lacked any others. That is a recipe for loss.

One of the persistent themes by those opposed to same-sex marriage on religious grounds is that this is a "Christian Country," and, therefore, Christianity and/or the Bible are the only sources for choosing marriage. The "Christian country" label hides the ball and begs the public policy question all at the same time.

HIDING THE BALL. The primary problem with the "Christian country" claim in this context is that it is factually misleading. As I explain above, politically powerful religious groups do passionately oppose it.[49] In truth, however, not all Christian or Jewish faiths oppose same-sex marriage. At the same time, various mainstream denominations are still working out their theological views on the issue. The Presbyterian Church (U.S.A.) has permitted the ordination of gay ministers since 2010, but the representatives at their 2012 annual meeting narrowly sustained the rule against same-sex unions, though not to put the issue completely to rest. They also decided to conduct a two-year church-wide study on the theology of marriage. Ministers who have openly defied the ban and expressed their intention to bless gay couples in their churches still risk censure.[50] The United Methodists have engaged in heated internal battles.[51] As a body, they have voted to reject same-sex marriages and affirmed their belief that homosexuality is inconsistent with the Bible. Meanwhile, many individual congregations continue to support same-sex unions with dozens of pastors in California presiding over such unions. In the face of that kind of internal rebellion, the church withdrew its original decision to sanction the California pastors.[52] This decision is not uniform throughout the entire United Methodist community, though. In December 2013, a Methodist lost his ministerial credentials because he performed his son's same-sex marriage.[53] As a result of presiding over the ceremony, the United Methodist Church in Pennsylvania denounced the minister's actions in hopes that it would set an example for other ministers.[54]

Like the Christians, the Jews are all over the place on this issue, and one cannot always use the believer's denomination to be certain of their position. Most Reform Jews favor same-sex unions, Conservatives are split, and most Orthodox are opposed, though there are some orthodox rabbis who are not opposed.[55] For instance, at the nation's largest gay and lesbian synagogue, Congregation Beth Simchat Torah in Manhattan, Rabbi Sharon Kleinbaum issued a call to all clergy, but particularly to rabbis, "to solemnize weddings without a marriage license" before New York recognized same-sex marriages.[56] When Conservative rabbi Jack Moline, whose synagogue is outside of Washington, D.C., explained the contradictory outlook of his faith, he said:

> [M]y confusion about gay marriage is . . . a conflict between two sets of values. If homosexuality is an orientation and not something that is environmentally conditioned or a matter of choice, then there must be a way for a sacred expression of intimacy for gays and lesbians, as there is for heterosexuals. On the other hand, you can't deny that the weight of our tradition is heavily against such an arrangement.[57]

Those resting on the "Christian country" formula may reply that they mean "Christian" in their sense, and that all others are not "true" Christians. Yet, that is simply incoherent in the United States' public arena, where the many Protestants (and Catholics) who in fact support gay unions are Christian in any normal sense of the term. No matter how diverse the group claiming that same-sex marriage is opposed to "Christian values," it obviously does not speak for all Christians in the United States on this issue. Therefore, the "Christian country" label is hollow even for those in the Judeo-Christian tradition. Finally, it is especially hollow for the millions of Americans that are not from that tradition, including Muslims, Buddhists, Unitarians, Hindus, Native Americans, Sikhs, Wiccans, Pagans and more.[58]

BEGGING THE QUESTION. "Christian" has so many connotations that invoking it leads to no particular theological and certainly no public policy conclusion. "Christian" can refer to the set of beliefs that are Catholic, or those that are Protestant, or those that are Evangelical, or all of these beliefs taken together. It encompasses disparate cultural world-views. For example, the Irish Catholics are Christian and so are the white Anglo-Saxon Protestants. "Christian" contains within itself powerful contradictions: the South African Dutch Reformed Church, which supplied the theology on which apartheid was built,[59] is Christian, and so was the Rev. Martin Luther King, Jr., who led the civil rights movement in the United States in the 1960s on Christian principles. Slavery in the United States was enforced with Christian maxims, like the following by Jefferson Davis, president of the Confederate States of America: "[Slavery] was established by decree of Almighty God . . . it is sanctioned in the Bible, in both Testaments, from Genesis to Revelation . . . it has existed in all ages, has been found among the people of the highest civilization, and in nations of the highest proficiency in the arts."[60] Truth be told, one can find individual biblical passages that support the practice. For example, Ephesians says:

> Slaves, be obedient to the men who are called your masters in this world, with deep respect and sincere loyalty, as you are obedient to Christ: not only when you are under their eye, as if you had only to please men, but because you are slaves of Christ and wholeheartedly do the will of God. Work hard and willingly, but not for the sake of men. You can be sure that everyone, whether a slave or a free man, will be properly rewarded by the Lord for whatever work he has done well.[61]

At the same time, Christians constructed the Underground Railroad that brought thousands of former slaves and their families to freedom.[62] The term "Christian" can equally refer to the harrowing torture of the Inquisition, the impetus behind the Salem witch trials, or Mother Teresa's work in Calcutta. Christianity is present in every one of these examples, which means it is an amorphous term that carries more political punch than one identifiable meaning. In fact, its current political force is built on an assumption that the Unites States is a monolithic and united Christian nation. There is no such thing – America has always been a collection of sects, not a homogeneous people of faith.

The United States is still not a Christian country in the sense those using the phrase want it to mean, because even if every possible meaning were packed into the term, it still would not encompass what this republican form of government aspires to. That is the achievement of the highest public good, which in turn, is determined by representatives who are delegated the responsibility to consider and then determine it in light of current knowledge and experienced problems – not a particular religious viewpoint or writing. It is not an overstatement to say that the phrase "Christian country" in the same-sex marriage context is no more and no less than a political grab for power, rather than a description of any single set of values that could or should determine public policy.

The hard work of this republican form of government cannot be avoided by posting a sign declaring "Christian" on the front lawn of the United States Capitol, or every state capitol. Representatives, in dialogue with the people, must forge the hard policy choices for every citizen, believer or nonbeliever, Jew, Muslim, Christian, or Wiccan. Their job is to define the social construct of marriage in a way that best serves the needs of the public, and all those who are affected by the marriage law, which is part of an intricate social web. The issues are extraordinarily complex: inheritance, legitimacy, children's rights, property ownership, and taxation, to name a few, and the task is unfortunately quite difficult. Resorting to phrases like "Christian country" does not begin to answer the question.

We in the United States are sometimes blind to what the world already sees. It is a simple fact that those who insist that marriage mirror their religious faith are content to impose their beliefs on others as though they lived in a theocracy. This is the sort of parochialism that makes what is a noble constitution in theory a laughing stock to the world. We look hypocritical, not to mention naive.

There is also great inconsistency in the misguided devotion to a unitary religious culture. Ironically, the same groups that push for their faith to determine public policy have pushed for federal commissions to chastise foreign governments like China for their intolerance of a wide variety of religious faiths.[63] The Catholic bishops, who have frequently asserted that public policy should be shaped solely by their religious principles, have criticized China's treatment of religious diversity as follows:

> The tools of U.S. diplomacy need to be brought to bear in a broad way to make China's religious prisoners of conscience an undeniable priority in U.S.–China relations. Forming policy to respond to China's violation of religious liberty is not just a matter of utilizing the sanctions available under the International Religious Liberty Act. Rather, it is a matter of making religious liberty a first-level concern of our whole diplomatic effort. Our European friends should be encouraged by all our ambassadors on a daily basis to join the U.S. initiative before the

U.N. Human Rights Commission. Trade representatives and business travelers, under State Department or other government auspices, ought to raise the concerns as their own in private talks with their counterparts. The U.S. ambassador to China should pose a question in his every meeting with the Chinese government, and so should his staff, whatever their formal role, whether military attaché or commercial officer.[64]

Whether they realize it or not, those who would define marriage solely by reference to their religious beliefs are asking for a governing order that is antithetical to what the Constitution was intended to accomplish. There were Christian theocracies not long before the founding of the United States, in particular in Britain, and they were the negative backdrops against which colonies were established here.[65] Queen Mary forced everyone to be Catholic and then Queen Elizabeth I forced everyone to be Protestant, and they took care of dissent by exterminating those who would not follow their belief mandate. The era when the definitions of Catholic and Protestant could be so pure as to draw an either/or distinction is long past. To now seek a "Christian" culture through the imposition of a supposed unitary religious viewpoint is nonsensical.

Many of the early American colonists departed Britain to escape theological mandates imposed on them by the European theocracies that blended sovereign and religious power. In this pluralist society, the pressure by a subset of Christians to push for a single moral vision under the heading of "Christian" cannot be characterized other than as a drive to institute a theocracy in their own image. In short, their arguments, which are intended to summon references to the flag, mom, and apple pie, in fact are quite dangerous to a free America.

The United States cannot craft social institutions on the basis of a particular belief system, even if it is some form of Christianity. The government has to look more broadly than the religious views of some citizens to choose the social construction of marriage that is most consistent with the public good. Thus, even if the heading "Christian country" were accurate, it is an inappropriate tool to use in order to shape legislation for all Americans.

First, the U.S. Supreme Court, when it held that private sexual conduct between consenting adults was protected by the right of privacy in *Lawrence v. Texas*,[66] explicitly stated that the decision did not extend to questions of marriage: "[The case] does not involve whether the government must give formal recognition to any relationship that homosexual persons seek to enter."[67] Justice Sandra Day O'Connor's concurrence also emphasized her conviction that distinguishing between homosexual and heterosexual sexual practices violated equal protection, because it was an irrational distinction between two similarly situated sets of adults. But that did not "mean that other laws distinguishing between heterosexuals and homosexuals would similarly fail." On her reasoning, the state may well assert a legitimate state interest in "preserving the traditional institution of marriage."[68] Justice Antonin Scalia, though, muddied the waters in his dissent, when he rolled out his parade of horribles: if the state could not outlaw sodomy between consenting adults, then "[s]tate laws against bigamy, same-sex marriage, adult incest, prostitution, masturbation, adultery, fornication, bestiality, and obscenity are ... called into question by [the Court's] decision; the Court makes no effort to cabin the scope of its decision to exclude them from its holding."[69]

Evangelical theology professor Harold O.J. Brown spun Justice Scalia's reasoning into a claim that with *Lawrence*, the Supreme Court "has in effect declared the nation pagan."[70] His reasoning is a classic illustration of the religious individual who judges public policy solely according to his own religious reference, and who expects it to reflect his particular religious worldview. The only possible government for him was a Judeo-Christian theocracy. On *Lawrence*, he wrote:

> What were those justices thinking? The man who wrote the majority opinion [Justice Anthony Kennedy] is a Roman Catholic. Does he not know that his church, his spiritual leader the pope, the Bible, and all of the church fathers up to the present, consider the behavior that he now protects an abominable sin? ... Do the two Jewish justices not know that their Torah rejects sodomy as an abomination? ... And the two women on the Court: by what perverted logic do they mock the role that God and nature have given to their sex in conjunction with the male – to bring children into the world in a matrimonial union. ... [71]

Justice Kennedy's decisions in *Lawrence* and *Romer v. Evans*,[72] where the Colorado constitutional amendment denying civil rights protections for homosexuals was held unconstitutional because it was based on nothing other than animus, showed him exercising his power as a Justice should. Not as a representative of the Pope, but rather a servant of the law of the United States. He has been a "Catholic Justice" in the tradition of President John F. Kennedy, who when asked whether he would rule according to the Church's law or the United States', stated:

> I believe in an America where the separation of church and state is absolute, where no Catholic prelate would tell the president (should he be Catholic) how to act, and no Protestant minister would tell his parishioners for whom to vote; where no church or church school is granted any public funds or political preference; and where no man is denied public office merely because his religion differs from the president who might appoint him or the people who might elect him.
>
> I believe in an America that is officially neither Catholic, Protestant nor Jewish; where no public official either requests or accepts instructions on public policy from the Pope, the National Council of Churches or any other ecclesiastical source; where no religious body seeks to impose its will directly or indirectly upon the general populace or the public acts of its officials; and where religious liberty is so indivisible that an act against one church is treated as an act against all.[73]

Now deceased, Brown apparently did not know that our Justices (and legislators) must act from neutral principles.

Second, the social construct of marriage is a state law question. That is the message of the Supreme Court's decision in *United States v. Windsor*, where the Court held that the federal government must defer to the states on the definition of marriage. The states are free to have an open and ongoing debate about the shape of marriage, which can take into account the religious views of every citizen, but the public policy discussion cannot be dictated solely by religious viewpoint. Responsible elected representatives must also, and even more so, consider how the parameters of state marriage law affect all those involved: the partners, the children, the generations beyond, and the society as a whole.

Third, there is a bedrock constitutional rule the same-sex opponents ignored: the government must have a secular reason to justify a law, at least one. When the only reason is religion the law fails. When the only reason is hate it is also unconstitutional. The second half of *Windsor* held that laws violate equality when a law is based on hatred. This portion of

Windsor has led to a cascade of decisions in favor of same-sex couples. The barriers are falling, in large part because the laws against same-sex marriage were based solely on religious beliefs, rather than neutral public policy.

As of this writing, the following states still have same-sex marriage bans. Expect the list to get shorter. Alabama, Alaska, Arizona, Arkansas, Colorado, Florida, Idaho, Indiana, Georgia, Indiana, Kansas, Kentucky (held unconstitutional but a stay is in place), Louisiana, Michigan, Mississippi, Missouri, Montana, Nebraska, Nevada, North Carolina, North Dakota, Ohio, Oklahoma (held unconstitutional, but stay is in place), Oregon, Pennsylvania, South Carolina, South Dakota, Tennessee, Texas (held unconstitutional but stay is in place), Utah (held unconstitutional, but a stay is in place), West Virginia, Wisconsin, Wyoming.

The many problems with polygamy, and why it is nothing like same-sex marriage

In the case of polygamous marriage, there are very few religious sects that advocate the practice. They are small in number and even smaller in political power in the United States; they lack the close relationships with those in power that the same-sex marriage opponents have started to enjoy over the last decade or so. Nor do they argue that the law should reflect their religious teaching. They do not suggest, as do the opponents of gay marriage, that every marriage should reflect their particular beliefs (in part because it is a nonstarter, I am sure). Rather, they argue that the First Amendment gives them the right to practice polygamy, despite the laws against it.

In the end though, the two sets of arguments by religious entities are quite similar. Both expect religious belief to direct public policy, and neither has a sufficient appreciation for the role of the legislature in achieving the public good. Their horizons are defined by their religious belief, and they transport those horizons into the public square as though they should delineate good and bad public policy by themselves. Yet, religious belief, no matter who holds it, or even how many hold it, cannot be the sole measuring rod for U.S. policy. This pluralist society is the result of the Constitution's best aspirations and for those who claim that they share the faith of the Framers to argue that the fruit of those early aspirations – peaceful religious diversity – is intolerable should be treated with some skepticism. The drive to power can wear religious garb just as easily as secular.

Well over a hundred years ago, when the Church of Jesus Christ of Latter-day Saints believed that polygamy on earth paved the way to heaven, the federal government outlawed the practice.[74] Polygamy is "[t]he condition or practice of having more than one spouse at one time."[75] The most common form of polygamy is polygyny, which is "the condition or practice of having more than one wife at one time."[76] The laws, however, outlawed multiple spouses of either gender. For purposes of this discussion, I will use "polygamy" to mean just that. It does not mean, by the way, "polyamory," the practice of having multiple sexual partners. When the Supreme Court decided *Lawrence v. Texas*, discussed above, it made it rather clear that the right of privacy protects personal sexual relations between consenting adults.[77] Thus, polyamory has been left to private choice. That does not mean it is the right choice from a moral perspective, but it does mean it is beyond the government's purview. "Polygamy," by contrast, implicates the larger social construct of marriage, not only the sexual relations between adults. For these purposes, the two universes need to be kept distinct.

As mentioned above, George Reynolds, a polygamist Mormon, challenged the federal law outlawing polygamy in the 1870s, arguing that because his actions in taking two wives were the result of religious belief, they were outside the force of the law. In other words, the anti-polygamy law might be okay as applied to someone who took two wives simply because he liked two women equally, but where a man's religious beliefs required taking multiple wives, then the government was powerless.

Essentially, Reynolds asked the Court to interpret the First Amendment to mean that belief and conduct are the same thing. That religious belief should be protected was not contested. The Court certainly had no problem in protecting the absolute freedom of conscience, but it refused to extend that unassailable protection to conduct.[78] In *Reynolds v. United States*, it uttered one of the most famous lines in free exercise cases: "Can a man excuse his practices to the contrary because of his religious belief? [To] permit this would be to make the professed doctrines of religious belief superior to the law of the land, and in effect to permit every citizen to become a law unto himself."[79] Common sense requires this reasoning.

Religious individuals harm the public good by violating the law no less (and no more) than any other entity breaking the law. As I will explain in Chapter 10, the touchstone in conduct cases must be harm or damage, not just a believer's perspective. No proper democracy exists that permits individuals to harm others at will simply because of their beliefs. The principle is often repeated in federal and state cases.

As Chapter 2 shows, a parent who allows a child to die of a medically treatable ailment does an identical harm to society as a parent who does it out of spite. In either case, society is robbed of that child's potential and talents. And society's quantum of suffering increases, because a child has been permitted to suffer when there were means to stop it. Just as no parent should be permitted to act to make a child a martyr, no adult is permitted to redefine marriage unilaterally. Marriage is a social construct that must be determined in light of neutral principles and the larger public good, not solely by the reflection of any particular group's religious beliefs. Here is where the polygamists' line of reasoning starts to look like the fundamentalists' argument against gay marriage. They expect to shape public law according to a religious litmus test, without reference to larger public good.

Canadian officials, whose constitution typically shares U.S. free exercise principles, intimated at one time that polygamy may be constitutionally protected and therefore the polygamy laws were unenforceable.[80] "Former Prime Minister Pierre Trudeau told us it wasn't the state's business and he implied that the rest of us shouldn't poke our noses in either."[81] But that view was rejected when the Canadian Supreme Court took up the issue in 2011.[82]

The contention raised by George Reynolds was no different from the pervasive argument in present times that religious conduct should be privileged vis-à-vis the law – simply because the cause is religious. For present purposes, Reynolds initiated a series of cases implementing a remarkably consistent and persistent principle: one's actions are measured by their effects and the law, not by their religious motivation. No one's conduct, with its capacity to harm others, is immune. In 1971, the U.S. Supreme Court in Gillette v. United States,[83] stated it as clearly as it has ever been stated: "Our cases do not at their farthest reach support the proposition that a stance of conscientious opposition relieves an objector from any colliding duty fixed by a democratic government."[84]

There is no question in the United States that polygamy is not constitutionally mandated. The arguments challenging the polygamy laws were first rejected in 1878, a result cemented in multiple federal and state decisions, ever since.[85] One 1955 Utah decision put it as plainly as possible:

> It was never intended or supposed that the amendment could be invoked as a *protection against legislation for the punishment of acts inimical to the peace, good order, and morals of society....* However free the exercise of religion may be, it must be subordinate to the criminal laws of the country, passed *with reference to actions regarded by general consent as properly the subjects of punitive legislation.*[86]

But to say there is no constitutional right to polygamy is not to say that the religious accommodation discussion is necessarily over.

There is never any harm in a free society re-examining the bases of public policy, even when that which is being examined has been entrenched since the beginning of the country. Tradition by itself cannot and should not determine whether the common good has been adequately served. When polygamy was first outlawed in the United States, it was considered, along with slavery, to be one of the "twin relics of barbarism."[87]

In this era, the polygamists are challenging the traditional marriage model, and saying essentially, "no harm, no foul." If consenting adults are willing to enter into polygamous relationships, it is a victimless crime, the reasoning goes. This is the classic libertarian position that holds that government should involve itself in the lives of individuals as minimally as possible, and that is enormously attractive in an era in which the Supreme Court has recognized a private right to choose sexual practices and partners in *Lawrence v. Texas*. But the link between *Lawrence* and marriage is weak, as I explain above. Consensual sexual practices involving adults constitute a category decidedly distinct from the definition of marriage, which determines legitimacy, inheritance, and numerous other legal consequences. The private sexual act can stay in the bedroom; the shape of marriage is an external decision, far removed from the bedroom – even if most marriages involve sex between partners.

Until recently, government officials in Canada and the United States have been extraordinarily diffident in prosecuting the crime of polygamy or even child or spouse abuses within such communities. For example, the Department of Justice did not actively pursue tailor-made Mann Act violations where underage girls were exchanged between FLDS colonies in Utah, Arizona, and Canada until the 2006 arrest of their prophet Warren Jeffs. Nearly 60 years ago, the U.S. Supreme Court held that the transport of girls and women in such circumstances violated the Mann Act and maintained that a free exercise "defense claims too much. If upheld, it would place beyond the law any act done under claim of religious sanction."[88] In contrast, there have been a number of Mann Act prosecutions that did not involve religion.[89] No prosecutor should choose between available prosecutions according to the religious status of the actor, though they often do.

Twenty-seven legislators asked the Arizona attorney general to prosecute criminal violations by polygamous communities, including rape, incest, and bigamy.[90] In response to the political pressure, within months a multi-use facility was established in the Arizona/Utah enclave, which was staffed by local and state officials and provided a place for victims to report abuse.[91] The FLDS harassed its believers who tried to take advantage of the facility to the point that it had to be shut down.

In Utah, it took the revelation of child abandonment discussed in Chapter 2 for Attorney General Shurtleff even to say he would consider taking action.[92] When the office distributed a manual for polygamy's victims, Tapestry Against Polygamy refused to assist in the distribution of the book, because it depicted polygamy as a "unique lifestyle," rather than a criminal act.[93] In early September 2004, however, action was taken through the Justice Department's Office of Violence Against Women, which established a grant of approximately $700,000 to assist domestic violence victims in rural and polygamous communities.[94]

Civil liberties groups, civil authorities, and other proponents of "religious liberty" for conduct seem to operate from the premise that a democratic society is obligated to ensure the perpetuation of religious groups. After the *Salt Lake Tribune* published an editorial saying "polygamy is inherently destructive,"[95] a letter to the editor argued that laws against polygamy in the 1800s might have obliterated the early Mormon Church, as though public policy should be chosen to preserve religious groups.[96] Government regulation is not supposed to ensure or foster the development of certain religions; the United States has fostered a busy marketplace in religion, in part because the government has been

constitutionally deterred from supporting or undermining religious institutions. A religious organization that has declining membership may
not and should not be able to demand government assistance or regulation to sustain itself. Andrea Moore-Emmett rightly responded to the
letter, saying that religion has proven remarkably resilient in the face
of government regulation of certain actions,[97] and therefore such concerns cannot drive the public policy determination. Rather, the government's obligation is to persist in choosing the public good over all other
concerns.

As the issue has become a front-page story, at least one academic has
defended polygamy on First Amendment grounds, and his reasoning
nicely illustrates how these arguments can run off the rails. Professor
Jonathan Turley in *USA Today* called the arguments against polygamy
by conservative groups fighting gay marriage hypocritical:

> Given this history and the long religious traditions [that had recognized
> polygamy at some point in history], it cannot be seriously denied that
> polygamy is a legitimate religious belief... if we yield to our impulse
> and single out one hated minority, the First Amendment becomes little
> more than hype and we become little more than hypocrites.[98]

That the belief is "legitimate," means nothing as a legal matter, because
under the First Amendment, all sincere religious beliefs – no matter how
outlandish – are legitimate, and the government may not draw such
a distinction between sincerely held beliefs. He then declares, "The
First Amendment was designed to protect the least popular and least
powerful among us."[99] This is the kind of overgeneralization that too
often substitutes for considered discussion of the First Amendment in
the United States, regrettably.

The First Amendment was not crafted to protect conduct that harms
others, even if the actor is unpopular or powerless. A small polygamous
and incestuous California sect was no doubt unpopular and politically
powerless, but the cult leader who is now accused of murdering his wives
and children (some of whom were both) was no more defensible than
any other mass murderer.[100] The First Amendment is simply irrelevant
to the legality of his conduct. If the government had directed the cult to
cease believing in polygamy or to stifle its speech about it because the
government found it unpalatable, Turley's analysis might have had some

bite, but it is completely beside the point when the issue is conduct, like polygamous marriage.

Moreover, it is important to point out that the FLDS has not been politically powerless. Like the ultra-Orthodox Jews in Brooklyn, they are a political force, because the religious leaders have dictated how the community will vote. Elected officials often abandon principle for such votes. There are not more prosecutions of FLDS men and women for child rape and abandonment, because the FLDS has exercised political power that has held back prosecutors in every state where they are located, with the notable exception of Texas.

Turley's main mistake was that he substituted the view of the religious individual for legal reasoning and, therefore, lost sight of the only relevant question: is the conduct harmful or beneficial? Indeed, his focus on the religious is so intense that he fails to take into account that bigamy and polygamy are not just religious practices, and that even the secular bigamists may harm society.[101] He frames the question incorrectly. The legitimate legal issue is not whether the religious viewpoint of certain believers is internally inconsistent, or even what any one group of believers holds true. The question for public policy is whether the practice of polygamy is consistent with what is best for society, period. As with so many public officials and representatives, he confuses a debate over belief with the debate over public policy. Both debates are welcome at the public round-table. Only the latter properly shapes the law. The government may not enter the former, but it is duty-bound to address the latter.

As mentioned above, reality star Kody Brown challenged Utah's polygamy laws and won a partial victory. They did not succeed in setting aside the polygamy law itself, but achieved two victories (the first of which I expect to be reversed on appeal). [102]

First, Brown persuaded the court that polygamy only occurs when a group of adults attempt to obtain more than one marriage license. The court ignored common law marriage, which occurs when couples hold themselves out as married for a given number of years. Second, the court ruled that adults have a right to cohabitate under *Lawrence v. Texas*.

Formerly polygamous wives argue that the typical religious polygamy community elevates certain men over all others and treats women and children as nothing more than property to accumulate.[103] In Chapter 2, I described polygamy's impact on children; it has also harmed women.

When underage girls are forced into marrying much older men in these communities, they are taken out of school, deprived of any means of future earning or self-support, and burdened with the expectation of bearing as many children as possible. From the perspective of any family court, where the reigning standard is the "best interest of the child," this formula violates many of the established criteria. No family court judge would choose the parent with these characteristics in a divorce case. It is a sentence for girls to a life of underachievement and, therefore, for a court to approve it is to violate equal protection.

The cost of such enormous families can prove to be too much for any one man, leading some polygamist men to support only their first wives, leaving all later wives (and their children) no option but state support.[104] Moreover, home schooling is favored in order to avoid the public school system, which could lead to discovery of their criminal acts. So mothers who have marginal educations themselves are teaching their children. These children would appear to be destined to be as undereducated as their mothers, despite federal legislation that purports to leave no child behind. When government refuses to prosecute the legal violations within these polygamous enclaves, it further isolates the women and leaves their children far behind the standardized goals set by the federal legislation.[105]

There is some debate whether this describes the natural propensities of polygamy, or whether only the bad polygamous actors get the attention of the public. Some of the wives from the FLDS Bountiful, British of Columbia commune have defended their lifestyle, saying that they enter the marriages freely, that the women are educated, and that there is no abuse.[106] There is also a Utah organization of polygamous women, Principle Voices of Polygamy, which defends the practice.[107]

Polygamy's defenders are not only Mormon fundamentalists. Mark Henkel is a self-proclaimed spokesman for a Christian polygamy advocacy group in Maine, who "cites biblical scripture and the polygamists' lifestyle of such Old Testament biblical figures as Abraham and King David as justification." He asserts he does not, however, support forced marriages and believes in the free choice of women to enter the arrangement.[108] Of course, there is only free choice when the girl is of age.

Legislators must consider whether the unbalanced numbers in a polygamous marriage institute an inherently unequal relationship and a tendency toward abuse of girls and abandonment of boys. While there are a certain number of people in the United States who argue that the above abuses are simply perversions of what can be a productive and happy relationship, others have seen in polygamy an internal contradiction with the rule of law and democracy. At the very least, male-dominated polygamy sends the message that only one man need satisfy multiple women, so that the women are not equal to the man. Naomi Schaefer Riley, who is a Fellow at the Ethics and Public Policy Center, in Washington, D.C., believes the latter, saying that it "corrupt(s) civil society as a whole, destroying education, individual rights and the rule of law – in other words the foundations of democratic governance."[109] Others, like political science professor Thomas Flanagan at the University of Calgary, Canada, are more blunt, arguing that polygamous societies are highly unequal and a deadly foe of constitutional government. He offers as proof that constitutional democracies have arisen only from monogamous societies.[110]

The facts of religious polygamy are the proper focus of any social and legislative reconsideration of marriage. The victims of polygamy should be heard, as should the continuing practitioners who would defend the practice. The typical defense by the men is that their religion demands it, and the government should have no power to regulate their religion. That should never be enough when there is such credible evidence of child abuse and neglect and such stark treatment of women as unequal partners in the community and marriage.

> Members of the Fundamentalist Church of Jesus Christ of Latter-day Saints believe that men must have at least three wives to reach heaven's highest echelon.[111] One leader elaborated by pointing out that it was a blessing for the women, because "the only way she could ever be happy was – that she would let her husband, a faithful man, rule over her. That was the only way back to Heavenly Father for the woman."[112] He was not quite as subtle when dealing with recalcitrant wives: "You can either live here and live in hell, and then when you die have eternal happiness. Or else, you can go out into the world and live in hell and die and even have more eternal hell."[113]

In underdeveloped regions of the world where polygamy is still widely practiced the problems are complex. Florence Butegwa, former regional director of Women in Law & Development in Africa (WiLDAF) has commented on the contradicting views of polygamy in Uganda, where women have organized "to demand the abolition of polygamy as a necessary step for protecting women's rights in marriage." At the same time, Muslim women, "either on their own volition or on the demands of their Islamic leaders," opposed the movement. "They liked polygamy, they [didn't] want it to go away." Their claims "provided the government with an escape route."[114] Similar campaigns against polygamy were started in other African nations, especially Nigeria, where The Campaign Against Polygamy & Women Oppression In Nigeria and Africa (CAPWONA), and the Total World Women Freedom Alliance (TOWWFA), believed that polygamous marriages were inherently unequal and lead to unhappiness for the women, but they also saw a larger issue involving the building blocks of the society.[115] Given the multitude of issues surrounding women's rights in Africa, including access to healthcare, child custody issues and basic property laws, Professor Mojubaolu Olu-funke Okome of Brooklyn College, CUNY, put it this way: "I don't think that many women in Nigeria think polygamy is a problem in and of itself. . . . the unjust treatment of a woman under the polygamous system may be a problem."[116]

Kenya recently set an example of the perils of polygamy when it legalized it. Women asked to have a say in the choice of other spouses, yet the law that passed handed men the power to choose later wives without notice to the first.[117] As the Supreme Court noted in *Reynolds*, polygamy is inherently patriarchal.

The notion that a religious heritage requires continued adherence in defiance of the law is undermined by the many mainstream Latter-Day Saints who have firmly rejected polygamy, and thrived, and by the millions of Muslims in the United States who have rejected polygamy as well. When the Black Muslim movement began in the United States in the 1970s, its adherents did not make polygamy an essential element, and it never has been. It has since divided into the American Society of Muslims and the Nation of Islam, both of which thrive despite rejecting polygamy.

While United States officials have been apt to turn the other way, international treaties have labeled polygamy as an inherently unequal relationship that violates fundamental principles of equality. For example, following the creation of the Convention for the Elimination of All Forms of Discrimination Against Women (CEDAW), the United Nations offered the following analysis: "Polygamous marriage contravenes a woman's right to equality with men, and can have such serious emotional and financial consequences for her and her dependents that such marriages ought to be discouraged and prohibited."[118]

Muslims who believe in polygamy would limit it to four wives per man, but also observe a requirement that the man set up the women and their children in separate housing with separate support. The financial side of these requirements can be a deterrent, but, as one man in Turkey said, polygamy itself invites men to use their wives as a "sign of power," because it is a symbol of wealth, power, and virility.[119] With so many wives, and a value placed on numbers of children, the Muslim culture can also contribute to fathers who are less than attentive. One man in Turkey said that he didn't recognize his own son on the street.

All of this is proper fodder for legislative consideration, including the experiences of those in the United States who have lived within the institution, the views of those who have left it, and the knowledge of the international community.

Under the constitutional arrangement, the states have the power to define marriage in each state. Only state legislatures, acting as elected representatives of all of the people, can engage in a wide-ranging and wide-eyed factual inquiry, consultation with experts here and abroad, and consideration of what this society needs marriage to accomplish. Courts are constrained to look at only the facts gathered for a case by the parties. That makes them far less superior in setting public policy.

To the extent the religious polygamists insist that the Constitution mandates permission for their practices, they are on quicksand. If they are arguing instead that polygamy is a socially beneficial practice that is capable of serving the public good, then they should make the case, but as the UN has observed, that is a case impossible to make.

Here, as elsewhere, elected officials – legislators, prosecutors, and Governors – need to be reminded that they are not in their positions of power to roll over for religious organizations that demand rights to do whatever their beliefs dictate. It is never enough for representatives to assert they are furthering religious liberty. The victims of polygamy need to be taken into account in such a calculus, just as the victims of clergy abuse and medical neglect need to be in the forefront of legislators' minds when they determine statutes of limitations on childhood sexual abuse, child abuse reporting, and medical neglect laws. The legislative mantra needs to be that conduct always has the potential to harm and that, as legislators, they are obligated to identify, forestall, and deter harm.

Before anyone agrees to overturn polygamous marriage, they should be required to read the stories of its many victims. The following are just a few:

- Dorothy Allred Solomon, *Daughter of the Saints: Growing Up in Polygamy*
- Carolyn Jessop, *Escape*
- Elissa Wall and Lisa Pulitzer, *Stolen Innocence: My Story of Growing Up in a Polygamous Sect, Becoming a Teenage Bride, and Breaking Free of Warren Jeffs*
- Daphne Bramham, *The Secret Lives of Saints: Child Brides and Lost Boys in a Polygamous Mormon Sect*
- Stephen Singular, *When Men Become Gods: Mormon Polygamist Warren Jeffs, His Cult of Fear, and the Women Who Fought Back*

Conclusion

I chose to focus this chapter on the two forms of marriage that have prompted recent religious debate and defenses. The reader, however, should not assume that marriage and religion issues end here. There is another arena in which the civil rights and safety of women have been at risk. The evangelical Christian movement has included a strain of believers who preach subservience of women to men. While they have the right to believe that this is Biblically required, such a belief can pave the way to abuse.[120]

Recently, Bill Gothard, the founder of the Advanced Training Institute, which at one time hosted stadium-sized gatherings of evangelical Christian families, was an avid promoter of a Bible-based relationship between a man and a woman. In *Meeting Your Husband's Seven Basic Needs: How to be a Godly Wife*, he lays out a laundry list of ways in which a wife should serve her husband, which includes an admonition to maintain her appearance: "A wife should dress to please her husband. She should have a joyful countenance and select clothing that draws attention to it. A wife should always be well groomed."[121] She must also "honor his leadership," make "appeals" not "demands," and be "grateful," among other attributes.

In 2014, Gothard was placed on administrative leave after he was credibly accused by many women and teen-age girls of sexual harassment.[122] Other victims of this trend have been speaking up. Coral Anika Thiess published *Bonshea: From Darkness to Light* in 2007 to tell the world about the abuse she suffered in a marriage governed by Gothard's principles. Similarly, the online organization, Recovering Grace, is a group of adults who were raised as children under the Advanced Training Institute, and Gothard's rules, who are motivated to help the significant number who were physically, sexually, and emotionally abused growing up.[123]

Like polygamy, this movement to put women in "their place" – under the control of men is an example of how religious entities can operate to empower men and undermine women's flourishing and safety. The Nigerian terrorist group Boko Haram, which abducted more than 300 teen-age girls from their school to sell them as wives, is different in degree, but not kind. The name of the group means "Western education is sinful," but its mission is to ensure that *girls* are not educated.[124]

4

RELIGIOUS LAND USE AND
RESIDENTIAL NEIGHBORHOODS

Part One covers many arenas wherein religious entities act as though the public interest pales in comparison to their agendas. In many circumstances, though, the average American has little idea how religious entities are harming others. In contrast, the disputes in this Chapter occur in Americans' own backyards.

Religious landowner impose intense challenges on local governments. They need worship space large enough to accommodate weekly (or biweekly) gatherings of a significant percentage of their members, and even bigger assemblies for holiday; they can also host schools, weddings, bar and bat mitzvahs, funerals, youth activities, and social services like Alcoholics Anonymous, blood drives, food kitches, and homeless shelters. Thus, a small building with minimal parking is ordinarily inadequate. In the era when these buildings were only used for worship and maybe a choir practice, despite their size, houses of worship were attractive residential neighbors. Church properties were like miniature parks of peaceful tranquility in residential neighborhoods – the grounds were pretty, the building was tasteful, and they were excellent neighbors. Parking, traffic, lights, and noise were not typical problems. That is no longer true as large religious projects are using extreme religious liberty arguments to wedge themselves into residential zones, and changing the character of the residential neighborhood.

From RFRA to RLUIPA: religious landowners obtain preferential treatment under the land use laws

RFRA was an enormous boon for religious entities intent on avoiding the law. In an interesting turn of events, it was a land use, historic preservation case that razed RFRA. The archbishop of San Antonio, Texas, sought to demolish the lovely St. Peter Catholic Church in Boerne, Texas, and to replace it with a box-like structure. The Boerne City Council responded by denying permission for complete demolition, because the mission-style church, built in 1923, was located in a historic preservation district, and in fact was a focal point of the district. The two parties began to negotiate over what percentage of the front of the church would be preserved when RFRA became law in November 1993. The archbishop filed a federal lawsuit claiming that RFRA permitted the church to avoid the city's historic preservation laws. In 1997, the Supreme Court held that Congress could not usurp state and local authority by this law with its breathtaking scope, and invalidated RFRA.[1] What was the result? The parties resumed negotiating and 80 percent of the church was retained, with the facade facing the historical district preserved and a beautiful addition on the back, beyond the sightlines from the historical district.[2] All of which is to point out that land use law is usually a matter of negotiating, and that reasonable parties typically sit on either side of the table. The federal law tipped the power balance in favor of the religious entity momentarily, but its invalidation righted the balance.

Religious entities, however, were not to be impeded by the Supreme Court's rejection of RFRA. They soldiered on to introduce RLPA, which would have had nearly the same scope, but which did not make it to the floor of the Senate, because of growing concerns about its real-world impact, especially on children. When the vast scope of RFRA and RLPA proved unconstitutional and then unpalatable to Congress, religious groups stripped the RLPA bill down to two categories: land use and prisons. The resulting statute was the Religious Land Use and Institutionalized Persons Act.[3] The acronym, RLUIPA, rhymes with chalupa.

Before RLUIPA, religious landowners in virtually every jurisdiction were simply landowners, required to abide by zoning and land use restrictions, with the concomitant market price for property and for obtaining zoning alterations. If their project was incompatible with the district, they would have to apply for a special-use permit or a variance, just like any other landowner. When they sought to institute a building project in a residential neighborhood, they had to weigh the costs of the land and construction; the likelihood the use would be limited because it was in a residential area; and the costs of obtaining a permit. They also had to take into account the views of the surrounding homeowners and families on the impact of their proposal. In other words, they were property owners with equal rights under the land use law with all other property owners, and they had to be good neighbors.

RFRA and then RLUIPA changed all that. In 2000, President Bill Clinton (who never met a religious cause he would not support as President),[4] signed RLUIPA, saying: "Today I am pleased to sign into law S.2869, the 'Religious Land Use and Institutionalized Persons Act of 2000,' which will provide important protections for religious exercise in America." Then he praised the usual suspects behind such legislation, Senators Hatch and Kennedy. (It has not been done yet, but one could write a book about their partnership benefiting religious entities both in public and under the table.) Not skipping a beat, he then thanked the religious groups, the Coalition for the Free Exercise of Religion, and the civil rights communities for "crafting this legislation." Current Supreme Court Justice, Elena Kagan, worked as counsel for President Clinton at the time and endorsed RLUIPA's attempted predecessor, RLPA, saying she was "the biggest fan" of the proposed act in the Clinton Administration.[5]

President Clinton went on to say: "Their work in passing this legislation once again demonstrates that people of all political bents and faiths can work together for a common purpose that benefits all Americans."[6] Translation: this was religious special interest legislation, drafted outside Congress and then passed because the members and the President believed the right people were behind it, not because they had determined independently that it was a good law for the people.

RLUIPA requires equal and fair treatment for religious landowners, which is not particularly remarkable, aside from the fact that one can fairly question why Congress would spend time on provisions that obviously mimic the Constitution.[7] But it also directs courts to treat land-use laws as applied to religious entities as though they were presumptively unconstitutional. Those provisions mandate the following: where the land use law imposes a substantial burden on a religious landowner's religious conduct, and the law is applied through an "individualized assessment," the government may not enforce its law unless it can prove the law was necessary and narrowly tailored.[8] In other words, Congress created a new "civil right" and a new forum – the federal courts – for churches burdened by land use laws. The RLUIPA regime has introduced the following scenario: a religious landowner who might not have attempted to impose an ambitious building project on a residential neighborhood or who would not have purchased a piece of property because it needed zoning that would be difficult to obtain, will change course 180 degrees. Congress displaced local zoning and planning authorities, and the federal judiciary, who had never heard land use cases unless there was a constitutional violation charged, became zoning board review courts. This is not a good scenario for homeowners or local governments. The balance of power in residential neighborhoods shifts to the religious landowners at the expense of the residential quality of the neighborhood. The untoward result is that homeowners have become second-class citizens to their religious neighbors, and federal courts meddle with land use law.

The reader may be thinking that religious entities might not take advantage of their superior status very often, because they are institutions of integrity or because the cost of federal litigation would lead them to bring RLUIPA claims only when the cost of the litigation could be justified. Unfortunately, they do.

The first reason – integrity – unfortunately does not wash, because the religious entities usually view their project as so superior to the needs of the neighbors that they feel justified in their elevated status. The statute establishes a terrible dynamic where religious landowners defend their special treatment on the ground that their goals are religious, as though the neighbors are all atheists (the likelihood of which, in this society, is low – only about 14 percent claim to be atheists or agnostics).[9] When the neighbors balk at the projected plans on neutral grounds, such as increased traffic, noise, and light, they are accused of being anti-xxx (the reader should fill in the blank of the religious affiliation of the landowner). RLUIPA has turned neighbor against neighbor and is one of the most religiously divisive laws ever enacted in the United States.

Nor does the cost of RLUIPA litigation typically deter religious landowners. The drafters of RLUIPA (the American Civil Liberties Union, the Department of Justice, and others) did not stop at providing "a legal weapon" no secular landowner could wield.[10] RLUIPA contains an "attorneys' fees" provision, which forces the government to pay the attorneys' fees for both sides if the government loses.[11] The attorneys' fees provision has magnified the special quality of RLUIPA for religious landowners, enticing them to file federal lawsuits they would not have dreamed of filing in the past.

In times of tight city and state budgets, the prospect of having to pay for federal litigation, which is always expensive, is daunting enough. But the specter of having to pay *both* sides' fees can be catastrophic to the local budget, especially where the locality's insurance carrier balks at covering RLUIPA litigation, as sometimes happens. Local authorities too often fold like a house of cards, regardless of the merits, because the economics so heavily favor the RLUIPA claimant.

The prospect of attorneys' fees also has encouraged interest groups and white-shoe law firms to bankroll land use litigation, making the litigation free for the religious entity (with a plan to seek millions in fees from the City as the price of settlement). Thus, for the religious landowner, no longer is cost a factor in deciding whether to go to federal court, and claims that religious landowners would never have pursued in the past have become attractive. Congress tipped the balance of power between the religious land developers and local governments in favor of the developers.

The religious landowners also have a strategic advantage in the federal courts, because, as the usual vague allegations of discrimination waft through the lawsuit, the federal court usually knows very little about typical zoning practices and rules. The churches have an uncanny ability to make standard, fair practices sound inherently prejudiced. In that poisoned atmosphere, cities then must argue that their laws were passed for a "compelling interest" by the "least restrictive means." It's a miracle if every house of worship does not obtain whatever it seeks through RLUIPA, because the atmospherics and the believers' arguments typically amount to a claim that they have a right to complete exemption from the law. RLUIPA, thus, is a win-win-win situation for religious landowners. They obtain new power against ordinary land use laws, they have the prospect of having their attorney's fees paid by the city, and with the expectation of fees whether they win or settle, interest group law firms, small boutique firms, and large, white-shoe law firms will work for free during the pendency of the case. All of the incentives work for the opportunistic religious landowner and against the local government, neighbors, and taxpayers.

A wide array of ambitious religious land use proposals have been asserted under the RLUIPA umbrella. A good number have not been outright winners, but RLUIPA still has levied heavy costs on neighbors, taxpayers, and local governments. Residential neighbors have had to fight incompatible land uses to keep their neighborhoods residential, and local governments have been saddled with the cost of such litigation even when the claim was not meritorious. It takes money to defend oneself in federal court.

If there is one thing that is sacrosanct in the United States, it is the belief that one's home is one's castle, and therefore the religious land use disputes pit one cherished ideal – religious liberty – against another – the American Dream of a nice home in a quiet neighborhood, where children can be safe. In 1974 the Supreme Court put it this way:

> A quiet place where yards are wide, people few, and motorcycles restricted are legitimate guidelines in a land use project addressed to family needs. . . . The police power is not confined to elimination of filth, stench, and unhealthy places. It is ample to lay out zones where family values, youth values, and the blessings of quiet seclusion and clean air make the area a sanctuary for people.[12]

Religious groups lobbying for preferential land use rights seem to have an odd blind spot on this core American value. They live in the culture, and surely many live in just such a setting. Yet, they seem surprised – or at least bemused – when their privileged status renders neighborhoods war zones.[13] Lawyer Anthony Picarello, who was with the Becket Fund and now is General Counsel of the United States Conference of Catholic Bishops, said it like this: "RLUIPA does not create 'two classes of citizens' across religious lines. Instead, it creates two classes of activities – land use that involves religious exercise, and land use that does not – and then reinforces the constitutional protection for all citizens who choose to use their land for religious exercise."[14] In other words, religious land is more valuable than anyone else's. Note also his sly use of the phrase "constitutional protection," as though RLUIPA is constitutionally required. It is not.

RLUIPA DOES NOT REPLICATE PRE-EXISTING FREE EXERCISE DOCTRINE OR REFLECT FIRST AMENDMENT CASE LAW. Lower courts have been hoodwinked into believing that RLUIPA is just a reiteration of the Free Exercise Clause, so no harm, no foul. The significant uptick in federal litigation over religious land use since RLUIPA's passage proves the opposite. The law was passed because religious landowners demanded more than the First Amendment requires. Enterprising defenders of the law, however, including some in the U.S. Department of Justice, hit upon a way to have their cake and eat it, too. Religious landowners are granted better treatment than ever before, but the law's defenders wave a wand as they chant that nothing has changed.

First, as I explain in Chapters 1 and 8, the least restrictive means test was never imposed on the government by the Court in the First Amendment free exercise cases. Even when there was a threat of discrimination, the Court's doctrine employed ordinary strict scrutiny. RLUIPA's invocation of the "least restrictive means" test distances it far from the First Amendment and especially in the land use context.

Second, before RFRA and RLUIPA imposed extreme religious liberty standards on land use laws to the benefit of religious entities, those same entities were required to follow generally applicable, neutral laws.[15] The clever trick is that RLUIPA imposes strict scrutiny on land use laws that involve "individualized assessment,"[16] because there are some Supreme Court free exercise cases that invalidate laws that employ "individualized assessment," or so they say. Then in every RLUIPA case, they argue that any application of a land use law entails an "individualized assessment," in the sense that each landowner's case is decided on its own facts. Trust me, this is crazy reasoning.

The Supreme Court has never treated case-by-case analysis as presumptively unconstitutional. That is tantamount to saying that every time a court decides a case by applying the law to the facts, its decision should be presumptively unconstitutional. What has happened is that the drafters of RLUIPA ingeniously included the term "individualized assessment," but they left off its modifier. That has permitted them to argue in a huge universe of cases (virtually any land use case) that RLUIPA is simply replicating free exercise law. It is masterful, wishful thinking, or just plain devious. "Individualized assessment," by itself, means "case by case." If government making individualized assessments makes the outcome presumptively unconstitutional, then every judicial decision in the United States is likely unconstitutional. That's just plain silly.

In the cases where government regulations employed individualized assessments and the Court treated the government's action as presumptively unconstitutional, the constitutional error was not case-by-case analysis, but rather the fact that government engaged in case-by-case analysis *of the reasons* for the requested exemption *and* treated religious reasons less well than secular reasons.[17] Where the government was willing to exempt some from its rules for secular reasons, but would not provide any relief for religious reasons, the court was suspicious of animus toward religion, and rightly so.

For example, there was no rational explanation for the Newark Police Department's rule that no officer could have facial hair unless he had a medical condition.[18] Those with religious reasons for facial hair were not accommodated. If the department's policies were not undermined by creating an exemption for the few with a medical problem, then they could not be harmed for the few that required a religious exemption.

Similarly, an unemployment compensation scheme that permitted people to take certain days off for secular reasons was unconstitutional when it rejected religious reasons to take those days off.[19] Again, if the general policy could tolerate the secular exceptions, it should tolerate the religious. It is the disparate treatment between secular and religious *reasons* for the exemption that justifies strict scrutiny, not the individualized assessment itself. Thus, RLUIPA goes significantly farther for religious entities than the Constitution does. Under settled constitutional principles, religious entities are bound by generally applicable, neutral laws, including land use laws, but now those laws are presumptively illegal under RLUIPA. It is a large net win for the religious.

Some of the lower courts that have addressed the issue so far, though, have fallen for the "individualized assessment" language. In the Eastern District of Pennsylvania, Judge Stewart Dalzell, saw the issue as obvious: "What Congress manifestly has done . . . is to codify the individualized assessments' jurisprudence in Free Exercise cases that originated with the Supreme Court's decision in *Sherbert v. Verner* [the individualized assessments' unemployment compensation case]."[20] The point was equally unremarkable to Magistrate Judge Holly Fitzsimmons, who stated that it is "'apparent that [RLUIPA] faithfully codifies the 'individual assessments' jurisprudence in the *Sherbert* through *Lukumi* line of cases.'"[21] They were wrong.

Keep in mind, however, that religious lobbyists did not enact extreme religious liberty statutes by themselves; that was done by legislators. And these legislators are the ones who need to be brought to account on these issues. It is one thing for an interest group to hide the other side of an issue, but it is a severe failure of responsibility for Congress (and state legislators) to miss the other side altogether. Moreover, in the land use arena, virtually every one of them has owned or owns a home, so it is not as though they needed special expertise to be able to foretell how private homeowners would feel when large houses of worship could destroy the residential quality of their neighborhoods. Members of Congress betrayed the vast majority of their constituents with RLUIPA.

The paradigm shift in houses of worship

There has been a paradigm shift in houses of worship in the United States. Unfortunately for their residential neighbors, although favorable for the recipients of their services, contemporary houses of worship are not the sleepy institutions they once were. They are now a locus for social services, as well as a center for worship and entertainment. These thriving religious entities need sizeable buildings, with seating for hundreds – sometimes thousands, and bring heavy traffic, intense parking needs, and even bus transportation into the neighborhood from off site. Problems arise when established houses of worship situated in residential neighborhoods attempt to compete with these new multipurpose churches or when large or growing congregations try to wedge a new campus into a neighborhood. The established church may seek to transform its existing grounds into parking lots as it adds buildings and services, or a new church may enter the real estate market and purchase five or six neighboring homes – often without telling the neighbors. A homeowner can go to sleep in a quiet residential enclave and wake up next door to a proposed 150-car parking lot.[22] The result of church expansion is too often that neighborhood streets where children once played roller hockey are now so busy that the parents are uneasy letting the children play in the front yard. Minimal traffic and the atmosphere it creates, after all, attract many families to their homes in the first place.[23]

The size of the congregation alone does not dictate how the house of worship will affect residential neighborhoods. There is also the question of what services will be provided. "Church on Sunday" is no longer the rule. The house of worship use that is carved into the memories of so many adults in the United States is gone. Houses of worship are, in fact, multiple-use social centers. The typical congregation may use its property for schools, weddings, funerals, receptions, social services like Alcoholics Anonymous, soup kitchens, homeless shelters, youth athletics and socials, and religious study. The worship program may include numerous elements as well, such as a summer religious camp; services on days other than the Sabbath; youth groups for elementary, junior high, and high school students; and multiple choirs. Hours of use skyrocket from less than a dozen to well over 60 in a single week, with the use generating a traffic pattern and accompanying noise and light more evocative of a grocery store than a home. "When viewed from an objective land use perspective (considering only the level of activity, not its substance) or from a traffic perspective, such a use begins to look more like a commercial facility than like the traditional neighborhood church."[24]

The phenomenon of the "megachurch" in the United States takes this trend to its logical extreme, with some campuses including child and senior day care, recreation centers, health clubs, bowling alleys, bookstores, coffee houses, hotels, home-repair assistance, and motion picture theaters.[25] There is one religious institution in Houston, Texas, that included a McDonald's.[26] These complexes are, in fact, self-contained communities for believers to go after work and on the weekends, where social and religious needs are satisfied simultaneously.

The final factor in this house-of-worship expansion is that many congregations have come to think of themselves as ministers to all, not just their own members, so there is competition among religious entities to provide a panoply of social services to those outside the congregation. The menu of services also serves to entice new members. According to one expert, "'American churches of all kinds are trying to do everything they can to enlarge their tent, be seen, be accessible.'"[27] It is a formula that seems to be working, because nondenominational, nontraditional churches are the fastest growing religious groups in the United States.[28]

When size and intense use combine to affect a residential neighborhood, previously friendly neighbors can become mutually hostile enemies. There are two conflicting dynamics happening at once. The religious entity is experiencing a heady and exciting period of expansion, and likely sees earthly hurdles as contrary to its divinely inspired religious movement. The neighbors are in a very different place. Typically, they have lived in the neighborhood for a long time, or they chose the neighborhood for its residential qualities, so the new building project is a serious threat to their happiness in their home and their reasonable expectations about their neighborhood. To make matters worse for everyone concerned, a home is often a family's largest financial, and emotional, investment; thus, when the character of the neighborhood and property values are threatened, homeowners understandably object. Typically, they really do not care if the expansion project will result in a bakery or a temple. "You could be a car dealership, a hospital, a university; it doesn't matter. Especially if it is in your neighborhood."[29]

Either way, they are losing much of what they value in their homes. Moreover, given the demographics of religion in the United States, the two sides are almost always religious, so any implied condescension from the new religious group can really hit a nerve, and even a whiff of a holier-than-thou attitude from the members can lead to a conflagration of bad feelings. Conversely, the landowners' attorneys are not shy about calling neighbors who oppose the project bigots. Isn't it interesting how when it comes to land use, the religious claim they are outnumbered and discriminated against, but when it comes to same-sex marriage, they insist this is a "Christian country" where the majority must rule, as I discuss in Chapter 3? My point is that the extreme religious liberty mindset teaches that the end always justifies the means.

Local government has found itself quite literally between a rock and a hard place on these issues. These intensely used properties wedged into residential neighborhoods challenge basic land use principles. Again and again, RLUIPA has forced local governments to abandon the neighbors' needs and expectations in favor of the religious applicant. In 2000, RLUIPA introduced three threats against local governments: federal litigation, attorneys' fees for the religious applicant, and Department of Justice oversight.

Too often, a pastor or developer finds a deal on a piece of property in a zone where their project is not permitted. Before RLUIPA, either they would keep looking or buy it on a contingency, which requires them to complete the sale only if they receive land use approvals. RLUIPA does not encourage thoughtful or careful dealings by religious purchasers. In one case, the pastor signed off on a purchase with no contingency, but little realistic likelihood the project would qualify under the land use code, which should have been his risk to assume, but RLUIPA forced the government's hand.[30]

RLUIPA is extreme religious liberty for landowners, which Congress had no idea would be a scourge for neighborhoods, cities, and taxpayers. I speak from experience as one who has been contacted by dozens, if not hundreds, of homeowners organized around the United States who have had remarkably similar experiences, and one who represents some of the cities involved in these disputes.

A home becomes a synagogue

In Los Angeles's beautiful Hancock Park neighborhood, an Orthodox Jewish shul, or synagogue, operated for decades out of Rabbi Chaim Baruch Rubin's home. The neighborhood is roughly 80 years old, and many of the homes have a distinctive Mediterranean look. For many years, the shul was attended by a small number of men, and the neighbors did not complain because they had no reason to. But then the rabbi passed away and the rabbi's son, Rabbi Chaim Baruch Rubin, took over and assumed control with a grander vision, which led to a legal dispute. First, he expanded the use of his father's home from a daily prayer meeting, or minyan, to a synagogue with a congregation attending weekly Sabbath services and holding bar and bat mitzvahs. Then, when this expanded use triggered resistance from the neighbors, he requested a variance to construct and operate what amounted to a full-service synagogue on another nearby property in the same neighborhood. Under existing law, there was virtually no question that this project was inconsistent with the city's land use laws. On the first round in 1996, before RLUIPA entered the picture, the city council explained that the use would have been unprecedented in Hancock Park:

> There are no other church or institutional uses on the residentially zoned properties within the notice radius for this action, this use would be precedent setting and compromise the 75 year maintenance and rec-ognized quality and sought after ambience of this historical residential neighborhood.[31]

The Los Angeles Superior Court emphatically agreed, saying that the synagogue "'would be a precedent setting encroachment of an institu-tional use in a single family area ... [that could] destabilize what has been a long standing, quality single-family residential neighborhood that has through constant efforts maintained its stable, high quality residential character.'"[32]

In response to the argument that the synagogue was convenient for its members, and therefore should receive this unprecedented treatment, the court held, "There are other locations within a reasonable walking distance from the subject site which could be used as a synagogue by right without the potential to impact and disturb the quiet enjoyment of the existing residential community."[33] The California Court of Appeals affirmed.[34]

In federal court, where the congregation appealed the city's decision on constitutional grounds, the court rejected all of their constitutional arguments and was ready to dismiss. Then, RLUIPA became law, grant-ing special privileges to religious landowners, and the city did an about-face on its settled and affirmed land use principles by entering into a secret Settlement Agreement that "accomplished the purpose sought by the Congregation in its 1996 conditional-use permit application – gain-ing official approval for property uses then taking place in violation of the Los Angeles Municipal Code."[35] The deal was cut with no notice to neighbors or public hearing.

In other words, this new federal law, which carried with it the threat of continuing federal court litigation, persuaded the City of Los Angeles to abandon its land use code, the Hancock Park homeowners, and grant the religious entity most of what it requested. Los Angeles put a few conditions on the use. For example, it required the synagogue to maintain the "residential character" of the neighborhood. That proved futile, as neighbors watched the small house on the small property being razed and then replaced with a building twice the size, which looks like a synagogue and overshadows its neighbors. It is so close to the property line that the homeowner on one side must close her curtains facing the synagogue.

The neighbors were outraged that their city's settled land use law could be discarded so abruptly and their neighborhood taken in precisely the opposite direction from what the law required. They were also angry that this land use applicant had been permitted to leap over the land use process. A significant number of them formed the League of Residential Neighborhood Advocates (LRNA) and filed a federal lawsuit, which was a highly unusual step for a homeowner's organization. The LRNA challenged the unilateral reversal and secret meeting as an abdication of the city's responsibility to follow its own laws, and alleged that it therefore violated due process.[36] In the interest of full disclosure, I represented them along with first-rate attorney Les Werlin. For purposes of this book, I seek only to describe the facts. In 2007, the federal Ninth Circuit agreed with LRNA's claim that the Settlement Agreement was invalid and unenforceable as it was in violation of state law.[37]

Following LRNA's victory in the Ninth Circuit, in February 2009 the Congregation re-entered the Los Angeles land use process and filed a conditional use permit to convert the residence into a house of worship. At first, it appeared that the previous denial would be replicated, because the use is so inconsistent with the area. Eight months later, the Zoning Administrator denied the permit, finding that the synagogue use of the residential property was merely a matter of convenience. The Central Area Planning Commission affirmed the denial in 2010.

Then RLUIPA strong-armed the process when the Congregation filed suit in federal court. Both parties moved for summary judgment. In

May 2013, the trial court found that the Los Angeles Municipal Code as applied to the Congregation violated RLUIPA, ordering that judgment be entered in favor of the Congregation.[38] Ultimately, the Congregation obtained everything it sought. There was no discrimination. Rather, Los Angeles's neutral and generally applicable zoning laws were swept aside for the benefit of this full-service house of worship. The city initially announced an intent to appeal the decision and had strong arguments. Then politics intervened. The block where the synagogue is located was redistricted. Before, it was located in the district of a council member who supported the City's land use law and the neighbors. Now, it is in the district of a council member who promised to support the synagogue against the neighborhood during his campaign. After the redistricting, the city caved and paid attorneys' fees of $950,000 to the congregation.

Neighborhood disputes also have the capacity to creep beyond their borders. The Hancock Park dispute is a classic example of the challenges imposed when a religious use increases in intensity and scope. Unfortunately, the ugliness of the dispute is typical as well. When the neighbors objected to the opening of this new facility, which would be intensely used, the congregation took offense. A press release was distributed in the neighborhood accusing those opposed to the building project as "anti-Jewish" and "anti-Semitic." The Congregation's response got the attention of other Jewish leaders, including a leading museum curator, who wrote a letter accusing the neighborhood of "hate." After he met with the synagogue's neighbors, many of whom are Jewish, he backtracked and said he was not calling the neighbors anti-Semitic, only intolerant. No homeowner walks away from such an exchange without feeling less happy about his or her choice of neighborhood.

This case is especially ironic, because Rabbi Rubin testified before Congress:

> Congregation Etz Chaim (Congregation or Etz Chaim) is a small group of Orthodox Jewish residents of Hancock Park who, for the last 30 years, have gathered together in one of two residences in Hancock Park for communal prayer. Orthodox Judaism requires that worshipers pray together, and that they walk to services on the Sabbath and on other holy days. Thus, in order to comply with the dictates of their faith, Orthodox Jews must have a house of worship within walking distance of their homes. Over the years, Etz Chaim has come to serve

the needs of many elderly and disabled Hancock Park residents, who, because of their disabilities, are physically unable to walk the mile or more round-trip to synagogues located in the commercial zone outside of Hancock Park. For years, these faithful congregants have attended services at Etz Chaim using their canes and walkers.[39]

He then described the current use as involving "40 members (with a high of sixty (60) members . . . [and] four bar mitzvah ceremonies," but then claimed that "[t]he only activities which take place at the residence are prayer services."[40] If one were inclined to read the testimony for its facts, one would quickly see that a minyan was on its way to becoming a full-service synagogue catering to families with children. That is a dramatic change in use. Denial of the emerging use is not evidence of discrimination. It is common sense.

Today, the truth rarely impedes those religious interests intent on obtaining special benefits from Congress and their willing accomplices, our elected representatives. In spite of its incomplete character, Rabbi Rubin's testimony has been repeatedly invoked as evidence of rank discrimination against benign neighborhood religious uses. Senators Orrin Hatch (R, UT) and Edward Kennedy (D, MA), in their joint statement, asserted that,

> [s]ometimes, zoning board members or neighborhood residents explicitly offer race or religion as the reason to exclude a proposed church, especially in cases of black churches and Jewish shuls and synagogues. More often, discrimination lurks behind such vague and universally applicable reasons as traffic, aesthetics, or 'not consistent with the city's land use plan.'[41]

In other words, it was the rare instance where overt discrimination could be identified in the land use process, but discrimination supposedly could be implied on the basis of "universally applicable reasons" for land use determinations. Thus, Congress pulled the discrimination rabbit out of the hat and transformed all zoning commissions and homeowners into bigots.

Despite no overt proof of discrimination, a city's decision to follow its settled land use law is typically twisted into a pretext for invidious discrimination, while the legitimate concerns of homeowners about traffic, aesthetics, and maintaining the character of the neighborhood are supposedly so trivial that to invoke them leads to the ineluctable conclusion that discrimination must be at play. It's a disturbing claim for two U.S. Senators to make about millions of their constituent homeowners without concrete proof, but it had legs, because it became *the* element of all of the hearings before Congress that undergirded RLUIPA in the eyes of the courts.

One professor went even further than the senators, claiming overt and not just implied religious discrimination, when he wrote that Los Angeles's "express reason for excluding a place of worship was that it wanted to exclude places of worship!"[42] Nothing but an overactive imagination intent on finding discrimination because it suits one's purposes can explain this characterization of Los Angeles's decisions in the Hancock Park case. It was the increasing intensity of use, not the religious character or identity of the gathering, that engendered the original denial, which was affirmed by the California courts.

The failure of Congress to delve beneath the surface of the discrimination talk is shameful. When Congress considered extreme religious liberty for landowners in 1999, only religious entities with vested interests were permitted to testify. I testified, but solely on constitutional issues. Groups like the National League of Cities and the International Municipal League asked to testify, but they were not invited to testify at the hearings. Then-New York Mayor Rudolph Giuliani asked to testify regarding New York City's concerns with the bill, but he was not invited, either. Nor was his letter in opposition put in the record. Sen. Patrick Moynihan (D, N.Y.), other land use officials, and zoning authorities who might have been able to give Congress the benefit of the other side of the issue were also excluded. No homeowner or homeowners' association that had tangled with an ambitious religious building project was permitted on the record. The religious lobbyists behind the scenes had no interest to educate Congress on land use, which has always belonged first and foremost to the local and state governments. Again, the fault lay in Congress, not self-interested lobbyists. Congress simply did not bother to inquire whether relieving religious entities of land use laws might well affect one's neighbors or community. It's an obvious question, but was never posed throughout the hearings.

The record contains many religious entities complaining about garden-variety land use laws along with weak anecdotes of discriminatory treatment. The problem with the discrimination claims was that there were virtually no cases to support their argument that Congress needed to intervene to aid religious landowners. In fact, the only secular – as in unbiased – study done to date supported the view that the claims to discrimination before Congress did not hold water because discrimination simply is not a typical feature in the land use process when religious entities are involved.[43] In the face of religious representatives from the Mormon Church, the Presbyterian Church, and the Roman Catholic Church, Congress treated their unsupported claims as gospel truth, and once the testimony was recorded in the *Congressional Record*, courts deferred to the claims as well because Congress had accepted them.[44] The first court to uphold RLUIPA's constitutionality simply quoted the one-sided conference report as though an independent, disinterested review of the record to ensure constitutional requirements were met was not the court's business (even though it is). It engaged in the follow-ing "analysis," which merely parrots Senators Hatch and Kennedy's joint statement: "The hearing record compiled massive evidence that this right is frequently violated."[45] This is bologna.

Thus, interest group politics built a case on gossamer threads, and voilá, religious landowners were freed from the land use laws that make neighbors good neighbors. As I said previously, the deficiency in the political process here is not only with the interest group's distorted or self-interested perspective. That is to be expected, especially if the proponents are religiously motivated in this era. But there is every reason to criticize elected representatives who kowtow to religious interests, and, as a result, fail to ask the simplest questions: for example, how does your land use proposal affect others, like neighbors? Had the question been posed, our elected representatives might have developed the political will to ask others – like their constituents – besides the religious groups about alleged discrimination. Perhaps then there might have been some fact finding, as opposed to posturing.

There is another fault line in this process. Congress has limited, enu-merated powers under the Constitution. Although it has attempted to take over virtually every area of governance, the Supreme Court has repeat-edly held that land use is one area that belongs to the state and local governments. For that reason, most members of Congress (and federal judges) are ignorant of *basic* land used principles. RLUIPA violates the separation of power between the states and the federal government, and it does so at the expense of taxpayers who also must underwrite federal litigation on issues that belong to them, and federal courts are incompetent to decide. Private property is the keystone to America – prosperity and success. When any landowner – religious or secular – receives or seemingly receives preferential treatment, there are bad feelings. Because city governments are supposed to ensure that residential neighborhoods remain peaceful and attractive to families, when they abandon those principles for religious entities, homeowners are betrayed.[46] The impact of these large operations on property values and residential character turn homeowners against religious entities way too often.[47] In the words of one reporter, although RLUIPA was only "intended to ease city zoning restrictions for religious institutions, the civil rights law has pitted neighbor versus neighbor and church versus state in areas nationwide."[48]

Religious entities often view their property as serving a higher purpose, which translates into insensitivity to the "earthly" values of their neighbors. The message is sent loud and clear that they believe the complaints of increased traffic deserve negligible attention. When homeowners appropriately object to bringing the homeless into the neighborhood for social services, because they fear for the safety of their children and the impact on property values, they are told that their values are misplaced. Right now, in Ventura, California, neighbors are dealing with a homeless shelter next to a residential neighborhood that rightly worries parents and the local government. RLUIPA is already being slung around by the believers as the sword it is.

From the religious perspective, the religious mission always transcends these mortal concerns. Sometimes a pastor will spearhead an ambitious building project, on the basis of a vision for the future, not just current numbers. For example, in Greensboro, North Carolina, Senior Pastor Jerry Shetler of the First Presbyterian Church said in 1995 that his plan to raze historic homes set on tree-lined streets for a parking lot and a hall large enough to accommodate basketball as well as banquets was not "necessitated by the congregation's growth in numbers, [but rather] the growth of the congregation in terms of its understanding of what it ought to be."[49]

At one conference I attended, a representative for a religious organization declared that he simply could not comprehend residential homeowners' objections to cars parked on the street on a regular basis. At the same time, a scholar declared that concerns about traffic and parking are simply pretexts for discrimination against religion, as though it is inconceivable that homeowners would take those issues seriously.[50] I guarantee that if they could not get out of their driveways or feared for the safety of their children because of traffic, they would change their tune.

The ingrained American prejudice in favor of religious projects was evident at a 1999 conference at the University of California, Davis School of Law, where one professor asserted the following as a fact: some neighbors to a new church "are hostile to religion and to churches, either in general or in certain manifestations. Some Americans are hostile to all religion. They believe it is irrational, superstitious, and harmful." He immediately qualified the statement, though, because it could not stand on its own: "This is the view of a small minority."[51] No joke.

Religious hostility does not, in fact, describe the attitudes of the vast majority of residential neighbors. For RLUIPA's advocates, the homeowners objecting to a law that would let churches off the hook for land use laws "brought a remarkable intensity and sense of entitlement to their desire to prevent the construction of churches."[52] The intensity is not "remarkable" at all. Had they ever attended just about any public hearing involving a building project affecting private homes, they would have witnessed the same passion, which is motivated by these homeowners' love of their neighborhood and families, not any hatred for any or all religions. Opposing development is not the same as hating religion.

It is notable that those on the side of the religious entities have been so far removed from the emotional, economic, and even spiritual value that American families invest in their homes. It is neither a *de minimis* nor throwaway value. This is where the family meets, where children live, and where personal traditions are built.[53] If the family is the fundamental building block in American society – as so many are claiming in the same-sex marriage debate – the home is simply an extension of those values. Yet, page after page of congressional testimony in support of federal religious liberty legislation criticizes how religious landowners are treated in the United States, without a single witness called to ask about the impact these religious building projects have on private homeowners. That is a severe failure of representation.

Given their worldview, there is a tendency for religious landowners to characterize run-of-the-mill zoning regulations and the costs of securing property and construction as an unacceptable burden on their free exercise of religion. Until the advent of extreme religious liberty, their land use was treated according to its impact, not the identity of the owner. For example, in Miami Beach, Florida, Naftali and Sarah Grosz lived in their home on property zoned for single-family residential use for a number of years. They bought the property with a deed restriction that explicitly limited their use to residential purposes and did not request rezoning. But they did have an "accessory structure" for which they asked and received permission to remodel for what they called "playroom use." As part of its approval, among other particulars, the city told them that the structure could not be used as a "religious institution." While the external features of the structure were not changed, the couple installed "benches to seat over 30 persons, Torahs, Arks, a Menorah, skull caps, an eternal light, numerous books, shawls, and other items of religious significance," all of which violated the city's ordinance against religious institutions in residential neighborhoods without permission.[54] The Grosz's sued the city in federal court, claiming the ordinance was an unconstitutional burden on their free exercise rights.[55] The U.S. Court of Appeals for the 11th Circuit rightly rejected their claims in 1983, because there is no justification in a residential neighborhood to treat the impact of a religious use as though it is any different from the impact of a nonreligious use. Here, a "playroom" would have yielded minimal use, while the shul was in constant use. The court quite rightly found there was no substantial burden on the family's free exercise of religion, saying:

> [W]e note that Miami Beach does not prohibit religious conduct per se. Rather, the City prohibits acts in furtherance of this conduct in certain geographical areas. . . . Appellees' home lies within four blocks of such a district. Appellees do not confront the limited choice of ceasing their conduct or incurring criminal liability. Alternatively, they may conduct the required services in suitably zoned areas, either by securing another site away from their current house or by making their home elsewhere in the city. We cannot know the exact impact upon Appellees, in terms of convenience, dollars or aesthetics, that a location change would entail. The burden imposed, though, plainly does not rise to the level of criminal liability, loss of livelihood, or denial of a

basic income sustaining public welfare benefit. In comparison to the religious infringements analyzed in previous free exercise cases the burden here stands towards the lower end of the spectrum.[56]

This is the sort of common sense reasoning that permeated the cases before RFRA and RLUIPA entered the picture.

Religious landowners, particularly with RLUIPA at their back, are unique because they are often persuaded that their building mission is transcendent, and, therefore, in the order of things, they should take precedence over competing earthly demands. To be sure, secular developers frequently have a "vision" for a project, but when religion enters the picture, that vision can become freighted with a sense of entitlement. For example, in one case, a church had sought permission to build an enormous worship center. Pastor Virgil Best couched the project in terms of religious mission, saying that it was their "mission that our congregation should be able to worship together."[57] The lawyer for the Grace United Methodist Church in Cheyenne, Wyoming, whichsought to add a 100-child day-care center to its building in a residential neighborhood, pointed to testimony from a church leader that "God called the group to build the daycare center."[58] Broward County's Primera Iglesia Bautista Hispana believed that its building plans were a "Godly mission" that was stymied by the county's zoning and land use restrictions, which they blamed for undermining the growth they sought.[59]

As a constitutional matter, ordinary zoning laws are just as much the religious landowner's responsibility as any other landowner's, and this is as it should be, because land use inescapably affects neighbors, the community, and the state. Zoning and land use laws exist to minimize the negative effects of any landowner's use of their property. "One of the general purposes of zoning is to ameliorate the impact of development on neighboring land and on the community as a whole."[60] Zoning, which is a 20th-century phenomenon, was made necessary to mediate disputes from increasingly concentrated populations, as the Supreme Court explained in 1926:

Until recent years, urban life was comparatively simple; but with the great increase and concentration of population, problems are developed, and constantly are developing, which require, and will continue to require, additional restrictions in respect of the use and occupation of private lands in urban communities. . . . Such regulations are sustained, under the complex conditions of our day, for reasons analogous to those which justify traffic regulations, which, before the advent of automobiles and rapid transit street railways, would have been condemned as fatally arbitrary and unreasonable.[61]

In contrast to the application of everyday land use laws to religious organizations, discrimination against a religious landowner is a free exercise violation. For example, if a zoning board or city intended to rid the community of a religious group, and therefore denied an otherwise appropriate variance simply because it disapproved of the landowner's beliefs, the purpose would violate the Establishment Cause, which prohibits laws that do not "have a secular legislative purpose."[62] It would also violate the Free Exercise Clause, which bars religious animus or hostility by the government.[63] Religious lobbyists argue that they are often subjected to discriminatory land use decisions, but "[t]he nearly universal experience of American congregations seeking government authorization to do something they want to do is one of facilitation rather than roadblock."[64]

For those familiar with the typical relationship between religious entities and the government in the United States, this should come as no surprise. In my experience at least, it is the rare city, town, or municipality that will not go out of its way to help a religious project go forward. The government will not turn its back on the community's master plan, ordinarily, but religious landowners seem to do significantly better than secular developers with similarly burdensome projects. As the *Smith* Court said:

> Values that are protected against government interference through enshrinement in the Bill of Rights are not thereby banished from the political process. Just as a society that believes in the negative protection accorded to the press by the First Amendment is likely to enact laws that affirmatively foster the dissemination of the printed word, so also a society that believes in the negative protection accorded to religious belief can be expected to be solicitous of that value in its legislation as well.[65]

There is a strong flavor of entitlement in the religious landowners' drive to avoid the typical expenses and hurdles faced by any ambitious building project, especially if that project seeks to insert itself into a residential neighborhood. The United States has fed into such a view by giving religious landowners property tax exemptions, which despite the enormous financial benefit, were upheld against Establishment Clause attack in 1970 because the practice had been in place since the beginning of the country's history.[66]

THE DISDAIN FOR HISTORIC PRESERVATION AND AESTHETICS IN LAND USE. Historic preservation has been treated as a burr in religious entities' saddles, because they often own older buildings that are eligible for historical designation. In New York City in 1986, St. Bartholomew's Church challenged the city's historical preservation laws, but the court found that there was no free exercise defense.[67] That decision spurred religious entities to lobby for exemptions from historical preservation and land use regulations, which they argue never serve a compelling interest.[68] Religious landowners also have been assisted by exemptions from historical preservation laws in California,[69] Pittsburgh,[70] and Rockwall, Texas, which revised its historic district boundaries to specifically exclude four churches so that they would not be burdened by the designation.[71] In 1992, the Washington Supreme Court, applying state constitutional law, determined that Seattle could not impose landmark designation on a church where it would have to seek approval for alterations, and the ordinance granted the city the right to determine which changes were religious in nature. Because the law was not neutral on its face, strict scrutiny applied, and the government failed to prove that historical preservation is a compelling interest.[72]

This is one of the more curious features of American society, actually. No one in Europe would dream of asserting that history is a second-class interest. There is history on every corner, oftentimes in the form of a cathedral, but in this relatively new country, there is less respect for history, and even less for preserving historical buildings. Thus, American courts tend to have little difficulty declaring that historic preservation is comparable to aesthetic preference, and that beauty is a second-order value as well. For example, one Oregon court flatly stated that "zoning for aesthetic purposes alone is not a valid exercise of police power, as land use restrictions designed solely for improvement of appearance of community do not tend to promote public health, safety, morals or general welfare of community."[73] A Washington state court also set the value of historic preservation and aesthetics well below the religious landowner's interests: "The City's interest in preservation of aesthetic and historic structures is not compelling and it does not justify the infringement of First Covenant's right to freely exercise religion. The possible loss of significant architectural elements is a price we must accept to guarantee the paramount right of religious freedom."[74]

In this environment, churches presume that historical preservation is not their responsibility. When the Trinity United Methodist Church in Opelika-Auburn, Alabama, was given the century-old Frederick-Whatley-Chapman house, it saw "it as a white elephant," which it hoped to sell to someone to move it from the lot.[75] If no one was willing to pay for the move, they planned to demolish it, even though the house has been described as one of the city's "most majestic and historic homes."[76] This is a story repeated frequently – the religious institution sees no moral or social problem with treating historical properties as throwaways and treats those who do place value in historical preservation as enemies of the good. Good government would inject the idea of the public good into this competition of interests and find means of serving everyone's interest. The best result in every land use dispute is the win-win result.

Religious day-care centers in residential neighborhoods

Before RFRA or RLUIPA became law, it was generally held that religious day-care centers in residential neighborhoods could be regulated as a distinct category from churches and nursery schools in churches.[77] They had to abide by density, signage, and other typical requirements for obtaining a special-use permit. For example, in Evanston, Illinois, in 1987, Love Church and its pastor, Marzell Gill, alleged that requiring them to file a detailed plan and an application fee for a special-use permit violated their free exercise rights. The court rejected their argument, because the express purpose of these requirements was plainly secular: to protect health, safety, morals, and welfare. The court explained:

> The burden this ordinance places on Love Church is merely financial.
> If the price is right, landlords can be found who will be willing to agree
> to a contingency clause. If all else failed, plaintiffs could rent without a

contingency clause. Economic burdens do not rise to a constitutionally impermissible infringement of freedom to worship.[78]

This was standard reasoning until 1993, when RFRA was passed. Then there was a return to sanity from 1997 to 2000, after RFRA was held unconstitutional. In 2000, this reasoning took another hit when RLUIPA was enacted.

Since RLUIPA appeared, cases have turned 180 degrees. Before, a zoning decision could be made according to the intensity of the use, so the law required cities to treat churches like all other landowners. It worked both ways for them. In California, for example, churches had no special privilege to be in any particular zoned district. Therefore, cities could zone churches to zones other than residential zones, in part because their intense use was incompatible with residential neighborhoods.[79] In other circumstances, it meant that a zoning authority could not treat a church any less well than other landowners in the same district, e.g., by adding a day-care facility. "Churches or religious associations are recognized and treated . . . as bodies entitled under any form of government, to enjoy the benefits of property, which property, like that of all other citizens, whether individuals, associations of individuals, or corporations, should be protected and secured to them by law."[80]

In Cheyenne, Wyoming, the Grace United Methodist Church proposed in 2001 to add a nonreligious 100-child day-care center in the heart of a settled residential neighborhood.[81] When the local authorities denied permission, the church appealed but the Board of Adjustment still rejected its claims, because it was not a use permitted in a residential district and it was "incompatible with community goals and the neighborhood."[82] A federal lawsuit soon followed, invoking RLUIPA. The federal trial court held that the church had failed to prove the zoning law placed a substantial burden on its religious conduct, and therefore they lost under RLUIPA. The Tenth Circuit affirmed the judgment of the District Court in 2005;[83] however, the court then granted plaintiff's petition for rehearing, which included challenging the District Court's jury instructions regarding RLUIPA.[84] The Tenth Circuit held that while the jury instructions regarding the substantial burden test were erroneous, it resulted in harmless error as "a reasonable juror could not have been misled to Grace United's detriment by Instruction 19" because the jury found that the Church failed to prove it was engaged in a sincere exercise of religion.[85] The First Amendment simply does not entitle the Church to special treatment so that it may operate a daycare exactly where it pleases while no one else can do the same. Although the First Amendment does not, RLUIPA can.

Bringing the homeless into a residential neighborhood

In the Pico-Union area of East Los Angeles, the Catholic Brothers of the Missionaries of Charity, which was founded by Mother Teresa, sought to bring a homeless shelter – operating three days a week during the day and serving approximately 40 adults – into the settled residential, historic neighborhood of Alvarado Terrace. In May 2001, neighbors started to notice beer cans on the ground and loitering by those coming to the shelter. The city did nothing on its own about the fact a homeless shelter was operating in a residential neighborhood without the necessary permits, which is typical. Cities generally do not extend themselves to find religious entities in violation of zoning laws. But when the neighbors complained, the city issued citations for the obvious zoning violations and asked that the use as a homeless shelter be moved to another, more compatible area. As often happens in these cases, the city scouted out more suitable sites for the religious organization, which is not necessary, but shows the city's good faith. The Brothers insisted their younger homeless needed the "safe haven" of a "residential environment." The group's leader, Brother James Walker, said, "This is how we worship . . . by helping the poorest of the poor."[86] The neighbors observed the residential quality of their neighborhood crumbling, as some witnessed drug deals near the shelter and endured the homeless knocking on their doors at night, looking for the shelter.

Instead of finding a middle ground, the Brothers filed an RLUIPA lawsuit in federal court, arguing that the city's order to move would be unduly burdensome on the homeless who came to the shelter and that such a move would be costly for them. At the trial-court level, the judge issued a tentative order finding that the city did not infringe on the Brothers' free exercise rights, but that it created a substantial burden on the Brothers' under RLUIPA.[87] The City did not appeal the merits.

The attempt to transform light religious use into congregational use

In Abington, Pennsylvania, a nunnery and then a monastery with nearly nonexistent traffic operated for years at the end of a quiet cul-de-sac. Indeed, the monastery was so quiet some of the neighbors thought the monks had all died. Then a thriving Reform Jewish congregation projected to encompass approximately 450 families, purchased the 10-acre parcel in 1999 for worship services, Hebrew classes, religious classes, the High Holy Days, religious meetings, bar and bat mitzvah services, wedding ceremonies, and other celebrations. The parking lot was to be expanded from 20 to a minimum of 137 spots.[88] The property was in a residential neighborhood, but the congregation argued it had a right to establish a synagogue at the site, because it had been previously dedicated to religious purposes. The zoning board rejected the claim, because the prior use was so dramatically different than the proposed use. Traffic studies indicated that the synagogue's proposed use would increase the number of cars daily from fewer than 10 to over 100,[89] which meant neighboring homeowners, who bought their homes because they were on this quiet cul-de-sac, faced the necessity of having to tell their children to stop playing street hockey and to watch for cars and strangers. If the project were approved, the character of the neighborhood would undergo a seismic shift.

Replacing the formerly light uses with a busy congregation would have undermined the residential character of the street. Judge Clarence Newcomer, of the district court, however, ruled initially that the congregation's constitutional rights were infringed on equal protection grounds."[90] The Court of Appeals for the Third Circuit reversed the trial court's equal protection reasoning, finding that standard land use principles had been applied, and it was sent back to the trial court for RLUIPA proceedings.

In order for an RLUIPA claim to go forward, the religious entity bears the threshold burden of showing that the land use law imposes a "substantial burden" on religious conduct. "Substantial burden" is a term of art, which has been employed in free exercise cases for decades. It means that if a law places a *de minimis* burden on religious conduct, there is no issue about religious liberty. Rather, the burden must "effect 'grave interference with important religious tenets or . . . affirmatively compel [congregants] to perform acts undeniably at odds with fundamental tenets of their religious beliefs.'"[91] Expense and inconvenience are not substantial burdens.[92] The congregation argued "that preventing a church from developing a particular property is in fact a substantial burden on free exercise."[93] In effect, the Abington congregation was arguing that it had a right to choose its location, which is to say that zoning was simply inapplicable to them under RLUIPA. Amazingly, Judge Newcomer agreed: "Evaluating the instant case with the understanding that the RLUIPA changed the standard for the type of burdens on free exercise that are actionable, and under the case law applying this definition, it is clear that the Ordinance and the denial of a variance to the Plaintiffs are substantial burdens on their free exercise rights."[94]

The congregation had available to it other alternative locations within the same jurisdiction, but it succeeded in proving that its religious beliefs were somehow burdened, as if it were being forced to change, because that particular property was being made unavailable. In effect, the court ruled that inconvenience was sufficient to prove there was a substantial burden on religious conduct. The court is wrong on the interpretation of "substantial burden," but this case illustrates how religious liberty discourse can get so off track in the United States, especially when RLUIPA enters the picture.

The means by which religious land use advocates have orchestrated the public record is quite evident in the Abington case. The neighbors objected to the changing quality of their neighborhood, but, from the beginning, the congregation's strategy was to insinuate that the denial was based on religious discrimination. The *Wall Street Journal* gave the Becket Fund space for an editorial addressing the issue in general, which also addressed the Abington case in particular: "The Philadelphia suburb of Abington Township refused to allow a Jewish congregation to move into a former Catholic convent, ruling that substituting Jewish worship for Catholic worship was not a 'continuing use' of the land."[95] Contrary to what the Becket Fund claimed, the use was not continuous, because the use was dramatically different regardless of religious identity. The congregation was asking to transform a property so quiet that neighbors did not know that monks still resided there into a full-service, large-scale religious complex that would multiply traffic by a factor of fifteen. What you have here is a religious advocate injecting interdenominational hatred into a context where it otherwise did not exist. If these are the tactics of those assisting religious landowners, presumably with their clients' consent, it is no wonder that divisive religious discord is being sown in residential neighborhoods in the wake of RLUIPA.

Eventually, the case settled, because the Congregation found other, more suitable property nearby, with the assistance of the Township. Thus, the cost of the litigation in time and money was an utter waste. But for RLUIPA, this amicable resolution would have occurred sooner.

This *Wall Street Journal* op-ed, also offered the following description of a pending case at the time:

> Across the country, laws inhospitable to religious organizations . . . have become quite typical. Consider: In Castle Hills, Texas, the city, in a recent court filing, referred to a Baptist church as a "cancer." Several years ago the city ran another house of worship out of town, ultimately moving into the space, taking down the cross and transforming the building into city hall.[96]

Sounds like a pretty awful city, doesn't it? It certainly rings of discrimination against religion. When federal judge Royal Furgeson decided the case, though, he found a very different picture. First, the city had "granted multiple special use permits to the [mentioned Baptist] Church in order to accomplish its goals for expansion." The city was not opposed to religious use at all, but rather was consistently concerned about the impact of intense uses on residential neighborhoods. In an insightful and well-written opinion, he stated that

> [T]his City struggles against size, not religious practice. Here, the undisputed facts reveal a long-lasting antagonism between Church and City that is rooted in a struggle over size of the Church and size and character of the surrounding neighborhood. There is no evidence here that the City harbors ill-will nor that the City means by its aggressive zoning decisions to alter or impede the religion in any way. Rather, the City means to halt this Church's growth, not spiritually, but geographically . . . [even though the] City refers to the Church as a cancer feeding upon healthy surrounding cells, [t]he Court's review of the evidence submitted by both parties . . . [shows that none of the City's conduct] rises to the level of religious discrimination or exclusion.[97]

The *Castle Hills Baptist Church v. City of Castle Hills* case illustrates how charges of discrimination can mask legitimate disputes over land use, and how RLUIPA fails to solve that very real, local problem as it injects ugly and unfair name-calling. In the case, the church was not permitted to add a parking lot, but was given the right to use a fourth story in a neighborhood zoned for two stories, and because it prevailed on that single issue, the city could have been liable for attorney's fees for the church's entire litigation.

Racing from the local land use authorities to federal court in RLUIPA cases

Before RLUIPA was enacted in 2000, cities, towns, municipalities and their organizations asked that RLUIPA include a provision that required landowners to exhaust the local land use process before RLUIPA could be invoked. They anticipated the specter of religious entities taking them straight to federal court – before they had a chance to fully investigate or finally rule on an application. They did not get the provision, although the legislative history does include the following: The "Act does not provide religious institutions with immunity from land use regulation, nor does it relieve religious institutions from applying for variances, special permits or exceptions, hardship approval, or other relief provisions in land use regulations, where available without discrimination or unfair delay."[98] As RLUIPA has worked its way through the courts, one of the questions that has required resolution (because Congress failed to be clear enough) concerns when a religious landowner may go to federal court with RLUIPA.

In general, the federal courts have held that an applicant may not avoid the land use process. That does not mean religious entities have not tried to avoid it. When they go to federal court before going through the process, they leapfrog the community and insert federal court oversight over an issue on which federal judges know very little generally.

In Morgan Hill, California, San Jose Christian College did not even bother to file a complete application for a zoning amendment to allow for the conversion of a hospital, grandfathered into a residential community, into an educational facility. The U.S. Court of Appeals for the Ninth Circuit correctly found that the process itself did not impose a substantial burden on the college.[99]

In the most extreme case to date of a religious applicant attempting to avoid local procedures involves the Rabbinical College of Tartikov, which seeks to impose a campus on the small bedroom community of Pomona, New York, whom I represent. It jumped into federal court without filing a single application for any of the many uses the complaint indicates may be intended, houses of worship, study halls, libraries, museums, or multi-family housing.[100] The College argued that it should not have to file an application or zoning permit where it alleged that it would have been futile to do so. The District Court held that the RLUIPA land use claim was unripe (and therefore the court lacks jurisdiction), because a developer must file at least one application, even if the developer claims discrimination. The court couched its decision in federalism concerns as follows:

> The Second Circuit has held that the final decision rule: (1) "aids in the development of a full record"; (2) ensures that a court "will . . . know precisely how a regulation will be applied to a particular parcel"; (3) recognizes the possibility that, by granting a variance, the administrative body "might provide the relief the property owner seeks without requiring judicial entanglement in constitutional disputes"; and (4) "evinces the judiciary's appreciation that land use disputes are uniquely matters of local concern more aptly suited for local resolution."[101]

The court, however, permitted the College to continue its challenge to three local laws that the college claimed were discriminatory. Since the filing of the complaint in federal court in July 10, 2007, the litigation is ongoing. Still, the College has filed not a single plan, and Pomona continues to have to litigate a case involving a hypothetical project.

RLUIPA is not limited to religious institutions; private homeowners have invoked it as well

In New Milford, Connecticut, Robert Murphy believed in praying at home with family and friends, holding weekly prayer meetings at his home.[102] Often, attendance reached or exceeded 50 people, and the guests stayed a number of hours every Sunday. The neighbors did not respond to the religious character of the meetings, but they did voice objections to increased traffic and parking problems. In response, Murphy asked for permission to install a parking lot on his property. He eventually withdrew the parking lot request, which made sense, given that a parking lot is not a typical accessory use for a single-family home. The Zoning Enforcement Officer counted 13 to 20 cars in the driveway, rear yard, or cul-de-sac on three separate occasions, and issued a cease-and-desist order for the intense use of the home to cease. This was not a "customary" use for a residential property, which is to say it was not "commonly, habitually, and by long practice established" as a use reasonably associated with a single-family home in an R-40 zone (which is a low-density, single-family zone that permits residences, farms, and associated accessory uses).

There were several options open to Murphy at that point. He could have filed an appeal with the zoning board of appeals in New Milford or he could have requested a variance. Either avenue was open. Instead, he chose to file directly in federal court on the basis of a single cease-and-desist order. Despite the undeveloped record and incomplete determination in New Milford, the magistrate judge, Holly Fitzsimmons, found in favor of the Murphys in 2003 in a 39-page opinion on a number of theories, and the zoning enforcement officer, Kathy Castagnetta, whom I represented, appealed. The Second Circuit vacated and remanded the district judgment with instructions to dismiss the complaint without prejudice holding that plaintiffs' claims were not ripe for judicial intervention.[103] The point here is not to debate the merits, but to point out how RLUIPA could transform a single zoning action taken by a town into costly federal litigation that lasts years. The rational taxpayer must wonder if it is worth it. The city is in an impossible position: it faces millions in attorneys' fees from the religious landowners' "pro bono" lawyers if it sticks to its local, generally applicable land use laws, and enraged neighbors if it abandons those principles to permit a use that is inconsistent with the law.

Mayors, city councils, cities, states, attorneys general, and governors should be aggressively attacking RLUIPA's invasion of an arena that, under the Constitution, belongs first and foremost to them. Why aren't they? The situation reminds me of the prosecutors who neglected to prosecute churches and clergy for child sex abuse for decades. Elected officials want to stay in office, and they perceive an attack on RLUIPA (or a state RFRA) as political suicide, because they treat believers as voting blocs. So far, the victims of RLUIPA, largely residential neighborhoods, are a silent and amorphous majority. If they organize and make their views known, it is possible that elected officials in this context might learn what the last Brooklyn District Attorney Hynes learned (as I discuss in Chapter 2): Times are changing. Pandering to the religious is not always a ticket to re-election.

The problem with RLUIPA, or any law that gives neighboring landowners different rights simply on the basis of religious status

The primary problem with RLUIPA is that it is unfair. It sows discord, by altering the balance between neighboring properties in the same zoned district. Residential homeowners who are faced with ambitious religious building plans have a strong claim that their right to the equal protection of the laws has been violated. The religious entity is attempting to do that which the homeowner may not, and in effect, there are two classes of citizens under RLUIPA and the state RFRAs. The first class is classified as "religious" and the second class envelops everyone else. It is fundamentally unfair, the many homeowners who have been in this situation will tell you.

Religious landowners could still receive special privileges in some states once RLUIPA is found unconstitutional, dramatically narrowed in scope, or repealed, as it should be

Nineteen states have some form of extreme privilege for religious entities to mold generally applicable, neutral laws into presumptively illegal laws when applied to them. They usually state that the government "may not substantially burden a person's exercise of religion, even if the burden results from a rule of general applicability, unless it demonstrates a compelling governmental interest that is 'the least restrictive means of furthering that compelling governmental interest.'" Seventeen states have legislative religious freedom restoration acts or state constitutional amendments that extend to land use. These are Alabama, Arizona, Connecticut, Florida, Idaho, Illinois, Kansas, Kentucky, Louisiana, Missouri, New Mexico, Pennsylvania, Rhode Island, South Carolina, Tennessee, Utah and Virginia.[104] At the same time, Oklahoma has a RFRA-like law, but which carves out specific exceptions to allow local governments to carry out generally applicable land use laws: "a governmental entity has no less authority to adopt or apply laws and regulations in a nondiscriminatory manner concerning zoning, land use planning, traffic management, urban nuisance, or historic preservation, than the authority of the governmental entity that existed under the law prior to the passage of this act."[105]

These state laws are like ticking time bombs, which have not yet been used extensively, but that will be ready for action if and when RLUIPA is held unconstitutional, restricted in scope to make it constitutional, or carved back by Congress. The Connecticut home prayer case discussed above, invoked not just RLUIPA, but also the Connecticut RFRA. Other cases have adverted to the mini-RFRAs, as well, but there are precious few decisions, because the theory is usually duplicative of RLUIPA at this point.

The conflict between religious land use and residential owners generated by the likes of RFRA, RLUIPA, and the state RFRAs entrenches on the most fundamental values of most Americans. Private property is the building block that permitted a massive middle class to be built and to have upward mobility. It broke the bonds of the aristocracy on property ownership, and equalized citizens in ways that no other innovation in the United States would. The private property norm brings into question the notion that entities should have different property rights simply because of their religious status. Real property is real property, and its use affects neighbors regardless whether the homeowner is having a Tupperware party or a prayer meeting, or a large building is hosting religious or secular child care.

Extreme religious liberty for land use also cuts to the heart of another cherished American principle: the belief in fair dealing. When churches get special privileges, their neighbors feel (and rightly so) that they have been cheated. It is fundamentally unfair to treat property owners in the same location differently because of their identities. It's a gut instinct for

Americans, and altering the balance between property owners has been divisive, to say the least.

The real property system in the United States established opportunity and equality. So long as religious entities insist on having special property rights, they will generate the backlash they are just now beginning to comprehend.

5

SCHOOLS

The early public school system did not take long to land in religious dispute, and religious accommodation conflicts continue today. Public schools were originally instituted by a Protestant majority and reflected Protestant religious viewpoints, including mandatory daily readings from the King James Bible. In the early 1820s, New York started funding schools, and by 1840, some Catholics were objecting to the Protestant religious curriculum. The Protestant majority protected its turf by denying funding to "sectarian" schools (as though the Protestant public schools were not sectarian), "including Baptist, Methodist and Catholic." Over the succeeding years, the political will to prevent funding for any schools other than the Protestants' was distilled into an anti-funding drive aimed mainly at Catholics.[1]

Some Christians in the United States might be tempted to latch onto the early Protestant practices in the schools as proof that the schools should now reintroduce prayer and religion in the schools. They argue that public education has been corrupted, because prayer and Bible reading were held unconstitutional. The now-deceased Rev. Jerry Falwell, following 9/11, remarked: "We have seen the course of secularism in our schools, and it is obviously time for a change. It is high time our nation once again favors its people of faith by allowing our public-school students to be exposed to prayer and the pursuit of faith."[2] Mississippi Governor Kirk Fordice opined: "'one day, I hope soon, it's not going to be legal to keep prayer out of public schools.'"[3] The Rev. Louis Farrakhan also has urged a return to prayer in the public schools: "Thomas Jefferson was rooted in the Gospel of Jesus Christ even though he didn't apply it to his slaves. Those Founding Fathers of this nation were God-fearing men [who would be displeased] if they could come back today and see that the children can't utter a prayer in school, that this nation has put God out and relegated God and religion to some back seat, when without God you have no government."[4] Conservative commentator Pat Buchanan also echoes these sentiments:

> How did America's Christians allow themselves to be dispossessed of a country their fathers had built for them? How did America come to be a nation where not only have all Christian prayers, pageants, holidays and holy days been purged from all government schools and public institutions, but secularism has taken over those schools, while Christians are mocked at Christmas in ways that would be declared hate crimes were it done to other religious faiths or ethnic minorities?[5]

Before embracing a return to the supposedly golden era of the public school system, though, it is worthwhile to consider how the early preference for the majority religion affected citizens. Instead of simply crafting good character among the students, it sowed religious conflict. Catholics legitimately objected to the use of the King James Bible, but Protestants "refused . . . to withdraw the King James Bible, which, although Protestant, no longer seemed to [them to] belong to any one church."[6] When the Protestants insisted on their own version, the Catholics walked away from the entire system and created their own, at their expense. The Catholic parochial school system that exists today is a result of that exchange. The disputes between Protestants and Catholics are not an indictment of public education. Rather, it is a reminder of the dangers of any one religious worldview dominating in the United States. This history is also the backdrop for the evolution from public schools into a network of public schools, private religious schools, private secular schools, and eventually home schooling. Parents today have a constitutional right to choose between the public schools and private education under the Supreme Court's decision in *Pierce v. Society of Sisters*, which is evidence of the principle of accommodation that permeates the American culture, as the Court noted in *Smith*.

The more diverse the U.S. student body has become, the more extraordinary are the claims that have arisen in the public schools. The United States is well past the era when it could be credibly claimed that the public schools can or should cater exclusively to a Judeo-Christian population. School districts face a dizzying menu of challenges from Sikhs to the Amish to the United Pentecostal Church, just to name a few, alongside the demands by powerful religious entities to introduce prayer and control content.

This chapter describes three areas of school regulation where religious entities have requested accommodation: antiviolence regulations, dress codes, and curriculum. Each request taken by itself may seem innocuous enough (leaving out the violence category), but the problem for the schools was nicely captured by U.S. Supreme Court Justice Robert Jackson in 1948:

> If we are to eliminate everything that is objectionable to any of these warring sects or inconsistent with any of their doctrines, we will leave public education in shreds. Nothing but educational confusion and a discrediting of the public school system can result from subjecting it to constant lawsuits.[7]

The challenge lies in the enormous assortment of religions in the United States. The accommodation question, as in every other context, cannot be adequately addressed by an examination of the believer's tenets and conduct, for they are not the only ones affected. When the issue is education, the other students, the educational mission, and the society as a whole that benefits from a well-educated citizenry all have a stake in the decision. Discipline and a controlled atmosphere necessary to educate young people would evaporate if there were slavish accommodation.

The court-ordered accommodations – under either the RFRA[8] or Wisconsin v. Yoder[9] – are difficult to harmonize with common sense, because the court is drawn into a sympathetic, even narcissistic, assessment of the believer and invited to discount society's interests in the light of this one believer. There is a tendency in these cases to minimize the actual impact the religious conduct has on the government interests necessary to create the conditions for a good education. For example, when a child carries a relatively small knife for religious purposes, it is easy to believe that this one accommodation will not hurt anyone – it's just a *de minimis* infringement of the no-weapons rule. But the child carrying the knife does not live in a vacuum, or in a constant state of grace. Here, as elsewhere, accommodation needs to be accomplished by a legislative body that can calculate the balance of harms within a broader context, not by a judge who may only consider the facts of the case before him or her.

These cases address only public and not private schools, because the First Amendment's free exercise guarantees only limit government action. But they have tremendous impact, because 90 percent of U.S. students attend public school.[10] The same free exercise formula is necessary here as in every other context: legislative accommodation must be consistent with the public good, and the legislature needs to consider all sides, because it imposes a larger perspective than any one religious believer, faith, or administrator.

Religious accommodation in conflict with preventing
violence in the public schools

WEAPONS. In the decade since the first edition of this book, there has been a tragic increase in gun violence in the schools. The Columbine High School tragedy occurred in 1999, and others followed in Santee, California in 2001, Omaha, Nebraska in 2011, and Sandy Hook, Connecticut, in 2012. The numbers keep increasing, with a school shooting, during school hours, occurring on average every two weeks in 2013.[11]

But there has also been a spike in violence with other weapons, including knives. For example, a student in Murrysville, Pennsylvania, recently attacked his classmates with two kitchen knives, resulting in over twenty being injured, and another student in Danvers, Massachusetts, used a box-cutter to threaten, rape, and then murder his high school teacher.[12] A survey conducted by the Center for Disease Control in 2011 indicated that 16.6% of high school students carried a weapon (gun, knife or club) to school on at least one day in the thirty days preceding the survey.[13] Of those students, 5.1% carried a gun to school on at least one day during those thirty days.[14] There is now a passionate national conversation about weapons in schools.

Sikh students in particular have requested religious accommodation to carry weapons in schools. In 1990, there were approximately 13,000 Sikhs in the United States; by 2001, there were 57,000,[15] and as of 2014 it is estimated that there are over 500,000.[16] Most of the roughly 20 million Sikhs in the world live in the Punjab region of India[17], which is in the northwest, near Pakistan, with significant populations in the United Kingdom and Canada, whose Sikh population now sits at over 800,000.[18] Devout Sikhs are initiated into the Khalsa, and wear the 5Ks, which are Kesh (uncut hair), Kara (a steel bracelet), Kanga (a wooden comb), Kaccha (distinctive underwear), and Kirpan (sword).[19] (Other, less-doctrinaire believers have moved toward Western style dress and hair.[20]) The Sikhs believe generally in mutual tolerance and respect. Even so, it should come as no surprise that the sword, or knife, they carry has caused consternation in the schools.

In the Sikh faith, kirpan (knives) are considered to be "ceremonial," and there is no set style, which means they can be only a few inches or as long as three feet. They are worn in a sheath over or under clothing.[21] While the rule is that they are only to be drawn if the person believes himself to be in a life and death situation, they are potentially lethal weapons, at times concealed, and at the ready in volatile circumstances.[22] Human nature being what it is, the kirpan have not been simply benign symbols of the Sikh faith.

The Sikhs live in the real world, where knives can be very dangerous. For example, two drug addicts (one of whom was a police officer's son) purchased some heroin in Delhi, India, and when they discovered it was mixed with other chemicals, returned, killed two of the dealers and injured a third with a kirpan.[23] This could just as easily happen in or near one of our schools.

There are many Sikhs in British Columbia, Canada, where the Sikh population has doubled in the past decade,[24] and provincial authorities have had their share of kirpan-related problems. A Toronto Sikh temple's high priest, Jatinder Singh, allegedly stabbed one of his members, Sarbjit Singh Sandhar, with a kirpan in the midst of a heated exchange regarding whether a Sikh holy book was available for a blessing ceremony. After Singh said none were available, a fight ensued, and Singh allegedly stabbed Sandhar in the chest, and then attempted to stab his neck as well. The priest claimed that his turban was knocked off, and therefore, he feared for his life (which would have justified the stabbing in the Sikh religion if not the secular law). The court did not find his claims credible, but later evidence was discovered that indicated someone else may have used his kirpan in the dispute, so that he was granted a new trial. Singh ultimately pleaded guilty to assault for stabbing the parishioner with his kirpan.[25]

In Toronto, Canada, Tarlochan Dhillon pulled his kirpan on a distant relative, Harvinder Virk, and stabbed him in the stomach. Dhillon was convicted of aggravated assault, but amazingly, while in custody, he objected to the prison authorities taking away his kirpan (and turban), but there was no question that an inmate could not have a knife in prison.[26] In another violent exchange, in Vancouver, fundamentalists believe in eating on the floor because it signifies all are equal, but others do not think it is necessary. The controversy (which was actually international in scope) turned into a battle royale at one Vancouver temple when a crowd gathered and some tried to bring tables and chairs into the temple. Many carried kirpan, and in the resulting melee, there were six injuries before the police could pry the two factions apart. One man's throat was slit, leading to charges of attempted murder.[27]

The school problems have arisen when Sikh children wear kirpans, typically strapped to their leg. The kirpan that have been the most troubling have been approximately seven inches long.[28] Every public school in the United States has a no-exceptions weapons ban at this point, so a conflict was inevitable.

In California, the Livingston Union School District refused to permit Rajinder, Sukhjinder, and Jaspreet Cheema, who were Khalsa-baptized Sikhs, to wear their kirpan to school. Under the Supreme Court's dominant free exercise jurisprudence, the school should have had no problem applying its neutral, generally applicable law to these children.[29] Indeed, it is highly unlikely that the case would have even been brought but for the fact that the RFRA encouraged claims to be brought challenging the free exercise of religion even when the customs are well beyond accepted practices. In the infamous *Cheema v. Thompson* case, the U.S. Court of Appeals for the Ninth Circuit held that the school had a compelling interest in safety, but it had not engaged in the "least restrictive means" of regulating the "ceremonial" knives, and therefore preliminarily enjoined the school district from preventing the Cheema children from coming to school with their kirpan.[30]

This is a classic case of a court with only the record of two parties before it, thinking only in terms of the needs of the believer, and letting the RFRA suspend common sense. According to Judges Betty Binns Fletcher and Cynthia Holcomb Hall, the school could not ban the knives simply because other students might be frightened; rather, it could only regulate them in response to "those [threats] which are reasonably related to a real threat," implying that other children's fears would have been irrational. The school district, according to the court, had failed to prove that "any of its students are afraid of or upset by kirpans." Under the RFRA, the school district had to avoid "all unnecessary burdens" on religious believers, so the Sikhs could not be prohibited from attending school with the knives, because the record showed no "school-related violence" from kirpan to date and some school districts had permitted kirpan if they were loosely basted to their sheaths or the blade was blunt with a rounded tip.[31] Only a flawed legal doctrine would lead a court out on such a weak limb. Seven-inch knives are knives, and children are unlikely to be safe in their presence.

Judge Charles Wiggins, in dissent, invoked a far more rational analysis, by thinking *beyond* the believer's perspective. The Sikh believer may sincerely believe that a kirpan is only a formality, not intended to be used as a weapon, but Judge Wiggins asked, not what the believer sincerely believed, but rather what was the impact of the conduct. He identified three categories of danger arising from a kirpan, even if the average Sikh child would not be likely to draw it on other children. First, there was the "abnormal, non-law-abiding Sikh child," which is to say that one must bring one's knowledge of the human race to bear on these questions, and there is no question that some children (and adults) do not follow the mores they are taught. Second, he noted that it is not only the child carrying the weapon who is a potential threat, but also a different child who could grab the kirpan to hurt others. Finally, he made the observation that the plaintiffs were children, who had only the

> maturity and judgment of children. Given that Sikhs are to use their kirpans in life-or-death situations, we would be forced to rely on school children to make the determination as to when their lives are at stake. Clearly, school officials need not knowingly expose the non-Sikh school children to such an unacceptable position of vulnerability.... [I]t is not clear that any feasible means exist to accommodate the Cheemas' need to carry kirpans.[32]

After RFRA was invalidated in *Boerne v. Flores,* and the proper free exercise rule was reinstated, the only legitimate forum for the Sikhs to obtain permission for their children to carry kirpans was in the legislature, where the costs and benefits of exempting children from the weapons bans could be weighed, and there could be intensive investigation of the issue. In fact, the sizable Sikh population in California persuaded the California legislature to pass just such a measure, proving once again the power of religious lobbyists to obtain exemptions, as the Supreme Court's *Smith* decision predicted. Luckily, the process did not end there. Governor Pete Wilson vetoed the exemption in 1994, saying "I am unwilling to authorize the carrying of knives on school grounds and abandon public safety to the resourcefulness of a thousand districts."[33] Thus, the system vetted the issue, and common sense prevailed.

In the *Cheema* case's Canadian counterpart, a trial court granted a Sikh student, Gurbaj Singh, the right to wear a wooden kirpan underneath his clothes and in a sheath with a fold that was then sealed so that it could not be drawn either intentionally or accidentally. The student was also required to maintain control of the kirpan. The appellate court reversed, because the "kirpan is intrinsically dangerous and the conditions imposed by the trial judge do not address all the risks.... [N]ot only the [school], but any students, would have to assume the risks associated with the presence of a kirpan. Firstly, the physical integrity of the entire school community is threatened by the presence of dangerous objects at school. Secondly, the perception of the climate of security can also be affected."[34] The decision then went up to the Supreme Court of Canada in 2006, which rejected the argument that kirpans are inherently dangerous; therefore, the appellate court's absolute prohibition on kirpans in schools was not justified. The Court discussed the special nature of the relationship between teachers and students in schools as a means of dealing with any situations that might arise as a result of allowing kirpans in schools. However, the Court did say that schools could impose restrictions, such as that the kirpans must be concealed under clothing, sewn into place, or held in a sheath.[35]

The question on many readers' minds, I imagine, will be: what is a Sikh family to do? The kirpan has a long tradition in the faith. History gives three answers. First, if the children must carry dangerous knives, the family may choose to send their children to religious schools (or to home school). Second, the religion might adjust to the legal requirements, as happened with the Mormons and polygamy in the United States, by jettisoning the practice for children. Third, there might be some attempt on the part of the faith to meet the law halfway either by exempting children from the requirement (at least during the school day) and/or making the knife ceremonial rather than dangerous. The latter option appears to be the path that is being followed.

Adult male Sikhs have had to adjust to the post-9/11 era. For example, no adult Sikh can fly with a knife and, therefore, must check a kirpan. This is a historical development that challenged Sikhs to either adjust their practices or to choose not to fly. Many have chosen to adapt. There has been adjustment on the other side as well. They may not bring the 7-inch kirpan into federal buildings, but can carry one with a blade shorter than 2.5.[36]

To be sure, it is not the business of the government to direct the Sikhs to alter their beliefs, but it is certainly within the government's purview to reject conduct – religious or not – that is inherently dangerous. Sikh families continue to pressure public schools to permit the knives, and have had some success. Again, though, there is a tendency to permit only those versions that are safe. Under pressure from Sikh families, the Detroit school system started permitting kirpan in 2011.[37] In 2012, some California districts began to permit them when the "parents agree to sign a statement that requires the kirpan ... to be worn under clothing, to have a blade dulled, to be soldered or sewn into its sheath so it cannot be removed and to have a blade that is 2½ inches or less."[38] If the knives are incapable of being used in violent ways, the accommodation makes sense.

GANG COLORS AND INSIGNIA. U.S. schools have struggled mightily to eradicate gangs in the schoolhouse. They are inherently violent and when given free rein in the schools, terrorize other students, foster drug trade, and commit other heinous crimes. Gangs appear to have become a permanent feature of the schools and inner cities. Recent studies indicate that nearly 10% of females and males aged eighteen to thirty are gang members.[39]

Schools have found that in order to reduce gang activity, they need to force students to remove gang identifications, for example, gang "colors," insignia, or jewelry containing gang symbols. These identifiers unite the gangs and cement the differences between rival gangs. "The primary consensus is that a gang is a group with social, racial, or ethnic ties that acts to further a criminal purpose."[40] The problem is that they alter their colors or symbols so that members are more difficult to detect by the authorities. One school board explained, "clothing which is identifiable as gang related changes frequently and is, therefore, often difficult to discern."[41] Frank Hutchins, the principal of the Horace Mann Junior High School in Baytown, Texas, expressed his alarm at the effects that gang apparel caused in his school:

> It wasn't subtle at all.... You'd see students dressed in black and red, for instance, clustering together in the mornings. Students said they were being told if they didn't wear a gang's "colors", they'd be jumped. Teachers noticed the increased presence on campus and said it was becoming disruptive in the classroom.[42]

A dress code was later instituted in an effort to combat gang violence.

This school was part of a movement among public schools nationwide to institute school uniforms or rigid dress codes to minimize the impact of gangs and school violence. A 1999 survey of school principals revealed that 85 percent wanted dress codes at their schools, and they cited the elimination of gang activity as one of the top motivations for instituting the policy.[43] President Bill Clinton urged the adoption of such policies to improve behavior and eradicate gang clothing in schools.[44] The Department of Education published a widely distributed "Manual on School Uniforms" that listed decreasing violence and gang affiliation in schools as important goals of instituting dress codes and cited several "Model School Uniform Policies" that appeared to have had an impact on the school environment. For example, after requiring uniforms in all elementary and middle schools, the Long Beach, California, schools saw a 36 percent decrease in overall crime and 50 percent fewer weapons offenses. Other schools commended by the Department of Education did not detail crime statistics, but all saw marked changes in the attitudes and educational environments at their schools.[45] By 2010, 76% of public schools had adopted a uniform or strict dress code policy,[46] with city schools about twice as likely to do so as compared to suburban, town, or rural schools.[47]

When schools restrict gang symbols, they can come into conflict with other students' religiously motivated conduct. In *Levon v. O'Rourke*, the Calumet City School District in Illinois was worried about gang activity at the school and in adjacent areas, and therefore considered imposing a dress code. Street gangs including the Latin Kings, Black Gangster Disciples, Black P Stones, and Insane Unknowns were known to be in the vicinity near the school. During the 1995–96 school year, the District asked students to wear blue "bottoms" and white "tops," but when compliance was low, instituted a mandatory dress code for the 1996–97 school year, because "[s]tudents' choice of clothing disrupts the learning environment where it may be representative or suggestive or [sic] gang affiliation, or activities. The Board of Education recognizes that gangs are present in the District's community and pose a real threat to the disruption of the schools." The policy also contained a religious and health accommodation provision as well, which authorized the principal discretion to accommodate the student's religious- or health-motivated conduct where there was a "genuine conflict" between the policy and the conduct.[48]

When the policy was under consideration, one mother, Kathryn Levon, in 1994 objected to the school board's policy, because jeans were more durable and the cost of a uniform was beyond her means. Two years later, she argued that it violated her parental rights and that it would not solve the gang nuisance. She had no legal argument until her objections transformed into religious arguments. In August 1996, she objected on numerous religious grounds, most drawn from the New or Old Testament of the Bible, one from the Rev. Martin Luther King, Jr., and another from the Rev. John Irvin. She argued that forcing her son to wear a uniform would be forcing her son to "adorn" himself a certain way, in violation of several Bible verses. Finally, she quoted an ancient proverb, "A monkey in silk is still a monkey." The board then offered to purchase a uniform for her son, Adam, which was refused, and after Adam was expelled for refusing to follow the code, the board offered him a uniform again, home tutoring, or tutoring in the public library. The parents declined, and Adam was not educated during the fall term.

Magistrate Judge Joan Lefkow found that the Levons failed to prove there was a substantial burden on their religious conduct, because their beliefs were not being coerced. The question was whether the parents were "'being prevented from engaging in religiously motivated conduct or expression,'"[49] and the court concluded that the burden placed by the school district was *de minimis*, and therefore could not rise to a free exercise violation (under RFRA or the Constitution). Furthermore, Mrs. Levon did not raise a religious argument until she learned of the statutory exemption on religious grounds, and did not object in the same manner to gym uniforms.

Evenhandedness is the hallmark of a constitutional policy. No school district may choose to enforce a rule against some students and not against others. When the district permits a child to avoid any rule, it better be prepared to permit other students that are similarly situated to avoid it as well, and if it permits abridgment for secular reasons, it must provide the same accommodation for sincere religious reasons. For example, in Biloxi, Mississippi, school officials refused to permit Jewish student, Ryan Green, to wear a Star of David necklace outside his clothing.[50] His grandmother had given it to him as a symbol of his heritage. On a unanimous vote, the school board supported a teacher who had ordered him to take it off, because students were forbidden from wearing any symbol that might be construed as a gang symbol. Gang insignia have included a six-pointed star, like the Star of David, as well as crosses and crucifixes.[51]

The constitutional problem arose, however, when the board decided to permit Christians to continue wearing crucifixes and crosses. Thus, not only is this a case where the rule was not so necessary that it could not be broken in some circumstances, but also the board was picking and choosing between religious symbols. That smacks of potential discrimination and justifies the courts' closest scrutiny of the school board's actions and purposes. After the ACLU initiated a lawsuit, the board properly reversed its position.

Dress codes in conflict with religious mandates (beyond gang issues)

Sometimes a school district will prohibit an article of clothing or jewelry because it is disruptive to the educational atmosphere. Overly short skirts, skimpy tank tops, and T-shirts with obscene messages fit into this category and show that instilling a dress code can be an appropriate means of encouraging the proper learning environment. The concept of "disruption," however, can also play into the marginalization of uncommon religions, but school districts are capable of learning from their mistakes. Rebecca Moreno was a student at the Waxahachie, Texas, High School, and her family was Wiccan. The Morenos explained Wiccan religion as a pagan religion that incorporates witchcraft, multiple gods and goddesses, and nature worship.[52] In 2001, when she was 15 years old, she wore a pentacle necklace, which is a five-pointed star that is a central symbol for the Wiccan religion. First, the school district banned it for its disruptive qualities. Then, Rebecca and the school compromised; she could wear it under her clothing. It needed to be concealed from the other students, because it scared the other students, who associated the pentacle with Satan worship and animal sacrifice. The school superintendent, Bobby Parker, wrote to the Morenos "While the Wiccan faith may not be the majority religion in our community, our board policies protect all faiths."[53] From a situation that threatened a lawsuit, the parties were able to land on a shared accommodation.

The dress code and apparel regulations do serve (when applied as they should be) important ends, including safety and maintaining a nurturing educational environment. RFRA robbed school districts of their power to enforce uniform dress codes, by making it likely that "schools generally may not prohibit the wearing of [religious] items," in the words of a memorandum to the schools on religious liberty in the schools in 1995 from U.S. Secretary of Education Richard Riley and Attorney General Janet Reno.[54]

A recurring contemporary problem here and abroad has been the conflict between school prohibitions on headgear and the Islamic belief that adolescent girls and women should wear a burka, niqab, hijab, khimar, or headscarf.[55] Headgear bans in the schools often exist because hats can detract from the educational atmosphere, may be used as gang reinforcement, and are preferred hiding places for contraband, such as drugs and weapons.[56] One can hardly fault any school district struggling with violence for the policy, and the First Amendment provides no defense to a neutral rule applied evenhandedly.

Even though the Constitution does not mandate the accommodation, the door always remains open, and various school districts have accommodated a variety of religious headgear, to their credit. For example, the Lafayette, Louisiana, school board with a no-hat rule permitted eight Rastafarian children to attend school, even though their religion required head coverings, or crowns (loose-knit circular hats, which typically are knitted red, yellow and green, which represents the Ethiopian flag), which are worn over dreadlocks.[57] In another case, a computer teacher at Antelope Valley College in Lancaster, California, ordered a student to remove her hijab, but she refused on religious reasons. The school policy was "no head-wear except knit caps in extremely cold whether" and "hair on male students should not descend below the bottom of the earlobe to touch the top of the collar in the back." The dean supported the student, the teacher quit, and that was the end of it.[58]

These dilemmas have not been limited to the United States, as Canadian schools have faced them as well. In 1994, Emilie Ouimet, age 12, was expelled from Ecole Louis Riel, a public high school, for wearing a hijab, but a year later, the Quebec Human Rights Commission ruled that public school dress codes banning the hijab violated the Charter.

The issue is different when the question is whether the religious clothing can be worn in the context of a nonpublic religious school. In 2003, Irene Waseem, 16, was expelled from College Charlemagne, a private Catholic girls' school, for wearing the hijab.[59] The different results lie in the fact that private schools have more latitude to impose beliefs and religious symbols in their schools. Dania Bali, a straight-A student at College Regina Assumpta, a private Catholic girls' school in north-end Montreal, was permitted to wear her hijab for two years, but then was expelled for wearing it. Upon consideration, the parents' committee voted unanimously to retain its strict school uniform policy of banning headwear, and the school's administration agreed. Despite her fellow students' support, Ms. Bali was told to remove her scarf or shop for a new school the following year. When she chose the latter, there were no further legal consequences.[60]

There is also a strong First Amendment defense where the rule is selectively enforced. A Muskogee, Oklahoma, school district had in place a rule against wearing "hats, caps, bandannas, plastic caps, and hoods on jackets inside the [school] building."[61] The policy was enforced against sixth-grader Nashala Hearn, who wore a hijab (a veil covering the head and chest) to the Benjamin Franklin Science Academy, by suspending her twice. Apparently, the school permitted some students to wear head coverings for secular purposes, at the same time it refused to let Nashala wear her niqab. The U.S. Department of Justice, which intervened after the family filed the lawsuit, reached a consent decree with the school district and condemned its actions, saying, the department "would not tolerate discrimination against Muslims or any other religious group.... [S]uch intolerance is un-American, and is morally despicable."[62] This is an archetypal case for explaining when the courts should strongly suspect unconstitutional purposes. Whenever the government has a rule, permits some exceptions, and prefers nonreligious reasons over religious reasons, the courts are justified in applying strict scrutiny. This is the sort of individualized assessment of the reasons for the conduct that calls for a presumption of unconstitutionality and strict scrutiny by the courts.[63]

After all, if the policy behind the hat ban is not severely undermined by those wearing hats for secular reasons, the religious individuals will not undermine it either. We do not have the benefit in this case of a fully developed trial record to know precisely what happened, but the terms of the consent decree are instructive. The decree required the district to permit Nashala to wear her niqab and to revise its dress code to permit headgear for a "bona fide religious reason." The accommodation was not absolute, however, as the district was instructed to consider requests for religious accommodation individually. The school could reject the request only where the claimed belief was not sincerely held and where to grant the accommodation would endanger "safety and security."[64] In addition, the district was ordered (1) to educate administrators, teachers, parents, and students on the new policy, which permitted head coverings in only three circumstances: doctor's orders, religious accommodation, and for a "special school activity"; (2) to certify compliance over a four-year period; and (3) to pay the Hearn family an undisclosed sum.[65] Had the school district enforced its headgear ban uniformly against all students, without reference to religion, the Department of Justice would have had no constitutional argument against the district. By its arbitrary actions, the district invited federal intervention.

France has followed a principle that forbids all religious and political symbols from the public schools, which includes headscarves. This is an apt place to show the differences between the French and the U.S. approaches to accommodation.

In the United States, as the Supreme Court noted in *Smith*, there is a value placed on encouraging a free marketplace of religion. Two First Amendment principles work together to let religion operate in a free and open market. The Free Exercise Clause prevents persecution based on religious belief that would rid the market of certain religious elements and the Establishment Clause prevents the government from supporting religion, which would torque the market away from actual demand toward government-managed demand. The result is not only a truly amazing variety of religious faiths, but also a fascinating blend in the public square which is filled with religious talk and images, juxtaposed with a government that does not itself take positions on religious belief in that square. The celebration of religious diversity that is at the heart of the First Amendment encourages accommodation, and so a flat ban on conduct tends to be undesirable if religious belief can be accommodated consistent with the public good. The problem in the United States in recent years is that too often the drive to accommodate religious conduct takes flight from common sense and public security.

The French appear to have the opposite inclination – a presumption against accommodation. As of March 15, 2004, it became illegal in France to wear clothing, insignia, or symbols that "conspicuously manifest a religious [or political] affiliation."[66] The directive applies across the board to all students, though some believe it was prompted by Muslim girls wearing headscarves to school,[67] at a time of large Muslim migration into France and resulting discord.[68]

The motive behind the French law would not have made it unconstitutional in the United States, because the law is neutral and generally applicable. But the political culture fostered by the First Amendment's robust protection of belief and speech has encouraged legislative accommodation. This attitude would have opened the door to the Islamists to persuade Parliament that headscarves could be worn without harm to the public good. For those in the United States who believe this country has reached the point of factually separating church and state and has eviscerated all traces of religion from public places, the French example provides an outstanding context for understanding that strict separation never was and likely never will capture the spirit of the U.S. Religion Clauses.

Hair length also has posed accommodation issues in U.S. schools, especially for Native Americans. The Alabama Coushatta Tribes of Texas and 12 Native American students challenged the hair-length regulations of the Big Sandy Independent School District in east Texas. A number of the students received in-school suspensions for refusing to cut their hair, because they believed in the context of their Native American and Christian beliefs that long hair was a "symbol of moral and spiritual strength," and was an integral part of the body's "oneness."[69] The school's hair code was enacted to "minimize disruptions attributable to personal appearance," to "foster an attitude of respect for authority," and to create a favorable impression of the district when its students participated in extracurricular activities elsewhere.[70] While acknowledging that the U.S. Court of Appeals for the Fifth Circuit had previously upheld a hair policy because it did not violate any fundamental rights, the Big Sandy court distinguished that case, because it did not implicate the free exercise of religion.[71] The students prevailed, because the case involved a combination of rights – free exercise, free speech, and equal protection – and the court examined the rule closely and presumed that the accommodation should be permitted. While I don't disagree with the result, this notion that multiple rights, which the *Smith* court called, "hybrid rights," justify heightened judicial scrutiny of a law is questionable. Some circuits have simply thrown up their hands trying to understand or apply it.[72] Where there are two rights, for example, and the government has not violated either individually, it makes no sense to conclude that their coexistence justifies treating the law as presumptively unconstitutional, so the approach in this decision is on shaky ground.

Yet, if there is any case that argues for judicial intervention in the legislative accommodation context, this might be the one. The students were not themselves disruptive, their hair did not block anyone's educational experience, and, in this day and age, surely no one was so distracted by the fact of its length so as to be unable to pay attention in class. The school district's refusal to accommodate them seems willful, if not just plain silly, and maybe the judge in this case got a whiff of discrimination that led him to find for the Native American students under as many theories as he could. Having said all that, however, the rule was generally applicable; it was found by the court to be neutral, and the district's policy was rational, so under the Constitution, the outcome should have been the opposite.

That would have left the tribe with the Texas legislature to obtain accommodation. Some will immediately shake their heads and assume that they have no chance, because they are a small group or because they lack political power, but the Native American Church obtained exemptions for religious use of peyote under the Texas drug laws.[73] Moreover, where the hair-length restriction is unevenly applied, so that only one group, like the Native Americans, is being punished for the infringement, the punishment would be unconstitutional.[74] Since the case was decided, the Texas RFRA was passed, so the outcome in favor of the students is secure.

The challenges of choosing a curriculum to fit all
religious viewpoints

My vote for the worst Religion Clause case in the United States goes to *Wisconsin v. Yoder*, which held that the Amish could avoid Wisconsin's compulsory education laws by removing their children from school after age 14, because the First Amendment granted Amish parents a right to remove the children from school.[75] As I will discuss in more detail in Part Two, I would deep-six it for its romantic, depiction of Amish life, its assumption that parental rights automatically trump any question about the children's needs or beliefs, and its judicially forced accommodation, which forestalled legislative debate or determination regarding whether permitting a significant number of children to forego higher education was consistent with their best interests or the public good. There is good reason to question that conclusion in a society where every other citizen is required to go to school at least until they are 16 (and therefore the Amish children are being disabled in terms of their future prospects) and where the political and social welfare of the country rests on well-educated and informed adults.

The *Yoder* case is also problematic in that the court believed it was legitimate to take into account whether the sect would continue to exist as it has for centuries. The government, including the courts, is required to take a neutral position in religious beliefs and existence. It is not appropriate for it to prop up religious groups or treat them as necessarily static. It is up to the faiths themselves to decide whether they will adjust to cultural developments, and only up to the government to serve the public good. The *Yoder* court's reasoning to protect the Amish lifestyle itself was unconstitutional.

The Yoder decision implicates the religious medical neglect cases. Should parents be permitted to deprive their children of medical treatment or education, when that deprivation could disable them permanently? These are not easy questions, though I would weigh the children's interests in health and education more weightily than they have been to date. In any event, the issues certainly were not resolved by the Court's love letter to the Amish in *Yoder*. The *Yoder* decision is emblematic of the social debate over curriculum. If students can be pulled from school altogether during the last two compulsory years, in order to pursue a solely agrarian education, why can't they be removed to solely study Torah or the Bible? The answer is that students needed then to be educated in the typical high school topics, including United States history, biology, and geometry to be better voters, to assess their government, and even to be better farmers. Today, in the technological society that has developed since *Yoder* was decided, it is utterly indefensible to defend an "agrarian" education as adequate. The Court should have left it up to the Wisconsin legislature to make the call.

EVOLUTION. Mainstream believers have incorporated the evolution science into their belief systems, while fundamentalists, who read the Bible literally, have not. The 1987 Supreme Court decision *Edwards v. Aguillard* held that a school policy of requiring creationism to be taught alongside evolution, known as the Balanced Treatment Act, violated the Establishment Clause, because the statute permitted government funds and power to achieve a religious purpose.[76]

These conflicts did not disappear after *Edwards* was decided. For example, the school board of a Wisconsin district revised its curriculum to allow the teaching of creationism.[77] In 2001, the Kansas State Board of Education restored the teaching of evolution to the curriculum after having controversially voted to remove it from public school science standards in 1999.[78] In 2002, 2,000 parents in Cobb County, Georgia (just outside Atlanta) presented a petition to school officials complaining that their science textbooks discussed evolution but not creationism. The schools responded by requiring science textbooks to contain an evolution warning sticker, that read: "This textbook contains material on evolution. Evolution is a theory, not a fact, regarding the origin of living things. This material should be approached with an open mind, studied carefully and critically considered." The ACLU and six parents filed an Establishment Clause challenge, saying that the stickers promoted creationism and discriminated against certain religions. During the bench trial, the judge asked, "How were teachers told to address questions or conflicts stemming from the disclaimer?" The school district's answer was troubling: the sticker was supposed to bring the students' attention to the fact that "there is a scientific discussion and there's a religious discussion, and we're going to have a scientific discussion." That made it sound as though the sole purpose of the stickers was to inject religion into the schools. Moreover, the district tried to use the pressure by the creationists to justify the schools' action, saying that the school "had an obligation to those who felt very strongly about this."[79] Private individuals may have any views they like, but a public school may not use those citizens' religious viewpoints to justify its policies. Accordingly, the court found the stickers unconstitutional. The school district appealed the case to the Eleventh Circuit, which vacated and remanded the case.[80] Ultimately, the case settled in 2006 on the following terms: the school district may not (1) reattach the stickers or any other statements regarding evolution; (2) make any disclaimers about evolution orally, in writing, or by other means; (3) excise or redact any materials in school science textbooks; or (4) violate state standards regarding the teaching of evolution. If the school district violates any of the 4 provisions, the case will be reopened.[81]

There is no apparent end to these attempts to insert theology into the classroom. Creationism's supporters changed the name of their belief to "intelligent design," and took a run at instituting such a curriculum in central Pennsylvania.[82] In 2004, the Dover Area School District adopted a policy that would allow for the following statement to be read in public school science classes:

> The Pennsylvania Academic Standards require students to learn about Darwin's Theory of Evolution and eventually to take a standardized test of which evolution is a part.
>
> Because Darwin's Theory is a theory, it continues to be tested as new evidence is discovered. The Theory is not a fact. Gaps in the Theory exist for which there is no evidence. A theory is defined as a well-tested explanation that unifies a broad range of observations.
>
> Intelligent Design is an explanation of the origin of life that differs from Darwin's view. The reference book, Of Pandas and People, is available for students who might be interested in gaining an understanding of what Intelligent Design actually involves.
>
> With respect to any theory, students are encouraged to keep an open mind. The school leaves the discussion of the Origins of Life to individual students and their families. As a Standards-driven district, class instruction focuses upon preparing students to achieve proficiency on Standards-based assessments.[83]

One month later, plaintiffs, including parents and teachers, filed suit alleging the policy violated the Establishment Clause.[84] The school board argued that the policy was passed "for the secular purpose of improving science education and to exercise critical thinking skills,"[85] but there was no evidence at trial that the board consulted scientific material, scientists, or scientific organizations.[86] Furthermore, the court found that the District failed to consider the views of the district's science teachers and only gathered legal advice from organizations with clear religious purposes.[87] The court ultimately agreed with plaintiffs' claims and permanently enjoined the district "from requiring teachers to denigrate or disparage the scientific theory of evolution, and from requiring teachers to refer to a religious, alternative theory" in order to preserve the separation of church and state.[88] Some state legislators persist in introducing intelligent design legislation, although their more recent efforts have failed. In 2013, Missouri attempted to pass two separate intelligent design bills, both of which failed in committee.[89]

HOMESCHOOLING. Some religious parents keep their children out of public *and* private schools to shoulder the responsibility for education themselves. One of the impetuses has been the rejection of the science of evolution by fundamentalists.[90] Homeschoolers are also escaping from the "secular" environment and curriculum in the public schools.[91] The Home School Legal Defense Association website makes this position quite clear:

> God has delegated the authority *and* responsibility to teach and raise children to the parents first. Parents can delegate their *authority* to teach and raise children to someone else, but they can never delegate their *responsibility* to teach their children to anyone else. God will hold parents responsible for what education their children receive (whether from teachers, books, projects, or peers). To whom much is given, much is required. We have a free choice in this country to *not* send our children to an ungodly public school – we will, all the more, be responsible. Remember, our children are dying souls entrusted to our care![92]

Two conflicts have arisen as a result. The first involves access to extracurricular programs while the second deals with how the state can ensure that each child is being adequately educated, in light of the overriding interest in an educated citizenry in a republican form of democracy (notwithstanding *Yoder*).

First, homeschooled children have asked to participate in the extracurricular activities typically offered by the public schools, despite the fact they are receiving their education at home. Of the 42 states[93] that have legislation or case law addressing access of private school or home school students to public school activities, 22 permit access.[94] In states without laws addressing the issue, the decision is generally left to individual schools and school districts to decide. Most states also have sports league associations for interscholastic sports, which have adopted bylaws that usually do not permit schools to allow a student's participation in these activities unless the student is enrolled full-time in the school.[95]

Second – and this is the greater challenge – is how to monitor each child's education. The states impose requirements on each public and private school to satisfy certain educational aims in each subject, so that the education of each child in the system is monitored and well documented. Paperwork goes back and forth between the school districts and the state, and the private schools and the state. In addition, there are state visits to each school, and there is statewide standardized testing – which determines whether each school is teaching the necessary curriculum adequately and whether individual students are achieving certain minimum standards. In contrast, the homeschooling context poses a difficult challenge for the states, because it is so difficult to monitor such students. It's a problem of enforcing some kind of reporting requirement, having the manpower to deal with the individual education of children outside the public and private school system, and the expense associated.

Homeschooling eliminates the efficiencies created by the school systems' ability to take on the administrative burdens of monitoring education child by child. In contrast, homeschooling parents find some state's reporting requirements onerous, invasive, and unnecessary. "Homeschooling parents are overburdened," says former HSLDA president Michael Farris.[96] Moreover, most believe that parents have the constitutional right to choose to educate their children as they wish. The Supreme Court has rejected the notion, however, that a child can be a "martyr" for his or her parents' faith, and held that "those who nurture [a child] and direct his destiny have the right and high duty to recognize and prepare him for additional obligations."[97]

The HSLDA is spearheading litigation in handpicked states to fight the burdens placed on parents by the states' education reporting requirements. For instance, in a pair of Pennsylvania cases, two families challenged the state's home education law under Pennsylvania's Religious Freedom Protection Act, claiming that the home education law imposed a substantial burden on the free exercise of their religion. Specifically, the plaintiffs challenged the provisions of the statute that require parents to notify the district that they are homeschooling their children, provide a detailed curriculum, submit homeschool students to regular testing, and have their program certified annually by the superintendent.[98]

The HSLDA's agenda is to deregulate education for homeschoolers, but complete deregulation is inconceivable in light of the importance of education in the United States. The school boards and state fought to defend the state education law vigorously and won at the District Court level, which culminated in a decision by the Third Circuit

Court of Appeals holding that Pennsylvania's home education law was constitutional.[99]

From a free exercise perspective, the issue presents the typical analytical hurdle in all accommodation cases: from the perspective of the individual believer, it seems like a *de minimis* burden on the state, but from the state's perspective, the individualized element in it poses nearly insuperable administrative and cost barriers. In general, no matter the prevailing standard, the government has won these sorts of cases. While homeschooling issues have not made their way to the Supreme Court yet, one can analogize to other cases for guidance on the appropriate principles.

For example, when the Amish challenged the requirement that they pay Social Security taxes, and the Supreme Court rejected the claim, saying "Congress drew a line in § 1402(g), exempting the self-employed Amish but not all persons working for an Amish employer. The tax imposed on employers to support the Social Security system must be uniformly applicable to all, except as Congress provides explicitly otherwise."[100] The same result accrued when Native American parents objected to the requirement that every child must have a Social Security number. They argued that, under their religious beliefs, the assignment of a unique Social Security number would "rob the spirit" of their daughter.[101] The Court held that the government's interest in the fair and efficient administration of the system trumped the family's interest in accommodation. Surely the same can and will be said about the administration of education to millions of children.

Under *Smith*, the analysis is straightforward – education laws (except in the rare instance) are neutral and generally applicable, which means the homeschoolers' best route for accommodation is in the state legislatures. And they have not done too badly, as they have obtained exemptions for participation in interscholastic activities, truancy laws, drivers' education requirements, and the necessity of having someone trained in CPR present. Some states have even enacted a special tax credit for them.

The public good calculus on this topic, though, is not limited to the state's interest in educating children, or the parents' right to determine their children's education. Children have rights as well. Where their level of education is inferior to their peers', children are disabled for later life. The state also has an obligation to protect children from abuse and neglect and the vast majority of abuse occurs in the home. Homeschooling removes one of the most effective means the state has of ensuring that children are not abused – the teachers, aides, counselors, and principals who see the children outside the home on a regular basis. For the state to fully deregulate homeschooling may well abdicate its responsibility toward children potentially at risk of abuse or neglect. This is not to say that homeschoolers abuse children anymore than do other parents (unfortunately, the amount of abuse never reaches zero), but rather that children who are being homeschooled do not have the additional layer of protection of a teacher or principal, who has a mandatory obligation to report any abuse. It is just a fact that these children are at a higher risk of abuse.[102] Many homeschoolers would respond that their children engage in extracurricular activities, so their children are seen by other adults; the question is whether they are adults with a legal obligation to report perceived abuse.

All of which is to say that the question of legislative accommodation for the homeschoolers is complicated. There are weighty issues on both sides. It should be crystal clear that no court has the tools or powers necessary to determine the right balance between the competing interests of the children, the parents, and the public. These are issues that need public debate and legislative consideration that are beyond pandering to religious lobbyists.

CHOICE OF READING SERIES. There can be no more likely stage for conflict between religious parents and the schools than in the choice of a reading curriculum. It is impossible to teach reading without substantive content, and religious parents have had objections to a wide range of materials, including the fantasy materials at the heart of the following case.

Parents in Wheaton, Illinois, challenged an elementary school's adoption of the Impressions Reading Series, which encourages reading skills, using the works of C. S. Lewis, A. A. Milne, Dr. Seuss, Ray Bradbury, L. Frank Baum, Maurice Sendak, and other authors. The parents argued that the series established a religion of "superior beings exercising power over human beings by imposing rules of conduct, with the promise and threat of future rewards and punishments," and that it "indoctrinates children in values directly opposed to their Christian beliefs by teaching tricks, despair, deceit, parental disrespect and by denigrating Christian symbols and holidays."[103] A contrary view of the series was put forth by, among others, the Institute for First Amendment Studies, which filed an amicus brief in the case:

> The Impressions reading series employs the whole language approach to language arts instruction. Many fundamentalists believe the whole language method is a deliberate scheme on behalf of the National Education Association to produce functional illiterates, thus creating a dependent society susceptible to a one-world government. Believing that phonics is the only correct way to learn to read, they find inventive ways to reject whole language curricula.[104]

The parents lost on both Religion Clause theories, as they should have. The court listed certain types of activities in the schools that had been held to violate the Establishment Clause, each of them involved the school sending a rather clear message to the students about what they should believe: for example, inviting clergy to offer prayers at graduation, daily Bible readings or recitation of the Lord's Prayer, distribution of Gideon Bibles to public school students, posting the Ten Commandments in classrooms, excluding evolution science or requiring it be taught along with creation science, beginning school assemblies with prayer, and "teaching a Transcendental Meditation course that includes a ceremony involving offerings to a deity." In comparison, the courts have not been eager to invalidate the use of particular books in the public schools, whether they were novels, textbooks, other reading series, or even the Bible when employed for literary or historical purposes.[105]

The court struggled to identify what religion was allegedly being established in the series, which appeared to the court to be no more than a "collection of exercises in 'make-believe' designed to develop and encourage the use of imagination and reading skills in children that are the staple of traditional public elementary school education."[106] In a refreshingly frank passage, the court vehemently rejected the notion that fantasy and make-believe amounted to a "pagan" religion, asking,

> [W]hat would become of elementary education, public or private, without works such as these and scores and scores of others that serve to

expand the minds of young children and develop their sense of creativity? With that off our chest, we can now properly dispose of the parents' claim within the structure of the 'Lemon test.'[107]

The court found a "clear secular purpose" in the choice of "fantasy and 'make-believe' to hold a student's attention" and to develop the child's creative side, and that despite the presence of a few stories employing witches and goblins, the series "fit the norm."[108] Nor did the court find that the series had the effect of furthering a religion, because some of the stories employed imaginative characters, some were consistent with Protestantism and Catholicism, and overall the series simply improved reading skills. Finally, there was no entanglement with religion where the school board chose the series, because that is a standard school board activity.

The parents lost on their free exercise claim as well, because there was no coercion of the parents or the children's religious beliefs and the school's interest was extremely important. The same result accrued when a mother of four challenged the Holt, Rinehart, and Winston reading series, because her children were not permitted to abstain from using the series, which is used in many schools.[109] The court distinguished *Yoder* in that it "rested on such a singular set of facts" that it did not announce a general rule. Unlike the Amish parents in *Yoder*, the parents in the present case wanted their children to acquire the necessary skills to live in modern society, and it was not impossible to reconcile the religious requirements with the aim of public education.[110]

The Texas legislature tried to insert religion into its curriculum with its policy of using textbooks steeped in Christian precepts. Starting in 2009, Texas legislators sought to "water down" the Texas science and history curriculums by "placing a conservative stamp" on textbooks, "stressing the superiority of American capitalism, questioning the Founding Fathers' commitment to a purely secular government and presenting Republican political philosophies in a more positive light."[111] The latest battle in 2013 surrounded the adoption of environmental and biology textbooks. After much debate among members of the State Board of Education panel on how climate change and evolutionist theories should be taught, science eventually prevailed and popular, factually sufficient textbooks were adopted into the curriculum.[112] Subsequent to this battle, the Texas Board of Education changed the policies for curriculum implementation to give teachers priority and limit citizen review.[113]

COEDUCATIONAL CLASSES. Intellectual content is not the only arena where parents have objected to a school's curriculum. In McLean County, Illinois, children of the United Pentecostal Church objected to having to attend coed physical education classes, because of the "immodest apparel" worn.[114] The 1979 decision was predetermined by the *Yoder* Court's troubling reasoning, as it evidences every bit as much concern about preserving the religious entity's future as it does the government interest at stake:

> Given the abundant support in the record that modest dress is a traditional way of life of the plaintiffs, the compulsory attendance at a coeducational physical education class is in sharp conflict with the fundamental mode of life mandated by the Pentecostal religion. . . . Under the present facts there is, through coeducational physical education, daily exposure of the children to worldly influences in terms of attitudes and values of dress contrary to their religious beliefs. This exposure . . . substantially interferes with the religious development of the Pentecostal children and their integration into the way of life of the Pentecostal faith community at the crucial adolescent stage of development. These two effects of the way this Illinois statute has been construed contravenes the basic religious tenets and practice of the Pentecostal Church, both as to parents and the children.[115]

The students suggested that they be permitted to have sex-segregated physical education or individual physical education, but the court added a third option, providing them an exemption from physical education altogether. The court obviously had some discomfort about its holding, because it stated more than once that it was "not telling the school system or these defendants what they must do; only what they may not do."[116] Then the court did indeed indicate the accommodation it preferred, without serious investigation into the state's interest. It expressly disavowed forcing the district to provide the students' suggested sex-segregated or individual physical education (P.E.), saying that its holding simply meant the students could not be forced to go to the coeducational P.E. In effect, the judge mandated at a very minimum, the exemption he earlier suggested. The decision is a product of its era, which placed courts in the impossible position of adjudicating constitutional rights and crafting exemptions that call for legislative judgment.

Conclusion

Schools have a strong responsibility to enforce fair rules evenhandedly, to keep the atmosphere positive for learning, and to ensure children's health and safety. These are not easy issues, but they are critical to the protection of our next generation, and to ensure an adequate level of education. There is room for accommodation in this arena, but there is also a need to act in the best interests of all children and the larger society.

6

THE PRISONS AND THE MILITARY

Prison administrators' jobs have become more complex since RFRA was first enacted in 1993 along with the advent of international terror and increasingly violent gangs. Both phenomena have roots in religion, and, therefore, extreme religious liberty has hit the federal and state prison systems hard.

The fanatical Muslim terrorist networks within United States borders before September 11, 2001, were an undetected cancer spreading through the system. But they were hard at work: a bomb exploded in the World Trade Center basement in 1993. Our own prisons – and the military – have been potential breeding grounds for them. It took the annihilation of almost 3,000 victims from abroad and the U.S., and the World Trade Center – two of the tallest buildings in the world – for

Americans to realize that there was a religious movement intent on their destruction.

In the aftermath of September 11, it quickly became apparent that Muslim chaplains in the prisons and the military were in a strategic position to recruit, train, and indoctrinate those individuals who were open or vulnerable to an approach. Like the pedophiles discussed in Chapter 2, terrorists seek out individuals who are vulnerable to their overtures – those who are isolated from family and friends – and then they play on their insecurities. The same is true for extremist gangs. John Pistole, the former head of the FBI's counterterrorism division in 2003, and now the Administrator of the Transportation Security Administration, summarized the problem in the prisons:

> Inmates are often ostracized, abandoned by, or isolated from their family and friends, leaving them susceptible to recruitment. Membership in the various radical groups offers inmates protection, positions of influence and a network they can correspond with both inside and outside of prison.[1]

Paradoxically, inmates gravitate to gangs and terrorist cells for safety and a sense of belonging. The fact is that violent religious extremists in prisons have been a problem for ages, and this is just a new iteration. We were not paying close attention to the Islamic terrorists before they struck on September 11. The country as a whole, however, was becoming increasingly aware of the existence of white supremacists preaching hatred and violence, for example, the Aryan Brotherhood, Ku Klux Klan, World Church of the Creator, Arizona Aryan Brotherhood, Aryan Circle, and Aryan Brotherhood of Texas, among others. The two movements – violent gangs and terrorist cells – are archetypes for chaos and criminal activity in arenas where security and order is paramount.

For legal purposes, the problem with these groups is not what they believe, as distasteful as that may be. As in every other venue in the United States, they have every right to believe whatever they choose. Rather, conduct is the trigger for the law to enter the picture. The challenge for prison authorities and the larger society from white supremacists or fanatical Muslims is that their beliefs lead them to take illegal action – whether advocating the violent overthrow of the government or taking concrete steps to that end. Often, their beliefs or membership in violent societies is proof of likelihood of illegal action. Whether Muslim extremists or white supremacists are involved, the potential for violence is not hypothetical.

The Aryan Brotherhood: intolerance and violence spread through the prisons

The Aryan Brotherhood (AB) is a particularly scary organization that started in California prisons in the early 1960s for the purpose of protecting white inmates from the black and Mexican prison gangs.[2] In 1967, the name Aryan Brotherhood was chosen; later, it became known also as the Brand. At first, the members had to be part Irish to join – hence the identifying clover tattoo, often with the religious symbol, 666, the "mark of the beast," in the middle. Their other identifying symbol is the swastika, which designates the wearer as an outlaw. The organization originally was intended to help whites, but it eventually devolved into a racist group interested solely in its own power – to kill, deal in drugs, run prostitution rings and extortion rackets, control gambling, and dominate entire prison populations. They killed with their bare hands in maximum-security prisons and ordered hits from solitary confinement. Assistant U.S. Attorney Gregory Jessner reportedly assessed the AB as the "most murderous criminal organization in the United States," capable of dividing the prison population into "predators and prey."[3]

The AB recruited the strong and the ruthless, and demanded single-minded devotion to other members even into death. In the 1970s, when AB members started to be incarcerated for federal crimes in the federal prisons, the AB's influence spread beyond state prison boundaries. By 1982, the FBI estimated that there were about 100 AB in California's prisons and 100–160 in federal prisons, and when they came up for parole or discharge, they took their gang membership to the outside. Once out, they were obligated to look out for the interests of the others inside; otherwise, they would be killed if and when they reentered the prison system. Those interests included supplying drugs and killing people on the outside. The AB became so powerful at one point that it was thought that it controlled elements of organized crime. Its ethos was no different;

an AB instruction manual said the act of killing "is like having sex" and becomes extremely rewarding, because "it's a holy cause."[4]

An extensive federal investigation of the AB resulted in numerous arrests and in July 2006, four leaders were convicted of murder, racketeering, and conspiracy.[5] Their power had at least been momentarily decimated, but another gang was waiting in the wings, the white supremacist Nazi Low Riders, to take over the prison drug trade, the assaults and murders of black or Latino gang members, and on the outside, authorities saw a decisive escalation in drug dealing, physical assaults, and home robberies. It took four full-time police officers and four full-time agents from the FBI plus assistance from the Federal Bureau of Alcohol, Tobacco, Firearms, and Explosives, the California Department of Corrections, the county sheriff's department, and three other local police departments to slow them down.[6] The move induced members to drop out of the Nazi Lower Rider gang and to cooperate. The Aryan Brotherhood were not long deterred, though, and are now estimated to have 20,000 members in the prisons, where they are responsible for almost 20% of the murders in the prisons where they are incarcerated.[7]

The evil within the prisons and the evil on the outside

Religious prisoners have rights to worship and observance under Supreme Court doctrine, RFRA (which applies to federal prisons) and RLUIPA (which applies to local and state prisons). Because of their incarceration, and the inability to attend ordinary worship services, prisoners experience "exceptional government-created burdens on private religious exercise."[8] In fact, prisons support religious observance generally, because it is usually beneficial to prison safety and peace in most instances. This is not always true.

The history of the AB highlights one of the reasons why it is absolutely essential that violent gangs are suppressed in prison: many of their members eventually get out, and when they do, they can become a menace to society. The notorious and horrific killing of James Byrd, Jr., in 1998 in Jasper, Texas, by Lawrence Russell Brewer, John King, and Shawn Berry is one example. The three of them had been in prison before, where King and Berry had joined a white supremacist gang, the Confederate Knights of America. By the time they were released, each had a number of alarming tattoos, and had become out-and-out racists. They had been misfits, and now they belonged. And when they got out, an assistant district attorney explained, "They brought their prison life out with them."9 The three white men picked up Byrd, who was African-American, in their pickup truck, took him to a secluded area, and used a chain to attach him to the back of their truck after spray-painting his face black. Then they dragged him until his body came apart, and he eventually died. Brewer and King were sentenced to the death penalty, while Berry, the driver, received life in prison. Prison gangs had prepared them to kill Byrd.

Both radical Muslims and white supremacist groups, like the AB, have confounded standard penological practices. In general, when a group of inmates becomes trouble, the best way to deal with the problem is to disperse them throughout the system. Unfortunately, that can be the equivalent of blowing on a dandelion puff in the summer, with the seeds spreading far and wide, and eventually generating more weeds. In the case of the AB, the dispersal mechanism meant that they expanded their empire from California to Texas, Illinois, Kansas, Pennsylvania, and Georgia.

Radical Islamic recruitment in the prisons

The radical Islamist cells in the prisons pose a threat to Jews in particular and Americans generally. While serving time in a California prison, Kevin James formed the Jam'iyyat Ul-Islam Is-Saheeh gang, and recruited members for a terrorist plot against military installations, Jewish synagogues, and Israeli government facilities. The plot was orchestrated by the gang while they are still in prison. After the FBI, with the assistance of several other agencies, uncovered the plan, James was indicted and convicted for conspiring to wage war against the United States.[10] He was sentenced in 2009 to sixteen years and is currently serving his sentence.

James Cromitie and two co-conspirators converted to radical Islam in prison, hatched a plan to attack synagogues, and were charged with planning to bomb Bronx synagogues as part of a terror plot. Their convictions and sentences were upheld on appeal in 2013.[11] They confirm the terror experts' view that prison "is a cauldron for Islamic radicalism."[12]

According to expert Mark Hamm, who conducted a study for the National Institute of Justice on the Kevin James case and the issue of terrorist recruitment in American prisons, "Prisoners – especially those in gangs – have long recruited other inmates to act as their collaborators upon release. James, however, was the first gang member to radicalize inmates into joining a prison gang with a terrorist agenda."[3] The study found that:

- Although only a very small percentage of converts turn radical beliefs into terrorist action, the James case is not an isolated event. Gang intelligence officers in Florida and California reported having uncovered potential terrorist plots inside prisons.
- Prisoners who convert to a non-Judeo-Christian religion are primarily searching for meaning and identity. In most cases, the conversion experience makes a meaningful contribution to prisoner rehabilitation.
- Radicalization in prisons is linked to prison gangs.
- Inmate leadership is the most important factor in prisoner radicalization.[14]

Another terrorist expert, Steven Emerson, has been a fierce critic of the federal Bureau of Prisons' (BOP) handling of terrorist recruitment in prisons. Part of the problem for the federal prisons is that RFRA imposes an extreme burden on them to accommodate all religious faiths. Administrators inside the system complain bitterly about its additional burdens, but they are not allowed to publicly criticize RFRA or challenge its constitutionality. Many state prison authorities feel the same way about RLUIPA, but are also silenced by Attorneys General and governors pandering to religion as they seek higher office. Emerson rejects the religious defenses in these cases, saying in 2009 that

Congress needs to impose new rules that force BOP to mandate and operate strict investigations of those who preach in the prisons and the material they are allowed to import.

Wahhabist literature, Muslim Brotherhood tracts calling for Jihad, Saudi produced Qurans that exude hatred for Jews and Christians – all of this continues to flow into federal and local prisons unhampered.

> To those who say this is a violation of the free practice of religion or free speech, that is pure nonsense: Like government officials who are denied clearances based on background checks, Islamic chaplains who do not pass certain clearance standards can also be denied the right to enter prisons. That does not stop them from practicing their religion; it only stops them from spreading their ideology in government institutions.[15]

When President Obama suggested moving the jihadists in Guantánamo Bay to United States prisons, Emerson responded that this would be a debacle for American prisons, which were already ineffectively dealing with terrorist recruitment in the prisons, saying,

> [t]he Guantánamo prisoners will be looked up [sic] as jihadi rock stars and each one could potentially produce a hundred new ticking time bombs ultimately walking the streets of America. Although the President tried to reassure us that no inmate has ever escaped from a super maximum security prison, what about the newly indoctrinated jihadists among the existing inmates who will be certainly released after their terms are up?[16]

Congress has refused to permit the detainees to be sent to the United States (though it has permitted them to be sent to other countries that will accept them).[17] The problem is not abating. In the United States, Muslims constitute approximately five percent of the federal prison population and Islamic conversion appears to be outpacing other faiths.[18]

French prisons have witnessed the same phenomenon with Muslim extremist inmates, as their numbers have swelled. One inmate told *Le Monde*, the Paris daily, that French prisons had "become the cradle of the future jihad."[19] British prisons are also struggling, as radicals are targeting "young inmates in prison."[20]

Islamic imam recruitment in the federal prisons

Prisoners are not the only problem. So are radical imams. The lead Muslim chaplain in New York state prisons at the time, Warith Deen Umar, believed the 9/11 hijackers were martyrs. In a 2004 speech, he said:

> Brothers, be prepared to fight, be prepared to die, be prepared to kill. It's a part of the deen, and this ain't your brother just saying this, this

is history, this is Quran, nobody can deny it. and we need to let the enemies know.[21]

Muslim chaplain recruitment has been worrying for a number of years now. It is not terribly difficult for an extremist to fall through the cracks of the system, especially when there is a shortage of clerics in a particular faith.

Some claim that the prison conduits for Muslim chaplains have kept moderates out, so that only radical imams would be within prison walls. Thus, the prisons' paid chaplains were in a position to reach the disaffected prisoners that would be susceptible to their anti-society and anti-United States rhetoric. Prisoners already are on the outs with the general society and the government, so these are fertile grounds for radical Muslim chaplains to recruit. Furthermore, conversions of recruits from non-Muslim backgrounds are crucial to the terrorists' plans, because they are more capable of "blending in" and have Western passports.[22]

According to Senator Charles Schumer (D, N.Y.), "These imams flood the prisons with anti-American, pro-bin Laden videos, literature, sermons and tapes." They "seek to create a radicalized cadre of felons." The dedication of the terrorists to their cause is single-minded, and the initiation of imams into the federal prisons was accomplished by a man with connections to the extremist Muslim Brotherhood. Abdurahman Alamoudi started the American Muslim Council and was responsible for vetting chaplain candidates for the military from 1993 to 1998, even though he (1) publicly asserted that the 1993 World Trade Center attackers were treated "harshly and with vengeance, and to a large extent, because they were Muslim"; (2) defended Hamas's "good work" and its need to "resort to some kind of violence" as well as Hezbollah; and (3) in 1996, spoke to the convention of the Islamic Association of Palestine in the following terms:

> It depends on me and you, either we do it now or we do it after a hundred years, but this country will become a Muslim country. And I [think] if we are outside this country we can say, oh, Allah, destroy America, but once we are here, our mission in this country is to change it.[23]

Alamoudi was arrested in September 2003 for serving as an intermediary between Libyan officials and Saudi dissidents. Although he was not charged in connection to the alleged plot to kill Crown Prince Abdullah, the prosecutors referred to it as a reason to give him the maximum sentence.[24] He was sentenced to 23 years in federal prison after "admitting that he pocketed nearly $1 million and used it to pay conspirators in the plot, which sources said came close to succeeding before it was broken up by Saudi intelligence officials."[25]

Three organizations have been said to be responsible for placing imams in the federal prisons: the Graduate School of Islamic and Social Sciences (GSISS), the Islamic Society of North America (ISNA), and the American Muslim Armed Forces and Veteran Council. The Bureau of Prisons (BOP) has said that only ISNA has been an official endorser of imams, although the GSISS is where most of the Muslim chaplain candidates have been trained.[26] Although the groups have denied links with terrorist networks, Professor of Islamic Studies at Harvard University Ali Asani said that the ISNA and the GSISS are "ultraconservative, ultra-orthodox," and out of touch with the moderate Muslims in the United States.[27]

And the problem has not been solely confined to federal prisons. In New York, prison authorities had to boot a longtime chaplain recruiter when he told the *Wall Street Journal* that the September 11 terrorists were actually martyrs. There was even a lawsuit brought by Shiite Muslim inmates in New York, arguing that moderate imams were not available to them.

One of the roots of the problem appears to be a shortage of Muslim clerics. Department of Justice inspector general Glenn A. Fine explained why a shortage could further the terrorist agenda: "Without a sufficient number of Muslim chaplains on staff... inmates are much more likely to lead their own religious services, distort Islam and espouse extremist beliefs."[28] After being instructed to investigate the issue, the Office of the Inspector General identified some troubling problems in the recruitment of chaplains in the federal prisons, which still persisted after the BOP tried to ameliorate concerns.

The problems identified were:

• Review of candidates did not include a review of their belief systems to see if they were inconsistent with prison security policies;

- An inadequate exchange of information between the Bureau of Prisons and the FBI;
- Since the federal government was no longer accepting recommendations from national Islamic organizations, imam hiring had come to a standstill, leading to a shortage;
- The BOP was not using imams already in the system to help screen potential candidates;
- There was inadequate supervision of the messages delivered by imams;
- There was a lack of supervision of Islamic services by BOP employees;
- There was inadequate supervision of imams by correctional officers within the prisons.[29]

The first problem the inspector general identified, that the government had not inquired into the beliefs of potential imams, probably raises constitutional red flags for some. Belief, after all, is *absolutely* protected under the Constitution. This issue, however, does not involve pure belief or even pure speech. The relevant question is whether the imam advocates the violent overthrow of the U.S. government and its people. That is not mere speech; it is speech directed at inciting illegal action, which is a category of speech that can be regulated. Authorities do not have to wait for the illegal action to occur before putting a stop to it. Outside the prisons, such speech is strongly protected unless the violence is imminent, under *Brandenburg v. Ohio*,[30] which expanded the protection for speech advocating illegal action.

The prison context, however, and its strong potential for producing antisocial or criminal behavior, argues in favor of relaxing the protections required by *Brandenburg*. Arguments have been advanced that weigh against suppressing terrorist speech on websites, because it is impossible to determine whether the danger is imminent.[31] Yet, the prison context increases the likelihood of violence inside and outside the prison significantly, and therefore such speech demands monitoring and even suppression.

Some chaplains have blamed the growth in radical Muslims in the prisons on inmates as opposed to clerical persuasion. This may be true, due to the shortage of Muslim clerics. The Federal Bureau of Prisons has a rule that "inmates are not permitted to lead religious programs."[32] The problem, though, is that when there are inadequate clerics, inmates do lead religious services if they are to have them at all, and so the practice has become a staple of federal prison life.

Whatever the source of recruitment, there is no question that prisons worldwide have become breeding grounds for terrorists. Richard Reid, who was convicted of attempting to detonate an American Airlines flight from Paris to Miami with a bomb in his shoe, found Islam through radical clerics in a British prison, where some have said the amount of Islamic literature far outpaces Christian literature.[33] The French prisons, with half of their population Muslim, have had extensive problems with controlling terrorists. And Jose Padilla, who attempted to set off a "dirty" bomb in the United States, was converted to radical Islam in a Broward County, Florida, prison and later drawn into al-Qaeda. Padilla's case made it to the U.S. Supreme Court, but they did not reach the merits for procedural reasons.[34]

Not only are radical Muslim clerics recruiting new members inside the prisons, but those who are already imprisoned also have tried to orchestrate further terror from inside, not unlike the Mafia don who tries to arrange a hit while incarcerated. Abdel Rahman, who helped orchestrate the 1993 attack on the World Trade Center and was incarcerated in a federal prison in Rochester, Minnesota, tried to foment more terror in April 2002. It is alleged that he used his attorney and translator to pass messages to his followers, including calling for the end to a cease-fire in Egypt and new terrorist attacks by his followers in a terrorist network called the "Islamic Group," which is said to be responsible for the deaths of dozens of Western tourists visiting the pyramids at Luxor in 1997.[35] The nature of extremism is such that when the criminal is arrested and put into prison, he can still generate hatred within the prison walls by writing, teaching, and inculcating new recruits. While it is a cliché in the United States that a Mafia don or FLDS prophet might be pulling the strings of his organization from inside the prison walls, the notion that terrorism can be arranged from inside is disconcerting. It may be surprising, but it is a fact.

Since 9/11, scholars on the prevalence of Islam in prisons have diverged on opposite ends of the spectrum: one side takes the stance that Muslims in prison are a breeding ground for terrorism, while the other disputes any significant relationship between prisoner conversions to Islam and terrorism.[36] One study concludes:

> [E]vidence suggests that there is some credibility to both the reassuring and the alarmist perspectives on prisoner radicalization in America. And this presents a conundrum. On one hand, signs of radicalization include positive personal behavior. For the overwhelming majority of inmates who convert to Islam and other non-traditional faiths during incarceration, the experience helps prisoners learn self-discipline and interact with other inmates and staff in a positive manner, thereby making a meaningful contribution to the reformation process. On the other hand, from the crucible of positive behavior comes the potential for ideologically-inspired criminality. In the rarest of cases, conversion may incite terrorism. On this highly circumscribed basis, then, U.S. prisons are vulnerable to prisoner radicalization and terrorist groups that infiltrate, recruit, and operate behind the walls.[37]

The law of religious accommodation in the prisons

The Supreme Court has been deferential in the prison and military contexts, because it has viewed the courts as incapable of assessing security threats or needs regarding prisons or national security. Thus, they have given the executive branches of the federal and state governments wide berth to keep order. In the Court's own words, "'courts are ill equipped to deal with the increasingly urgent problems of prison administration and reform.'"[38] In these contexts, the branch most capable of assessing the issue – the executive – has been given the power to do so, with minimal restrictions. Prison regulations have been subject rationality review under *O'Lone v. Estate of Shabazz* and to intermediate-level scrutiny under *Turner v. Safley*,[39] which means the prisoner must first show that the law imposes a substantial burden on his religious practice, and then the prison administrator need only show that the regulation was created for a "legitimate penological" objective.[40] This latter test left room for reasonable accommodations, like no-pork diets (which are required by a number of faiths), but it did not force prison authorities to either sacrifice security for any prisoner's beliefs or divert precious resources to repeated federal litigation.

That is, until RFRA and RLUIPA were enacted, which turned generally applicable, neutral prison regulations into presumptively illegal regulations. A hair length and facial hair regulation applied across the board in a prison could no longer be presumed to be legal, at least until the prisoners litigated the issue through the federal courts and the government carried its burden of proving that the grooming policy existed for a compelling interest (security) and there was no other less restrictive way to serve the same end. It is an expensive process borne by taxpayers, with questionable utility.

The Religious Land Use and Institutionalized Persons Act

As I discuss in more detail in the Introduction and Chapter One, RFRA was held unconstitutional in 1997. Congress followed with a new RFRA for federal law and RLUIPA to challenge state and local land use law and institutionalized persons law. The impact of RFRA and RLUIPA on the prisons is hard to overestimate. Under the First Amendment, the Court traditionally deferred to prison authorities, particularly on issues of prison administration and security. The extreme religious liberty formula is the farthest removed from the constitutional standard in the prison context.

In 2000, President Bill Clinton signed RLUIPA and launched another litigation attack on prison authorities. The prison side of RLUIPA received so little attention in the form of hearings and testimony that it is virtually impossible to divine what existing problem it was intended to redress. Two men testified in support of it: Charles Colson (the now-deceased ex-convict from the Nixon administration's Watergate scandal, who then found religion in prison), who founded the conservative Christian Prison Fellowship Ministries, and Isaac M. Jaroslawicz of the Aleph Institute, which assists state and federal prisons to accommodate Jewish inmates.

Both emphasized how important religion can be to rehabilitation, as they led members to believe that the religious influences helped by RLUIPA would all be beneficial. What they meant was that their faiths were good for rehabilitation. If RLUIPA or RFRA could constitutionally only empower those faiths that in fact further rehabilitation, that would be one thing. But as a constitutional matter, no law may impose denominational preferences. So it is all or nothing – expand rights beyond the First Amendment's requirements for the destructive as well as constructive religions, or do it for neither. RFRA has even been invoked by the Guantanamo detainees.

Neither Colson nor Jaroslawicz addressed the myriad problems posed by expanding free exercise rights beyond constitutional boundaries for gangs, white supremacists, rabid racists, or terrorists. Nor did they talk about the impact on the prison system of subjecting the state and federal prison systems to the potential for lawsuits from every corner, whether the faith aided rehabilitation or impeded it. Nor did the members ask.

Neither Colson nor Jaroslawicz provided much in the way of justifying the imposition of extreme standards on every prison regulation. Colson objected to the Supreme Court's free exercise jurisprudence that left accommodation to the legislatures, saying, "We *want* judges to handle these questions and we want them to use the legal standard that imposed strict scrutiny on every prison regulation."[41] Of course he did, because then the believer is the primary focus of the case and the public good is proportionally discounted. At this point, there is no question that the Court has settled on a free exercise doctrine that Colson did not approve, and he had the right to have his own views, but that debate is and should be settled. Religious entities are subject to neutral, generally applicable laws. As is typical in the circumstances, he did not offer actual proof of any actual religious suppression in the prisons that justified RLUIPA's imposition on the prisons. Instead, Colson invoked the need for extreme religious liberty in the prisons as an accepted fact for which no proof was necessary. Given the members' typical pandering to religious entities, it was not.

Jaroslawicz presented the only "hard" evidence when he argued that Jewish prisoners are not adequately accommodated in the prisons. Some of the examples he raised did not justify an RLUIPA, because they involved overt discrimination against Jews, which is unconstitutional under both Religion Clauses. For example, he stated that the Michigan Department of Corrections had banned Chanukah candles at every prison, because of concerns for fire safety. If the rule against fire had been enforced against every prisoner, the inmate would not have had a free exercise claim, but "smoking, cooking, and votive candles were all still allowed."[42] Thus, the Free Exercise Clause's entrenched rule against singling out religions would be triggered, and RLUIPA was, at best, duplicative.

He also criticized the prisons for inadequately protecting Jews from hostile anti-Semitic inmates, of which there are many. He said there were instances where a Jewish inmate was beaten and then placed in "administrative segregation," which means "solitary confinement," for his safety. But the aggressors continued to "roam free." Finally, he claimed pervasive anti-Semitic treatment from prison chaplains against Jews throughout the Texas system. All of these examples would be subject to strict scrutiny under the Religion Clauses, and therefore RLUIPA was not necessary.

But Jaroslawicz did object to at least one neutral, generally applicable practice in state prisons: the practice of providing accommodation for certain faiths only at some of the prisons. In other words, not every Michigan facility offered kosher food, but at least some would.[43] His objection was that the locations of the prisons providing the kosher food were not desirable, because they were far from family. But one is hard-pressed to fully understand the objection. Prisoners have never had a right to "choose" their prison location. While a state may permit them to suggest a preference, they are assigned where the state or federal government decides. This fact was recently seen in the case of Cameron Douglas, son of actor Michael Douglas, who requested a facility in New Jersey, but instead was assigned to one in Pennsylvania. It is also a puzzling objection in light of Jaroslawicz's earlier stated concerns about Jews being isolated and placed in danger; bringing them together is surely better than dispersing them so that they are completely isolated from others of their own faith. Essentially, he was demanding RLUIPA be passed, not because there was no accommodation, but so that Jewish prisoners could insist on having accommodation at the prison closest to their families. Where is the burden on religion here? It seems more a matter of prisoner preferences. If that is why RLUIPA was needed, it is a slender reed on which to hang such a heavy and costly burden on prison systems and taxpayers. To my knowledge, no such case has been brought under RFRA or RLUIPA, which underscores the thinness of this justification for it.

One actual conflict between religious needs and prison security Jaroslawicz described was the refusal in Michigan to permit the Aleph Institute to ship matzos (unleavened bread) into high-security facilities during Passover, when Jews are not permitted to eat any other kind of bread. The system's general rule was that no "outside" foods were permitted, because they open the door to contraband. At the same time, the system did not provide the matzos itself, and therefore Jewish inmates were forced to violate their religious beliefs during Passover. The rule is constitutional.

Enter RLUIPA, however, and matzos become a federal case. RLUIPA puts the prison authorities on the defensive, having to prove that forbidding such shipments serves a compelling interest. It does, but the taxpayers must pay a high cost in federal litigation to make the point. But then there is the hardest part of the extreme free exercise regime for the government: it must also prove that denying access to the outside matzos is the least restrictive means as applied to this religious believer to serve its compelling interest in safety in a high-security prison. The case now turns into a policy debate, with the inmate arguing for his preferred policy, the prison having to rebut whatever the prisoner suggests, and the court in the position of making a policy judgment whether the prison can afford (in loss of security and funds) to make the matzos available.

It is easy to imagine a "less restrictive" rule than the refusal to permit the matzos to be brought in via outside suppliers. RLUIPA leads the court to look solely at this large institution with its large budget and one believer, making it easy to conclude that changing the practice for one is feasible.

But no prison would or should make such a decision for just one inmate. There are many factors to consider. For example, the prison must consider how changing the policy would affect its budget and staffing; who, administratively, is responsible for keeping track of when matzos are made available, and which matzos are most religiously acceptable to the believers; and, inevitably, if they do this for one prisoner, what other holiday-specific food items must also be made available for other believers in the future on specific dates. For example, fish on Fridays during Lent for Catholics?

And given that RFRA and RLUIPA require accommodation even if the belief is not central to the religion, which holiday-specific foods does RLUIPA deliver? Lamb for Christians on Easter or Muslims on the Eids? Hot cross buns for Fat Tuesday, before Lent begins? In the absence of a constitutional violation, why should taxpayers foot the bill for such requests? More importantly, RLUIPA should not be forcing taxpayers to underwrite such litigation for both sides.

A few were allowed to speak during congressional hearings preceding RLUPIA against the prison provisions of RLUIPA. Unlike the land use side of RLUIPA, where no government official or land use expert was permitted to testify or even to explain the operation of local land use law vis-à-vis houses of worship, there was a semblance of balance and fair-minded consideration of the issues on the prison side, as abbreviated as it was.[44]

Ohio solicitor Jeffrey Sutton (now a federal appellate judge on the Sixth Circuit) was permitted to testify that prisons should have been exempted from the Religious Liberty Protection Act (RLPA), the failed, predecessor bill to RLUIPA. The Ohio Corrections Department's experience with RFRA led him to offer the following: The RFRA "cases included such bizarre claims as demands for recognition of the right to burn Bibles, the right to possess and distribute racist literature, the right to engage in animal sacrifices, and the right to group martial arts classes." It also forced prison authorities to spend a great deal of time on issues that had been settled in the courts already.[45]

Even more troublesome, though, was the fact that prisoners "exploited" RFRA to "insulate illicit, even dangerous, activities from official scrutiny." Nationwide, "white supremacist inmates suddenly converted to obscure or eccentric religions, then demanded that officials recognize their religious gatherings and practices under RFRA... and recruited 'religious volunteers' to bring drugs and prostitutes into Lorton prison" – a District of Columbia facility located in Virginia. He cited the example of the Wyoming prison that permitted Luciferian inmates unsupervised group services to burn Bibles and hymnals, which led to significant smoke damage throughout the facilities. Sutton also pointed out that RFRA forced chaplains to shift their focus from providing religious services to litigation, because the inmates came to view the chaplains as the "enforcers" of RFRA, rather than a spiritual resource.[46] His implicit point was that prisons are already financially strapped and under siege from serious internal security problems. To pile on RLUIPA made no sense.

When RFRA was under consideration, Sen. Harry Reid (D, Nev.) offered an amendment on the Senate floor that would have prohibited the application of RFRA to incarcerated individuals, in part because he believed prisoners had become far too litigious. But it was too late in the process, which meant RFRA was enacted without the exception. He later expressed concerns regarding the impact of the later-introduced RLPA and RLUIPA on prisons, because corrections officers had contacted him and expressed sincere concern about their own and the public's security:

> AFSCME recently alerted their corrections officer membership that this legislation was coming up for a vote, and was deluged with phone calls from members expressing their distress about how this bill might affect their ability to maintain security and protect the safety of the public. As you can well imagine, getting inmates to comply with security measures in prison is no easy task. Many prisoners will use any excuse to avoid searches and to evade security measures instituted to protect prison personnel and the general public from harm.[47]

Sen. Strom Thurmond (R, S.C.) expressed similar concerns in testimony following RLUIPA's passage by Congress but before President Clinton signed it into law, and added that "inmates have used religion as a cover to organize prison uprisings, get drugs into prison, promote gang activity, and interfere in important prison health regulations. Additional legal protections will make it much harder for corrections officials to control these abuses of religious rights."[48] Despite these legitimate concerns, members of Congress did not inquire further. It is a perfect example of the phenomenon where Congress resolutely serves religious entities by deferring to religious lobbyists without taking into account the questions implicating the larger public good – and the many other interests implicated by these questions.

Unbelievably, Reid dropped these concerns and supported RLUIPA on a promise that Sen. Orrin Hatch (R, Utah) would hold hearings a year *after* its enactment, to which state officials would be invited to assess how it had worked in practice. Anyone who knows anything about legislation knows that once a law is passed, it is virtually impossible to repeal it, so the promise of post-enactment hearings seems hardly adequate to Reid's concerns. He was also mollified by the notion that he and Senator Hatch would ask the General Accounting Office to conduct a detailed study of its effect on prisons.[49] Neither has been done.

It appears that, but for Colson (and Jaroslawicz to a lesser extent) and his desire to position Prison Fellowship Ministries to proselytize conservative Christianity in prisons across the country, RLUIPA might only have addressed land use, and not prisons. What is desperately needed in Congress is some member who can rise above religious lobbying to secure the larger good – members that at least ask if there is another side to an issue raised by a religious entity.

RLUIPA's prison provisions were challenged as a violation of the separation of church and state in 2005. A unanimous Supreme Court upheld them in *Cutter v. Wilkinson*, on the reasoning that prisoners experience extraordinary potential barriers to worship, because of their incarceration, but with a repeated warning from the Justices that they expected the courts to be duly deferential to prison authorities regarding prison security.[50] It was an interesting opinion in its narrowness. It clearly intended to speak only to the prison provisions, with an explicit note that the Court was not deciding the constitutionality of the land use side of RLUIPA, and a concurrence by Justice Thomas questioning Congress's power to enact RLUIPA in the first place. We shall see how serious the *Cutter* Court was about taking prison security seriously when it decides the Arkansas facial hair case, *Holt v. Hobbs*, in the 2014 Term.

The challenge of accommodating religious prisoners

Prison wardens welcome peaceful religions within their walls, because they can assist with rehabilitation.[51] The same cannot be said for white supremacist religions that preach violence or Islamic fanatics, who advocate the end of the United States. Given the high percentage of religious believers in the United States, prison officials are in all likelihood religious themselves, so the notion that there is antireligious sentiment in the prisons is hard to prove. New York City corrections commissioner Martin Horn nicely captured the difficulties faced by prison authorities: "The vast majority of inmates have genuine faith needs, and the professional standards of prison and jail administration call for the respect of honestly held faith beliefs. But there are no lack of examples of inmates who will misuse it."[52]

For those not familiar with prison administration, the requests for religious accommodation by prisoners may seem innocuous, taken one by one. This fellow needs a kosher diet, and that woman needs a crucifix, while another needs long hair. And these issues typically arise in the context of a case, so it appears that it is a simple request by a sincere individual or small group of individuals. The global impact on the prisons is lost in the context of the particular case, but that larger context is what the prison administrator *must* take into account. Prisons can only operate successfully where each prisoner perceives he or she is being treated just like any other prisoner, where discipline is tight and predictable, and where a routine is set. And it is not just a problem of logistics; it is expensive for a significant number of inmates to be accommodated.

How much trouble can religious accommodation be? The answer is that it can be enormously problematic, when one multiplies religions, religious practices, and the individual variations on each and then sets them in the context of a prison that must ensure security and order within a typically tight budget. (The First Amendment contemplates the absolute right to believe, which has no "mainstream religion" or "settled religious practice" element, so the breadth of protected religious belief is infinite.) The following is a list of some of the requested accommodations in state and federal prisons to give the reader a sense of the scope of the issue. It is far from inclusive.

Accommodation request	Religion
Diet restrictions	
• Vegan	African Hebrew Israelite
• Vegetarian diet	Buddhist
• Protein tablets	Buddhist
• Vegetarian diet	Jehovah's Witness (not required for most)
• Vegetarian (no meat/eggs)	Hindu
• Kosher diet*	Orthodox Jew
• Diet – no pork; halal† meat only	Muslim
• No pork or shellfish	Seventh-day Adventist
• Dairy vegetarian most of year; fast of milk and water	Ethiopian Orthodox Tewahido Church

* A kosher diet basically prohibits pork and shellfish, and the consumption of milk and meat together.

† "Halal" meat has been killed according to religious rituals. Kosher meat satisfies the halal requirement.

Accommodation request	Religion
Diet restrictions (continued)	
• I-tal diet[‡]	Rastafarian
• Biblically derived diet[§]	Nation of Islam
• Fish and unleavened bread during Lent	Catholic
• Steak and sherry every Friday	CONS (Church of the New Song)
Grooming/dress restrictions	
• No haircut	Hindu, Native America
• No haircut; beard	Sikh
• Beard	Muslim
• Muslim cellmate	Muslim
• Muslim head covering in prison yard (already allowed in prayer services)	Muslim
• Dreadlocks and hat	Rastafarian
• Beard longer than allowed	Rastafarian
• Headband	Native American
• Metal cross	Protestant
• Religious medal	Odinis
• Bow ties during religious service	Nation of Islam
• Tallow-free soap and conditioner	Buddhist
• Sidelocks	Orthodox Hasidic Jew
• Worship in the nude	Technicians of the Sacred (Neo-African faith)
Literature	
• Racist literature	Christian Identity, Church of the Creater
• Noncensored religious texts	Hebrew Israelite Faith
• Texts	Taoism

‡ Fresh, unprocessed fruit, vegetables, fish, juices and grains.
§ Permits whole wheat or rye bread; fruit, and fruit pies with brown sugar and whole wheat flour; navy beans, soy beans, kale, peas, collard greens, turnip greens, sweet or white potatoes, some fish, and cream cheese. No lima beans, pork, fried or hard-baked foods, cornbread, freshly cooked bread, pancakes and syrup, nuts, halibut, catfish, carp, eel, oyster, lobster, crab, clam, shrimp, and snail.

Accommodation request	Religion
Literature (continued)	
• Religious materials	Moorish Science Temple of America
• Access to banned literature	Asatru, Church of Jesus Christ Christian, Wiccan, Satanist, Nation of Islam
• Scripture – NPKA Book of Blotar	Odinist
• Racist literature, redacted	Hebrew Israelite
• Satanic Bible	Satanist
• Aryan Nation literature	Aryan Nation
• Religious comic books	Fundamentalist Christian
• Literature and numerological devices	Nation of Gods and Earths, or Five Percent Nation (roots in Black Islam)
• Bible – specific version	Variety of Christian denominations
Miscellaneous	
• Evergreen tree, sauna, charm necklace with Thor's hammer, small stone altar in cell, cauldron, drinking horn, branch, Viking-type swords made of soft wood	Odinist
• Sweat lodge*	Native American
• Wild-bird feathers	Native American
• Permission to cast spells/curses	Wiccan
• Tarot cards	Wiccan
• Proper disposal of blood after drawn for medical testing	Jehovah's Witness (fundamentalist)
• Refusal to take tuberculosis test	Rastafarian, Muslim
• Placement only with Caucasians	Christian Separatist Church Society
• Worship separate from Sunni Muslims	Shi'ite Muslims
• Worship separate from Shi'ites	Sunni Muslims

* A building made of branches in which rocks are heated so that participants have a sauna-like effect, which is a location for medicine and pipe ceremonies and prayer.

Accommodation request	Religion
Miscellaneous (continued)	
• Muslim cellmate	Muslim
• Right not to be classified as a Security Threat Group, which designates violent prisons gangs	Five Percent Nation
• Medicine pouch	Native American Church
• Spiritual necklace	Native American Church
• Weekly Jumu'ah prayer	Muslim
• Prayer oil (in or outside cell)	Muslim
• Candles, incense	Muslim
• Religious talismans	Muslim
• Bible burning	Luciferian
• Writing paper, newspaper, more access to spiritual adviser	Wotanist
• Menorah for Hanukah	Jew
• Tefillin*	Orthodox Jew
• Not filling out standard form to obtain kosher meal	Orthodox Jew
• Wine for communion	Catholic
• Personal counseling, worship service, Bible study, ministers	Pentecostal
• Prayer rug	Muslim
• Spiritual adviser, well-rounded research library in cell, Bible in yard for proselytization	Fundamentalist Christian Separatist
• Denominational pin, shirt, separate services	Christian Identity Church
• Cleric from outside prison to conduct services	Muslim
• Weekly group meetings	Atheist
• Oils, powders, incense, candles, religious Botanicals, stones, Talisman, Charm bags	Voodoo/Egyptian Freemasonry
• Better Protestant programming	Baptist

* Small leather boxes with prayer scrolls inside that are tied with leather straps to the foreheads and forearms while praying.

Accommodation request	Religion
Miscellaneous (continued)	
• Observance of Muslim holidays not recognized by Sunni/Shi'ites	Nation of Islam
• Embrace and kiss wife	Christian
• Change of name after being born again	Universal Life Church
• Kirpan (knife)	Sikh

If this chart does not look daunting enough, inmates change faith in prison and sometimes combine several into their own personal blend. The state of Washington has dealt with this by permitting each individual prisoner to claim up to three faiths. Most prisons try to accommodate at least some religious diets – within the parameters of affordability, good nutrition, and feasibility. Typically, there will be a kosher option, a vegetarian option, and/or a no-pork option. The fine differences between the different versions of vegetarianism are nearly impossible to match. Some Hindus will not eat any food resulting from an animal's suffering, which means no meat, eggs, animal by-products, or honey, while dairy products are acceptable. Jains add to the Hindu diet a restriction on any food resulting from the suffering of plants, for instance, root vegetables like potatoes, and microorganisms. For some Buddhists, eating meat is forbidden, and the larger the animal, the worse the karma; but fish is lower on the animal kingdom scale and therefore may be eaten. The Seventh-day Adventist believer is not a vegetarian per se but will not eat pork or shellfish, while Muslims tend not to eat pork. Putting together a nutritionally balanced diet for all of these beliefs at once is quite challenging, to say the least. That is why some systems concentrate certain faiths in particular prisons so that they can accommodate that group as efficiently as possible. But all of these factors can take a backseat when RFRA or RLUIPA enter the picture, and force the balance of policies in favor of an individual prisoner.

Prisoners have demanded rights to kosher food and won in Texas[53] prisons; vegetarian food and won in Pennsylvania[54] prisons; and halal food and won in Oklahoma[55] prisons. They have lost on kosher food in Florida,[56] Kansas,[57] Pennsylvania,[58] and Texas[59] prisons; vegan food in New York[60] prisons; and halal food in Arkansas[61] prisons.

Grooming policies also come into conflict with a fair number of religious practices. Typically, prisons regulate hair length and beard length, because both, if long enough, can be used to hide contraband, including drugs and weapons. The rule is obviously passed for a compelling interest – security in the prisons. A number of faiths are burdened by such a regulation. Native Americans often believe that hair should only be cut in sorrow. Rastafarians believe in wearing long dreadlocks and beards. The Muslim faith requires men to have beards. Like long hair and beards, head coverings also are convenient places for drugs and weapons, and similarly regulated.

If the grooming policy is applied across the board, it is constitutional, despite the burdens on religious believers, under the reasoning of *Smith*, *O'Lone v. Estate of Shabazz*, and *Turner v. Safley*. Prison authorities get into trouble, though, if they do not apply the principle evenhandedly. If the policy can be abridged by one prisoner, the claim to security has lost force. RLUIPA changes the balance, though, because even neutral, generally applicable grooming policies can be attacked. The results are all over the place, as one would expect from a law that has a requirement that the law be tailored to the believer. Muslims and Native Americans have won grooming cases against prisons in Texas and California.[62] African Hebrew Israelites of Jerusalem, Assemblies of Yahweh, Rastafarian, and Muslim believers in Illinois, Arkansas, and Virginia have lost.[63] In March 2014, the Supreme Court granted certiorari for an appeal from the Eighth Circuit in *Holt v. Hobbs*, a case challenging the Arkansas Department of Corrections' inmate facial grooming policy.[64]

Religious objects are a very difficult category for the prison authorities to handle. The key problem is that prisoners are so clever at crafting just about anything into a weapon. The metal from crosses and crucifixes can be shaped into a shank. One or two headbands can be an effective garrote. Whether wood or metal, a menorah can be fashioned into an offensive weapon. And the sweat lodge requested by some Native Americans involving a fire within a structure built with branches, with fire's obvious potential for harm, has been accommodated, though it requires additional guards and ample grounds on which to place it.

Space requirements – the need for a place for worship, or to be near or away from certain other groups – can be especially difficult when the variety of religions in the prison reaches a certain quantum of faiths. Prisons have to scramble to find enough worship spaces, appropriate rooms for each particular group, and additional guards. They also have to guard against worship spaces being used for gang or terrorist activity.

Each of these practices can be the basis of a federal lawsuit under RFRA or RLUIPA. So long as the inmate is sincere about the belief, or the prison lacks the evidence to challenge sincerity, the court must consider the request for accommodation of the prison's regulation under a standard that presumes the regulation is illegal.

These sincere requests are difficult enough, but the prisons also face an uphill battle against the cunning and cleverness of many inmates.

New religions in prison

One of the more serious problems for prisons facing extreme religious liberty guarantees is that a significant number of inmates are sorely tempted to claim religious privilege for what is, in fact, a secular desire. It is not out of the realm of possibility that a Christian inmate who thinks the kosher food looks better than what he is eating will insist that he has had a sudden conversion to Judaism. Or that a prisoner will claim that his religion requires an exercise mat and free time every day at 4:00 P.M. But the prize goes to the Church of the New Song (CONS).

The CONS was founded in the early 1970s by a federal inmate, Harry Theriault, who said it was a "game." And what a game it is. This "religion" requires a prisoner to be served Harvey's Bristol Crème and steak every Friday at 5:00 P.M.[65] As one can imagine, it quickly gained recruits. This is a classic case of a group testing the waters with insincere claims of religious devotion. Common sense should have sent their free exercise claims packing. While no prisoner has yet won the right to steak and sherry on Fridays, the courts have been dealing with their claims ever since.

Unfortunately, though, their original claims aired in the 1970s when the Supreme Court's free exercise jurisprudence bent over backward for believers to the detriment of the public good, and a court actually held that CONS was a religion deserving protection under the First

Amendment.[66] It is, to be sure, an embarrassing moment for the U.S. Court of Appeals for the Eighth Circuit, which reasoned as follows:

> After careful consideration of the entire record we are satisfied that the district court's judgment that The Church of the New Song is a religion within the ambit of the First Amendment is based on find-ings that are not clearly erroneous and that no error of law appears. Further there is insufficient evidence in this record to establish [the] contention that [CONS'] beliefs are not sincere and genuinely felt. It also appears that [CONS] have not been allowed a fair and meaningful opportunity to freely exercise their religion in the same degree as other inmates, Protestant and Catholic.[67]

The good news (if one thinks of common sense as a virtue) is that another court refused to fall for the legal ploy, and held that:

> The beliefs professed by [CONS] are not sincerely held and do not in their own scheme of things constitute a 'religion' nor are they sincerely of a "religious" character.... The so-called "Church of the New Song" does not meet the criteria adopted by this Court in its analysis above to entitle it to First Amendment protection as a religion. It is clearly a sham designed and calculated to obtain favored treatment for its members incarcerated in various prisons and has no measurable following outside Federal Penitentiaries.[68]

Hear, hear.

Thirty years after the Eighth Circuit recognized CONS as a religion, the church brought a new free exercise claim. The lawsuit was brought when prison authorities at the Iowa State Penitentiary in Fort Madison refused to deliver trays of food for the CONS' "celebration of life" to inmates who were in lock-up during the banquet. Apparently, the other believers were able to eat their celebration feast together, so the only CONS believers at issue were in lock-up. In any event, a federal law-suit was filed on behalf of these locked-up inmates who were denied participation in the "celebration of life." Thirty years into this charade, the judges of the Eighth Circuit were bound by the previous decision, but they seemed to have gotten some perspective. Judge Pasco M. Bow-man, writing the opinion for himself and Judges William Jay Riley and Lavenski R. Smith, had to "suspend disbelief" to get through the case.[69]

When prisoners create religions, there can be some chaos in the institution of their traditions. CONS is an excellent example. During the Iowa litigation, at first, the "celebration of life" (1) was a spring festivity, saluting nature's renewal of life; (2) then it was a party to celebrate the day CONS was founded; (3) and then it was the same as the Sacred Unity Feast mentioned in their religious text, the Paratestament. The court perused the Paratestament carefully, and was forced to conclude that it could not be the same as the Sacred Unity Feast, because the latter only happens after "the hundred and forty-four thousand Revelation ministers have been sealed as prophesied." Since it was "apparent to the court that the hundred and forty-four thousand Revelation ministers had not yet been sealed," no Sacred Unity Feast could be held.[70] Further perusal of the scripture led the court to conclude that this was not a religiously mandated celebration and therefore no free exercise rights would accrue.

But on the off chance that the Supreme Court might consider reversing its reasoning I suppose, the court persevered to explain why, even if the celebration were religiously mandated, the prison authorities could refuse to deliver the trays of food to lock-up. The penitentiary argued that there was no way for it to prevent contraband from traveling in or on the trays, in part because health regulations prohibited them from handling the food. In fact, CONS helped to make the penitentiary's case, because before the celebration of life denial, CONS members "sent contraband into the lock-up unit through a variety of illicit methods."[71] So the court had to conclude the state had more than carried its burden, and, besides, the "celebration-of-life" feast itself had no particular dietary requirements, so the deprivation of the trays did not affect the CONS's beliefs.

It is a silly "church" and a funny case, to be sure. But it is also deeply troubling. The CONS's testimony regarding the meaning of the so-called "celebration of life" was confused and muddled, probably because they were making it up as they went along. When that first court declared them a legitimate, protected religion, they won. They successfully played the system. The fact that they won recognition as a religion from a federal court taught them that conning the correctional system works, and that the Constitution protects the con game. That's some rehabilitative message. Demanding proof of sincerity about religious belief and practices is not antireligious, as perhaps the first court believed; rather, it keeps the system honest, the results just, and the First Amendment legitimate.

A new phenomenon: religious prisons

Two cultural forces have come together to create "religious prisons" in the United States. First, there has been a persistent belief that religion, as a whole, is good for people, and inmates in particular.[72] There appears to be an increasing amount of evidence that suggests that some religious programming in the prisons can reduce the recidivism rate.[73]

Second, certain religious entities have gained remarkable power in the political sphere, which leads politicians to desire to be identified with religious projects and to grant religious entities what they request. The combination of a Pollyanna-like attitude regarding religion and religion's political power make it an opiate for elected representatives. It is an addictive mix that paralyzes their common sense and disables their otherwise natural cynicism about lobbyists in general. When Chuck Colson importuned a Republican-dominated Congress to include prisons under RFRA and RLUIPA, the members were all too happy to oblige. At one point, there was even a rumor that the goal was to get RLUIPA passed by Easter! To state the matter modestly, the temptation to make religion a centerpiece of the prison experience is quite strong in the United States at this time. These religious prisons offer mass accommodation, at least for some believers, but especially Christians.

There are two types of religious prisons. First, there is the Iowa model, which has been tried in Texas, Kansas, and Minnesota as well, where, Colson's Prison Fellowship Ministries, employing its "Christ-centered" approach, takes over a wing of a prison at state cost. Second, there is the Florida model, where the system designates certain prisons as religious, gives inmates a choice to go and a choice to leave, and the religious activities are funded by private, religious entities. As a constitutional matter, the former is on much shakier ground than the latter.

The Iowa experiment is Christian at its core. Prison Fellowship Ministries takes over a wing of a prison and sets up shop, hoping to convert as many prisoners as possible. A report on National Public Radio indicated that they call the cells the "God Pod," and the Warden describes them: "The doors are wooden. One of the differences you notice, the doors are unlocked as you come in. Cell doors are unlocked. They can come and go by their schedule." The NPR Reporter then elaborated on the system:

> The men can stay up longer. They see more visitors. But they also have a more disciplined regimen: no TV except for the news, up for prayer and worship at 6 A.M., Bible study several hours a day, as well as vocational training, workshops, mentoring programs, all by Christians. It is, in fact, a virtual drenching in evangelical Christianity.[74]

The cost of the extra programming has been defrayed by the state revenue from all inmates' phone calls.

Iowa was sued by the ACLU and another suit was filed by Americans United for the Separation of Church and State.[75] In 2007, the Eighth Circuit in large part upheld the District Court's decision finding that the InnerChange Freedom Initiative, the religious program at Iowa's Newton Correctional Facility, violated the Establishment Clause, but because of the fact it was financed by other inmates' phone calls.[76] Iowa changed the funding scheme, but eventually the program was discontinued. It is still in place in other states.[77]

The Iowa system is reminiscent of the attempts to get Christian prayer back into the public schools; a nostalgic attempt to construct a Christian country in the context of contrary constitutional principles. Those principles do not permit the government to single out any one religious viewpoint for good or for bad, or to have the effect of advancing religion, or of government endorsement of religion, or excessive entanglement of church and state. One could even say that in a prison context, where privileges and open cell doors are rare, and therefore a tremendous incentive to do whatever it takes to get them, it is akin to coercion to become Christian (or at least to participate in Christian activities). In an interesting twist, the organization that fought for strict scrutiny of all prison regulations will have its sectarian program in the prisons subjected to strict scrutiny as well. The difference is that the prison regulations were neutral and generally applicable and therefore did not deserve searching judicial review, while there is every reason to assume that a state prison with a "God Pod" paid for by the state is probably unconstitutional. In the words of the Supreme Court, "when we are presented with a state law granting a denominational preference, our precedents demand that we treat the law as suspect and that we apply strict scrutiny in adjudging its constitutionality."[78]

Then there is the Florida model, which is being tried or considered in a number of states, where certain prisons have been designated as "faith based," and theoretically, all faiths are welcome. Inmates who have a certain level of good behavior within the system as a whole are eligible to go to the faith-based alternative for the last 36 months of their incarceration. While there, they are taught basic life skills, like writing a résumé and opening a checking account, by religious volunteers, and in the evenings, there is frequent religious programming. In addition, every morning, there are Christian devotions available to whoever desires to attend.

The Florida system is distinctive from the Iowa model in that the rehabilitative programming and staffing are supplied by religious groups from outside the prison. Instead of the government providing financial support for religious mission, the religious groups are donating money and services to a state system. This is an especially interesting phenomenon in light of sociology professor Mark Chaves's book, *Congregations in America*, which documents that religious groups spend relatively little on social services. In his words,

> [F]or the vast majority of congregations, social services constitute a minor and peripheral aspect of their organizational activities, taking up only small amounts of their resources and involving only small numbers of people. We fundamentally misunderstand congregations if we imagine that this sort of activity is now, was ever, or will ever be central to their activities.[79]

So the Florida experiment, with its intensive labor from church members and fairly significant costs, does seem to break new ground.

Like other religious phenomena in the United States, it is easy to be led down the path of thinking that the religious program is all for the good. There is an underbelly to the program, however, and that is that minority religions are not getting adequate attention. It is almost exclusively a Christian system, and in Florida, at least, it seems predestined to be a Christian system. It is at the mercy of the believers who live near the prison, and therefore any prisoner from outside the community who does not share its faith may well receive lesser religious instruction and worship than the others. The lopsided nature of the program in Florida has been accentuated by the fact that last year Florida slashed funds for chaplains and staff dramatically, making it ever more difficult to serve a wide variety of believers. The combination of the dependency on the local believers and the state's reduction in its professional chaplaincy make it all too likely that one prisoner has rightly assessed the situation: "You know, in the manual you would read that all religions are reverenced, but it's understood it's under Christian dictatorship."[80] The details are troubling: there was only one visit from a Muslim cleric in a year, while everyone is urged to participate in the Christian so-called "devotions" on a daily basis. Thus, the ACLU of Florida's executive director may well have a point: Governor Jeb Bush is "willing to improve conditions in prison facilities only for those inmates that are willing to accept religious proselytizing."[81] Like the Iowa model, though, the rational prisoner desires the placement, because there is more liberty, more education, and even more entertainment – so members of smaller faiths may be coerced – certainly induced – into signing up for a program that is predominantly Christian. Some of those from minority religions do not complain about the faith-based environment, though, because it is simply quieter than the average prison.[82]

With the many seemingly intractable problems in most prisons, the temptation to treat the religious prisons as a cure-all is strong. Such wishful thinking probably accounts for the simultaneous reduction in the size of the chaplaincy at the same time the programs opened. But prison systems cannot suddenly dispose of sensible criminology principles, according to most experts. For example, as important as constructive religion may be in reducing the recidivism rate, religious programming should not replace other factors that are also known to help, including counseling, drug and alcohol abuse treatment, and job instruction. One critique of these plans is that they are jerry-rigged to make the religious effect look more powerful than it really is. For recidivism to be reduced, the most difficult criminals need to be included, but these programs cherry-pick the believers who already have a good track record. Thus, the program's positive impact on recidivism may be a chimera. It may be that the success of the Florida program, at least, has more to do with its job training and life-skills courses than it does with religion, and those assessing these programs need to be hardheaded in making such determinations. If recidivism rates are reduced, that will save states many dollars while the general public is served by a reduction in criminal activity. If they do not, and the system has jettisoned the core criminological methods to rehabilitate prisoners, the people of the state of Florida will be in worse shape than they were when the program was introduced.

Like RFRA and RLUIPA, these are experiments in accommodating and meeting religious prisoners' needs. Also like RLUIPA, there is good reason to worry whether the government is acting in a neutral and even-handed manner toward particular religions or religion in general. If it strays from the path of neutrality, the Establishment Clause will raise barriers to the program, and prisons will either have to adjust or abandon these attempts. It is too early to tell how they will operate over the long term, but as of 2007 there were similar programs in place in Texas, Kansas, Minnesota, Arkansas, and Missouri.[83] But there is every reason to watch them with care, as their models have spread quickly through the state prison systems desperate to contain costs and reduce recidivism. The religious groups behind these programs have taken on some enormous social problems, and it is not just religious practice that is at stake, but also the general welfare of the society as a whole.

Religion in the military

There have been numerous complaints of evangelical military leaders at the Air Force Academy proselytizing to the cadets, leading to the formation of the Military Religious Freedom Foundation (MRFF) to fight attempts in the military to indoctrinate recruits and officer candidates in particular faiths. The MRFF was founded by a Jewish cadet who found the evangelical atmosphere suffocating and an affront to the separation of church and state.[84] The Air Force responded to this significant problem by establishing guidelines that forbid proselytizing except by chaplains. Under pressure from evangelical Christians, they softened the restrictions, permitting proselytizing in private conversations. The Chaplain Alliance for Religious Liberty has argued there is nothing wrong with a commander endorsing a religious gathering, but even evangelical professors at the Academy have responded that a "suggestion" from a commander is actually an order in the military.[85] The problem is not isolated to the Air Force Academy, but has been more intense there, in part because of its location in Colorado, which is home to a number of evangelical Christian organizations.

The government must tread a fine line between the free exercise rights of all members of the military and the separation of church and state. For example, a former evangelical Protestant minister in the U.S. Navy sued the Secretary of the Navy, alleging constructive discharge in violation of free speech, free exercise, RFRA, and the Establishment Clause. However, the court found that because the minister had resigned voluntarily, he lacked standing to bring the constitutional claims.[86] Similarly, two military chaplains filed suit against the Department of Veterans Affairs in November 2013, alleging that they were harassed and forced out of the VA Chaplain program as a result of quoting scripture and praying. The case is still pending.[87] As a result of the government shutdown in fall 2013, a Catholic priest, considered a civilian and non-essential personnel under his contract with the Department of Defense, was furloughed. He filed suit against the Department of Defense for violation of his First Amendment rights. He was reinstated the next day, but the complaint was not dismissed so as to ensure that civilian priests would not be removed in the event of future government shutdowns.[88]

Another issue that has plagued the military is chaplain selection, particularly when it comes to Muslim chaplains in the era of fanatical Islamic terrorism. Official chaplains must be ordained clergy, nominated by their denomination. They must have completed a post-baccalaureate degree in theology or a related field from an approved institution. The graduate degree must require at least 72 credit hours, and the institution must be accredited by the American Council on Education or must meet Department of Defense approval guidelines for unaccredited institutions.[89] Chaplains must meet all of the other criteria required for commission as an officer of the armed forces. Chaplains are selected from approved denominations based on quotas, which are calculated based on the needs of the services and the general population.[90] The armed services, however, are not always able to fill a need with a full-time chaplain. Under these circumstances, at least as of 1983 (when the military could not fill its requirements from the ranks of its chaplains), it relied on auxiliary chaplains who are appointed on an annual basis and whose function is purely religious. They must have ecclesiastic endorsement

214 / GOD VS. THE GAVEL

and must be approved by the chief of chaplains. If auxiliary chaplains are not available, then the military can contract with individual religious organizations to provide chaplain services, and these requirements are much looser. The organization is supposed to be a "recognized religious institution," and the institution can appoint the individuals who will provide the services.[91]

According to the military, the government itself may not choose clergy, because of constitutional limitations, and therefore the religious groups choose their own representatives when a chaplaincy is open. Filling Muslim chaplaincy spots without introducing dangerous elements into the system has been more difficult than it is with other faiths, because Islam is so decentralized, which leads the government to rely on the views of "grassroots Muslim groups" rather than established leaders to fill the positions.[92]

Some might ask whether a government-sponsored chaplaincy is constitutional. It obviously features the government paying for religious worship. Perhaps it should be privatized. Numerous reasons, though, can be listed to justify it, not the least of which is that the military cannot operate securely if it is not evaluating those in close contact with their soldiers. To privatize the chaplaincy service altogether (and therefore avoid the government payment issue) would present serious problems for national security, especially in an era of terror.[93]

The conflict between military requirements and religious dress requirements

The military always has been given broad latitude to enforce the rules it believes are necessary for order, discipline, and defense of the country. The courts have not felt institutionally competent to take on the question whether this uniform or that practice is necessary to ensure a strong military. Those decisions belong in the hands of the executive, from the Supreme Court's perspective. Thus, any accommodation by the military will have to come through Congress, and it has.

In the 1980s, the Air Force prohibited its officers from wearing headgear other than that which was officially authorized by Air Force rules. S. Simcha Goldman was an Orthodox Jew who was required by his religious beliefs to wear his yarmulke while on duty, as a clinical psychologist. He had worn it for several years with no disciplinary proceedings, but he was reported, and then told he could not wear the yarmulke with his uniform outside the hospital. Goldman rejected the order, saying that the free exercise of religion trumped the military regulation.

He won at the trial court, but the court of appeals reversed, and the Supreme Court agreed. Only two months and a few days after oral argument, in an opinion written by then-Justice William Rehnquist, and joined by Chief Justice Warren Burger and Justices Byron White, Lewis Powell, and John Paul Stevens (which was a politically diverse group), the court refused to second-guess the military's determinations regarding dress regulations. The regulation was reasonable and evenhanded, and accorded with the military's "perceived need for uniformity."[94] Despite the obvious burden on religious conduct, the court found no First Amendment guarantee to alter military uniform requirements. The court did not need to say it, but there was obviously no *obligation* for the Air Force to refuse to let Goldman wear the yarmulke, which left open legislative accommodation, upon due consideration of the need for uniformity in these circumstances.

In a telling dissent, Justice William Brennan, joined by Justice Thurgood Marshall, argued that the court had "abdicate[d] its role as principal expositor of the Constitution and protector of individual liberties in favor of credulous deference to unsupported assertions of military necessity."[95] The dissenters simply did not buy the claimed interest in uniformity, and would have penalized the Air Force, because it had yet to explain why a "neat and conservative yarmulke" was inconsistent with the uniform. Justice Harry Blackmun dissented separately to say that the Air Force had not convinced him that its interests were harmed by the yarmulke and he wanted to know why the service could not accommodate not only Goldman but also those with "indistinguishable requests for religious exemptions," so he would not have stopped with an exemption for yarmulkes, but would have used the Constitution to impose a uniform exemption policy in other circumstances as well.[96] Justice Sandra Day O'Connor, joined by Justice Marshall, also dissented, because she was not persuaded there was any threat at all to discipline or esprit de corps by an accommodation – she has always stood by judicial accommodation.[97] Every dissent was a quintessential example of legislative reasoning – carried out by unelected justices. The dangers of permitting courts to engage in such weighing is painfully evident, as each of the three dissents had a different accommodation in mind. A legislature would have been forced to examine all the choices, compromise, and find a single accommodation that was in the best interest of the public.

Now, the typical tale of the Free Exercise Clause in the United States would have many decrying the *Goldman v. Weinberger* decision as a sellout to the military, or an abdication of First Amendment principles, or an utterly unfair imposition of majority dress practices on a minority religion that could not protect itself in the political process. That is the standard story, and plenty were critical. According to one commentator, "in fact, there was no support offered by the government for its claims other than the bare assertion of military judgment and the abstract interest in military preparedness, duty, and discipline. . . . Yet for the *Goldman* Court, the abstract military interest and the military's judgment of reasonableness were constitutionally sufficient."[98]

But that is not the end of the story. When the Court refused to carve an accommodation out of a neutral and generally applicable regulation, the fight was taken to the halls of Congress. And guess what? Congress enacted an exemption for religious headgear,[99] and so Orthodox Jews (and other religious believers) may now wear religious headgear in many circumstances. The accommodation makes a lot of sense if one looks at the whole picture. What makes the most sense, though, is that the court declined to impose its limited knowledge of military uniform needs through a tortured reading of the Free Exercise Clause, and instead let the issue migrate to the political branch, where it was most appropriately addressed.

Such headgear accommodation, though, has its limits, as it must. A Sikh man insisted on wearing a turban, which is required by his religion, with his uniform – even when a helmet was required. The U.S. Court of Appeals for the Ninth Circuit held that the military had the right to court-martial someone who will only wear a turban in combat.[100] Under pressure imposed in part by RFRA, the military further expanded the religious headgear accommodation in 2014 to the benefit of Sikhs, and now permits turbans in a number of scenarios, thought not all.[101] No doubt religious entities will continue to push for more accommodations from the military with RFRA at their back.

Conclusion

Courts are not as institutionally competent to determine permissive religious accommodation in the prisons or the military as are the executive and legislative branches. Before RFRA and RLUIPA, the courts applying the First Amendment deferred to prison officials on issues of security. Inmates enjoyed significant protection, however, under *Turner v. Safley*, which accorded them rights unless it would violate a "legitimate penologolical interest," and the rule against government control of belief and against discrimination based on belief. That is the right balance. Congress's decision with RFRA and RLUIPA to alter the standard dramatically by making all prison regulations substantially burdening any religious inmate's religious conduct presumptively illegal is hard to defend.

The record is too slim to justify the interference with the extraordinarily difficult job of running a prison. It is also telling that even though no members of Congress raised substantive concerns about any other regime governed by RFRA when it was first enacted, there was genuine concern about the impact on prisons on the part of Sen. Reid, a Democrat, and, after RLUIPA was passed, from Sen. Thurmond, a Republican. Sen. Hatch promised to have hearings on RLUIPA's impact on the prisons a year after passage, which led Sen. Reid to withdraw his opposition. They never happened.

Perhaps the latest RFRA lawsuit involving United States prisons will get Congress's attention. Guantánamo Bay detainees who were found not to be enemy combatants are suing the federal government on several theories, including the Alien Tort Statute and RFRA. In other words, they are arguing that RFRA affords them free exercise rights against the neutral, generally applicable laws in place at Guantánamo Bay, and demanding an injunction that would prevent prison officials from feeding inmates against their own will.[102] This is one of the best examples yet of how RFRA's blind exemption formula leads to cases no one remotely imagined when it was passed.

If Congress were not captured by religious interests, it would at least study the effects and costs of RFRA and RLUIPA in three main categories: (1) are there increased threats to security imposed by providing extreme protection; (2) what are the costs to taxpayers of RFRA and RLUIPA litigation; and (3) how have RFRA and RLUIPA mandated accommodations that have affected state and federal prison budgets. To do this responsibly, they would have to seek information from the federal and state prison authorities and experts. They should have done that twenty years ago, but it is never too late.

The Supreme Court also has routinely deferred to the military in constitutional cases, because it does not find itself institutionally competent to second-guess the executive on national defense and military preparedness. This has not meant necessary suppression. As the yarmulke case makes clear, accommodation can be achieved in the legislative process, even when the group is a smaller religion and even when the Supreme Court has refused to craft a constitutional rule for the believer. Judicial deference to the military and to the prisons is not the end of religious liberty; it's just ordered liberty.

7

THE RIGHT TO DISCRIMINATE

"**Discrimination**" is a dirty word, and discrimination by religious entities is counterintuitive when one is inclined to believe that religion is always a force for good. Religious entities have had a prickly relationship with the anti-discrimination laws. Many hold views or choose clergy according to criteria that contravene civil rights laws: sometimes the religious entity wins, sometimes not.

Race discrimination has been particularly difficult for religious entities to achieve without consequences. For example, Bob Jones University, which prohibited interracial dating, was notified by the Internal Revenue Service that its tax-exempt status would be revoked because of its violation of the federal civil rights laws prohibiting racial discrimination.[1] The university argued vigorously that it was a private organization that should be able to believe anything, and that tax-exempt status should not turn on its views on racism. At the Supreme Court, the University was supported by the American Baptist Churches, Center for Law and Religious Freedom of the Christian Legal Society, the National Association of Evangelicals, and Congressman Trent Lott (R-Miss.).[2] The Supreme Court rejected their arguments, saying that "the Government has a fundamental, overriding interest in eradicating racial discrimination in education. . . . That governmental interest substantially outweighs whatever burden denial of tax benefits places on petitioners' exercise of their religious beliefs."[3] Taxation is not the only arena wherein religious institutions are forbidden to discriminate on the basis of race. A religious organization that is selling, renting, or limiting the occupancy of property (in a noncommercial context) may choose to deal only with those who share the same religion, unless membership "is restricted on account of race, color, or national origin."[4]

The prohibition on race discrimination by the religious is not absolute, however. In 2012, in *Hosanna Tabor Evangelical Lutheran Church and School v. E.E.O.C.*, the Supreme Court held that the First Amendment immunizes religious organizations from the civil rights laws in their selection of clergy and ministers. The Court did not say that race discrimination is off-limits.[5] Thus, at least when it comes to clergy and ministers, religious entities can discriminate according to race, color, religion, sex, national origin, disability, age, and pregnancy.

Religious institutions and believers have clashed with the anti-discrimination laws in two primary arenas: employment and housing. There is also a third wave, which is a revival of one of America's darkest eras, hearkening back to the Jim Crow race policies before the civil rights laws: religious believers are refusing to deal with homosexuals in the marketplace and are fighting to get extreme religious liberty rights so they can deny service based on their religious beliefs. Some of the proposed state RFRAs were motivated by a desire to protect believers from having to do business with homosexuals but in fact would have paved the way to discrimination by believers on the basis of race, gender, disability, sexual orientation, alienage, and religion.[6] Others have targeted same-sex couples.[7] So far, all except Mississippi's were pulled back due to the effective lobbying of civil rights groups and public pressure.

The Right to Discriminate in Employment

There are two means by which religious entities can avoid discrimination claims in hiring. There is a First Amendment doctrine called the "ministerial exception," which covers ordained clergy and ministers, and there are statutes that apply to all other employees.

THE FIRST AMENDMENT AND THE MINISTERIAL EXCEPTION. The First Amendment's "ministerial exception" immunizes employment decisions regarding ordained clergy and ministers from the civil rights laws. Beginning in 1972, courts recognized what would become known as the "ministerial exception,"[8] which grants religious employees wide latitude to choose clergy and ministers. The earliest court to address it derived its interpretation of the First Amendment from the following idea: "[t]he relationship between an organized church and its ministers is its lifeblood. . . . Matters touching this relationship must necessarily be recognized as of prime ecclesiastical concern."[9]

The religious institutions that have succeeded in these cases have done so in no small part because it is intuitive, in light of history, that they must be able to use their own criteria to select clergy. It is difficult to find a religion that does not place some kind of restriction on its clergy, which a secular employer could not. Catholics have only male priests; some conservative Christians do not permit divorced or unwed women in the pulpit; Orthodox Jews only permit men to become rabbis, though Reform, Conservative, and Reconstructionist congregations also permit women; and many denominations would not permit a homosexual to hold a clergy position, though this is an evolving issue.

In 2012, a unanimous Supreme Court decided *Hosanna-Tabor Evangelical Lutheran Church and School v. EEOC*,[10] in which the Court upheld the lower courts' long-time construction of a "ministerial exception," whereby the "Religion Clauses bar the government from interfering with the decision of a religious group to fire one of its ministers."[11] The case answered the question whether there is such a doctrine, but left a number of issues open.

Cheryl Perich was a teacher at the church's school, who was classified as a "called" teacher, which meant she took at least eight courses of theological instruction, obtained the endorsement of the local Synod district, and passed an oral exam. She was primarily a teacher of secular subjects, including math, language arts, social studies, science, gym, art, and music, but she also taught a religion class four days each week, led students in prayer and devotional exercises each day, and attended a weekly school-wide chapel service. Once she was "called," she also received the title, "Minister of Religion, Commissioned." Her duties were no different, however, than the duties of a lay teacher.

Perich developed narcolepsy and, thus, needed to take a leave of absence for treatment starting in June 2004. In January 2005, she informed the school her health was improving, and that she would return the next month. She arrived at school on February 22 but the school had hired another teacher in the interim and asked her to leave. She responded that she had consulted a lawyer and would sue for her rights, which she did. The Church defended itself, saying that she had violated their beliefs by pursuing legal action, because they believed "that Christians should resolve their disputes internally."[12] In other words, the Church claimed it did not believe in the American system of justice for its believers. That issue fell to the wayside, though, because the Court found that the First Amendment absolved Hosanna-Tabor from the ADA's limitations.

The Court could have limited the exception to ordained clergy, which at least would have provided a bright line rule, but the Justices declined to limit the religious entities' right to discriminate. Instead, the Court held that the First Amendment protected more than "the head of a religious congregation," and was "reluctant . . . to adopt a rigid formula for deciding when an employee qualifies as a minister."[13] They believed it was "enough for us to conclude, in this our first case involving the ministerial exception, that the exception covers Perich, given all the circumstances of her employment."[14] Thus, ministerial exception cases will be fact-intensive for employees who are not ordained clergy, which means there are many unanswered questions. For example, are all church youth group leaders, or parochial school teachers, or religious school coaches, or worship organists ministers? Is a retired member of the clergy, hired as an independent consultant on growing a congregation, a minister?

While there will be many cases that may be difficult to predict after *Hosanna-Tabor*, there are plenty of other older cases that were decided consistently with its principles. For example, in one gender discrimination lawsuit, Sandy Williams, an ordained minister in the

Episcopal Church, alleged that she was discriminated against on the basis of gender (a brand of discrimination not mandated by the Church's belief system). After she told the church that she believed she was receiving disparate treatment, she was constructively discharged – the hostile work environment and gender discrimination and the diocese's unwillingness to do anything made her feel that she had no choice other than to resign.[15] Looking at the facts, the whole affair seems patently unfair. This woman pointed out an injustice, which is actually contrary to the church's beliefs, and then she appears to have been treated to the very treatment she had complained about! In a secular setting, that would be illegal. But in the religious setting, the court held that the ministerial exception shielded the church from any liability for retaliatory discharge.[16] That is where the ministerial exception leads.

Refinements of the Lower Courts' Ministerial Exception Built into the Hosanna-Tabor Decision

The Court chose a middle ground. First, some lower courts had held that the ministerial exception creates such a zone of liberty around religious entities that it is jurisdictional and, therefore, the courts cannot even hear such cases. The Court obviously rejected such a theory, as it left each case to be decided on its facts.

Second, other courts had held that the ministerial exception privilege is not triggered unless the religious organization's decision is based on a religious belief. That would have reduced the number of cases in which religious organizations could succeed. On this interpretation, Hosanna-Tabor could not have fired Perich with impunity unless it believed that clergy cannot be disabled. Or, to turn to the Church's asserted defense, if in fact it did not really believe that pursuing legal recourse is sinful, it could not have benefitted from the ministerial exception. The Court, however, rejected a requirement that the firing be related to a religious belief, saying, "The purpose of the exception is not to safeguard a church's decision to fire a minister only when it is made for a religious reason. The exception instead ensures that the authority to select and control who will minister to the faithful . . . "[17] Thus, earlier, troubling, cases were actually correct: the firing of a Catholic priest allegedly based on invidious race discrimination was immune from a civil rights attack, as was the firing of a female University Chaplain, even though neither decision was based on a religious belief that required the discrimination.[18]

The Court also refused to adopt autonomy as its theory of religious liberty, and pointed toward legal theories other than discrimination to make the point that its theory was not one that grants religious organizations autonomy from the law. I submitted an amicus brief on behalf of Bishopaccountability.org, the Cardozo Advocates for Kids, Child Protection Project, The Foundation to Abolish Child Sex Abuse, Jewish Board of Advocates for Children, Inc., Kidsafe Foundation, The National Black Church Initiative, The National Center for Victims of Crime, Survivors for Justice, and the Survivors Network of Those Abused by Priests in the Hosanna-Tabor case for two primary purposes.[19] First, the organizations were concerned that the decision could inadvertently interfere with cases involving clergy sex abuse. Second, they were concerned that religious entities, particularly the Catholic and Mormon bishops, were pushing a theory of "autonomy" from the law, which the organizations believe is dangerous to children and others harmed by religious organizations. Thus, we raised the fact that the Court had never adopted "autonomy" as a theory of religious liberty in any case, and the Court did not in fact use the term. Nor was the Court's reasoning, which left open other legal disputes including contract and tort suits involving employees, consistent with the demands for autonomy.

Interestingly, a concurrence authored by Justice Alito and joined only by Justice Kagan, did embrace autonomy from the law for religious organizations.[20] It was a surprise to see these two Justices, with their differences on so many issues, banding together for the purpose of immunizing believers from the law. It is worth noting that Justice Kagan was Associate White House Counsel between 1995 and 1996, and then Deputy Assistant to the President, Domestic Policy Council (DPC), between 1997 and 1999. The DPC would have had jurisdiction over RFRA, because it oversees the implementation of the President's domestic policy agenda among the different federal offices and agencies. In an exchange of emails, she warned that Vice President Gore should not support RFRA at the time (which was during the RLPA hearings). Even though she was RFRA's "biggest fan" in the White House, she cautioned that otherwise "you'll have a gay/lesbian firestorm on your hands." She added that a meeting was planned with gay and religious groups to find a solution.

"We'll let you know," she wrote, "as soon as it's safe to go back in the water."[21] Little did she know that the RFRA formula, would later be the model inviting the states to license businesses to discriminate, as I discuss in the Epilogue.

Plenty of laws still control the religious employer-minister relationship after *Hosanna-Tabor*. In response to concerns expressed by the E.E.O.C. and Perich, the Court noted that *Hosanna-Tabor* itself had rejected the notion that the "exception could protect religious organizations from liability for retaliating against employees for reporting criminal misconduct or for testifying before a grand jury or in a criminal trial."[22] In other words, employees would not be able to be fired under this theory if they did the right thing by participating in the criminal justice process. The Court further disavowed a holding that the right would create "'unfettered discretion' to violate employment laws,"[23] e.g., child labor laws. The exception is limited to suits "by or on behalf of ministers themselves," and does not forestall "breach of contract" actions. Finally, the Court distinguished cases involving "tortious conduct by their religious employers,"[24] i.e., clergy sex abuse cases.

The ministerial exemption may be limited in other ways as well. Before *Hosanna-Tabor* was decided, theories of breach of contract and fiduciary duty permitted seminarian Christopher McKelvey's claims against the Philadelphia Archdiocese to go forward. Its dictum may actually reserve those theories for future plaintiffs. McKelvey planned to be a priest in the Camden, New Jersey, diocese, which offered to pay for his college and seminary education and, in its papers to him, emphasized the priestly requirement of celibacy. McKelvey made it through college and then headed for the St. Charles Borromeo Seminary near Philadelphia, where he lost enthusiasm for his career path when he allegedly was on the receiving end of repeated homosexual advances from other seminarians and priests, including propositions to engage in homosexual acts, to discuss masturbation, and to accompany them to gay bars. According to McKelvey, he was further demoralized when he reported the sexual harassment up the chain of command, and expecting his supervisors to enforce the vow of chastity, instead received hostile responses. When he did not return from a leave of absence, the archdiocese terminated his candidacy and sent him a bill for his education expenses in the amount of $69,002.57.[25] He sued.

226 / GOD VS. THE GAVEL

The Diocese argued in response only one theory: the courts were barred from taking the case at all on the ground that the First Amendment prohibited the courts from intervening in the dispute, because it involved the relationship between a church and its clergy (or, in this case, potential clergy). On its theory (and this tack is attempted in cases across the country in any number of contexts, including clergy abuse), the ministerial exception shielded the church from *any* claims involving a clergy member. The trial court agreed, and the intermediate appellate court agreed. In a unanimous opinion, the New Jersey Supreme Court did not agree, and ruled in favor of McKelvey. According to the court, the problem with the lower courts' reasoning was that it was too clumsy. The First Amendment might preclude the courts from settling internal disputes over the meaning of religious dogma, or might prohibit the courts from getting involved in rendering interpretations of the church's beliefs. But the First Amendment did not stand in the way of claims invoking neutral principles of law where the analysis could be accomplished in secular terms. Far from creating an impenetrable wall around religious organizations' decisions regarding clergy, the court instructed the lower New Jersey courts that they were required to examine each element of each claim to determine whether the claim could be proved and analyzed using secular principles. The court quoted a decision by the U.S. Court of Appeals for the Fifth Circuit that accurately characterizes the law and explains why so many claims of ministerial privilege can be adjudicated:

> The First Amendment does not categorically insulate religious relationships from judicial scrutiny, for to do so would necessarily extend constitutional protection to the secular components of these relationships.... The constitutional guarantee of religious freedom cannot be construed to protect secular beliefs and behavior, even when they comprise part of an otherwise religious relationship.... To hold otherwise would impermissibly place a religious leader in a preferred position in our society.[26]

McKelvey, therefore, was permitted to go forward on theories of breach of contract and breach of fiduciary duty. The parties settled the case after it was remanded for a trial. Because the Supreme Court did not rule that the ministerial exception is jurisdictional, these issues will be capable of being raised in further cases.

It must be emphasized, though, that the restrictions on the law's ability to make religious organizations accountable for their actions toward their religious employees should have no force when the case involves a harmed third party. The ministerial exception only applies, when it does apply, in an employment dispute brought by the religious employee against the employer. The language in some cases about the right of the organization to choose, hire, retain, and fire whomever it pleases on religious grounds does not immunize the religious organizations from laws that protect third parties. Therefore, tort and criminal laws retain their force in clergy sexual abuse and medical neglect cases brought by victims. The court is not being asked in such a case to determine religious criteria, or clergy fitness *qua* clergy, but rather to assess whether the actions taken by the religious organization violate neutral criminal or tort principles. An organization can use any religious criteria it desires to choose clergy, but when it places anyone under its control it knows to be a pedophile within easy reach of children, it has endangered the welfare of children, among other crimes, and acted negligently on a number of theories. This distinction is crucial if religious institutions are to be deterred from putting their interests ahead of society's interests.

One aspect of the ministerial exception seems very unfair. The people who take positions with religious organizations are unlikely to expect to be unfairly discriminated against, and, as Americans, likely to believe that such discrimination would be illegal. That was certainly the sentiment of the many religious employees who have filed discrimination claims only to bump up against the ministerial exception. I have spoken with many of them and they were shocked to learn that religious organizations have a constitutional right to engage in invidious discrimination.

There is a solution that they deserve, which I recommended to the United States Commission on Civil Rights at its hearing on these issues.[27] If these employees cannot have the benefit of the anti-discrimination laws, then religious employers should be required to disclose to them at the time of hiring that they are considered either clergy or ministers for the purpose of the ministerial exception and, therefore, they do not have rights against discrimination based on race, color, gender, national origin, disability, age, or pregnancy. Just because an organization says someone is a "minister," won't make them one, as the *Hosanna-Tabor* opinion held, so there may be employees who are told they have no rights, who do. But that is better than so many employees assuming they have rights only to find in the face of invidious discrimination they do not.

ANTI-DISCRIMINATION STATUTES AND EMPLOYEES OTHER THAN MINISTERS. There are a slew of federal anti-discrimination laws that apply to private entities, including religious entities. Title VII of the Civil Rights Act of 1964 outlaws discrimination in employment by private entities with fifteen or more employees, based on "race, color, religion, sex or, national origin."[28] The Americans with Disabilities Act (ADA) outlaws discrimination by private entities with fifteen or more employees based on "physical or mental disabilities."[29] The Age Discrimination in Employment Act (ADEA) applies to private entities that have over twenty employees and outlaws refusing or failing to hire an individual based on age, or otherwise discriminating against or segregating the individual in compensation or terms of employment.[30] The Pregnancy Discrimination Act (PDA) amended Title VII to forbid discrimination by employers with 15 or more employees against women "affected by pregnancy, childbirth, or related medical conditions . . ."[31]

Title VII recognizes an exception for *religious organizations* in that they may hire based on religious belief though they are still obligated not to discriminate under the other prohibited categories.[32] It defines a religious organization as a "religious corporation, association, educational institution, or society with respect to the employment of individuals of a particular religion to perform work connected with the carrying on by such corporation, association, educational institution, or society of its activities."[33] To summarize, only religious organizations may discriminate based on religion, and even religious organizations cannot discriminate on the basis of race or the other categories, *unless* the employee is clergy or a minister.

When the Title VII exception for religious organizations to discriminate based on religious belief is invoked, three issues tend to arise: (1) whether the defendant is a religious or really a secular organization[34]; (2) whether the plaintiff works in a religious or secular capacity[35]; and (3) whether the reason for the employment action was based on religious belief, including whether Title VII imposes a substantial or a *de minimis* burden on that belief.[36] If any of these three criteria are not satisfied, the organization loses and must obey all of the restrictions imposed by Title VII.

The Equal Employment Opportunity Commission (EEOC) has developed criteria for answering the first question whether an organization is religious or not:

> whether the entity is not for profit, whether its day-to-day operations are religious (e.g., are the services the entity performs, the product it produces, or the educational curriculum it provides directed toward propagation of the religion?); whether the entity's articles of incorporation or other pertinent documents state a religious purpose; whether it is owned, affiliated with or financially supported by a formally religious entity such as a church or other religious organization; whether a formally religious entity participates in the management, for instance by having representatives on the board of trustees; whether the entity holds itself out to the public as secular or sectarian; whether the entity regularly includes prayer or other forms of worship in its activities; whether it includes religious instruction in its curriculum, to the extent it is an educational institution; and whether its membership is made up of coreligionists.[37]

The close cases under this reasoning have involved, e.g., a Jewish community center, which was found to be non-religious, and a non-profit school.

The second recurring issue is whether the employee is actually a religious employee or an employee of a religious institution performing secular duties. For example, the Southwestern Baptist Theological Seminary won and lost its attempt to avoid an investigation by the Equal Employment Opportunity Commission regarding its employees.[38] While those performing ministerial tasks were not protected by the anti-discrimination laws, the court found that at least four support personnel who performed non-ministerial duties (yet were also ordained ministers) were "not entitled to ministerial status," and therefore their discrimination claims could go forward. In another case finding that accommodation was not required because the employee was not a religious employee for these purposes, the Pacific Press Publishing Association, a non-profit publishing house in California associated with the Seventh-day Adventist Church, was accused of engaging in gender and marital-status discrimination. Its policy was to pay employees according to sex and marital status, which led an unmarried secretary, Lorna Tobler, to bring charges of sexual discrimination (and retaliation) against the company. The U.S. Court of Appeals for the Ninth Circuit held the press liable for discrimination, because Tobler's duties did not go to the heart of the religious organization's operations, and the First Amendment was not implicated, because the impact of applying the anti-discrimination laws in this case on its religious belief was *de minimis*, especially when compared with the government's interest.[39]

The third common issue is whether the reason for the employment decision was based on a religious or a secular motivation. Only religious reasons enjoy the benefit of the exemption under Title VII. This element sharply contrasts from the ministerial exception as the Court in *Hosanna Tabor* held that there need be no proof that the discrimination against clergy or a minister is based on a religious belief. Therefore, a church that believes that ministers should only be male, but no beliefs related to race, can discriminate at will based on race as well.

Before RFRA and the state RFRAs, the range of permissible discrimination extended from clergy and ministers to religious reasons in religious entities involving other employees. Extreme religious liberty, however, has changed the playing field, with for-profit business owners pursuing the right to discriminate against their employees and their customers.

RFRA and the Right of For-Profit, Nonreligious
Businesses to Discriminate

RFRA has tempted for-profit, nonreligious business owners to claim a right to discriminate against their employees. As I discuss in more detail in the Epilogue, Hobby Lobby and many other companies, which are frankly for-profit and nonreligious under any ordinary reasoning, are demanded the right under RFRA to exclude women's reproductive health care according to their religious lights. These are entities that may not discriminate on the basis of gender or religion under Title VII and state and local laws. It would be unthinkable for them to be able to refuse to hire women or pay them the same as men based on their religious beliefs. Health care benefits are simply a part of the compensation package and, therefore, these claims are a form of discrimination against their employees based on gender and religion. This was a new wrinkle in the

RFRA universe, and in June 2014, the Court held that RFRA handed companies the power to impose their owners' religious beliefs on their employees' health care plans. These businesses' novel demands were accompanied at the same time by conservative Christian groups, like the Alliance Defending Freedom, lobbying the states to expand state RFRAs to "accommodate" businesses for the purpose of discriminating against their customers.

The State RFRAs and the Right of Businesses to Discriminate Against Customers?

There was a time in the United States when the Jim Crow laws prevented blacks from sitting at the same lunch counters as whites, or using the same restrooms. They were buttressed by everyone in the culture, which was heavily religious. The Civil Rights Act of 1964 changed that. The presumption has been that businesses may not discriminate in the marketplace, and must provide their services without discrimination. The Jim Crow mentality, however, has reared its ugly head again.

As same-sex marriage has spread across the country, some business owners have complained about having to do business with homosexuals. For example, a photographer in New Mexico complained that she did not want to photograph a gay marriage because the marriage violated her religious beliefs, and was sued under the state's public accommodations laws. After she lost,[40] conservative religious lobbyists raced to a number of states with the bright idea of expanding state RFRAs so that private businesses and individuals could refuse to do business with anyone they chose, based on religious belief. Up to this point, all RFRAs, including RLUIPA, were limited to actions against the government.

This is as extreme as religious liberty gets, and civil rights groups finally mobilized against these aggressive religious liberty laws and entered the fray. They played a pivotal role in halting the progress of such perilous bills in Maine,[41] Kansas,[42] South Dakota,[43] Ohio,[44] and Idaho[45] One bill did make it through both houses in Arizona, though, before Gov. Jan Brewer vetoed it.[46]

Arizona's expansive language would have created opportunities for discrimination by businesses owned by believers based on sexual orientation, race, gender, alienage, and disability. If not vetoed by the governor,

Arizona would have had a law that re-enacted the Jim Crow laws. White supremacist business owners would have been revitalized along with those who are anti-homosexual. This exercise was an important lesson in how far believers will push the formulae available. RFRA started us down this path. Mississippi picked up where Arizona left off, enacting a state RFRA in 2014 that opens the door for business owners to invoke their religious beliefs to discriminate. For more on this topic, see the Epilogue.

The Right to Discriminate in Housing

In the United States, there are religious home or apartment owners who have dutiful scruples about letting their property be used by unmarried couples, gay couples, and/or unwed mothers. They have not fared terribly well under the fair housing laws, in no small part because the availability of shelter is one of the primary needs of humans.

The housing discrimination issue played a pivotal role during the passage of RFRA, its invalidation, and then RLUIPA. When RFRA was first proposed in 1990 and then passed for the first time in 1993, it was next to impossible to find anyone who objected to it, including initially myself. What could possibly have been wrong with more religious liberty? Indeed, those behind the law were on what seemed like a noble crusade. Senators Orrin Hatch (R-Utah) and Edward Kennedy (D-Mass.), who frequently teamed up for religious entities, spoke in elegiac terms about their mission. They were the literal saviors of religious liberty, or so they said. Senator Kennedy proclaimed, "Few issues are more fundamental to our country. America was founded as a land of religious freedom and a haven from religious persecution. Two centuries later, that founding principle has been endangered."[47] As I discuss in Chapter One, the ACLU, a proponent of fair housing laws, did not initially perceive that RFRA would be at cross-purposes with the fair housing laws.

RLUIPA could have been stretched to cover the fair-housing laws, a result many conservative organizations would have hailed. Its legislative history, though, disavows any intent to reach that far.[48] Indeed, the ACLU may well have been at the helm of drafting RLUIPA in order to ensure that the new bill did not reach housing discrimination claims.

The first state fair housing law was passed in California in 1959, with the federal Fair Housing Act (FHA) passed in 1968.[49] By 2005, 49 states and the District of Columbia had enacted laws prohibiting discrimination in the housing market. Most mirror the FHA and prohibit it on the basis of race, color, national origin, religion, sex, familial status, or handicap. Others are broader and encompass age, military status, sexual orientation, genetic disposition or carrier status, HIV status, gender identity, and source of income.[50] Approximately half of the states prohibit discrimination in housing based on marital status; while a decade ago only a handful prohibit it based on sexual orientation, now nearly half the states also prohibit discrimination in housing based on sexual orientation.[51]

There are many interests at stake in these cases. Like the land use cases discussed in Chapter 4, they implicate the right to determine how private property is used. In those lawsuits, religious landowners chafe at residential restrictions. In these cases, they battle the government's strong interest in ensuring that all citizens are treated fairly in the housing market, where shelter is a human necessity. The courts also have tended to reject the religious landlord's religious defense, in part because they are not required by law to rent apartments or participate in the housing market. Thus, the law does not operate to place any burden on the landlord, who has voluntarily chosen to become a landlord.[52] They can avoid the burden.

One principle in this context, though, has tended to work in religious landlords' favor, and that is they have exercised a right to choose to sell their non-commercial property to fellow believers, rather than outsiders. For example, St. Monica's Catholic parish near Milwaukee, Wisconsin, decided to sell a house it owned, and Michael and Barbara Bachman, who were Jewish, made an offer. In response, the parish pulled the house off the market and asked if any of its parishioners were interested. When none were, the parish sold it to a Catholic couple at a price higher than the Bachmans had offered, with financing terms that may have made the Bachman deal the better offer for the parish. The Bachmans sued under the Fair Housing Act, claiming ancestral discrimination. St. Monica's prevailed. The U.S. Court of Appeals for the Seventh Circuit upheld the verdict, because the jury had been permitted to consider two mutually exclusive possibilities: either the refusal to sell rested solely on anti-Semitism, or the congregation's decision had nothing to do with their ancestral heritage.[53] The court held that the defendants were entitled to this jury instruction, because even if the parish did in fact give a preference to Catholics, this alone would only be *evidence of* discrimination against Jews, not explicit discrimination against Jews.[54]

In contrast, religious landlords have found it difficult to impose their religious criteria on prospective tenants for four reasons. First, even where the landlord succeeds in arguing that he or she has a free exercise right at issue, some courts have found that removing discrimination in this context is a compelling state interest.[55] This ground, though, is not entirely settled. With a RFRA in place (or strong state constitutional free exercise guarantees), courts have had to consider whether preventing marital status discrimination serves a compelling interest, and the results are not consistent across the board.[56] The newest cases involve discrimination based on sexual orientation, in which, the same-sex couples fare better in states where same-sex marriage is recognized.

Second, the harm that results from the exercise of these beliefs directly affects the victims of the discrimination. It is neither indirect nor insignificant.[57]

Third, there is no substantial burden on the religious entity's actual religious beliefs, because there is either no burden or only a *de minimis* burden.[58]

Finally, there is no other means of achieving the government's goal of eliminating discrimination on the basis of marital status, or sexual orientation, other than imposing the laws on all – even the religious landlords.[59]

The Fair Housing Act was enacted to ensure that individuals were not excluded from the housing market on the basis of impermissible categories. It was not intended to make it possible for religious groups to force a neutral, generally applicable housing system to meet their beliefs. For example, four Orthodox Jewish students at Yale College brought an interesting lawsuit invoking the federal Fair Housing Act, though in the end it was not successful. They argued that Yale's coeducational dormitories, where all unmarried freshmen and sophomores were required to live, violated their religious belief in sexual modesty. The U.S. Court of Appeals for the Second Circuit held that the dormitory policies had been disclosed well before the students came to campus and, moreover, the FHA was not designed to accommodate the plaintiffs' unique religious beliefs.

> Significantly, plaintiffs do not claim that defendants adopted their policy because of animus toward Orthodox Jews or that they grant exemptions to other religious groups or to students lacking a religious affiliation in a manner different from the exemption process for Orthodox Jews. Because plaintiffs seek exclusion from housing and not inclusion, they do not state an FHA claim. The purpose of the FHA is to promote integration and root out segregation, not to facilitate exclusion.[60]

There have been cases, though, where religious landlords have been able to engage in religiously-motivated discrimination – by arguing that the governmental interest in the free exercise of religion trumps any state interest in protecting unmarried couples from discrimination. In Minnesota, Susan Parsons agreed to rent a house from landlord Layle French. Shortly thereafter, French learned that Parsons would be living with her fiancé. A member of the Evangelical Free Church, French believed that an unmarried couple living together gives the "appearance of evil" and raised a religious defense to Parsons's action under the Minnesota Human Rights Act. The Supreme Court of Minnesota held that the state constitution's protection of religious beliefs exempted the landlord from compliance with the fair-housing provisions.[61] In California, a landlord turned down two prospective tenants as soon as she learned that they were unmarried and planned to cohabitate. A devout Roman Catholic, the landlord believed that premarital sex was a sin and believed that renting the apartment to the couple would in itself be a sin. The Court of Appeals of California held that the landlord was entitled to an exemption from the fair-housing claim, because the constitutional interest in free exercise of religion was substantially greater than the state's lesser interest in eradicating discrimination against unmarried couples.[62]

This is an area of law in the United States that is not settled, at least with respect to discrimination involving marital status and sexual orientation. There is no consensus among state laws on these two categories, and the federal fair-housing laws do not adequately address them.

Conclusion

Religious believers have demanded the right to discriminate in three arenas: employment of ministers, housing, and to avoid doing business with homosexuals or same-sex couples. The first issue is governed by the ministerial exception under the First Amendment and is in cement. The second is in flux. The third is in its infancy.

PART TWO

THE HISTORY AND DOCTRINE BEHIND COMMON-SENSE RELIGIOUS LIBERTY

ORDERED LIBERTY: RELIGIOUS LIBERTY AT THE SUPREME COURT

The free exercise cases

The Supreme Court's consistent approach to free exercise has held that religious belief is absolutely protected, but religious conduct is subject to duly enacted laws. Why not follow the logic of libertarianism and extend the absolute freedom of belief to conduct? It is obvious. While beliefs harm no one, conduct can. In the words of Thomas Jefferson, "The legitimate powers of government extend to such acts only as are injurious to others. But it does me no injury for my neighbor to say there are twenty gods, or no God. It neither picks my pocket nor breaks my leg."[1]

This is a fundamental principle that unites the Free Speech and Free Exercise Clauses, and that rests on the republican form of government at the base of the constitutional order. John Stuart Mill explained it as follows: "The fact of living in society renders it indispensable that each should be bound to observe a certain line of conduct toward the rest."[2] Once one understands the no-harm rule[3] and its distinguished pedigree, autonomy from the law for religious believers and organizations appears foolhardy.

The framing generation did not believe religious actors deserved unlimited license to act. They even had a name for too much liberty: "licentiousness."[4] It was commonplace for state constitutions and the framing generation to expect that safety, peace, and order would trump religiously motivated conduct. In fact, all liberty in the Constitution generally is couched in a larger concern about the public good and may legitimately be limited when the public good demands.

One of the more challenging concepts to teach is that the "liberty" in the Bill of Rights is nowhere close to absolute, but rather must give way to a number of societal interests. There is only one absolute right in the entire Constitution, and that is the absolute right to believe whatever one chooses, under the First Amendment. After that, every other right can be trumped by government interests when those interests are strong enough. The Second Amendment's right to "bear arms" does not mean that any criminal may own any gun he or she desires. Rather, the government has broad latitude to regulate gun ownership, especially when the owner has a criminal record. A homeowner's Fourth Amendment right of privacy, which prohibits searches and seizures without permission, is far from absolute. Where the police have "reasonable suspicion," they may enter even without the homeowner's permission. The Fifth Amendment right not to be "deprived of life [or] liberty" does not mean that the government may not take a traitor's life or impose a prison sentence on a criminal. When the government interest is strong enough, it can take both life and liberty. The "right to a speedy trial" in the Sixth Amendment does not mean the trial must take place the same day as the indictment, but rather at some reasonable time in the future.

Republicanism, which is the United States' representative form of government, is built on the belief that humans entering society must agree to (1) delegate their lawmaking to representatives and (2) create a system that is geared toward achieving the public good. Absolute freedom of religious conduct would give clergy carte blanche to abuse children;

it would permit white supremacist prisoners to engage in race-based violence in the prisons; and the Church of Heroin to open on every street corner. For all but the most libertarian, such a culture is intolerable, and therefore liberty must be ordered liberty, and that means the public good must be able to trump the demands of religious actors.[5] The rapist that attacks a child deserves lengthy time in prison, whether he is a priest or a layman. To paraphrase Gertrude Stein, a harm is a harm is a harm.

If a legislature finds an injury is significant enough to prohibit, religious entities that commit the same harm should be as culpable as every other citizen. (The one exception would be where the legislature has made a considered decision that exempting the religious entity is consistent with the public good, an approach I will discuss in detail in Chapter 10.)

From 1878 until 1963, the Court held religious actors accountable for their conduct.

Beginning in 1963, the Supreme Court – in a select set of cases – edged toward giving believers a right to trump the law because their conduct was religiously motivated. The first variation appeared in the *Sherbert* case, where the state had an unemployment compensation scheme that treated religious and secular reasons differently. As I discuss in the Introduction, an employee, Adell Sherbert, was fired and denied unemployment compensation for attending church, when she could have received it for going to a doctor's appointment. The Court required South Carolina to explain its different treatment of religion and secular reasons with a "compelling interest." It couldn't, and, therefore, Sherbert won. This was a defensible development, because the government's toleration of exceptions in the first place undermined its argument that the system could not operate with both secular and religious reasons.

A single, disastrous diversion from the Court's doctrine occurred in 1973 with the *Yoder* case discussed in the Introduction. There a neutral law that applied to everyone equally was struck down when the Court ran the state's interests through the wringer and imposed a heavy burden on the state to justify the law. This introduction of strict scrutiny for a generally applicable, neutral law did not displace the dominant view so much as it awkwardly inserted itself into the jurisprudence in this one case.

Despite the paucity of cases that have followed the *Yoder* reasoning and its internal inconsistency with the Court's primary free exercise principles, it became the favored approach among many academics and believers. By the time the Court righted the jurisprudence in 1990, there was a widespread fallacy that religious entities need not answer to any law but the most necessary.

The First Amendment's Free Exercise Clause

When the Court decided its first case interpreting the Free Exercise Clause in 1879, *Reynolds v. United States*,[6] the Court upheld the federal law outlawing polygamy in the Utah Territory, and articulated what would eventually become the settled doctrine for the free exercise of religion: religious belief is absolutely protected, but religious conduct is subject to the rule of law. The *Reynolds* Court quoted Thomas Jefferson: "The legislative powers of the government reach actions only, and not opinions."[7] The fact that the conduct arose from belief did not immunize the actor from the force of the law.

The Court's reasoning rested on a larger theory of the relationship between a citizen and society. Individuals could not be given an unfettered right to act according to their own dictates, for otherwise the society would disintegrate into a collection of narcissistic individuals, and the total would be decidedly smaller than the sum of its parts. In the Court's words:

> Can a man excuse his practices to the contrary because of his religious belief? To permit this would be to make the professed doctrines of religious belief superior to the law of the land, and in effect to permit every citizen to become a law unto himself. Government could exist only in name under such circumstances.[8]

The Court thereby relied on the long-recognized principle in representative democracies that individual rights are crucial, but they do not extend to harming another.[9] For Jefferson, as the *Reynolds* Court noted, there was a comfortable relationship between natural rights and the law, because he was "convinced [man] has no natural right in opposition to his social duties."[10] In other words, the rights of humans were never absolute, but rather were shaped to honor the necessity of social order and duty. Whether or not one believes in natural rights, once the social compact is in place and individuals must coexist with others, rights are to be measured against the backdrop of the public good and according to how one's actions affect others.

Jefferson in turn had echoed the influential 17th century British political philosopher John Locke. As a starting point, Locke advocated a robust right of conscience, or belief.[11] He then argued that "God is the true proprietor" and therefore human beings could not "belong to one another, i.e., [they were] independently valuable."[12] From this precept, Locke derived a general "no-harm" principle: individuals were not to "take away, or impair the life, or what tends to the preservation of the life, the liberty, health, limb, or goods of another."[13] For Locke, then, individuals joining together in society had a general liberty of conscience, or belief, but the state legitimately restrained those actions that harmed others. The *Reynolds* Court formulated the Jeffersonian/Lockean theory of religion and government as follows: "Congress was deprived of all legislative power over mere opinion, but was left free to reach actions that were in violation of social duties or subversive of good order."[14]

The *Reynolds* Court was not only looking backward, however. Its holding also reflects the views of the most influential philosopher of the 19th century in the English-speaking world, John Stuart Mill, who died only a few years before *Reynolds* was decided. A defender of individual liberty, Mill set forth the following maxims:

> [F]irst, that the individual is not accountable to society for his actions, in so far as these concern the interests of no person but himself.... Secondly, that for such actions as are prejudicial to the interests of others, the individual is accountable, and may be subjected either to social or to legal punishments, if society is of opinion that the one or the other is requisite for its protection.[15]

This is a precise explanation of the Court's free exercise jurisprudence in the main.

Another way to approach the Court's free exercise jurisprudence is to examine the oft-repeated concept of "ordered liberty," which appears across the constitutional spectrum.[16] Liberty by itself was not valued at the time of the Constitution's framing, at the time of *Reynolds*, nor has it been the focus of the Supreme Court's subsequent rulings on religious liberty. The framing generation feared the licentiousness and anarchy that arises from pure liberty and thus did not institute sheer libertarianism, but rather liberty anchored in the necessity of order. They believed that in the absence of order, there is no real liberty, but rather only a clash of individual wills. The influential Rev. John Witherspoon, president of the College of New Jersey, who signed the Declaration of Independence, served in the Continental Congress and trained James Madison and other Framers on governance principles,[17] put it this way: the "true notion of liberty is the prevalence of law and order, and the security of individuals," and therefore an "object of civil laws is, limiting citizens in the exercise of their rights, so that they may not be injurious to one another, but that the public good may be promoted."[18]

In cases involving religious conduct, the Court has kept in view the fact that religious individuals and institutions are firmly situated within the context of a society that entails mutual obligations.[19] Isolationism or pure libertarianism or autonomy cannot be squared with this worldview.

The Court's approach, with all of its distinguished support in history and philosophy, also has had lasting power, because it redounds in common sense. Even if the Court were inclined to recognize an individualistic right to do whatever one believes, the practical result would be anarchy. The strong libertarian position proposes what cannot be accomplished: the utter solitude of a single believer, or the complete isolation of a religious group that can act without affecting others.

Some would point to *Yoder*,[20] discussed in the Introduction and Chapter Five, for the proposition that religious entities have a constitutional right to be isolated, and to shape education in a way that sends children back to the religious community. In that case, the Court was willing to let the Amish operate independently of the public good in an opinion that was a paean to their way of life, and that failed to consider the children's needs, as Justice Douglas pointed out.[21] *Yoder*, however, stands by itself, and is later explained by the Court as a case that is more easily interpreted in terms of parental rights than in terms of what religious entities owe to the public good.[22] In fact, as discussed previously, *Yoder* was wrongly decided. If religious children were to be exempted from the public school system, that decision belonged in the hands of the legislature, not the courts. In any event, if there were any question that the Court did not intend to shield the Amish in particular from the rule of law, ten years later the Court held that they were required to pay into the social security system for their employees even though they did not believe in doing so.[23]

Harmful religious conduct is a zero-sum game; the more liberty the religious actor has, the more at risk are those who could be hurt by his conduct. Even the arch-libertarian Robert Nozick has had to concede that there must be "side constraints" on the libertarian's behavior, because of the potential for harm to others.[24] From the beginning of the U.S. constitutional experiment, the joinder of liberty and order meant that religious liberty was not irresponsible individualism, but rather an element of the public good. Some liberty can and should be absolute and still consistent with the preservation of order – the liberty of belief. Other liberty cannot be absolute if the right level of order is to be preserved – the liberty of conduct.

The two principles governing regulations affecting religious conduct

The Court has recognized two coordinate principles in its free exercise cases. The first is that religious entities, just as much as any other citizen, can be prohibited from harming others and thus can be made to obey a myriad of laws, including narcotics laws, bureaucratic requirements, child labor laws, tort laws, anti-polygamy laws, property laws, and tax laws. The Court simply has not recognized in the vast majority of its cases a right to trump duly enacted laws for religious reasons.

By the same token, religious entities may not be subjected to laws that are hostile or motivated by animus toward religion in general or any sect in particular. "The fullest realization of true religious liberty [includes a rule that the government may] effect no favoritism among sects or between religion and nonreligion. . . . "[25] If a law applies to all those who are capable of the harm, the legislature has acted to ban a harm, not to single out any particular group or individual. The cases are legion that permit the believer to be subject to such laws. Where the law does not cover all those who produce the same harm, however, questions arise regarding whether the law was passed to prevent a particular harm or to burden certain specific entities. Where the law targets a religious organization or religion in general – and particularly if animus or hostility can be discerned through the language of the law – the Court has been disinclined to uphold the law.

If the law discriminates against a religious organization or religion in general, that law is constitutionally suspect, and therefore rightly subject to close judicial scrutiny.[26] Thus, the dominant approach has been to couple the application of the rule of law to religious entities, with a strong rule against discrimination aimed at particular religious sects, or religion in general.

The First Amendment cases applying neutral laws to religious entities

The Court has routinely upheld laws that have been passed for the general public good and without reference to religion. As I explained earlier, these are known as "neutral, generally applicable laws." In *Reynolds*, the Court sustained the federal anti-polygamy law that governed the Utah Territory. The law was neutral on its face – it outlawed polygamy by anyone, regardless of belief.

Reynolds was more complicated than the run-of-the-mill case involving neutral, generally applicable law. While *Reynolds* involved a law that applied to everyone and was written in neutral language, it was common knowledge that the motivation behind the law was to suppress the Mormon growth in the Northwest.[27] Some have pointed to the fact the Mormons were disproportionately impacted by the law, because they were they only practicing polygamists. Some have argued, then, that the anti-polygamy law violated the anti-persecution principle. They are wrong, because the law does not single out a particular group, but instead prohibits anyone—religious or not—from engaging in polygamy, and it does so after every state in the union outlawed polygamy. The objection to the law because the Mormons were engaged in the practice sounds a lot like the Catholic bishops' objections to the national sweep of laws creating more opportunities for justice for victims of child sex abuse. Just because they have covered up abuse does not mean that laws that make it more difficult to do so are unconstitutional.

Under the Court's approach, had the law singled out the Mormons, the law would have been unconstitutional. A law singling out Mormons would have indicated that Congress was not concerned about the harm generated by polygamy, but rather was trying to suppress their beliefs. Disparate impact is not enough to scuttle a law, or even to subject it to close judicial scrutiny. Where the language is neutral and the sweep of the law captures everyone now or in the future engaged in the same conduct generating the same harm, it is constitutional. In short, harm is harm, even when a religious entity is disproportionately responsible for inflicting that harm.

The Court's reasoning rests on a judgment about institutional competence: one branch of government is best equipped to assess the public good, and that is the legislature, because it is the most capable of surveying and studying social issues – a legislature can call hearings, appoint expert commissions, and order extensive studies. Courts are incapable of examining the public good in any comprehensive way, because they are limited by the Constitution's "Case and Controversy" requirement to the facts and arguments before them.[28] The executive lacks the multiple contacts with the polity that makes for a more accurate assessment of the public's interest (even if the public's view is not always the equivalent of the public good) and is too capable of acting unilaterally to ensure that deliberation over the public good has taken place.

Because the legislature is superior to the courts and the executive in assessing the public good, where the legislature has spoken in language that is unambiguous, the Court has refused to look behind that language to ferret out improper motive. If the law identifies a harm and it punishes everyone that causes that harm, the law stands. Indeed, the disparate impact argument that would have scuttled the anti-polygamy law in *Reynolds* is a red herring. If an action is harmful to society without reference to the identity of the one who has acted, the fact that only a religious organization engages in that action does not change the calculus of harm.

This reasoning has led the Court to sustain a wide variety of laws that burden religiously motivated conduct. The Amish lost their bid to avoid paying the Social Security taxes for their employees that every other employer must pay.[29] Bob Jones University was not permitted to retain its tax-exempt status if it violated the racial anti-discrimination laws, a rule that applied to all who sought tax-exempt status.[30] The Tony and Susan Alamo Foundation, a nonprofit religious foundation, was required to observe the Fair Labor Standards Act.[31] A United States Air Force captain who was an Orthodox Jew and an ordained rabbi could be prohibited from wearing his yarmulke indoors under a general regulation that banned all headgear not officially part of the uniform.[32] A welfare applicant who did not believe in assigning Social Security numbers to children was required to do so, along with all other applicants for benefits, in order to obtain the benefits.[33] The Northwest Indian Cemetery Protective Association did not have a constitutional right to stop the federal government's neutral plans for federal lands even though it believed the land was sacred.[34] Members of the Church of Scientology were subjected to the tax rules regarding any and all charitable contributions and were not allowed to claim as a deduction contributions for which they received a quid pro quo.[35] Jimmy Swaggart Ministries was required to honor California's generally applicable sales and use taxes on the sale of its religious materials.[36] Religious prisoners could not avoid work detail on Friday afternoons.[37] And drug counselors could be denied unemployment compensation for violating the state's laws banning the use of the hallucinogen peyote, even though it was used as part of a religious ritual, which was the same penalty that would have been accorded any other employee within the state.[38]

Whatever one thinks of the outcome of any one these free exercise cases, they are remarkably consistent in their theory and the application of that theory. They show a dominant jurisprudence of republicanism and ordered liberty.

The last case mentioned – involving drug counselors who used hallucinogens during a religious ritual, were fired and then denied unemployment compensation – is *Employment Division v. Smith*. As I described previously, two drug counselors were employed by a nonprofit company. They ingested an illegal drug, peyote, as part of a Native American Church service, and were fired for engaging in work-related misconduct. There was little dispute that their religious beliefs were sincerely held or that the Native American Church uses peyote in its religious services. But drug counselors were not supposed to use illegal drugs, and they had. When they applied to the state for unemployment compensation, they were denied for having engaged in work-related misconduct. Following the denial, they argued that the First Amendment forbade the state from denying unemployment compensation when the conduct that led to their firing was religiously motivated.

The *Smith* majority evaluated the case against the entire spectrum of its free exercise precedents, and accurately concluded that under the Free Exercise Clause, "the approach in accord with the vast majority of our precedents, is to hold the [strict scrutiny] test inapplicable to [free exercise] cases" involving neutral, generally applicable laws.[39] For the

Court, the case was essentially a case of first impression in that it involved a demand for accommodation where the underlying religious conduct was illegal, which distinguished it from the preceding cases.[40]

Since it was decided over twenty years ago, many commentators, both scholarly and otherwise, have characterized *Smith* as a dramatic, unjustified departure from previous free exercise cases. This interpretation of the case is so prevalent that many treat it within and outside the field as obvious truth. It is false. But religious lobbyists rode this false characterization right over to Congress to obtain RFRA.

The lobbyists argued that *Smith* was controlled by two cases: *Sherbert v. Verner,*[41] and *Wisconsin v. Yoder.*[42] This misleading interpretation, led by preeminent legal academics, and echoed by religious lobbyists, shoved to the side the likes of *Reynolds v. United States,*[43] *Braunfeld v. Brown,*[44] *United States v. Lee,*[45] *Gillette v. United States,*[46] and other important cases. As with all lobbyists, they highlighted for Congress what they wanted members to see and swept under the rug anything that hurt their cause.

The claim that *Smith* was a far departure from accepted doctrine was used to castigate the Court unfairly and then to launch the first extreme free exercise statute, RFRA,[47] its state counterparts,[48] and RLUIPA.[49] That this disturbing reconfiguration of power within the United States was prompted by a misleading analysis of a single Supreme Court decision should make Americans not just unhappy, but angry.

Smith is a landmark case, in part because it generated tremendous resistance in the law schools and among intellectuals and, therefore, a great deal of publicity, but more importantly, because it marked the Court's self-conscious decision to survey its free exercise jurisprudence and choose the dominant approach. According to the Court, the "vast majority" of its free exercise cases had deferred to legislative judgments on public policy, where the law was "generally applicable" and "neutral."[50] The Court was positively correct in its assessment of its own jurisprudence.

The cases involving laws that treated religion with animus or hostility

Under the First Amendment, strict scrutiny has been reserved for a small number of cases – those involving laws that target religion or exhibit animus or hostility toward religion. That is to say, where there is reason to suspect invidious discrimination, the government's actions are subject to close examination. The Court articulated the principle in 1997 as follows: "The Free Exercise Clause commits government itself to religious tolerance, and upon even slight suspicion that proposals for state intervention stem from animosity to religion or distrust of its practices, all officials must pause to remember their own high duty to the Constitution and to the rights it secures." In effect, the Court was describing "the fundamental" principle of the First Amendment as the "nonpersecution principle."[51]

In point of fact, the Court has not needed to address a large number of laws that discriminate against believers in the United States. That is because the United States and its legislatures have been generous toward religious entities. As the Court noted in *Smith*, "a society that believes in the negative protection accorded to religious belief can be expected to be solicitous of that value in its legislation."[52]

The leading decision addressing when strict scrutiny should be applied against laws that substantially burden religion is *Church of Lukumi Babalu Aye v. City of Hialeah*,[53] which was decided three years after *Smith* and mere months before RFRA was signed into law. There, the city passed an ordinance outlawing the "sacrifice" of animals. The Court looked to whether every actor that slaughtered an animal received the same treatment, and concluded that the law was not generally applicable: the Santerians could not slaughter animals as part of their worship service, but others could, e.g., kosher butchers. Because the Santerians were targeted, the Court mandated strict scrutiny for the law, which the Court held was not generally applicable. The church's lawyer argued to the Supreme Court that the law should fail because the government had not proved a compelling interest in the least restrictive means. The city lost, but not on the standard proposed by the church. The Court applied ordinary strict scrutiny, and, consistent with all former cases, did not invoke the "least restrictive means" test.

The Court also has applied strict scrutiny to cases in which the government treated religious reasons less favorably than secular ones. In *Sherbert v. Verner*, the Court addressed the question whether a Sabbatarian could obtain unemployment compensation after refusing to work on her Sabbath, Saturday. The South Carolina Unemployment Compensation Act "provide[d] that, to be eligible for benefits, a claimant must be 'able to work and . . . available for work'; and, further, that a claimant is ineligible for benefits 'if . . . [s]he has failed, without good cause . . . to accept available suitable work when offered [her] by the employment office or the employer. . . . '" It appears that the state's application of the "good cause" requirement is what bothered the Court. "Good cause" was used to permit exceptions to the law for valid secular reasons but not for religious reasons. The state's willingness to engage in an individualized determination that permitted secular reasons to justify missing work, but not religious ones, led the Court to apply strict scrutiny and hold the statute unconstitutional.

Sherbert controlled the next few unemployment compensation cases. *Thomas v. Review Bd. of Ind. Employment Sec. Div.* involved a man who quit his job at a foundry after being transferred to a division that manufactured armaments, claiming "his religious beliefs prevented him from participating in the production of war materials." The state denied his unemployment claim "by applying disqualifying provisions of the Indiana Employment Security Act," which prohibited any "individual who has voluntarily left his employment without good cause" from receiving benefits.[54] The Supreme Court reversed. *Hobbie v. Unemployment Appeals Commission of Florida* involved a woman whose "employer discharged her when she refused to work certain scheduled hours because of sincerely held religious convictions adopted after beginning employment." Florida's unemployment compensation scheme provided benefits only "to persons who become 'unemployed through no fault of their own.'"[55] The Supreme Court invalidated the law. *Frazee v. Ill. Dep't of Employment Sec.* involved a man who turned down a temporary position "because the job would have required him to work on Sunday" and he told the employer that, "as a Christian, he could not work on 'the Lord's day.'" Unlike the appellant in *Sherbert*, "Frazee was not a member of an established religious sect or church, nor did he claim that his refusal to work resulted from a 'tenet, belief or teaching of an established religious body.'" Even so, the Court found that "Frazee's refusal was based on a sincerely held religious belief" and therefore he was entitled to "invoke First Amendment protection."[56]

Sherbert was widely criticized after it was first announced,[57] because it was such a departure from earlier free exercise cases, but by the late 1970s, a chorus of approval began.[58] The rule, at least as it was later interpreted in *Smith*, makes sense in that where the government permits exemptions from its laws for secular reasons, but denies them for religious reasons, one might suspect anti-religious animus. Therefore, it is defensible to say that such laws should be treated as presumptively unconstitutional, i.e., subjected to strict scrutiny.

But this reasoning is a far cry from the notion that neutral, generally applicable laws should be accorded strict scrutiny. The notion that all neutral, generally applicable laws are presumptively unconstitutional when applied to religious entities opens the door to the most extreme arguments. That is why the Supreme Court did not extend strict scrutiny to cases involving neutral, generally applicable laws except for one.

When read together, *Smith* and *Lukumi* identified two pivotal principles: (1) the courts are to apply a default rule in favor of upholding duly enacted, neutral, and generally applicable laws to all conduct, even if religious; and (2) that default rule is only overcome in the face of evidence of targeting religion for negative treatment.

The misfit case: Strict scrutiny for a generally applicable,
neutral law affecting religious conduct

The outlier case is *Wisconsin v. Yoder*,[59] which I discuss in Chapter 5, but think the facts are worth repeating here to make the point of how extreme the Court's reasoning was. In *Yoder*, the religious claimants were Amish and Mennonite parents, who argued that the compulsory education laws that required children to attend school through age 16 violated their religious principles, which required students to leave school and turn to an agrarian way of life several years early. They also argued that the state law was a threat to their religious way of life, which required them to be "aloof from the world" and had been in place for 300 years. Even though the Wisconsin law was neutral on its face, and generally applicable, the Court applied strict scrutiny, and held that it violated the Free Exercise Clause, because the state had failed to prove a compelling interest in having Amish children go to school until age 16. Chief Justice Burger wrote for the majority:

> Wisconsin's interest in compelling the school attendance of Amish children to age 16 emerges as somewhat less substantial than requiring

such attendance for children generally.... There is no intimation that the Amish employment of their children on family farms is in any way deleterious to their health or that Amish parents exploit children at tender years.[60]

In effect, the Court carved out an exemption from Wisconsin's generally applicable, neutral law solely for the Amish. *Yoder* would be the only case in which the Court applied strict scrutiny to a neutral, generally applicable law.

Had the Court ruled differently in *Yoder*, the Amish would have had to approach their state legislatures to avoid upper-level compulsory education for their children. Instead of the courts imposing their views of public policy on the people, the legislature could have considered and weighed the many competing interests, including the value of religious liberty, the best interests of children, and society's need for a well-educated citizenry. The Court's decision preempted such a debate, and permitted the Amish to make their arguments divorced from any serious consideration of the public good. If one reads *Yoder* with some care, it becomes quite obvious that the Court took it upon itself to preserve a religious way of life regardless of the society's assessment of the public good, that is, to prefer the religious to the legislative. That in itself should have been reason to revisit *Yoder*. But this was also the Court, after all, that decided *Bowers v. Hardwick*, where it used Anglo-American religious reasons to uphold laws against sodomy.

Even though *Yoder* was an anomaly, many in the academy and religious organizations wanted it to be the rule for all cases. Professors Ellis West and William Marshall stood alone for a significant period of time in their defense of the rule of law.[61] In 1990, just after the Court had chosen between the two competing approaches in its free exercise cases in the *Smith* decision, then-University of Chicago Law School professor Michael McConnell set forth a historical argument mandating exemptions for religious actors from legislative enactments.[62] To be fair to Professor McConnell, I will let him describe his conclusions:

> The conclusions of this [article] are (1) that exemptions were seen as a constitutionally permissible means for protecting religious freedom, (2) that constitutionally compelled exemptions were within the contemplation of the framers and ratifiers as a possible interpretation of

the free exercise clause, and (3) that exemptions were consonant with the popular American understanding of the interrelation between the claims of a limited government and a sovereign God. While the historical evidence may not be unequivocal (it seldom is), it does, on balance, support *Sherbert*'s interpretation of the free exercise clause.[63]

Thus, his conclusion was not that he had found evidence for mandatory accommodation, but rather that mandatory accommodation was not inconsistent with the Framers' views. Even prominent scholars who have examined the record with his conclusions in mind have soundly rejected McConnell's milquetoast endorsement of mandatory accommodation.[64] Though I will not retread their potent criticisms, it is important to note that McConnell's thesis was deeply at odds with the reigning theological views during the historical era he examined. Calvinism dominated the culture at the time of the framing, and its tenets required obedience to duly enacted laws unless the law dictated that religious entities abandon their religious beliefs.[65] Many preachers at the time repeatedly urged their believers to obey the rule of law, to such an extent that one can make a case that the rule of law in the United States was instituted in large part from the pulpit.[66]

For the 18th-century preachers, the horizon under which legislatures were to make legitimate law was the public good, as opposed to individual freedom at the expense of the common good. For example, in 1747, Charles Chauncy declared that civil "rulers . . . have an undoubted right to make and execute laws, for the public good."[67]

A separate problem with McConnell's suggestion of mandatory accommodation was that it had not been applied in so many contexts for so many years; his thesis could not explain why his approach had been rejected (or forgotten) until *Yoder* in 1972. If the history supported mandatory exemption, even if weakly, as he suggested, then what had the Court been thinking from 1878 to 1990, aside from the lone decision in *Yoder*?

For the Justices, who viewed *Smith* as a case of first impression, it was an appropriate opportunity to review its entire free exercise jurisprudence to assess it and apply it to this new set of facts. The *Yoder* reasoning called for strict scrutiny of Oregon's neutral, generally applicable unemployment compensation and narcotics laws. That is precisely what the drug counselors' lawyers argued.[68] In other words, they said that the Oregon laws should have been treated as presumptively unconstitutional. They also pressed the argument that this was just another unemployment compensation case and all of those cases had employed strict scrutiny.

But the case was more in sync with the Court's other free exercise cases, where the courts would not second-guess a neutral, generally applicable law. Unlike *Sherbert*, this case did not involve the government treating secular reasons for acting better than religious reasons. The Oregon laws were truly neutral and generally applicable. That argument was pressed heavily by Oregon's Attorney General David Frohnmayer.[69]

During the Court's confidential Conference following the parties' oral arguments, Justice Stevens questioned *Yoder* itself, saying it was "all wrong."[70] The Justices also viewed *Smith* as a case of first impression, because the *Sherbert* line of unemployment compensation cases involved religiously motivated conduct that was *legal*, e.g., attending church. The case asked them to decide how to approach a free exercise claim where the believers' underlying religiously motivated conduct was illegal.[71]

It should have come as no surprise to the scholars of religious liberty or the public that the Court chose the latter. The Court correctly explained: "We have never held that an individual's religious beliefs excuse him from compliance with an otherwise valid law prohibiting conduct that the State is free to regulate." Thus, neutral and generally applicable laws with the "incidental effect" of burdening religious conduct do not offend the First Amendment.[72]

The Court did not close its decision with a simple rejection of the *Yoder* approach, but rather also fit its religion clause jurisprudence into the larger structure of the Constitution and society. The message of the opinion was that Alfred Smith and Galen Black had come to the wrong institution. Religious entities were not required to abandon their desire to engage in particular religious conduct; they could not, however, find their solution in the courts. They were directed to the legislature, where they would have to justify their request for exemption to the body charged with assessing and choosing public policy. The Court explained that discourse would not necessarily disfavor religious entities in this society:

Values that are protected against government interference through enshrinement in the Bill of Rights are not thereby banished from the political process. Just as a society that believes in the negative protection accorded to the press by the First Amendment is likely to enact laws that affirmatively foster the dissemination of the printed word, so also a society that believes in the negative protection accorded to religious belief can be expected to be solicitous of that value in its legislation as well.[73]

Some decried the notion that religious entities could be thrown into the political process,[74] but one purpose of this book is to illustrate how deeply entrenched religious entities have been in the political sphere and especially the legislative process before and after *Smith*. They are pervasive and powerful, which is why they have scored RFRA, RLUIPA, and the state RFRAs.

In the U.S., religious entities do not stand on the political sidelines. For the Court, that conflict was better debated under the horizon of the public good in the legislature than in the rarified atmosphere of a courtroom. The Free Exercise Clause would not be permitted to absolve religious entities of social and legal obligations: "[T]he right of free exercise does not relieve an individual of the obligation to comply with a 'valid and neutral law of general applicability on the ground that the law proscribes (or prescribes) conduct that his religion prescribes (or proscribes)."[75]

With respect to *Yoder*, the Court's attempt to incorporate the decision into its overarching jurisprudence was less convincing. The Court labeled it a "hybrid rights" case where the rights of parents were being combined with the potential for free exercise rights against otherwise neutral laws, giving rise to presumptive unconstitutionality. The reasoning of *Yoder* was directly at odds with the reasoning in *Smith*, however, and a more straightforward assessment would have overruled *Yoder*.

When the Justices were discussing *Smith* in Conference, *Yoder* was questioned and criticized.[76] For very good reason, the Court's preservation of the reasoning in *Yoder* and its introduction of a "hybrid rights" approach has been rejected as unworkable in the lower courts.[77] As I discuss in Chapter 4, if a law does not deserve strict scrutiny under any single constitutional provision, it makes little sense to impose strict scrutiny simply because two weak constitutional claims are invoked. Two weak rights do not amount to a strong constitutional right.

In my view, the Court should have explicitly reversed *Yoder's* irrational protection of the Amish way of life, rather than devising the further problematic "hybrid rights" theory. Had the Court *done so*, we might well not have RFRA or its progeny today.

RFRA's History

After *Smith* was decided, religious lobbyists and academics mislead-ingly asserted that the Court had overturned a long-settled doctrine that required strict scrutiny of any law, no matter how neutral, that substan-tially burdened religious conduct.[78] Even though it wasn't true, one well-known church/state scholar declared that *Smith* was "inconsistent with the original intent, inconsistent with the constitutional text, incon-sistent with doctrine under other constitutional clauses, and inconsistent with precedent."[79] Another wrote that the *Smith* Court's "use of prece-dent is troubling, bordering on the shocking."[80] Yet another said the *Smith* Court "chose... to promote an advocacy of intolerance."[81] The echoes continued with another saying that *Smith* illustrated "judicial willingness to distort precedents to destroy traditional concepts of indi-vidual liberty."[82] According to another, "[T]he Court wanted to reach its result in the worst way, and it succeeded" and in so doing "'depublished' the free exercise clause."[83] It is not hyperbole to say they were all wrong. *Smith* was no tsunami in free exercise law; it was simply a reaffirmation of cornerstone constitutional principles.

The fault for the intense response to the *Smith* decision does not rest entirely on those who misread the previous cases. In part, the Court invited the heated response to *Smith*, by reaching an issue that was neither briefed nor argued. The petitioners Black and Smith and their supporters in the academy believed the case only addressed how *Sher-bert's* strict scrutiny applied, not whether it applied at all. Why? Because *Smith* was an unemployment law case and the four preceding unem-ployment cases starting with *Sherbert* had applied strict scrutiny to the benefit of the religious entity. In the pigeonhole mentality that frequently infects constitutional thinking, many expected the Court to reach for the prior unemployment cases and those cases alone, and then to dis-pose of the case with little effort. That the Court would look beyond the unemployment compensation aspect of the case to its free exercise cases in other contexts and ultimately to the larger question of whether a generally applicable, neutral law is binding on religious entities was unexpected.

In hindsight, the Court might have laid the groundwork for the deci-sion by asking for re-briefing and re-argument, which is the usual proce-dure when the Justices perceive a new and potentially dispositive issue in a case already under consideration.[84] There was no emergency that blocked the Court from holding the case over for the next Term. Instead, the Court moved forward without warning. There was not even any intimation from the bench at oral argument that the members were preparing to comprehensively review the entirety of its free exercise jurisprudence.[85] Even those like Professor William Marshall, who had defended the rule of law approach before *Smith*, castigated the Court: "The opinion is . . . a paradigmatic example of judicial overreaching. The holding extends beyond the facts of the case, the lower court's decision on the issue, and even the briefs of the parties. In fact, it appears that the Court framed the free exercise issue in virtually the broadest terms possible in order to allow it to reach its landmark result."[86]

It might have been better had the members in the majority in *Smith*-Justices Antonin Scalia, Byron White, John Paul Stevens, Anthony Kennedy, and Chief Justice William Rehnquist – let the parties and those watching know that they were ready to repudiate the misfit approach in *Yoder* in favor of a clear affirmation of ordered liberty. If there ever were a need for the venting function of the First Amendment's Free Speech Clause, this was it. In the end, though, these procedural objections do not render its substantive analysis wrong.

Even so, Congress listened to the religious entities and the law professors and within four months of the *Smith* decision, held hearings to castigate the Supreme Court.[87] Religious groups, believing they had lost more than they actually had, turned to Congress to deliver what they claimed was their constitutional right: a "return" to strict scrutiny of every law in every free exercise case. This rhetoric was riddled with mistaken understandings of the Court's free exercise doctrine to date. To unpack what actually happened, I offer the following chart of the differences between the Court's free exercise doctrine, RFRA, RLUIPA, and the state RFRAs. The most important element to understand is that the "least restrictive means" test in RFRA. RLUIPA, and the state RFRAs was nowhere to be found in the Court's First Amendment free exercise cases.

In essence, with RFRA, Congress brazenly stepped into the shoes of the Court. RFRA'S drafters selected the constitutional standards they preferred and required them to be applied in every circumstance where the Court had ruled they should not be. RFRA is Congress's attempt to concoct its own free exercise clause out of the Court's constitutional doctrine. The following chart should help to explain the differences:

The Never-Ending Spiral of Extreme Religious Liberty

1.   1878-present
Ordered Liberty Under the Constitution, First Amendment, Free Exercise Clause
Employment Division v. Smith, 494 U.S. 872 (1990)
Church of Lukumi Babalu Aye v. City of Hialeah, 508 U.S. 520 (1993)
Rules: a. Believer must prove law imposes a substantial burden.
        b. A neutral, generally applicable law is constitutional unless irrational.
        c. If law is not neutral or not generally applicable, ordinary strict scrutiny applies: the government must prove a compelling interest and that the law is narrowly tailored
        d. the right is only good against the government (state action)

2.   1972
Wisconsin v. Yoder, 406 U.S. 205 (1972)
Rules: a. Believer must prove a substantial burden
        b. Only case where a neutral, generally applicable law is subjected to strict scrutiny
        c. Government must prove a compelling interest and that the law is narrowly tailored

3.   1993
Religious Freedom Restoration Act of 1993
Rules: a. Believer must prove a substantial burden

        b. Government must prove a neutral, generally applicable law serves a compelling interest

        c. Narrow tailoring is replaced by the more extreme "least restrictive means"

        d. Relief permitted only "against a government"

4. 2000
Amendments to Religious Freedom Restoration Act (further expansion of rights for believers)
Rules: a. Expands definition of "religious exercise" to be: "any exercise of religion, whether or not compelled by, or central to, a system of religious belief," including "the use, building, conversion of real property for the purpose of religious exercise" so long as the person, assembly, or institution "uses or intends to use the property for that purpose."

5. 2000
Religious Land Use and Institutionalized Persons Act
Rules: a. Believer must prove a substantial burden

        b. Government must prove a neutral, generally applicable land use or prison law serves a compelling interest

        c. Narrow tailoring is replaced by the more extreme "least restrictive means"

        d. Relief permitted only "against a government"

If you compare the Court's articulation of strict scrutiny and RFRA's formula in the chart, it becomes apparent that the Coalition borrowed free exercise doctrine up to the point it could hand religious lobbyists the maximum benefit under the existing free exercise cases, but the religious lobbyists were not even satisfied with that. RFRA further piles on the least restrictive means test, which is never applied in the free exercise cases, and requires the courts to tightly mold the law to fit the believer.

"Religious Freedom Restoration Act" was a brilliant name for this new invention. Everyone wants "religious freedom" and by calling it a "restoration," it provided a level of comfort to members. One cannot "restore" a standard that never existed before, however, and RFRA's application of a compelling interest test coupled with a least restrictive means test to neutral, generally applicable laws is novel, to put it mildly. It is also irrational. In truth, RFRA was an attempt to overrule the Court's constitutional interpretation, and to say otherwise is to engage in high-level intellectual gymnastics divorced from the text, history, and fundamental common sense.

Proof of RFRA's power to mislead continues to pile up. The Alliance Defending Freedom and other conservative religious groups have fought to spread the contagion of RFRA to the states in 2014, and have failed to educate the members on what the bills actually mean. One Ohio member withdrew his RFRA bill after learning it would lead to discrimination against homosexuals and same-sex couples, saying, "'What we did want [with a state RFRA], what the intent was, was to protect our First Amendment religious rights.'"[88] Senator David Burns of Maine sponsored a similar state RFRA in Maine, though it was rejected by the Maine Senate. In support of the bill, Sen. Burns claimed, "'This is not a partisan issue, it's an American issue.'"[89] These state RFRA sponsors apparently had no idea that their own bill went well beyond First Amendment doctrine! I doff my hat to whoever created the name, though it would be best for the entire country if they were not called upon again to name a statute, given its power to mislead.

The political tactics adopted by the Coalition for the Free Exercise of Religion that led to its slide through Congress

At the beginning, civil rights groups fell for the rhetoric and joined the religious groups; they were oblivious to how it would be invoked to undermine civil rights, foment discrimination, and hurt the vulnerable. On its surface, it seemed like a harmless, do-good law. Why? Because they didn't understand the legalese, and were never told the specific policies the religious groups intended to attack with it. The only member of Congress to suggest an amendment was Sen. Harry Reid, who understood that it would impose new burdens on the country's prisons.[90] The amendment went nowhere.

The hearings were filled with vitriol aimed at the Court, and with members of Congress castigating the author of *Smith*, Justice Scalia, in particular. The same tactic was used among academics. It was as though Scalia had singlehandedly destroyed religious liberty. To this day, those who despise *Smith* talk about it in terms of, what "Scalia wrote," or "Scalia said." In fact, the Justices who joined Scalia – Chief Justice Rehnquist, and Justices Kennedy, White, and Stevens – had sided with its approach even before *Smith*, but castigating Justice Scalia was part of the public relations attack on *Smith*.

While RFRA was percolating in Congress, the case of *Church of Lukumi Babalu Aye v. City of Hialeah* was advancing in the federal courts. The Supreme Court heard the case on Nov. 4, 1992 and decided it on June 11, 1993. The irony is bountiful. The religious lobbyists were testifying in Congress in favor of RFRA's extreme standard as though it had always been the First Amendment standard in every case, whether or not the law was neutral and generally applicable. Across the street, at the Court, the litigators for the Church of Lukumi were trying to persuade the Court to adopt the extreme RFRA standard in a case of alleged discrimination. Five months before RFRA was signed into law by President Clinton, the Court announced the *Lukumi* decision, and refused to embrace the RFRA standard the the Church of Lukumi demanded of the Court and the religious lobbyists sought in Congress. The church lost at the Court, while the lobbyists won in Congress. But no one changed the title of RFRA from "Restoration" to "Transformation" as honesty would have required.

The Court ruled that if a law is neutral and generally applicable, as in *Smith*, rationality review applies, not strict scrutiny. But if a law is not neutral or not generally applicable, strict scrutiny applies, which requires the government to prove a compelling interest and narrow tailoring (not that it was the least restrictive means for this believer). The city lost on the standard, but, tragically, Congress paid no need to the Court's articulation, again, of the First Amendment's standard, and instead forged ahead to enact a standard that was no restoration.

After three years of hearings in which the members of the House and Senate denounced the Court (in over 450 pages of the Congressional Record) for abandoning a doctrine that had never been applied in free exercise cases, Congress passed RFRA, which established what *Smith's* detractors claimed (incorrectly) the preceding doctrine had required.

It is not an exaggeration to say that the law professors' and religious lobbyists' inaccurate representations of the prior case law led Congress down the wrong path. Congress was persuaded that it was standard free exercise doctrine to subject every single law to strict scrutiny, an approach the Supreme Court had never even broached, let alone reached and that social security entails imposition on the government of the least restrictive means test. But all of the blame cannot be placed at the feet of the lobbyists.

Congress did not do its homework, and deserves the vast majority of the blame for RFRA and its perhaps unintended, but destructive impact. No one discussed how this new legal device would apply in clergy sex abuse cases, or medical neglect cases, or cases involving polygamy or corporal punishment. There was no testimony about whether for-profit companies – say like Wal-Mart or McDonald's – would be able to invoke RFRA to avoid their legal obligations to their employees. There was certainly no discussion of the fact that a number of religious groups hoped to use it to trump the Fair Housing Act so as to keep renters whose beliefs differed from theirs from moving into their apartment buildings, particularly if they were single mothers, unmarried couples, or same-sex couples. Nor was there in 1993 any discussion of how the RFRA formulation would make it easier to discriminate against homosexuals and women. Or of the possibility that employers might find it useful to carve up medical benefits according to their religious beliefs. Yet, these are all problems the law has actually faced prompted its enactment.

In *Smith*, the Court encouraged believers to go to the legislatures for relief from an otherwise constitutional law that imposes a burden on religious practice. For example, the Court pointed approvingly to state law exemptions for the use of peyote from generally applicable drug laws.[91] And, in fact, a number of states and the federal government would follow suit after *Smith*, in effect proving the efficacy of the Court's approach for religious entities. But those positive developments for religious liberty after *Smith* were lost in the maelstrom of invective against it. In a move that was fueled by the endemic misinterpretations of the Court's pre-*Smith* jurisprudence and, to be frank, political opportunism, the religious entities looked to Congress to reverse the Court's doctrine. Ironically, the religious organizations did precisely what *Smith*'s detractors seemed to believe they either could not or should not: they petitioned the most powerful legislature in the country, Congress, and they obtained what they sought. In effect, they proved the political feasibility of the *Smith* Court's political theory.

With *Smith*, the Court had articulated the relationship between religious entities, the government, and society. Its constitutional vision was based on fundamental principles of republican democracy, the public good, and the rule that no one should harm another. The statute that was generated in the wake of *Smith* – RFRA – raised the corollary question whether Congress could unilaterally rearrange the relationship between religious entities, the law, and the public good. If so, then the larger republican and democratic principles at the base of *Smith* could be abandoned in favor of permitting religious entities to avoid most generally applicable, neutral laws. It would take the decision addressing RFRA – *City of Boerne v. Flores* – to vindicate the bedrock republican principles that justify and require subjecting religious entities to the generally applicable, neutral laws that govern everyone else.

The Court Considers RFRA

From the 1960s into the 1990s, law schools taught two constitutional principles that were largely unquestioned; one might even say they were articles of faith. First, no government could enforce a law against a religious believer unless the government could prove that its law was passed for a compelling interest.[92] Second, Congress held the power to increase constitutional rights at will.[93] A generation of law students was taught that these principles were self-evident from the Constitution and Supreme Court cases.

In 1990, the U.S. Supreme Court rejected the first principle, and in 1997, it rejected the second. Many perceived a revolution at the Court, but it was not. In fact, in both categories, the four decades between 1960 and 2000 were a time when the Court straddled sometimes-conflicting doctrinal approaches. Facing an either/or choice in each category, the Court in the 1990s did not so much invent new doctrines as it chose to excise doctrines that were causing friction. A 1997 Supreme Court case confirmed that the Court had made a definitive choice in each area. That case is *City of Boerne v. Flores*.[94]

The two issues in *Boerne* – free exercise protection and the power of Congress – typically belong in separate constitutional domains. The first rests on interpretation of the Free Exercise Clause, while the latter requires interpretation of Congress's powers, including Section 5 of the Fourteenth Amendment. Indeed, a conventional view would place the first under the heading of "individual rights," and the second under "congressional power," and therefore it is customary to teach them in separate constitutional law classes. This is a fault line in the law schools' approach, because it obscures the fact that every right is situated within a larger constitutional structure. Republican representative democracy – not to mention much theology and moral philosophy from John Locke to John Stuart Mill to Robert Nozick – rests on the assumption that no individual has the right to harm others, and therefore it limits rights a fortiori. When law schools, and their graduates, divorce rights from their structural context, they treat rights as a pure libertarian would: without reference to the rights holders' obligations to society. While the nation's law schools inculcated this mistake for decades, the Supreme Court has not made this mistake in the vast majority of its cases.

Free exercise and even disestablishment theories too often have focused on religious entities by themselves, as though their well-being or their liberty alone is an appropriate proxy for the general public good. That is certainly how the topic was taught in most law schools. This focus on religious entities and their corresponding interests and concerns is myopic and antidemocratic, and has led some legislatures to grant legislative exemptions for child neglect and physical abuse and some courts to refuse to hold churches accountable for their criminal and tortious actions, which are plainly in conflict with the public good. There is no simple equation between the needs of religious entities and the public good.

The two domains were unavoidably united – like the overlapping areas in a Venn diagram – in the *Boerne* case, because the congressional enactment at issue involved congressional deregulation of religious conduct. The overlap required the Court, in a single opinion, to speak simultaneously to the scope of the rights under the Free Exercise Clause and the power of Congress to alter those rights. The result was a remarkably comprehensive theory of the role of religion in the polity, both as a private force and as a political actor.

The congressional power cases before Boerne v. Flores

From the 1930s until 1995, the Supreme Court systematically deferred to congressional exercises of power. The result was an unaccountable, headstrong Congress that sincerely believed it held plenary power over all issues, despite the plain meaning of the Constitution's structure and language limiting its powers. The federalism component of the Constitution disappeared through inattention, and Congress's power subsumed the states'. By 1995, the Court began to see the problems attendant upon an unaccountable Congress, and gingerly began to draw some boundaries around what had become an arena with no limits. The Court's reinstitution of federalism brought to the foreground the inherent limits of Congress's power, vis-à-vis the states. Congress was supposed to be an institution of enumerated powers, not plenary power. Initially, the Court was accused of being insular, harsh, and unsympathetic to civil rights.[95] For others, the Court was simply power hungry,[96] but in fact the cases have been moderate in trend, with the Court striking the most outrageous reaches for federal power, including the Religious Freedom Restoration Act, as it has upheld the Family Medical Leave Act[97] and Title II of the Americans with Disability Act.[98] RFRA and *City of Boerne v. Flores* arrived at the Court in this era of revived federalism. Thus, the Court was predisposed to ask whether Congress constitutionally held the power it exercised.

RFRA Violates the Separation of Power

RFRA dramatically increases the rights of religious believers against all laws, as compared to the First Amendment. Therefore, the Court in *Boerne* had to address what power Congress holds to expand rights of religious liberty against either the federal or state governments.

First, the Court rejected the notion that Congress could create new constitutional rights against the federal government through its enumerated powers. There simply was no such power. That should have spelled the end of RFRA permanently, and had Congress not had the chutzpah to "amend" RFRA so it only applied to federal law in 2000, we would not have to deal with it today.

The open question in the case then was whether perhaps Congress could create new rights against the states through Section 5 of the Fourteenth Amendment. As discussed below, the Court held that even Sec. 5 did not create such an opportunity against the states. Therefore, the only path to RFRA should have been through a constitutional amendment. In other words, RFRA is just plain unconstitutional.

The background behind the Section 5 cases leading up to Boerne

Beginning in the late 1950s and the 1960s, the United States witnessed an explosive growth in federal civil rights law. Congress passed increasingly expansive civil rights acts.[99] The attorney general enforced these new laws in the face of strong opposition in the states.[100] And the Supreme Court dramatically expanded the protections afforded under the Equal Protection Clause in the wake of its landmark 1954 case, *Brown v. Board of Education*.[101] The Court struck down laws forbidding interracial marriage[102] and interracial cohabitation,[103] and requiring ballots to indicate the race of candidates.[104] It overturned convictions for disturbing the peace by sitting at race-reserved lunch counters,[105] for refusing to sit in a courtroom's segregated section,[106] and for murder where there was prima facie evidence of discrimination in grand and petit jury selection.[107] The Court also expanded the power of Congress under the Commerce Clause to prohibit racial discrimination in motels,[108] expanded the definition of state action by defining a private restaurant as a state actor where the restaurant leased public space and was maintained with public funds,[109] and by including in the definition of state action any agency of the state taking action.[110] Finally, the Court refused to permit private discrimination in housing.[111]

It was a time of cataclysmic but positive social change for the rights of minorities. As between the states and the federal government, there was no question that the federal government was the protector of liberty.

When the federal government freed minorities from the oppressive discrimination under which they had labored for two centuries in the United
States, it was a noble enterprise. The federal government was liberating
an oppressed people, and in the process unmasking the depth of the
entrenched racial discrimination in the country. While the United States
deserves plenty of criticism for its Constitution's early acquiescence in
slavery and then its failure to end discrimination for decades following
the Civil War and the Reconstruction era, the 1960s civil rights era was
impressive.

Inevitably, the reasoning of expanding rights found its way into other
doctrines. It certainly influenced Justice Brennan's push to expand the
rights of religious entities starting with *Sherbert* in 1963. The equal protection issues and the free exercise issues, though, were on completely
different planes. Minorities were demanding, and obtaining – at least
from the federal government – equal rights with all others under the law.
They were asking for a level playing field, but the religious entities were
starting from a constitutional doctrine that mandated equality to start and
wanted more: privileges beyond equal treatment.

The religious entities did not request equality, but rather the right
to trump the law, to be treated better than others who were similarly
situated and governed by the same law. Thus, while the Court's work for
minorities was heroic, its decision to abandon the rule of law for religious
entities was a serious mistake, for which the United States continues to
pay in terms of harm to children, the inculcation of terrorism in the
prisons, and the dilution of private property rights. Like the free exercise cases, the congressional power cases beginning in the 1960s sprang
from an environment conducive to altering the law and veered off the
right course until the 1990s. The deference to the federal government –
which was earned by its valiant and successful fight for civil rights for
minorities – was transformed into a dogmatic belief in the unassailability
of whatever Congress attempted. The result was an engraved invitation
to congressional overreaching.

The RFRA was invalidated in *City of Boerne v. Flores* on the ground
that it violated the separation of powers, was beyond Congress's power,
violated Article V's constitutional amendment procedures, and violated
federalism. In *Boerne*, a church in little Boerne, Texas, applied for a
demolition permit in a historic preservation district. As typically happens

in land use cases, the parties discussed a middle ground, e.g., preserving some of the building, while permitting demolition of that which was beyond the historic district's sight line. Instead of reaching a compromise, however, the church filed a federal lawsuit invoking RFRA and argued the City's historic preservation laws did not govern its actions.

The case posed the question: what precise power did Congress have to construct constitutional rights?

The Court's answer shocked the academy and, more important, Congress: Congress could enforce the guarantees of the 14th Amendment, including the incorporated bill of rights, but it could not unilaterally create and expand upon constitutional rights. In other words, for the Constitution to change, it had to be amended via Article V and its onerous requirement[112] of a two-thirds vote in Congress followed by ratification by three-fourths of the states – not by a simple majority vote in both houses of Congress. As four members of the Court had explained in dissent in *EEOC v. Wyoming*,[113] at the apex of Congress's power, "[a]llowing Congress to protect constitutional rights statutorily that it has independently defined fundamentally alters our scheme of government."[114]

The academy was so entrenched in its belief that Congress could set the level of constitutional rights at will, that it had coined a phrase to explain it: Congress had the power, they said, to "ratchet" up rights.[115] This novel power was defended on the ground that it was a "one-way ratchet,"[116] so no rights could be diminished by Congress, but they could be increased at will. If that was Congress's proper role, then RFRA was a no-brainer, or so they thought. It dramatically expanded the rights of religious entities, and certainly did not diminish them.

For that reason, RFRA's legislative history includes precious little discussion of Congress's power to enact it, despite the number of pages devoted to it in the Congressional Record. If the prominent law professors were not concerned about congressional power, one can be certain that the members of Congress were even less so. The basic justification for RFRA was provided by a single law professor, who described it as "[a]n attempt to create a statutory right to the free exercise of religion, pursuant to Congress' power under Section 5 of the Fourteenth Amendment to enforce the Fourteenth Amendment and therefore presumably to enforce all the rights incorporated in the Fourteenth Amendment."[117]

The leading case regarding Congress's power under Section 5 of the 14th Amendment was *Katzenbach v. Morgan*.[118] Like *Sherbert*, which took the Free Exercise Clause astray, the controversial *Katzenbach v. Morgan*, was written by Justice Brennan, who was appointed by a Republican administration, but who became one of the most libertarian Justices. He was not an ideologue, but rather pursued his libertarian agenda pragmatically. He typically altered the Court's direction not by overruling previous precedents, but rather by doing what he did in both *Sherbert* and *Katzenbach*: engrafting onto the existing doctrine a new branch that sent the doctrine in a new direction. He was very good at crafting a change in emphasis that would then alter doctrine, outcomes, and eventually the theory.

In *Katzenbach*, the Court addressed the constitutionality of the Voting Rights Act of 1965, Section 4, which prohibited the states from excluding any voter on the ground that he or she could not speak or write English. The law affected several hundred thousand immigrants from Puerto Rico in New York. Registered voters in New York City brought suit, arguing that Section 4 was unconstitutional, because Congress lacked the power to override their voting laws, which required English proficiency. The question was plain, even if the answer was somewhat complicated: what power did Congress have to pass Section 4 of the Voting Rights Act of 1965?

Justice Brennan provided two rationales to uphold the act. First, Congress was simply enforcing constitutional guarantees against the states pursuant to Section 5 of the 14th Amendment, which states: "Congress shall have power to enforce, by appropriate legislation, the provisions of this article."[119] The Constitution forbade discrimination on the basis of race or origin, and therefore Congress was enforcing the guarantee to equal treatment. The problem with that analysis, however, was that the Court previously had held that there was no constitutional right that forbade English proficiency requirements.[120] Therefore, Congress was requiring the states to do more than the Constitution required, and the states argued that such an expansive requirement violated the reserved rights of the states in the Constitution.

Justice Brennan explained this expansion as Congress exercising its "prophylactic" power.[121] Where the states had engaged in persistent constitutional violations, Congress was given broad latitude to force the states to tow a more difficult line than the Constitution required. There was no question that the discrimination at issue was widespread, intransigent, and persistent. In an earlier case, the Court had characterized the congressional record for the Voting Rights Act as follows:

> Two points emerge vividly from the voluminous legislative history of the [Voting Rights] Act contained in the committee hearings and floor debates. First: Congress felt itself confronted by an insidious and pervasive evil, which had been perpetrated in certain parts of our country through unremitting and ingenious defiance of the Constitution. Second: Congress concluded that the unsuccessful remedies, which it had prescribed in the past, would have to be replaced by sterner and more elaborate measures in order to satisfy the clear commands of the Fifteenth Amendment.[122]

The prophylactic power made sense in the face of the studied recalcitrance to equal protection guarantees in the South and parts of the North during the 1950s. If state governments decided to flout the Constitution's requirements over and over again, Congress had the power to hold them to even stricter conduct than the Constitution required in order to get them to obey the Constitution. This reading of Congress's power under Section 5 was not controversial.

More controversial was the second *Katzenbach* rationale. Justice Brennan introduced a new element to assess congressional power – the so-called "ratchet theory," which would have permitted Congress to expand the constitutional right itself by simple majority vote. The theory was criticized by Justice John Marshall Harlan, in dissent, who accused Justice Brennan of expanding congressional power too far: "In effect the Court reads § 5 of the Fourteenth Amendment as giving Congress the power to define the substantive scope of the Amendment."[123] Harlan reasoned that if Congress had unilateral power to alter the scope of constitutional rights that it could decrease as well as increase them. Brennan dismissed in a footnote Harlan's logical deduction that the power to set rights included the power to diminish them.[124]

From 1966 to 1990 (only three years shy of *Sherbert*'s reign), the Court had available a theory that would provide Congress considerable new power.

As indicated earlier, the ratchet-up theory became quite popular in the law schools, and many legal scholars came to accept that Congress did indeed have such a power. Professor Archibald Cox explained the force of the ratchet theory as follows:

> The etymological meaning of section 5 may favor the narrower reading. Literally, "to enforce" means to compel performance of the obligations imposed; but the linguistic argument lost much of its force once the South Carolina and Morgan cases decided that the power to enforce embraces any measure appropriate to effectuating the performance of the state's constitutional duty.[125]

There was not universal acceptance, however. Professor William Cohen of Stanford Law School criticized the theory in 1977 in the *Stanford Law Review* as follows:

> Justice Brennan's "ratchet" interpretation of section 5 presents two problems. First, it does not satisfactorily explain why Congress may move the due process or equal protection handle in only one direction.... The second and more significant problem with the ratchet theory is the difficulty in determining the direction in which the handle is turning.[126]

But it also suffered from an ivory tower assessment of liberty. Increasing the liberty to act for one almost always means a diminution of liberty for someone else. This is a zero-sum game.

In the free exercise context, Brennan had been able to insert the novel reasoning of *Sherbert* into a small number of cases involving virtually identical facts. While this was not a striking accomplishment, he was less successful in propagating the ratchet theory in the Court's cases. Unlike *Sherbert*'s new rule in the free exercise context, this new congressional power theory was never the dispositive basis for any Supreme Court decision.[127] Even in *Katzenbach*, it was only an alternative basis for decision. During the same term as *Katzenbach*, and a few months before it was decided, the Court held that Congress could not "attack evils not comprehended by the Fifteenth Amendment" and therefore devalued the currency of the ratchet theory – at least with respect to a similar amendment – several months before it appeared. Five members of the Court rejected the theory in 1970 in *Oregon v. Mitchell*,[128] which then-Justice Rehnquist pointed out in *City of Rome v. United States*.[129]

In *Oregon v. Mitchell*,[130] for which admittedly one needs a scorecard to know precisely what was held and who on the Court reached the holding, five justices agreed to some limits on congressional power under Section 5; as was stated in the dissent to *EEOC v. Wyoming*, there was a "limitation on the extent to which Congress may substitute its own judgment for that of the states and assume this Court's 'role of final arbiter.'"[131] Thus, by the time *Boerne* arrived at the Court in 1996, there were two competing theories in Section 5 cases in circumstances where Congress forced states to toe a line more restrictive than the Constitution.

While the ratchet theory was never as widely accepted in the academy as the *Sherbert* approach to free exercise cases,[132] the bulk of law professors assumed that the RFRA would be upheld on the theory. And it did not appear to be wishful thinking, but rather a conviction that the ratchet theory was impregnable. Nor is there any indication that the members of Congress read their power any more narrowly than the ratchet theory would have afforded.

When Congress passed the RFRA, it forced the Court's hand on the Section 5 issue. The petitioner's certiorari petition specifically asked the Court to answer the question whether Justice Brennan's prophylactic power theory explained Congress's power under Section 5, or whether the ratchet theory did. Once the question was posed, academics became more circumspect than they had previously been, and a number argued against the ratchet theory. For example, Professors Eugene Gressman and Angela Carmella argued as follows:

> [O]ne can imagine other RFRA-like statutes [justified under the ratchet theory] that would (1) ratchet obscenity and pornography up to the status of free speech, which the Court has refused to do, (2) ratchet up the personal interest in reputation to the level of a constitutionally protected liberty interest, (3) ratchet up the right to an education to the status of a constitutionally protected right, subject to strict scrutiny, (4) ratchet up gender and sexual orientation to the highest levels of scrutiny, (5) define and ratchet up additional unenumerated privacy rights as yet unrecognized by the Court, or (6) restore and ratchet up those privileges and immunities of citizens of the United States that were destroyed by the Slaughterhouse Cases. In short, the RFRA model can be used by Congress to reform, destroy or restore a wide variety of

the Court's constitutional interpretations, thus putting Congress into the heart of the judicial function.[133]

The ratchet theory thus was an opportunity for tremendous mischief by a Congress that could alter constitutional rights on a sliding scale through simple majority vote. Indeed, in light of the practice in both Houses of Congress of using "unanimous consent," which permits the leaders to bring a bill to the floor with virtually no other members present and with no recorded vote, rights could be altered by a mere handful of the leadership in either House. The Court simply could not sign on to such a theory, because it was too far removed from the accepted constitutional practices surrounding rights. Moreover, it sidelined the Court in constitutional determinations. Accordingly, not a single member of the Court wrote approvingly of the ratchet theory in the landmark congressional power case, *City of Boerne v. Flores.*

City of Boerne v. Flores

After the sharp and even bitter criticism of *Smith*, the Supreme Court might well have thought better of its free exercise reasoning when it considered RFRA, and backtracked. That did not happen. The Court had another opportunity to alter its free exercise doctrine or to cast it in a different light, but the Court held firm on the rule requiring courts to apply neutral, generally applicable laws to religious entities and judged RFRA in light of that constitutional standard.

Congress's action in passing RFRA, however, reopened the door to religious entities that had sought to trump generally applicable, neutral laws. Indeed, it covered far more instances than Justice Brennan's theory had been permitted to: it applied strict scrutiny to every law in the country, state or federal, executive, legislative, or judicial, and past or present. I represented Boerne and in our opening brief characterized RFRA's scope as "breathtaking." Thus, while *Smith* might have reinstated with clarity the principle that religious entities are properly subject to neutral, generally applicable laws, RFRA threatened to alter the regime altogether and to place religious entities above a vast portion of the law.

This is not a book on congressional power so much as it is about religious accommodation, so I will not describe the Court's reasoning in *Boerne* at length, but suffice it to say that the Court plainly rejected Justice Brennan's ratchet theory:

> Congress' power under § 5, however, extends only to "enforcing" the provisions of the Fourteenth Amendment. . . . The design of the Amendment and the text of § 5 are inconsistent with the suggestion that Congress has the power to decree the substance of the Fourteenth Amendment's restrictions on the States. Legislation which alters the meaning of the Free Exercise Clause cannot be said to be enforcing the Clause. Congress does not enforce a constitutional right by changing what the right is. It has been given the power "to enforce," not the power to determine what constitutes a constitutional violation. Were it not so, what Congress would be enforcing would no longer be, in any meaningful sense, the "provisions of [the Fourteenth Amendment]."[134]

The prophylactic theory, thus, was embraced by itself. Congress could not hold the states to standards more stringent than the Constitution required unless there was proof of widespread and persisting constitutional violations in the states and the federal law was "congruent and proportional" to the degree of constitutional overstepping by the states. Thus, entrenched and invidious discrimination in the vast majority of circumstances across the states against religious entities might have justified RFRA's draconian requirements, but the Court saw no such set of facts, either through judicial notice or the congressional record supporting RFRA.

> While preventive rules are sometimes appropriate remedial measures, there must be a congruence between the means used and the ends to be achieved. . . . A comparison between RFRA and the Voting Rights Act is instructive. In contrast to the record which confronted Congress and the judiciary in the voting rights cases, RFRA's legislative record lacks examples of modern instances of generally applicable laws passed because of religious bigotry.[135]

But the record by itself was not dispositive. The central inquiry was whether Congress had acted in a way that was proportional to the constitutional harm identified. "Regardless of the state of the legislative record, RFRA cannot be considered remedial, preventive legislation, if those terms are to have any meaning. RFRA is so out of proportion to a supposed remedial or preventive object that it cannot be understood as responsive to, or designed to prevent, unconstitutional behavior."[136]

The case simultaneously thus rejected discordant sub-doctrines in both the free exercise and Section 5 contexts. First, the Court upheld *Smith* and refused to hold that strict scrutiny was mandated in free exercise cases involving neutral, generally applicable laws.

Second, the *Boerne* Court chose *Katzenbach*'s prophylactic theory and held that Congress could not give religious entities the right to across-the-board strict scrutiny in the absence of proof of widespread and persisting discrimination against religious entities – proof that the religious entities will never be able to accumulate, because of their significant though often underestimated power in the political sphere and because of the sheer numbers in the United States who are religious. (One of the purposes of this book is to bring to light the remarkable power of religious entities to obtain special treatment in the legislatures, even when they can harm others.)

Moreover, the Court did not limit its reasoning invalidating RFRA to states' rights under Sec. 5 of the Fourteenth Amendment. It also violates the separation of powers and Article V. The most obvious problem with RFRA, which its advocates never want to discuss, is that it features Congress unilaterally taking over the First Amendment's Free Exercise Clause, and, therefore, in reality is an amendment to the Constitution. With RFRA, Congress simply devised the free exercise constitutional standard it prefers, thereby making itself the appellate court of the Supreme Court. By enacting RFRA through a simple majority vote process, Congress also violated Article V, which requires supermajorities to ratify constitutional amendments.

The net result of the *Boerne* decision was to foreclose religious entities' arguments that religious motivation by itself should ever absolve religious actors of neutral laws governing their conduct.

Conclusion

It would be a mistake to think that *Boerne* was only a culmination of U.S. legal principles, because it was also an endpoint of the larger Anglo-American struggle between religious entities and secular authorities, a struggle that had proceeded for hundreds of years. Seemingly unbe-knownst to those lobbying for a religious liberty that undercut neutral, generally applicable laws and permitted religious entities to be above the law, the British government had vast experience in the field, and had rejected the rule they advocated. The next chapter will explain the centuries of history that put *Smith*, RFRA, and *Boerne* in proper perspective.

9

THE DECLINE OF CHURCH
AUTONOMY AND THE RISE OF THE
NO-HARM RULE

There has been an ongoing dialectic among religious entities, the law, and the public good in the West for centuries. This history begins with strong privileges for religious entities and moves toward a requirement that they may not have others anymore than anyone else. This play of power has yielded a legal construct that reflects lessons learned. As Justice Oliver Wendell Holmes said, "the life of the law has not been logic: it has been experience."

There was a time in Anglo-American history when established religious entities were sovereign and the clergy enjoyed special treatment under the law. It would have come as no surprise to anyone that the established religious institution was immune to the requirements of the law or that clergy were relieved of its requirements while all other citizens were not. A citizen could be put to death for raping a child, while a clergy member could commit the same crime and be sentenced to a year at a monastery.

That era, however, was centuries ago. Today, the rule in the United States is that every entity – including a religious entity – is subject to the law.

This chapter places the United States' religious liberty principles in historical context. The contemporary system – reaffirmed in *Employment Division v. Smith* and *Boerne v. Flores* – is not a 20th-century phenomenon, but rather the result of centuries of experience.

There are, of course, many reasons to invoke history: the purpose here is two-fold. First, this chapter is intended to show that there are two British antecedents that informed the U.S. system: (1) the robust – and then dwindling – special treatment of clergy and religious institutions in Britain, and (2) the burgeoning development of the secular common law there, followed by the growth of republicanism and the rule of law here. Both are critical to understanding today's rules for religious entities. Too often, the Supreme Court's decision in *Employment Division v. Smith*, holding that religious entities are subject to generally applicable and neutral laws, is treated as though *Smith* came out of the blue. Chapter 8 argues to the contrary, that it represented the dominant trend in the Supreme Court's jurisprudence; this chapter shows that it is the culmination of centuries of legal and social development. The decision was neither ad hoc nor accidental.

Second, this chapter is intended to put to rest the pervasive – but misguided – belief that religious liberty at the time of the framing meant that religious entities were superior to the law. The colonies and then the states picked up where Britain left off. This is not an originalist argument that the views of the Framers are binding today, or that intellectual history moves in a single straightforward progression. In the Anglo-American tradition, though, there is a value set on experimenting with different approaches to see what works best and then to adjust; experience has taught both Britain and the United States to reject special privileges for religious entities and to embrace the rule of law. The United States thus has the benefit of centuries of experimentation and the capacity to learn from past mistakes, which is the essence of the common law. *The plainest lesson to be taken from these hundreds of years of development is that even religious reasons are inadequate to justify harming others.*

Since the 12th century, when Henry II (1154–1189) took the first steps toward a common law by resisting a separate sphere of justice for clergy, the justifications for special treatment of religious entities have become increasingly hollow. Although it took centuries for Henry II's intended reforms to be fully effected, the logic of Henry's attempts to place clergy under the same justice system as all others was ineluctable: the victim of rape or murder by a clergy member is just as injured as the victim of an ordinary citizen. The injury demands proportional punishment, which is determined according to the harm, not the identity of the actor. Thus, the drive to avoid the law by contemporary religious entities is not a new development, but it is an anachronistic one.

The internal logic of Anglo-American common law has drawn the United States to the conclusion that the public good requires the deterrence and punishment of harmful actions, regardless of the identity of the actor. I will call this the no-harm principle.

Before the creation of the United States, churches did have autonomy from the law. The rights of religious institutions and their clergy were above those of ordinary citizens. From the 3rd to the 16th centuries in Britain, church autonomy was in fact the order of the day. The Roman Catholic Church was permitted to harbor fugitives from the law under the practice of "sanctuary." The church was co-sovereign with the state, and it instituted ecclesiastical courts that provided separate (and far more lenient) justice for the criminal acts of clergy, which came to be called the "benefit of clergy."

An introduction to the historical evolution from church autonomy to the no-harm rule

Going back at least to the 12th century, the Roman Catholic Church in Britain was a co-sovereign with the Crown, with both enjoying sovereign immunity. That meant they each also had their own judicial systems: the ecclesiastical and the common law. Two privileges – sanctuary and the benefit of the clergy – ensured that clergy (at least the clergy of the established church) were either beyond the reach of the law or held to lesser punishments than ordinary citizens. Experience with these immunities and the rise of the common law led to the abolition of these two privileges by the mid-16th century. In the 17th century, most civil and criminal matters were transferred from the ecclesiastical courts to the common law courts and the newly created courts of chancery. This triumph of the common law coincided with the rise of Puritanism, the interregnum, and the Restoration. During the 19th century, Parliament statutorily abolished most of the jurisdiction of the ecclesiastical courts. They retained jurisdiction only over discipline of clergy, certain types of sexual offenses committed by laypersons, and minor matters concerning worship services.[1]

By the mid-19th century, two forces came together to undermine religious entities' and believers' claims to privilege. First, the logic of the common law – that all similarly situated individuals should be governed by the same laws – overtook the earlier claims to privilege.[2] Second was the concept of "ordered liberty," and its corollary, the no-harm rule,[3] each of which opened the door to those who had been harmed to sue religious institutions for their tortious behavior.[4] In response to this development, the courts introduced the doctrine of charitable immunity, which protected the coffers of charitable institutions – including religious institutions – from such lawsuits.[5] Charitable immunity was abandoned in England even before it was ever entrenched and was honored in the United States only for a limited time.[6] It is now defunct in most jurisdictions in the United States, with some remaining caps on liability.[7] In sum, the fundamental fairness inherent in the common law led to an inevitable conclusion: even religious believers must be held accountable for the harm they cause.[8]

At the same time that these principles joined forces, the status of those who were most likely to be harmed by religious entities – children, women, and minorities – improved. Laws prohibiting illicit sex were among those laws expected to be enforced throughout society. As I have discussed previously, ministers and pastors themselves during the founding era preached the rule of law for religious believers from their pulpits. "Influential preacher John Leland removed 'licentious indulgence of the carnal appetite' from the sphere of religion, placing it squarely under control of 'human law.'"[9] As women, children, and minorities shifted from being the property of white male property owners to inherently valuable beings, the harm done to them became increasingly intolerable. It took both the legal developments and an expansion of civil rights to reach the full flowering of the no-harm rule in the United States.

Historical privileges that placed clergy and religious
institutions above the law

In Britain, there were three historical privileges that benefited religious individuals and entities: sanctuary, the benefit of clergy, and charitable immunity. All three privileges have been discarded or discredited. Analyzing this history provides crucial background for understanding that church autonomy today would be a throwback, not a step forward.

The U.S. Supreme Court has repudiated the spirit of these three principles, but they still haunt religious institution theories[10] and the legal tactics of religious institutions themselves.[11] It is important to learn and understand this history, because it formed the background for the Framers and for the early formation of the law governing religious institutions and individuals in the United States. It is also important because it uncovers past experiences with church autonomy that did not, and could not, withstand the growth of representative democracy and the rule of law in Britain and then in the United States.

The sanctuary privilege and the geographical sovereignty
of the Roman Catholic Church

As early as the third century A.D., secular authority recognized the ecclesiastical right to provide sanctuary, or protection, for those threatened by "private vengeance for alleged wrongdoing."[12] Sanctuary was intended to forestall blood feuds and the vigilantism of the times. Although secular governments tried to retain control over some categories of wrongdoers, the ecclesiastical authorities held full sway to determine whether and what kind of sanctuary would be made available. The church further refused to deliver anyone who was within its sanctuary unless promises were made that the wrongdoer would not be harmed.[13]

Seven centuries after the practice first appeared, the Crown created the chartered sanctuary, a form of asylum that was backed by the king but controlled by the church.[14] Chartered sanctuaries provided greater protection than church sanctuary, including a broader geographic and temporal scope, and a greater range of protected offenses. Fugitives hidden in chartered sanctuaries were governed by the church, and lived in a fugitive community, apart from the rest of the world.[15] Such sanctuaries could be quite large geographically. Secular authorities recognized this practice well into Tudor times. The sanctuary privilege shielded both laity and clergy, but clergy were often given special dispensation. The power of sanctuary was fortified by "fear of Divine vengeance," thus "when the Church said that those who sought her protection must be treated with leniency and mercy, and their lives and persons spared, no state or individual was strong enough or bold enough to refuse to comply."[16]

Sanctuary is a valuable tool to come to terms with the enormous power of the Roman Catholic Church at the time. It was sovereign in the sanctuary territories, which it ran as separate universes from the Crown's territory. The church created a quasi-citizenship for fugitives, determined if and what punishment it would permit, and answered to no one. As the Crown sought to enlarge its jurisdiction and attitudes about the proper role of the church changed, so too did secular deference to the practice of sanctuary. Beginning in 1467, the Crown began to reduce the types and locations of offenses covered by sanctuary and, by 1540, chartered sanctuary was abolished.[17] Sanctuary was completely repealed in 1623 by act of Parliament during the reign of James I, though the practice persisted unofficially with regard to service of process until the end of the 17th century.[18] By that time, the Crown found the separate justice system insupportable, because it made criminal punishment nonuniform.[19]

The end of sanctuary marked the end of the church's geographical control in Britain. But it did not signal the end of special treatment for the clergy; rather it was only one stage in the movement away from church autonomy toward the rule of law under the common law. "Despite its formal demise, the spirit of sanctuary lived on in the practice known as 'benefit of clergy,' which did not offer outright immunity, but served, when available, to mitigate the severity of secular law."[20]

The benefit of the clergy privilege and the juridical sovereignty of the Roman Catholic Church over its clergy

To understand the benefit of clergy principle, one must go back to 12th-century Britain. In that era, King Henry II succeeded the lax reign of King Stephen (1135–1154), who had permitted the barons and the Roman

Catholic Church to exercise overweening power. Henry II, who is known as the father of the common law, took on both the barons and the church, but ultimately failed to make the church and its clergy accountable to the general public good.[21]

From 1076, when William the Conqueror established the dual court system, until 1576, during the reign of Elizabeth I, the royal courts and the ecclesiastical courts shared jurisdiction over criminal law,[22] which brought conflict and dissension. Henry II saw the need to standardize criminal justice, and sought to bring clergy under the jurisdiction of the civil courts. But the succeeding scandal with Archbishop Thomas Becket derailed his plans and led to a system of special treatment of clergy criminals that lasted several centuries.

Under Stephen, the clergy had become accustomed to unaccountability to the civil, or royal, courts.[23] Henry II thought their privilege to be above the law was dangerous, and in 1164, he called a meeting with the bishops to require them to agree to observe the customary powers of the king in the area of criminal law.[24] Specifically, he demanded that criminal clerics be defrocked by the church and handed over to the civil courts:

> Henry II was too astute a ruler not to perceive the immense evils arising from [the special treatment for the church], and the limitation which it imposed upon the royal power by emancipating so large a class of his subjects from obedience to the laws of the realm. When in 1164 he endeavored, in the Constitutions of Clarendon, to set bounds to the privileges of the church, he therefore especially attacked the benefit of clergy, and declared that ecclesiastics were amenable to the royal jurisdiction.[25]

At first, the archbishop of Canterbury, Thomas Becket, agreed. Becket's approval was a victory for Henry, because the Canterbury bishopric was the most powerful prelate in Britain, second only to the Pope.[26] As archbishop, Becket had the power to excommunicate and was the cleric empowered to perform coronations in the event of a new king.[27] Thus, Becket's approval was crucial for the king's plans to unify the criminal justice system. To Henry's dismay, Becket reversed his position under pressure from other bishops.[28] As a result of the disagreement, Henry halted Becket's income and exiled him to France in 1164.[29]

Six years later, and anxious to secure succession, Henry sought to have his eldest surviving son crowned. Because Becket was in exile and therefore unavailable, Henry had Canterbury's ancient rival, the archbishop of York, preside over young Henry's coronation. Becket was enraged at the affront and, with papal backing, threatened to lay England under the ban of interdict.[30] He and Henry reached a truce, which allowed Becket to return to England in the autumn of 1170. The Sheriff of Kent accused Becket of returning to unseat Young Henry. Becket replied, "I have not the slightest intention of undoing the king's coronation. . . . But I have punished those who defied God and the prerogative of the church of Canterbury by usurping the right to consecrate him."[31] Despite the truce, just before returning to England, Becket raised Henry's ire by excommunicating all of the bishops who had participated in young Henry's coronation. It was after this incident that Henry declared in frustration to his assembled court, "Will no one rid me of this turbulent prelate?"[32]

In response to this furious statement, four of Henry's barons murdered Becket in Canterbury Cathedral on December 29, 1170. Although he publicly disavowed involvement with the murder, Henry was subsequently overcome with remorse and from his weakened position, retreated from his earlier plan to create one criminal court and acquiesced in the ecclesiastical courts' continuing jurisdiction over clerics accused of crimes.[33] In the aftermath of this feud, the practice known as benefit of clergy became entrenched.[34]

The benefit of clergy, or *privilegium clericale*, was often the difference between life and death for a criminal.[35] In the king's courts, capital punishment was mandated for all felonies.[36] In contrast, capital punishment was beyond the power of the ecclesiastical courts. Hence, clergy and laypeople could commit the same illegal actions, and the layperson's sentence would be death while the cleric's sentence would be defrocking, incarceration in a monastery, or forfeiture of belongings other than land.[37]

There were also procedural advantages for clergy members. Ecclesiastical trials of criminal matters were conducted by compurgation – the accused would take a formal oath that he was innocent of the crime and bring into court an "arbitrary" number of compurgators who would swear to their belief in his oath.[38] Acquittal was typical, because evidence was only adduced from the defense, and perjury by the defendant and com-purgators was routine.[39] In addition, the clergy were exonerated from all prior criminal acts upon conviction of a single crime.[40] Thus, the rape of a girl and the murder of her father – both perpetrated by a single cleric – could be reduced to a single crime and a single punishment of suspension from ministry for two years.[41] The same crimes by any other citizen would have been tried as separate crimes and death would have been the likely sentence for either or both. From this history, one can draw many interesting conclusions, but "the remarkable point is that the clergy should have been able to maintain for centuries a special priv-ilege in crime. This is a corollary to the magnitude and power of the church."[42]

Many laypeople, as well as Henry II, viewed the privilege for clergy as grossly unfair.[43] If clergy could avoid the death penalty, why couldn't laymen who had committed the identical crimes? This sense of funda-mental unfairness did not abolish the privilege, but rather caused it to be eventually extended beyond clergy to cover all first-time offenders.[44] Ironically, the extension of the privilege operated out of the same prin-ciple that would abolish special privileges for religion: identical actions should yield similar punishments, the measure of which must be degree of harm, not the identity or status of the offender.

The power of the religious institutions during the British monarchy was also evidenced by the existence of the "high courts" of the royal and ecclesiastical courts: the Star Chamber and the High Commission, respectively. They appeared during the reign of Henry VIII (1509–1547) and came to full flower under Elizabeth I (1558–1603). These were the "prerogative courts."[45] "The court of High Commission stood to the church and to the ordinary ecclesiastical courts somewhat in the same relation as the Council and Star Chamber stood to the state and the ordi-nary courts of the state, central and local."[46] Upon declaring himself the head of the church in England, Henry VIII used both courts to enforce spiritual uniformity on the people, a tradition followed by his succes-sors (whether Catholic or Protestant), until the courts were abolished in 1641.[47]

Under Elizabeth's reign, the lines between ecclesiastical justice and secular justice further blurred. By 1576, under Elizabeth I, the benefit of clergy privilege had been extended beyond clergy to all those who were literate (there was a time when only the clergy were literate), and therefore the benefit of the clergy was not only a means for the clergy to move their trials to the friendlier ecclesiastical courts, but it also became a tool for laypeople to reduce the likely sentence for a crime, even though they were being tried in secular courts.[48] It was assumed that a felony was "clergyable," that is, capable of preventing capital punishment, unless the Parliament explicitly stated otherwise. Eventually, during the latter half of the 16th century and the beginning of the 17th, the benefit became inapplicable to murder, rape, abduction, thefts of the person exceeding a shilling, burglary, highway robbery, stealing horses, and stealing from churches.[49]

Also in 1576, Parliament abolished the ecclesiastical courts' jurisdiction over crimes committed by clergy, roughly 400 years after Henry II tried and failed to do so.[50] At the same time, the "benefit of clergy" became a gambit to be invoked at sentencing for laypeople and clergy alike.[51] Parliament removed the criminal jurisdiction of the ecclesiastical courts because it perceived that the church had taken over a large portion of its criminal jurisdiction.[52] Moreover, the Crown was appalled at the level of perjury and corruption in the ecclesiastical courts:

> This scandalous prostitution of oaths, and the forms of justice, in the almost constant acquittal of felonious clerks by purgation, was the occasion, that, upon very heinous and notorious circumstances of guilt, the temporal courts would not trust the ordinary with the trial of an offender. . . . As, therefore, these mock trials took their rise from factious and popish tenets, tending to exempt one part of the nation from the general municipal law; it became high time, when the reformation was thoroughly established, to abolish so vain and impious a ceremony.[53]

As a result, Blackstone writes, the 1576 statute abolished the practice of purgation (and with it, the ecclesiastical courts' jurisdiction over clergy members who committed crimes), by directing that an offender who pled the benefit of clergy "was not to be delivered to the [ecclesiastic courts], as formerly," but instead was to be burned on the hand to show that he had used the privilege for a first-time felony, (a practice that became ceremonial in some cases) and, at the judge's discretion, could be sentenced to up to a year in prison.[54] The 1576 statute served two purposes: Parliament did away with the corrupt practice of trial by compurgation while it effectively enlarged the Crown's criminal jurisdiction at the expense of the ecclesiastical courts. The loss of ecclesiastical jurisdiction over crimes committed by clergy was significant, and not nearly as divisive as it had been in Henry II's and Becket's day.

In England and in the colonies, the benefit of clergy principle eventually became a tool for all defendants to avoid the death penalty. It was replaced by "transportation" away from the jurisdiction during the 18th century and ultimately abolished in the 19th century.[55] Moreover, early America did not recognize special, ecclesiastical courts for clergy that substituted for secular courts in criminal matters. Rather, clergy members were subject to the law of the secular courts as were all citizens.[56] The "benefit of clergy," therefore, did not confer any special benefit on clergy *qua* clergy in the colonies or later, the states. Instead, it was a tool for juries and judges to avoid the death penalty as applied to first-time felonies.[57]

The end of sanctuary, the end of benefit of clergy, and the end of a politically sovereign church signaled the demise of the structural mechanisms that had protected religious individuals or institutions from criminal liability in Britain. When the colonies were first established in the early 17th century, the settlers were part of a generation that had been ruled by Queen Elizabeth I, during whose reign the ecclesiastical courts were definitively removed from criminal jurisdiction. Neither the privileges nor the ecclesiastical courts made it across the Atlantic. Once the United States was established, the states did not reinvigorate the rejected British privileges. Instead, they picked up where Britain had left off and permitted the government to bring clergy under civil court authority[58] and religious institutions to account.[59]

A number of early American states followed this path. This exclusion from free exercise protection first appeared in the Charter of Rhode Island and Providence Plantations of 1663. An exclusion for "licentiousness" was reflected in a few other early state constitutions as well, but it became most prevalent during the nineteenth century. Most early constitutions also included exceptions to the free exercise of religion for peace and safety.[60] The current attempts by religious organizations to avoid criminal liability by invoking alleged privileges do have their roots in history, but they lost their moral and legal underpinnings long ago.

The charitable immunity experiment

Charitable immunity was a rule that protected the coffers of charitable organizations from actions in tort. Unlike sanctuary and the benefit of clergy, it was not a privilege limited to churches or clergy. Rather, it was intended to shield volunteer or charitable associations in general.[61] The doctrine of charitable immunity protected charitable organizations from tort lawsuits, which meant that victims could not bring successful tort claims against the employees of those organizations.[62]

It appears to have developed based on a variety of justifications. The doctrine, originally developed in England in 1846, was based on a trust theory "that the funds of the charity are not to be diverted from the purposes intended by their donors and applied to the payment of liabilities in tort."[63] Another theory offered was that since charities do not gain or benefit from the services they offer, they could not be held liable under the doctrine of respondeat superior for works done on their behalf. A third justification was that the recipients of charity assume the risk of negligence when they accept the benefit, thereby waiving their right to sue. It was also argued that the acts of charitable organizations are analogous to municipalities and therefore, charities deserve the protection that governmental immunity offers. Finally, public policy – fueled by a fear that people and institutions working to better society would no longer contribute if they were liable for actions associated with that work – justified charitable immunity.[64]

The latter, public policy, argument was especially forceful in late 19th-century America. When public charities first emerged in the United States, they were foundering institutions run only on an experimental basis. Any substantial judgment against them would have led to their demise, or at the very least, discouraged contributions. In an effort to foster their growth and thus benefit to the public, most state courts adopted the policy of shielding charities from tort liability.[65]

In England, the charitable immunity rule did not involve religious institutions specifically. In the United States, the definition of a charitable organization eventually reached beyond the traditional non-profit groups that aided the poor to include hospitals, schools, and churches. At its height, the immunity provided complete protection against any damage awards and therefore made charitable organization's coffers autonomous from any countervailing social responsibility. In a minority of jurisdictions, immunity extended only to certain persons or certain sources of the organization's income (trust funds and donations).[66]

The now disfavored doctrine entered the British common law in 1846, as dictum in the House of Lords' decision in *The Feoffees of Heriot's Hospital v. Ross*: "To give damages out of a trust fund would not be to apply it to those objects whom the author of the fund had in view, but would be to divert it to a completely different purpose." The case was an action for damages for wrongful exclusion from the benefits of the charity, not for any personal injury inflicted in its operation.[67] By the time the doctrine became entrenched in the American courts, it was no longer good law in England.[68] By 1871, after only twenty-five years of experience with the doctrine, the English courts rejected it on the ground that it made no sense to hold charities blameless for the harm they caused. As a 1909 case characterized it: "It is now well settled that a public body is liable for the negligence of its servants in the same way as private individuals would be liable in similar circumstances."[69]

Massachusetts was the first state to adopt the doctrine of charitable immunity in *McDonald v. Massachusetts General Hospital*,[70] with many other state courts following suit. By 1900, seven state supreme courts followed suit, with another thirty-three joining the charitable immunity movement by 1938.[71]

By the early 20th century, American scholars and courts considered charitable immunity a faulty doctrine based on a weak foundation.[72] In *Georgetown College v. Hughes*, one of the first American cases rejecting charitable immunity, the court characterized it as an "anomaly," stating that "[t]he doctrine of immunity of charitable corporations found its way into the law . . . through misconception or misapplication of previously established principles."[73] Even defenders of limited liability for charitable organizations recognize that the "traditional rationales for denying *all* tort recovery against charitable organizations cannot withstand close scrutiny."[74] The reasoning is irrefutable: when the law is intended to redress harm and charitable institutions are intended to assist those in need, permitting them to avoid liability for the harm they cause is perverse.

Some vestiges of the doctrine remain, with several states still recognizing the doctrine and/or instituting a cap on damages, as opposed to complete immunity. While it has been thought appropriate to hold charitable organizations accountable for the actions of their employees, their liability for volunteers has been contested.[75] But, all in all, nonprofits have not been able to sustain an argument for avoiding all of their obligations to those they hurt.

Like the benefit of clergy and sanctuary, charitable immunity was vulnerable to the burgeoning value that all citizens who act in the same way should be subject to the same law. As in Britain, in the United States, charitable immunity has been nullified because it makes little sense. The three benefits these could not withstand modern beliefs in fairness, deterrence, and accountability.

The Reformation's influence on the rejection of special privileges for religion

The Reformation also bolstered the arguments against special legal treatment for religious entities, when co-sovereigns, the Church and the Crown fought over jurisdiction.[76] In the 13th century, the gap between them widened when secular lawyers replaced ecclesiastics on the benches of the common law courts.[77] Yet they rested on similar grounds. The rival courts were separate systems of law, differed in many of their rules and derived their force from different sovereigns,[78] but they were based on the same philosophical foundation – "the will of God expressed through authority" – whether ecclesiastical or royal.[79] So long as the one ground existed to justify each, there was little question of separate identities between Church and Crown. There was a single whole under God, though its elements were often in tension.

All this changed with the Reformation in the 16th century. The attack on the authority of the church was in effect an attack on the whole medieval system of law. Thus, religion was no longer universally considered the basis of civil government, and the premises of the common law firmly gained ascendancy over ecclesiastical law.[80]

The scope of ecclesiastical jurisdiction began to decline at the outset of the Reformation, reflecting a "basic shift in attitude towards the proper role of the Church in men's lives."[81] The end of benefit of clergy, which shifted power away from ecclesiastical courts and toward civil courts, led to a corresponding decline in the sovereign authority of the established church in Britain.[82] It became clear that a "shift in the balance of power" to secular authority at the expense of the ecclesiastical "had to be carried out in the context of legal competition and compromise."[83] The ecclesiastical courts continued to exercise jurisdiction over some matters that had been in their purview since the medieval period, such as tithing, probate, marriage, defamation, and cases involving "mortal sins" such as fornication and adultery.[84] The increasing entrenchment of the common law,[85] the Roman Catholic Church's loss of moral authority during the Reformation,[86] and the subsequent growth of Protestantism with its emphasis on accountability[87] reduced the ecclesiastical courts' power and undermined whatever argument the Church once had to be sovereign or to have its clergy immune from the criminal law.

The Star Chamber and the High Commission

During the Tudor and Stuart years, 1485–1714,[88] the Crown engaged in a systematic suppression of religious dissent and the persecution of those whose beliefs differed from those of the established church. In 1526, Henry VIII divided his king's council into two branches: a privy council to consider domestic and foreign policy issues, which came to be known as the Star Chamber, and the court of High Commission, to address ecclesiastical issues. When Henry VIII officially became the head of the church eight years later in 1534,[89] he was able to use both branches, also referred to as prerogative courts, to exercise control over religious belief and practice. The unification of church and state made "any deviation from the new religious order a threat to royal supremacy."[90] Thus, heresy and treason became indistinguishable as the Star Chamber cases involving "sedition" or "subversion" and the High Commission cases involving "heresy" worked in tandem to rid Britain of religious dissenters. "Those who continued to support the authority of the pope, Henry VIII sent to the executioner's chopping block; those who preached new doctrines he sent to the fires at Smithfield."[91]

Henry VIII's successors carried on his practices. His son, Edward VI (1547–1553), was only ten years old when he ascended to the throne on Henry's death in 1547, but the dukes of Somerset and Northumberland ruled in his name, and both promoted Protestantism as the established and sole religion of the realm.[92] The Catholic Queen Mary (1553–1558) ruled in a country dominated by Protestants,[93] whom she believed invited divine retribution on her reign for their heresy.[94] She atoned by burning hundreds of Protestants at the stake, including Bishops Cranmer, Ridley, and Latimer, during her short reign.[95]

Protestant Elizabeth I gained control of a country divided by religion. To reunite the country, she ruthlessly suppressed Catholicism (she was excommunicated by the Pope in 1570[96]) through her enforcement of the Acts of Supremacy and Uniformity, which she employed the High Commission to institute, and through her use of the Tower of London to execute heretics.[97] After centuries of sovereign control in Britain, the Catholic Church found itself in the 1570s instructing Catholics to avoid Anglican worship services and to attend their own "despite the penalties for doing so."[98] James I (1603–1625) and Charles I (1625–1649) avidly suppressed religious opposition. Only five years before the end of James I's reign, in 1620, the Mayflower pilgrims sailed for America.[99] Throughout his reign, Charles I aggressively suppressed Puritans.[100] Abuses by the Star Chamber and the High Commission were legion, and thousands of British citizens left for the American colonies (and the Netherlands), bringing with them certain knowledge of the consequences that result when a government joined forces with a single religion. After refusing to convene Parliament from 1629 until 1640, Charles I finally did so; the Puritans then seized power and soon thereafter abolished the prerogative courts (the Star Chamber and High Commission) and their abusive practices, which were,[101] "no longer compatible with liberty."[102] In addition, in a dramatic move forward for the common law, the ecclesiastical courts were deprived of *all* criminal jurisdiction, the entirety of which was placed in common law courts.[103]

The Crown did not respond to the Reformation by embracing religious pluralism. Rather, each British monarch, no longer bound to share power with one church, chose between Roman Catholicism and Protestantism, and forced her subjects to follow suit.

The Tower of London was an essential tool for the inculcation of the established religion of the realm. It was employed by Queen Mary to imprison and execute Protestants, after she revived the heresy laws at the end of 1554. The first Protestant martyr was publicly burned in 1555.[104] Between 250 and 300 were burned alive, while hundreds more were imprisoned.[105] Her successor, Queen Elizabeth I, used similar techniques to ward off Catholic Europe and those who refused to attend Church of England services by incarcerating bishops, archbishops, and others for years.[106] "There were as many executions of Catholics under Elizabeth as there were Protestants under Mary, though over a reign nine times as long."[107] James I continued to use the Tower as a prison, as the Tudors had done.[108] This was the era of the United States' early colonization.

In 1643, Parliamentarians seized control of the Tower during the Civil War. Throughout the Restoration, the Tower's function as a state prison declined and it became a military headquarters and munitions store-house. The last execution was in 1747, long after the first wave of emi-grants left for the New World in the late 16th and early 17th centuries. Indeed, the first permanently established settlement in the United States, in Jamestown, Virginia, was established a mere four years after the end of Queen Elizabeth's reign.[109]

The Bloody Tower, as it is often called, is a monument to the British history of religious dominance and intolerance. It was unquestionably stamped on the mind-set of any British subject at the time, and scores of them emigrated to the New World. The founding generation and the Framers thought about organized religion in this British context and did not have to leap to reach the conclusions that granting governing power to religion could be dangerous and that religious individuals and entities needed to be curbed by just laws. The signal innovation in the United States was religious pluralism, with each state, or smaller jurisdic-tion, establishing its own church or establishing multiple churches. The resulting variety of religious sects was an important step on the way to the privatization of religion in the United States, which in turn contributed to the treatment of religious entities as accountable citizens rather than sovereigns.

Influences on the Framers that informed the First Amendment

No one was more aware of the capacity of religious institutions to harm the public good than the framing generation, many of whom escaped England and its cruel religious hegemony.[110] The Reformation, which spawned a multiplicity of sects in tension with the established church, ended only twenty years before the first emigrants started across the

Atlantic.[111] Thus "[w]hen English settlers first sailed for America in 1584, they carried with them a faith worked out over fifty years of religious turbulence."[112] This turbulence continued well into the next century. Religious persecution in Britain only abated when the Puritans rose to power and disbanded the Star Chamber and the High Commission in 1641.[113] To be sure, the colonists did not swear off of established churches or persecution of nonbelievers or false believers immediately, but such principles were neither instituted nor praised in the federal Constitution. Rather, the federal Constitution, including the Bill of Rights, weighed heavily against both, in some measure because of the framing genera-tion's knowledge of the abuses that had gone before.

The influence of the Inquisition on the framers

While drafting the Constitution, Madison – and the Framers in general – had the despotic practices of the Catholic Inquisitors stamped on their political consciousness, a fact proven by Madison's direct reference to the Inquisition in his *Memorial and Remonstrance*, where he argued against state payment of certain Christian educators as follows:

> Because the proposed establishment is a departure from the generous policy, which, offering an asylum to the persecuted and oppressed of every Nation and Religion, promised a lustre to our country, and an accession to the number of its citizens. What a melancholy mark is the Bill of sudden degeneracy? Instead of holding forth an Asylum to the persecuted, it is itself a signal of persecution. It degrades from the equal rank of Citizens all those whose opinions in Religion do not bend to those of the Legislative authority. Distant as it may be in its present form from the Inquisition, it differs from it only in degree. The one is the first step, the other the last in the career of intolerance. The magnanimous sufferer under this cruel scourge in foreign Regions, must view the Bill as a Beacon on our Coast, warning him to seek some other haven, where liberty and philanthropy in their due extent, may offer a more certain response from his Troubles.[114]

There is little question that the excesses of the Inquisition (1184–1834), which encompassed the Spanish Inquisition (1474–1834), as well as the public executions of those whose faith differed from the Crown in England (1531–1689) and the excesses generated by the unity of power between the monarchies and organized religion, were part of the calculus the framing generation used to calibrate the need for government, the reach of religious liberty, and the need to make religious institutions accountable to the public good. Nor can there be any question that they believed in placing legal limitations on the religious institutions, because the Framers knew at a visceral level that religious institutions were not worthy of blind trust.

Religious organizations are complex institutions that are run and staffed by humans, who are inherently imperfect. That is, after all, the world view on which the constitutional scheme is based. According to the Framers, humans are inherently likely to abuse whatever power they hold. They hoped that a structured society based on the rule of law, and a structured Constitution pitting various power centers against each other, could forestall the inevitable temptations to abuse power.[115] Indeed, Madison's mentor, the Rev. John Witherspoon, president of the College of New Jersey, which later became Princeton University, explained the history of the United States in the context of the Inquisition:

> [A]t the time of the Reformation when religion began to revive, nothing contributed more to facilitate its reception and increase its progress than the violence of its persecutors. Their cruelty and the patience of the sufferers naturally disposed men to examine and weigh the cause to which they adhered with so much constancy and resolution. At the same time also, when they were persecuted in one city, they fled to another and carried the discoveries of Popish fraud to every part of the world. It was by some of those who were persecuted in Germany that the light of the Reformation was brought so early into Britain.

> [T]he violent persecution which many eminent Christians met with in England from their brethren, who called themselves Protestants, drove them in great numbers to a distant part of the New World where the light of the gospel and true religion were unknown.[116]

Under the reign of Pope Gregory IX, in response to the spread of "heretic" beliefs, Roman Catholic bishops conducted medieval "inquisitions" designed to rid France, Germany, and Italy of non-Catholics. Because these events influenced the framing generation's perception of the qualities of religious organizations, it is important to understand their history. Investigation of heresy was traditionally the duty of the bishops.[117]

The Inquisition, then known as the Holy Office, is perhaps best known for convicting Galileo at trial in 1633 for his "dangerous" scientific beliefs.[118] Most Inquisition trials resulted in a guilty verdict, and those convicted faced a myriad of horrific punishments as well as fines, imprisonment, and death.[119]

The Spanish Inquisition was independent of the medieval Inquisition, but it was also part of the history that the framing generation would have known and used to judge contemporary ideas. The purpose of the Spanish Inquisition was to discover and punish converted Jews (and later Muslims) who were insincere.[120] It was established in 1478 by King Ferdinand and Queen Isabella with the reluctant approval of Pope Sixtus IV.[121] The institution was entirely controlled by the Spanish crown – the pope's only check on the Inquisition was in naming and appointing the nominees to be inquisitors.[122] In 1483, the Spanish Crown created a new royal council of the Supreme and General Inquisition to expand the operation of the Inquisition throughout Spain. The notorious Tomas de Torquemada was named inquisitor general, who was the head of the council, responsible for creating branches of the Inquisition in various cities by establishing local tribunals.[123] The Spanish Inquisition was not finally abolished until 1834, nearly sixty years after the Declaration of Independence was signed.[124]

The early move toward religious pluralism

In Britain in 1662, during the Restoration, Anglicans and Presbyterians attempted to form a national British church, but the effort failed. Parliament passed a new Act of Uniformity, and Presbyterian ministers who refused to conform to Anglicanism were expelled from their congregations.[125] Dissenting Protestant worship became legal in 1689, but the dissenters were not allowed to hold property to construct churches unless they were subject to the oversight of the Court of Chancery. Not until 1791 were Catholics given parity with other Protestant dissenters. The inability of the established Anglican Church to answer to the public good when dealing with issues involving taxation, tithing, local government, marriage, education, and charity led to the assumption of civil jurisdiction over those issues. It was the measuring stick of the public good that transformed Britain from a country with only one recognized religion to one of religious liberty. "English pluralism was the result of a gradual wearing away of a unitary system through concessions made because it seemed right to make them."[126]

Like Britain, the United States did not begin as a fully pluralistic and tolerant society. The early colonies and then some of the states, with the exception of Pennsylvania, had established churches with corresponding privileges for members and disabilities for dissenters. There was no Tower of London or Star Chamber and High Commission to force the established church's beliefs upon others, but there were the Salem witch trials, anti-blasphemy laws, and a blending of governing and religious authority. Massachusetts did not tolerate religious dissenters, leading Anne Hutchinson and Roger Williams to escape to Rhode Island. The establishments, such as they were, gave way not long after the Constitution and then the Bill of Rights were ratified.

The Establishment Clause is testimony to the founding generation's rational fear of overweening, concentrated religious power and of the mischief that can be fostered by religious institutions, particularly when they are sovereign. It cannot be, as some argue, a rule solely intended to protect religious entities.[127] The history leading up to the founding of United States and the Protestant cast of governance theories at the time undermines such attempts to treat religion as though it is not a dangerous and potent social force that must be limited, just as the state must be.

The Protestant influence on the framing generation

The dominant mindset of the early Americans was Protestant.[128] At its most fundamental level, all Protestantism incorporates the view that religious individuals and institutions have the capacity to stray from a holy path into the path of evil.[129] For Protestants, individuals are locked into original sin. According to John Calvin, who, along with Martin Luther, sparked the Reformation and Protestantism, there was never a moment in history when humans could be blindly trusted to be, or do, good:

> [L]et us hold this as an undoubted truth which no siege engines can shake: the mind of man has been so completely estranged from God's righteousness that it conceives, desires, and undertakes, only that which is impious, perverted, foul, impure, and infamous. The heart is so

steeped in the poison of sin, that it can breathe out nothing but a loathsome stench. But if some men occasionally make a show of good, their minds nevertheless ever remain enveloped in hypocrisy and deceitful craft, and their hearts bound by inner perversity.[130]

Thus, Calvin counseled in favor of a diligent surveillance of one's own actions and the actions of others at the same time he endorsed the value of the law (both biblical and secular) to guide human behavior away from its propensity to do wrong.[131] Granted, no human could ever live up to all of the law's demands, but laws were valuable as a checking measure nonetheless.

Protestantism equally discounted the likelihood that a religious institution could be trusted on its own to serve the public good. "[Protestantism] is essentially an attempt to check the tendency to corruption and degradation which attacks every institutional religion."[132] The early Protestants, after all, were the Catholic dissenters who eventually rejected the 16th-century Roman Catholic Church for its malignant ways.[133] The belief that the Catholic Church had led the Christian Church down evil paths was a fervently held belief at the time of the framing as well, with John Adams identifying the "worst tyranny ever invented" as "the Romish superstition."[134]

The attitude of the framing generation on this subject differed little from Calvin's description of the 16th-century Roman Church's hubris and unaccountability:

> Because of the primacy of the Roman Church, they say, no one has the right to review the judgments of this See. Likewise: as judge it will be judged neither by emperor, nor by kings, nor by all the clergy, nor by the people. This is the very height of imperiousness for one man to set himself up as judge of all, and suffer himself to obey the judgment of none. But what if he exercise tyranny over God's people? If he scatter and lay waste Christ's Kingdom? If he throw the whole church into confusion? If he turn the pastoral office into robbery? Nay, though he be utterly wicked, he denies he is bound to give an accounting.[135]

The solution for the wayward path of the Catholic Church, at least according to Calvin, was proper government, a need the early Presbyterians (and Calvinists), identified both in the society and the Church:

Man's depraved apostate Condition renders Government needful.
Needful both in the State and in the Church. In the former without
Government Anarchy wou'd soon take place with all its wild and dire
Effects and Men wou'd be like the Fishes of the Sea where the greater
devour the less. Nor is Govern[men]t in the Church less needful than
in the State and this for the same Reason.[136]

The framing generation and the development of the no-harm principle

There is nearly universal agreement that a no-harm rule undergirds and
justifies criminal, tort, and regulatory laws.[137] The no-harm rule was a
notion articulated by John Locke in the 17th century, widely shared by
the framing generation in the 18th century, and entrenched in modern
philosophy and law by John Stuart Mill,[138] who was the most influential
philosopher in the 19th-century English-speaking world. He set forth the
following maxims, which came to be known collectively as the Harm
Principle:

> [F]irst, that the individual is not accountable to society for his actions,
> in so far as these concern the interests of no person but himself. . . .
> Secondly, that for such actions as are prejudicial to the interests of
> others, the individual is accountable, and may be subjected either to
> social or to legal punishments, if society is of opinion that the one or
> the other is requisite for its protection.[139]

Mill thereby restated the Lockean principle in a way that honed it down
to a no-harm rule itself. It is a firm rejection of autonomy from the laws
that protect others from harm.

He also advocated absolute dominion over one's mind, which entailed
tolerance of conflicting beliefs: "If all mankind minus one, were of one
opinion, and only one person were of the contrary opinion, mankind
would be no more justified in silencing that one person, than he, if
he had the power, would be justified in silencing mankind."[140] The
universe of actions was divided into two categories: those that will not
harm others and those that will. The former should not be regulated,
and the latter should.

In the 20th century, the no-harm principle was further elaborated by
H. L. A. Hart and Joel Feinberg. H. L. A. Hart stated in the 1960s that the
line to be drawn between legitimate laws and illegitimate laws rested on

the Harm Principle.[141] Joel Feinberg further developed the theory.[142] By the latter half of the 20th century, the no-harm rule was widely accepted as the best justification for criminal, tort, and regulatory laws. It remains the dominant approach.

As discussed in Chapter 8, Locke believed in a robust right of conscience, but also that belief must be coupled with the obligation not to harm others through one's actions. The no-harm principle is part and parcel of the core principle of ordered liberty embedded in republicanism: the maximal amount of liberty is calibrated to achieve the minimal amount of harm.[143] Order must be fitted with liberty.

Locke's no-harm principle was taken as a commonplace during the era of the framing. Thomas Jefferson famously explained, "the legitimate powers of government extend to such acts only as are injurious to others. But it does me no injury for my neighbour to say there are twenty gods, or no God. It neither picks my pocket nor breaks my leg."[144] Freedom of belief and "free argument and debate" were essential human rights, but when those "principles break out into overt acts against peace and good order" it is the "rightful purpose[] of civil government, for its officers to interfere."[145] Jefferson articulated the same principle when he wrote to James Madison in 1788 to outline the rights he thought necessary to include in a bill of rights. He backed a bill of rights, but he was also conscious that rights had the capacity to "do evil." Thus, he explained what the "freedom of religion" in the bill of rights would (and would not) accomplish: "The declaration that religious faith shall be unpunished, does not give impunity to criminal acts dictated by religious error."[146]

James Madison – drafter of the First Amendment – equally recognized the right to complete freedom of belief: "Religious bondage shackles and debilitates the mind and unfits it for every noble enterprise, every expanded project."[147] He admired the tolerance of religious beliefs in Pennsylvania, which exhibited a "liberal, catholic, and equitable way of thinking as to the rights of Conscience."[148] His discussions of "conscience" were discussions about belief, and not conduct.

Madison was particularly harsh regarding the potential abuses of power by religious institutions and especially their clergy. When backed by state authority, he declared, the clergy "tend to great ignorance and corruption, all of which facilitate the execution of mischievous projects." He castigated some believers at the time: "Poverty and luxury prevail among all sorts: pride, ignorance, and knavery among the priesthood, and vice and wickedness among the laity. . . . That diabolical, Hell-conceived principle of persecution rages among some, and to their eternal infamy, the clergy can furnish their quota of imps for such business."[149] Obviously, Jefferson and Madison envisioned the potential for great harm to the public good when a religious entity abuses power.[150] For this reason, neither they nor their fellow citizens ever contemplated absolute liberty for religious organizations. In fact, the primary assumption at the Constitutional Convention – and it is the most important principle that has contributed to the Constitution's success – was that every individual and every institution holding power was likely to abuse that power and therefore must be checked.[151]

Many in the framing era were also distrustful of religious organizations and clerics. The Deists at the time, like Jefferson, believed in Christ, but were unwilling to align themselves with the theology of any particular organized religion because, in their eyes, most theologies were a corruption of Christianity.[152] Jefferson famously excised portions of the Bible he found unacceptable to create his own creed.[153] Thus, Jefferson declared, "To the corruptions of Christianity, I am indeed opposed; but not to the genuine precepts of Jesus himself."[154] The Deists dominated the universities, and had a disproportionate effect on the culture compared to their numbers. Among Christians other than the Deists, anticlericalism also was an entrenched viewpoint.[155]

The Protestant mindset, and its interpretation of the violent history of religion in Europe, holds relevance for understanding the legal system that emerged in early America. It is no accident that the rise of Protestantism, its elemental rejection of the Roman Catholic Church, and its affirmation of the sinfulness of all humans – including and especially those who were clerics – coincided with the demise of the ecclesiastical courts and the benefit of clergy.[156]

Protestant theology, the reformed branch in particular, has long rested on a deep mistrust of human nature rooted in original sin, which has led to the necessity of government and a no-harm rule.[157] In fact, the Calvinist-Presbyterian branch of reformed theology contributed to the construction of the U.S. Constitution's emphasis on checks and balances, separation of power, and the necessary division of power between state and federal governments.[158] This starting point is shared by the Framers, Catholic Social Thought, and reformed theology. All three equally value the rule of no harm, that is, the necessity of deterring all citizens and institutions from harming others. For Protestant theology, government rightly exists to serve the common good, and that good is served best when the potential to do harm is restrained through duly enacted laws.

One particularly relevant idea in Protestant theology is the theory of "sphere sovereignty" introduced by a reformed theologian, Abraham Kuyper, in the late 19th century.[159] Under sphere sovereignty (or authority as some have suggested), church and state (and the arts and business, among other social organizations) each have their own sovereign base, but each also has a distinctive role. "[T]he *telos* of the state is the common good."[160] Thus, the distinctive role of the state is to "prevent the spheres from infringing upon one another, and it may use compulsion when necessary to maintain order."[161] He further explained:

> The cogwheels of all these spheres engage each other, and precisely through that interaction emerges the rich, multifaceted multiformity of human life. Hence also rises the danger that one sphere in life may encroach on its neighbour like a sticky wheel that shears off one cog after another until the whole operation is disrupted. Hence also the raison d'être for the special sphere of authority that emerged in the State. It must provide for sound mutual interaction among the various spheres, insofar as they are externally manifest, and keep them within just limits.[162]

This oversight role includes the power to protect the powerless in every sphere.[163] Thus, no sphere is considered immune from the sovereignty or power of another, but rather each sphere is to exercise its authority according to its own *telos*. Moreover, the state holds the authority to "intervene when the authorities in other spheres *are manifestly abusing their power*."[164]

The just criticism of the sphere sovereignty theory is that it is fuzzy at the boundaries, and it does not fully articulate the specific role of either the state or the religious institution.[165] Its value, however, lies in its articulation of the *role* of government vis-à-vis the church. It is not at all a stretch to claim that the powers identified are those undergirding the no-harm doctrine: the state is a neutral arbiter that ensures peace and protects the powerless. The state that chooses church autonomy is at odds with this notion.

Religious attitudes toward obedience to the rule of law in the framing generation

The dominant view at the time of the framing was that the rule of law was to be applied to religious individuals and institutions.[166] As the experiments with democracy around the world in the last thirty years have taught, the rule of law cannot operate without the widespread acceptance of this principle among the people.[167] During the latter half of the 18th century, such acceptance in this country was significantly furthered by sermons in a wide range of Protestant churches – Baptist, Presbyterian, Congregational, and Episcopalian.[168]

Whether religious believers would be subject to the general laws of the new country was a topic that was frequently on the minds of preachers in the latter half of the 18th century. Their sermons, as well as the governing documents of their churches, show the religious leaders of 18th-century society articulating a fairly cohesive vision for the coexistence of God's law and civil law. I do not intend to overstate the consistency of their claims, because there were dissenting, minority views and not every preacher adopted every tenet discussed here. Nevertheless, there was a generally accepted view that was sufficiently repeated to justify the claim that it was an important and formative element in the social mix.

To be sure, the ideas that the various sermons set forth are consistent with and can even plausibly be traced to not only theology but also to political philosophy of the time. In particular, many of the sermons reference the work of John Locke. In any event, religious leaders at the time of the formation of the Constitution conveyed a vision to their members: congregants were urged by their religious leaders to follow the rule of law on a number of grounds.

The discussion of religion and the rule of law in the pulpit was usually preceded by an acknowledgment of the existence of two concurrent realms, one civil, one religious, each with a rightful pull on the citizen. While the argument for the superiority of God's obligations is made, a number of ministers assert that the civil law is, in fact, a form of God's law. Believers were not to focus solely on their private understanding of what God asks of them individually, but rather, as part of their Christian practice, to take into account the good of the whole in their obedience to the law. Preachers also argued, in the larger picture, that obedience to the civil law is necessary for the realization of true liberty and that the freedom of religion does not extend to conduct beyond worship. Far from the overly simplified assumption that conflicting laws automatically should give way to religious claims, 18th-century religious leaders cautioned their members of the perils to the broader society of failing to follow the law.

Respected clergymen tended to be well-educated, and were the political and social leaders of their day. There was no national government or identity, so elected officials were limited geographically to a particular state or city. But many of the clergy were itinerant, often crossing state boundaries and delivering political and social news from state to state. The two elements – travel across state lines and high regard – made them formidable influences immediately before, during, and after the Revolution right up through the Constitutional Convention. Thus, it is well worth one's time to examine what they had to say about the law and religious entities at the time.

In 18th-century sermons, there was a repeated emphasis on the existence of two concurrent and distinguishable realms of power: church and state. Each was to have its rightful, limited claim on human conduct and mutual boundaries.[169]

Civil law made legitimate claims on religious believers when civil law operated in the proper realm. For example, Elisha Williams in 1744 stated that "obedience is due to civil rulers in those cases wherein they have power to command, and does not call for it any farther." In other words, according to Williams, "[t]he ground of obedience cannot be extended beyond the ground of that authority to which obedience is required."[170] The proper ground included the preservation of "life, liberty, money, lands, houses, family, and the like."[171] Three years later, Charles Chauncy echoed that civil "rulers . . . have an undoubted right to make and execute laws, for the publick [sic] good."[172] The horizon under which legislatures were to make law was the public good. According to John Lathrop, "[I]f the essential parts of any system of civil government are found to be inconsistent with the general good, the end of government requires that such bad systems should be demolished, and a new one formed, by which the public weal shall be more effectually secured."[173]

The two domains were coterminous and mutually exclusive. Thus, civil government's proper realm ended when it attempted to "establish any religion" by instituting or requiring "articles of faith, creeds, forms of worship or church government [in part because] . . . these things have no relation to the ends of civil society."[174]

To be sure, the clergy did not intend to rubber stamp the rule of any civil government per se, but rather only that government that flows directly or indirectly from the people and that is obligated to the public good. The law that binds is the law derived as follows:

> [R]eason teaches men to join in society, to unite together into a com-
> monwealth under some form or other, to make a body of laws agree-
> able to the law of nature, and institute one common power to see
> them observed. It is they who thus united together, *viz.* the people,
> who make and alone have right to make the laws that are to take place
> among them; or which comes to the same thing, appoint those who
> shall make them, and who shall see them executed. For every man has
> an equal right to the preservation of his person and property; and so an
> equal right to establish a law, or to nominate the makers and executors
> of the laws which are the guardians both of person and property.[175]

For at least one preacher in 1784, the fact that citizens legitimized the government by choosing their rulers led to the conclusion that such rulers were to be obeyed.[176]

Part of this shared vision depends on a notion of differentiation between church and state. But it is not a total separation that forces the believer to choose one sphere over the other, but rather a distinction of spheres, each with a legitimate, concurrent, and strong pull on the believer's allegiance. Thus, the free exercise of religion was to be pursued not in isolation but rather in "so far as may be consistent with the civil rights of society."[177] Taking the image of concurrent but distinguishable realms to its logical end, Isaac Backus reasoned that when each is functioning properly within its own realm, "the effects are happy, and they do not at all interfere with each other." The key to such happiness lies in their separate spheres, with "mischiefs" ensuing whenever "these two kinds of government . . . have been confounded together."[178]

The one realm reinforced allegiance to the other, and thus the obligation to obey the civil law was treated as part of the Christian's obligation.

Peace was to be achieved when men lived under these two authoritative regimes, because Christians "are taught to obey [civil] magistracy."[179] Thus, the allegiance to the Christian Church carried with it an allegiance to laws duly enacted by those who were appointed by the people and entrusted with serving the public good.[180]

The 18th-century preachers' reasons to obey the civil law

Far from urging civil disobedience, many 18th-century sermons exhorted believers to obey the civil law. There are three reasons offered by the clergy to obey the law. First, the law is given by God and therefore the believer must obey. Second, the rule of law serves the good of the whole. Third, which is a subset of the second justification, true or real liberty cannot be achieved in the absence of the rule of law functioning in a system appointed by the people.

First, for many of the preachers in the 18th century, God was present in both types of government – civil and ecclesiastical – in the sense that God has instituted government and that reason is founded in God. In a strong challenge to the notion that church and state are completely separate, Charles Chauncy in 1747 rejected the notion that civil government is purely a "humane constitution." Rather, civil government arises out of reason and therefore is "essentially founded on the will of God. For the voice of reason is the voice of God." Indeed, God's hand is in the very institution of civil government.[181]

Applying these grounding principles, Elizur Goodrich preached in 1787 that "transgress[ing] the laws of society . . . [will] expose ourselves to the high displeasure of Almighty God."[182] In other words, the obligation to obey the law is not merely based on principles of reason, but rather is a directive from God.

Second, in contemporary debate, the argument is oft raised that churches and their believers have a right to be left alone by the law, to isolate themselves from the community, in effect. Indeed, one of the most common justifications used to defend mandatory judicial exemptions is that the law should leave religious believers alone. In other words, no regulation affecting religion should be the baseline.[183] That was not the framing generation's vision.

This is a worldview that would have been alien to the religious leaders of the latter half of the 18th-century. It is as though history is being read through the anachronistic prism of Brandeis's famous 20th-century argument for the "right to be let alone."[184] By contrast, in the 18th-century sermons, there was a strong focus on the importance of believers contributing to the greater good and the community at large. In Nathaniel Eells's words in 1743, "We are not made for our selves alone, but we are made to help in making the World better."[185] Parishioners were exhorted to "promot[e] the public peace and happiness," not just their private salvation. The failure to submit to the "just commands of the civil authority" was contrary to God's will and worked "an injury . . . to the community."[186]

On these terms, there would be no true liberty, but rather only anarchy, in the isolationist Brandeis-like vision. Thus, "[p]ublic good is not a term opposed to the good of individuals; on the contrary, it is the good of every individual collected."[187] The Protestant preachers rejected the notion that Christians can live apart from society, isolated and not responsible for the common good. "'Let regard be had only to the good of the whole' was the constant exhortation by publicists and clergy."[188]

To secure true liberty, Christians were to be part of the tapestry of the society, contributing to its highest ends: peace, welfare, and security. "True liberty was 'natural liberty restrained in such manner, as to render society one great family; where every one must consult his neighbour's happiness, as well as his own.'"[189] Isaac Backus further explained the principle as follows: "Each rational soul, as he is a part of the whole system of rational beings, so it was and is, both his duty and his liberty to regard the good of the whole in all his actions."[190]

As parts of the fabric of society, Christians had obligations to ensure that the greater good was secured to the society as a whole in many categories. In Jonas Clarke's words:

> In a word, as by the social compact, the whole is engaged for the protection and defense of the life, liberty and property of each individual; so each individual owes all that he hath, even life itself, to the support, protection and defence of the whole, when the exigencies of the state require it. And no man, whether in authority or subordination, can justly excuse himself from any duty, service or exertions, in peace or war, that may be necessary for the publick peace, liberty, safety or defense, when lawfully and constitutionally called thereto.[191]

The alternative to this vision was anarchy, division, and war. Thus, God's directive to seek peace was to be achieved by the body of Christians operating as a community together pursuing the common good.

Late in the 18th century, Jonathan Edwards reaffirmed this view of Christian community with an obligation to the common good: "it especially becomes this [Christian family], visibly to unite, and expressly to agree together in prayer to God for the common prosperity."[192] Under this understanding, believers were obliged not simply to look after their own interests and to follow duly enacted law, but rather to embrace the needs of the polity as a whole as part of the Christian mission here on earth.

Third, real liberty was to be achieved through obedience to law as well as the good of the whole. John Witherspoon taught his students, a number of whom later became Framers, including James Madison, at the Presbyterian College of New Jersey, now Princeton University, that the "true notion of liberty is the prevalence of law and order, and the security of individuals."[193] The various 18th-century sermons state that liberty from the law of a legitimate government is no liberty at all. Government is necessary and obedience to just laws is necessary for there to be "real liberty." Indeed, "it is so far from being necessary for any man to give up any part of his real liberty in order to submit to government, that all nations have found it necessary to submit to some government in order to enjoy any liberty and security at all."[194]

The peace and good order imposed by a just government, that is, one chosen by the people, was not to be undermined by the religious believer.

> [W]hen a man adopts such notions as, in their practice, counteract the peace and good order of society, he then perverts and abuses the original liberty of man, and were he to suffer for thus disturbing the peace of the community, and injuring his fellow-citizens, his punishment would be inflicted not for the exercise of a virtuous principle of conscience, but for violating that universal law of rectitude and benevolence which was intended to prevent one man from injuring another.[195]

Thus, the laws ensuring peace, tranquility, and order obligated the believer and trumped counter-instincts for the purpose of achieving the fullest liberty. "It is true, the interests of society require subordination, but this deprives none of liberty, but helps all to enjoy it better."[196]

Finally, the framing generation believed that conduct, even when religiously motivated, could be regulated by the state in the interest of others. One of the most interesting aspects of the sermons, taken as a whole, is that they are consistent in naming the arenas over which the church has complete control as they leave the achievement of peace and order to the civil government. The churches' domain included the "power to make or ordain articles of faith, creeds, forms of worship or church government."[197] Conversely, "[t]he duty of magistrates is not to judge of the divinity or tendency of doctrines"[198] but rather to constrain actions that harm others and the public good. "[D]isturbers . . . ought to be punished."[199]

The ecclesiastical domain ended and the civil domain appropriately held sway when the beliefs, faith, worship, and church governance turned into "overt acts of violence [or effect]."[200] So even when overt acts involved the subject areas of ecclesiastical government, the civil authority permissibly dominated. Thus, religious defenses to a wide range of antisocial conduct, such as "murder, theft, adultery, false witness, and injuring our neighbor, either in person, name, or estate" were immoral or irreligious or both.[201] One sermon explained as follows:

> A Shaking-Quaker, in a violent manner, cast his wife into a mill-pond in cold weather; his plea was, that God ordered him so to do. Now the question is, Ought he not to be punished as much as if he had done the deed in anger? Was not the abuse to the woman as great? Could the magistrate perfectly know whether it was God, Satan, or ill-will, that prompted him to do the deed? The answers to these questions are easy.

> In the year of 1784, Matthew Womble, of Virginia, killed his wife and four sons, in obedience to the Shining One . . . to merit heaven by the action. . . . Neither his motive, which was obedience, nor his object, which was the salvation of his soul had any weight on the jury.[202]

In other words, actions taken in contravention of public peace and safety, under a civil government chosen by the people, left the perpetrator, even if a religious believer, vulnerable to civil action.[203]

The subjects of the kingdom of Christ, claim no exemption from the just authority of the magistrate, by virtue of their relation to it. Rather they yield a ready and cheerful obedience, not only for wrath, but also for conscience sake. And should any of them violate the laws of the state, they are to be punished as other men.[204]

The portrait of society painted by the sermons of the 18th century brought Christians from a wide sweep of denominations under a shared horizon of working toward the public good in concert with the government, a task that required obedience to duly enacted law governing actions. Backus captured this worldview when he explained that religious believers had "an unalienable right to act in all religious affairs according to the full persuasion of his own mind, where others are not injured thereby."[205]

In sum, the no-harm principle was widely accepted, especially among religious believers, clergy, and political leaders at the time of the framing. The arguments[206] that have been made for a mandatory constitutional right to avoid the application of the law to religious conduct simply cannot be supported.[207] Religious autonomy – in the sense of an independent power to act outside the law – was not part of the Framers' intent or of the framing generation's understanding, not to mention the vast majority – and the best – of the Supreme Court's free exercise jurisprudence.[208]

As Justice Scalia reasoned in his concurrence in *Boerne*, the most plausible reading of early free exercise enactments is a "virtual restatement of *Smith*."[209] He correctly pointed to the many state constitutional provisos that imposed the public interest in safety, health, and welfare on religious conduct. These important public safeguards transcended absolute liberty from the beginning in the United States:

> Religious exercise shall be permitted *so long as it does not violate general laws governing conduct*. The "provisos" in the enactments negate a license to act in a manner "unfaithful to the Lord Proprietary" (Maryland Act Concerning Religion of 1649), or "behave" in other than a "peaceable and quiet" manner (Rhode Island Charter of 1663), or "disturb the public peace" (New Hampshire Constitution), or interfere with the "peace [and] safety of the State" (New York, Maryland, and Georgia Constitutions), or "demean" oneself in other than a "peaceable and orderly manner" (Northwest Ordinance of 1787). See *post*, at 8–12. At the time these provisos were enacted, keeping "peace" and "order" seems to have meant, precisely, obeying the laws.[210]

In fact, "[e]very breach of law is against the peace."[211]

Scalia was correct. The framing generation believed that too much liberty was as bad as no liberty. Nineteenth and early twentieth century writings and cases equated "licentiousness" with the variety of illicit sex activities – adultery, child sex abuse, and polygamy or bigamy. Dictionaries also defined "licentious" as "dissolution" or "sexual immorality."[212]

According to historian John Philip Reid, those in the eighteenth century "had as great a duty to oppose licentiousness as to defend liberty."[213] Historian Bernard Bailyn further explained that

> [t]he very idea of liberty was bound up with the preservation of this balance of forces. For political liberty, as opposed to the theoretical liberty that existed in a state of nature, was traditionally known to be "a natural power of doing or not doing whatever we have in mind" so long as that doing was "consistent with the rules of virtue and the established laws of the society to which we belong"; it was "a power of acting agreeable to the laws which are made and enacted by the consent of the PEOPLE, and in no ways inconsistent with the natural rights of a single person, or the good of the society."[214]

This treatment of religious liberty as a middle ground between the public good and the believer is healthy.

Conclusion

The notion of "religious autonomy" is dangerous and outdated. The elimination of religious sovereign power made religious institutions private, and therefore on a more equal footing with other private entities. As such, they must be checked by the law. The constitutionally relevant question is not what is best for any church – indeed that question is forbidden by the neutrality principle underlying the Establishment Clause.[215] The proper question instead is whether the liberty accorded believers is consonant with the no-harm principle. If so, the public good has been properly served, because both liberty and order have been taken into account. If not, the public good – and therefore the constitutional order – has been subverted. As the no-harm principle has developed over the centuries, it has become an insuperable barrier for the claim that the Constitution can or should place religious believers above the law.

The current revelations of worldwide childhood sexual abuse by clergy, when combined with the concomitant secret knowledge of their individual religious institutions, reinforce what the founders of this country knew in the 17th and 18th centuries: religious entities often will abuse what power they have. To set aside the law for them without consideration of the public good is to choose liberty at the expense of order and to make society responsible for the harm they can cause. The right free exercise doctrine gives a wide berth to religious belief, but follows the rule that no American may act in ways that harm others without consequence.

10

THE PATH TO THE PUBLIC GOOD

Were all religious institutions and individuals always beneficial to the public, this book would not be needed. The rule would be plain: religious liberty is absolute. Religious entities would not need to be deterred from criminal or tortious behavior. The purpose of this book is to alert the public to extreme demands for religious liberty, which threaten many in the United States, and our society as a whole.

The logistics of the landmark *Boerne v. Flores*[1] case, discussed in Chapter 8, brought me into contact with the many groups that lobby against damaging religious conduct, such as the American Academy of Pediatrics, Children's Healthcare Is a Legal Duty (CHILD), district attorneys, and state regulatory agencies, among many others. Getting to know them educated me in two ways. First, I learned that my original theory of free exercise that would have excused religious entities from the vast majority of laws was patently absurd. It was a product of the ivory tower – a theory based on ignorance of religious conduct. I came to recognize that I (like many Americans) was a Pollyanna when it came to religion.

Second, I came to see what I could not see before. Religious conduct in the United States (and around the world) had an underbelly few knew about, fewer discussed, and even fewer raised in the public square. It was Aristotle who said: "We have to learn before we can do . . . we learn by doing."[2] My experience with RFRA – which covered every law in the United States and therefore affected every possible victim of religious entities – forced my eyes open and led me to comprehend that the widespread cultural presupposition that religion is inherently and always good for society is naïve and dangerous. The "religion" that should be freed from legal constraints was a chimera: beautiful and comforting, but false. In the initial analysis, a theory of religious liberty cannot sustain itself unless it factors in the possibility of heinous harms by religious individuals and institutions, some of which are detailed in Part One.

It is a simple fact that religious entities are not invariably beneficial. As Part One shows, religious entities can be responsible for lethal medical neglect of children, childhood sexual abuse, the takeover of neighboring property owners' rights under the zoning laws, and discrimination against women and homosexuals, among other conduct. Unfortunately, religion is often used (or misused) to harm others. These behaviors are intolerable in a civil and civilized society, and the state must have the power to deter and punish them. The right default rule subjects the religious to general constraints on harmful behavior.

The hard question that has been at the heart of the religious debate since the 1960s is when, if ever, a religious individual or institution should be given freedom from the neutral, general law. As explained in Chapter 8, the typical rule at the Supreme Court has been that neutral, general laws apply to everyone, religious or not. And that is the correct default rule.

Misguided or misinformed Americans have argued that the law should not encumber religious conduct unless it is an extremely important law. For them, *Wisconsin v. Yoder*[3] was rightly decided, and the courts should scrutinize the legislature's enactments to determine whether they are important enough to trump religious conduct. The net result is unacceptable: religious entities have broad sway to violate the vast majority of laws and the courts determine which legislation is important and which is not, according to their own lights. For those who understand the capacity of religious individuals and institutions to hurt others, the notion that religious entities ought to trump all but the most necessary laws is morally wrong. Moreover, the courts are not equipped to make relative determinations about social policy regulating conduct.

Even so, it is the rare individual who would jettison religious liberty altogether. Some modern scholars have tried, by reducing religious liberty to equality. Nonetheless, that approach fails to take into account the potent and distinctive drive of religious belief in every human society and its distinctive value for society. While the courts should not have the power to pick and choose between the laws that affect religious conduct, there should be some mechanism that allows the government to take into account the inherent value of religious liberty and weigh that value against the impact on the public good of letting the religious entity avoid the law. If an exemption will not harm others, it should be provided – by a legislature.

This final chapter lays out the three necessary conditions for legitimate religious accommodation. Religious conduct should only be exempt from neutral, general laws when (1) duly enacted by a legislature, not decreed by a court; (2) debated under the harsh glare of public scrutiny; and (3) consistent with the larger public good. Where the burden on religious conduct can be lifted by the legislature with only *de minimis* harm to the public, there is good reason to accommodate the religious conduct. But where the religious conduct significantly harms others, accommodation is not consistent with the public good, and the exemption is likely a legislative sellout that shortchanges important interests in society and that violates the Establishment Clause. This is the permissive accommodation rule that fits with the larger constitutional scheme and honors both religious liberty and the obligation of the government to protect citizens from harm. It is the Supreme Court's interpretation of the First Amendment.

Religious conduct in the context of the Constitution's structure

Freedom of religion is an integral part of the Constitution, not a principle somehow divorced from the rest of the document. The same underlying principles that drove the Framers' other choices also set in motion their placement of religion within American society. Any theory of the First Amendment that fails to take into account the Constitution's larger structure is incomplete.

One principle infused throughout the Constitution is distrust of the powerful. The Framers believed that every individual and every institution holding power was likely to abuse that power.[4] They did not trust the King, the executive, the legislatures, nor the people, and therefore no single entity could be trusted to govern. Distrust led the Framers to the checks and balances that are now so familiar. The three branches – legislative, executive, and judicial – were to check each other, and the federal and state governments were mutual checks.[5]

It should come as no surprise that the Framers started from a position of distrust. The years between the Declaration of Independence and the Constitutional Convention were years of disillusionment. The Declaration was an ebullient Enlightenment document that reflected the freed colonists' optimism about the future after breaking ties with the British monarchy and Parliament. There was widespread hope and expectation that they would institute the first truly successful republican form of government the world had seen. The Articles of Confederation established thirteen separate states, asserting, "Each state retains its sovereignty, freedom, and independence, and every power, jurisdiction, and right, which is not by this Confederation expressly delegated to the United States, in Congress assembled."[6] Because the Continental Congress had no power to force states to do other than they desired, the Articles recognized thirteen wholly independent sovereigns. To say that the state governments that followed did not deliver on the Declaration's hopes is to severely understate the matter. Because of their distrust of the king, the newly formed states disabled their governors and therefore placed virtually all governing authority into the hands of the state legislatures.

That move would teach them the hard lesson that unchecked power is abused power. In the face of crushing trade and monetary problems, the states were incapable of acting in the interest of the public and even more incapable of coordinating themselves, thus provoking the ineffectual Continental Congress to eventually disband in the mid-1780s.[7] The result was that the unchecked state legislatures descended into vortices of corruption that rendered laws for individuals but failed abysmally to address the pressing needs of the times, from mass forfeitures to a lack of stable currency to a failure of trade or military coordination.[8] The result was a descent into discord between the states, as the early Americans came to distrust the governing structures they had built. The fall from high hopes to failure led to desperate measures. The famous Shays' Rebellion (where distinguished Revolutionary veterans took up arms against their own relatively new state governments) was just one symptom of the severe failure of governance.[9] The Framers gathered at the Constitutional Convention, because a more suitable government was necessary, and the focus of the debate was on how to stem the human impulse to abuse power in ways that harm the public interest.[10] The Constitution's republican, or representative, structure was chosen and crafted for the purpose of making representatives accountable to the public good.[11]

As if the post-Revolutionary disappointments would not have been enough, the framing generation was predisposed to distrust the exercise of power by humans, because so many were Protestant and a significant percentage of those were Calvinist. Protestantism rested on the premise that governing institutions, even the Church, were capable of being corrupted. The Calvinists, whose theological worldview was dominant at the time,[12] held the paradoxical belief that all men were corrupt but that their inclinations to abuse power could be deterred by well-crafted governing structures. Calvin himself suggested fixing the corrupt Catholic Church in the 16th century by transforming it from an absolute monarchy into a representative structure, where the people would have some say over their ministers.[13]

When the First Amendment was amended to the Constitution, the same principle of distrust found its way into the document. The First Amendment's Establishment Clause, which states: "Congress shall make no law respecting an establishment of religion . . . "[14], is an explicit check on the power of religion in the political sphere. Conversely, it is also a limit on the power of government in the religious sphere. At a minimum, it means no religious institution should hold governing power.

The separation of church and state seeks a balance of power. Following the historical developments detailed in Chapter 9, the Framers made a conscious decision that religion and the state could not be co-sovereigns.[15] The combination of their power was the definition of tyranny.[16] This principle is a bellwether for freedom. Leading Middle

East scholar Bernard Lewis explained it as follows: "Separation [of church and state] . . . was designed to prevent two things: the use of religion by the state to reinforce and extend its authority and the use of state power by the clergy to impose their doctrines and rules on others."[17]

By denying religion the constitutional authority to rule, the Constitution privatized religion. There would be two sovereigns, but they were secular governments: the state and the federal. That does not mean that religion lost social power. It could and would still occupy the bully pulpit and use its influence among the people and in the legislatures to shape public policy, but it could not be government itself.

The Establishment Clause's prohibition of religious sovereignty is inadequate by itself to ensure that religious entities do not undermine the public good. By privatizing religion and protecting the right of conscience, the First Amendment instigated a teeming marketplace of belief. Religious views compete with other religious views in the public square, and influence not only the people but also government and public policy. The privatization of religion also raised an important issue. If they were not sovereign and therefore could not be checked by the Constitution's internal structures (like the three branches and the two sovereigns – state and federal – established), what would keep any one or any group of religions from harming others or taking over the country? The answer is that religious entities must be checked as are all other private entities – by the rule of law.

The end, perhaps the inexorable, result of the privatization of religion in the United States is the rule that religious conduct is properly subject to "neutral principles of law."[18] The Supreme Court in 1971 explained the principle as follows: "Our cases do not at their farthest reach support the proposition that a stance of conscientious opposition relieves an objector from any colliding duty fixed by a democratic government."[19] In other words, when a democratic government passes a law, that law is as binding on religious conduct as it is on secular conduct.

Some will persist in asking: if religious freedom is a precious right in the United States, why force religious believers to be governed by laws that conflict with their beliefs? The answer is that the duties created by a democratic government – via its laws – are created for the purpose of furthering the public good, which is served when bad actors are deterred from harming others and punished if they do. When religious believers avoid laws enacted in light of the public good, they undermine the public policy that led to the law. Every civilized society recognizes the rule of no harm, and none can afford to give individuals the right to harm others just because they are religiously motivated.

Those who would place religious believers above or outside the law start at the wrong end when they begin their analysis – and certainly when they end it – with only a discussion of what the religious entity needs or demands.[20] The constitutionally relevant question is not what is best for any single religious entity or believer. Indeed, that question is forbidden by the neutrality principle underlying the Establishment Clause.[21] Instead, lawmakers should consider whether the liberty accorded is consonant with the no-harm rule. If it is, the public good is being properly served. If not, the public good, and therefore the constitutional order, has been subverted. Both values – liberty and no harm to others – are absolutely necessary elements of any First Amendment calculus. The no-harm rule is a restatement of the Supreme Court's rule – from *Reynolds v. United States* to *Gillette v. United States* to *Employment Div. v. Smith and Boerne v. Flores* – that the First Amendment subjects religious entities to neutral, generally applicable laws.

By "no harm" I do not mean zero harm, but rather harm that is not significant. It is not that religious actors can't affect others in any way, which would be nonsensical, but rather that they may not be permitted, more than anyone else, to inflict significant harm against others.

The typical answer by the believers to this analysis is that legislatures often pass laws that are nonsensical, unnecessary, and just plain political, so why should religious entities have to curtail their religious conduct in the face of such laws? Moreover, the explosive growth in regulation since the time of the framing surely argues against applying the law to religious believers, because there is a lot more law now than there was then. Therefore religious believers are more burdened by laws today than they were in the past, or so the argument goes.

The questions are fair and deserve a response, but they do not lead to the conclusion that we should institute legal autonomy for believers. In a perfect world, with legislatures operating as the Framers intended them to, legislatures are focused on the public good and only enact laws to serve the public good. In that perfect world, legislators make independent judgments in the interest of the public good. Moreover, they only enact laws that actually serve a public interest. Were the world and legislators perfect, the application of neutral laws to religious entities would be justified in every instance.

This is far from a perfect world, however, and lawmakers have passed laws that are ill-conceived, RFRA being chief among them. Moreover, the impact of a law often cannot be assessed until the law is in place, so a well-intentioned law may generate effects that were not considered when it was passed. For these reasons, religious believers who find their religiously motivated conduct substantially burdened by a law should be able to ask for relief. That is not to say they have a constitutional right to relief. Most laws are intended to prevent or deter some harm, so letting a religious entity violate the law at will may well harm others. It is up to the discretion of the legislature, which has the tools – including the power to commission studies, investigate issues, and hold public hearings – to consider the accommodation request in light of the public interest.

When approached by the religious believer or institution, the legislature can consider anew the need for the law, including what harm it was intended to prevent, and then assess the impact a religious believer's exemption would have on others and society as a whole. It is a matter of line drawing. When the harm to others is *de minimis* with the exemption, religious believers should be granted the exemption.

There are numerous exemptions that pass this test. The peyote exemptions are an example of well-crafted relief. Many state and federal exemptions lift the drug laws to permit individuals to use peyote for religious purposes. Peyote is used during Native American Church ceremonies and was the conduct at stake in *Smith*. The *Smith* Court condoned peyote exemptions as it made clear they were not constitutionally required.[22] The Drug Enforcement Agency's dossier on the drug notes that, "While peyote produced rich visual hallucinations that were important to the native peyote cults, the full spectrum of effects served as a chemically induced model of mental illness."[23] If used recreationally, users could be a danger to others if they operated machinery, or drove a car, or cared for children. Therefore, both the federal and state governments are well within their power to prohibit it, and the limitation can be applied to religious entities. That was in fact an implicit holding of *Smith*.

At the same time, peyote is a drug that is not widely abused, because it frequently fails to produce the desired effect and not infrequently leaves its users with a headache or nausea. Nor do small amounts trigger addiction. The difficulty involved in peyote cultivation makes it highly unlikely that its use could become widespread. The federal government grants licenses to harvest and distribute peyote for purposes of sacramental use.[24] Unlike heroin, cocaine, or methamphetamine, an exemption for peyote is unlikely to increase the number of addicts or to foster an illegal drug trade independent of the religious purpose. Moreover, it is used for religious purposes in overnight ceremonies, and therefore it is unlikely religious users will drive while impaired. By permitting religious believers to use it for their ceremonies, the state is still adequately protecting others from harm. Were it discovered that peyote is being given to children, though, which could harm their health, further consideration and legislation would be justified.

A second example of a praiseworthy exemption is the exemption for the sacred use of communion wine during the United States' doomed-to-failure attempt to prohibit alcohol during Prohibition.[25] The small amounts of wine used during communion did not introduce the harm to society that Prohibition was designed to prevent. Proponents of the Eighteenth Amendment such as Carry Nation and East Coast industrialists pointed to improved worker reliability, morals, and family life to justify the total prohibition on alcohol.[26] The religious use of wine was no threat to those principles.

Finally, the federal government has provided an exemption from the military draft since the earliest years of the republic, for those who have a conscientious objection to war.[27] Quakers during the earliest conflicts dissented from military duty.[28] The exemption has been upheld for religious as well as nonreligious objectors[29] and most recently exempted a Coptic Orthodox Church member.[30] Such objectors are not relieved of government service during wartime altogether, but rather are required "to perform . . . such civilian work contributing to the maintenance of the national health, safety, or interest as the local board pursuant to Presidential regulations may deem appropriate."[31] Congress's determination is respectful of religious beliefs, but just as important, it is also an accommodation that is consistent with the larger public good. Religious entities are not permitted to use their religious beliefs to avoid their obligation to serve the war effort, but rather are moved to other positions that will accomplish the same end through different work. That is good for the religious believer, but it also is good for the country.

Contrary to popular belief, in the United States, the legislature is not a majoritarian institution

The most common objection to the Supreme Court's doctrine of permissive accommodation is that the legislature will do nothing for minority religions. That objection, though, stems from a pervasive, but false understanding of representative democracy in the United States and from an underestimation of the power religious entities wield. So-called "minority religions" are not necessarily or even usually consigned to a life of belief divorced from action in the United States. To understand why, it is necessary to explain the main features of the U.S. representative form of government.

At the Constitutional Convention, Pennsylvania's James Wilson, perhaps the most brilliant man there, opined that he could not abandon "his judgment to any supposed objections that might arise among the people," because he had been charged with doing what was in their interest. His frame of reference in crafting the Constitution was the public good, not public sentiment. He wondered aloud, "what he should say to his constituents in case they should call upon him to tell them why he sacrificed his own Judgment in a case where they authorized him to exercise it?" If he told them he was simply "flatter[ing] their prejudices" he expected them to "retort: did you suppose the people of [Pennsylvania] had not good sense enough to receive a good Government?"[32] In short, he was sent to the Convention to reach a result in the public's interest, not according to the public's predilections at the time. This is a good description of what elected representatives in the United States are supposed to do.

The system simultaneously frees the representatives to do what is best for the country – even if the people do not fully comprehend the issues or agree on the course taken – but it also imposes the difficult burden on elected representatives to make independent decisions in the larger public interest. They are accountable for *results*, not following orders. For the representative, it would be less complicated to follow the dictates of his or her constituents. Because representatives are the trustees of the people's interest, though, and are supposed to take into account far more than the majority's preferences, history – not numbers – is the ultimate judge of any elected official in the United States.

Majorities elect representatives, but after the election, those representatives have substantial latitude to listen to minority interests and in fact do.[33] The legislature is constructed so that legislators are not subject to the unfettered will of the people, but rather free to do what they believe is right, even when the majority disagrees. "Republican liberty signifies government in pursuit of the common good, where no citizen is subjected to the unfettered will of another. The central meaning of republican government since Cicero has been legislation for the 'res publica' or common good of the people."[34]

As proof that U.S. citizens continue to believe in republicanism, and independent elected representatives' accountability, one of the most common complaints about Congress is that it is "captured" by special interests, which are not representative of the people and which operate within their own narrow self-interest. This objection is commonly raised by those who believe their representatives have a duty to consider a larger public good than any one entity's entreaties.

For example, a significant majority of the American public in the 1960s was prejudiced against racial minorities. The South practiced an entrenched racism that is shocking to our children. Blacks were relegated to particular restaurants, restrooms, and occupations. Numerous states imposed "poll taxes," "grandfather clauses," or literacy requirements for the very purpose of excluding racial minorities from the voting booth.[35] In the wake of *Brown v. Board of Education*,[36] in which the Supreme Court required the desegregation of public schools, public officials and townspeople took extreme measures, including closing down public schools, to avoid the Court's mandate.[37] The racial war was played out on the television every night. Racism was not limited to the South, of course. Desegregation had to be court-ordered in Boston,[38] Denver,[39] and Detroit,[40] and Latinos found themselves blocked from the voting booth in New York, because they did not speak English.[41] Many states had bans on interracial marriage until these laws were declared unconstitutional in 1967.[42] Race-based housing discrimination was given a judicial imprimatur in 1948,[43] but was declared unconstitutional two decades later.[44] The majority was prejudiced, but the federal government still fought discrimination, as discussed in Chapter 8.

There is a form of democracy where legislation is driven by majorities, but it is not the constitutional order in the United States. It is called direct or pure democracy, where citizens themselves make the law through simple majority vote. The most familiar example is the town-meeting style government of some New England towns, for example, Marshfield, Massachusetts.[45] The Framers were certainly familiar with such a brand of democracy, in New England as well as Greece. But this form of government was definitively rejected by them, because they deeply distrusted what they considered "mob rule," a view that was informed by the experiences under the Articles of Confederation and the state constitutions that gave the people the right to instruct their representatives. Instead, they opted for representative democracy, wherein the people choose representatives, but do not control their public policy decisions during the term of office.[46] The end result is that majorities do not control legislation.

To be a representative in the U.S. system requires courage and vision, because it is the representative who is responsible for the quality of the common good, and who will therefore be judged accordingly. They have to choose between popularity and good results, which is a real choice, because good results will make them popular even if in the short term they are not. Minorities do well in this system. The work of the brilliant political scientist Mancur Olson showed that cohesive minorities with a clear message fare significantly better in a legislature than do amorphous majorities – a political fact that is now widely accepted.[47] This political fact is why lobbyists representing the disabled, and homosexuals, and racial minorities have done as well as they have at both the state and federal level. If majorities of citizens drove legislative results, none of those reforms would have been likely, because each places a burden on some powerful element in the majority. There is no religious "majority" in the United States. Every religion, even the largest – Roman Catholicism – has only a minority of Americans as members. The issue is not size, anyway, but rather political influence. That is something religious groups have in abundance as they have proven with RFRA, RLUIPA, and the state RFRAs.

Representative democracy opens the door for small
as well as powerful religions

For the following reasons, the oppressed minority religion argument is a red herring. First, the use of the term "minority," which conjures up invidious discrimination, is misleading. Even Protestantism, taken as a whole, which would encompass a vast number of faiths, is a dwindling majority, and will not be a "majority religion" in the very near future.[48]

Second, as Part One illustrated, smaller religions have done quite well in obtaining exemptions in the legislatures – sometimes too well – thereby weakening the argument significantly.[49] The often-stated concern that the courts are the better institution to secure religious liberty because religious groups can't navigate the legislative process is poppycock.

Third, as discussed above, it is a misconception to think of the U.S. republican form of government as a majoritarian system. Political scientists now accept as fact that minorities with a coherent message even tend to fare better in the legislative process than unorganized majorities.[50]

Fourth, the argument seems to be that small religions will be subject to covert and inevitable discrimination, but that is already redressed by the Religion Clauses, which prohibit discrimination. For example, any law specifically singling out a particular religious organization for detrimental treatment is unconstitutional. Besides, as a matter of fact, in the legislative process, the scale has definitely been weighted on the side favoring smaller religions, who have obtained the various exemptions and special treatment detailed in Part One, including the Native American Church, purportedly harmed by the *Smith* decision, Christian Scientists, and a slew of employers who don't believe in contraception. In addition, there is some insurance against discrimination under the *Smith* formulation favoring neutral, generally applicable laws, which drives legislatures toward general prohibitions. Where the legislature has decided that particular actions are unacceptable, because they generate certain harm and issued a blanket prohibition on the action, there is some insurance that the legislature has not acted out of discriminatory motive. The willingness to burden all actors with the law means that the legislature is concerned about the harm, not the identity of the actor.

Fifth, the constitutional culture weighs against such discrimination, at least as compared to other Western democracies. The most entrenched constitutional right in the United States is the absolute right to believe anything at all. The result is the most pluralistic religious culture in history, with new faiths appearing all the time.[51] In that context, unusual faiths are a commonplace in the American experience, and hardly an automatic target for negative treatment by the legislature. Add to that a history that never recognized a national established religion and such discrimination seems even less likely. In the United States, no particular religion has ever been able to obtain singular privileges for itself, and therefore all religions are "outside" the government. The same cannot be said for Europe, where new or upstart religions have experienced difficulties. "Although many European constitutions ostensibly grant rights to religious minorities, the existence of dominant religions in the European States forces the remaining confessions into a hierarchy, the bottom tier of which may only legally exercise those rights by engaging in practices that conform to the doctrines of the dominant religions."[52]

Even then, perhaps there is a risk that some small, politically powerless religions that are incapable of putting together a coherent message for the legislature or incapable of enlisting the support of mainstream religions may well have problems obtaining exemptions. The system does not generate perfect results, no matter how exemptions are handled. But the perfect should not be permitted to be the enemy of the good. In the end, the *Smith* Court correctly weighed the alternatives in this scenario as follows:

> It may fairly be said that leaving accommodation to the political process will place at a relative disadvantage those religious practices that are not widely engaged in; but that unavoidable consequence of democratic government must be preferred to a system in which each conscience is a law unto itself or in which judges weigh the social importance of all laws against the centrality of all religious beliefs.[53]

The legislature is the most institutionally competent to hear the concerns of the burdened religious entities and to make the determination whether relieving them of an obligation to a particular law is consistent with the public good. Thus, the route for those individuals and institutions that find their religious conduct at odds with the prevailing law lies beyond the courts. The Supreme Court in *Smith* made it clear that religious entities may ask for legislative exemptions narrowly tailored to their religious practices.[54] If a religious entity can persuade a legislature (that is doing its job and serving the public good) that exempting it from the law will not harm the public good, then an exemption is consistent with ordered democracy.[55] If not, then the religious entity is rightly prevented from doing the harm proscribed by the legislature. The Supreme Court's free exercise doctrine is just plain common sense.

The entry of extreme religious liberty

The *Smith* Court said, "Our decisions reveal that the [correct] reading [of the Free Exercise Clause] is . . . [that] [w]e have never held that an individual's religious beliefs excuse him from compliance with an otherwise valid law prohibiting conduct that the State is free to regulate."[56]

Many scholars and religious organizations roundly criticized the *Smith* Court's reaffirmation of the rule of law for religious entities on the theory that it was introducing a regime of tyranny. They, however, manufactured religion's enemies. Everyone in this culture takes religion seriously, because they must, for good and for bad. Millions of Americans are believers and that includes our elected representatives, many of whom slavishly defer to religious entities. Republican and Democratic Presidents curry the favor of religious leaders, as do legislators. President Obama's unwillingness to budge on the application of the Affordable Care Act's contraceptive mandate to for-profit companies, even if owned by religious believers, was the exception that proves the rule.

Eighty-five percent of the country professes some sort of religious belief.[57] Even atheists, agnostics, and humanists have to take religion very seriously, because it affects so many elements of their lives.

Smith's detractors are also fundamentally wrong about the conflict between religions. On the one hand, this society has done a remarkable job of welcoming an ever-growing and enormous collection of religions – literally tens if not hundreds of thousands. But on the other hand, because of the nature of religious faith and its truth claims, there is always the potential for conflict between religious believers. The United States has not had a religious war, because of the separation of church and state.

In fact, conflicts are heightened as religious entities are given more power to trump the laws that govern everyone else. For example, RLUIPA has led to religious tensions heretofore absent from the land use process. The land use arguments lead to deep divisions between neighbors, because the odds are overwhelming that the neighbors objecting are religious in their own right and resent being told that their values are necessarily in conflict with "higher principles" or that they are opposed to any particular religion simply because they value their neighborhood's relative peace, safety, and aesthetics – all elements of the American dream. The bad feelings do not disappear once the case has been concluded, and too often, the religious division that was not there before the religious landowner invoked RLUIPA to trump his neighbor's property rights becomes a marked characteristic of the neighborhood. The likelihood in these scenarios – given the depth of the feeling on both sides – is that the neighborhood will become mono-religious or that an invisible divide between one religion and every other will make itself visible in times of political upheaval.

Others responded to *Smith* with a full-dress parade of horribles, which are worth repeating here, because they bring into focus the Chicken Little quality of the post-*Smith* hysteria:

> Consider the fact that employment discrimination laws could force the Roman Catholic Church to hire female priests, if there are no free exercise exemptions from generally applicable laws. Or that historic preservation laws could prevent churches from making theologically significant alterations to their structures. Or that prisons will not have to serve kosher or hallel food to Jewish or Moslem prisoners. Or that Jewish high school athletes may be forbidden to wear yarmulkes and thus excluded from inter-scholastic sports. Or that churches with a religious objection to unrepentant homosexuality will be required to retain an openly gay individual as church organist, parochial school teacher, or even a pastor. Or that public school students will be forced to attend sex education classes contrary to their faith. Or that religious sermons on issues of political significance could lead to revocation of tax exemptions. Or that Catholic doctors in public hospitals could be fired if they refuse to perform abortions. Or that Orthodox Jews could be required to cease and desist from sexual segregation of their places of worship.[58]

More than twenty years into *Smith's* reintroduction of the rule of law for religious entities, this list is more imagination than fact. Not only that, but it is based on a false assumption that the United States is hostile to religion. It is not, and the sky has not fallen. To my knowledge, no conservative church has been required to hire an organist or music director who was openly gay, and religious institutions have been permitted to deny employment to homosexuals. For example, Catholic schools in Pennsylvania and Washington State were permitted to fire teachers for marrying same-sex partners.[59] Nor has the government entered orthodox temples and required the men to sit with the women. Churches have avoided landmarking laws that affect liturgy.[60] State legislatures have permitted children to opt out of sex education courses.[61] Courts have held that prison officials' refusal to provide kosher or Muslim diets was unreasonable (before and after RLUIPA).[62] Finally, all but for-profit corporations obtained exemptions from the contraception mandate in the Affordable Care Act, even though the medications are extremely important to many women's health.[63] No yarmulke-wearing athletes have been barred from the field. Religious storeowners have been permitted to impose a modest dress code inside their establishments. And since 2000, federal law exempts doctors with religious objections from being required to perform abortions.[64]

The issue regarding whether churches should be able to support particular political candidates and retain their tax-exempt status does not involve the impact of *Smith*. Rather, there is a federal law that does deny tax-exempt status when churches support political candidates.[65] The purpose of the law was to ensure that political action committees could not avoid taxes under the ruse of being a nonprofit, charitable organization. While the purpose made some sense, the impact on the political speech of religious institutions is not good for them or for society. U.S. citizens are better off knowing which candidates are being backed by particular religious powers, because religious entities are extremely active in the political process, and the people deserve to know which interests in the society are pressuring which representatives and on which issues. If nothing else, this book should make clear why backroom deals for religious institutions are just as inconsistent with the public good as backroom deals that favor businesses or other interest groups.

In 1990, Stephen Carter published *The Culture of Disbelief: How American Law and Politics Trivialize Religious Devotion*, which argued that religious interests were being sidelined in the United States. He stated: "there is much depressing evidence that the religious voice is required to stay out of the public square."[66] The book was an influential bestseller, and even appears in the hand of President William Jefferson Clinton in Yale University's portrait of him. The problem with Professor Carter's thesis was that religious institutions are not politically powerless, and his thesis has aided them to exercise political power while appearing to be socially weak. Carter, of course, is not the only person who has argued that U.S. culture has been "secularized."[67] It's a dominant refrain that fosters religious entities' political agendas rather nicely. In the midst of the rhetoric regarding secularization, it is easy to assume that religious institutions are either politically dormant or that they are politically ineffective, and therefore to think they need the courts to grant exemptions from the law. Neither is accurate. Jerry Falwell's Moral Majority in the 1970s was just one example of the many efforts by religious entities to influence politics. In light of the political realities, I would back a Sunshine Law that would repeal the prohibition and encourage religious institutions to make their political agendas as public as possible, for reasons that should be apparent from Part One.[68]

The basic problem with the anti-*Smith* agenda is that it assumes that legislatures are inclined to suppress religious liberty, that religious lobbyists are weak in the legislative process, and that there are strong lobbies to achieve the anti-religion ends presumed. In fact, the contrary is true. Religious entities are uncannily able to obtain what they seek in the legislative context and legislators are all too often their sycophants. As the *Smith* Court stated, "a society that believes in the negative protection accorded to religious belief can be expected to be solicitous of that value in its legislation as well."[69] Thus, the assumption among those opposing *Smith* that legislative accommodation would result in no accommodation was simply inaccurate. That is why Senator Hatch's declaration that without RFRA there would be no "basis to challenge Government regulations which infringe on the rights to the free exercise of religion" cannot be taken seriously.[70] It is political hyperbole, and no more.

The Court's antagonists have argued that *Smith* was wrong, because the Free Exercise Clause is supposed to provide protection for those who lack "the ability to protect themselves in the political sphere" and for anyone who might find him or herself "caught in conflict with our secular political culture." The religious entity as a weakling in the legislative process is simply not persuasive for all the reasons presented in this chapter. *Smith's* opponents also talk about "our secular political culture."[71] What exactly is that? In the United States, the culture is not divorced from religion. Far from it. Religious lobbyists draft, push, and oppose legislation in every legislature in the country. Religion informs the beliefs of the vast majority of citizens and their leaders; the history of ideas that fed the culture's political institutions are rooted in no small part in a variety of theological constructs; and there is a healthy and vital public debate about religion and its role in society. Major newspapers have religion pages and religion news reporters, the radio air waves and cable television are filled with religious messages and political opinions, and the war on terror has trained our attention – whether we like it or not – on the radical Islamists' fanaticism and their theological worldview. Religion is quite literally inescapable. Some have argued that religious reasons should not be part of the debate over public policy.[72] It's an interesting theory, but utterly impossible. Religion cannot be avoided. There is no community without a house of worship, and typically there are many in any one town. There are approximately 345,000 congregations in the United States,[73] and almost 318 million people.[74] That is roughly one house of worship for every 920 people. Religion is everywhere, and any atheist will tell you that it is impossible to inhabit a "secular" political environment in the United States.

In sum, the passionate objections to *Smith* have turned out to be more passion than fact. More than twenty years later, there has been no decline in religious liberty or in religion's political power.

Free exercise is best pursued just as the Smith Court described

There are three principles that make the Supreme Court's described system legitimate and worthy.

(1) There is an appropriate role for the courts and the legislatures.
There are some who see little functional difference between law made by

a court and law made by a legislature. That is particularly true in the religious liberty context, where one scholar argues: "If there is nothing wrong with statutory commands of the sovereign that make exceptions from generally applicable laws in cases of conflict with religious conscience, then there should be nothing wrong with constitutional commands of the same sort."[75] This reasoning makes one of the cardinal errors of those who argue in favor of the extreme religious liberty statutes. Their perspective is that so long as the believer can obtain what they seek, then the process is irrelevant. In effect, the only relevant question is whether the religious believer obtains the accommodation. This formulation encourages religious narcissism and leaves out the good of others and the society.

The courts routinely defer to legislative judgment to avoid inserting their policy preferences into the law; that is in fact a canon of constitutional interpretation. But they also have established markers that trigger concern of a constitutional violation and the need to abandon their ordinary deference. In the case of free exercise, the Court looks for the following to justify its interference with the legislative process through the application of strict scrutiny: (1) evidence of discrimination or animus against religion, which would indicate the law is not neutral; (2) evidence that a law is not generally applicable, but rather crafted to apply solely to this religious entity; or (3) evidence that a law affords secular reasons for exceptions to a law but not religious reasons. The courts apply a similar version of this approach and internal reasoning to one constitutional right after another, including equal protection, free speech, and others. This framing of the issue is appropriate to the courts' powers and capacities.

Under the Constitution's structure, the legislative process is definitively different from a court's, and legislative statutory commands are dramatically different from a judicial decree. The judicial process is a packaged affair with strict limitations on the latitude of the judge to make policy determinations. In contrast, the legislative process is at its very best when it engages in wide-ranging debate and investigation that can determine social policy out of a universe of options.

In contrast, courts may only consider the claims of the parties before them and only the record introduced by the parties. To a significant degree, the parties control the court's (and especially the less experienced clerk's) worldview. Their facts – and only their facts – are relevant in the case. That is why activists look for "test cases," that is, those cases that present the facts as they would like the court to think are typical. The judicial system is also binary, with only two sides before the Court, but not everyone potentially affected. It is true that in some cases, outside interests can expand the judge's understanding of the underlying social issues by filing amicus, or friend of the court, briefs, but that is rarely done at the trial level, and the practice does not grant the amicus standing to engage in briefing on the merits or oral argument.

Nor does the court have the prerogative to decide issues beyond those presented. It is constrained in its examination of the law by the issues raised by the parties, procedural rules including evidence limits, and jurisdictional issues like standing or ripeness. A judge is not supposed to decide legal issues that are not presented in that particular case (as much as he or she might like to do so).

Judges are also in a fundamentally different position than are legislators. A judge is required to be open-minded, to be evenhanded, and to read the law as the legislature intended or the Constitution commands. The symbol of the judicial system, seen in courtrooms throughout the United States, is blindfolded Lady Justice. According to the American Bar Association (ABA) Model Rules of Professional Conduct and Code of Judicial Conduct,

> A judge shall perform judicial duties without bias or prejudice. A judge shall not, in the performance of judicial duties, by words or conduct manifest bias or prejudice, including but not limited to bias or prejudice based upon race, sex, religion, national origin, disability, age, sexual orientation or socioeconomic status, and shall not permit staff, court officials and others subject to the judge's direction and control to do so."[76]

Thus,

> Each justice or judge of the United States shall take the following oath or affirmation before performing the duties of his office: "I,_, do solemnly swear (or affirm) that I will administer justice without respect to persons, and do equal right to the poor and to the rich, and that I will faithfully and impartially discharge and perform all the duties

incumbent upon me as under the Constitution and laws of the United States. So help me God.[77]

And where there is a particular case raising the specter of a judge's bias, there are rules that demand recusal: "Any justice, judge, or magistrate [magistrate judge] of the United States shall disqualify himself in any proceeding in which his impartiality might reasonably be questioned."[78] By comparison, the legislature has unlimited latitude to frame the issues (over which it has legitimate power), to determine the extent of its investigation, and to take a position. Both fact-finding *and* lawmaking are at the prerogative of the legislator.

Assuming it is making law within its constitutional powers, Congress can consider laws already in place, laws enacted by other legislatures, by other countries, and laws never before imagined by anyone else. Indeed, members may even decide to investigate a social problem in depth before deciding whether any law is needed and before anyone anywhere has considered such a law. They have at their disposal the power to subpoena witnesses, to hold extensive hearings, to commission studies, and to elicit the views of any expert, citizen, or constituent. A legislature sets its own parameters for consideration.

A further value of enlisting legislative judgment for permissive accommodation (as opposed to judicial judgment) is that the legislature has the power to repeal the laws that it finds are noxious in practice. Precedent has not nearly the pull that it has in the judicial arena. Thus, judgments about relative harm can be revisited and reweighed. The power to repeal legislation reflects the human nature of regulation – it is always based on imperfect understanding and capable of being viewed through different lenses at a later time.[79] After a generally applicable law is passed, those burdened by it in practice can still request an exemption, and can show how the law operated in fact. That is the history of peyote exemptions. Conversely, when an exemption renders more harm than originally understood, it can be rescinded. This is the story in many states, where exemptions for clergy from mandatory child sex abuse reporting were repealed in the wake of the scandals mentioned in Chapter 2.[80]

(2) *Legislative accommodation should be debated under the harsh glare of public scrutiny*. Legislatures are competent to grant permissive accommodation and many religious entities are quite familiar with the legislative process. But the public good is often sacrificed in favor of religious entities, as can be seen in the states that provide religious exemptions to excuse the death of a child from the failure to obtain medical treatment.[81] Too often, such deals are made in the back halls of the legislative rotunda, rather than in the harsh glare of public scrutiny. This is what I call "silent" accommodation.

As I discussed in Chapter 2, the Followers of Christ Church in Oregon allowed three children to die of medical neglect in 1998. When authorities investigated and they discovered a large cemetery of children, both prosecutors and the public became concerned.[82] When prosecutors sought to bring them to justice, only then did they learn about the religious defenses to felonies in their state.[83] The original exemption had been granted without publicity. Once the consequences were made real and in the newspapers (consequences that could have been easily imagined had legislators done their job and considered the larger public good in the course of granting the exemption in the first place) and children were dead, the public discussion that should have taken place in the first instance began. Rita Swan, along with other child advocates, worked hard to educate legislators and the public about the realities of religious medical neglect and the dangers to children.

Then the faith-healing lobbyists leapt into action. What was their argument? That the Constitution guaranteed their right to religious freedom, and that freedom entailed a right to choose prayer over medical treatment for even very sick children. As a result, in 1999, some but not all exemptions from criminal liability were repealed. For several years, the group did not permit other children to die, but that ended, and in 2011, Oregon eliminated spiritual treatment as a defense to all criminal charges.[84]

The states have required professionals to report child abuse to civil authorities. Many states, unbeknownst to the public at large, also granted clergy an exemption from the requirement – even though clergy are often in a good position to know whether a child is in trouble. Subsequently, those who had the most knowledge about childhood sexual abuse at the hands of trusted clergy were under no obligation to report it, and the abuse continued with further abuse and new victims. It is an issue that was not a part of the public debate until thousands of Catholic Church victims were revealed within the last decade. Once again, had legislatures asked what best served the public good under the public spotlight rather than provide a silent exemption, some of this harm might have been prevented.

RFRA is probably the best example of the phenomenon of silent (as well as blind) exemptions. It was both impenetrable on its surface, making it a blind exemption, but it was also silent because there was no legislative discourse about its actual impact. It is a law that disabled the vast majority of laws in the United States as they applied to religious entities, but prompted virtually no concern in the House or the Senate. Late in the process, there were some passing comments about its impact on prisons, but no investigation was initiated to determine the likely actual impact on prison order. There was no debate about children who die from religiously motivated medical neglect, or from physical abuse in fundamentalist work camps and unlicensed child care centers. Or about the fair housing laws or schools. Because Congress did not ask the hard questions about the public good, members and the public did not understand that so many potential victims were in harm's way. They raced to pander to the religious, as they embraced the opportunity to reverse the Supreme Court's First Amendment doctrine.

RFRA's progeny also spawned numerous silent exemption statutes. The Pennsylvania Religious Freedom Protection Act of 2002, for example, was passed without hearings and as quickly as possible so as to avoid opposition. Holding a single hearing should have prompted a public debate, because by the time it was passed, a great deal was known about the negative impact of RFRA and its progeny.

(3) *The accommodation should be consistent with the public good.*
An exemption is not legitimate unless it is the product of deliberation over both religious liberty *and* the public interest. Yet, the very latitude that permits legislators to make judgments about the public good also creates the conditions for them to act without taking into account the public good. Representation is an enormous power and responsibility. The legislator receives the power from the people to make laws without popular veto and without mindless deference to the majority, so that he can consider the public good. The question is whether he will. We know he will listen to the religious entity.

This is the typical image of the legislator: captured by special interests and incapable of acting in the public's interest. It is a caricature, to be sure, but it is also too often true when it comes to religion. As discussed above, legislatures are engineered to hear messages from cohesive groups even if they are small. The lobbyist for a minority, therefore, is not necessarily at the disadvantage of large majorities. This quality in the legislative process in fact supports permissive legislative accommodation, because there is no reason to assume minority religions will not be heard. As discussed above, plenty have been heard and accommodated.

Their implicit argument, however, is that other and possibly less savory, interests will drown out the religious lobbyist. This rests on an assumption that religious liberty is not valued by elected representatives. That cannot be supported. The very existence of RFRA and its progeny – which affect every law and therefore a vast majority of the interests in the United States – disproves the point, as do many of the exemptions examined in Part One. As Justice Antonin Scalia said in *Smith*, "a society that believes in the negative protection accorded to religious belief can be expected to be solicitous of that value in its legislation."[85] Such a large percentage of Americans attest to religious belief – nearly 85 percent – that the objection of weakness in the political process is based more on social myth than reality.[86]

In part, that myth is constructed by indefensible presuppositions about religious entities in the political sphere. There was a widespread, though often undeveloped, assumption that religious entities are above the dirtiness of the legislative, political process. They supposedly operated at a higher and purer level. In point of fact, religious entities are a potent and vocal presence in the legislative and political process and know how to operate the levers as well as any other lobbyist. Their success in obtaining exemptions, e.g., that immunize from prosecution those faith-healing parents who let their children die of treatable medical ailments, speak for themselves. They pressure legislators on abortion, the death penalty, welfare, tax issues, foreign affairs, the environment, and child sex abuse statutes of limitation, to name only a few. Moreover, many religious leaders wield the kind of social power that makes them just as desirable A-list invitees as any member of Congress or state legislature, meaning that politicians and religious leaders associate outside the legislative arena.

That familiarity greases the way for them to request and obtain exemptions. But, even those without A-list status have the capacity to influence the legislative process. I have no doubt the popular Pope Francis will also wield significant influence on public policy.

Representatives hear the religious entities' requests (sometimes because they share the same religion), and they respond eagerly even when the conduct will harm others. Why? Because elected officials have (incorrectly) assumed that religious leaders necessarily represent the voting blocs. They defer to bishops, rabbis, and even fundamentalist Mormon prophets to secure votes. It is a disgrace. What legislator would even grant a meeting with a group asking for the right to avoid prosecution if they let children die or for the right to avoid liability for putting children within reach of known pedophiles? Is there a legislator in the country that would entertain a proposal to permit secular motion picture theaters to avoid land use laws?

The real question is whether they will consider the larger public interest. To reach a legitimate exemption, the legislature may not merely hear the religious entities' request and grant it. That would be the essence of the establishment of religion – the government ceding its responsibility to the people to religious interests. Instead, the legitimate exemption should be a product of the legislature exercising its power and responsibility to consider the effect on the public if the religious entity is permitted to avoid the law.

Legislators would do well to pay attention to current polling showing that they defer to religious leaders on immoral issues at their peril.[87] They should also learn from former Brooklyn D.A. Charles Hynes, who lost re-election when it became well-known he had assisted his ultra-Orthodox Jewish constituents in keeping child sex abuse secret.[88]

All legislative judgments should include consideration of the public interest; such consideration is essential for exemptions, because it proves that the exemption is not a handout to religion that sells out the public's interest. The Establishment Clause forbids blind exemptions – those that are granted because the recipient is religious and not because the larger public good is benefited by it.

More recently, one state after another is being pushed by religious lobbyists to expand the RFRA formula to empower believers to avoid the law even more easily. This latest push reduces the initial burden on the believer as it deletes the word "substantial" from the substantial burden test.[89] Therefore, a believer who is suffering a *de minimis* burden on his, her, or its religious practice can file a lawsuit and demand that the law should not apply unless the government bears its heavy burden of proof. These new, aggressive iterations of mini-RFRAs is part of extreme religious liberty spiralling out of control.

The Never-Ending Spiral of Extreme Religious Liberty

1.   1878-present
Ordered Liberty Under the Constitution, First Amendment, Free Exercise Clause
Employment Division v. Smith, 494 U.S. 872 (1990)
Church of Lukumi Babalu Aye v. City of Hialeah, 508 U.S. 520 (1993)
Rules: a. Believer must prove law imposes a substantial burden.
b. A neutral, generally applicable law is constitutional unless irrational.
c. If law is not neutral or not generally applicable, ordinary strict scrutiny applies: the government must prove a compelling interest and that the law is narrowly tailored
d. the right is only good against the government (state action)

2.   1972
Wisconsin v. Yoder, 406 U.S. 205 (1972)
Rules: a. Believer must prove a substantial burden
b. Only case where a neutral, generally applicable law is subjected to strict scrutiny

    c. Government must prove a compelling interest and that the law is narrowly tailored

3. 1993

Religious Freedom Restoration Act of 1993

Rules: a. Believer must prove a substantial burden
- b. Government must prove a neutral, generally applicable law serves a compelling interest
- c. Narrow tailoring is replaced by the more extreme "least restrictive means"
- d. Relief permitted only "against a government"

4. 2000

Amendments to Religious Freedom Restoration Act (further expansion of rights for believers)

Rules: a. Expands definition of "religious exercise" to be: "any exercise of religion, whether or not compelled by, or central to, a system of religious belief," including "the use, building, conversion of real property for the purpose of religious exercise" so long as the person, assembly, or institution "uses or intends to use the property for that purpose."

5. 2000

Religious Land Use and Institutionalized Persons Act

Rules: a. Believer must prove a substantial burden
- b. Government must prove a neutral, generally applicable land use or prison law serves a compelling interest
- c. Narrow tailoring is replaced by the more extreme "least restrictive means"
- d. Relief permitted only "against a government"

State RFRA Developments That Undermine Neutral, Generally Applicable Laws

Source	Capabilities/Power/Interpreted to
AZ, FL, IL, LA, SC, TX	standard state RFRA
AL, CT	would have deleted or deletes "substantial" from "substantial burden"
RI, NM, MO	removed "substantial burden" and replaced with "restrict"
ID, KS, KY, OK, PA, TN, VA	adds to government's burden: clear and convincing evidence
MS	expands to include suits between private parties
MS	applies to businesses
MS	works against homosexuals or same-sex couples

The better path than RFRA is *Smith*. True, legislators have enacted some extreme exemptions, but at least they have the virtue of being on the public record and identified beyond the trail of a single case. Moreover, at least individual exemption requests inform legislators so they understand what is being requested. As Americans become more savvy about what religious believers demand behind closed doors in the state and federal rotundas, they will make it more difficult for elected representatives to do the wrong thing. RFRA banks on getting religious entities special privileges behind a veil of feel-good rhetoric.

I am not saying that legislators always get it right. Far from it! But when they are involved, and the issues are not behind closed doors, public policy can be rationally crafted. The debate can extend beyond the individuals in front of a court. I categorically condemn the Idaho legislature, which recently halted consideration of a bill to deter faith-healing parents from letting their children die. Rep. Christy Perry fought the bill to protect the parents' religious freedom, saying, "This is about religious beliefs, the belief God is in charge of whether they live, and God is in charge of whether they die."[90] I disagree and believe the state has more responsibility to protect these live children than the fetuses in the abortion debates, but at least, given this was aired in the legislature through an introduced bill, we know who was responsible for choosing adults' religious liberty over their children's lives. That is an issue that citizens can challenge and pursue in the future. It's the opacity of the RFRAs that makes them especially dangerous.

The legitimate religious accommodation can be characterized as follows: (1) it follows a judicial finding that the First Amendment is violated; or (2) it is enacted by a politically accountable legislature charged with consideration of the public good; it is not a blind exemption, but rather one that takes into account the public's interest; and it is not a silent exemption, but occurs in the crucible of public debate.

Conclusion

Some might respond to this book by asking why the entire system of religious liberty should be built on a presumption that religious organizations and individuals will harm the public good. That's just perverse, they say. And they might add, while the examples in the first part of this book are disturbing, to be sure, they are the exceptions that prove the rule. A few bad apples are no reason to burden every religious group with the vast number of laws in the United States, or so the argument goes. This instinct is understandable. Because if religion is capable of enough immoral or evil acts that it deserves only limited liberty, then it may seem like there is little hope for society. Pretending believers are all good actors, though, is patently dangerous.

When self-deception leads the United States to give religious conduct a berth that results in intolerable harm were it perpetrated by any other entity, this country proves that religion can be the "opiate of the masses."[91] The Marxist wholesale jettisoning of religion was a doomed social experiment, but Marx was indisputably correct that religion is too often an excuse for sloppy thinking and delusional optimism. Such blind trust is an abdication of social responsibility that will in the end undermine the culture altogether. We don't do religious entities or believers any favors by giving them a pass on their illegal or immoral behavior.

The rule of law is a canopy of mutual protection reached through legitimate legislative processes, under which all members of the society must abide by the same rules and observe the rule of no harm to others. The public good is diminished when individuals may use their personal beliefs to avoid the law at the expense of others.

The burden should rest on the religious believer demanding exemption from a law to prove that his or her conduct is not harmful to the society and individuals within it. To date, the primary obstacles to the proper function of these principles have been judicial activism and overly deferential legislatures. Too many ill-considered exemptions have been granted, and too many RFRAs passed, solely because the one demanding the exemption was religious and the legislator abdicated his or her responsibilities.

The United States' system, though it started on the right track, has been derailed in recent decades into a system of possessive individualism – the "conception of the individual as essentially the proprietor of his own person or capacities, owing nothing to society for them."[92] Religious entities have argued either that the laws are too onerous *for them* or that the default rule should be complete deregulation. They have coined a phrase to describe their view of religion and the society within which it resides: church autonomy.[93] This libertine agenda has persuaded legislatures to permit religious entities to trump the public good by permitting them to avoid accountability. It is a triumph of the urge to power, in Nietzsche's sense, not a sacred right.[94]

The mindset in the United States regarding religion must change if there is ever to be true liberty as the framing generation wisely understood it. The culprits in the cases that I described in Part One are not the religious entities lobbying for privileges without regard to their victims, but, rather, the legislators that pander to religion and the voters who do not hold those legislators accountable. There is an expectation that lobbyists pursue their own narrow interests, regardless of public good or the needs of others. Part One of this book demonstrated that this principle applies emphatically to religious entities. Legislators are supposed to stand between lobbyists and the larger public good, and they owe the people the duty of investigating who will be harmed by *any* lobbyist's demand. With the RFRAs, legislators abandoned their constituents' and America's needs.

A vigorous, public legislative deliberation is just as crucial, and sometimes more crucial, in the context of religious demands, as it is in any secular context. The United States must abandon its adolescent belief in the inevitable goodness of every religious entity and instead demand an accounting when religious entities seek to avoid the laws that govern everyone else. This is not so much a matter of distrusting religious entities as it is an invitation for common sense return to religious liberty.

The Never-Ending Spiral of Extreme Religious Liberty

1. **1878-present**
Ordered Liberty Under the Constitution, First Amendment, Free Exercise Clause
Employment Division v. Smith, 494 U.S. 872 (1990)
Church of Lukumi Babalu Aye v. City of Hialeah, 508 U.S. 520 (1993)
Rules: a. Believer must prove law imposes a substantial burden.
     b. A neutral, generally applicable law is constitutional unless irrational.
     c. If law is not neutral or not generally applicable, ordinary strict scrutiny applies: the government must prove a compelling interest and that the law is narrowly tailored
     d. the right is only good against the government (state action)

2. **1972**
Wisconsin v. Yoder, 406 U.S. 205 (1972)
Rules: a. Believer must prove a substantial burden
     b. Only case where a neutral, generally applicable law is subjected to strict scrutiny
     c. Government must prove a compelling interest and that the law is narrowly tailored

3. **1993**
Religious Freedom Restoration Act of 1993
Rules: a. Believer must prove a substantial burden
     b. Government must prove a neutral, generally applicable law serves a compelling interest
     c. Narrow tailoring is replaced by the more extreme "least restrictive means"
     d. Relief permitted only "against a government"

4. **2000**
Amendments to Religious Freedom Restoration Act (further expansion of rights for believers)
Rules: a. Expands definition of "religious exercise" to be: "any exercise of religion, whether or not compelled by, or central to, a system of religious belief," including "the use, building, conversion of real property for the purpose of religious exercise" so long as the person, assembly, or institution "uses or intends to use the property for that purpose."

5. **2000**
Religious Land Use and Institutionalized Persons Act
Rules: a. Believer must prove a substantial burden
     b. Government must prove a neutral, generally applicable land use or prison law serves a compelling interest
     c. Narrow tailoring is replaced by the more extreme "least restrictive means"
     d. Relief permitted only "against a government"

State RFRA Developments That Undermine Neutral, Generally Applicable Laws

Source	Capabilities/Power/Interpreted to
AZ, FL, IL, LA, SC, TX	standard state RFRA
AL, CT	would have deleted or deletes "substantial" from "substantial burden"
RI, NM, MO	removed "substantial burden" and replaced with "restrict"
ID, KS, KY, OK, PA, TN, VA	adds to government's burden: clear and convincing evidence
MS	expands to include suits between private parties
MS	applies to businesses
MS	works against homosexuals or same-sex couples

EPILOGUE: FOLLOW THE MONEY

As with everything else in American society, it pays to follow the money.

There is no natural limit on believers' sense of entitlement today, and it now extends to the free market, business, and money. RFRA was launched because legislators supposedly would not accommodate Native American Church use of peyote after *Smith*. Its creators were wrong about that, but the RFRA ethos contributed toward the narcissistic sense of entitlement that soon exceeded any supposed lack of religious liberty for the plaintiffs in *Smith*.

The original RFRA's legislative history contained a few anecdotes about individual Hmong and Orthodox Jews objecting to the autopsies states require when there is a suspicious death.[1] The Hmong believe that the physical invasion inherent in conducting an autopsy inhibits the body's path to the afterlife,[2] and "unnecessary" autopsies violate Orthodox Jewish beliefs, because the Talmud forbids "mutilating" the dead.[3] Then Congress was told that extreme religious liberty for land use was necessary to help a minyan (a small group of Jewish men meeting to pray each morning) meeting in a home in a residential neighborhood, because they must walk[4] and so that houses of worship could be built without discrimination.[5] RFRA, RLUIPA, and the state RFRAs are sold as though underdog believers needed Congress's assistance. The deep irony, of course, is that while the politically powerful mainstream members of the Coalition for the Free Exercise of Religion demanded RFRA in Congress, the little Native American Church was winning peyote exemptions in legislatures across the country.

As the charts in Chapter 8 and Chapter 10 show, believers have pushed persistently to expand the already expansive scope of RFRA in the federal and state legislatures. Losses under this extreme standard are an argument to them that they need even more latitude to break the law. What does this tell us? That the goal here is dominion by religious believers, over all laws. Those behind the move want to make it nearly impossible for the government to enforce laws against believers who want autonomy.

Twenty years later, for-profit businesses are striding into the arena. They want RFRAs to mold the free market to their faith. Some do not want to do business with homosexuals; others with same-sex couples; and others believe they are entitled to exclude women's medical care from their health care plans based on their religious beliefs. In other words, we started with allegedly defenseless believers and here we are, twenty years later, with for-profit corporations and large religious corporations demanding a "right" to mold the marketplace however they see fit.

Hobby Lobby and the RFRA and RLPA Legislative History

The passionate opponents to universal health care, or, as they dubbed it, Obamacare, joined forces with religious conservatives to deploy RFRA to carry their fight forward after they lost in Congress. Encouraged by the Roman Catholic bishops, who have chosen not only to fight abortion but also to launch a public offensive against contraception, owners of every conceivable type of organization argued that RFRA accords them the right to avoid the Affordable Care Act's wellness requirement that women be afforded comprehensive reproductive health care, including but not limited to contraceptives, anemia screening, gestational diabetes testing, STD screening, breast and cervical cancer testing, and urinary tract infection and tobacco use screening.[6] The Affordable Care Act itself includes an exemption for churches and frankly religious groups: "(i) a member of a recognized religious sect or division thereof..., and (ii) an adherent of established tenets or teachings of such sect or division "[7] as well as a religious employer, defined as one that "(1) has the inculcation of religious values as its purpose; (2) primarily employs persons who share its religious tenets; (3) primarily serves persons who share its religious tenets; and (4) is a non-profit organization described in a provision of the Internal Revenue Code that refers to churches, their integrated auxiliaries, conventions or associations of churches, and to the exclusively religious activities of any religious order."[8]

Under pressure from the bishops, the Obama Administration expanded the exemption to include religious nonprofits like the University of Notre Dame.[9] For these groups, they need only fill out a form informing their insurance issuer and plan administrator (if self-insured) that they do not believe in the use of contraception, "self-certify[ing]" that they are a nonprofit, religious organization[10] to obtain an exception to the contraceptive mandate.[11]

This left only for-profit, nonreligious corporations covered by the contraception mandate. They invoked RFRA, and they won.

To put things in perspective, it is worthwhile to know the facts about the highly successful Hobby Lobby company that led the charge. It has annual revenues of $3.3 billion[12] and describes itself as follows:

> We have 595 stores across the nation that average 55,000 square feet and offer more than 67,000 crafting and home decor products. Hobby Lobby is listed as a major private corporation in *Forbes* and *Fortunes* list of America's largest private companies.[13]

It is not the type of claimant the drafters of RFRA had in mind, to put it mildly. Americans need to understand what Hobby Lobby and the Supreme Court have done to the fabric of the United States.

First, Hobby Lobby is a nonreligious, for-profit corporation, by definition. In the United States, we have a public free market in goods and a private sphere of religious exercise. Large corporations like Exxon or Wal-Mart have never been considered religious entities that have free exercise rights. True, there is a regulation involving religion and large corporations, which is Title VII, but it *forbids* corporations from discriminating on religion against their employees – it doesn't create free exercise rights for nonreligious corporations! As discussed in Chapter 7, Title VII does afford certain religious organizations the right to discriminate on the basis of religion, to a:

> religious corporation, association, educational institution, or society with respect to the employment of individuals of a particular religion

to perform work connected with the carrying on by such corporation, association, educational institution, or society of its activities.[14]

From this list, and without RFRA in the picture, Hobby Lobby would need to be a "religious corporation" to be free of Title VII's application. So, what is a religious corporation? According to established case law, it is one whose "purpose and character are primarily religious."[15] Under any ordinary reading of these criteria, more fully laid out in Chapter 7, Hobby Lobby is a nonreligious corporation for American free enterprise purposes. Its owners may be religious, but that does not make its enterprise religious. Its "67,000 crafting and home décor products" are not religious in nature, but are sold to make a profit.

The need to divide the marketplace into religious versus nonreligious and for profit vs. nonprofit entities is reflected in settled corporate law. The amicus brief for the Supreme Court in the *Hobby Lobby* case on behalf of corporate and criminal law professors explained,

> The first principle of corporate law is that for-profit corporations are entities that possess legal interests and a legal identity of their own – one separate and distinct from their shareholders . . . Allowing a corporation, through either shareholder vote or board resolution, to take on and assert the religious beliefs of its shareholders in order to avoid having to comply with a generally-applicable law with a secular purpose is fundamentally at odds with the entire concept of incorporation . . . If this Court were to agree that, as a matter of federal law, shareholders holding a control bloc of shares in a corporation may essentially transfer their religious beliefs to the corporation, the results could be overwhelming. Federal courts faced with RFRA and Free Exercise Clause lawsuits would be forced to resolve questions about what degree of ownership constitutes "control." They would also be forced to resolve difficult questions about the "legitimacy" of controlling shareholders' efforts to imbue the corporation with a religious identity.[16]

To protect the public:

> The separateness between shareholders and the corporation that they own (or, in this case, own and control) is essential to promote investment, innovation, job generation, and the orderly conduct of business . . . Adoption by this Court of a "values pass-through" theory here would be disruptive to business and generate costly litigation. It would encourage intrafamilial and intergenerational disputes. It would also

encourage subterfuge by corporations seeking to obtain a competitive advantage.[17]

This distinction has been part and parcel of creating our teeming, free market in goods, has quelled the Balkanization that has afflicted other countries, and has encouraged the peaceful coexistence of a wide array of believers in this diverse country.

Therefore, when Hobby Lobby and Conestoga Wood and others ginned up RFRA arguments against the Affordable Care Act, I was frankly shocked. Had I missed some huge element of the RFRA history, where everyone agreed that a for-profit, nonreligious corporation could invoke RFRA against the government? One of RFRA's longtime proponents, the Christian Legal Society, asserted to the Supreme Court that RFRA was always applicable to large, for-profit nonreligious corporations, like Hobby Lobby. Yet, there is no precedent in American history that would accord free exercise rights to a for-profit corporate behemoth like Hobby Lobby. And there is legislative history of the current RFRA that indicates that a company like Hobby Lobby can't have religious beliefs *by its nature*.

There is nothing in the original legislative history of RFRA that even hints at rights for for-profit corporations. As I explained earlier, the legislative history mostly featured complaints about *Smith* and a purportedly clueless or evil (take your pick) Supreme Court, with a couple of anecdotes about autopsies thrown in. After RFRA was held unconstitutional in *Boerne*, the Coalition returned to Congress and asked for another bite of the extreme religious liberty apple. Congress then considered the Religious Liberty Protection Act, which was intended to be RFRA redux.

During RLPA's proceedings, the ACLU and members like New York Congressman Jerry Nadler raised the concern whether it would create a defense for believers against the civil rights laws. Why? Because there were a handful of cases where believers who owned apartment buildings had argued that RFRA trumped the fair housing laws and, therefore, they had a right to discriminate against unmarried couples. All of those lawsuits involved enforcement of the fair housing laws by the Equal Employment Opportunity Commission (EEOC) or its state counterpart against individual landlords.[18]

By 1997, after the Court declared RFRA unconstitutional, many groups were aligned to defeat RLPA, including the ACLU, children's groups, cities, and other government entities, because once RFRA was in operation, its opacity receded as actual cases revealed its perils. The argument they raised that gained the most traction was that it would be used to defeat state and local anti-discrimination laws. (As usual, children's interests received lip service from members but did not get the traction that adult interests did.) Congressman Nadler offered a Solomonic amendment to prevent the evisceration of the civil rights laws, which would have permitted small businesses to invoke RFRA to overcome state and local civil rights laws, but would have prevented large corporations from invoking RFRA. Hobby Lobby would have been out of luck under Nadler's amendment. The amendment did not pass, and neither did RLPA.

During the debate over Nadler's proposed RLPA amendment there are a number of revealing moments, which show that the members viewed corporations like Hobby Lobby as incapable of having religious rights "by their nature." For example, when debating the amendment, Nadler explained that it

> recognizes that religious rights are rights that belong to individuals and to religious assemblies and institutions. *General Motors does not have sincerely held religious beliefs, by its nature.*[19] (emphasis added)

Rep. Charles Canady, the primary House sponsor, who opposed Nadler's amendment, agreed on the "nature" of large, for-profit, nonreligious corporations, saying,

> I do not think that General Motors or Exxon Corporation or any other such large corporation . . . could come within a mile of showing that anything that was done would substantially infringe on their religious beliefs. *They do not have a religious belief.* They do not have a religious practice. *It is not in the nature of such to have such religious beliefs or practices.*[20] (emphasis added)

Thus, regardless of whether they were for or against the Nadler amendment, they were in agreement that large, for-profit, nonreligious corporations simply don't have free exercise rights by their very natures. Thus, they cannot even bring a claim under RFRA. Their claims are non-starters.

This same distinction between commercial entities and religious entities was reflected in the legislative history regarding land use.

> ... the use, building, or conversion of real property for religious purposes is religious exercise of the person or entity that intends to use the property for that purpose. It is only the use, building, or conversion for religious purposes that is protected, and not other uses or portions of the same property. Thus, if a commercial enterprise builds a chapel in one wing of the building, the chapel is protected if the owner is sincere about its religious purposes, but the commercial enterprise is not protected. Similarly if religious services are conducted once a week in a building otherwise devoted to secular commerce, the religious services may be protected but the secular commerce is not.[21]

On this reasoning, the secular, commerce part of a business is simply not protected.

Discussion then ensued during the spring of 2000 over enacting a version of RFRA (the bill that will not die) just for local and state land use and prisons, RLUIPA. The opposition continued, and at the end of July, RLUIPA's opponents were informed that there would be hearings on the bill in September. We all breathed a sigh of relief.

On that same day, July 27, 2000, leadership covertly enacted RLUIPA as the summer recess was called, by the ubiquitous and nefarious "unanimous consent" in both houses. Opposing members, who were already on the way home, did not know it was enacted until the groups opposed contacted them. Welcome to gotcha politics for believers.

RLUIPA came packaged with amendments to RFRA to limit it to federal law. When the new RLUIPA + RFRA bill was passed, Canady explained that there was no reason to be concerned about the potential impact on the civil rights laws:

> [RLPA] as you may recall, had some people concerned with some civil rights implications. Those concerns have been allayed. They are not present in this bill. The Leadership Conference on Civil Rights and the American Civil Liberties Union, both of which had concerns about last year's bill, both support this bill.[22]

It makes no sense that the civil rights groups' concerns about RLPA would be allayed if the new bill were going to affect civil rights. So how is it that the new RFRA, limited to federal law, would not undermine federal civil rights, primarily Title VII?

First, they obviously believed that the large, for-profit, nonreligious corporations discussed above are not religious by nature and, therefore, *couldn't* bring a RFRA claim. Further, they assumed that no company could obtain RFRA rights for their commercial practices.

Second, Title VII's exemption for religious faith for religious organizations forestalled Nadler's concern about kosher butchers. They also assumed (probably too optimistically) that co-religionists would not sue each other for civil rights violations.

Third, Title VII only applies to companies that have over 15 employees for 20 or more weeks each year.[23] Therefore, the small companies with under 15 employees aren't covered by the federal civil rights laws, which would include the Kosher butchers in New York (if they were not already included under Title VII's exemption) Nadler had in mind. Nadler's amendment only protected companies with 5 or fewer employees, so Title VII is even better (from the perspective of the believers).

However one slices it, the RFRA legislative history did not support Hobby Lobby's claim. It is the epitome of the thriving, large, for-profit, nonreligious corporation. Moreover, its claim under RFRA involves its commercial activity of providing benefits to its employees, not its owners personal religious practices. Regardless of what its owners or founders believe, their for-profit business is much more like Exxon than it is like a house of worship.

When the Supreme Court interpreted RFRA to protect Hobby Lobby, it transformed the vast majority of corporations into religious actors. The Court held for another day the question whether RFRA protects publicly traded corporations, but held that closely-held corporations can have religious beliefs that trigger RFRA's extreme regime.

Hobby Lobby had argued that it should receive the benefit of RFRA because it's a family business with owners and board members, and they are religious. So is 80% of the American public.[24] Similarly, it argued that RFRA applied because the company was closely held, but once again, that describes most corporations. When Hobby Lobby won, the decision restructured the corporate order in the United States.

The fiscal results are impossible to predict, because three roads lay open once the decision was reached. First, the immediate effect of the decision left the female employees covering their own emergency contraception. Second, the Court indicated that the government should or could replicate the same accommodation for for-profit nonreligious businesses like Hobby Lobby as it had for religious nonprofits like Notre Dame, which would mean the insurer would cover the cost of the contraception, not the employee. Third, the Court suggested that to relieve Hobby Lobby of the burden of being complicit in its employees' private reproductive health care decisions, the government (aka taxpayers) could simply pick up the tab. Thus, Hobby Lobby's accommodation shifts the cost either to its employees, its insurers, or the rest of us.

Businesses Seek State RFRA Amendments to Discriminate and the Ability to Invoke It Against Customers

The RFRA formula showed its true colors when the Alliance Defending Freedom and other ultra-conservative organizations opposed to same-sex marriage started pushing state RFRA amendments that would permit for-profit businesses to use RFRA as a defense in lawsuits by customers denied services. Yes, they actually thought it would be a good idea to revive the Jim Crow laws of the Deep South that permitted lunch counters to refuse service to blacks. Now, they defend this as not really like Jim Crow, because, according to their most articulate defenders, race discrimination is worse than sexual orientation discrimination.

It all started when a wedding photographer in New Mexico refused to photograph a same-sex marriage, and was sued under the public accommodations law. When sued by the customer, the photographer raised the state RFRA as a defense. She lost when the New Mexico Supreme Court ruled that the state RFRA did not apply in a case between two private parties, as the New Mexico government was not a party to the case.[25] That prompted anti-gay marriage groups to push laws in the states, including Kansas and Arizona, to ensure that businesses with religious owners would not have to deal with gay couples (or homosexuals). In Kansas, the amendment was a flat-out exemption for individuals and religious entities from having to deal with any "any marriage, domestic partnership, civil union or similar arrangement" that would be contrary to "sincerely held" religious beliefs.[26] The Arizona law did not provide an outright exemption for such businesses, but expanded the categories of discrimination to include not just sexual orientation, but also race and gender, among others.[27]

These laws also would have expanded the RFRAs from laws that permitted believers to raised RFRA against the government to lawsuits between private parties. Businesses wanted to be able to use it as a shield against gay customers. The federal RFRA plainly applies only to cases where a believer is suing or being sued by the government. It imposes the burden of proving a compelling interest and the least restrictive means on "the government" and it affords judicial relief "against a government."[28] RLUIPA also has language the makes it clear that every case must involve the government.[29] This language is buttressed by commentary at the time. For example, Professor Michael McConnell, a staunch supporter of extreme religious liberty, decried the *Boerne* decision with a list of horribles, each of which involves the government, and not a dispute between private parties.[30]

The proposed state expansions of the RFRA formula to disputes between private parties are a tendentious and ominous warning of religious discord to come. The Kansas bill provided on this score:

> . . . No individual or religious entity shall be required . . . to:
>
> (A) provide any services, accommodations, advantages, facilities, goods, or privileges; provide counseling, adoption, foster care and other social services; or provide employment or employment benefits, related to, or related to the celebration of, any marriage, domestic partnership, civil union or similar arrangement.
> (B) solemnize any marriage, domestic partnership, civil union or similar arrangement; or
> (C) treat any marriage, domestic partnership, civil union or similar arrangement as valid.[31]

The Arizona bill stated:

> 'A person whose religious exercise is burdened in violation of this section may assert that violation as a claim or defense in a judicial proceeding, and obtain appropriate relief against a government, regardless of whether the government is a party to the proceeding. The person asserting such a claim or defense may obtain appropriate relief.[32]

Other states considered variations of the Kansas and Arizona bills, including Hawaii, Georgia, Idaho, Ohio, Oklahoma, Maine, Missouri, South Dakota, and Tennessee, but only Mississippi actually enacted a RFRA

A Sampling of Religious Groups That Would Discriminate If Given an Opening Under the Law[1]

Name	Belief in a Nutshell
Aryan Nation (aka Church of Jesus Christ Christian)	White Christian supremacists
Nation of Islam	Black separatists, anti-Semitic, anti-LGBT
Westboro Baptist Church (fundamentalist Christian)	Anti-LGBT, anti-Semitic
America's Promise Ministry	Christian Identity[1]/white supremacist
Church of the Creator (a.k.a. The Creativity Movement)	White supremacist, white separatist
Church of the National Knights of the Ku Klux Klan	Christian white supremacists and separatists white supremacist, female-submissive, polygamist, homophobic, anti-secular government totalitarianism
Kingdom Identity Ministries	Christian Identity/white supremacist
Restored Church of God (formerly part of Worldwide Church of God)	Anti-LGBT, Anti-miscegenation
Satmar/Hasidic Jews	Women as submissive, strict gender separation, anti-secular gov't, anti LGBT
Ultra Orthodox Jews (Haredi) – Zionists	Women as submissive, strict gender separation, anti-LGBT
Kinism	Christian white-separatist

[1] Christian Identity is a far-right wing radical extremist Christian theology which advocates belief that all non-whites are "soulless sub-humans" and Jews as "satanic or cursed by God" and believes that "judgment day will arrive in form of a sanctified race war" which must be prepared for. Christian Identity is also the theology followed and advanced by most members of Aryan Brotherhood prison gangs. Southern Poverty Law Center, Intelligence Files, Groups, http://www.splcenter.org/get-informed/intelligence-files/groups

that opens the door to discrimination by private business owners, because Mississippi law defines "person" in a way that includes for-profit corporations.. Knowing the tenacity of religious lobbyists, though, who view their proposals as not just great policy but God's mandate, it is worth pausing for a moment to consider just which religious organizations Arizona's bill might have helped.

Milwaukee Archdiocese Bankruptcy and RFRA

When Catholic dioceses face lawsuits from the sex abuse victims of their priests, it has become *de rigeuer* to file for Chapter 11, voluntary bankruptcy to protect assets.[33] The Milwaukee bankruptcy is the first where the Archdiocese has argued that RFRA shields it from the fraudulent conveyance laws. The case is pending, and I represent the creditors for purposes of RFRA and the First Amendment, so I will not pursue it here, except to say that, in general, the invocation of RFRA in the archdiocesan bankruptcies shows how far we have departed from RFRA's roots. A statute that was purportedly needed to help the Hmong and Orthodox Jews deal with autopsy requirements, and elderly men to get to their daily prayer services, has become a tool the powerful invoke against their own victims and, in Hobby Lobby's case, their employees.

For the survivors of abuse, it is a cruel irony that as they are put through the wringer of federal bankruptcy law desperately trying to obtain some justice, the institution that made their abuse possible can claim RFRA as a shield against them. While no member of Congress or President ever has taken up the victims' righteous cause, they blindly enacted RFRA not once, but twice. As the Irish and Australian governments dig deep to unearth and excise the cancer of clergy sex abuse in their countries, the federal government of the United States has acted as though these victims are not our own American children, as though it never happened. Cruelly, Congress delivered yet another tool for their continuing victimization with RFRA.

Conclusion

What do we do about extreme religious liberty? Educate the public and they will let elected representatives know that they are not remote-controlled by their clergy, not slavishly devoted to religious institutions that betray our children and our values, and that they believe in fairness and justice first and foremost. Educate legislators about the harm religious actors can wreak, and then refuse to vote for them when they give religious actors a pass to harm others.

Then repeal RFRA, RLUIPA, and the state RFRAs. Let the First Amendment stand as the beacon of liberty it was before these false statutes obscured the truth and set Americans on a self-righteous search for self-centered narcissism. We have never needed ordered liberty more than we do now.

FOREWORD TO THE 2005 EDITION

Judge Edward R. Becker, for whom I clerked, was one of the "greats" to use one of his own favorite phrases. He was a brilliant jurist with a practical bent. But he also had a big heart, and knew your cousins, whoever you were. Sadly, he passed away May 19, 2006. Judge Becker graciously agreed to write the following Foreword for the first edition, and I continue to be very grateful. He is sorely missed.

Marci A. Hamilton, March 4, 2014

The role of religion in a free society, once a subject of benign and lofty discourse, has become a raging controversy in both the private and public arenas. While few in America challenge the multifarious benefits of religion to the individual believer and to society as a whole, there are sharply divergent views as to the extent to which notions of religious liberty immunize religious conduct from sanction when it interferes with public health, safety, and welfare.

In recent years, religious entities, often with the assistance of legislatures and courts, have advocated a presumptive constitutional right to avoid the law pursuant to the federal and state free exercise of religion guarantees, arguing that the First Amendment, the Due Process Clause, and separation of powers render them immune from some legal requirements and precepts. Opponents of these initiatives have responded that this approach is at odds with American culture and legal tradition.

In this volume, Professor Marci Hamilton, one of the nation's leading legal scholars and one of the premier authorities on the Constitution's Religion Clauses, tackles these issues in depth and with gusto. Her dominant theme is that the temptation to treat religion as an unalloyed good is a belief one can embrace only at one's peril. Building upon her already prolific body of work, she proceeds from the baseline of the "no-harm principle" – that no person or entity can act in ways that harm others without consequence – which she demonstrates was widely shared by the Framers' generation. After establishing, with impressive documentation, that, despite their generally beneficent effect, religious entities can be responsible for many harms, for example, lethal medical neglect of children, childhood sexual abuse, the takeover of neighboring property owners' rights under the zoning laws, and the undermining of laws against discrimination, she forcefully argues that the burden rests on the religious believers demanding exemption from a law to prove that the conduct sought to be immunized is not harmful to the society and individuals within it. Referencing the precept of *Employment Div. v. Smith* that "the [correct] reading [of the Free Exercise Clause] is . . . an individual's religious beliefs do not excuse him from compliance with an otherwise valid law prohibiting conduct that the State is free to regulate," Professor Hamilton engages the scholarship of Professor Laycock and Professor (now Judge) McConnell and that of others who have criticized this holding. She argues that these scholars have misconstrued the jurisprudence of the Religion Clauses and that their defense of the Religious Freedom Restoration Act (overruled by *City of Boerne v. Flores*) and the Religious Land Use and Institutionalized Persons Act (RLUIPA) is flawed.

Whatever the reader's take on these issues may be, he or she will be edified by Professor Hamilton's exegesis of the history, jurisprudence, and policy considerations that inform the debate. This is a truly important, if provocative, work that is essential reading for anyone who wishes to delve beneath the surface of the contemporary battle over religion and values.

The Hon. Edward R. Becker
United States Court of Appeals

NOTES

Introduction: The Wages of RFRA

1. Burwell v. Hobby Lobby Stores, Inc., No. 13-354, slip op. (U.S. June 30, 2014).
2. United States v. Lee, 455 U.S. 252 (1982) (emphasis added).
3. *Lee*, 455 U.S. at 261.
4. Jimmy Swaggart Ministries v. Equalization Bd. of Calif., 493 U.S. 378 (1990).
5. Lyng v. Northwest Indian Cemetery Protective Ass'n, 485 U.S. 439 (1988).
6. Braunfeld v. Brown, 366 U.S. 599 (1961).
7. Bowen v. Roy, 476 U.S. 693 (1986).
8. Braunfeld v. Brown, 366 U.S. 599, 603–04 (1961).
9. Church of Lukumi Babalu Aye v. City of Hialeah, 508 U.S. 520 (1993).
10. Sherbert v. Verner, 374 U.S. 398 (1963).
11. Wisconsin v. Yoder, 406 U.S. 205, 209–213 (1972).
12. Employment Div. v. Smith, 494 U.S. 872 (1990).
13. Reynolds v. United States, 98 U.S. (8 Otto.) 145, 164 (1878).
14. 42 U.S.C. § 2000cc et seq. (2012).
15. Kate Tracy, *Bill Gothard Relieved of Duties During Sexual Harassment Investigation*, CHRISTIANITY TODAY (Feb. 28, 2014), http://www.christianity today.com/gleanings/2014/february/bill-gothard-relieved-of-duties-during-sexual-harassment-in.html.
16. Mark Chaves, *The Decline of American Religion?*, ARDA GUIDING PAPER SERIES (2011), *available at* http://www.thearda.com/rrh/papers/guidingpapers/Chaves.pdf.

1. The Problem

1. *See* NAT'L CTR. FOR CHARITABLE STATISTICS, QUICK FACTS ABOUT NONPROFITS, *available at* http://nccs.urban.org/statistics/quickfacts.cfm.

2. Gary Strauss, *Religious Groups Mobilize Aid to Phillipines for Tyhpoon Haiyan Victims*, HUFFINGTON POST (Nov. 14, 2013), http://www.huffingtonpost .com/2013/11/14/religious-groups-aid_n_4275766.html.

3. *See generally* HAROLD KOENIG, M.D., THE HEALING POWER OF FAITH (1999).

4. U.S. COMM'N ON INT'L RELIGIOUS FREEDOM, ANNUAL REPORT 2013 30 (2013), *available at* http://www.uscirf.gov/sites/default/files/resources/2013%20USCIRF %20Annual%20Report%20(2).pdf.

5. *Background: Persecution of Falun Gong in China*, FRIENDS OF FALUN GONG, http://www. http://fofg.org/the-persecution/background-persecution-of- falun-gong-in-china (last visited Apr. 18, 2014).

6. THOMAS LUM, CONG. RESEARCH SERV., RS 20333, CHINA AND "FALUN GONG" 6 (Cong. Research Serv. 2001), *available at* http://www.globalsecurity.org/military/ library/report/crs/RS20333.pdf (last visited Aug. 23, 2004).

> In 2002, the commission reviewed a second report on Falun Gong, which included updates on events in China including the self-immolation of six practitioners in Tiannanmen Square, new tactics of practitioners to bolster recognition of their cause, and the continuing crackdown by the Chinese Government. These events led Congress to institute two resolutions condemning China for its poor human rights record, and calling upon the PRC to cease its persecution of Falun Gong practitioners.

Id. at 4–6. In 2003, the Congressional Report noted that, "Government authorities continue to repress spiritual groups, including the Falun Gong spiritual movement, chiefly through the use of anti-cult laws." CONG.-EXEC. COMM. ON CHINA, 108TH CONG., ANNUAL REP. 1 (Comm. Print 2003). *See also* AMNESTY INT'L, AMNESTY INTERNATIONAL REPORT 2012: THE STATE OF THE WORLD'S HUMAN RIGHTS, CHINA 108–09 (2012), *available at* http://files.amnesty.org/air12/air_2012_ full_en.pdf.

7. *Id.*

8. *See* Ivan Andreyev, *The Catacomb Church in the Soviet Union*, ORTHODOX LIFE (Mar.–Apr. 1951), *available at* http://www.holycross-hermitage.com/pages/ Orthodox_Life/CatacornbChurch.htm (last visited Aug. 20, 2004). *See also* Anatoly Andreevich Krasikov, *Church State Relationships in Russia: Yesterday, Today, and Tomorrow, in* THE LAW OF RELIGIOUS IDENTITY: MODELS FOR POST-COMMUNISM 153, 161–68 (András Sajó & Shlomo Avineri eds., 1999).

9. *See generally* Ronald A. Christaldi, *The Shamrock and the Crown: A Historic Analysis of the Framework Document and Prospects for Peace in Ireland*, 5 J. TRANSNAT'L L. & POL'Y 123, 124–52 (1995).

10. W. WARD ET AL., THE CAMBRIDGE MODERN HISTORY 650 (1934); CHARLES H. LEA, A HISTORY OF THE INQUISITION OF SPAIN 173–74 (1907), *available at* http:// libro.uca.edu/lea1/1lea.htm (last visited Sept. 13, 2004).

11. *See* J. H. HEXTER, PARLIAMENT AND LIBERTY FROM THE REIGN OF ELIZABETH TO THE ENGLISH CIVIL WAR 4–5 (1992) ("During the century long rule of [the Tudors] a few hundred martyrs or zealots lost their lives by hanging, burning, or

beheading. More numerous were the victims who had taken up arms on religious grounds against their Tudor rulers of whatever religious persuasion.").

12. AMIT GUPTA & KAIA LEATHER, CONG. RESEARCH SERV., RL 31481, KASHMIR RECENT DEVELOPMENTS AND U.S. CONCERNS 2 (Cong. Research Serv. 2002), *available at* http://www.fas.org/man/crs/RL31481.pdf (last visited Aug. 23, 2003).

13. Unlike similar trials in Europe that were run by the Church itself, the Salem witch trials were handled in ostensibly secular courts. *See* RICHARD WEISMAN, WITCHCRAFT, MAGIC, AND RELIGION IN SEVENTEENTH-CENTURY MASSACHUSETTS 12–14 (1984). Nevertheless, Puritan beliefs and colonial clergy played an important role in the witchcraft statutes, trials, and subsequent executions. *Id.* at 23–29.

14. The Muslim Brotherhood was founded in Egypt in 1928 by Hassan al-Bana. *See* Stephen Kinzer, *Muslim Scholar Loses U.S. Visa as Query Is Raised*, N.Y. TIMES, Aug. 26, 2004, at A14.

15. *See generally* ANDREA MOORE-EMMETT, GOD'S BROTHEL (2004).

16. *See* Janna C. Merrick, Symposium, *Spiritual Healing, Sick Kids and the Law: Inequities in the American Healthcare System*, 29 AM. J. L. & MED. 269, 273 (2003) ("Christian Science deaths from diabetes and malignancy were twice the national average.").

17. 494 U.S. 872 (1990), *superseded by statute*, Religious Land Use and Institutionalized Persons Act of 2000, Pub. L. No. 106–274, *as recognized in* Sossamon v. Texas, 131 S. Ct. 1651 (2011).

18. 103 CONG. REC. S14461, 14466 (1993) (statement of Sen. Dole).

19. 42 U.S.C. § 2000cc et seq. (2012).

20. Wisconsin v. Yoder, 406 U.S. 205, 215 (1972).

21. Bd. of Trs. v. Fox, 492 U.S. 469, 477–78 (1989).

22. Fullilove v. Klutznick, 448 U.S. 448, 507 (1980) (Powell, J., concurring).

23. 139 CONG. REC. S2822 (1993).

24. 139 CONG. REC. D1315 (daily ed. Nov. 16, 1993); Malcolm Gladwell, *At Least 5 Die, 500 Hurt as Explosion Rips Garage under World Trade Center; Bomb Suspected in Midday Blast*, WASH. POST, Feb. 27, 1993, at A1.

25. Owen Bowcott, *The Nine Victims of IRA Bomb Aimed at Loyalist Paramilitaries*, GUARDIAN (LONDON), Oct. 25, 1993, at 1; List of Terrorist Incidents.

26. 139 CONG. REC. S14350 (statement of Sen. Hatch).

27. Coalition for Religious Freedom Calls on Supreme Court to Uphold Constitutionality of Religious Freedom Restoration Act, *available at* http://www.ajcongress.org/pages/RELS1997/JAN97REL/jan_005.htm (last visited Nov. 14, 2004).

28. City of Boerne v. Flores, 521 U.S. 507 (1997).

29. TEX. CIV. PRAC. & REM. CODE A. § 110.010 (Vernon 2001).

30. CONS. STATE. ANN. § 2406(b) (West 2004).

31. Christopher C. Lund, *Religious Liberty After Gonzales: A Look at State RFRA's*, 55 S. DAKOTA L. REV. 466, 475 (2010) (California & Maryland); Electa Draper, *Focus on the Family Withdrawing Religious-Liberty Ballot Initiative*, DENVER POST (May 4, 2012), http://www.denverpost.com/breakingnews/ci_

20553204/focus-family-withdrawing-religious-liberty-ballot-initiative; Doug Grow, *Message from North Dakota Voters on Religion Has National Implications*, MINNPOST (June 15, 2012), http://www.minnpost.com/politics-policy/2012/06/message-north-dakota-voters-religion-has-national-implications (North Dakota).

32. There are also some states that apply ordinary strict scrutiny under the state constitution's free exercise provision, but rarely are these protections as extreme as RFRA's formula.

33. H.B. 279, 2013 Leg., Reg. Sess. (Ky. 2013).

34. McCreary County, Ky. v. ACLU of Ky., 545 U.S. 844 (2005); Santa Fe Indep. Sch. Dist. v. Doe, 530 U.S. 290 (2000); Cnty. of Allegheny v. ACLU, Greater Pittsburgh Chapter, 492 U.S. 573 (1989).

35. *Religious Freedom Restoration Act of 1991: Hearings on H.R. 2797 Before the Subcomm. on Civil and Constitutional Rights of the H. Comm. on the Judiciary*, 102d Cong. 65 (1992) (statement of Nadine Strossen, President, and Robert S. Peck, Legislative Counsel, American Civil Liberties Union).

36. *Religious Liberty Protection Act of 1999: Hearing on H.R. 1691 Before the Subcomm. on the Constitution of the H. Committee on the Judiciary*, 106th Cong. 81 (1999) (statement of Christopher E. Anders, Legislative Counsel, American Civil Liberties Union).

37. Br. of American Civil Liberties Union et al., as Amici Curiae in Support of the Government, Sebelius v. Hobby Lobby Stores, Inc., No. 13–354 and Conestoga Wood Specialties Corp. v. Sebelius, No. 13–356.

38. Marci A. Hamilton, *The Belief/Conduct Paradigm in the Supreme Court's Free Exercise Jurisprudence: A Theological Account of the Failure to Protect Religious Conduct*, 54 OHIO ST. L.J. 713, 794 (1993).

39. The enormous amount of information that has come out of the Los Angeles Archdiocese about clergy sex abuse was not due to the government's efforts, but rather to the civil lawyers who were able to bring lawsuits for the victims after the statute of limitations was lifted during 2003, making it possible for hundreds of victims whose meritorious claims had been shut out of court to obtain justice. *See generally* Marci A. Hamilton, *Justice Denied: What America Must Do to Protect Its Children* (Cambridge University Press 2007).

2. Children

1. Kathleen Alaimo, *Historical Roots of Children's Rights in Europe and the United States*, in CHILDREN AS EQUALS: EXPLORING THE RIGHTS OF THE CHILD 3 (Kathleen Alaimo & Brian Klug eds., 2002) ("If adults take responsibility for the protection of children, doesn't that potentially limit their freedom?").

2. For purposes of this book, I will use "pedophile" as a term encompassing both pedophiles and ephebophiles. Technically, a pedophile is defined as "[a] person who over at least a 6 month period has recurrent, intense sexually arousing fantasies, sexual urges, or behaviors involving sexual activity with a prepubescent child or children (age 13 years or younger)." AMERICAN PSYCHIATRIC ASSOCIATION,

DIAGNOSTIC AND STATISTICAL MANUAL OF MENTAL DISORDERS (4th ed. 1994). "Adults who sexually interact with adolescents are called ephebophiles. However, there is neither a medical definition nor a medical diagnosis for this group." Gene G. Abel, M.D., & Nora Harlow, *The Abel and Harlow Child Molestation Prevention Study* 4 (updated 2002), *in* THE STOP CHILD MOLESTATION BOOK (2001), *available at* http://www.childmolestationprevention.org/pdfs/study.pdf (last visited Feb. 14, 2014).

3. *See, e.g.,* Scott Mendelson, *The Lasting Damage of Child Abuse,* HUFFINGTON POST (Dec. 31, 2013, 1:48 PM), http://www.huffingtonpost.com/scott-mendelson-md/the-lasting-damage-of-chi_b_4515918.html; Joseph Nowinski, *Childhood Trauma and Adult Alcohol Abuse: Shedding Light on the Connection,* HUFFINGTON POST (July 22, 2013, 10:01 AM), http://www.huffingtonpost.com/joseph-nowinski-phd/alcohol-abuse_b_3595743.html.

4. *See* Dylan Farrow, *An Open Letter from Dylan Farrow,* N.Y. TIMES KRISTOF BLOG (Feb. 1, 2014, 3:04 PM), http://kristof.blogs.nytimes.com/2014/02/01/an-open-letter-from-dylan-farrow; Genaro C. Armas & Marc Levy, *Sandusky Is Arrested on New Sex Abuse Charges,* WASH. POST, Dec. 8, 2011, at D05.

5. *See* Bill Bowen, *Is There a Problem?,* http://www.silentlambs.org/answers/isthereaproblem.htm (last visited Feb. 14, 2014).

6. REPORT OF THE GRAND JURY, IN RE CNTY. INVESTIGATING GRAND JURY XXIII, Misc. No. 0009901–2008 (Feb. 10, 2011), *available at* http://www.phila.gov/districtattorney/PDFs/clergyAbuse2-finalReport.pdf (last visited Feb. 14, 2014); REPORT OF THE GRAND JURY, IN RE CNTY. INVESTIGATING GRAND JURY, Misc. No. 03–00–239 (Sept. 15, 2005), *available at* http://www.bishop-accountability.org/reports/2005_09_21_Philly_GrandJury/Grand_Jury_Report.pdf (last visited Feb. 14, 2014).

7. Rev. Michael Peterson, F. Ray Mouton & Rev. Thomas P. Doyle, *The Problem of Sexual Molestation by Roman Catholic Clergy: Meeting the Problem in a Comprehensive and Responsible Manner* 2, 10 (1984) (confidential report on Catholic clergy abuse directed to bishops) (on file with author), *also available at* http://natcath.org/NCR_Online/archives2/2002b/051702/051702a.htm (last visited Feb. 14, 2014) (hereinafter *Problem of Sexual Molestation by Roman Catholic-Clergy*).

8. *Id.* at 3, 4, 11, 88.

9. *See* generally BISHOPACCOUNTABILITY.ORG, http://www.bishop-account ability.org (last visited Feb. 14, 2014); Committee on the Rights of the Child, *Concluding Observations on the Report Submitted by the Holy See Under Article 12, Paragraph 1, of the Optional Protocol to the Convention on the Rights of the Child on the Sale of Children, Child Prostitution and Child Pornography,* U.N. CONVENTION ON THE RIGHTS OF THE CHILD (Jan. 31, 2014), *available at* http://tbinternet.ohchr.org/Treaties/CRC-OP-SC/Shared%20Documents/VAT/CRC_C_OPSC_VAT_CO_1_16307_E.pdf; Jeff Waters, *Victoria Government Moves Swiftly to Implement Recommendations of Abuse Inquiry,* ABC NEWS (Nov. 13, 2013, 2:23 PM), http://www.abc.net.au/news/2013-11-13/inquiry-recommnends-making-failure-to-report-sexual-abuse/5088212; Henry McDonald,

"Endemic" Rape and Abuse of Irish Children in Catholic Care, Inquiry Finds,
GUARDIAN (May 20, 2009), http://www.theguardian.com/world/2009/may/20/
irish-catholic-schools-child-abuse-claims.

10. Estimates range from 10,000 to 100,000. Sociologist and Catholic priest
Andrew Greeley predicted that there are probably 100,000 clergy-abuse victims
in the United States. *See* Andrew M. Greeley, *How Serious Is the Problem of
Sexual Abuse by Clergy?*, AMERICA, Mar. 20, 1993, at 6, *available at* http://www
.bishop-accountability.org/resources/resource-files/timeline/1993-03-20-Greeley-
HowSerious-1.htm (last visited Feb. 14, 2014) ("A not unreasonable estimate of the
victim population would then be well in excess of 100,000, each one a human
being who has suffered a terrible personal tragedy."); NAT'L REVIEW BD. FOR THE
PROTECTION OF CHILDREN AND YOUNG PEOPLE, A REPORT ON THE CRISIS IN
THE CATHOLIC CHURCH IN THE UNITED STATES 23 (2004) (hereinafter REPORT
ON THE CRISIS IN THE CATHOLIC CHURCH), *available at* http://www.bishop-
accountability.org/usccb/causesandcontext/2004-02-27-CC-Report.pdf (last visited Feb. 14, 2014).

11. Mark Donald, *Judging Amy?*; *Jehovah's Witnesses Sued for Allegedly Protecting Members Who Abuse*, 20 TEXAS LAWYER 1 (May 3, 2004) (hereinafter *Judging
Amy?*) (quoting Fort Worth lawyer Kimberlee Norris, who said she "talked to
my 1,500th alleged victim in March 28, 2003 . . . After I reached 2000, I stopped
counting."); *see also* www.silentlambs.org (website that assists survivors of Jehovah's Witness abuse, run by a former church elder, Bill Bowen). *See, e.g.,* Oren
Yaniv & Larry McShane, 103 *Prison for More Than a Century B'Klyn Victim Cheers
Sentence: Says Abuser Stole Her Innocence*, N.Y. DAILY NEWS, Jan. 23, 2013, at 6;
Jehovah's Witnesses Told to Pay in Abuse Case, N.Y. TIMES, June 18, 2012, at A14.

12. *See* Susan Edelman, *Brooklyn DA Reveals New Details on Nearly 100
Orthodox Sex Abuse Cases*, N.Y. POST (May 20, 2012), http://nypost.com/2012/05/
20/brooklyn-da-reveals-new-details-on-nearly-100-orthodox-sex-abuse-cases; Zoë
Blackler, *Brooklyn DA Accused of Failing to Tackle Orthodox Jews' Cover-Up
of Sex Abuse*, GUARDIAN (Mar. 29, 2012, 2:13 PM), http://www.theguardian.com/
world/2012/mar/29/brooklyn-da-orthodox-jews-cover-up.

13. *See* Rich Calder & Josh Saul, *Fight for the Future: Hynes Is Trounced After
24 Yrs. as DA*, N.Y. POST, Sept. 11, 2013, at 8.

14. In 1980, two news organizations won Pulitzer Prizes for their reporting
about the financial misdealings of religious institutions. Bette Swenson Orsini
and Charles Stafford of the *St. Petersburg (Fla.) Times* won the Pulitzer for
National Reporting "for their investigation of the Church of Scientology," which
is available at http://www.lermanet.com/scientologynews/sptimes/spt-series-index
.htm (last visited Feb. 14, 2014). The same year, the *Gannett News Service* won the
Pulitzer for Public Service for "its series on financial contributions to the Pauline
Fathers." The Pulitzer Board Presents, *The Pulitzer Prize Winners of 1980, available at* http://archive.is/s9Ino (last visited Feb. 14, 2014). In 1988, The Charlotte
(N.C.) *Observer* won the Public Service Pulitzer "for revealing misuse of funds
by the PTL television ministry through persistent coverage conducted in the face
of a massive campaign by PTL to discredit the newspaper." The Pulitzer Board

Presents, *The Pulitzer Prize Winners of 1988, available at* http://archive.is/sZs7h (last visited Feb. 14, 2014).

15. *See* JASON BERRY, LEAD US NOT INTO TEMPTATION: CATHOLIC PRIESTS AND THE SEXUAL ABUSE OF CHILDREN (1992); JASON BERRY & GERALD RENNER, VOWS OF SILENCE: THE ABUSE OF POWER IN THE PAPACY OF JOHN PAUL II (2004).

16. *See* Susan Hogan-Albach, *Years of Conflict,* DALLAS MORNING NEWS, June 10, 2002, at 10A.

17. FRANK BRUNI & ELINOR BURKETT, A GOSPEL OF SHAME: CHILDREN, SEXUAL ABUSE, AND THE CATHOLIC CHURCH 98–101 (1993).

18. *Problem of Sexual Molestation by Roman Catholic Clergy, supra* note 7, at 7 (detailing press outlets actively pursuing the issue at the time).

19. *See generally* BILL WRIGHT DZIECH & JUDGE CHARLES B. SCHUDSON, ON TRIAL: AMERICA'S COURTS AND THEIR TREATMENT OF SEXUALLY ABUSED CHILDREN 10–11 (1989).

20. *Federal Assistance to States to Prevent the Abuse of Children in Child Care Facilities: Hearings on S. 521 and S. 1924 Before the Senate Judiciary Committee,* 98th Cong. 30 (Apr. 11 and Sept. 18, 1984) (statement of Melvin D. Mercer and Kenneth V. Lanning).

21. Melinda Beck & Tessa Namuth, *An Epidemic of Child Abuse,* NEWSWEEK, Aug. 20, 1984, at 44.

22. Russell Watson et al., *A Hidden Epidemic,* NEWSWEEK, May 14, 1984, at 32.

23. Glen Martin & Delfin Vigil, *Study Reveals Clergy Abuse Figures,* S.F. CHRON., Feb. 2, 2004, at A1.

24. Greeley, *supra* note 10.

25. REPORT ON THE CRISIS IN THE CATHOLIC CHURCH, *supra* note 10, at 23.

26. The American Academy of Pediatrics (AAP) has been a staunch advocate for children at risk of medical neglect. *See* American Academy of Pediatrics, *Religious Exemptions from Child Abuse Statutes,* 81 PEDIATRICS 169 (1988). The AAP has a Child Abuse and Neglect home page, *available at* http://www2.aap.org/sections/childabuseneglect (last visited Feb. 14, 2014). AAP also filed an amicus brief, along with other health organizations, opposing Medicare and Medicaid reimbursement for institutions run primarily by Christian Scientists (because the practice encourages faith healers to deny children appropriate medical care). *See* Brief of the American Academy of Pediatrics, the American Medical Association, the Iowa Medical Society, and the American Nurses Association as Amicus Curiae in Support of Petitioners, Children's Healthcare Is a Legal Duty, Inc. v. Min De Parle, 212 F.3d 1084 (8th Cir. 2000). AAP is also on the record opposing state exemptions for parents who have denied medical care to their children for religious reasons. *See* Press Release, American Academy of Pediatrics, *Pediatricians File Brief in Prayer vs. Medical Care Case* (Dec. 29, 1998) (on file with author).

27. *See* Bronson v. Swensen, 500 F.3d 1099, 1102 (10th Cir. 2007) (holding that Plaintiffs lacked standing to sue Defendant marriage clerk by arguing that Utah's criminal provision banning polygamy was unconstitutional).

28. Brown v. Buhman, 947 F. Supp. 2d 1170 (D. Utah 2013).

29. *Federal Assistance to States to Prevent the Abuse of Children in Child Care Facilities: Hearings on S. 521 and S. 1924 Before the Senate Judiciary Comm.*, 98th Cong. 29 (Apr. 11 and Sept. 18, 1984) (statement of Melvin D. Mercer and Kenneth V. Lanning); *Federal Assistance to States to Prevent the Abuse of Children in Child Care Facilities: Hearings on S. 521 and S. 1924 Before the Senate Judiciary Comm.*, 98th Cong. 29 (Apr. 11 & Sept. 18, 1984) (statement of Melvin D. Mercer and Kenneth V. Lanning); *see also id.* at 26 (oral testimony).

30. *Id.* at 31.

31. *Id.* at 30 (according to Dr. Ann Burgess). *See also* KENNETH V. LANNING, CHILD MOLESTERS: A BEHAVIORAL ANALYSIS 18–19 (3d ed. 1992), *available at* http://www.skeptictank.org/nc70.pdf (last visited Feb. 14, 2014).

32. Ralph Ranalli, *A Curious Twist in Geoghan Case*, BOSTON GLOBE, Oct. 25, 2003, at B3.

33. Ralph Ranalli, *Priests in Church Scandal Barred*, BOSTON GLOBE, May 7, 2004, at B1. NAMBLA is an organization which advocates for ending age-of-consent laws. According to its website, it promotes "the rights of youth as well as adults to choose the partners with whom they wish to share and enjoy their bodies." *See Who We Are*, NAMBLA, http://nambla.org/welcome.html (last visited Feb 14, 2014).

34. Leary v. Geoghan, No. 2001-J-0688, 2001 WL 1902391, at *1 (Mass. App. Ct. Dec. 21, 2001) (affirming trial court decision that First Amendment did not bar discovery of Church files).

35. Brief for Church of Jesus Christ of Latter-day Saints as Amicus Curiae Supporting Respondents, Ramani v. Segelstein (Nev. Oct. 5, 2009) (No. 49341).

36. *See* Malicki v. Doe, 814 So. 2d 347, 351 n.2 (Fla. 2002); State v. Young, 974 So. 2d 601, 613 (Fla. Dist. Ct. App. 2008); Melanie H. v. Defendant Doe, No. 04–1596-WQH-(WMc), slip op. at 8 (S.D. Cal. Dec. 20, 2005); Perry v. Johnston, No. 4:09-CV-105, 2009 U.S. Dist. LEXIS 74706, at *11 (E.D. Mo. Aug. 24, 2009); Martinelli v. Bridgeport Roman Catholic Diocesan Corp., 196 F.3d 409, 431 (2d Cir. 1999); N.H. v. Presbyterian Church, 998 P.2d 592, 602 (Okla. 1999); Young v. Gelineau, No. 03–1302, 2007 WL 3236736 (R.I. Super. Sept. 20, 2007); Roman Catholic Diocese of Jackson v. Morrison, 905 So. 2d 1213 (Miss. 2005); Olson v. First Church of Nazarene, 661 N.W.2d 254 (Minn. Ct. App. 2003); Odenthal v. Minnesota Conference of Seventh-Day Adventists, 649 N.W.2d 426 (Minn. 2002); Rashedi v. General Bd. of Church of Nazarene, 54 P.3d 349 (Ariz. Ct. App. 2002); Doe v. Evans, 814 So. 2d 370, 371 (Fla. 2002); Redwing v. Catholic Bishop for Diocese of Memphis, 363 S.W.3d 436 (Tenn. 2012).

37. Hella Winston, *Weberman Abuse Case Exposes Role of Shadowy "Modesty Committees,"* JEWISH WEEK (Dec. 11, 2012), http://www.thejewishweek.com/news/new-york-news/weberman-abuse-case-exposes-role-shadowy-modesty-committees (last visited Feb. 13, 2014). *See also* Sharon Otterman, *Abuse Verdict Topples a Hasidic Wall of Secrecy*, N.Y. TIMES, Dec. 11, 2012, at A1.

38. Marci A. Hamilton, *Sex Abuse and Lawlessness in the Ultra-Orthodox Community*, http://verdict.justia.com/author/hamilton.

39. Videotape: "Jennifer Chapin Detailing Childhood Sexual Abuse by Monsignor Francis" (on file with author).

40. *See* William Lobdell & Jean Guccione, *Church to Pay $3 Million in Rape*, L.A. TIMES, Jan. 24, 2004, at B1.

41. Glen Martin & Delfin Vigil, *Study Reveals Clergy Abuse Figures*, S.F. CHRON., Feb. 2, 2004, at A1.

42. Charles Burress, *CA Woman Makes Plea to Victims of Clergy Abuse*, S.F. CHRON., Jan. 26, 2004, at B2.

43. *Id.*

44. *See, e.g.*, Steven Yaccino & Michael Paulson, *In Files, a History of Sexual Abuse by Priests in Chicago Archdiocese*, N.Y. TIMES, Jan. 22, 2014, at A10; Dana Bartholomew, Barbara Jones & Brenda Gazzar, *Release of Priests' Personnel Files Called Step Closer to Truth*, L.A. DAILY NEWS, Jan. 22, 2013 (discussing the release of personnel files from the Los Angeles Archdiocese after Cardinal Roger Mahony was stripped of his duties).

45. Ralph Ranalli, *Reardon Victims Still Wait for Help: Diocese Yet to Pay for Sex Abuse Care*, BOSTON GLOBE, June 16, 2003, at B1.

46. Eric Convey, *Reardon Victim Settles YMCA Claim for $35G*, BOSTON HERALD, July 19, 2003, at 10.

47. Kevin Cullen & Stephen Kurkjian, *Church in an $85 Million Accord*, BOSTON GLOBE, Sept. 10, 2003, at A1.

48. Fernanda Santos, *Parishioners: Priest Heard about Abuse*, EAGLE-TRIBUNE (Haverhill, Mass.), Feb. 1, 2002, at 1; Tom Mashberg, *Records: Molesters Advised Other Abusers*, BOSTON HERALD, June 6, 2002, at 28.

49. Richard Pérez-Peña, *Christian School Faulted for Halting Abuse Study*, N.Y. TIMES (Feb. 11, 2014), http://www.nytimes.com/2014/02/12/education/christian-school-faulted-for-halting-abuse-study.html?_r=0.

50. Parks v. Kownacki, 737 N.E.2d 287, 290–91, 296 (Ill. 2000).

51. WIS. STAT. ANN. § 990.06 (2013) provides:

In any case when a limitation or period of time prescribed in any act which shall be repealed for the acquiring of any right, or barring of any remedy, or for any other purpose shall have begun to run before such repeal and the repealing act shall provide any limitation or period of time for such purpose, such latter limitation or period shall apply only to such rights or remedies as shall accrue subsequently to the time when the repealing act shall take effect, and the act repealed shall be held to continue in force and be operative to determine all such limitations and periods of time which shall have previously begun to run unless such repealing act shall otherwise expressly provide.

52. Laurie Goodstein & Jodi Wilgoren, *2 Paths, No Easy Solution on Abusive Priests*, N.Y. TIMES, Mar. 3, 2002, at 1 (hereinafter *2 Paths, No Easy Solution*). *See also* Tim O'Neil, *Man Accused in Abuse Cases in Southern Illinois Removed from Priesthood*, ST. LOUIS POST-DISPATCH (Feb. 7, 2013, 4:07 PM),

http://www.stltoday.com/news/local/raymond-kownacki-subject-of-abuse-cases-in-southern-illinois-removed/article_be4393da-e50e-50e4-af85-0738f79f69f0.html.

53. Robert Goodrich, *Retired Priest Named in New Sex Abuse Case*, St. Louis Post-Dispatch, Sept. 26, 2003, at B1.

54. *See* Wisniewski v. Kownacki, 851 N.E.2d 1243 (Ill. 2006).

55. *See* Jesse Bogan, *Sex Abuse Victim Iis Ppaid $6.3 Million by Belleville Diocese*, St. Louis Post-Dispatch (Aug. 11, 2011, 12:02 AM), http://www.stltoday.com/news/local/crime-and-courts/article_29ee3e11-f79e-570f-95cb-8d1e17fee518.html.

56. *See* Kiera Feldman, *Sexual Assault at God's Harvard*, New Republic (Feb. 17, 2014), http://www.newrepublic.com/article/116623/sexual-assault-patrick-henry-college-gods-harvard.

57. Sarah Barringer Gordon, The Mormon Question 1 (2002). The federal law banning polygamy, 12 Stat. 501, passed by Congress in 1862, was upheld against attack by a Mormon man in *Reynolds v. United States*, 98 U.S. 145, 167 (1879).

58. *See The Doctrine and Covenants: Section 132*, *in* The Church of Jesus Christ of Latter-day Saints, the Scriptures (Internet Edition), *available at* http://www.lds.org/scriptures/dc-testament/dc/132?lang=eng (last visited Feb. 14, 2014). *See also* John Krakauer, Under the Banner of Heaven 255 (2003) (hereinafter Under the Banner of Heaven) (Fundamentalist Mormons "pointed out that *D&C* 132 was still an accepted part of the Mormon scripture (and indeed still is today)").

59. *Texas: Polygamist Leader Gets Life Sentence*, N.Y. Times, Aug. 10, 2011, at A15.

60. *See* Jim Dalrymple, *Polygamous Town Leaders, Feds Fight Over First Amendment*, Salt Lake Trib., Oct. 5, 2013.

61. Complaint, Jeffs v. Jeffs, et al., ¶¶ 22–24 (Utah 3d Jud. Dist. Ct. 2004) (on file with author).

62. Karen Brooks, *Polygamists Accused of Rape*, Dallas Morning News, July 31, 2004, at 5A.

63. Complaint, Jeffs v. Jeffs, ¶¶ 25–28.

64. *See* Ben Winslow, *"Lost Boys" Drop FLDS Lawsuit*, Deseret Morning News (Mar. 19, 2008), http://www.deseretnews.com/article/695263008/Lost-Boys-dropping-lawsuit-against-Jeffs-FLDS-Church.html?pg=all.

65. Texas Dep't of Family and Protective Servs., Eldorado Investigation 4, 7 (2008), *available at* http://www.dfps.state.tx.us/documents/about/pdf/2008-12-22_Eldorado.pdf. *See also* Ben Winslow, *FLDS Report Says 12 Girls Married Underage*, Deseret Morning News, Dec. 24, 2008, at A01; Marci A. Hamilton, *Taking Stock of the 2008 Intervention at the Texas Fundamentalist Latter-day Saints Compound on Its One-Year Anniversary: The Lessons We Must Learn to Effectively Protect Children in the Future*, Findlaw.com (Apr. 16, 2009), http://writ.news.findlaw.com/hamilton/20090416.html.

66. *See Fundamentalist Church of Jesus Christ of Latter-day Saints Fast Facts*, CNN (Oct. 31, 2013, 2:09 PM), http://www.cnn.com/2013/10/31/us/fundamentalist-church-of-jesus-christ-of-latter-day-saints-fast-facts/.

67. *In re* Tex. Dep't of Family and Protective Servs., 255 S.W.3d 613 (Tex. 2008).

68. Referred to in *Estimates: Ministry of Families and Children: Official Report of Debates of the Legislative Assembly* 36th Parl., 4th Sess. 16,937–38 (B. C. Hansard) (June 28, 2000) (statement of Hon. G. Mann Brewin, questioned by B. McKinnon), *available at* http://www.leg.bc.ca/hansard/36th4th/H00628p.HTM (last visited Feb. 14, 2014).

69. *Id.* at 16938.

70. *See Polygamy in Canada: Hunting Bountiful: Ending a Half Century of Exploitation*, ECONOMIST, July 10, 2004, at 3 ("[I]nertia stems from a case in 1992 when police recommended that two Bountiful men be charged with polygamy. But the crown attorney's office declined to do so, following legal advice that conviction was impossible because the guarantee of religious freedom in Canada's Charter of Rights and Freedoms renders the law against polygamy unconstitutional."); *see also Complaint to BC Human Rights Tribunal* (May 19, 2004) (describing Canadian government officials' failure to enforce the law against polygamy, because it "*may* be unconstitutional").

71. Letter from Seven Complainants, former wives or concubines at Bountiful commune, to Tribunal Members, B.C. Human Rights Tribunal 1 (May 19, 2004) (on file with author). The complainants request anonymity as a condition of participation in tribunal proceedings. For that reason, I will not publish their names.

72. *Id.*

73. *See Polygamy, Exploitation Charges Considered in Bountiful Case*, CBC NEWS (July 10, 2013, 2:39 PM), http://www.cbc.ca/news/canada/british-columbia/polygamy-exploitation-charges-considered-in-bountiful-case-1.1320741.

74. ANDREA MOORE-EMMETT, GOD'S BROTHEL 172 (2004); *see also* UNDER THE BANNER OF HEAVEN, *supra* note 57, at 25 (quoting the polygamous police chief of Colorado City).

75. Complaint at 5, United States v. Town of Colorado City (June 21, 2012) (No. 3_12CV08123), 2012 WL 2354466.

76. *Connie Chung Tonight: Witnesses Abused? Church Accused of Failing Children* (CNN television broadcast, Aug. 24, 2002), *transcript available at* http://www.watchtowerinformationservice.org/sexual-child-abuse/transcript-of-cnn-connie-chung-tonight-program-witnesses-abused-church-accused-of-failing-children (last visited Feb. 14, 2014).

77. *See, e.g., Judging Amy?*, *supra* note 11 ("According to scripture [Deuteronomy 19:15], for a person to be disciplined, there needs to be at least two witnesses to substantiate the charge or an admission of sin."); Dennis O'Brien, *Another Church Facing Charges of Sexual Abuse: Former Jehovah's Witness Leader to Be Tried on Sex Offenses, Attempted Rape*, BALT. SUN, May 21, 2002, at B1 (hereinafter *Another Church Facing Charges of Sexual Abuse*).

78. CAL. CIV. PROC. CODE § 340.1 (West 2013). In fact, the window was opened for civil and criminal statutes alike, but the Supreme Court held the retroactive effect of the revival of the criminal charges was unconstitutional in *Stogner v. California*, 539 U.S. 607 (2003). California opened a second year-long window for victims who had pressed criminal charges before *Stogner* forced their cases to be

dismissed, so that they can file civil claims against those who caused and aided and abetted childhood sexual abuse. CAL. CIV. PROC. CODE § 340.1(c) (West 2013).

79. *Connie Chung Tonight: Witnesses Abused?, supra* note 76.

80. Meyer v. Lindala, 675 N.W.2d 635, 641 (Minn. Ct. App. 2004), *review denied*, 2004 Minn. LEXIS 308 (Minn., May 26, 2004) (quoting Lundman v. McKown, 530 N.W.2d 807, 826 (Minn. App. 1995)).

81. *See* Bowen, *Is There a Problem?, supra* note 5.

82. *Another Church Facing Charges of Sexual Abuse, supra* note 77.

83. *See* Bowen, *Is There a Problem?, supra* note 5.

84. *See* Bryan R. v. Watchtower Bible & Tract Soc'y of New York, 738 A.2d 839 (Me. 1999), *cert. denied*, 528 U.S. 1189 (2000); Rees v. Watchtower Bible & Tract Soc'y of New York, No. CV-98–60, 1998 Me. Super. LEXIS 211 (Me. Super. Ct. Aug. 18, 1998); Anderson v. Watchtower Bible and Tract Soc'y of New York, Inc., No. 2004–01066, 2007 WL 161035, at *1 (Tenn. Ct. App. Jan. 19, 2007), *cert denied*, 552 U.S. 891 (2007); *see also* Swanson v. Roman Catholic Bishop, 692 A.2d 441 (Me. 1997) (involving sexual activity between a priest and an adult woman).

85. Decorso v. Watchtower Bible & Tract Soc'y of New York, 829 A.2d 38 (Conn. App. Ct. 2003).

86. *See, e.g.*, Abrams v. Watchtower Bible and Tract Soc'y of New York, Inc., 715 N.E.2d 798 (Ill. App. Ct. 1999), *appeal denied*, 186 Ill.2d 565 (1999) (holding that the court was deprived of jurisdiction to adjudicate a complaint involving ecclesiastical principles and doctrines); Anderson v. Watchtower Bible and Tract Soc'y of New York, Inc., No. 2004–01066, 2007 WL 161035, at *1 (Tenn. Ct. App. Jan. 19, 2007), *cert. denied*, 552 U.S. 891 (2007) (holding that the trial court erred in not dismissing the plaintiffs' claims because the First Amendment prohibited secular courts from interfering with "purely religious matters").

87. Bryan R., 738 A.2d at 848.

88. Church of the Lukumi Babalu Aye, Inc. v. City of Hialeah, 508 U.S. 520, 531 (1993); Bollard v. California Province of the Society of Jesus, 196 F.3d 940, 947–48 (9th Cir. 1999); Martinelli v. Bridgeport Roman Catholic Diocesan Corp., 196 F.3d 409, 431–32 (2d Cir. 1999); Sanders v. Casa View Baptist Church, 134 F.3d 331, 335–36 (5th Cir. 1998), *cert. denied*, Baucum v. Sanders, 525 U.S. 868 (1998); Dausch v. Rykse, 52 F.3d 1425, 1428 (7th Cir. 1994); Doe v. Liberatore, 478 F. Supp. 2d 742, 773 (M.D. Pa. 2007); Melanie H. v. Defendant Doe, No. 04–1596-WQH-(WMc), slip op. at 25 (S.D. Cal. Dec. 20, 2005); Doe v. Archdiocese of Denver, 413 F. Supp. 2d 1187, 1194–95 (D. Colo. 2006); Dolquist v. Heartland Presbytery, 342 F. Supp. 2d 996, 1007 (D. Kan. 2004); Ehrens v. Lutheran Church-Missouri Synod, 269 F. Supp. 2d 328, 332–33 (S.D.N.Y. 2003); Smith v. Raleigh Dist. of the North Carolina Conf. of the United Methodist Church, 63 F. Supp. 2d 694, 705 (E.D.N.C. 1999); Doe v. Hartz, 52 F. Supp. 2d 1027, 1065 n.7 (N.D. Iowa 1999); Smith v. O'Connell, 986 F. Supp. 73, 77 (D. R.I. 1997); Rashedi v. General Bd. of Church of the Nazarene, 54 P.3d 349, 354 (Ariz. Ct. App. 2002), *rev. denied*, No. CV-03–0049-PR, 2003 Ariz. LEXIS 100 (Ariz. 2003); Moses v. Diocese of Colorado, 863 P.2d 310, 319–21 (Colo. 1993), *cert. denied*, 511 U.S. 1137 (1994); Carnesi v. Ferry Pass United Methodist Church, 826 So. 2d 954, 955 (Fla. 2002), *cert. denied*, 537 U.S. 1190 (2003); Malicki v. Doe, 814 So. 2d 347, 351 n.2, 357–58,

360–62 (Fla. 2002); Fortin v. Roman Catholic Bishop of Portland, 871 A.2d 1208, 1232 (Me. 2005); Petrell v. Shaw, 902 N.E.2d 401, 406 (Mass. 2009); Odenthal v. Minnesota Conference of Seventh-Day Adventists, 649 N.W.2d 426, 436 (Minn. 2002); Roman Catholic Diocese v. Morrison, 905 So. 2d 1213, 1242–43 (Miss. 2005); McKelvey v. Pierce, 800 A.2d 840, 850, 857–58 (N.J. 2002); F.G. v. MacDonell, 696 A.2d 697, 701 (N.J. 1997); Strock v. Pressnell, 527 N.E.2d 1235, 1237 (Ohio 1988); Redwing v. Catholic Bishops for the Diocese of Memphis, 363 S.W.3d 436 (Tenn. 2012); Turner v. Roman Catholic Diocese of Burlington, 987 A.2d 960, 972–73 (Vt. 2009); C.J.C. v. Corporation of the Catholic Bishop, 985 P.2d 262, 277 (Wash. 1999). *See also* James G. Dwyer, *A Taxonomy of Children's Existing Rights in State Decision Making About Their Relationships*, 11 Wm. & Mary Bill Rts. J. 845, 850 (2003).

89. Gibson v. Brewer, 952 S.W.2d 239, 243–44 (Mo. 1997) (upholding trial court's dismissal of all claims against Brewer, dismissing 4 of Plaintiff's claims against the Diocese for failure to state a claim, and reversing trial court's dismissal of the plaintiff's claim against the Diocese for intentional failure to supervise clergy).

90. *Id.* at 247.

91. David Chaifetz, *Sharing the Secret That's Haunted My Soul*, Jewish Week (Mar. 28, 2013), http://www.thejewishweek.com/news/new-york-news/sharing-secret-thats-haunted-my-soul?page=1&favtitle=Sharing%20The%20Secret%20 That%E2%80%99s%20Haunted%20My%20Soul.

92. *Id.*

93. Marci A. Hamilton, *The Rules against Scandal and What They Mean for the First Amendment's Religion Clauses*, 69 Md. L. Rev. 101 (2009).

94. Michael Wilson, *Judge Orders Mormons to Provide Sex-Abuse Records*, Oregonian, Feb. 9, 2001, at D1.

95. Gustav Niehbur, *Mormons Paying $3 Million to Settle Sex Abuse Case*, N.Y. Times, Sept. 5, 2001, at A14.

96. Franco v. The Church of Jesus Christ of Latter-day Saints, 21 P.3d 198 (Utah 2001).

97. Andrea Albright, *Minister Pleads Guilty in Second County*, Topeka Capital J. (Kan.), Dec. 11, 2001.

98. Chris Grenz, *Minister Sentenced to Five Years*, Topeka Capital J. (Kan.), Dec. 6, 2001.

99. *Man Jailed on Internet Sex Charges*, Pittsburgh Post-Gazette, Aug. 28, 1995, at D2.

100. *Sentence in Molestation*, Wash. Post, Feb. 1, 1996, at B3.

101. Peter Wilkinson, *The Life and Death of the Chosen One*, Rolling Stone, June 30, 2005, at 114, *available at* http://www.xfamily.org/index.php/Rolling_Stone:_The_Life_and_Death_of_the_Chosen_One.

102. Marci A. Hamilton, Justice Denied: What America Must Do to Protect Its Children (2008).

103. Allie Bidwell, *50 Years After Vaccine Creation, Measles Still Threaten U.S.*, U.S. News (Dec. 5, 2013), http://www.usnews.com/news/articles/2013/12/05/50-years-after-vaccine-creation-measles-still-threatens-us.

104. Lauren Silverman, *Texas Megachurch At Center of Measles Outbreak*, NPR (Sept. 1, 2013, 8:11 AM), http://www.npr.org/2013/09/01/217746942/texas-megachurch-at-center-of-measles-outbreak.

105. *See, e.g.*, Thomas Zambito, *Queens Parents Who Oppose Vaccination on Religious Grounds Asking Judge to Knock Down City Policy*, N.Y. DAILY NEWS (Feb. 8, 2012, 2:11 AM), http://www.nydailynews.com/life-style/health/queens-parents-oppose-vaccination-religious-grounds-judge-knock-city-policy-article-1.1018973; J. D. Wallace, *Vail Explains Whooping Cough Measures to Parents*, TUCSON NEWS NOW (Dec. 13, 2013, 12:36 AM), http://www.tucsonnewsnow.com/story/24210615/vail-explains-whooping-cough-measures-to-parents.

106. Saad B. Omer et al., *Legislative Challenges to School Immunization Mandates*, J. AMERICAN MEDICAL ASSOC. (Feb. 11, 2014), http://jama.jamanetwork.com/article.aspx?articleid=1829670.

107. MISS. CODE ANN. § 41-23-27 (2013) (upheld as constitutional in the face of free exercise challenge in Brown v. Stone, 378 So. 2d 218 (Miss. 1979), *cert. denied*, 449 U.S. 887 (1980)); W. VA. CODE § 16-3-4 (2013); *see also* State v. Riddle, 168 W. Va. 429, 439) (1981) (upholding conviction of parents for failing to send children to school in face of free exercise challenge, and citing for support the mandatory immunization statute as an "urgent public policy"). *See also States with Religious and Philosophical Exemptions from School Immunization Requirements*, NAT'L CONFERENCE OF STATE LEGISLATURES, http://www.ncsl.org/research/health/school-immunization-exemption-state-laws.aspx (last visited Feb. 15, 2014).

108. *See* CHILD, Inc., *Religious Exemptions from Healthcare for Children*, http://www.childrenshealthcare.org (last visited Feb. 4, 2014).

109. P.L. 93-247 (Jan. 31, 1974) did not, on its face, require an exemption. However, it was interpreted to mean that by the Department of Health and Human Services. This was corrected when Congress subsequently amended the Bill in 1983. *See* 48 Fed. Reg. 3698 (Jan. 26, 1983) (codified at 45CFR § 1340.2). 42 U.S.C. § 5106i(a)(2) (2012), enacted in 1983, provides: "Nothing in this Act . . . shall be construed . . . to require that a State find, or to prohibit a State from finding, abuse or neglect in cases in which a parent or legal guardian relies solely or partially upon spiritual means rather than medical treatment, in accordance with the religious beliefs of the parent or legal guardian."

110. *See, e.g., In re* Green, 292 A.2d 387 (Pa. 1972) (refusing to appointment a guardian for a boy suffering from paralytic scolios, whose Jehovah's Witness mother refused to consent to corrective surgery that would require a blood transfusion and holding that "as between a parent and the state, the state does not have an interest of sufficient magnitude outweighing a parent's religious beliefs when the child's life is *not immediately imperiled* by his physical condition") (emphasis in original).

111. Prince v. Massachusetts, 321 U.S. 158, 170 (1944).

112. For a list of religious exemptions for felonies and misdemeanors by state, see *Religious Exemptions from Health Care for Children*, CHILDREN'S HEALTH CARE IS A LEGAL DUTY, INC., http://childrenshealthcare.org/?page_id=24#Exemptions (last visited Feb. 14, 2014).

113. *See, e.g., Walker*, 47 Cal. 3d at 131 n. 11 (describing lobbying activities of Christian Scientists in California); CAROLINE FRASER, GOD'S PERFECT CHILD: LIVING AND DYING IN THE CHRISTIAN SCIENCE CHURCH 282 (1999) (hereinafter GOD'S PERFECT CHILD).

114. Most religious exemptions are worded in general terms that would extend to any religious believer relying on faith rather than medicine, but there are statutes that have been crafted solely with the Christian Scientists in mind. *See* Children's Healthcare Is a Legal Duty, Inc. v. Vladeck, 938 F. Supp. 1466 (D. Minn. 1996) (holding 42 U.S.C. § 1395x(e) and 42 U.S.C. § 1395x(y)(1) (2012), which explicitly referred to Christian Science practices, as unconstitutional). After the church-specific law was found unconstitutional, Congress responded by passing a broader regulation, that was not sect specific, although virtually no other religious organization would satisfy the description. The regulations, 42 U.S.C.S. § 1395x(ss)(1) and 42 U.S.C.S. § 1395i–5(a)(2), have been held constitutional since they are not facially discriminatory and a permissible accommodation of religion. Children's Healthcare Is a Legal Duty, Inc. v. De Parle, 212 F.3d 1084 (8th Cir. 2000), *cert. denied*, 532 U.S. 957 (2001).

115. *See* 26 U.S.C.A. § 5000(d)(2)(A) (West).

116. MARY BAKER EDDY, SCIENCE AND HEALTH 120, 1 (1994) (hereinafter SCIENCE AND HEALTH).

117. GOD'S PERFECT CHILD, *supra* note 113, at 337.

118. *Spiritual Healing – A Family Affair*, CHRISTIAN SCI. SENTINEL, July 23, 2001, at 7.

119. *See, e.g.*, Lundman v. McKown, 530 N.W.2d 807, 819 (Minn. Ct. App. 1995), *cert. denied*, 516 U.S. 1099 (1996) ("Appellants [including Christian Science Church] challenge the existence of a duty of care and a breach of that duty.").

120. *See id.* at 814–15 (When child was not admitted to Christian Science Nursing Home because he was under 16, his mother considered taking him to the hospital. She dismissed this idea after the nursing home "proposed hiring a private Christian Science nurse to come to the McKown home."); *see also What Is a Christian Science Practitioner?*, CHRISTIAN SCI. SENTINEL, Aug. 30, 2004, at 13 (answer of Jon Benzon, practitioner, to the question "Have you ever refused to give someone treatment?" Benson responded: "Yes, though rarely.... I realized that Christian Science treatment was being asked for to 'hedge their bets,' so to speak, while the patient was also relying on medical treatment."); *id.* at 18 ("What should the patient's role be when you are praying for him or her?" Practitioner Leide Lessa responded: "A patient needs to be sincere. And I can feel it clearly when this is not the case."); ROBERT PEEL, SPIRITUAL HEALING IN A SCIENTIFIC AGE 34 (1987) (hereinafter SPIRITUAL HEALING IN A SCIENTIFIC AGE) ("Christian Science treatment and medicine do not mix well.").

121. Mary Trammell, *A Prayer-First Approach to Healthcare*, CHRISTIAN SCI. SENTINEL, July 23, 2001, at 1.

122. SCIENCE AND HEALTH, *supra* note 116, at 4.

123. *Spiritual Healing – A Family Affair*, CHRISTIAN SCI. SENTINEL, July 23, 2001, at 7 (quoting Christian Science practitioner Richard Biever).

124. GOD'S PERFECT CHILD, *supra* note 113, at 329. Practitioners pray for the sick, while nurses tend to their physical needs.

125. SPIRITUAL HEALING IN A SCIENTIFIC AGE, *supra* note 120, at 151.

126. *See* Janna C. Merrick, *Christian Science Healing of Minor Children: Spiritual Exemption Statutes, First Amendment Rights, and Fair Notice*, 10 ISSUES IN L. & MED. 321 (1994).

127. Some have asserted that the Christian Scientists were the only organization that asked for the rule. They did not testify, but that is no indication of whether they sought the rule behind the scenes. *See id.* at 330 (between 1967 and 1974 "the church began a widespread lobbying effort to enact laws that would protect its members from future prosecutions").

128. *See, e.g.*, Michael Higgins, *Boy's Death Puts Religious Exemption in Spotlight*, CHI. TRIB., Sept. 5, 2003, at C18 ("Forty-one states, including Illinois, have exemptions in their civil laws, such as those governing when child welfare officials can remove a child from a home.... Some of the laws stem from lobbying by Christian Science Church members, many of whom use prayer instead of science-based medicine."); *see also* Gayle White, *Variety of Faiths Make Views Known at Capitol*, ATLANTA J.-CONST., Feb. 16, 2002, at 2B.

129. Seth M. Asser, M.D., & Rita Swan, *Child Fatalities from Religion-Motivated Medical Neglect*, 101 PEDIATRICS 625 (1998).

130. *See* Dirk Johnson, *Trials Loom For Parents Who Embraced Faith Over Medicine*, N.Y. TIMES, Jan. 21, 2009, at A23.

131. State v. Neumann, 832 N.W.2d 560, 583–84 (Wis. 2013).

132. *See* 1995 Or. Laws 657 (H.B. 2492). Other states have similar statutes. *See* ARK. CODE ANN. § 5–10–101(a)(9) (2013) (affirmative defense for capital murder); W. VA. CODE § 61–8D-2(d) (2013) (same).

133. The investigation, by Oregon's medical examiner, showed that at least 21 of the 78 children who died since 1955 probably would have survived with medical treatment. Mark Larabee & Peter D. Sleeth, *Followers Children Needed Medical Care, Experts Say*, CLEVELAND PLAIN DEALER, June 28, 1998, at 21A.

134. Mark Larabee, *Bill Aims to Lift All Oregon Religious Shields*, OREGONIAN, Jan. 22, 1999, at C6.

135. OR. REV. STAT. § 163.115(4) (2013).

136. Rita Swan, *Victory in Oregon*, CHILD, Nov. 2011, at 1, 6, *available at* http://childrenshealthcare.org/wp-content/uploads/2010/10/2011-01-fnl.pdf

137. Arthur Caplan, *Children's Health Can't Be Left to Faith Alone*, NBC NEWS (Mar. 31, 2008), http://www.nbcnews.com/id/23885944/ns/health/#.UvK6DXlN1uY.

138. *Id.*

139. William McCall, *Faith Healing Father Gets 60-day Sentence*, KATU.com (July 31, 2009), http://www.katu.com/news/local/52220642.html.

140. *See* Ryan Smith, *Mixed Blessing: Parents Beat Manslaughter Charge in Baby's "Faith Healing" Death*, CBS NEWS (July 24, 2009, 6:45 AM),

http://www.cbsnews.com/news/mixed-blessing-parents-beat-manslaughter-charge-in-babys-faith-healing-death.

141. *See* Nicole Dungca, *Jeffrey and Marci Beagley Sentenced to 16 Months of Prison for Their Son's Faith-Healing Death*, CLACKAMAS CNTY. NEWS (Mar. 8, 2010, 12:40 PM), http://www.oregonlive.com/clackamascounty/index.ssf/2010/03/jeffrey_and_marci_beagley_sent.html.

142. State v. Beagley, 305 P.3d 147, 155 (Or. 2013) (finding that the jury was "correctly informed that defendants' religious beliefs were not a defense").

143. *See* Isolde Raftery, *Changes in Oregon Law Put Faith-Healing Parents on Trial*, N.Y. TIMES, May 30, 2011, at A14.

144. *See* Steve Mayes, *Dale and Shannon Hickman Receive 6-Year Sentence, Harshest Yet for Faith-Healing Church*, OREGONIAN, Oct. 31, 2011.

145. Harriet Hall, *Faith Healing: Religious Freedom vs. Child Protection*, SCIENCE-BASED MEDICINE (Nov. 19, 2013), http://www.sciencebasedmedicine.org/faith-healing-religious-freedom-vs-child-protection/

146. John Miller, *Faith-Healing: Parent's Religious Right or Felony?*, CDA PRESS (Jan. 16, 2014), http://m.cdapress.com/news/local_news/article_c8b07ofc-8211-11e3-825d-001a4bcf887a.html?mode=jqm.

147. *Walker*, 47 Cal. 3d at 118–19, 138–39, 141.

148. Lawrence J. Goodrich, *Christian Scientist's Case Settled in California*, CHRISTIAN SCI. MONITOR, June 25, 1990, at 8.

149. *See generally* MANSLAUGHTER WORKING GROUP, REPORT TO THE (U.S. SENTENCING GUIDELINE) COMMISSION (1997), *available at* http://www.ussc.gov/Research/Working_Group_Reports/Miscellaneous/19971215_Manslaughter_Report.pdf (last visited Feb. 14, 2014) (discussing median sentences for involuntary manslaughter).

150. *Lundman*, 530 N.W.2d at 813–15. The Minnesota Supreme Court reversed the punitive damage award, but allowed the compensatory damages (reduced by the trial court to $1.5 million) to stand. *Id.* at 832.

151. *Id.* at 817, 819, 825.

152. *Id.* at 816, 832.

153. "Today, many LDS women and men are involved in health care practice and research. Church members, who are advised to seek medical assistance from competent licensed physicians, generally believe that advances in medical science and health care have come though the inspiration of the Lord." Cecil O. Samuelson, Jr., *Medical Practices, in* 2 ENCYCLOPEDIA OF MORMONISM 875 (1992), *available at* http://contentdm.lib.byu.edu/cdm/compoundobject/collection/EoM/id/4391/show/3912 (last visited Feb. 14, 2014). The faith does prescribe a health regimen: "[T]he code encourages eating grains, fruits, vegetables, and herbs, but strongly discourages using tobacco and consuming alcohol, tea, and coffee. In addition, practicing Latter-day Saints forgo food for 24 hours once a month as a fast." Church of Jesus Christ of Latter-day Saints, *Why Mormons Make Good Neighbors*, NEWSROOM (July 9, 2012), http://www.mormonnewsroom.org/article/why-mormons-make-good-neighbors.

154. Katy Kelly, *A Dangerous Parent Trap*, U.S. NEWS & WORLD REP., Oct. 13, 2003, at 12.

155. *MRI Abnormal in Boy Whose Parents Reject Chemotherapy*, CHI. TRIB., Sept. 28, 2003, at 20.

156. *Couple Missing After Fleeing with Sick Son*, CHI. TRIB., Aug. 21, 2003, at 20.

157. *Utah Won't Force Parents to Treat Son*, MILWAUKEE J. SENTINEL, Sept. 30, 2003, at 4A; Amy Joi Bryson, *Parental Rights Gain Momentum in Senate*, DESERET MORNING NEWS (Salt Lake City), Feb. 1, 2005.

158. Dave Wedge, *Cult Mom Acquitted in Baby's Starving Death*, BOSTON HERALD, Feb. 4, 2004, at 8.

159. Marie Szaniszlo, *Cultist's Guilty Plea Expected for Vision That Starved Baby*, BOSTON HERALD, Feb. 10, 2004, at 12.

160. Dave Wedge, *Jury Finds Cult Dad Guilty of Killing Son*, BOSTON HERALD, June 15, 2002, at 1.

161. Joseph Slobodzian, *Parents Who Prayed for Child to Stand Trial*, PHILA. INQUIRER (Oct. 8, 2009), http://articles.philly.com/2009-10-08/news/25272321_1_first-century-gospel-church-church-school-faith-tabernacle-congregation.

162. Tom Waring, *Parents Will Be Tried in Infant Death*, NE. TIMES (Aug. 14, 2013), http://www.bsmphilly.com/2013/aug/14/schaible-child-death-8-142/#.Uu3KkqWqzjQ.

163. Joseph A. Slobodzian, *No-Contest Plea by Parents in Faith-Healing Death of 2d Child*, PHILLY.COM (Nov. 16, 2013), http://articles.philly.com/2013-11-16/news/44117262_1_herbert-schaible-no-contest-plea-bacterial-pneumonia.

164. MaryClare Dale, *Herbert Schaible, Catherine Schaible Sentencing: Faith Healers Face Prison Time for Son's Death*, HUFFINGTON POST (Feb. 19, 2014, 4:25 AM), http://www.huffingtonpost.com/2014/02/19/herbert-schaible-catherine-schaible-sentencing-faith-healing_n_4813638.html?ncid=edlinkusaolp00000009.

165. Ted McDonough, *Lost Boys Found: How the Plight of Several Young Men Became a Legal Battle to Bring Down a Polygamous Sect*, SALT LAKE WEEKLY, Sept. 23, 2004, at 22.

166. *Id.; see also* Pamela Manson, *"Lost Boys" File Suit Against FLDS Church*, SALT LAKE TRIB., Aug. 28, 2004, at B1.

167. *See* Derrick Nunnally, *Minister Gets 30 Months in Boy's Death*, MILWAUKEE J. SENTINEL, Aug. 18, 2004, at 1B.

168. Wisconsin v. Hemphill, No. 2005AP1350-CR (Ct. App. Wisc. Aug. 15, 2006), *available at* http://www.wicourts.gov/ca/opinion/DisplayDocument.html?content=html&seqNo=26207.

169. Commonwealth v. McBurrows, 2001 PA Super. 164, 779 A.2d 509 (2001), *appeal denied*, 815 A.2d 632 (Pa. 2002), *cert. denied*, 124 S.Ct. 60 (2003).

170. Keith Herbert, *Pastor Is Sentenced in Beating*, PHILA. INQUIRER, Aug. 28, 2004.

171. Jim Vertuno, *Two on Trial in Bible Studies Beating*, ASSOC. PRESS, Dec. 3, 2003.

172. Claire Osborn, *Brothers Get Prison Terms for Beating*, AUSTIN AMERICAN-STATESMAN (Tex.), Dec. 13, 2003, at B1.

173. David Cheifetz, *Sharing the Secret That's Haunted My Soul*, JEWISH WEEK (Mar. 28, 2013), http://www.thejewishweek.com/news/new-york-news/sharing-secret-thats-haunted-my-soul. *See also* Jamie Schram, William J. Gorta & Chuck Bennett, *Oh, No, Uncle Joe! – Counselor Charged in Kid-Sex Case*, N.Y. POST, Mar. 5, 2011, at 7.

174. Associated Press, *Church Members Sentenced on Abuse Charges*, LAWRENCE J.-WORLD (Kan.), Jan. 7, 2004.

175. Associated Press, *Case Involved Restraining Kids with Belts, Cords*, TOPEKA CAPITAL-J. (Kan.), Feb. 8, 2004.

176. Associated Press, *Church Members Sentenced*, *supra* note 173.

177. *See* Richard Greer, *Preacher Convicted in Whipping Faces Jail for Directing DeKalb Church Beating*, ATLANTA J.-CONST., June 5, 1993, at 1B.

178. Steve Visser & Jill Young Miller, *Strong Words End Church Trial*, ATLANTA J.-CONST., Oct. 15, 2002, at 1B.

179. Jill Young Miller, *House of Prayer's Preacher Leaves Jail*, ATLANTA J.-CONST., Jan. 26, 2003, at 7C.

180. Steve Visser, *Minister Sentenced to 2 Years*, ATLANTA J.-CONST., Aug. 26, 2003, at 3B.

181. Michael Ferraresi, *Teen Reach Founder Fires Back at State*, ARIZ. REPUBLIC, Apr. 3, 2004, at 1B.

182. The decision was affirmed. Teen Reach's license was revoked in 2004 and it appears that it has been unable to obtain a new license. Arizona State Dep't of Econ. Sec'y v. Teen Reach et al., CV2004–009905 (Ariz. Civil Ct. Maricopa Cnty., Apr. 1, 2005).

183. As of February 2014, the bill has not yet been passed into law.

184. ARIZ. REV. STAT. ANN. § 36–897.04 (2013).

185. *Parent Information*, MISSOURI DEP'T OF HEALTH & SENIOR SERVS., http://www.thejewishweek.com/news/new-york-news/sharing-secret-thats-haunted-my-soul (last visited Feb. 9, 2014).

186. Cara Connelly, *Former Students, Prosecutors Question Methods of Some "Tough Love" Schools*, KY3 NEWS (Springfield, Mo.), Apr. 30, 2004, *available at* http://www.nospank.net/n-l88r.htm.

187. MO. REV. STAT. § 210.254 (2013).

188. Paul Pinkham, *Is Camp Salvation or Ruin? Children's Home Again Defends Itself Against Abuse Complaints*, FLORIDA TIMES-UNION, July 13, 2003, at B1.

189. Paul Pinkham, *Second Lawsuit Alleges Abuse at Camp: Harvest Baptist Church Runs Camp for Troubled Youths*, FLORIDA TIMES-UNION, June 7, 2003, at B1; *see also* Pinkham, *Is Camp Salvation or Ruin?*, *supra* note 188.

190. Jessie-Lynne Kerr, *Law & Disorder: Church Settles Abuse Suit*, FLORIDA TIMES-UNION, Nov. 8, 2003, at B3.

191. Pinkham, *Is Camp Salvation or Ruin?*, *supra* note 187.

192. Pinkham, *Second Lawsuit Alleges Abuse at Camp*, *supra* note 188.

193. Pinkham, *Is Camp Salvation or Ruin?*, *supra* note 187.

194. *See generally* NAT'L ASS'N FOR REGULATORY ADMIN. & THE CHILDREN'S FOUNDATION, 2004 FAMILY CHILD CARE LICENSING STUDY (2004).

195. MO. REV. STAT. § 210.211(1)(5), (2) (2013). The other states with complete exemptions are: Alabama (ALA. CODE § 38–7–3 (2013)); Arkansas (ARK. CODE ANN. §§ 20–78–206, 209(a), 9–28–402 (2013)); Florida (FLA. STAT. ANN. § 402.316 (West 2013)); Indiana (IND. CODE ANN. § 12–17.2–2–8(5) (West 2013)); North Carolina (N.C. GEN. STAT. § 131D–10.4(1) (2013)); Vermont (VT. STAT. ANN. tit. 33, § 3502(b)(3) (2013)). Some states exclude religiously operated child care from the definition of "child care" and provide the exemption that way. *See, e.g.*, Michigan (MICH. COMP. LAWS § 722.111(1)(e) (2013)); New Hampshire (N.H. REV. STAT. ANN. §170-E:3(I)(d) (2007)); New Jersey (N.J. STAT. ANN. § 30:5B-3(b)(3) (West 2013)). Ohio is slightly different, because the exemption only applies where the parent, guardian or custodian is participating in religious services on the same premises. *See* OHIO REV. CODE ANN. § 5104.02(B) (LexisNexis 2013)).

196. *See* INDIANA FAMILY AND SOCIAL SERVICES ADMINISTRATION ET AL., THE ABC'S OF A CHILD CARE BUSINESS 3–4 (3d ed. 2002) (contrasting the requirements of licensed facilities with those of facilities registered by ministries to illustrate this point); *see also* Vermont State Auditor, Review of Child Care Licensing and Registration by the Child Care Services Division of the Department of Social and Rehabilitation Services (Dec. 18, 1997), *available at* http://auditor.vermont .gov/sites/auditor/files/child%20care%20licensing.pdf (last visited Feb. 14, 2014) (explaining the distinction in Vermont's dual system).

197. The states are: Delaware (DEL. CODE ANN. tit. 31, § 343 (2007)); Kansas (KAN. STAT. ANN. § 65–501 (2013)); Maryland (MD. CODE ANN., FAM. LAW § 5–509 (West 2012)); Michigan (MICH. COMP. LAWS § 722.111 (2013) which only exempts from licensing "[a] facility operated by a religious organization where children are cared for not more than 3 hours while persons responsible for the children are attending religious services"); Oklahoma (OKLA. STAT. tit. 10, § 403 (2013)); Washington (WASH. REV. CODE § 74.15.090 (2013) with an exception only for Native American tribes).

198. ALA. CONST. art. I, § 3.01; ARIZ. REV. STAT. ANN. §§ 41–1493 to -1493.02 (2013); CONN. GEN. STAT. § 52–571b (2013); FLA. STAT. ANN. §§ 761.01–.05 (West 2013); IDAHO CODE ANN. §§ 73–401 to 404 (2013); 775 ILL. COMP. STAT. ANN. 35/5 (2013); N.M. STAT. ANN. §§ 28–22–1 to -5 (West 2012); OKLA. STAT. tit. 51, §§ 251–258 (2013); 71 PA. CONS. STAT. ANN. §§ 2401–2407 (West 2012); R.I. GEN. LAWS §§ 42–80.1–1 to .1–4 (2013); S.C. CODE ANN. §§ 1–32–10 to -60 (2013); TEX. CIV. PRAC. & REM. CODE ANN. §§ 110.001 to .012 (West 2013).

199. Pritzlaff v. Archdiocese of Milwaukee, 533 N.W.2d 780 (Wis. 1995); Colosimo v. Roman Catholic Bishop of Salt Lake City, 156 P.3d 806 (Utah 2007); Gibson v Brewer, 852 S.W.2d 239 (Mo. 1997).

200. Barbara Baird, *Youth Groups Fear Specter of Sexual Abuse*, L.A. TIMES, Sept. 25, 1988, at 4 (quoting psychiatrist and sexual abuse expert, "most of those identified [accused] as molesters are never booked; most of those who are booked are dismissed without charges. And any charges are often negotiated down so that

they are not recognizable as a sexual crime. The effective child molester will be active all his life without attracting accusations. Only the inept losers get caught.").

201. 2 *Paths, No Easy Solution, supra* note 51.

3. Marriage

1. Goodridge v. Dep't of Pub. Health, 440 Mass. 309, 313–14 (2003).

2. *Id.* at 320–21.

3. Opinions of the Justices to the Senate, 440 Mass. 1201, 1205–06 (2004).

4. Varnum v. Brien, 763 N.W.2d 862 (Iowa 2009).

5. These states include: California (2013), Connecticut (2008), Delaware (2013), District of Columbia (2010), Hawaii (2013), Illinois (2014), Maine (2012), Maryland (2013), Minnesota (2013), New Hampshire (2010), New Jersey (2013), New Mexico (2013), New York (2011), Rhode Island (2013), Vermont (2009), and Washington (2012). HUMAN RIGHTS CAMPAIGN, MARRIAGE EQUALITY AND OTHER RELATIONSHIP RECOGNITION LAWS (2014), *available at* http://www.hrc.org/files/assets/resources/marriage_equality_1-14-2014.pdf.

6. These states include: Alabama (2006), Arizona (2008), Arkansas (2004), Colorado (2006), Florida (2008), Georgia (2004), Idaho (2006), Kansas (2005), Kentucky (2004), Louisiana (2004), Michigan (2004), Mississippi (2004), Missouri (2004), Montana (2004), North Carolina (2012), North Dakota (2004), Ohio (2004), Oklahoma (2004), Oregon (2004), South Carolina (2006), South Dakota (2006), Tennessee (2006), Texas (2005), Utah (2004), Virginia (2006), and Wisconsin (2006). MARRIAGE EQUALITY AND OTHER RELATIONSHIP RECOGNITION LAWS, *supra* note 5.

7. *See* Terence Neilan, *High Court in Massachusetts Rules Gays Have Right to Marry*, N.Y. TIMES (Nov. 18, 2003), http://www.nytimes.com/2003/11/18/national/18CND-GAYS.html; *see also* Pam Belluck, *Same-sex Marriage: The Overview*, N.Y. TIMES, Nov. 19, 2003, at A1 (quoting Tony Perkins of the Family Research Council: "[I]t is inexcusable for this court to force the state Legislature to 'fix' its state constitution to make it comport with the pro-homosexual agenda of four court justices.").

8. *Reactions to the Massachusetts Supreme Court Ruling*, BELIEFNET, http://www.beliefnet.com/News/2003/11/Reactions-To-The-Massachusetts-Supreme-Court-Ruling.aspx?p=2 (last visited Feb. 23, 2014) (quoting Brian Fahling, Senior Trial Attorney, AFA [American Family Association] Center for Law & Policy).

9. Elizabeth Mehren, *Mass. High Court Backs Gay Marriage*, L.A. TIMES, Nov. 19, 2003, at A1 (quoting Roberta Combs, President, Christian Coalition of America).

10. 1 U.S.C. § 7 (2012) ("In determining the meaning of any Act of Congress, or of any ruling, regulation, or interpretation of the various administrative bureaus and agencies of the United States, the word "marriage" means only a legal union between one man and one woman as husband and wife, and the word "spouse"

refers only to a person of the opposite sex who is a husband or a wife."); 28 U.S.C. § 1738C (2012) ("No State, territory, or possession of the United States, or Indian tribe, shall be required to give effect to any public act, record, or judicial proceeding of any other State, territory, possession, or tribe respecting a relationship between persons of the same sex that is treated as a marriage under the laws of such other State, territory, possession, or tribe, or a right or claim arising from such relationship.")

11. United States v. Windsor, 133 S. Ct. 2675 (2013).

12. *Windsor*, 133 S. Ct. at 2680.

13. *Id.* at 2693 ("In determining whether a law is motived by an improper animus or purpose, '[d]iscriminations of an unusual character' especially require careful consideration. . . . DOMA cannot survive under these principles.")

14. Kitchen v. Herbert, No. 2:13-cv-217, 2013 WL 6697874 (D. Utah Dec. 20, 2013).

15. Jack Healy & Adam Liptak, *Justices' Halt to Gay Marriage Leaves Utah Couples in Limbo*, N.Y. TIMES, Jan. 7, 2014, at A1.

16. Bishop v. U.S. ex rel. Holder, No. 04-CV-848-TCK-TLW, 2014 WL 116013 (N.D. Okla. Jan. 14, 2014).

17. De Leon v. Perry, No. SA-13-CA-00982-OLG, 2014 WL 715741 (W.D. Tex. Feb. 26, 2014); Bostic v. Rainey, No. 2:13cv395, 2014 WL 561978 (E.D. Va. Feb. 13, 2014); Bourke v. Beshear, No. 3:13-CV-750-H, 2014 WL 556729 (W.D. Ky. Feb. 12, 2014).

18. *See* Marriage Protection Amendment, H.R.J. Res. 106, 108th Cong. (2004), *available at* http://thomas.loc.gov/cgi-bin/query/z?c108:H.J.res.106:; H.R.J. Res. 56, 108th Cong. (2003), *available at* http://thomas.loc.gov/cgi-bin/query/z?c108: H.J.RES.56.IH:; *see also* Marriage Protection Act of 2004, H.R. 3313, 108th Cong. (passed in the House of Representatives on July 22, 2004).

19. "The Musgrave Federal Marriage Amendment": Hearing Before the Subcomm. on the Constitution of the House Comm. on the Judiciary, 108th Cong. (2003) (statement of Rep. Marilyn Musgrave), *available at* http://www.gpo.gov/fdsys/pkg/CHRG-108hhrg93656/html/CHRG-108hhrg93656.htm). The proposed Federal Marriage Amendment resolution stated: "Marriage in the United States shall consist only of the union of a man and a woman. Neither this Constitution or the constitution of any State, nor state or federal law, shall be construed to require that marital status or the legal incidents thereof be conferred upon unmarried couples or groups." H.R.J. Res. 56.

20. "Limiting Federal Court Jurisdiction to Protect Marriage for the States": Hearing Before the Subcomm. on the Constitution of the House Comm. on the Judiciary, 108th Cong. (2004) (statement of former Rep. William E. Dannemeyer), *available at* http://commdocs.house.gov/committees/judiciary/hju94458.000/hju94458_of.htm. There were 19 Senator co-sponsors to the joint resolution to amend the Constitution to forbid gay marriage (S.J.RES.40), and 131 Representatives (H.J.RES.56).

21. Robert P. George, *One Man and One Woman*, WALL STREET J., Nov. 28, 2003 at A8.

22. United States v. Reynolds, 98 U.S. 145 (1878).

23. *Reynolds*, 98 U.S. at 166.

24. Bd. of Ed. of Kiryas Joel Village Sch. Dist. v. Grumet, 512 U.S. 687, 703 (1994).

25. *Reynolds*, 98 U.S. at 165–66.

26. *See* Complaint, Bronson v. Swensen, 394 F.Supp.2d 1329 (D. Utah 2005) (No. 2:04CV00021 TS), 2004 WL 3462279; *National Briefs: Polygamist's Appeal Based on Gay Sex Ruling*, HOUSTON CHRON., Dec. 2, 2003, at A17.

27. *See* Angie Welling, *Green's Conviction Is Upheld by Ruling*, DESERET MORNING NEWS (Salt Lake City), Sept. 4, 2004, http://www.deseretnews.com/article/595089043/Greens-conviction-is-upheld-by-ruling.html?pg=all.

28. Bronson v. Swensen, 500 F.3d 1099 (10th Cir. 2007).

29. State v. Green, 99 P.3d 820 (2004).

30. Brown v. Buhman, 947 F. Supp. 2d 1170 (D. Utah 2013).

31. John Schwartz, *Is Polygamy the Next Frontier?*, DAILY LIFE (Jan. 12, 2014, 11:55 PM), http://www.dailylife.com.au/life-and-love/real-life/is-polygamy-the-next-frontier-20140110-30ljz.html.

32. Testimony of Carolyn Jessop, Senate Judiciary Committee, (July 24, 2008), http://www.judiciary.senate.gov/hearings/testimony.cfm?id=e655f9e2809e5476862f735da13ed24c&wit_id=e655f9e2809e5476862f735da13ed24c-3-3.

33. Press Release, Alliance for Marriage, Introduction of the Federal Marriage Amendment in Congress (May 15, 2002) (on file with author).

34. Hollingsworth v. Perry, 133 S. Ct. 2652 (2013).

35. Chris Cillizza & Sean Sullivan, *How Proposition 8 Passed in California – And Why It Wouldn't Today*, WASH. POST (Mar. 26, 2013), http://www.washingtonpost.com/blogs/the-fix/wp/2013/03/26/how-proposition-8-passed-in-california-and-why-it-wouldnt-today.

36. *Nationally Acclaimed Pastor Rick Warren Announces Support for Proposition*, PR NEWSWIRE, Oct. 24, 2008.

37. Jessica Garrison, *Churches Plan a Big Push Against Same-Sex Marriage*, L.A. TIMES, Aug. 24, 2008.

38. *Protecting Family Values*, ALLIANCE DEFENSE FUND, http://www.alliancedefensefund.org/issues/familyvalues.php (last visited Oct. 15, 2004).

39. *See* Alan Cooperman, *Opponents Of Gay Marriage Divided*, WASH. POST, Nov. 29, 2003, at A1 (interviewing Matt Daniels, President of Alliance for Marriage); *see also* Mathew D. Staver, Esq. et al., Letter on Behalf of The Liberty Counsel, *The Federal Marriage Amendment Preserves Marriage as the Union of One Man and One Woman and is Consistent with Constitutional Jurisprudence and Federalism*, July 10, 2004, *available at* http://www.lc.org/marriage/fma_memo_senate_071004.pdf; *Editorial: Call Congress Now; Urge Support for Marriage Amendment During Sept. 30 Vote*, BAPTIST PRESS, Sept. 24, 2004, *available at* http://www.bpnews.net/bpnews.asp?ID=19174.

40. *See* Press Release, Cardinal Adam Maida, Archbishop of Detroit, An Open Letter to Michigan's United States Senators [Levin and Stabenow], July 2, 2004 (on

file with author). Orthodox Jews also support the Amendment. *See* Press Release, Union of Orthodox Jewish Congregations of America, Union Of Orthodox Jewish Congregations Supports Constitutional Marriage Amendment, July 13, 2004 (on file with author).

41. Todd Hertz, *Christian Conservatives Split on Federal Marriage Amendment*, CHRISTIANITYTODAY.COM (June 1, 2002), http://www.christianitytoday.com/ct/2002/123/43.0.html (discussing divide among Christian conservatives whether FMA was adequate to ensure there would be no marriages in the United States other than heterosexual).

42. *See, e.g.*, HUMAN RIGHTS CAMPAIGN, http://www.hrc.org (last visited Oct. 12, 2004). *See also* Amicus Curiae Brief of Coalition for the Protection of Marriage in Support of Hollingsworth and Bipartisan Legal Advisory Group Addressing the Merits and Supporting Reversal, Hollingsworth v. Perry, 133 S. Ct. 2652 (2013) (No. 12–144) and Windsor v. United States, 133 S. Ct. 2675 (2013) (No. 12–307), 2013 WL 1780812.

43. Brief for Amici Curiae Leadership Conference on Civil and Human Rights, Bar Associations and Public Interest and Legal Service Organizations in Support of Respondent Edith Windsor, *Windsor*, 2013 WL 769334.

44. Brief of Amicus Curiae American Sociological Association in Support of Respondent Kristin M. Perry and Respondent Edith Schlain Windsor, *Hollingsworth* and *Windsor*, 2013 WL 840004.

45. Brief Amicus Curiae of the American Jewish Committee in Support of the Individual Respondents on the Merits, *Hollingsworth* and *Windsor*, 2013 WL 4737187.

46. *The UAA Joins in Filing Amicus Briefs in Support of Marriage Equality*, UNITARIAN UNIVERSALIST ASS'N OF CONGREGATIONS (Mar. 20, 2013), http://www.uua.org/news/pressroom/pressreleases/284789.shtml.

47. *LGBT in the Church*, THE EPISCOPAL CHURCH, http://www.episcopalchurch.org/page/lgbt-church (last visited Feb. 13, 2014).

48. The largest study is the Australian Study of Child Health in Same-Sex Families. UNIV. OF MELBOURNE, THE AUSTRALIAN STUDY OF CHILD HEALTH IN SAME-SEX FAMILIES: INTERIM REPORT (2013), *available at* http://mccaugheycentre.unimelb.edu.au/__data/assets/pdf_file/0008/786806/simon_report_.pdf. *See also* Ellen C. Perrin & Benjamin S. Siegel, *Promoting the Well-Being of Children Whose Parents Are Gay or Lesbian*, AM. ACAD. OF PEDIATRICS, http://pediatrics.aappublications.org/content/early/2013/03/18/peds.2013-0377 (last visited Feb. 20, 2014).

49. Brief of Amici Curiae United States Conference of Catholic Bishops; National Association of Evangelicals; The Church of Jesus Christ of Latter-day Saints; The Ethics & Religious Liberty Commission of the Southern Baptist Convention; and Lutheran Church-Missouri Synod in Support of Defendants-Appellants and Supporting Reversal, Kitchen v. Herbert, 961 F.Supp.2d 1181 (D. Utah 2013) (Nos. 13–4178, 14–5003, 14–5006).

50. Jerry L. Van Marter, *GAPJC Upholds Spahr Rebuke for Performing Same-Gender Weddings*, PRESBYTERIAN CHURCH (USA) (Feb. 22, 2012), http://www.pcusa.org/news/2012/2/22/gapjc-upholds-spahr-rebuke-performing-same-gender-.

See also G. Jeffrey MacDonald, *Presbyterian Church Rejects Same-Sex Marriage*, Christian Sci. Monitor (July 7, 2012), http://www.csmonitor.com/USA/Society/2012/0707/Presbyterian-church-rejects-same-sex-marriage.

51. Rachel Zoll, *Methodists in Crisis over Gay Marriage, Church Law*, Huffington Post (Feb. 9, 2014, 3:42 PM), http://www.wral.com/methodists-in-crisis-over-gay-marriage-church-law/13373571.

52. Matt Smith, *A Quiet Struggle Within the Gay Marriage Fight*, N.Y. Times (Feb. 18, 2012), http://www.nytimes.com/2012/02/19/us/within-gay-marriage-battle-a-quiet-struggle-in-churches.html?pagewanted=all&_r=0.

53. Laurie Goodstein, *Defrocking of Minister Widens Split over Gays*, N.Y. Times (Dec. 19, 2013), http://www.nytimes.com/2013/12/20/us/methodist-pastor-defrocked-over-gay-marriage-service.html?_r=0.

54. *Id.*

55. *See Stances of Faith on LGBT Issues: Judaism*, Human Rights Campaign, https://www.hrc.org/resources/entry/stances-of-faiths-on-lgbt-issues-judaism (last visited Feb. 13, 2014).

56. MacDonald, *supra* note 50.

57. *Id.*

58. U.S. Census Bureau, Self-Described Religious Identification of Adult Population: 1990, 2001 and 2008 (2012), *available at* http://www.census.gov/compendia/statab/2012/tables/12s0075.pdf.

59. *See* Richard Cameron Blake & Lonn Litchfield, *Religious Freedom in Southern Africa: The Developing Jurisprudence*, 1998 B.Y.U. L. Rev. 515, 521 (1998) ("The Dutch Reformed Church (known in Afrikaans as Nederduitse Gereformeerde Kerk (NGK)) provided the moral and philosophical underpinnings for Nationalist apartheid policies. It also gave support to particular laws and made statements supporting the government's actions.").

60. Dunbar Rowland, 1 Jefferson Davis 286 (1923).

61. *Ephesians* 6:5–9 (Jerusalem Bible).

62. *See* William H. Seibert, The Underground Railroad from Slavery to Freedom 93–99 (1968) (discussing the role of Quakers and Methodists in the crusade against slavery).

63. For example, the Christian Legal Society was part of a coalition supporting the Freedom from Religious Persecution Act of 1998, H.R. 2431, 105th Cong. H3, 267–69 (May 14, 1998), during the same year they supported the Religious Liberty and Charitable Donation Protection Act of 1998, H.R. 2604, 105th Cong. H4,001 (June 3, 1998).

64. U.S. Comm'n on Int'l Religious Freedom, Annual Report 2013 (2013), *available at* http://www.uscirf.gov/sites/default/files/resources/2013%20USCIRF%20Annual%20Report%20(2).pdf. *See also* Policy Responses to the Denial and Restriction of Religious Liberty in the People's Republic of China: Hearing Before the United States Commission on International Religious Freedom (Mar. 16, 2002) (Prepared Statement of Rev. Drew Christiansen, S.J., Woodstock Theological Center [Georgetown University] Washington, D.C.), *available at* http://www.uscirf.gov/hearings/16maroo/christiansenPT.php3.

65. *See* HAROLD J. BERMAN, LAW AND REVOLUTION II: THE IMPACT OF THE PROTESTANT REFORMATIONS ON THE WESTERN LEGAL TRADITION 209–10, 215–16 (2003) (between 1630 and 1640, an estimated twenty thousand religious dissenters fled to the Massachusetts Bay Colony, and a similar number emigrated to the Netherlands); *see also* 1 WILLIAM S. HOLDSWORTH, A HISTORY OF ENGLISH LAW (7th ed. 1956); ROBERT E. RODES, JR., LAW AND MODERNIZATION IN THE CHURCH OF ENGLAND: CHARLES II TO THE WELFARE STATE 81 (1991).

66. 539 U.S. 558 (2003).

67. *Id.* at 578.

68. *Id.*

69. *Id.* at 590 (Scalia, J., dissenting).

70. Harold O. J. Brown, *A Decisive Turn to Paganism*, CHRISTIANITYTODAY.COM (Aug. 1, 2004), http://www.christianitytoday.com/ct/2004/008/24.39.html.

71. *Id.*

72. 517 U.S. 620 (1996).

73. *JFK's Speech on His Religion*, NAT'L PUB. RADIO (Dec. 5, 2007), http://www .npr.org/templates/story/story.php?storyId=16920600.

74. Anti-Polygamy Acts (the Morrill Act), ch. 126, 12 Stat. 501 (1862) (repealed 1910). The only reference to polygamy in the current U.S. Code deals with immigration law (Inadmissible aliens include "Practicing polygamists. Any immigrant who is coming to the United States to practice polygamy is inadmissible." 8 U.S.C.S. § 1182 (a)(10)(A) (2004)).

75. AMERICAN HERITAGE DICTIONARY OF THE ENGLISH LANGUAGE (5th ed. 2013), *available at* http://ahdictionary.com/word/search.html?q=polygamy &submit.x=61&submit.y=18.

76. AMERICAN HERITAGE DICTIONARY OF THE ENGLISH LANGUAGE (4th ed. 2000), *available at* http://ahdictionary.com/word/search.html?q=polygyny& submit.x=38&submit.y=24.

77. Lawrence v. Texas, 539 U.S. 558, 578 (2003).

78. *Reynolds* 98 U.S. at 166 ("Laws are made for the government of actions, and while they cannot interfere with mere religious belief and opinions, they may with practices.").

79. *Id.* at 166–76.

80. *Hunting Bountiful: Ending Half a Century of Exploitation*, ECONOMIST (London), July 8, 2004.

81. Daphne Bramham, *Editorial: See No Evil, Hear No Evil, Speak No Evil: Local People and Politicians Are Uncomfortable That Police and State Are Opening the Closed Doors at Bountiful*, VANCOUVER SUN (B.C.), Aug. 21, 2004 at C7.

82. Reference re: Section 293 of the Criminal Code of Canada, 2011 B.C.S.C 1588, *available at* http://www.courts.gov.bc.ca/jdb-txt/SC/11/15/2011BCSC1588 .htm.

83. 401 U.S. 437 (1971).

84. *Id.* at 461.

85. *See, e.g.*, Davis v. Beason, 133 U.S. 333, 348 (1890); *Reynolds*, 98 U.S. at 166; White v. United States, No. 01–4225, 41 F. App'x. 325, 326 (10th Cir. May 23, 2002);

Potter v. Murray City, 760 F.2d 1065, 1070 (10th Cir 1985); In re State in Interest of Black, 283 P.2d 887, 903–04 (Utah 1955); State v. Barlow, 153 P.2d 647, 653 (Utah 1944); United States v. Snow, 9 P. 697, 700–01 (Utah 1886).

86. *Black*, 283 P.2d at 904 (emphasis in original).

87. *Republican Platform of 1856, in* 1 NATIONAL PARTY PLATFORMS 1840–1972 27, 27 (Kirk H. Porter & Donald B. Johnson eds., 5th ed. 1975).

88. Cleveland v. United States, 329 U.S. 14, 20 (1946).

89. *See, e.g.,* United States v. Cole, 262 F.3d 704 (8th Cir. 2001); United States v. Draper, No. 98–10082, 1999 U.S. App. LEXIS 10990 (9th Cir. May 25, 1999); United States v. Niece, No. 93–5011, 1993 U.S. App. LEXIS 27327 (6th Cir. Oct. 19, 1993).

90. Joseph A. Reaves, *Troubles Dogging Polygamy Prophet,* ARIZONA REPUBLIC, Aug. 1, 2004, at 1A (listing "key dates" for FLDS).

91. Amanda J. Crawford, *Polygamy Town Gets Outside Aid,* ARIZONA REPUBLIC, Aug. 10, 2004, at B3.

92. *See, e.g.,* Brooke Adams, *Polygamy's "Lost Boys" Need Not Walk Alone,* SALT LAKE TRIB., Aug. 1, 2004, at B1; Nancy Perkins, *FLDS Church, Leaders Sued by 6 "Lost Boys",* DESERET MORNING NEWS (Salt Lake City), Aug. 28, 2004; Patty Henetz, *Krakauer Still Vexed by FLDS,* DESERET MORNING NEWS (July 31, 2004), http://www.deseretnews.com/article/595081003/Krakauer-still-vexed-by-FLDS.html?pg=all.

93. Travis Reed, *Group Calls Utah Soft on Polygamy,* FLORENCE NEWS (Ariz.), July 15, 2004, *available at* http://www.zwire.com/site/news.cfm?newsid=12354937&BRD=1817&PAG=461&dept_id=222076&rfi=8.

94. Patrice St. Germain, *Utah Gets Grant for Rural Communities: Money Will Be Used to Help Domestic Violence Victims in Polygamous Colonies,* SPECTRUM (St. George, Utah), Aug. 31, 2004.

95. *Editorial: More Perfect Unions,* SALT LAKE TRIB., Aug. 15, 2004.

96. Brian Barnard, *Public Forum Letters,* SALT LAKE TRIB., Aug. 22, 2004.

97. Andrea Moore-Emmett, *Inherently Destructive,* SALT LAKE TRIB., Aug. 31, 2004, at A12.

98. Jonathan Turley, *Polygamy Laws Expose Our Own Hypocrisy; Rights Should Be Based on Principle, Not Popularity,* USA TODAY, Oct. 4, 2004, at A13.

99. *Id.*

100. *Judge Upholds Charges Against Wesson,* L.A. TIMES, Apr. 13, 2004 at B7 ("Police said Wesson engaged in a lifestyle of incest and polygamy, fathering children with his own daughters and nieces. They allege that he held total control over his family and likened himself to God.").

101. *See, e.g.,* In re Conduct of Kirkman, 830 P.2d 206, 207 (Or. 1992) (disbarring a judge accused of bigamy and saying "These were not 'victimless' crimes. The accused's duplicity existed over a period of years, causing injury and humiliation to both of his families."); John Ellement, *Bigamist Sentenced for Theft of Funds,* BOS. GLOBE, Feb. 27, 2003, at B2; Lateef Mungin, *Alleged Bigamist May Have Fled to Tennessee,* ATLANTA J.-CONST., Nov. 5, 2003, at J4 (describing allegations against Anthony Glenn Owens, "who may have been married to at least

nine women at the same time" and married the "women to steal money from them.").

102. *Brown*, 947 F. Supp. 2d 1170.

103. Tapestry Against Polygamy was the pioneering group formed by formerly polygamous wives to fight polygamy, but is no longer in existence. Currently, the Sound Choices Coalition is working on these issues. SOUND CHOICES COALITION, http://sound-choices.com (last visited Feb. 13, 2014). *See also* Kristen Andersen, *Former 'Sister Wife': Polygamy Was 'Like Living with Adultery on a Daily Basis'*, LIFESITENEWS.COM (Feb. 11, 2013, 4:56 PM), http://www.lifesitenews.com/former-sister-wife-polygamy-was-like-living-with-adultery-on-a-daily-basis.html; Hemant Mehta, *Confessions of an Ex-Mormon Ex-Polygamist Ex-Wife*, PATHEOS.COM FRIENDLY ATHEIST BLOG (Aug. 4, 2012), http://www.patheos.com/blogs/friendlyatheist/2012/08/04/confessions-of-an-ex-mormon-ex-polygamist-ex-wife; *Wife Speaks Out Against Polygamy*, CNN NEWSROOM BLOG (July 2, 2012, 4:09 AM), http://newsroom.blogs.cnn.com/2012/07/02/wife-speaks-out-against-polygamy.

104. *See, e.g.*, ANDREA MOORE-EMMETT, GOD'S BROTHEL: THE EXTORTION OF SEX FOR SALVATION IN CONTEMPORARY MORMON AND CHRISTIAN FUNDAMENTALIST POLYGAMY AND THE STORIES OF 18 WOMEN WHO ESCAPED 138 (2004); TODD COMPTON, IN SACRED LONELINESS: THE PLURAL WIVES OF JOSEPH SMITH 199 (1997).

105. No Child Left Behind Act of 2001, 20 U.S.C. §§ 6301 et seq. (2012). "The purpose of this title is to ensure that all children have a fair, equal, and significant opportunity to obtain a high-quality education and reach, at a minimum, proficiency on challenging State academic achievement standards and state academic assessments." 20 U.S.C. § 6301.

106. Mike D'Amour, *Sect Wives Defend Lives: Women Say Polygamy Choice Is Theirs*, CALGARY SUN, July 29, 2004, at 4.

107. *See* Brooke Adams, *Plural Wives Defend Lifestyle*, SALT LAKE TRIB., Feb. 13, 2004, at C1. *See also* MARY BATCHELOR, ET AL., VOICES IN HARMONY: CONTEMPORARY WOMEN CELEBRATE PLURAL MARRIAGE (2000) (a collection of essays by women who are living in polygamous marriages supporting their lifestyle); Catherine Elsworth, *Investigation Launched into Polygamous Sect Dubbed "Canada's Dirty Little Secret*," DAILY TELEGRAPH (London), Aug. 5, 2004, at 14.

108. Rasheed Oluwa, *In Marriage, Three's a Crowd – And a Crime*, POUGHKEEPSIE J., Apr. 28, 2003, at A1.

109. Naomi Schaefer Riley, *Yes, Polygamy Is Everybody's Business*, L.A. TIMES, Feb. 9, 2004, at 11.

110. *See* Nicholas Bala and Rebecca Jaremko Bromwich, *Context and Inclusivity in Canada's Evolving Definition of the Family*, 16 INT'L J. L. POL'Y & FAM. 145, 169 (2002) (quoting Flanagan: "'the historical record shows that monogamy, like private property, is indispensable to constitutional democracy . . . Constitutional government has emerged only in societies where monogamy was the legally enforced, or at least the commonly observed, social norm . . . The modern adoption of

constitutional democracy in non-Western societies such as Japan and India has been accompanied by the parallel acceptance of monogamy. Those regions of the world where polygamy is still practiced . . . are precisely the areas where constitutional democracy has made the least progress.'").

111. *See* John Dougherty, *Double Exposure: Arizona's Finally Followed Utah's Lead and Launched Serious Action to Stop Abuses by Polygamists*, Phoenix New Times, Dec. 25, 2003; *see also* Mark Havnes, *Hildale Polygamist Guilty of Unlawful Sex, Bigamy*, Salt Lake Trib., Aug. 15, 2003, at A1 ("FLDS members believe taking plural wives is a direct commandment from God, to be followed even if it means violating civil law.").

112. John Dougherty, *Blasphemous Backlash*, Phoenix New Times, Jan. 29, 2004.

113. John Dougherty, *Bound by Fear: Polygamy in Arizona*, Phoenix New Times, Mar. 13, 2003 (reporting what Ruth Stubbs says Jeffs told her when she considered leaving the sect).

114. Dorothy L. Hodgson, *Women's Rights as Human Rights: Women in Law and Development in Africa (WiLDAF)*, 49 Africa Today 3 (2002).

115. Campaign Against Polygamy & Women Oppression In Nigeria and Africa, http://www.tk-one.com (last visited Oct. 24, 2004) (explaining the beliefs of the organization; Campaign against Polygamy and Women Oppression International (CAPWOI) *Discouraging polygamy through education, advocacy and support.* http://www.polygamystop.org/ (last visited May 5, 2014).

116. Traci Mayette, Interview, *A Conversation with Dr. Mojubaolu Olufunke Okome*, *reprinted in* 10:2 Africa Update Newletter (2003), http://web.ccsu.edu/afstudy/upd10-2.html#interview (last visited Feb. 22, 2014).

117. Laura Stampler, *Kenyan President Signs Polygamy Law*, Time (April 29, 2014).

118. Comm. on the Elimination of Discrimination Against Women, *General Recommendation 21 on Equality in Marriage and Family Relations*, 13th Sess., at 14, U.N. Doc. A/49/38 (1994). President Jimmy Carter signed it on July 17, 1980, but the Senate never ratified it. "Both last fall and for years beforehand, the vigilance of Sen. Jesse Helms (R-NC), a longtime opponent of measures that compromise U.S. sovereignty, was the dominant reason why CEDAW never came up for ratification." Melana Zyla Vickers, The Federalist Soc'y for Law and Pub. Pol'y Studies, The Convention on the Elimination of All Forms of Discrimination Against Women: A Leading Example of What's Wrong With International Law 2 (2007), *available at* http://www.fed-soc.org/doclib/20070325_CEDAWvic.pdf.

119. Dan Bilefsky, *Polygamy Fosters Culture Clashes (and Regrets) in Turkey*, N.Y. Times (July 10, 2006), http://www.nytimes.com/2006/07/10/world/europe/10turkey.html?fta=y&_r=0.

120. Lynn Beisner, *How Christian Purity Culture Enabled My Step Dad to Sexually Abuse Me*, Alternet.org (April 24, 2014) http://www.alternet.org/how-christian-purity-culture-enabled-my-step-dad-sexually-abuse-me (last visited April 26, 2014).

121. *How Can I Meet My Husband's Basic Needs?*, Inst. in Basic Life Principles, http://iblp.org/questions/how-can-i-meet-my-husbands-basic-needs (last visited Mar. 3, 2014).

122. Kate Tracy, *Bill Gothard Resigns Amid Sexual Harassment Investigation*,
ChristianityToday.com (Feb. 28, 2014), http://www.christianitytoday.com/
gleanings/2014/february/bill-gothard-relieved-of-duties-during-sexual-harassment-
in.html.

123. *Our Mission*, Recovering Grace, http://www.recoveringgrace.org/
our-mission (last visited Mar. 3, 2014).

124. Michelle Faul, *Boko Haram Leader Says He Will Sell Kidnapped Girls*,
USA Today (May 5, 2014) http://www.usatoday.com/story/news/world/2014/05/05/
protester-1st-lady-orders-arrests/8715751/

4. Religious Land Use and Residential Neighborhoods

1. City of Boerne v. Flores, 521 U.S. 507 (1997).

2. Amy Dorsett, *1997 Year in Review: Trees, Traffic Among Top Issues*, San
Antonio Express-News (Tex.), Jan. 1, 1998, at 1S.

3. 42 U.S.C. § 2000cc *et seq.* (2012).

4. *See generally* Marci A. Hamilton, *Religion and the Law in the Clinton Era:
An Anti-Madisonian Legacy*, 63 L. & Contemp. Probs. 359 (2000).

5. Melissa Rogers, *Free Exercise Flip? Kagan, Stevens, and the Future of Religious
Freedom*, Brookings (June 23, 2010), http://www.brookings.edu/research/papers/
2010/06/23-kagan-rogers.

6. Presidential Statement on Signing the Religious Land Use and Institutionalized Persons Act of 2000, 36 Weekly Comp. Pres. Doc. 2168 (Sept. 22, 2000).

7. 42 U.S.C. § 2000cc(b) provides:

> (1) Equal terms. No government shall impose or implement a land use
> regulation in a manner that treats a religious assembly or institution on less
> than equal terms with a nonreligious assembly or institution.
>
> (2) Nondiscrimination. No government shall impose or implement a
> land use regulation that discriminates against any assembly or institution on
> the basis of religion or religious denomination.
>
> (3) Exclusions and limits. No government shall impose or implement a
> land use regulation that
>> (A) totally excludes religious assemblies from a jurisdiction; or
>> (B) unreasonably limits religious assemblies, institutions, or struc-
>> tures within a jurisdiction.

42 U.S.C. § 2000cc(b).

8. *Id.* § 2000cc(a).

9. Barry A. Kosmin, Egon Mayer & Ariela Keysar, American Religious
Identification Survey of 2001, *available at* http://www.gc.cuny.edu/CUNY-
GC/media/CUNY-Graduate-Center/PDF/ARIS/ARIS-PDF-version.pdf (last vis-
ited Feb. 8, 2014) (conducted by City University of New York).

10. City of Boerne v. Flores, 521 U.S. 507, 537 (Stevens, J., concurring).

11. 42 U.S.C. § 1988 provides, in pertinent part: "In any action or proceeding to enforce a provision of . . . the Religious Land Use and Institutionalized Persons Act of 2000 . . . the court, in its discretion, may allow the prevailing party, other than the United States, a reasonable attorney's fee as part of the costs." 42 U.S.C. § 1988(b).

12. Vill. of Belle Terre v. Boraas, 416 U.S. 1, 9 (1974).

13. Allison B. Cohen, *Neighbors Divided*, L.A. TIMES (Apr. 25, 2004) [hereinafter *Neighbors Divided*], http://articles.latimes.com/2004/apr/25/realestate/re-zoning25 (last visited Feb. 15, 2014). ("There is such greater emphasis on land in California. . . . You don't see these kinds of cases in North Dakota. Most of the time this is about neighbors' NIMBYism and churches' abilities to worship." (quoting Roman Storzer, attorney for the Becket Fund)).

14. Anthony R. Picarello, Jr., *RLUIPA Is Constitutional*, 56 PLAN. & ENVTL. J. 3 (2004), *available at* http://www.becketfund.org/other/RLUIPA%20Is%20Constitutional.pdf (last visited Oct. 31, 2004).

15. Locke v. Davey, 540 U.S. 712, 720 (2004).

16. 42 U.S.C. § 2000cc(a)(2)(C) provides:

This subsection applies in any case in which . . . the substantial burden is imposed in the implementation of a land use regulation or system of land use regulations, under which a government makes, or has in place formal or informal procedures or practices that permit the government to make, individualized assessments of the proposed uses for the property involved.

42 U.S.C. § 2000cc(a)(2)(C) (2012).

17. The lead case employing this reasoning is *Sherbert v. Verner*, 374 U.S. 398, 404 (1963).

18. *See* F.O.P. Newark Lodge No. 12 v. City of Newark, 170 F.3d 359 (3d Cir. 1999).

19. *See* Sherbert v. Verner, 374 U.S. 398 (1963).

20. Freedom Baptist Church of Del. Cnty. v. Twp. of Middletown, 204 F. Supp. 2d 857, 868 (E.D. Pa. 2002).

21. Murphy v. Zoning Comm'n, 289 F. Supp. 2d 87, 119 (D. Conn. 2003) (citation omitted); *see also* Guru Nanak Sikh Soc'y v. Cnty. of Sutter, 326 F. Supp. 2d 1140, 1155 (E.D. Cal. 2003) ("Relying on RLUIPA's legislative history, several courts have concluded that 'these provisions codify existing Equal Protection Clause and Free Exercise Clause jurisprudence.'" (quoting Petra Presbyterian Church v. Vill. of Northbrook, 2003 WL 22048089, at *11 (N.D. Ill. Aug., 29, 2003)); *Freedom Baptist Church of Del. Cnty.*, 204 F. Supp. 2d at 869, *supra* note 20 (Sections (b)(1) and (b)(3) of RLUIPA "codify existing Supreme Court decisions under the Free Exercise and Establishment Clauses of the First Amendment as well as under the Equal Protection Clause of the Fourteenth Amendment.").

22. ZONING AND LAND USE CONTROLS § 40.03 (Matthew Bender 2002).

23. *Neighbors Divided*, *supra* note 13.

24. ZONING AND LAND USE CONTROLS, *supra* note 15.

25. *See generally* SCOTT THUMMA, EXPLORING THE MEGACHURCH PHENOMENA: THEIR CHARACTERISTICS AND CULTURAL CONTEXT (Hartford Inst. for Relig. Research 2000), *available at* http://hirr.hartsem.edu/bookshelf/thumma_article2.html (last visited Feb. 1, 2014); *see also* Patricia Leigh Brown, *Megachurches as Minitowns*, N.Y. TIMES, May 9, 2002, at F1; Gustav Niebuhr, *Where Religion Gets a Big Dose of Shopping-Mall Culture*, N.Y. TIMES, Apr. 16, 1995, at A1; Lisa Shafer & Jack Brown, *Church Center's Profile Brings Fears: Bensalems Christian Life Complex Goes Far Beyond Sunday Services. Some Say it Oversteps*, PHILA. INQUIRER, May 14, 1999, at B1 [hereinafter *Church Center's Profile Brings Fears*].

26. Haya El Nasser, *Megachurches Clash with Critics Next Door*, USA TODAY, Sept. 23, 2002, at 1A (discussing Brentwood Baptist Church in Houston, Texas).

27. Daniel B. Wood, *Cathedral Reflects a New Vision of Church*, CHRISTIAN SCI. MONITOR, Sept. 9, 2002, at 3 (quoting religious architecture expert Jeanne Kilde of Macalester College in St. Paul, Minn.).

28. *See* David A. Roozen, *Denominations Grow as Individuals Join Congregations, in* CHURCH AND DENOMINATIONAL GROWTH 20–28 (1993), *available at* http://hirr.hartsem.edu/bookshelf/Church&Denomgrowth/ch&dngrw-ch1.pdf (last visited Feb. 1, 2014); C. Kirk Hadaway, *Is Evangelistic Activity Related to Church Growth?, in* CHURCH AND DENOMINATIONAL GROWTH 178–80 (1993), *available at* http://hirr.hartsem.edu/bookshelf/Church&Denomgrowth/ch&dngrw-ch8.pdf (last visited Feb. 1, 2014).

29. *See Church Center's Profile Brings Fears, supra* note 18 (quoting John Vaughan, Church Growth Today, which studies growth and decline of new and established churches).

30. *See* Int'l Church of Foursquare Gospel v. City of San Leandro, 673 F.3d 1059 (9th Cir. 2011), *cert. denied*, 132 S.Ct. 251 (2011); Petition for Writ of Certiorari, Int'l Church of Foursquare Gospel v. City of San Leandro, 132 S. Ct. 251 (2011) (No. 11–106), 2011 WL 3151262; *see also* Tom Abate, *City to Pay Faith Fellowship $2.3 Million to Settle Suit*, SAN LEANDRO PATCH (Sept. 25, 2012, 1:32 PM), http://sanleandro.patch.com/groups/politics-and-elections/p/city-to-pay-faith-fellowship-2-3-million-to-settle-suit; Press Release, City of San Leandro, City of San Leandro and International Church of Four Square Gospel Resolve Lawsuit (Sept. 25, 2012), *available at* http://www.sanleandro.org/civica/press/display.asp?layout=1&Entry=190.

31. Quoted in Plaintiffs' Second Amended Complaint, LRNA v. Los Angeles, Case No. CV-03–4890-HLH (C.D. Cal. Filed May 6, 2004).

32. *See* Complaint, League of Residential Neighborhood Advocates v. Los Angeles, Case No. CV-03–4890-HLH, at ¶ 13 (C.D. Cal. Filed July 10, 2003), *available at* http://www.thelrna.org/pdfs/hancockparklawsuit.pdf (last visited Feb. 8, 2014) (quoting Congregation Etz Chaim v. City of Los Angeles, No. BC192517 (L.A. Sup. Ct.)).

33. *Id.*

34. *Id.* ¶ 14.

35. Congregation Etz Chaim v. City of Los Angeles, 371 F.3d 1122, 1129 (2004) (Aldisert, J., dissenting).

36. I represented the neighbors in that litigation. *See* Order Granting Motion to Dismiss on Second Amended Complaint League of Residential Neighborhood Advocates v. City of Los Angeles, No. CV 03–4890 (CAS) (C.D. Cal. Jul. 15, 2004), *available at* http://www.thelrna.org/pdfs/071404.pdf (last visited Feb. 1, 2014).

37. League of Residential Neighborhood Advocates v. City of Los Angeles, 498 F.3d 1052 (9th Cir. 2007).

38. Order Granting Summary Judgment in Congregation Etz Chaim v. City of Los Angeles, No. 2:10-cv-01587 (C.D. Cal. May 15, 2013), *available at* http://www .thelrna.org/pdfs/05152013.pdf (last visited Feb. 8, 2014) (order granting summary judgment).

39. *The Religious Liberty Protection Act of 1998; Hearing Before the House Judiciary Comm.*, 105th Cong. (Feb. 26, 1998) (statement of Rabbi Chaim Baruch Rubin).

40. *Id.*

41. *Religious Land Use and Institutionalized Persons Act*, 105th CONG. REC. S7, 774–75 (July 27, 2000) (joint statement of Sen. Kennedy & Sen. Hatch).

42. Douglas Laycock, *State RFRAs and Land Use Regulation*, 32 U.C. DAVIS L. REV. 755, 779 (1999).

43. *See* MARK CHAVES, CONGREGATIONS IN AMERICA (2004) [hereinafter CONGREGATIONS IN AMERICA]; Mark Chaves & William Tsitsos, *Are Congregations Constrained by Government? Empirical Results from the National Congregations Study*, 42 J. CHURCH & STATE 335, 342 (2000) [hereinafter Chaves & Tsitsos].

44. *See generally*, Marci A. Hamilton, *Federalism and the Public Good: The True Story Behind the Religious Land Use and Institutionalized Persons Act*, 78 IND. L.J. 311 (2003).

45. Freedom Baptist Church v. Twp. of Middletown, 204 F. Supp. 2d 857, 862 (E.D. Pa. 2002).

46. Nasser, *supra* note 19.

47. Vanessa Ho, *Mainline Religions Dwindle as Megachurches Gain Ground*, SEATTLE POST-INTELLIGENCER, Mar. 18, 2002, at A1.

48. *Neighbors Divided, supra* note 13.

49. Justin Catanos, *What Form Faith?*, NEWS & RECORD (Greensboro, N.C.), May 14, 1995, at A1.

50. Laycock, *supra* note 35, at 755, 776, 780.

51. *Id.* at 760.

52. *Id.* at 758.

53. *See* John I. Gilderbloom & John P. Markham, *The Impact of Homeownership on Political Beliefs*, 73 SOC. FORCES 1589, 1592 (1995) ("Research has also shown that homeowners are more likely to be involved in community political activities, to be more neighborly, to be members of church or community organizations, and to be more aware of local affairs." (internal citations omitted)).

54. Grosz v. Miami Beach, 721 F.2d 729, 730 (11th Cir. 1983).

55. *Id.* at 732.

56. *Id.* at 739.

57. *Neighbors Divided, supra* note 13.

58. Juan Otero & Veronique Pluviose-Fenton, *City of Cheyenne, Wyo., Wins Religious Land Use Case,* NATION'S CITIES WEEKLY, June 23, 2003, at 3.

59. Terry Sheridan, *Federal Law Invoked as Pastor in Broward Fights County Zoning,* BROWARD DAILY BUS. REV. (Fla.), Apr. 15, 2003, at A1.

60. ZONING AND LAND USE CONTROLS, *supra* note 15, at § 5.01; *see also id.* § 34.02 ("Two additional valid objectives of zoning enabling legislation are prevention of overcrowding of land and ensuring against undue concentration of population.").

61. Euclid v. Ambler Realty Co., 272 U.S. 365, 367–68 (1926).

62. Lemon v. Kurtzman, 403 U.S. 602, 612 (1971).

63. *See* Locke v. Davey, 540 U.S. 712, 720 (2004); Church of Lukumi Babalu Aye v. City of Hialeah, 508 U.S. 520, 532–33 (1993); Emp't Div. v. Smith, 494 U.S. 872, 877 (1990).

64. Chaves & Tsitsos, *supra* note 36.

65. *Smith,* 494 U.S. at 890.

66. Walz v. Tax Comm'n of New York, 397 U.S. 664 (1970).

67. St. Bartholomew's Church v. City of New York, 914 F.2d 348 (2d Cir. 1990).

68. Keeler v. Mayor & City Council of Cumberland, 940 F. Supp. 879, 886 (1996).

69. *See* East Bay Asian Local Dev. Corp. v. California, 24 Cal. 4th 693 (2000), *cert. denied,* 532 U.S. 1008 (2001) (upholding Cal. Gov't Code §§ 25373, 37361 "which have the effect of granting an exemption from landmark preservation laws to noncommercial property owned by a religious organization that objects to landmark designation and determines in a public forum that the organization would suffer a substantial hardship if the property were designated a historic landmark").

70. Tom Barnes, *Council Shelters Religious Building,* PITTSBURGH POST-GAZETTE, Feb. 26, 2003, at B3.

71. Judy Evans, *District Approved, Minus Churches,* DALLAS MORNING NEWS, May 8, 2002, at 1R.

72. First Covenant Church v. City of Seattle, 840 P.2d 174 (Wash. 1992).

73. Oregon City v. Hartke, 400 P.2d 255, 261 (1965).

74. *First Covenant Church,* 840 P.2d at 185.

75. Editorial, *So Glorious, Yet So Vulnerable,* OPELIKA-AUBURN NEWS (Ala.), Aug. 23, 2000.

76. Paul Davis, *Auburn Shows Its Prowess in Handling a Real Emergency,* OPELIKA-AUBURN NEWS (Ala.), Aug. 20, 2000.

77. Cohen v. City of Des Plaines, 8 F.3d 484 (7th Cir. 1993); Abram v. Fayetteville, 661 S.W.2d 371 (Ark. 1983); Rose Lees Hardy Home & Sch. Assoc. v. Dist. of Columbia Bd. of Zoning Adjustment, 324 A.2d 701 (D.C. Ct. App. 1974); State v. Maxwell, 617 P.2d 816 (Haw. 1980); Yusuf v. Villa Park, 458 N.E.2d 575 (Ill. App. Ct. 1983) *overruled on other grounds as recognized in* Gallik v. Cnty. of Lake, 335

Ill. App. 3d 325, 326, 781 N.E.2d 522, 523 (Ill. App. Ct. 2002); Congregation Beth
Yitzchok v. Ramapo, 593 F. Supp. 655 (S.D.N.Y. 1984); Medford Assembly of God
v. Medford, 695 P.2d 1379 (Ore. Ct. App. 1985); Heard v. Dallas, 456 S.W.2d 440
(Tex. Ct. Civ. App. 1970).

78. Love Church v. City of Evanston, 671 F. Supp. 508, 513 (N.D. Ill. 1987).

79. See Roman Catholic Welfare Corp. v. Piedmont, 45 Cal. 2d 325 (Cal. 1955).

80. Harvest Christian Ctr. v. Zoning Appeals Bd., 55 Va. Cir. 279, 284 (Va. Cir.
Ct. 2001) (quoting Trustees v. Guthrie, 86 Va. 125, 140–41 (1889)).

81. Grace United Methodist Church v. City of Cheyenne, 235 F. Supp. 2d 1186
(D. Wyo. 2002) aff'd, 427 F.3d 775 (10th Cir. 2005), reh'g granted, opinion vacated,
451 F.3d 643 (10th Cir. 2006).

82. Id. at 1190.

83. Grace United, 427 F.3d 775, reh'g granted, opinion vacated, 451 F.3d 643
(10th Cir. 2006).

84. Grace United, 451 F.3d 643.

85. Grace United, 427 F.3d at 797.

86. Neighbors Divided, supra note 13.

87. See Order, Missionaries of Charity, Brothers v. City of Los Angeles, No. CV
01–08115-SVW (C.D. Cal. July 11, 2003).

88. Along with local counsel, I represented the township in this case. Congregation Kol Ami v. Abington Twp., No. 01-1919, 2004 U.S. Dist. LEXIS 16397, at
*9 (E.D. Pa. Aug. 12, 2004); Congregation Kol Ami v. Abington Twp., 309 F.3d
120 (3d Cir. 2002).

89. Congregation Kol Ami v. Abington Twp., 161 F.Supp. 2d 432, 435 (E.D. Pa.
2001).

90. Id. at 437.

91. Civil Liberties for Urban Believers v. City of Chicago, 342 F.3d 752, 766 (7th
Cir. 2003) (internal citations omitted); Bethel Baptist Church v. United States, 822
F.2d 1334, 1339 (3d Cir. 1987).

92. See Braunfeld v. Brown, 366 U.S. 599, 605 (1961); Civil Liberties for Urban
Believers, 342 F.3d at 762; Grosz v. Miami Beach, 721 F.2d 729, 736 (citing Braunfeld, 336 U.S. 599).

93. Congregation Kol Ami v. Abington Twp., CIV.A. 01-1919, 2004 WL 1837037
(E.D. Pa. Aug. 17, 2004) amended on denial of reconsideration, 01-1919, 2004 WL
2137819 (E.D. Pa. Sept. 21, 2004).

94. Id. at *29.

95. Patrick Korten, Vice President, Becket Fund for Religious Liberty, Churches
Don't Stand a Prayer, WALL ST. J., Jan. 22, 2003, at A14.

96. Id.

97. Castle Hills Baptist Church v. City of Castle Hills, No. SA-01-CA-1149-RF,
2004 WL 546792, at *4, *13–14 (W. D. Tex. Mar. 17, 2004).

98. 146 CONG. REC. S7,776 (daily ed. July 27, 2000) (joint statement of Sen.r
Hatch & Sen. Kennedy).

99. San Jose Christian Coll. v. City of Morgan Hill, 360 F.3d 1024,1035 (9th
Cir. 2004).

100. Congregation Rabbinical Coll. of Tartikov, Inc. v. Vill. of Pomona, No. 07-CV-6304(KMK), 2013 WL 66473 (S.D.N.Y. Jan. 4, 2013).

101. *Id.* at *18.

102. Murphy v. Zoning Comm'n, 289 F. Supp. 2d 87 (D. Conn. 2003), *vacated sub nom*, Murphy v. New Milford Zoning Comm'n, 402 F.3d 342 (2d Cir. 2005).

103. *Id.* at 344–45.

104. *See* Ala. Const. amend. 622 (2012) (enacted 1999), Ariz. Rev. Stat. Ann. § 41-1493.01 (2013) (enacted 1999), Conn. Gen. Stat. § 52–571b (2013) (enacted 1993), Fla. Stat. § 761.03 (2013) (enacted 1998), Idaho Code Ann. § 73–402 (2013) (enacted 2000), 775 Ill. Comp. Stat. 35/1 et seq. (2013) (enacted 1998), Kan. Stat. Ann. § 60-5301 (2013) (enacted 2013), Ky. Rev. Stat. Ann. § 446.350 (West 2013) (enacted 2013), La. Rev. Stat. Ann. § 13:5231-42 (2013) (enacted 2010), Mo. Ann. Stat. §§ 1.302-.307 (2013) (enacted 2003) N.M. Stat. Ann. § 28–22–3 (2013) (enacted 2000), 71 Pa. Cons. Stat. § 2401 *et seq.* (2013) (enacted 2002), R.I. Gen. Laws § 42–80.1–3 (2013) (enacted 1993), S.C. Code Ann. § 1–32–40 (2013) (enacted 1999), Tenn. Code Ann. § 4-1-407 (2013) (enacted 2009), Utah Code Ann. §§63L-5-101-403 (2013) (enacted 2008), Va. Code Ann. §§ 57-1-2.02 (2013) (enacted 2007) respectively.

105. *See* Okla. Stat. tit. 51, § 258 (2013) (enacted 2000).

5. Schools

1. Philip Hamburger, Separation of Church and State 219–20, 222, 283, 310 (2002).

2. Rev. Jerry Falwell, *Defending Prayer in School*, WND Commentary (Oct. 27, 2001, 1:00 AM), http://www.worldnetdaily.com/news/article.asp?ARTICLE_ID=25107.

3. *Id.*

4. The Hon. Minister Louis Farrakhan, *Atonement: The Road to Peace*, The Final Call, Oct. 29, 2001, http://www.finalcall.com/columns/mlf/mlf-atonement10–30–2001.htm.

5. Pat Buchanan, *Whose Country Is It, Anyway?*, Creators.com (Dec. 27, 2011), http://www.creators.com/opinion/pat-buchanan/whose-country-is-it-anyway-11–12–27.html.

6. Hamburger, *supra* note 1, at 223.

7. Illinois *ex rel.* McCollum v. Bd. of Educ., 333 U.S. 203, 235 (1948) (Jackson, J., concurring).

8. 42 U.S.C. § 2000bb (2012).

9. 406 U.S. 205 (1972).

10. *Private and Other Nonpublic Schools and the Nation's Report Card*, Nat'l Center for Educ. Stats., http://nces.ed.gov/nationsreportcard/about/nonpublicschools.aspx (last visited Feb. 22, 2014).

11. Brandy Zadrozny, *The School Shootings You Didn't Hear About – One Every Two Weeks Since Newtown*, The Daily Beast (Dec. 12, 2013),

http://www.thedailybeast.com/articles/2013/12/12/the-school-shootings-you-didn-t-hear-about-one-every-two-weeks-since-newtown.html.

12. Wesley Lowery, *Rape, Robbery Also Alleged in Teacher's Slaying: Essex Grand Jury Indicts Danvers Student, 14*, BOSTON GLOBE, Nov. 22, 2013, at A. Greg Botelho and Rande Iaboni, *Complaint: School stabbing suspect said, 'I have more people to kill'*, http://www.cnn.com/2014/04/25/justice/pennsylvania-school-stabbing/(last visited April 28, 2014).

13. CTR. FOR DISEASE CONTROL AND PREVENTION, U.S. DEP'T OF HEALTH & HUMAN SERVS., YOUTH RISK BEHAVIOR SURVEILLANCE – UNITED STATES, 2011 55 (2012), *available at* http://www.cdc.gov/mmwr/pdf/ss/ss6104.pdf.

14. *Id.*

15. GRADUATE CTR.OF THE CITY UNIV. OF N.Y., AMERICAN RELIGIOUS IDENTIFICATION SURVEY, STATISTICAL ABSTRACT OF THE UNITED STATES 67 (2003).

16. *The Sikh Community Today*, THE PLURALISM PROJECT: HARVARD UNIVERSITY, *available at* http://www.pluralism.org/religion/sikhism/america/community (last visited Feb. 15, 2014).

17. *The Global Religious Landscape*, PEW RESEARCH, http://www.pewforum.org/2012/12/18/global-religious-landscape-other/#spotlight (last visited Apr. 20, 2014).

18. *2011 National Household Survey: Data Tables*, STATS. CANADA, http://www12.statcan.gc.ca/nhs-enm/2011/dp-pd/dt-td/Rp-eng.cfm?LANG=E&APATH=3&DETAIL=0&DIM=0&FL=A&FREE=0&GC=0&GID=0&GK=0&GRP=0&PID=105399&PRID=0&PTYPE=105277&S=0&SHOWALL=0&SUB=0&Temporal=2013&THEME=95&VID=0&VNAMEE=&VNAMEF (last updated Jan. 13, 2014); *2011 Religion by Ethnic Group*, OFF. OF NAT'L STATS., *available at* http://www.ons.gov.uk/ons/search/index.html?newquery=sikh (last visited Feb. 15, 2014).

19. W. H. MCLEOD, THE SIKHS: HISTORY, RELIGION, AND SOCIETY 45, 142 (1989). Women are admitted into the Khalsa as well as men, though they rarely wear the turban. In theory, women are regarded as the equals of men. However, actual practice falls short of the claim. *See* W. H. MCLEOD, WHO IS A SIKH? 108–09 (1989) [hereinafter WHO IS A SIKH?].

20. *See* WHO IS A SIKH?, *supra* note 19, at 112–14 (1989); *see also* Michael Rollins, *Sikhs Bring Talent, Strife to New Home: Worship Practices Divide the Community of Immigrants to British Columbia*, OREGONIAN, Aug. 29, 1999, at A22.

21. Sandeep Singh Brar, *Understanding the Kirpan for Non-Sikhs*, http://www.sikhs.org/art12.htm (last visited Feb. 15, 2014).

22. *See* Cheema v. Thompson, No. 94–16097, 1994 U.S. App. LEXIS 24160, at *16 (9th Cir. 1994) (Wiggins, J., dissenting); Clifford Krauss, *A Sikh Boy's Little Dagger Sets Off a Mighty Din*, N.Y. TIMES, June 5, 2002, at A4 (stating that kirpan in "Sikh faith symbolizes the sovereignty of man and serves as a reminder to go to the defense of others in distress").

23. Global News Wire, *Punjab Cop's Son Held for Murder*, TIMES (India), May 27, 2003.

24. *Sikh Population Nearly Doubles in a Decade in Canadian City*, HINDUSTAN TIMES (May 9, 2013), http://www.hindustantimes.com/punjab/punjab abroadcanada/sikh-population-nearly-doubles-in-a-decade-in-canadian-city/article1-1057428.aspx.

25. Wendy Darroch, *Temple Priest Found Guilty in Stabbing with Dagger*, TORONTO STAR, May 26, 1989, at A22. Singh was to be sentenced July 18, 1989, but he was granted a new trial when evidence emerged that another person may have grabbed the kirpan from him and used it in the stabbing. *Priest Gets New Trial in Stabbing*, TORONTO STAR, Sept. 8, 1989, at A21. Singh admitted his role in the stabbing and pleaded guilty to the lesser charge of assault. Wendy Darroch, *Sikh Priest Jailed for Dagger Attack*, TORONTO STAR, Feb. 27, 1990, at A8.

26. Paula Schuck, *Sikh Gets 30 Days for Stabbing Relative with Ceremonial Knife*, TORONTO STAR, July 30, 1997, at B1.

27. Sudarsan Raghavan, Sikhs Experience Violence over Custom of Temple Meals, PHILA. INQUIRER, Mar. 24, 1999; Michael Rollins, *Sikhs Bring Talent, Strife to New Home: Worship Practices Divide the Community of Immigrants to British Columbia*, OREGONIAN, Aug. 29, 1999, at A22.

28. Cheema v. Thompson, No. 94–16097, 1994 U.S. App. LEXIS 24160 (9th Cir. 1994); Multani v. Commission Scolaire Marguerite-Bourgeoys, [2004] 241 D.L.R. 336 (Can.).

29. For further explanation, *see infra* Part Two, Chapters 8 and 10.

30. Cheema, 1994 U.S. App. LEXIS 24160, at *11.

31. *Id.* at *9, 11.

32. *Id.* at *16–17.

33. Greg Lucas, *Wilson Veto for Knives at School*, S.F. CHRON., Oct. 1, 1994, at A19.

34. Multani, 241 D.L.R. at 359.

35. [2006] 1 S.C.R. 256 (Can.), available at http://www.law.yale.edu/documents/pdf/Intellectual_Life/Multani_v._Comm._scolaire_Marguerite-Bourgeoys.pdf (last visited April 28, 2014).

36. NAT'L PROTE. AND PROGRAMS DIRECTORATE, DEP'T OF HOMELAND SEC'Y, PROHIBITED ITEMS PROGRAM 23 (2012), *available at* https://www.dhs.gov/sites/default/files/publications/foia/prohibited-items-program-nppd-fps-directive-15.9.3.1.pdf.

37. *Compromise Allows Sikh Daggers in Public School*, AMS. UNITED FOR SEPARATION OF CHURCH AND ST., https://www.au.org/church-state/march-2011-church-state/au-bulletin/compromise-allows-sikh-daggers-in-public-school (last visited Feb. 22, 2014).

38. Sandra Stokely, *Jurupa Valley: New Policy Allows Dagger-Like Objects on Campus*, PRESS ENTERPRISE (Nov. 19, 2012, 9:44 PM), http://www.pe.com/local-news/riverside-county/riverside/riverside-headlines-index/20121119-jurupa-valley-new-policy-allows-dagger-like-objects-on-campus.ece.

39. *Girl Gangs: Female Members on Love and Motherhood*, HUFFINGTON POST (Feb. 8, 2014, 10:45 AM), http://www.huffingtonpost.com/2012/03/06/girl-gangs_n_1323865.html (excerpt from Jorja Leap, Jumped In).

40. Jeffrey J. Mayer, *Individual Moral Responsibility and the Criminalization of Youth Gangs*, 28 WAKE FOREST L. REV. 943, 951 (1993).

41. Levon v. O'Rourke, No. 96C 7304, 1996 U.S. Dist. LEXIS 19378, at *4–5 (N. D. Ill. Dec. 24, 1996).

42. Cindy Horswell, *Gangs Get a Dressing Down: New Policy at Baytown Junior High School Limits Colors, Sports Attire*, HOUSTON CHRON., Mar. 28, 1992, at A1.

43. Todd A. DeMitchell, Richard Fossey & Casey Cobb, *Dress Codes in the Public Schools: Principals, Policies, and Precepts* 29 J. L. & EDUC. 31, 44–45 (2000).

44. *Uniform Policy: East High School Bets on Dress for Success*, COLUMBUS DISPATCH (Ohio), Jan. 19, 1997, at B2.

45. EDUC. RES. INFO. CTR., U.S. DEP'T OF EDUC., MANUAL ON SCHOOL UNIFORMS (1996), *available at* http://files.eric.ed.gov/fulltext/ED387947.pdf.

46. *Indicators of School Crime and Safety: 2012*, NAT'L CENTER FOR EDUC. STATS., http://nces.ed.gov/programs/crimeindicators/crimeindicators2012/tables/table_20_1.asp (last visited Feb. 22, 2014).

47. *Fast Facts*, NAT'L CENTER FOR EDUC STATS., http://nces.ed.gov/fastfacts/display.asp?id=50 (last visited Feb. 22, 2014).

48. Levon v. O'Rourke, No. 96-C-7304, 1996 U.S. Dist. LEXIS 19378, at *4–5, *12, *4, *5, *8 (N. D. Ill. Dec. 24, 1996).

49. *Levon*, 1996 U.S. Dist. LEXIS 19378, at *22 (quoting Sasnett v. Sullivan, 91 F.3d 1018, 1022 (7th Cir. 1996)).

50. Press Release, American Civil Liberties Union, Jewish Student to Wear Star of David Pendant as Mississippi School Board Reverses Policy (Aug. 24, 1999) (on file with author), [hereinafter Press Release, ACLU].

51. Olesen v. Bd. of Educ. of Sch. Dist. No. 228, 676 F. Supp. 820, 821 (N.D. Ill. 1987) (describing the use of crosses and six-pointed stars by the Simon City Royals, a large Bremen High School gang). The court dismissed the complaint against the Board's policy prohibiting the wearing or display of any gang symbol and Bremen's specific prohibition against the wearing of earrings by male students. *Id.* at 823. Press Release, ACLU, *supra* note 50.

52. *Student Agrees to Hide Wiccan Symbol, Is Readmitted to Classes*, ABILENE REP.-NEWS, (Sep. 5, 2002), *available at* http://lubbockonline.com/stories/090502/upd_075–3871.shtml.

53. Derek H. Davis, *Reacting to France's Ban: Headscarves and Other Religious Attire in American Public Schools*, J. CHURCH & STATE, Apr. 1, 2004, at 221 [hereinafter *Reacting to France's Ban*].

54. *Id.*

55. *See* Heather Rabkin, *[A Closer Look]: Wearing Hijab Provides Protection, Liberation*, THE DAILY BRUIN, (Oct. 20, 2004), http://dailybruin.com/2004/10/19/a-closer-look-wearing-hijab-pr/. A burka (also known as burqa or burqua) is either a veil tied over a headscarf or full burka (also called Afghan burka or chador), a top to bottom garment, which also covers the face. Hijab is a head cover worn by Islamic women. Niqab is a face veil worn by Islamic women, together with the hijab. Khimar is literally a covering – a headscarf.

56. *Reacting to France's Ban, supra* note 53 (Candace Ahlfinger speaking for the Waxahachie High School, said, "When we disrupt the educational progress of other students by wearing disruptive clothing, disruptive jewelry, disruptive hairstyles, whatever is disruptive, we are not only hurting one student, we are hurting all.").

57. *See* Press Release, American Civil Liberties Union, ACLU Says Louisiana Dress Code Denies Rastafarian Children the Right to an Education (Sept. 18, 2000), *available at* https://www.aclu.org/free-speech/aclu-says-louisiana-dress-code-denies-rastafarian-children-right-education; *see also* Aarika Mack, *Louisiana School District Relents, Allows Rastafarian Students' Dreadlocks, Caps,* FREEDOMFORUM.ORG (Sept. 25, 2000), http://www.freedomforum.org/templates/document.asp?documentID=3630.

58. *Reacting to France's Ban, supra* note 53.

59. Sheema Khan, *Why Does a Head Scarf Have Us Tied Up in Knots?,* GLOBE & MAIL (Ca.), Sept. 26, 2003, at A27, *available at* http://www.theglobeandmail.com/globe-debate/why-does-a-head-scarf-have-us-tied-up-in-knots/article772678.

60. *See* Irwin Block, *2nd Muslim Told to Shed Hijab or Leave School,* MONTREAL GAZETTE, Dec. 4, 1994, at A3; *see also* Khan, *supra* note 59.

61. *Reacting to France's Ban, supra* note 53.

62. Jim Myers, *Settlement Announced in Suit over Head Scarf,* TULSA WORLD, May 20, 2004, at A1.

63. Locke v. Davey, 540 U.S. 712 (2004); Church of Lukumi Babalu Aye, Inc. v. Hialeah, 508 U.S. 520 (1993); Emp't Div., Dep't of Human Res. of Or. v. Smith, 494 U.S. 872 (1990); Sherbert v. Verner, 374 U.S. 398 (1963).

64. Myers, *supra* note 62.

65. *See* Press Release, U.S. Dep't of Justice, Justice Department Reaches Settlement Agreement with Oklahoma School District in Muslim Student Headscarf Case (May 19, 2004), *available at* http://www.justice.gov/opa/pr/2004/May/04_crt_343.htm; *Judge Signs Settlement in Hijab Lawsuit,* TULSA AREA NEWS, May 21, 2004, http://www.teamtulsa.com/news/local/l5020.shtml.

66. Law No. 2004–228 of Mar. 15, 2004, J.O., Mar. 17, 2004, p. 5190, *available at* http://www.legifrance.gouv.fr/WAspad/UnTexteDeJorf?numjo=MENX0400001L.

67. *See* Elaine Sciolino, *Ban on Head Scarves Takes Effect in France,* N.Y. TIMES, Sept. 3, 2004, at A8.

68. *See* Suzanne Daley, *Europe Wary of Wider Doors for Immigrants,* N.Y. TIMES, Oct. 20, 2001, at A3.

69. Alabama & Coushatta Tribes of Tex. v. Trs. of the Big Sandy Indep. Sch. Dist., 817 F. Supp. 1319, 1324–25 (1993), *remanded,* 20 F.3d 469 (5th Cir. 1994); *see also* Chalifoux v. New Caney Indep. Sch. Dist., 976 F. Supp. 659 (S.D. Tex. 1997) (holding that the heightened level of scrutiny used in hybrid cases applies).

70. Alabama & Coushatta Tribes, 817 F. Supp. at 1323–24.

71. Karr v. Schmidt, 460 F.2d 609 (5th Cir. 1972), *cert. denied,* 409 U.S. 989 (1972).

72. *See* Knight v. Conn. Dep't of Pub. Health, 275 F.3d 156 (2d Cir. 2001) (holding in the context of claims involving free exercise and free speech that Smith's language relating to hybrid claims is nonbinding dictum); Kissinger v. Bd. of Trustees of the Ohio State Univ., Coll. of Veterinary Med., 5 F.3d 177 (6th Cir. 1993) (declining to apply the hybrid rights theory as "completely illogical"). The following Circuits, while not rejecting the hybrid rights theory outright, have not applied strict scrutiny in these cases: Civil Liberties for Urban Believers v. City of Chicago, 342 F.3d 752 (7th Cir. 2003), *cert. denied*, 124 S. Ct. 2816 (2004) (requiring a colorable claim of infringement of a specific constitutional right in addition to the free exercise claim); Miller v. Reed, 176 F.3d 1202 (9th Cir. 1999) (same); Swanson v. Guthrie Indep. Sch. Dist. No. I–L, 135 F.3d 694 (10th Cir. 1998) (same); EEOC v. Catholic Univ. of Am., 83 F.3d 455 (D.C. Cir. 1996) (requiring an independently viable claim of infringement of a companion right in addition to the free exercise claim); Brown v. Hot, Sexy & Safer Prods., 68 F.3d 525 (1st Cir. 1995), *cert. denied*, 516 U.S. 1159 (1996) (same).

73. Tex. Health & Safety Code Ann. § 481.111(a) (West 2004) ("The provisions of this chapter relating to the possession and distribution of peyote do not apply to the use of peyote by a member of the Native American Church in bona fide religious ceremonies of the church.").

74. Sch. Dist. No. 11-J v. Howell, 517 P.2d 422 (Colo. Ct. App. 1973) held that an application permitting noncompliance with school hair regulation was discriminatory where such application applied only to Indians.

75. Wisconsin v. Yoder, 406 U.S. 205 (1972).

76. *See* Judith G. McMullen, *Behind Closed Doors: Should States Regulate Homeschooling?*, 54 S.C.L. Rev. 75, 78 (2002) (noting that religious beliefs are the impetus for homeschooling in approximately 85% of cases, where "'[t]hese parents believe that God has given them the responsibility and the authority to educate their children. . . . Since they are called by God to be the primary teachers of their children and to apply God's word to each and every subject, they believe it would be a sin for them to delegate this authority to another school system.'" (quoting Christopher J. Klicka, The Right to Home School 2–3 (2d ed. 1998).

77. Edwards v. Aguillard, 482 U.S. 578 (1987).

78. Susanne Quick, *Theories Other Than Evolution to Be Taught in Grantsburg: Some Academics Say Move Is an Attempt to Discount Evolution, Promote Other Ideas*, Milwaukee J. Sentinel, Nov. 6, 2004, at A1.

79. John W. Fountain, *Kansas Puts Evolution Back into Public Schools*, N.Y. Times, Feb. 15, 2001, at A18.

80. Ariel Hart, *Judge in Georgia Orders Anti-Evolution Stickers Removed from Textbooks*, N.Y. Times, Jan. 14, 2005, at A16.

81. Selman v. Cobb Cnty. Sch. Dist., 449 F.3d 1320 (11th Cir. 2006).

82. *See Selman v. Cobb County School District*, Ams. United for Separation of Church And St., https://www.au.org/our-work/legal/lawsuits/selman-v-cobb-county-school-district (last visited Feb. 23, 2014).

83. Kitzmiller v. Dover Area Sch. Dist., 400 F. Supp. 2d 707 (M.D. Pa. 2005).

84. *Id.* at 708–09.

85. *Id.* at 709.

86. *Id.* at 762.

87. *Id.* at 763.

88. *Id.*

89. *Id.* at 766.

90. *See Antievolution Bills Die in Missouri*, NAT'L CENTER. FOR SCI. EDUC. (May 20, 2013), http://ncse.com/news/2013/05/antievolution-bills-die-missouri-0014848.

91. *See* James G. Dwyer, *The Children We Abandon: Religious Exemptions to Child Welfare and Educational Laws as Denials of Equal Protection to Children of Religious Objectors*, 74 N.C. L. REV. 1321, 1350 (1996) ("Approximately one million children in this country are in home schools, and the most common reason parents have for choosing this option is religious opposition to the content and manner of instruction in public schools.").

92. Christopher Klicka, *Biblical Reasons to Home School*, NAT'L CENTER. FOR HOME EDUC., HSLDA (May 17, 1999), http://www.hslda.org/docs/nche/000000/00000069.asp.

93. HSLDA, STATE LAWS CONCERNING PARTICIPATION OF HOMESCHOOL STUDENTS IN PUBLIC SCHOOL ACTIVITIES(2013), http://www.hslda.org/docs/nche/Issues/E/Equal_Access.pdf.

94. Liesl Den, *Homeschool Students Fight to Play on Public School Teams*, PARENTS HOMESCHOOL DEN BLOG (June 20, 2013, 2:30 PM), http://www.parents.com/blogs/homeschool-den/2013/06/20/must-read/homeschool-students-fight-to-play-on-public-school-teams; *Sports and Public School Classes*, HSLDA, http://www.hslda.org/docs/nche/issues/s/state_sports.asp (last visited Feb. 22, 2014).

95. STATE LAWS CONCERNING PARTICIPATION OF HOMESCHOOL STUDENTS IN PUBLIC SCHOOL ACTIVITIES, *supra* note 94.

96. *Pennsylvania – Homeschoolers Religious Freedom Case Can Proceed*, http://www.hslda.org/hs/state/pa/200408060.asp (last visited Apr. 21, 2014).

97. Pierce v. Soc'y of the Sisters of the Holy Names of Jesus & Mary, 268 U.S. 510, 535 (1925).

98. *See* Jesse Abrams-Morley, *Family to Appeal Home-School Ruling: A Judge Ordered Tomas and Babette Hankin to Show the District What Their Kids Are Learning*, BUCKS COUNTY. COURIER TIMES, June 7, 2006, at A1; Paula Reed Ward, *Home School Parents Sue State over Religious Freedom*, PITTSBURGH POST-GAZETTE, Oct. 11, 2004, at B1.

99. Combs v. Homer-Ctr Sch. Dist., 540 F.3d 231 (3d Cir. 2008).

100. United States v. Lee, 455 U.S. 252, 261 (1982).

101. Bowen v. Roy, 476 U.S. 693, 696 (1986).

102. *A Dark Side to Home Schooling*, CBS NEWS (Oct. 13, 2003, 1:50 PM), http://www.cbsnews.com/news/a-dark-side-to-home-schooling; *Home Schooling Nightmares*, CBS NEWS (Oct. 14, 2003), http://www.cbsnews.com/news/home-schooling-nightmares. *See also* Chip Lupu, *The Separation of Powers and*

the Protection of Children, 61 U. Chi. L. Rev. 1317 (1994) (children are best protected by having multiple, competing, and separate sources of authority and advice).

103. Fleischfresser v. Dirs. of Sch. Dist. 200, 15 F.3d 680, 683 (7th Cir. 1994).

104. Press Release, Institute for First Amendment Studies, Institute Joins Impressions Case (Sept. 1992) (on file with author).

105. Fleischfresser, 15 F.3d at 686–87.

106. *Id.* at 688.

107. *Id.*

108. *Id.*

109. Mozert v. Hawkins Cnty. Bd. of Educ., 827 F.2d 1058 (6th Cir. 1987), *cert. denied*, 484 U.S. 1066 (1988); *see also* Frances R. A. Paterson, *The Politics of Phonics*, 15 J. CURRICULUM & SUPERVISION 179 (2000) (describing the pattern of lawsuits "[f]rom 1986 to 1994, [in which] *Impressions* was challenged in at least 74 school districts in 16 states").

110. Mozert, 827 F.2d at 1067.

111. James C. McKinley, Jr., *Texas Conservatives Win Curriculum Change*, N.Y. TIMES, Mar. 13, 2010, at A10.

112. Motoko Rich, *Texas Education Board Flags Biology Textbook over Evolution Concerns*, N.Y. TIMES, Nov. 22, 2013, at A1; Texas Freedom Network, *How Science Won in the Texas Textbook Battle* TFN INSIDER http://tfninsider.org/2013/11/25/how-science-won-in-the-texas-textbook-battle (last visited Feb. 15, 2014); *Breaking News, Texas Review Panel Rejects Creationist Objections to Pearson Biology Textbook*, TFN *Insider available at* http://tfninsider.org/2013/12/17/breaking-news-texas-review-panel-rejects-creationist-objections-to-pearson-biology-textbook (last visited Feb. 15, 2014).

113. Scott Neuman, *Texas Overhauls Textbook Approval to Ease Tensions over Evolution*, NAT'L PUB. RADIO (Feb. 1, 2014), http://www.npr.org/blogs/thetwo-way/2014/02/01/269962257/texas-overhauls-textbook-approval-to-ease-tensions-over-evolution.

114. Moody v. Cronin, 484 F. Supp. 270 (C.D. Ill. 1979).

115. *Id.* at 276.

116. *Id.* at 277.

6. The Prisons and the Military

1. Dan Mihalopoulos, *U.S. Probes Jail Ministry for Muslims*, CHI. TRIB., Aug. 10, 2003, at 1 (quoting Dan Pistole) (hereinafter *U.S. Probes Jail Ministry for Muslims*); *see also* ANTI-DEFAMATION LEAGUE, DANGEROUS CONVICTIONS: AN INTRODUCTION TO EXTREMIST ACTIVITIES IN PRISONS, TOPICS IN EXTREMISM 25–26 (2002), *also available at* http://www.adl.org/learn/Ext_Terr/dangerous_convictions .pdf (last visited Nov. 8, 2004) (hereinafter DANGEROUS CONVICTIONS).

2. Facts regarding the Aryan Brotherhood have been gathered from FEDERAL BUREAU OF INVESTIGATION, ARYAN BROTHERHOOD, file number 183–7396 [hereinafter ARYAN BROTHERHOOD] (obtained through the Freedom of Information and

Privacy Acts), *available at* http://archive.org/stream/AryanBrotherhoodFbiFile/ aryanbro1_djvu.txt (last visited Feb. 25, 2014); David Grann, *The Brand*, New Yorker, Feb. 16 & 23, 2004, at 156 [hereinafter *The Brand*].

3. *The Brand*, *supra* note 2, at 158, 171.

4. *Id.* at 160.

5. Tori Richards, *Aryan Brotherhood Leaders Are Convicted in Murders*, N.Y. Times, July 29, 2006, at A11.

6. Andrew Blankstein, *Task Force Thwarts Prison Gang's Growing Reach*, L.A. Times, Jan. 30, 2004, at B2.

7. Michael Kelley, *America's 11 Most Powerful Prison Gangs*, Bus. Insider (Feb. 1, 2014, 12:14 PM), http://www.businessinsider.com/most-dangerous-prison-gangs-in-the-us-2014-2?op=1.

8. Cutter v. Wilkinson, 544 U.S. 709, 720 (2005).

9. Dangerous Convictions, *supra* note 1, at 3.

10. Press Release, FBI, Man Who Formed Terrorist Group That Plotted Attacks on Military and Jewish Facilities Sentenced to 16 Years in Federal Prison (Mar. 6, 2009), *available at* http://www.fbi.gov/losangeles/press-releases/ 2009/la030609ausa.htm (last visited Feb. 25, 2014).

11. United States v. Cromitie, 727 F.3d 194 (2d Cir. 2013).

12. Joseph Abrams, *Homegrown Terror Suspects Turned Toward Radicalism in U.S. Prisons*, Fox News (May 22, 2009), http://www.foxnews.com/story/2009/05/ 22/homegrown-terror-suspects-turned-toward-radicalism-in-us-prisons.

13. Mark S. Hamm, *Prisoner Radicalization: Assessing the Threat in U.S. Correctional Institutions*, Nat'l Inst. of Just. (Oct. 27, 2008), http://www.nij.gov/ journals/261/Pages/prisoner-radicalization.aspx.

14. *Id.*

15. Stephen Emerson, *Radicals in Our Prisons*, N.Y. Post (May 23, 2009, 3:51 PM), http://nypost.com/2009/05/23/radicals-in-our-prisons.

16. *Id.*

17. National Defense Authorization Act for Fiscal Year 2014, H.R. 1960, 113th Cong. (2013)

18. Pew Forum, Pew Research & Public Life Project, Religion In Prisons – A 50 State Survey of Prison Chaplains (Mar. 22, 2012), *available at* http:// www.pewforum.org/2012/03/22/prison-chaplains-exec.

19. Frank Viviano, *Future Terrorists Train in Prison*, S.F. Chron., Nov. 3, 2001, at A5; Alexandria Sage, *France Struggles to Fight Radical Islam in Its Jails*, Reuters (May 7, 2013, 1:35 PM), http://www.reuters.com/article/2013/05/ 07/us-france-radicalisation-insight-idUSBRE9460OQ20130507.

20. Martin Nevans & Duncan Gardham, *Radical Muslims "Target Young Inmates in Prison,"* Telegraph (Feb. 6, 2012, 8:00 AM), http://www.telegraph .co.uk/news/uknews/terrorism-in-the-uk/9062960/Radical-Muslims-target-young-inmates-in-prison.html.

21. Emerson, *supra* note 15.

22. *Terrorist Recruitment and Infiltration in the United States: Prisons and Military as an Operational Base: Hearing before the Senate Comm. on the Judiciary*,

108th Cong. (Oct. 14, 2003) [hereinafter Waller] (testimony of Dr. Michael Waller), *available at* http://www.judiciary.senate.gov/meetings/terrorist-recruitment-and-infiltration-in-the-united-states-prisons-and-military-as-an-operational-base (last visited Feb. 25, 2014).

23. *U.S. Probes Jail Ministry for Muslims, supra* note 1.

24. *Activist Gets 23 Years for Libyan Dealings,* Chi. Trib., Oct. 16, 2004, at C15.

25. Jerry Markon, *Muslim Activist Sentenced to 23 Years for Libya Contacts,* Wash. Post, Oct. 16, 2004, at A17.

26. Laurie Goodstein, *Pentagon Says It Will Review Chaplain Policy,* N.Y. Times, Sept. 28, 2003, at 1.

27. Markon, *supra* note 25.

28. Jerry Seper, *Prisons Breeding Ground for Terror: Moderate Muslim Chaplains in Short Supply, Justice Report Warns,* Wash. Times, May 6, 2004, at A11.

29. *See* Office of the Inspector General, U.S. Dep't of Justice, A Review of the Bureau of Prisons' Selection of Muslim Religious Services Providers (2004), *available at* http://www.usdoj.gov/oig/special/0404/final.pdf (last visited Feb. 25, 2014) (hereinafter Selection of Muslim Religious Services Providers).

30. Brandenburg v. Ohio, 395 U.S. 444 (1969).

31. John P. Cronan, *The Next Challenge for the First Amendment: The Framework for an Internet Incitement Standard,* 51 Cath. U. L. Rev. 425 (2002).

32. Selection of Muslim Religious Services Providers, *supra* note 29, at 8–9 (quoting BOP Technical Resource Manual 014.1).

33. Waller, *supra* note 22.

34. Rumsfeld v. Padilla, 124 S. Ct. 2711, 2717–18 (2004).

35. *See* Julia Preston, *Staten Island Phone Lets U.S. Eavesdrop on Global Militants,* N.Y. Times, Oct. 2, 2004, at A1.

36. Mark S. Hamm, Terrorist Recruitment in American Correctional Institutions: An Exploratory Study of Non-Traditional Faith Groups Final Report 24–26 (2007), *available at* https://www.ncjrs.gov/pdffiles1/nij/grants/220957.pdf.

37. *Id.* at 111.

38. Turner v. Safley, 482 U.S. 78, 84 (1987) (quoting Procunier v. Martinez, 416 U.S. 396, 405 (1974)).

39. O'Lone v. Estate of Shabazz, 482 U.S. 342 (1987); Turner v. Safley, 482 U.S. at 78.

40. *Id.* at 89.

41. *Protecting Religious Freedom After Boerne v. Flores: Hearing Before the Subcomm. on the Constitution of the House Comm. on the Judiciary,* 105th Cong. (July 14, 1997) (testimony of Charles W. Colson), *available at* http://www.justice.gov/jmd/ls/legislative_histories/pl106-274/hear-55-1-1997.pdf (last visited Feb. 25, 2014).

42. *The Need for Federal Protection of Religious Freedom After Boerne v. Flores: Hearing Before the House Comm. on the Judiciary,* 105th Cong. (Mar. 26, 1998) (testimony of Isaac M. Jaroslawicz), *available at* http://commdocs.house.gov/committees/judiciary/hju57227.000/hju57227_0f.htm (last visited Feb. 25, 2014).

43. *Id.*

44. One of the reasons for the lack of opposition to the land use side existed because the attorneys general, who tend to be politically ambitious, would not lobby against religious institutions seeking land use preferences, in part because these issues are local headaches, not state headaches, and also because religious individuals vote but, as is often said, prisoners do not vote.

45. *Protecting Religious Freedom After Boerne v. Flores: Hearing Before the Subcomm. on the Constitution of the House Comm. on the Judiciary,* 105th Cong. (July 14, 1997) (testimony of Jeffrey Sutton) (hereinafter Jeffrey Sutton), *available at* http://www.justice.gov/jmd/ls/legislative_histories/pl106-274/hear-55-1-1997.pdf (last visited Feb. 25, 2014).

46. *Id.*

47. 146 CONG. REC. S7774, 7779 (daily ed. July 27, 2000) (statement of Sen. Reid) (hereinafter Sen. Reid).

48. 146 CONG. REC. S7991 (daily ed. Sept. 5, 2000) (statement of Sen. Thurmond).

49. Sen. Reid, *supra* note 47.

50. Cutter v. Wilkinson, 544 U.S.709 (2005).

51. *See* THOMAS P. O'CONNOR & NATHANIEL J. PALLONE, RELIGION, THE COMMUNITY, AND THE REHABILITATION OF CRIMINAL OFFENDERS (2003); Stephen T. Hall, *Faith-Based Cognitive Programs in Corrections,* AM. CORR. CHAPLAINS ASS'N (Dec. 2003), http://www.correctionalchaplains.org/faith-based/page1.html (last visited Feb. 25, 2014); Robert Toll, *How a Multifaith Chaplaincy Program Operates in a County Detention Facility,* AM. CORR. CHAPLAINS ASS'N, http://www.correctionalchaplains.org/articles/01-02-2004.html (last visited Feb. 25, 2014); Oregon Dep't of Corr. Transitional Servs. Div., *Spirituality, Religion and What Works: Religious Outcomes This Side of Heaven, available at* http://www.oregon .gov/doc/OMR/pages/religious_services/rs_article2.aspx (last visited Feb. 25, 2014).

52. Adam Hochberg, *All Things Considered: Series of Lawsuits Calling for More Religious Freedoms for Prisoners* (National Public Radio broadcast, July 10, 2003), *available at* 2003 WL 5581034.

53. *See* Moussazdeh v. Tex. Dep't of Criminal Justice, 703 F.3d 781, 796 (5th Cir. 2012) (holding that RLUIPA "commands that [the Texas Department of Criminal Justice] adopt [a less restrictive means for Jewish prisoner to keep kosher].") *reh'g denied,* 708 F.3d 487 (5th Cir. 2013).

54. *See* Daley v. Lappin, No. 12–3393, 2014 WL 306932, at *5 (3d Cir. Jan. 29, 2014) (holding District Court erred in dismissing Rastafarian inmate's request to follow Ital diet under RFRA, and remanding).

55. *See* Abdulhaseeb v. Calbone, 600 F.3d 1301 (10th Cir. 2010) (holding that Muslim prisoner established that his religious exercise was substantially burdened when denied a halal diet and halal meat for a particular Islamic feast).

56. *See* Gardner v. Riska, 444 F. App'x 353, 355 (11th Cir. 2011) (denying Florida prisoner's request for kosher food because by purchasing non-kosher food from the prison canteen numerous times in the past, under § 3 of RLUIPA, he failed to

meet his burden of "demonstrat[ing] that he sincerely believes that a Kosher diet is important to the free exercise of his religion").

57. *See* Strope v. Cummings, 381 F. App'x 878, 880–81 (10th Cir. 2010) (holding that "deficiencies" in Jewish prisoner's kosher diet, including less varied meals, less seasonal fruit and vegetables, and occasional wilted or rotten items, did not constitute a substantial burden under RLUIPA on prisoner's free exercise of his religion).

58. *See* Kretchmar v. Beard, 241 F. App'x 863, 865 (3d Cir. 2007) (holding that prison's decision to continue providing Jewish prisoner with kosher food that was not hot, as requested, did not substantially burden prisoner's constitutional rights under RLUIPA).

59. *See* Baranowski v. Hart, 486 F.3d 112, 125 (5th Cir. 2007) (holding that Texas state prison's policies of not providing kosher food for a Jewish inmate in order to preserve order and avoid prisoner jealousy were "compelling government interests" under RLUIPA and were not required).

60. *See* Jova v. Smith, 582 F.3d 410, 417 (2d Cir. 2009) (holding that state prison's denial of individualized meals prepared by Tulukeesh adherents for prisoners of the Tulukeesh religion was justified by administrative burden of doing so, but ruling against prison on grounds of not providing least restrictive alternative for prisoner's general vegan dietary needs, and remanding for further fact-finding on this issue).

61. *See* Patel v. U.S. Bureau of Prisons, 515 F.3d 807, 815 (8th Cir. 2008) (holding that Muslim prisoner was not substantially burdened in his ability to keep a diet consistent with his religious beliefs when prison provided him with vegetarian food).

62. *See* Garner v. Kennedy, 713 F.3d 237 (5th Cir. 2013) (holding that state prison did not carry burden of showing prohibition of Muslim prisoner's quarter-inch beard was the least restrictive means of promoting its compelling government interest in security); Warsoldier v. Woodford, 418 F.3d 989, 1001 (9th Cir. 2005) (allowing Native American prisoner's RLUIPA claim against California prison's hair grooming policy to proceed to the merits).

63. *See* Lewis v. Sternes, 712 F.3d 1083 (7th Cir. 2013) (finding that prison officials did not violate RLUIPA by denying request by inmate, a member of the African Hebrew Israelites of Jerusalem, for a religious accommodation to wear dreadlocks); Fegans v. Norris, 537 F.3d 897, 907–08 (8th Cir. 2008) (finding that prison policy prohibiting prisoners – including Plaintiff, a follower of Assemblies of Yahweh religion – from wearing hair below collar and from growing beard did not violate RLUIPA); McRae v. Johnson, 261 F. App'x 554 (4th Cir. 2008) (finding that Virginia prison's grooming policy did not violate RLUIPA as applied to five inmate plaintiffs, two Rastafarians and three Muslims, because of prison's compelling interests in hygiene and security, among other concerns).

64. *Holt v. Hobbs*, 509 F. App'x 561 (8th Cir. 2013) *cert. granted*, 134 S. Ct. 1490 (2014) *cert. limited*, 134 S. Ct. 1512 (2014)

65. Theriault v. Silber, 453 F. Supp. 254, 260 (W.D. Tex. 1978), *appeal dismissed*, 579 F.2d 302 (5th Cir. 1978), *cert. denied*, 440 U.S. 917 (1979); *see also* PAUL W.

Keve, Prisons and the American Conscience: A History of U.S. Federal
Corrections 211–12 (1991).

66. Remmers v. Brewer, 494 F.2d 1277 (8th Cir. 1974) (per curiam), *cert. denied,*
419 U.S. 1012 (1974).

67. *Id.* at 1278.

68. *Theriault,* 453 F. Supp. at 264.

69. Goff v. Graves, 362 F.3d 543, 547 (8th Cir. 2004).

70. *Id.* at 548.

71. *Id.* at 549.

72. *See* Yehuda M. Braunstein, Note, *Will Jewish Prisoners Be Boerne Again?
Legislative Responses to City of Boerne v. Flores,* 66 Fordham L. Rev. 2333, 2379
(1998) (arguing that state RFRAs are necessary in part because "Religion in prison
is the most effective form of prisoner rehabilitation . . ."); *see also* O'Lone v. Estate
of Shabazz, 482 U.S. 342, 368 (1987) (Brennan, J., dissenting) ("Incarceration by its
nature denies a prisoner participation in the larger human community. To deny
the opportunity to affirm membership in a spiritual community, however, may
extinguish an inmate's last source of hope for dignity and redemption."); Barnett
v. Rodgers, 410 F.2d 995, 1002 (D.C. Cir. 1969) ("Religion in prison subserves the
rehabilitative function by providing an area within which the inmate may reclaim
his dignity and reassert his individuality.").

73. Tim Padgett, *When God Is the Warden: The Nation's First Faith-Based
Prison Mixes Religion and Rehab – And Stirs Up Controversy,* TIME, June 7, 2004,
at 50.

74. Barbara Bradley, *Morning Edition: "Morning Edition" Visits Bible-Based
Prison Program* (National Public Radio broadcast, Sept. 7, 2001).

75. The Americans United for Separation of Church and State's complaint is available online at http://www.clearinghouse.net/chDocs/public/PC-IA-
0025-0002.pdf (last visited Feb. 25, 2014).

76. Ams. United for Separation of Church and State v. Prison Fellowship Ministries, Inc., 509 F.3d 406 (8th Cir. 2007).

77. Sasha Volokh, *Do Faith-Based Prisons Work?,* Wash. Post (Feb. 10, 2014),
http://www.washingtonpost.com/news/volokh-conspiracy/wp/2014/02/10/do-faith-
based-prisons-work/.

78. Larson v. Valente, 456 U.S. 228, 246 (1982).

79. *See* Mark Chaves, Congregations in America 93 (2004).

80. Alan Cooperman, *An Infusion of Religious Funds in Fla. Prisons,* Wash.
Post, Apr. 25, 2004, at A1.

81. Megan O'Matz, *Taking the Bible Behind Bars: Evangelical Christians Mobilize for Two Campaigns Aimed at Carrying the Gospel of Jesus Christ into State
Prisons,* Sun-Sentinel (Ft. Lauderdale, Fla.), Apr. 17, 2004, at 1B.

82. Carlos Campos, *Faith Behind Bars Programs Aim to Uplift, But Foes Say
State Oversteps Bounds,* Atlanta J.-Const., Aug. 22, 2004, at C4.

83. David Crary, *Faith-Based Prisons Multiply,* USA Today (Oct. 13, 2007),
http://usatoday30.usatoday.com/news/religion/2007-10-13-prisons_n.htm.

84. *See* Chris Lisee, *Air Force Academy: Proselytizing and Religious Freedom Debate on School Campus,* Huffington Post (July 17, 2012, 1:16 AM),

http://www.huffingtonpost.com/2012/07/17/air-force-academy-religion-proselytism_ n_1678092.html.

85. *Id.*

86. Veitch v. England, 471 F.3d 124 (D.C. Cir. 2006).

87. Conservative Baptist Ass'n of Am., Inc. v. Shinseki (D.C. Cir. 2013), *available at* http://johnwellslaw.com/files/CBAmericaComplaint.a13.pdf (last visited Feb. 27, 2014).

88. *Father Ray Leonard Sues DOD and Wins After Government Shuts Down Catholic Religious Services on Base*, HUFFINGTON POST (Oct. 16, 2013), http://www .huffingtonpost.com/2013/10/16/father-ray-leonard-sues-dod-catholic-shutdown_ n_4108731.html.

89. Department of Defense Instruction 1304.28 § 6.1.5 (June 11, 2004).

90. *See* William T. Cavanaugh, Jr., *The United States Military Chaplaincy Program: Another Seam in the Fabric of Our Society?*, 59 NOTRE DAME L. REV. 181, 191–92 (1983).

91. *See* Julie B. Kaplan, *Military Mirrors on the Wall: Nonestablishment and the Military Chaplaincy*, 95 YALE L.J. 1210, 1217–18 (1983).

92. *Id.*

93. For further analysis, *see id.* at 1211–12 n.13, and Katcoff v. Marsh, 755 F.2d 223 (2d Cir. 1985).

94. Goldman v. Weinberger, 475 U.S. 503, 510 (1986).

95. *Id.* at 514 (Brennan, J., dissenting).

96. *Id.* at 524 (Blackmun, J., dissenting).

97. *See id.* at 528–33 (O'Connor, J., dissenting).

98. C. Thomas Dienes, *When the First Amendment Is Not Preferred: The Military and Other "Special Contexts,"* 56 U. CIN. L. REV. 779, 804 (1988).

99. *See* 10 U.S.C. § 774 (2012).

100. Sherwood v. Brown, 619 F.2d 479 (9th Cir. 1980).

101. Scott Neuman, *Pentagon Relaxes Uniform Rules to Allow Religious Headgear*, NPR (Jan. 23, 2014), *available at* http://www.npr.org/blogs/thetwo-way/2014/ 01/23/265230702/pentagon-relaxes-uniform-rules-to-allow-religious-headgear.

102. Petition for Writ of Habeas Corpus and Complaint for Declatory and Injunctive Relief, Bacha v. Bush, No. 105CV02349, 2005 WL 6342497 (D.D.C. Dec. 8, 2005).

7. The Right to Discriminate

1. I.R.C. § 501 (2012). *Exemption from Tax on Corporations, Certain Trusts, Etc.* IRS Rev. Rul. 71–447 ("A private school that does not have a racially nondiscriminatory policy as to students does not qualify for exemption.").

2. Bob Jones Univ. v United States, 461 U.S. 574, 576 (1983).

3. *Id.* at 604.

4. 42 U.S.C. § 3607 states:

Religious organization or private club exemption (a) Nothing in this title shall prohibit a religious organization, association, or society, or any non-profit institution or organization operated, supervised or controlled by or in conjunction with a religious organization, association, or society, from limiting the sale, rental or occupancy of dwellings which it owns or operates for other than a commercial purpose to persons of the same religion, or from giving preference to such persons, unless membership in such religion is restricted on account of race, color, or national origin. Nor shall anything in this title prohibit a private club not in fact open to the public, which as an incident to its primary purpose or purposes provides lodgings which it owns or operates for other than a commercial purpose, from limiting the rental or occupancy of such lodgings to its members or from giving preference to its members.

5. Hosanna Tabor Evangelical Lutheran Church & Sch. v. E.E.O.C., 132 S. Ct. 694 (2012).

6. *See* S.B. 1062, 51st Leg., 2d Reg. Sess. (Ariz. 2014).

7. H.B. 2453, 58th Leg., Reg. Sess. (Kan. 2014).

8. Vigars v. Valley Christian Ctr., 805 F. Supp. 802 (N.D. Cal. 1992) (distinguishing between exemption permitted where firing was based on adulterous relationship that violated religious tenets, but not permitted if firing was based on pregnancy, which was not proscribed by religious beliefs); Janet S. Belcove-Shalin, *Ministerial Exception and Title VII Claims: Case Law Grid Analysis*, 2 NEV. L.J. 86, 87 (2002). ("This historical [McClure] holding provided a constitutional mooring for what is variously referred to as "'the ministerial exception'" . . . "and what has been construed as a blanket exemption from Title VII judicial review of the employment relationship between a religious organization and its clergy.") (internal footnotes omitted).

9. McClure v. Salvation Army, 460 F.2d 553, 558–59 (5th Cir. 1972). On appeal, the 5th Circuit held the Free Exercise Clause of the First Amendment precluded the district court from exercising jurisdiction over the minister's claims.

10. 132 S. Ct. 694 (2012).

11. *Id.* at 702, 706. Hosanna-Tabor Evangelical Lutheran Church & Sch. v. E.E.O.C., 132 S. Ct. 694, 702, 706 (2012).

12. *Id.* at 701.

13. *Id.* at 707.

14. *Id.*

15. Williams v. Episcopal Diocese of Mass., No. 2000-03294B, 2001 WL 721453 (Sup. Ct. Mass. June 8, 2001), *aff'd*, 766 N.E.2d 820 (Mass. 2002). 676 F.2d at 1289.

16. Williams v. Episcopal Diocese, 13 Mass. L. Rep. Rptr.. 289 (Mass. Sup. Ct. 2001). *Id.*

17. Hosanna-Tabor, 132 S. Ct. at 709.

18. Rweyemamu v. Cote, 520 F.3d 198 (2d Cir. 2008); Petruska v. Gannon Univ., 462 F.3d 294 (3d Cir. 2006).

19. Brief for Bishopaccountability.org et al. as Amici Curiae in Supporting of Respondents, Hosanna-Tabor Evangelical Lutheran Church & Sch. v. E.E.O.C., 132 S. Ct. 694 (2012) (No. 10–553), *available at* http://www.americanbar.org/content/dam/aba/publishing/previewbriefs/Other_Brief_Updates/10–553-respondentamcu10grpsagainstchildabuse.authcheckdam.pdf.

20. Hosanna-Tabor, 132 S. Ct. at 712 (Alito, J., concurring).

21. Amy Goldstein, *Kagan's Newly Released E-mails Reveal Confident Voice in Clinton White House*, WASH. POST (June 19, 2010), http://www.washingtonpost.com/wp-dyn/content/article/2010/06/18/AR2010061805618.html.

22. Hosanna-Tabor, 132 S. Ct. at 710.

23. *Id.* (citation omitted).

24. *Id.*

25. McKelvey v. Pierce, 800 A.2d 840 (N.J. 2002).

26. *Id.* at 857 (quoting Sanders v. Casa View Baptist Church, 134 F.2d 331, 335–36 (5th Cir. 1998)).

27. U.S. COMM'N ON CIVIL RIGHTS, Briefing, *Peaceful Coexistence? Reconciling Non-Discrimination Principles with Civil Liberties*, U.S. COMM'N ON CIVIL RIGHTS U.S. Commission on Civil Rights (Mar. 22, 2013), (*available at* http://www.usccr.gov/calendar/trnscrpt/Peaceful-Coexistence-Briefing-Transcript_03–22–13.pdf).

28. 42 U.S.C. §§ 2000e, 2000e-2 (2012).

29. 42 U.S.C. § 12101 *et seq.* (2012).

30. 29 U.S.C. §§ 621–34 (2012).

31. Pregnancy Discrimination Act of 1978, Pub. L. No. 95–555, 92 Stat. 2076.

32. 42 U.S.C. § 2000e-1. The Age Discrimination in Employment Act (ADEA) does not have a religious exception. *See, e.g.,* De Marco v. Holy Cross High Sch., 4 F.3d 166, 173 (2d Cir. 1993).

33. 42 U.S.C. § 2000e-1.

34. *See, e.g.,* Killinger v. Samford Univ., 113 F.3d 196 (11th Cir. 1997) (considering numerous factors, found that the university is a religious institution); E.E.O.C. v. Kamehameha Sch./Bishop Estate, 990F.2d 458, 460 (9th Cir. 1993) (when the statute is properly and narrowly construed, a religious school does not count as a religious organization); E.E.O.C. v. Townley Eng'g & Mfg. Co., 675 F. Supp. 566 (D. Ariz. 1987) (for-profit corporation whose articles of incorporation made no reference to religion not entitled to Title VII exemption).

35. *See, e.g.,* Bryce v. Episcopal Church in the Diocese of Colo., 289 F.3d 648 (10th Cir. 2002) (court will not take jurisdiction where claim involves fired gay youth minister whose lifestyle was prohibited by church doctrine); EEOC v. Sw. Baptist Theological Seminary, 651 F.2d 277, 283 (5th Cir. 1981); Smith v. Raleigh Dist. of the N.C. Conf. of the United Methodist Church, 63 F. Supp. 2d 694, 706 (D. N.C. 1999) (hostile environment claim goes forward where employees performed nonreligious tasks); Guinan v. Roman Catholic Archdiocese, 42 F. Supp. 2d 849, 852–53 (S.D. Ind. 1998) (ministerial exception inapplicable in ADEA case where teacher did not function in a ministerial capacity).

The Supreme Court upheld Title VII's exemption for religion and interpreted the idea of "religious employee" broadly, so that a janitor in a religious organization could be denied the right to sue for discrimination. Corp. of Presiding Bishop of Church of Jesus Christ of Latter-day Saints v. Amos, 483 U.S. 327 (1987).

36. *See, e.g.,* Elvig v. Calvin Presbyterian Church, 375 F.3d 951, 958 (9th Cir. 2004) (holding the claims could not proceed in civil court because that would

involve an inquiry into the Church decisions of who shall be a minister); Bollard v. Cal. Province of the Soc'y of Jesus, 196 F.3d 940,947 (9th Cir. 1999) (allowing the case to proceed because "the Jesuits do not offer a religious justification for the harassment Bollard alleges" and, hence, there is no danger in secular courts passing judgment on religious beliefs or doctrine); Cline v. Catholic Diocese, 206 F.3d 615, 658 (6th Cir. 1999) (Title VII and ministerial exception did not protect the Church from claim based on firing of unwed pregnant woman because the Church cannot discriminate based on pregnancy, which is clearly discrimination based on sex); E.E.O.C. v. Pac. Press Pub. Ass'n, 676 F.2d 1272,1279 (9th Cir. 1992) (married female employee's suit against pay according to gender and marital status permitted to go forward, because *de minimis* burden on religious belief); E.E.O.C. v. Fremont Christian Sch., 781 F.2d 1362,1368 (9th Cir. 1986) (finding *de minimis* burden on religious belief where Christian school provided health insurance only to "heads of households"); Dolquist v. Heartland Presbytery, No. 03–2150-KHV, 2004 U.S. Dist. LEXIS 21888 (D. Kan. Oct. 28, 2004); Smith, 63 F. Supp. 2d at 710 (hostile environment claims go forward where they do not intrude upon defendant church's spiritual functions).

37. Letter from Reed L. Russell, Legal Counsel of the Equal Employment Opportunity Commission, to Kevin Cummings, Branch Chief, Business and Trade Services, Dep't of Homeland Security (Dec. 28, 2007), *available at* http://www.eeoc.gov/eeoc/foia/letters/2007/religious_organization_exception_dec_28_2007.html

38. Sw. Baptist Theological Seminary, 651 F.2d at 284.

39. Pac. Press Pub. Ass'n, 676 F.2d at 1278 (Title VII, sec. 702 applies only to employees whose duties "go to the heart of the church's function").

40. Elane Photography, LLC v. Willock, 309 P.3d 53 (N.M. 2013).

41. L.D. 1428, 126th Leg., 1st Reg. Sess. (Me. 2013)

42. H.B. 2453, Leg. Sess. 2014 (Kan.).

43. S.B. 128, 89th Leg. Assemb. (S.D. 2014).

44. H.B. 376, 130th Gen Assemb., Reg. Sess. (Ohio 2013–2014).

45. H.B. 426, 62d Leg., 2d Reg. Sess. (Idaho 2014).

46. S.B. 1062, 51st Leg., 2d Reg. Sess. (Ariz. 2014). Gov. Brewer vetoed the bill on February 26, 2014. Catherine E. Shoichet & Hallmah Abdullah, *Arizona Gov. Brewer Vetoes Controversial Anti-Gay Bill, SB 1062*, CNN (Feb. 26, 2014), http://www.cnn.com/2014/02/26/politics/arizona-brewer-bill/.

47. 139 Cong. Rec. S2822 (daily ed. Mar. 11, 1993).

48. "[A]pparently there has been some question about the potential effect of S. 2869 on State and local civil rights laws, such as fair housing laws. Although prior legislative proposals implicated civil rights laws in a way that concerned the Department, we believe S. 2869 cannot and should not be construed to require exemptions from such laws." 146 Cong. Rec. S7774 (2000) (letter from Robert Raben, Asst. Att'y Gen.); *see also id.* (letter from Melissa Rogers, General Counsel, Baptist Joint Committee on Public Affairs) ("We greatly appreciate the work of the bill's sponsors in drafting the consensus legislation that will provide important new

protections for the freedom of religious exercise without the harmful consequences for civil rights laws.").

49. 42 U.S.C. § 3601 et seq. (2012); 1959 Cal. Stat. 4074; see Maureen E. Markey, *The Price of Landlord's "Free" Exercise of Religion: Tenant's Right to Discrimination Free Housing and Privacy*, 22 FORDHAM URB. L.J. 699, 746 (1995).

50. David A. Thomas, *Fixing Up Fair Housing Laws: Are We Ready for Reform?*, 53 S.C. L. REV. 7, 50 n. 297 (2001); *State and Local Fair Housing Enforcement Laws*, THE LEADERSHIP CONF. ON CIV. & HUM. RIGHTS, http://www.civilrights .org/fairhousing/laws/state-laws.html (last visited Feb. 16, 2014).

51. Those in the latter category include: CA, CO, CT, DC, DE, HI, IL, IA, ME, MD, MA, MN, NE, NH, NJ, NM, NY, OR, RI, WA, VT, and WI. *LGBT Housing Discrimination*, U.S. DEP'T OF HOUSING AND URBAN DEVELOPMENT, http://portal.hud.gov/hudportal/HUD?src=/program_offices/ fair_housing_equal_opp/LGBT_Housing_Discrimination (last visited Feb. 17, 2014).

52. Smith v. Fair Emp't & Hous. Comm'n, 913 P.2d 909, 926–27 (Cal. 1996); McCready v. Hoffius, 586 N.W. 2d 723, 729 (Mich. 1998). This case was vacated in part in 459 Mich. 235 (1999). *See* Woods v. Real Renters Ltd., No. 01 Civ. 0269(MHD), 2007 WL 656907 (S.D.N.Y. Mar. 1, 2007); Stephanie Hammond Knutson, Note, *The Religious Landlord and the Conflict Between Free Exercise Rights and Housing Discrimination Laws – Which Interest Prevails?*, 47 HASTINGS L.J. 1669, 1716–17 (1996).); Michael P. Seng, *The Fair Housing Act and Religious Freedom*, 11 TEX. J. ON C.L. & C.R. 1, 11 (2005).

53. Bachman v. St. Monica's Congregation, 902 F.2d 1259 (7th Cir. 1990), *reh'g denied*, 902 F.2d 1259 (1990).

54. *Id.* at 1262.

55. Swanner v. Anchorage Equal Rights Comm'n, 874 P.2d. 274, 280 n. 8 (Alaska 1994) (per curiam); *McCready*, 586 N.W. 2d at 730 ("A compelling state interest in eradicating discrimination in real estate transactions justifies the burden on their beliefs"); *cf.* Att'y Gen. v. Desilets, 636 N.E.2d 233 (Mass. 1994), (recognizing a compelling interest test, but stating, "[t]he general objective of eliminating discrimination of all kinds referred to in the relevant version of § 4 (6) ('race, religious creed, color, national origin, sex, age, ancestry or marital status') cannot alone provide a compelling State interest that justifies the application of that section in disregard of the defendants' right to free exercise of their religion"); *see also* David M. Forman, *A Room for "Adam and Steve" at Mrs. Murphy's Bed and Breakfast: Avoiding the Sin of Inhospitality in Places of Public Accommodation*, 23 COLUM. J. GENDER & L. 326 (2012); Seng, *supra* note 54.

56. *Compare Swanner*, 874 P.2d at 274 *and McCready*, 586 N.W. 2d at 729 *with* Swanner v. Anchorage Equal Rights Comm'n, 513 U.S. 979 (1994) (Thomas, J., dissenting from denial of certiorari), Donahue v. Fair Emp't & Hous.Comm'n., 2 Cal. Rptr. 2d 32 (Ct. App. 1991), *and* State *ex rel* Cooper v. French, 460 N.W. 2d 2 (Minn. 1990). *Compare In re* Marriage Cases, 183 P.3d 384 (Cal. 2008) *and* Strauss

v. Horton, 207 P.3d 48 (Cal. 2009) *with* Dean v. District of Columbia, 653 A.2d 307 (D.C. Cir. 1995).

57. *Swanner*, 874 P.2d at 282–83; *McCready*, 586 N.W. 2d at 729 (explaining that the Michigan legislature determined the need for equal access to housing regardless of marital status so fundamental as to require the passing of the Civil Rights Act).

58. Smith v. Fair Emp't & Hous. Comm'n, 913 P.2d 909, 929 (Cal. 1996).

59. *Swanner*, 874 P.2d at 280, n. 9; *McCready*, 586 N.W. 2d at 730. *See also* Shawn Clancy, Note, *The Queer Truth: The Need to Update Title VII to Include Sexual Orientation*, 37 J. LEGIS. 119 (2011); Courtney G. Joslin, *Windsor, Federalism, and Family Equality*, 113 COLUM. L. REV. SIDEBAR 156 (2013).

60. Hack v. Fellows of Yale Coll., 237 F.3d 81, 89, 90 (2d Cir. 2000), *abrogated in part by* Swierkiewicz v. Sorema N.A., 534 U.S. 506 (2002).

61. State *ex rel* Cooper, 460 N.W.2d at 4–5, 8, 11.

62. *Donahue*, 2 Cal. Rptr. 2d at 50.

8. Ordered Liberty: Religious Liberty at the Supreme Court

1. THOMAS JEFFERSON, *Notes on the State of Virginia* (1787), *in* 2 THE WRITINGS OF THOMAS JEFFERSON 221 (Albert Ellery Bergh ed., 1905).

2. JOHN STUART MILL, ON LIBERTY, *reprinted in* Vol. XXV, Part 2 THE HARVARD CLASSICS (1909–14), *available at* http://www.bartleby.com/25/2/4.html.

3. As I discuss in Chapter One, by "no-harm," I mean no significant harm.

4. *See* City of Boerne v. Flores, 521 U.S. 507, 541 (1997) (Scalia, J., concurring); *see also* Marci A. Hamilton, *The "Licentiousness" in Religious Organizations and Why it is Not Protected Under Religious Liberty Constitutional Provisions*, 18 WM. & MARY BILL RTS. J. 953 (2010).

5. This is true in the history leading up to the Constitution, and in Supreme Court cases across the spectrum of constitutional topics. *See Boerne*, 521 U.S. at 539–41 (Scalia, J., concurring) ("Religious exercise shall be permitted *so long as it does not violate general laws governing conduct*") (emphasis in original) (citing the Maryland Act Concerning Religion of 1649, negating a license to act in a manner "unfaithful to the Lord Proprietary"; the Rhode Island Charter of 1663, requiring people to "behave" in other than a "peaceable and quiet" manner; the earliest New York, Maryland, and Georgia Constitutions prohibiting interference with the "peace [and] safety of the State"; the first New Hampshire Constitution forbidding anyone from "disturbing the public peace"; the Northwest Ordinance of 1787 prohibiting citizens from "demean[ing]" oneself in other than a "peaceable and orderly manner."); BERNARD BAILYN, THE IDEOLOGICAL ORIGINS OF THE AMERICAN REVOLUTION 77 (1967) ("Liberty, that is, was the capacity to exercise 'natural rights' within limits set, not by the mere will or desire of men in power but by nonarbitrary law – law enacted by legislatures containing within them the proper balance of forces"); GORDON S. WOOD, THE CREATION OF THE AMERICAN REPUBLIC 1776–87 60–61 (1969). The importance of "ordered liberty" in Supreme Court jurisprudence cannot be overstated. *See infra* note 18.

6. 98 U.S. 145 (1879).

7. *Reynolds*, 98 U.S. at 164 (quoting 8 JEFFERSON WORKS 113).

8. *Reynolds*, 98 U.S. at 166–67.

9. I have called it the no-harm principle. *See* Marci A. Hamilton, *Religious Institutions, the No-Harm Doctrine, and the Public Good*, 2004 BYU. L. REV. 1099 (2004).

10. *Reynolds*, 98 U.S. at 164 (quoting 8 JEFFERSON WORKS 113).

11. JOHN LOCKE, A LETTER CONCERNING RELIGIOUS TOLERATION 50 (Bobbs-Merrill 2d ed. 1955) (1689) ("[L]iberty of conscience is every man's natural right, equally belonging to dissenters as to themselves; . . . nobody ought to be compelled in matters of religion either by law or force. The establishment of this one thing would take away all ground of complaints and tumults upon account of conscience.").

12. *See* JOHN LOCKE, TWO TREATISES OF GOVERNMENT (Mark Goldie ed. 1993) (1689) [hereinafter LOCKE, TWO TREATISES], in which he discusses a "no-harm" principle ("If human beings belong to God, they cannot belong to one another, or even to themselves. Since God is the true proprietor, no one else has the right to damage or destroy his property"). *See also* Russell L. Caplan, *The History and Meaning of the Ninth Amendment*, 69 VA. L. REV. 223, 230 (1983) ("Under [Locke's] theory, individuals are born into a 'state of nature,' that is, without organized government, and agree out of "strong Obligations of Necessity, Convenience, and Inclination" to live in political communities. In so contracting, individuals must give up some of their natural rights so that the rest of those rights may be more effectively secured. The sole legitimate purpose of government, therefore, is the good of the contracting parties – the public. Accordingly, government has a right only to act for the benefit of the governed, to protect its citizens from rebellion within and invasion without.").

13. LOCKE, TWO TREATISES, *supra* note 12, at 164; *see also* Caplan, *supra* note 12, at 230.

14. *Reynolds*, 98 U.S. at 164.

15. MILL, ON LIBERTY, *supra* note 2.

16. *See* Chavez v. Martinez, 538 U.S. 760 (2003); Sell v. United States, 539 U.S. 166 (2003); Tyler v. Cain, 533 U.S. 656 (2001); County of Sacramento v. Lewis, 523 U.S. 833 (1998); O'Dell v. Netherland, 521 U.S. 151 (1997); Kansas v. Hendricks, 521 U.S. 346 (1997); Washington v. Glucksberg, 521 U.S. 702 (1997); Carlisle v. United States, 517 U.S. 416 (1996); Goeke v. Branch, 514 U.S. 115 (1995); Graham v. Collins, 506 U.S. 461 (1993); Gilmore v. Taylor, 508 U.S. 333 (1993); Riggins v. Nevada, 504 U.S. 127 (1992); Milkovich v. Lorain Journal Co., 497 U.S. 1 (1990); Butler v. McKellar, 494 U.S. 407 (1990); Teague v. Lane, 489 U.S. 288 (1989); Michael H. v. Gerald D., 491 U.S. 110 (1989); Stanford v. Kentucky, 492 U.S. 361 (1989), *abrogated by* Roper v. Simmons, 543 U.S. 551 (2005); Yates v. Aiken, 484 U.S. 211 (1988); United States v. Salerno, 481 U.S. 739 (1987); Bowen v. Roy, 476 U.S. 693 (1986); Memphis Cmty. Sch. Dist. v. Stachura, 477 U.S. 299 (1986); Dun & Bradstreet, Inc. v. Greenmoss Builders, 472 U.S. 749 (1985); United States v. Bagley, 473 U.S. 667 (1985); Kolender v. Lawson, 461 U.S. 352 (1983); Whalen v.

Roe, 429 U.S. 589 (1977); Ingraham v. Wright, 430 U.S. 651 (1977); Moore v. City of East Cleveland, 431 U.S. 494 (1977); Paul v. Davis, 424 U.S. 693 (1976); Stone v. Powell, 428 U.S. 465 (1976); United States v. Janis, 428 U.S. 433 (1976); Gertz v. Robert Welch, Inc., 418 U.S. 323 (1974); Roe v. Wade, 410 U.S. 113 (1973); Paris Adult Theatre I v. Slaton, 413 U.S. 49 (1973); Wisconsin v. Yoder, 406 U.S. 205 (1972); Williams v. United States, 401 U.S. 646 (1971) (plurality opinion); Coolidge v. New Hampshire, 403 U.S. 443 (1971); Duncan v. State of La., 391 U.S. 145 (1968); Tehan v. U.S. ex rel. Shott, 382 U.S. 406 (1966); Gideon v. Wainwright, 372 U.S. 335 (1963); Ker v. Cal., 374 U.S. 23 (1963); Mapp v. Ohio, 367 U.S. 643 (1961); Elkins v. United States, 364 U.S. 206 (1960); Ohio v. Price, 364 U.S. 263 (1960) (per curiam); Bartkus v. Illinois, 359 U.S. 121 (1959); Napue v. Illinois, 360 U.S. 264 (1959); Rochin v. California, 342 U.S. 165 (1952); Leland v. Oregon, 343 U.S. 790 (1952); Stefanelli v. Minard, 342 U.S. 117 (1951); Kovacs v. Cooper, 336 U.S. 77 (1949); Bute v. Illinois, 333 U.S. 640 (1948); Screws v. United States, 325 U.S. 91 (1945).

17. *See generally* THE WORKS OF JOHN WITHERSPOON, LECTURES ON MORAL PHILOSOPHY (1805).

18. 7 THE WORKS OF JOHN WITHERSPOON 100, 148 (1805). Witherspoon, a signer of the Declaration of Independence and president of Princeton, was influential in the development of many of the Framers, including James Madison.

19. Lee v. Weisman, 505 U.S. 577, 590–91 (1992) ("To endure the speech of false ideas or offensive content and then to counter it is part of learning how to live in a pluralistic society, a society which insists upon open discourse towards the end of a tolerant citizenry. And tolerance presupposes some mutuality of obligation."); Emp't Div. v. Smith, 494 U.S. 872, 879 (1990) ("the right of free exercise does not relieve an individual of the obligation to comply with a 'valid and neutral law of general applicability on the ground that the law proscribes (or prescribes) conduct that his religion prescribes (or proscribes).'" (quoting United States v. Lee, 455 U.S. 252, 263 n.3 (1982) (Stevens, J., concurring))).

20. *Yoder*, 406 U.S. 205 (1972).

21. *Id.* at 245.

22. *Smith*, 494 U.S. at 881.

23. *Lee*, 455 U.S. at 259–60.

24. ROBERT NOZICK, ANARCHY, STATE, AND UTOPIA 32–35 (1974).

25. Church of the Lukumi Babalu Aye, Inc. v. City of Hialeah, 508 U.S. 520, 547 (1993).

26. Abington Sch. Dist. v. Schempp, 374 U.S. 203, 305 (1963) (Goldberg, J., concurring).

27. SARAH BARRINGER GORDON, THE MORMON QUESTION: POLYGAMY AND CONSTITUTIONAL CONFLICT IN NINETEENTH CENTURY AMERICA 157 (2002).

28. U.S. CONST. art. III, § 2 states:

> The judicial power shall extend to all cases, in law and equity, arising under this Constitution, the laws of the United States, and treaties made, or which shall be made, under their authority . . . to controversies to which the United

States shall be a party; – to controversies between two or more states; – between a state and citizens of another state; – between citizens of different states; – between citizens of the same state claiming lands under grants of different states, and between a state, or the citizens thereof, and foreign states, citizens or subjects.

29. *Lee*, 455 U.S. at 259–60.

30. Bob Jones Univ. v. United States, 461 U.S. 574, 604 (1983).

31. Tony & Susan Alamo Found. v. Sec'y of Labor, 471 U.S. 290, 306 (1985).

32. Goldman v. Weinberger, 475 U.S. 503, 509–10 (1986).

33. Bowen v. Roy, 476 U.S. 693, 700–01 (1986).

34. Lyng v. Northwest Indian Cemetery Protective Ass'n, 485 U.S. 439, 452 (1988).

35. Hernandez v. Comm'r, 490 U.S. 680, 683 (1989), *reh'g denied*, 492 U.S. 933 (1989).

36. Jimmy Swaggart Ministries v. Bd. of Equalization, 493 U.S. 378, 394 (1990).

37. O'Lone v. Estate of Shabazz, 482 U.S. 342, 345 (1987).

38. Emp't Div. v. Smith, 494 U.S. 872, 885 (1990). In addition to this list of cases in which the Court upheld neutral, generally applicable laws against free exercise challenges, the Court also refused to read into the requirements of the civil rights act a duty to accommodate Sabbatarians. *See* Trans World Airlines v. Hardison, 432 U.S. 63, 81 (1977) ("It would be anomalous to conclude that by 'reasonable accommodation' Congress meant that an employer must deny the shift and job preference of some employees, as well as deprive them of their contractual rights, in order to accommodate or prefer the religious needs of others, and we conclude that Title VII does not require an employer to go that far."). This is especially interesting in light of the fact that the only arena wherein the Court consistently found free exercise violations between 1963 and 1990 involved Sabbatarians challenging the laws governing unemployment compensation. *See, e.g.,* Sherbert v. Verner, 374 U.S. 398, 398 (1963); *see also* Frazee v. Ill. Dep't of Emp't Sec., 489 U.S. 829 (1989).

39. *Smith*, 494 U.S at 885.

40. Marci A. Hamilton, Employment Division v. Smith *at the Supreme Court: The Justices, The Litigants, and the Doctrinal Discourse*, 32 CARDOZO L. REV. 1671, 1673 (2011).

41. 374 U.S. 398, 406 (1963) (finding denial of unemployment benefits unconstitutionally burdened plaintiff's free exercise by forcing a choice between abandoning Saturday religious practice or forfeiting benefits, but noting the statute excepted those worshipping on Sundays from having to make the same choice).

42. 406 U.S. 205 (1972).

43. 98 U.S. 145, 165–66 (1878).

44. 366 U.S. 599 (1961).

45. 455 U.S. 252, 261 (1982).

46. 401 U.S. 437, 443–44 (1971).

47. 42 U.S.C. §§ 2000bb-1 to 2000bb-4 (2012). RFRA was declared unconstitutional as applied to the states in *City of Boerne v. Flores*, 521 U.S. 507 (1997).

48. Ala. Const. art. I, § 3.01 (burden); Ariz. Rev. Stat. Ann. §§ 41-1493 to -1493.02 (2013) (substantial burden); Conn. Gen. Stat. § 52-571b (2013) (burden); Fla. Stat. Ann. §§ 761.01–761.05 (West 2013) (substantial burden); Idaho Code Ann. §§ 73-401 to -404 (2013) (substantial burden); 775 Ill. Comp. Stat. Ann. 35/1-99 (2013) (substantial burden); La. Rev. Stat. Ann. §§ 13:5231–:5242 (2013) (substantial burden); Mo. Rev. Stat. §§ 1.302–1.307 (2013) (restrictions on religious liberty); Okla. Stat. tit. 51, §§ 251–258 (2013) (substantial burden); 71 Pa. Cons. Stat. §§ 2401–2407 (West 2013) (substantial burden); R.I. Gen. Laws §§ 42-80.1-1 to -4 (2013) (restrictions on religious liberty); S.C. Code Ann. §§ 1-32-10 to -60 (2013) (substantial burden); Tenn. Code Ann. § 4-1-407 (2013) (substantial burden); Tex. Civ. Prac. & Rem. Code Ann. §§ 110.001–110.012 (West 2013) (substantial burden); Utah Code Ann. §§ 63L-5-101 to -403 (LexisNexis 2013) (substantial burden; land use only); Va. Code Ann. §§ 57-1 to -2.02 (2013) (substantial burden); N.M. Stat. Ann. §§ 28-22-1 to -5 (West 2012) (restrictions on religious liberty).

49. 42 U.S.C. §§ 2000cc to 2000cc-5 (2012). I discuss the serious constitutional faults of RLUIPA in Marci A. Hamilton, *The Constitutional Limitations on Congress's Power over Local Land Use: Why the Religious Land Use and Institutionalized Persons Act Is Unconstitutional*, 2 Alb. Gov't L. Rev. 366 (2009).

50. Emp't Div. v. Smith, 494 U.S. 872, 878–79, 885.

51. Church of the Lukumi Babalu Aye, Inc. v. City of Hialeah, 508 U.S. 520, 523, 547 (1993) (internal citations omitted).

52. *Smith*, 494 U.S. at 890.

53. *Lukumi*, 508 U.S. 520.

54. *Thomas*, 450 U.S. at 709 & n.1 (quoting Ind. Code § 22-4-15-1 (1978)).

55. *Hobbie*, 480 U.S. 136, 137–38 (quoting Fla. Stat. § 443.021 (1985)).

56. *Frazee*, 489 U.S. 829, 830–31, 834 (quoting Frazee v. Ill. Dep't of Emp't Sec., 512 N.E.2d 789 (Ill. App. Ct. 1987)).

57. *See, e.g.*, J. Morris Clark, *Guidelines for the Free Exercise Clause*, 83 Harv. L. Rev. 327, 329 (1969) ("In common sense terms the *Sherbert* decision seems correct enough.... Yet by its holding that some religious practices are protected even from laws not intended to affect the communicative aspects of belief, *Sherbert* introduced a new range of complexity into the free exercise clause."); Jonathan Weiss, *Privilege, Posture and Protection: "Religion" in the Law*, 73 Yale L.J. 593 (1964).

58. *See generally* Kent Greenawalt, *Religion as a Concept in Constitutional Law*, 72 Calif. L. Rev. 753 (1984); Philip E. Johnson, *Concepts and Compromise in First Amendment Religious Doctrine*, 72 Calif. L. Rev. 817 (1984); Note, *Toward a Constitutional Definition of Religion*, 91 Harv. L. Rev. 1056, 1077–82 (1978) (discussing and rejecting criticisms of Sherbert).

59. 406 U.S. 205 (1972).

60. *Id.* at 228–29.

61. *See* William P. Marshall, *The Case Against the Constitutionally Compelled Free Exercise Exemption*, 40 Case W. Res. L. Rev. 357 (1989–1990); Ellis West, *The Case Against a Right to Religious-Based Exemptions*, 4 Notre Dame J.L. Ethics & Pub. Pol'y 591, 624 (1989) (rejecting constitutionally compelled exemptions,

but not legislative exemptions). The historical case against mandatory exemptions was initiated in the well-respected article, Philip A. Hamburger, *A Constitutional Right of Religious Exemption: An Historical Perspective*, 60 GEO. WASH. L. REV. 915 (1992).

62. Michael W. McConnell, *The Origins and Historical Understanding of Free Exercise of Religion*, 103 HARV. L. REV. 1409, 1516 (1990).

63. *Id.* at 1415.

64. *See generally* Frederick M. Gedicks, *An Unfirm Foundation: The Regrettable Indefensibility of Religious Exemptions*, 20 U. ARK. LITTLE ROCK L. REV. 555, 574 (1998) ("[T]he historical moment for exemptions has come and gone. There no longer exists a plausible explanation of why religious believers – and only believers – are constitutionally entitled to be excused from complying with otherwise legitimate laws that burden practices."); Hamburger, *supra* note 61; Marshall, *supra* note 61; West, *supra* note 61, at 624 (rejecting constitutionally compelled exemptions, but not legislative exemptions); *see also* Frederick Mark Gedicks, *Towards a Defensible Free Exercise Doctrine*, 68 Geo. Wash. L. Rev. 925, 950–51 (2000) ("[I]n the long run, no effective defense is possible [for judicially mandated exemptions]. To the extent that a residuum of religious exemptions persists under state law, ... I say enjoy them while they last.").

65. *See, e.g.,* II JOHN CALVIN, INSTITUTES OF THE CHRISTIAN RELIGION, bk. IV, ch. XX, § 32, at 1520:

> But in that obedience which we have shown to be due the authority of rulers, we are always to make this exception, indeed, to observe it as primary, that such obedience is never to lead us away from obedience to him.

66. *See* Marci A. Hamilton, *Religion, the Rule of Law, and the Good of the Whole: A View from the Clergy*, 18 J.L. & POL. 387, 396–408 (2002).

67. POLITICAL SERMONS OF THE AMERICAN FOUNDING ERA, 1730–1805, at 147–48 (Ellis Sandoz ed., 1991) (Charles Chauncy 1747).

68. *See* Oral Argument, Emp't Div. v. Smith, 494 U.S. 872, *available at* 1989 U.S. TRANS LEXIS 94, at *36. Respondents argued that, "it is our belief that the state cannot meet any of the burdens in this case. The compelling state interest is the regulation of drug abuse generally, but we do not have any evidence in this case that peyote has been abused or that it contributes to the drug abuse problem. In fact, all of the evidence is to the contrary. We have the findings, for instance, of the federal agency charged with enforcement of the drug laws in this country, which found that and concluded that the religious use of peyote by the Native American Church does not cause a law enforcement problem in this country." *Id.*

69. *See* Reply Brief for Petitioners, *Smith*, No. 88–1213, 1989 WL 1126854 ("Unlike *Yoder*, the practice at issue here directly affects physical and mental health. The State's health interests in preventing the use of peyote is no different from its interests in preventing the use of mescaline, psilocybin, and LSD, all of which have substantially the same hallucinogenic properties as peyote. Unlike the Amish's practices, the state cannot accommodate religiously motivated drug

use without substantially compromising its interests in the health and safety of its citizens." (footnote omitted)).

70. Hamilton, *supra* note 40, at 1682.

71. *Id.* at 1683.

72. *Smith*, 494 U.S. at 878–79.

73. *Id.* at 890.

74. *See, e.g.*, James D. Gordon III, *Free Exercise on the Mountaintop*, 79 CALIF. L. REV. 91, 110 (1991) (calling *Smith*'s invocation of exemptions, "Small comfort. 'Discrete and insular minorities' often cannot protect themselves adequately in the legislative process. The right to practice one's religion should not be reduced to a question of political influence, completely subject to the whims of transient and shifting majorities." (quoting United States v. Carolene Prods. Co., 304 U.S. 144, 153 n.4 (1938))); Douglas Laycock, *The Remnants of Free Exercise*, 1990 SUP. CT. REV. 1,15 (criticizing Smith's reliance on exemptions in part because "Legislators are under no obligation to be principled. Subject only to their oath to uphold the Constitution, they are free to reflect majority prejudices, to respond to the squeakiest wheel among minorities, to trade votes and make compromises, and to ignore problems that have no votes in them."); Michael W. McConnell, *Free Exercise Revisionism and the Smith Decision*, 57 U. CHI. L. REV. 1109, 1129 (1990) [hereinafter McConnell, *Free Exercise Revisionism*] ("The rhetoric of [*Smith*] is certainly impolitic, leaving the Court open to the charge of abandoning its traditional role as protector of minority rights against majoritarian oppression.").

75. *Smith*, 494 U.S. at 879 (quoting United States v. Lee, 455 U.S. 252, 263 n.3 (1982) (Stevens, J., concurring)).

76. Hamilton, *supra* note 40, at 1682.

77. *See, e.g.*, Knight v. Conn. Dep't of Pub. Health, 275 F.3d 156, 167 (2d Cir. 2001) ("The allegation that a state action that regulates public conduct infringes on more than one of a public employee's constitutional rights does not warrant more heightened scrutiny than each claim would warrant when viewed separately."); Swanson by & Through Swanson v. Guthrie Indep. Sch. Dist. No. I–L, 135 F.3d 694, 699 (10th Cir. 1998) ("It is difficult to delineate the exact contours of the hybrid-rights theory discussed in Smith. As we discuss below, however, we believe that simply raising such a claim is not a talisman that automatically leads to the application of the compelling-interest test. We must examine the claimed infringements on the party's claimed rights to determine whether either the claimed rights or the claimed infringements are genuine."); Kissinger v. Bd. of Trustees of Ohio State Univ., 5 F.3d 177, 180 (6th Cir. 1993) ("We do not see how a state regulation would violate the Free Exercise Clause if it implicates other constitutional rights but would not violate the free Exercise Clause if it did not implicate other constitutional rights.... At least until the Supreme Court holds that legal standards under the Free Exercise Clause vary depending on whether other constitutional rights are implicated, we will not use a stricter legal standard . . . to evaluate generally applicable, exceptionless state regulations under the Free Exercise Clause.").

78. *Smith*, 494 U.S. at 907 (Blackmun, J., dissenting) ("This Court over the years painstakingly has developed a consistent and exacting standard to test the constitutionality of a state statute that burdens the free exercise of religion. Such a statute may stand only if the law in general, and the State's refusal to allow a religious exemption in particular, are justified by a compelling interest that cannot be served by less restrictive means.").

79. Douglas Laycock, *The Supreme Court's Assault on Free Exercise, and the Amicus Brief that Was Never Filed*, 8 J.L. & RELIGION 99, 102 (1990).

80. McConnell, *Free Exercise Revisionism*, *supra* note 74, at 1120.

81. Steven D. Smith, *Free Exercise Doctrine and the Discourse of Disrespect*, 65 U. COLO. L. REV. 519, 575 (1994).

82. Harry F. Tepker, Jr., *Hallucinations of Neutrality in the Oregon Peyote Case*, 16 AM. INDIAN L. REV. 1 (1991).

83. Gordon, *supra* note 74, at 114–15.

84. ROBERT L. STERN, ET. AL., SUPREME COURT PRACTICE 313–14 (8th ed. 2002).

85. The following colloquy from the oral argument is telling:

QUESTION [BY JUSTICE]: I mean, we granted certiorari on the question presented, which is whether the Free Exercise Clause of the First Amendment protects a person's religiously motivated use of peyote from the reach of the state's general criminal law prohibition. And you say maybe it is not so much a question of criminal law, but you agree that the First Amendment issue is here.

. . .

MR. DORSAY: Yes, but we think it is disposed of, and we need to keep reemphasizing this by *Sherbert* and *Thomas*, that the criminality is irrelevant. If the criminality is relevant, we still believe that the state has not met their test under the First Amendment. And I would be glad to move to that issue. Transcript of Oral Argument in Smith, 494 U.S. 872, 1989 U.S. TRANS LEXIS 94, at *35–42.

86. William P. Marshall, *In Defense of Smith and Free Exercise Revisionism*, 58 U. CHI. L. REV. 308, 308–09 (1991).

87. *See Religious Freedom Restoration Act of 1990: Hearing before the Subcomm. on Civil and Constitutional Rights of the H. Comm. on the Judiciary*, 101st Cong., 2d Sess. (1990).

88. *Area Rep. Kills Religious-Freedom Bill*, CINCINNATI.COM (Feb. 26, 2014, 8:57 PM), http://news.cincinnati.com/article/20140226/NEWS010801/302260112/SW-Ohioan-kills-religious-freedom-bill-cites-AZ-controversy.

89. Steve Mistler, *Maine Senate Rejects "Religious Freedom" Bill*, KENNEBEC J. (Feb. 18, 2014), *available at* http://rfraperils.com/2014/02/18/maine-senate-rejects-religious-freedom-bill-kennebec-journal/.

90. The one exception was Sen. Harry Reid of Nevada, who, in the final stages before RFRA was passed, requested an amendment to exempt the prisons. The

amendment failed. *See* 139 Cong. Rec. S14, 461–68 (daily ed. Oct. 27, 1993); 139 Cong. Rec. S14, 350–68 (daily ed. Oct. 26, 1993).

91. Emp't Div. v. Smith, 494 U.S. 872, 890.

92. Wisconsin v. Yoder, 406 U.S. 205, 221 (1972); Sherbert v. Verner, 374 U.S. 398, 406–07 (1963).

93. Katzenbach v. Morgan, 384 U.S. 641, 652 (1966).

94. In the interest of full disclosure, I represented the City of Boerne, Texas, in *City of Boerne v. Flores*, 521 U.S. 507 (1997), in which the City prevailed. My personal involvement in the case, however, is only tangentially relevant to the doctrinal analysis in this chapter. The City of Boerne, Texas was settled by German immigrants and is pronounced Ber-knee.

95. Robert C. Post & Reva B. Siegel, *Equal Protection by Law: Federal Anti-discrimination Legislation After* Morrison *and* Kimel, 110 YALE L.J. 441 (2000).

96. Larry D. Kramer, *No Surprise. It's an Activist Court*, N.Y. TIMES, Dec. 12, 2000, at A33. (in referring to *Boerne*, "But perhaps the most *audacious* instance of judicial activism is the way the court has extended the doctrine of judicial review itself.").

97. Nev. Dep't of Human Res. v. Hibbs, 538 U.S. 721 (2003).

98. Tennessee v. Lane, 541 U.S. 509 (2004).

99. Voting Rights Act of 1965, PL 89–110, 79 Stat. 437; Civil Rights Act of 1964, PL 88–352, 78 Stat. 241; Civil Rights Act of 1960, PL 86–449, 74 Stat. 86; Civil Rights Act of 1957, PL 85–315, 71 Stat. 634.

100. 42 U.S.C. § 2000b states:

> Whenever the Attorney General receives a complaint in writing signed by an individual to the effect that he is being deprived of or threatened with the loss of his right to the equal protection of the laws, on account of his race, color, religion, or national origin, by being denied equal utilization of any public facility which is owned, operated, or managed by or on behalf of any State or subdivision thereof, other than a public school or public college as defined in section 2000c of this title, and the Attorney General believes the complaint is meritorious and certifies that the signer or signers of such complaint are unable, in his judgment, to initiate and maintain appropriate legal proceedings for relief and that the institution of an action will materially further the orderly progress of desegregation in public facilities, the Attorney General is authorized to institute for or in the name of the United States a civil action in any appropriate district court of the United States against such parties and for such relief as may be appropriate, and such court shall have and shall exercise jurisdiction of proceedings instituted pursuant to this section. The Attorney General may implead as defendants such additional parties as are or become necessary to the grant of effective relief hereunder.

Similar language was included in all previous versions of the Civil Rights Act.

101. 347 U.S. 873 (1954).

102. Loving v. Virginia, 388 U.S. 1 (1967).

103. McLaughlin v. Florida, 379 U.S. 184 (1964).

104. Anderson v. Martin, 375 U.S. 399 (1964).

105. Garner v. Louisiana, 368 U.S. 157 (1961); *see also* Bell v. Maryland, 378 U.S. 226 (1963) (public accommodation law supersedes criminal trespass law used to convict African-American students who participated in a "sit-in" at private restaurant that refused to serve them).

106. Johnson v. Virginia, 373 U.S. 61 (1963).

107. Whitus v. Georgia, 385 U.S. 545 (1967).

108. Heart of Atlanta Motel v. United States, 379 U.S. 241 (1964).

109. Burton v. Wilmington Parking Auth., 365 U.S. 715 (1961).

110. Cooper v. Aaron, 358 U.S. 1 (1958).

111. Reitman v. Mulkey, 387 U.S. 369 (1967).

112. U.S. CONST. art. V provides:

The Congress, whenever two thirds of both Houses shall deem it necessary, shall propose Amendments to this Constitution, or, on the Application of the Legislatures of two thirds of the several States, shall call a Convention for proposing Amendments, which, in either Case, shall be valid to all Intents and Purposes, as Part of this Constitution, when ratified by the Legislatures of three fourths of the several States, or by Conventions in three fourths thereof, as the one or the other Mode of Ratification may be proposed by the Congress; Provided that no Amendment which may be made prior to the Year One thousand eight hundred and eight shall in any Manner affect the first and fourth Clauses in the Ninth Section of the first Article; and that no State, without its Consent, shall be deprived of its equal Suffrage in the Senate.

113. EEOC v. Wyoming, 460 U.S. 226 (1983).

114. *Id.* at 262 (Burger, C.J., dissenting).

115. William Cohen, *Congressional Power to Interpret Due Process and Equal Protection*, 27 STAN. L. REV. 603, 606 (1975).

116. *See id.* at 614; *see also* Matt Pawa, Comment, *When the Supreme Court Restricts Constitutional Rights, Can Congress Save Us? An Examination of Section 5 of the Fourteenth Amendment*, 141 U. PA. L. REV. 1029, 1062 (1993). *But see generally* Lawrence H. Tribe, *A Constitution We Are Amending: In Defense of a Restrained Judicial Role*, 97 HARV. L. REV. 433 (1983).

117. *See* 103 Cong. Rec. S6,867 (1994) (statement of Sen. Cochran quoting Douglas Laycock).

118. 384 U.S. 641 (1966).

119. U.S. CONST. amend. XIV, § 5.

120. Lassiter v. Northhampton Cnty. Bd. of Elections, 360 U.S. 45, 51–53 (1959).

121. While not using the term "prophylactic" explicitly in this opinion, the term was part of the jurisprudence that Brennan subscribed to at the time. *See, e.g.,* Estes v. State of Texas, 381 U.S. 532, 616 (1965) (White, J. dissenting, in which Brennan, J. joins) ("Serious threats to constitutional rights in some instances justify

a prophylactic rule dispensing with the necessity of showing specific prejudice in a particular case.").

122. South Carolina v. Katzenbach, 383 U.S. 301, 309 (1966), *abrogated by* Shelby Cnty. v. Holder, 133 S. Ct. 2612 (2013).

123. *Katzenbach*, 383 U.S. at 668 (Harlan, J., dissenting).

124. *Id.* at 651 n.10.

125. Archibald Cox, *Foreword: Constitutional Adjudication and the Promotion of Human Rights*, 80 HARV. L. REV. 91, 110–11 (1966).

126. Cohen, *supra* note 115, at 606–07.

127. Eugene Gressman & Angela C. Carmella, *The RFRA Revision of the Free Exercise Clause*, 57 OHIO ST. L.J. 65, 118–19 (1996) ("The 'ratchet theory,' which at the time of its birth in *Morgan* led to a spirited dissent by Justices Harlan and Stewart, has never been revisited, followed, or clarified by the Court.").

128. 400 U.S. 112 (1970), *superseded by constitutional amendment as stated in* Johnson v. Governor of Fla., 405 F.3d 1214 (11th Cir. 2005) (en banc).

129. 446 U.S. 156, 220–21 (1980), *abrogated by* Shelby Cnty. v. Holder, 133 S. Ct. 2612 (2013).

130. 400 U.S. 112 (1970), *superseded by constitutional amendment as stated in* Johnson, 405 F. 3d 1214.

131. 460 U.S. 226, 262 (quoting Oregon v. Mitchell, 400 U.S. 112, 205 (1970)), *abrogated as stated in* New York v. United States, 505 U.S. 144 (1992).

132. Gressman & Carmella, *supra* note 127, at 131–32.

133. *Id.* at 118–19; *see also* Daniel O. Conkle, *The Religious Freedom Restoration Act: The Constitutional Significance of an Unconstitutional Statute*, 56 MONT. L. REV. 39, 46 (1995).

134. City of Boerne v. Flores, 521 U.S. 507, 519 (1997).

135. *Id.* at 530.

136. *Id.* at 532.

9. The Decline of Church Autonomy and the Rise of the No-Harm Rule

1. HAROLD J. BERMAN, LAW AND REVOLUTION: THE FORMATION OF THE WESTERN LEGAL TRADITION 267 (1983) (hereinafter BERMAN, LAW AND REVOLUTION).

2. A. R. HOGUE, ORIGINS OF THE COMMON LAW 5, 186–90 (1966).

3. See *infra* notes 146–153 and accompanying text (discussing no-harm principle in works of John Locke, James Madison, and Thomas Jefferson).

4. *See, e.g.*, Craigdallie v. Aikman, 1 Dow 1, 3 Eng. Rep. 601 (H. L. 1813) (Scot.); The Reverend G. H. Forbes, of the Scotch Episcopal Church v. The Right Reverend Bishop Eden, Primus of the Scotch Episcopal Church, L. R. 1 Sc. 568 (1867) ("Per Lord Colonsay: A Court of Law will not interfere with the rules of a voluntary association, *unless to protect some civil right or interest which is said to be infringed by their operation.*") (emphasis added).

5. The Feoffees of Heriot's Hospital v. Ross, 1846, 12Clark & Fin. 507, 8 Eng. Rep. 1508 (introducing the doctrine of charitable immunity); Duncan v. Findlater, 1839, 6Clark & Fin. 894, 7 Eng.Rep. 934 (similar dicta from the same judge in this

earlier case); Holliday v. St. Leonard, 1861, 11 C.B., N.S., 192 (following Duncan's case); McDonald v. Massachusetts Gen. Hosp., 1876, 120 Mass. 432, 21 Am.Rep. 529 (first American case adopting the charitable immunity rule of Holliday's case); Perry v. House of Refuge, 1885, 63 Md. 20, 52 Am.Rep. 495 (charitable immunity rule of Heriot's case adopted by Maryland).

6. *See* Bradley C. Canon & Dean Jaros, *The Impact of Changes in Judicial Doctrine: The Abrogation of Charitable Immunity*, 13 LAW & SOC'Y REV. 969, 971 (1979).

7. *See, e.g.*, Robert F. Cochran, Jr., *Church Freedom and Accountability in Sexual Exploitation Cases: The Possibility of Both Through Limited Strict Liability*, 21 J. CONTEMP. LEGAL ISSUES 429, 429 (2013); Elizabeth Stewart Poisson, Comment, *The Impropriety of Statutory Caps on Pain and Suffering Damages in the Medical Liability System*, 82 N. C. L. REV. 759 (2004); M. King Hill III & Katherine D. Williams, *State Laws Limiting Liability for Noneconomic Damages: How Courts Have Dealt with the Related Legal and Medical Issues in Asbestos Personal Injury Cases*, 27 U. BALT. L. REV. 317 (1998); Nancy L. Manzer, Note, *Tort Reform Legislation: A Systematic Evaluation of Caps on Damages and Limitations on Joint and Several Liability*, 73 CORNELL L. REV. 628 (1988); George L. Priest, *The Current Insurance Crisis and Modern Tort Law*, 96 YALE L.J. 1521, 1587–88 (1987).

8. *See, e.g.*, Michel Rosenfeld, *The Rule of Law and the Legitimacy of Constitutional Democracy*, 74 S. CAL. L. REV. 1307, 1345–46 (2001) (noting that that the common law "is grounded in a common well of values, a widely shared sense of justice and fairness, and dedication to elaborating a pragmatically oriented, empirically based working legal order that insures stability through steadfast adherence to core principles."); *id.* at 1349 ("At least under certain propitious circumstances, therefore, the rule of law can promote both predictability and fairness; this seems equally possible in an Anglo-American common law setting as in a continental civil law system."); Charles H. Koch, Jr., *Envisioning a Global Legal Culture*, 25 MICH J. INT'L L.J. 1, 54 (2003) ("the common law judge is charged with applying the 'law' in order to render individual fairness, but is also committed to treating like cases alike.")

9. Marci A. Hamilton, *The "Licentiousness" in Religious Organizations and Why It Is Not Protected Under Religious Liberty Constitutional Provisions*, 18 Wm. & Mary Bill Rts. J. 953, 973 (2010)

10. *See* Locke v. Davey, 540 U.S. 712, 1309 (2004); City of Boerne v. Flores, 521 U.S. 507 (1997); Employment Div. v. Smith, 494 U.S. 872 (1990); Jimmy Swaggart Ministries v. Bd. of Equalization, 493 U.S. 378 (1990); Braunfeld v. Brown, 366 U.S. 599 (1961); Reynolds v. U.S., 98 U.S. 145 (1878).

11. Religious institutions being sued or prosecuted for childhood sexual abuse have repeatedly asserted so-called "privileges" over the law, claiming that they need not provide internal documents, despite their relevance. The Catholic Church has asserted numerous privileges that purportedly prevent the state from seeing employee files in grand jury proceedings. *See, e.g.*, William Lobdell and Jean Guccione, *A Novel Tack by Cardinal*, L.A. TIMES, Mar. 14, 2004, at A1.

12. Wayne A. Logan, *Criminal Law Sanctuaries*, 38 Harv. C.R. – C.L. L. Rev. 321, 323–24 (2003). The practice of sanctuary may date back much farther. The Bible explicitly mentions sanctuary three times and temples in ancient Greece afforded sanctuary to criminals. *Id.* Roman temples, on the other hand, offered only a temporary refuge before turning criminals over to civil authorities. *Id.* at 324.

13. *See* Norman MacLaren Trenholme, The Right of Sanctuary in England: A Study in Institutional History 5, 325 (1903).

14. *Id.* at 47.

15. *See* Logan, *supra* note 12, at 326.

16. *See* Trenholme, *supra* note 13, at 43 (noting that, during the 13th and 14th centuries, the law forced clergymen to surrender to ecclesiastical courts for "spiritual offenses" and to secular authorities for common law crimes. Once in the secular courts, however, they would be permitted to invoke the benefit of clergy, which sent them to the ecclesiastical courts, where they escaped the most severe punishments).

17. *See* Logan, *supra* note 12, at 328.

18. Stephen, *infra* note 82, at 491–92.

19. *See* Logan, *supra* note 12, at 329.

20. *Id.*

21. *See* C. Warren Hollister, The Making of England: 55 b.c. to 1399 149–50, 162–64 (7th ed. 1996); Richard Barber, Henry Plantagent 30, 106–10 (1967).

22. *See* Edward A. Freeman, 4 The History of the Norman Conquest of England: Its Causes and Results 392 (1871); George W. Dalzell, Benefit of Clergy in America & Related Matters 13 (1955); Hollister, *supra* note 21, at 115. William the Conqueror divided the ecclesiastical courts from the secular courts, decreeing that "no bishop or archdeacon shall any longer hold pleas involving episcopal laws in the hundred [court]," that instead bishops were to maintain separate courts of their own in which to try civil matters such as marriage, wills, and debts, and criminal offenses committed by or upon all members of the church. Richard Winston, Thomas Becket 17 (1967) (quoting H. I. Stubbs, Historical Introductions to the Rolls Series (ed. Arthur Hassell, 1902)). In the 12th and 13th centuries, canon law claimed jurisdiction over criminal and civil cases arising out of sin and breach of faith, as well as over clerics and church property; secular law had jurisdiction over criminal and civil cases arising out of seisin of freehold land and breach of the king's peace. *See* Berman, Law and Revolution, *supra* note 1, at 516.

23. *See* Peter D. Jason, *The Courts Christian in Medieval England*, 37 Cath. Law. 339, 342 n. 27 (1997) (citing Z. N. Brooke, The English Church and the Papacy 188–89 (1968)) ("Overall, Stephen failed to preserve the barrier against papal authority over the English Church. Therefore, when Henry II succeeded Stephen, he was faced with the challenge of overcoming the increased authority of the Church.").

24. Unless otherwise noted, the account of the feud between Henry II and Thomas Becket in the following paragraphs can be found in HOLLISTER, *supra* note 21, at 160–64; BARBER, *supra* note 21, at 110–21; WINSTON, *supra* note 22, at 166–91, 318–21.

25. HENRY C. LEA, STUDIES IN CHURCH HISTORY 187 (1869).

26. *See* HOLLISTER, *supra* note 21, at 161.

27. *See* WINSTON, *supra* note 22, at 319–20.

28. *See* HOLLISTER, *supra* note 21, at 162; BARBER, *supra* note 21, at 110–11; WINSTON, *supra* note 22, at 167–68. As archbishop of Canterbury, (who had previously served as Henry's royal chancellor) was the head of the English Church, responsible for the crowning of kings and direct relations with Rome. *See* HOLLISTER, *supra* note 21, at 161–63.

29. Henry ordered Becket to stand trial in the royal court for various offenses allegedly committed when he was Henry's chancellor. Claiming clerical immunity from royal jurisdiction, Becket fled the country to appeal his case to the pope, which violated the prohibition of unlicensed appeals to Rome. *See* HOLLISTER, *supra* note 21, at 162; BARBER, *supra* note 21, at 116–21; WINSTON, *supra* note 22, at 175–91.

30. *See* BERMAN, LAW AND REVOLUTION, *supra* note 1, at 262 ("Interdict was a partial or total suspension of public services and sacraments; it could extend to one or more persons or to a whole locality or kingdom.").

31. *See* WINSTON, *supra* note 22, at 319–20 (quoting 3 MATERIALS FOR THE HISTORY OF THOMAS BECKET, ARCHBISHOP OF CANTERBURY 119 [James Craigie Robertson, ed. 1875]).

32. *See* HOLLISTER, *supra* note 21, at 163; BARBER, *supra* note 21, at 140–41; WINSTON, *supra* note 22, at 302–05.

33. *See* HOLLISTER, *supra* note 21, at 163–64; BARBER, *supra* note 21, at 161–65; WINSTON, *supra* note 22, at 375.

34. *See* 2 THE REPORTS OF JOHN SPELMAN 327 (J.H. Baker ed. 1978) (stating that benefit of clergy appeared in 1170).

35. DALZELL, *supra* note 22, at 11.

36. *See* Phillip M. Spector, *The Sentencing Rule of Lenity*, 33 U. TOL. L. REV. 511, 515 (2002).

37. *See* DALZELL, *supra* note 22, at 11 ("church tribunal could not enter a 'judgment of blood," i.e., a capital sentence or an attainder").

38. R. H. HELMHOLZ, THE SPIRIT OF THE CLASSICAL CANON LAW 158–59 (1996).

39. DALZELL, *supra* note 22, at 11; R. H. HELMHOLZ, *Crime, Compurgation and the Church Courts*, in CANON LAW AND THE LAW OF ENGLAND 137 (1987) ("Too many accused persons successfully underwent purgation for the method to inspire confidence as a factfinding device . . . Almost every person who came before the ecclesiastical courts accused of theft, murder, or other secular offense, and who went on to purgation, did so successfully.").

40. DALZELL, *supra* note 22, at 11.

41. *See* Spector, *supra* note 36, at 515.

42. DALZELL, *supra* note 22, at 13.

43. *Id.* at 12 ("From the tie of the first Plantagenet the toleration of a class of privileged criminals was persistently assailed as iniquitous."). *See also* LEA, *supra* note 24, at 186–91.

44. *See* Spector, *supra* note 36, at 515 n. 22 (noting that in 1350, the privilege was statutorily extended to "all manner of clerks, as well secular as religious."). This statute was intended to extend the privilege to "inferior Orders" of the clergy rather than to laypersons. *Id.* Judges nonetheless interpreted "secular clerks" to include all literate males. *Id.* at 515.

45. Frank Riebli, Note, *The Spectre of Star Chamber: The Role of an Ancient English Tribunal in the Supreme Court's Self-Incrimination Jurisprudence*, 29 HASTINGS CONST. L.Q. 807, 826 (2002).

46. 1 WILLIAM S. HOLDSWORTH, A HISTORY OF ENGLISH LAW 608 (A.L. Goodhart & H.G. Hanbury eds., 7th ed. 1956).

47. *Id.* at 605–08.

48. *Id.* at 24.

49. John H. Langbein, *Shaping the Eighteenth Century Criminal Trial: A View from the Ryder Sources*, 50 U. CHI. L. REV. 1, 40, 45 (1983).

50. *See* DALZELL, *supra* note 22, at 24 (discussing 18 Eliz., ch. 7, §§ 2–3 (1576)).

51. Langbein, *supra* note 49, at 38 n. 147 (1983) (citing 18 Eliz., ch. 7, §§ 23 (1576)), *discussed in* WILLIAM BLACKSTONE, 4 COMMENTARIES ON THE LAWS OF ENGLAND 368 (Sir George Tucker, ed., 1803); J. F. STEPHEN, *infra* note 82, at 462.

52. *See* Spector, *supra* note 36, at 516.

53. BLACKSTONE, *supra* note 51, at 368–69.

54. *Id.* at 36.

55. DALZELL, *supra* note 22, at 49.

56. E. MORGAN, ROGER WILLIAMS: THE CHURCH AND THE STATE 67 (1967). Because there were no high officials of the Anglican church in the New World, there were no ecclesiastical courts. Matters still subject to ecclesiastical jurisdiction in England – marriage, divorce, probate – became purely civil matters in the colonies. *Id.*

57. Langbein, *supra* note 49, at 38.

58. *See, e.g.*, Craigdallie v. Aikman, 1 Dow 1, 3 Eng. Rep. 601 (1813); The Reverend G. H. Forbes, of the Scotch Episcopal Church v. The Right Reverend Bishop Eden, Primus of the Scotch Episcopal Church, L.R. 1 Sc&Div 568 (1867).

59. *See, e.g.*, Craigdallie, The Reverend G. H. Forbes, 1 Dow 1, 3 Eng. Rep. 601 (1813).

60. Marci A. Hamilton, *The "Licentiousness" in Religious Organizations and Why It Is Not Protected Under Religious Liberty Constitutional Provisions*, *supra* note 9 at 972 (2010).

61. *See* Canon & Jaros, *supra* note 6, at 971–72. Charitable organizations are those that serve the public, not just their members. *See* Tremper, *infra* note 62, at 408–09.

62. *See* Charles Robert Tremper, *Compensation for Harm from Charitable Activity*, 76 CORNELL L. REV. 401, 401–02 (1991); Canon & Jaros, *supra* note 6, at 971.

63. RESTATEMENT (SECOND) OF TORTS § 895E (1979); *See also* McDonald v. Massachusetts, 120 Mass. 432, 434–35 (1876).

64. RESTATEMENT (SECOND) OF TORTS § 895E (1979).

65. *See* Benjamin S. Birnbaum, Comment, Cashman v. Merident Hosp., 169 Atl. 915 (Conn.), 14 B.U. L. REV. 477, 478 (1934).

66. Canon & Jaros, *supra* note 6, at 971.

67. The Feoffees of Heriot's Hosp. v. Ross, 12Clark & Fin. 507, 8 Eng. Rep. (1508).

68. *Id. See also* Mersey Docks Trustees v. Gibbs, L.R. 1 H.L. 93 (1866); Foreman v. Mayor of Canterbury, L.R. 6 Q.B. 214 (1871).

69. Hillyer v. St. Bartholomew's Hosp., (1909) 2 K.B. 820.

70. 67. 120 Mass. 432, 21 Am. Rep. 529 (1876), *overruled in part by* Colby v. Carney Hospital, 254 N.E.2d 407, 408 (Mass. 1969) stating:

> In the past on many occasions we have declined to renounce the defence of charitable immunity set forth in McDonald v. Massachusetts Gen. Hosp., 120 Mass. 432. Now it appears that only three or four States still adhere to the doctrine.... Accordingly, we take this occasion to give adequate warning that the next time we are squarely confronted by a legal question respecting the charitable immunity doctrine it is our intention to abolish it.

71. Canon & Jaros, *supra* note 6, at 971.

72. Tremper, *supra* note 63, at n. 107 (describing rejected theories behind charitable immunity).

73. 130F.2d 810, 815 (D.C. Cir. 1942).

74. NONPROFIT RISK MANAGEMENT CENTER, STATE LIABILITY LAWS FOR CHARITABLE ORGANIZATIONS AND VOLUNTEERS 8 (2010), *available at* http://www.nonprofitrisk.org/downloads/state-liability.pdf (last viewed Feb. 13, 2014).

75. In 1997, Congress enacted the Volunteer Protection Act, 42 U.S.C. § 14501 et. seq., which immunizes volunteers from tort liability in certain, limited circumstances. The majority of state statutes follow this approach, with the VPA preempting those state laws that protect volunteers more narrowly. 42 U.S.C. § 14502. Rep. Inglis (S.C.), one of the bill sponsors, stated on the floor of the House of Representatives that:

> [T]here are 124 separate charitable organizations that support this legislation very strongly. They range from the American Association of University Women to the American Heart Association, to the American Red Cross, to the American Symphony Orchestra League, to B'nai Brith International, the Girl Scout Council USA, the National Association of Retired Federal Employees, the National Easter Seal Society, the Salvation Army, Save the Children, United Way, the YMCA. Any national organization that one can think of probably is a strong supporter of this legislation.

105 CONG. REC. H.R. 911, H3097 (daily ed. May 21, 1997) (statement of Rep. Inglis), *available at* http://thomas.loc.gov (last viewed Mar. 8, 2004).

76. HOLDSWORTH, *supra* note 46, at 584 ("As the state grew into conscious life it was inevitable that occasions for disputes between the temporal and spiritual powers should arise.").

77. *Id.* (noting that, "from that time on, the professional jealousy of the common lawyers led them to restrict the jurisdiction of the ecclesiastical courts whenever it was possible to restrict it.").

78. *Id.* at 587.

79. THEODORE F.T. PLUCKNETT, A CONCISE HISTORY OF THE COMMON LAW 41 (1929).

80. *Id.* (noting that, by the time Edward VI (1547–1553), the Reformation was used as a political weapon against Rome, and after the brief reign of Catholic Mary (1554–1558), Elizabeth made the Reformation "the permanent basis of English political and religious life.")

81. R. H. HELMHOLZ, CANON LAW AND THE LAW OF ENGLAND 320–21 (1997); *See also id.* at 316–17 (ecclesiastical jurisdiction over testamentary debt and probate began a slow decline in the mid-16th century; R. H. HELMHOLZ, IN SELECT CASES ON DEFAMATION TO 1600 xxxvii–xli (Selden Soc'y No. 101, 1985) (royal courts began to prohibit the church courts from hearing defamation cases involving secular crimes and began to hear such cases on their own in the 16th century); Edward P. Steegmann, Note, *Of History and Due Process*, 63 IND. L.J. 369, 397 (1988) (citing J. F. STEPHEN, 2 A HISTORY OF THE CRIMINAL LAW OF ENGLAND, ch. 25) (London 1883) (sodomy made a secular offense by statute in 1533)); Jeremy D. Weinstein, Note, *Adultery, Law, and the State: A History*, 31 HASTINGS L.J. 195, 225 (1986) (citing W. BLACKSTONE, 4 COMMENTARIES 64–65) (Puritans of the Commonwealth made adultery a capital offense in 1650, although this was nullified in 1660 with the Restoration). Conversely, the Church retained jurisdiction over other matters well beyond the Reformation. *See, e.g.*, R. H. HELMHOLZ, MARRIAGE LITIGATION IN MEDIEVAL ENGLAND 3 (1974) (jurisdiction over marriage and marital disputes not withdrawn from the Church until 1857); R. H. HELMHOLZ, CANON LAW AND THE LAW OF ENGLAND 210 (1997) (jurisdiction over bastardy litigation not withdrawn until the nineteenth century).

82. In 1576, the ecclesiastical courts were relieved of their jurisdiction over clergy who committed crimes. DALZELL, *supra* note 22, at 24 (discussing 18 Eliz., ch. 7, §§ 2–3 (1576)). In 1641, the Puritan-dominated Long Parliament abolished all criminal jurisdiction of the ecclesiastical courts. *See* HOLDSWORTH, *supra* note 46, at 611.

83. *See* BERMAN, LAW AND REVOLUTION, *supra* note 1, at 268.

84. *Id.* at 266–67.

85. *See* PLUCKNETT, *supra* note 80, at 43–44, 46; *see generally* R. H. HELMHOLZ, *Canon Law and the English Common Law*, in CANON LAW AND THE LAW OF ENGLAND 2 (discussing approaches to the relationship between the two systems during the rise of the common law).

86. *See* HOLDSWORTH, *supra* note 46, at 588 ("The wealth and corruption of the church, and more particularly the abuses of the ecclesiastical courts, were exciting extreme unpopularity."); FRANK LAMBERT, THE FOUNDING FATHERS AND THE PLACE OF RELIGION IN AMERICA 34–35 (2003) ("Whether or not the Church . . . was in as deplorable condition as its critics made out is beside the point; the fact is, widespread opinion that it was corrupt constituted the greater reality that shaped events."); WILL DURANT, THE REFORMATION: A HISTORY OF EUROPEAN CIVILIZATION FROM WYCLIF TO CALVIN, 1300–1564, 1584 (1957) (hereinafter DURANT, THE REFORMATION) (referring to "the collapse of the spiritual and moral authority of the priesthood.").

87. Of the Reformers, John Calvin in particular addressed the faults of the 16th-century Catholic Church as a problem in the structure of the church, with his primary concern being the lack of accountability of the clergy to the members or the higher good. It was his view that the Church had deviated from the ancient church's structures of accountability. *See, e.g.*, II JOHN CALVIN, INSTITUTES OF THE CHRISTIAN RELIGION, bk. IV, ch. IV, §§ 1–2, at 1068–70 (describing ancient practice of electing bishops and their accountability to "the assembly of his brethren"); *id.* at bk. IV, ch. VII, § 21, at 1141 (criticizing contemporary pope for ruling in a "tyrannical fashion" and considering "his own whim as law. . . . [I]t is utterly abhorrent not only to a sense of piety but also of humanity.").

88. *See* CHEYNEY, *infra* note 113, at 383–84.

89. "The Act of [26 Henry VIII. C.I.] recognized the king as 'the only Supreme Head in earth of the church of England,' having full power to correct all 'errors, heresies, abuses, offences, contempts, and enormities,' which by any manner of spiritual authority ought to be reformed; and the form of oath taken under the provisions of this Act denied to the Pope any other authority than that of Bishop of Rome." HOLDSWORTH, *supra* note 46, at 591–92 (citing Report of Ecclesiastical Commission 1883, 72). The ecclesiastical authorities lost all power save that granted by the King, and ecclesiastical judges need no longer needed to be clerics, a move that displaced Rome's canon law. *Id.* at 592.

90. Leonard W. Levy, Origins of the Fifth Amendment 69 (1986).

91. Riebli, *supra* note 45, at 826 (quoting LEVY, *supra* note 91).

92. *See* DURANT, THE REFORMATION, *supra* note 87, at 579 (Somerset "favored a Protestant policy"); *Id.* at 581, 585 (noting that in 1550, under Warwick (who was made duke of Northumberland in 1551), "the protectorate was now definitely Protestant."); *Id.* at 585 ("Religious persecution, so long of heretics by Catholics, was now in England, as in Switzerland and Lutheran Germany, of heretics and Catholics by Protestants.").

93. Although "numerically a minority," the Protestants were "financially powerful," and nearly every influential family held property taken from the Catholic Church. *See* DURANT, THE REFORMATION, *supra* note 87, at 590; *id.* at 588 (London, however, was a "half-Protestant city").

94. *See id.* at 595 ("To her simple faith these heresies seemed mortal crimes, far worse than treason.").

95. *Id.* at 598 ("[Cranmer's] death marked the zenith of the persecution. Some 300 persons died in its course, 273 of them in the last four years of her reign.").

96. Robert E. Rodes, Jr., Law and Modernization in the Church of England: Charles II to the Welfare State 81 (1991).

97. Holdsworth writes:

> The Act of Supremacy (26 Henry VIII. C.I.) recognized the king as 'the only Supreme Head in earth of the church of England,' having full power to correct all 'errors, heresies, abuses, offences, contempts, and enormities,' which by any manner of spiritual authority ought to be reformed; and the form of oath taken under the provisions of this Act denied to the Pope any other authority than that of Bishop of Rome.

HOLDSWORTH, *supra* note 46, at 591–92 (citing Report of Ecclesiastical Commission 1883, 72).

98. RODES, JR., *supra* note 97, at 81.

99. 7 THE CAMBRIDGE MODERN HISTORY 13 (W. Ward, et al. eds., 1934).

100. Riebli, *supra* note 45, at 826.

101. *See* BERMAN, LAW AND REVOLUTION II, *infra* note 111, at 104, and accompanying text.

102. HOLDSWORTH, *supra* note 46, at 597.

103. *Id.* at 611; BERMAN, LAW AND REVOLUTION, *supra* note 1, at 113.

104. 2 THE CAMBRIDGE MODERN HISTORY 532–33 (W. Ward, et al. eds., 1934).

105. CHEYNEY, *infra* note 113, at 325; DURANT, THE REFORMATION, *supra* note 87, at 598. The official website of the British monarchy places the figure at 300 executed in three years. *See Mary I*, THE OFFICIAL WEBSITE OF THE BRITISH MONARCHY, http://www.royal.gov.uk/HistoryoftheMonarchy/Kingsand QueensofEngland/TheTudors/MaryI.aspx (last visited Feb. 6, 2014).

106. 2 THE CAMBRIDGE MODERN HISTORY 586 (W. Ward, et al. eds., 1934).

107. *See* John Coffey, Persecution and Toleration in Protestant England: 1558–1689 169–70 (2000).

108. *See* RUSSELL CHAMBERLIN, THE TOWER OF LONDON 68–71 (1989).

109. *See id.* at 78.

110. *See* Harold J. Berman, Law and Revolution II: The Impact of the Protestant Reformations on the Western Legal Tradition 209–10, 215–16 (2003) (hereinafter BERMAN, LAW AND REVOLUTION II). Between 1630 and 1640, an estimated 20,000 religious dissenters fled to the Massachusetts Bay Colony, and a similar number emigrated to the Netherlands. *Id.* at 216.

111. *See infra* note 132.

112. LAMBERT, *supra* note 87, at 38–39. Early attempts at colonization were unsuccessful – settlements founded in Virginia between 1585 and 1587, and again in 1602, were either abandoned or destroyed. *See* Edward P. Cheyney, A SHORT HISTORY OF ENGLAND 354–55 (1919). Jamestown, founded in 1607 in Virginia, was the first permanent English settlement in America. *Id.* at 403.

113. HOLDSWORTH, *supra* note 46, at 611.

114. James Madison, *Memorial and Remonstrance, in* 8 THE PAPERS OF JAMES MADISON, at 301–02 (William T. Hutchinson, et al. eds., 1962).

115. *See generally* CHRISTIAN PERSPECTIVES, *infra* note 152 (discussing the paradox of hope and distrust at the base of constitutional vision).

116. THE SELECTED WRITINGS OF JOHN WITHERSPOON: LANDMARKS IN RHETORIC AND PUBLIC ADDRESS 135–36 (Thomas Miller ed., 1990). Witherspoon, whose stamp on the Constitution is visible, was also mentor to a number of other Framers. *See generally* MARCI A. HAMILTON, WHY THE PEOPLE DO NOT RULE (unpublished manuscript, on file with the author).

117. WILL DURANT, THE AGE OF FAITH: A HISTORY OF MEDIEVAL CIVILIZATION -CHRISTIAN, ISLAMIC, AND JUDAIC – FROM CONSTANTINE TO DANTE: A.D. 325–1300 779 (1950) (hereinafter DURANT, THE AGE OF FAITH).

118. *See* WADE ROWLAND, GALILEO'S MISTAKE: A NEW LOOK AT THE EPIC CONFRONTATION BETWEEN GALILEO AND THE CHURCH (2003).

119. *See* DURANT, THE AGE OF FAITH, *supra* note 118, at 782.

120. *Id.* at 208–09 (1957).

121. 2 THE CAMBRIDGE MODERN HISTORY 650 (W. Ward, et al. eds., 1934).

122. *See* DURANT, THE AGE OF FAITH, *supra* note 118, at 209.

123. *See* JOHN EDWARD LONGHURST, THE AGE OF TORQUEMADA 85 (1964), *available at* http://libro.uca.edu/torquemada/torquemada.htm (last visited Apr. 25, 2004).

124. *See* CHARLES H. LEA, 4 A HISTORY OF THE INQUISITION OF SPAIN 467–68 (1907) (Spanish Inquisition ended in 1834); 7 THE CAMBRIDGE MODERN HISTORY 208–09 (W. Ward, et al. eds., 1934) (Declaration of Independence signed in 1776).

125. *See* RODES, JR., *supra* note 97, at 87. The original Act of Uniformity, passed by the Elizabeth's Parliament in 1571, required that all Church of England prayers, services, and rites conform to the Book of Common Prayer. *See* LAMBERT, *supra* note 87, at 40.

126. RODES, JR., *supra* note 97, at 88–89, 93,147.

127. Carl H. Esbeck, Symposium, *The Church-State Settlement in the Early American Republic*, 2004 B.Y.U. L. REV. 1385 (2004).

128. *See* Marci A. Hamilton, *Religion, the Rule of Law, and the Good of the Whole: A View from the Clergy*, 18 J.L. & POL. 387, 394, n.22 (2002) (hereinafter Hamilton, *Religion, the Rule of Law, and the Good of the Whole*); *See also* ALICE M. BALDWIN, THE NEW ENGLAND CLERGY AND THE AMERICAN REVOLUTION 22–31 (2d ed. 1965) (detailing the social impact of the works of New England clergy before 1763); FRANCIS J. BREMER, SHAPING NEW ENGLAND: PURITAN CLERGYMEN IN SEVENTEENTH CENTURY ENGLAND AND NEW ENGLAND 82–88 (1994) (noting the influence of the clergy on education and government in 17th-century New England); BERNARD BAILYN, THE IDEOLOGICAL ORIGINS OF THE AMERICAN REVOLUTION 246–50 (1967) (discussing the predominant religions in the colonies before the Revolutionary War); GORDON S. WOOD, THE AMERICAN REVOLUTION: A HISTORY 129–35 (2002) (detailing impact of Protestant ministers at the forefront of the Revolutionary movement); James T. McHugh, *A Liberal Theocracy: Philosophy,*

Theology, and Utah Constitutional Law, 60 ALB. L. REV. 1515, 1520 n. 16 (1997) (citing ALICE M. BALDWIN, THE NEW ENGLAND CLERGY AND THE AMERICAN REVOLUTION 22–31 (2d ed. 1965) which details the social impact of the works of New England clergy before 1763)).

129. The Reformation was instituted by Martin Luther and John Calvin, because they believed that the Roman Catholic Church had turned away from all that is holy and become infested with evil. II JOHN CALVIN, INSTITUTES OF THE CHRISTIAN RELIGION, bk. IV, §§ 21–30, at 1141, 1144, 1147 (referring to "corruption of the present-day-papacy"; "kingdom of Antichrist"; "moral abandonment of the popes"). They were Church insiders, who initially acted in order to reform the Church itself, but the Church proved incapable of sufficiently rapid change to avoid having many of its members leave the Church to follow Luther, Calvin, or other reformation leaders, into new churches. The instinct to schism, in response to the perceptions of corruption, has never left the Protestant movement, which has resulted in the thousands of modern-day sects that continue to divide. *See generally* STEVE BRUCE, A HOUSE DIVIDED: PROTESTANTISM, SCHISM, AND SECULARIZATION (1990).

130. I CALVIN: INSTITUTES OF THE CHRISTIAN RELIGION, bk. II, ch. V, § 19, at 340 (John T. McNeill ed., 1975).

131. Calvin wrote that the "principal use" of the law was to help believers know the will of God and to incite them to obedience:

[The law] is the best instrument for enabling them daily to learn with greater truth and certainty what the will of the Lord is. . . . Then, because we need not doctrine merely, but exhortation also, the servant of God will derive this further advantage of from the Law: by frequently meditating upon it, he will be excited to obedience, and confirmed in it, and so drawn away form the slippery paths of sin.

I CALVIN: INSTITUTES OF THE CHRISTIAN RELIGION, bk. II, ch. VII, § 12 at 360–61 ("Even the believers have need of the law."). The depravity of humans, however, never made obedience to the law alone sufficient to ensure redemption. *Id.* at § 3, 351–52.

132. REV. WILLIAM RALPH INGE, PROTESTANTISM 3–5 (1927). *See also* 1 EMILE G. LEONARD, A HISTORY OF PROTESTANTISM: THE REFORMATION 316 (H. H. Rowley ed., Joyce M. H. Reid trans., 1965) (noting that Farel agreed with Luther in condemning institutionalism, saying "sects, organizations and institutions are born of the flesh"); 1 REV. J. A. WYLIE, THE HISTORY OF PROTESTANTISM 2 (London, Cassell, Petter & Galpin) ("[Protestants] replaced the authority of the Infallibility with the authority of the Word of God. The long and dismal obscuration of centuries they dispelled, that the twin stars of liberty and knowledge might shine forth . . . and human society . . . might, after its halt of a thousand years, resume its march towards a higher goal").

133. *See* DURANT, THE REFORMATION, *supra* note 87, at 329–33. On the eve of the Reformation in Germany, the Catholic Church was rife with abuses: there had been a breakdown of monastic discipline and clerical celibacy, greedy ecclesiastical authorities increased clerical rents, incomes, and taxes; the higher ecclesiastical

orders brazenly displayed their wealth, to the chagrin of the people; "mercenary abuse of sacred things" was common; and hush money was often sent to Rome.

134. *See* CHARLES P. HANSON, NECESSARY VIRTUE: THE PRAGMATIC ORIGINS OF RELIGIOUS LIBERTY IN NEW ENGLAND 11 (1998); *see generally* PHILIP HAMBURGER, THE SEPARATION OF CHURCH AND STATE (2003).

135. II John Calvin, Institutes of the Christian Religion, *supra* note 88, at bk. IV, ch. 7, § 19.

136. Leonard J. Kramer, *Presbyterians Approach the American Revolution*, 31 J. PRESBYTERIAN HIST. SOC. 71, 72 (1953) (quoting minutes of the Synod of New England, 1776–82).

137. *See, e.g.*, Richard A. Epstein, *The Harm Principle – And How It Grew*, 45 U. TORONTO L.J. 369, 370–71 (1995).

138. *See* M.N.S. SELLERS, AMERICAN REPUBLICANISM 133–41 (1994); M.N.S. SELLERS, THE SACRED FIRE OF LIBERTY 101–02 (1998).

139. JOHN STUART MILL, ON LIBERTY 87 (David Spitz ed., 1975).

140. *Id* at 11,18.

141. *See generally* H. L. A. HART, LAW, LIBERTY, AND MORALITY (1962); RICHARD A. EPSTEIN, PRINCIPLES FOR A FREE SOCIETY: RECONCILING INDIVIDUAL LIBERTY WITH THE COMMON GOOD (1998). Hart believed that "[r]ecognition of individual liberty as a value involves, as a minimum, acceptance of the principle that the individual may do what he wants, even if others are distressed when they learn what it is that he does – unless, of course, there are other good grounds for forbidding it." *Id.*

142. *See generally* JOEL FEINBERG, THE EXPRESSIVE FUNCTION OF PUNISHMENT, IN DOING AND DESERVING (1970); Joel Feinberg, THE MORAL LIMITS OF CRIMINAL LAW 214 (1988).

143. *See* Angela C. Carmella, *The Protection of Children and Young People: Catholic and Constitutional Visions of Responsible Freedom*, 44 B.C. L. REV. 1031, 1044 (2003) ("There is one condition attached to all exercises of freedom: that the use of the freedom will not breach minimal responsibilities owed to the larger society as those responsibilities are embodied in legitimate laws.").

144. Thomas Jefferson, *Notes on the State of Virginia* (1787), *in* 2 THE WRITINGS OF THOMAS JEFFERSON, at 221 (Albert Ellery Bergh ed., 1905).

145. Thomas Jefferson, *An Act for Establishing Religious Freedom, Passed in the Assembly of Virginia in the Beginning of the Year 1786, in* 2 THE WRITINGS OF THOMAS JEFFERSON, *supra* note 145, at 312. On the absolute right to believe, *see also* Letter to Benjamin Rush, *infra* note 155, at 381 (referring to "the common right of independent opinion, by answering questions of faith, which the laws have left between god and himself").

146. Letter from Thomas Jefferson to James Madison (July 31, 1788), *in* THE PAPERS OF THOMAS JEFFERSON (Julian P. Boyd, et al. eds., 1950).

147. ADRIENNE KOCH, MADISON'S "ADVICE TO MY COUNTRY" 15 (1966) (quoting James Madison).

148. Letter from James Madison to William Bradford (Apr. 1, 1774), *in* 1 THE PAPERS OF JAMES MADISON, at 112–13 (William T. Hutchinson, et al. eds., 1962).

149. Letter from James Madison to William Bradford (Jan. 24, 1774), *in* 1 THE PAPERS OF JAMES MADISON, *supra* note 149, at 112–13, 106.

150. *See, e.g.*, JAMES MADISON, *Memorial and Remonstrance, in* 8 THE PAPERS OF JAMES MADISON, *supra* note 149, at 301–02 ("Because experience witnesseth that ecclesiastical establishments, instead of maintaining the purity and efficacy of Religion, have had a contrary operation. During almost fifteen centuries has the legal establishment of Christianity been on trial. What have been its fruits? More or less in all places, pride and indolence in the Clergy, ignorance and servility in the laity, in both, superstition, bigotry and persecution"); Jefferson, *supra* note 146, at 221–22 ("Had not the Roman government permitted free enquiry, Christianity could never have been introduced. Had not free enquiry been indulged, at the aera of the reformation, the corruptions of Christianity could not have been purged away. If it be restrained now, the present corruptions will be protected, and new ones encouraged.").

151. *See generally* Marci A. Hamilton, *The Calvinist Paradox of Distrust and Hope at the Constitutional Convention, in* CHRISTIAN PERSPECTIVES ON LEGAL THOUGHT (Michael. W. McConnell et al. eds., 2001) (hereinafter CHRISTIAN PERSPECTIVES).

152. KERRY S. WALTERS, THE AMERICAN DEISTS: VOICES OF REASON AND DISSENT IN THE EARLY REPUBLIC 106–40 (1992). Jefferson, of course, was not solitary in his beliefs. Deists dominated the colleges during the latter 18th century. *Id.*

153. *See* FAWN M. BRODIE, THOMAS JEFFERSON: AN INTIMATE HISTORY 372 (1974).

154. Letter from Thomas Jefferson to Benjamin Rush, (Apr. 21, 1803), *in* 10 THE WRITINGS OF THOMAS JEFFERSON, 380 (Albert Ellery Bergh, ed., 1905).

155. *See generally* HAMBURGER, SEPARATION OF CHURCH AND STATE, *supra* note 135.

156. *See* R. H. HELMHOLZ, THE SPIRIT OF THE CLASSICAL CANON LAW 316–21 (1996); 1 WILLIAM S. HOLDSWORTH, A HISTORY OF ENGLISH LAW 588 (A.L. Goodhart & H.G. Hanbury eds., 7th ed. 1956); WILL DURANT, THE REFORMATION: A HISTORY OF EUROPEAN CIVILIZATION FROM WYCLIF TO CALVIN 1300–1564, at 584 (1957).

157. The Reformation was instituted by Martin Luther and John Calvin because they believed that the Roman Catholic Church had turned away from all that is holy and become infested with evil. *See, e.g.*, 2 JOHN CALVIN, INSTITUTES OF THE CHRISTIAN RELIGION, bk. IV, ch. IV, 1–2, at 1141, 1144, 1147 (referring to "corruption of the present-day papacy"; "kingdom of Antichrist"; and "moral abandonment of the popes"). They were Church insiders who initially acted in order to reform the Church itself, but the Church proved incapable of sufficiently rapid change to avoid having many of its members leave the Church to follow Luther, Calvin, or other reformation leaders into new churches. The instinct to schism, in response to the perceptions of corruption, has never left the Protestant movement, resulting in the thousands of modern-day sects that continue to divide. *See generally* STEVE BRUCE, A HOUSE DIVIDED: PROTESTANTISM, SCHISM, AND SECULARIZATION (1990).

158. Hamilton, *supra* note 152.

159. Frederick Nymeyer, *A Great Netherlander Who Had One Answer to the Problem of 'Liberty' Destroying Liberty, Namely Sphere Sovereignty*, in PROGRESSIVE CALVINISM (Feb. 1956).

160. David H. McIlroy, *Subsidiarity and Sphere Sovereignty: Christian Reflections on the Size, Shape and Scope of Government*, 45 J. CHURCH & STATE 739, 759 (2003).

161. *Id.* at 754–55.

162. Abraham Kuyper, *Sphere Sovereignty*, New Church Speech, October 20, 1880 (cited in McIlroy, *supra* note 161, at 755).

163. *Id.*; ABRAHAM KUYPER, LECTURES ON CALVINISM 124–25 (William B. Eerdmans ed., 1987) (1898–99), *available at* http://www.kuyper.org/stone/lecture4.html (last visited May 28, 2004).

164. McIlroy, *supra* note 161, at 757–59; *see also* JOHAN D. VAN DER VYVER, SPHERE SOVEREIGNTY OF RELIGIOUS INSTITUTIONS: A CONTEMPORARY CALVINISTIC THEORY OF CHURCH-STATE RELATIONS, at 24 (1999), *available at* http://www.uni-trier.de/~ievr/konferenz/papers/vanvyver.pdf (last visited Mar. 8, 2004) ("Persons engaged in government [have] the right and an obligation to scrutinize the conduct of their subjects.... Unbecoming conduct should not escape the power of the sword simply because it was committed in the name of religion.").

165. *See* Johan D. van der Vyver, Review, *Culture and Equality: An Egalitarian Critique of Multiculturalism: By Brian Barry*, 17 CONN. J. INT'L L. 323, 329 (2002).

166. *See generally* Hamilton, *Religion, the Rule of Law, and the Good of the Whole*, *supra* note 129.

167. Cass R. Sunstein, *American Advice and New Constitutions*, 1 CHI. J. INT'L L. 173, 178 (2000) (noting that while we cannot overestimate the significance of the constitutional text, we also cannot underestimate the "need for a culture that is committed, first to the rule of law and constitutional limitations"); Guillermo Garcia-Montufar & Elvira Martinez Coco *Antecedents, Perspectives, and Projections of a Legal Project about Religious Liberty in Peru*, 1999 B.Y.U. L. REV. 503; *Central Eastern European Law Initiative*, AMERICAN BAR ASSOC., http://www.abanet.org/ceeli/home.html (last visited June 10, 2004) (ABA/CEELI "advances the rule of law in the world by supporting the legal reform process in Central and Eastern Europe and the New Independent States of the former Soviet Union").

168. To be sure, many of the sermons used in this chapter were delivered by Calvinists, who would have a predisposition to the virtues of the rule of law. These views, however, were not exclusive to Calvinists, and appealed to Calvinists of all sorts, including Congregationalists, Anglicans, and Presbyterians, as well as the many Baptists influenced by Calvinist perspectives. *See, e.g.*, GREGORY A. WILLS, DEMOCRATIC RELIGION: FREEDOM, AUTHORITY, AND CHURCH DISCIPLINE IN THE BAPTIST SOUTH, 1785–1900 103 (1997); *see also* ROBERT BAYLOR SEMPLE, THE HISTORY OF THE BAPTISTS OF VIRGINIA 60 (1810).

169. Unless otherwise indicated, sermons are drawn from Ellis Sandoz's extremely useful collection, POLITICAL SERMONS OF THE AMERICAN FOUNDING ERA, 1730–1805 (Ellis Sandoz ed., 1991) (hereinafter POLITICAL SERMONS). *Id.*

at 334–35 (Isaac Backus 1773) ("God has appointed two kinds of government in the world, which are distinct in their nature, and ought never to be confounded together; one of which is called civil, the other ecclesiastical government."). *See also* HAMBURGER, SEPARATION OF CHURCH AND STATES *supra* note 135, at 21 (stating that Christians "often took for granted that church and state were distinct institutions, with different jurisdictions and powers").

170. POLITICAL SERMONS, *supra* note 170, at 80 (Elisha Williams 1774); *See also id.* at 81–82 (urging obedience to laws involving "those things which are the objects of the civil magistrate's power, *viz.* the civil interests of the people" but not on "matters of religion").

171. *Id.* at 58; *see also id.* at 337 (Isaac Backus 1773) ("the state is armed with the sword to guard the peace, and the civil rights of all persons and societies, and to punish those who violate the same"); Jonas Clarke, A Sermon 29 (1781), *cited in* Phillip A. Hamburger, A *Constitutional Right of Religious Exemption: An Historical Perspective*, 60 GEO. WASH. L. REV. 915, at 943 n. 112 (1992) ("[A]s by the social compact, the whole is engaged for the protection and defense of the life, liberty and property of each individual").

172. POLITICAL SERMONS, *supra* note 170, at 147–48 (Charles Chauncey 1747).

173. HARRY S. STOUT, THE NEW ENGLAND SOUL: PREACHING AND RELIGIOUS CULTURE IN COLONIAL NEW ENGLAND 273 (1986).

174. POLITICAL SERMONS, *supra* note 170, at 72, 67.

175. *Id.* at 58; *see also id.* at 1064 (Israel Evans 1791) ("*We the people* are the source of all legislative authority.").

176. Gersham C. Lyman, A Sermon 12, 19 (1784), *cited in* Hamburger, *Constitutional Right of Religious Exemption*, *supra* note 172, at 942 n. 112 ("It is a most inconsistent and distracted piece of conduct, to set up rulers, and then disobey their just & needful laws.").

177. A *Declaration of Certain Fundamental Rights and Liberties of the Protestant Episcopal Church of Maryland*, *in* 1 ANSON P. STOKES, CHURCH AND STATE IN THE UNITED STATES 741 (1950), *cited in* Hamburger, *Constitutional Right of Religious Exemption*, *supra* note 172, at 935 n. 84. *See also* NOAH HOBART, CIVIL GOVERNMENT THE FOUNDATION OF SOCIAL HAPPINESS 42 (1751), *cited in* Hamburger, *Constitutional Right of Religious Exemption*, *supra* note 172, at 942 n. 96 (stating that the government should not "inflict temporal Punishments" for ecclesiastical errors that "do not affect the Peace and Happiness of Civil Society").

178. POLITICAL SERMONS, *supra* note 170, at 337 (Isaac Backus 1773).

179. Samuel Stillman, A Sermon 20, 27–28 (Mass. Election sermon, 1779), *cited in* Hamburger, *Constitutional Right of Religious Exemption*, *supra* note 172, at 942 n. 111; *see also* THE CONSTITUTION OF THE PRESBYTERIAN CHURCH IN THE UNITED STATES OF AMERICA (adopted 1788).

180. THE CONSTITUTION OF THE REFORMED DUTCH CHURCH, IN THE UNITED STATES OF AMERICA 190 (1793), *cited in* Hamburger, A *Constitutional Right of Religious Exemption*, *supra* note 172, at 942 n. 111 (1992).

181. POLITICAL SERMONS, *supra* note 170, at 143 (Charles Chauncy 1747), *id.* at 335 (Isaac Backus 1773) ("God has appointed two kinds of government.").

182. *Id.* at 922 (Elizur Goodrich 1787); *see also* AARON HUTCHINSON, A WELL TEMPERED SELF-LOVE A RULE OF CONDUCT TOWARDS OTHERS 37–38 (1779) ("it is folly and stupidity for a man to plead conscience for breaking the moral law, which is a transcript of the moral perfections of God, and written upon the hearts of all by nature."); GORDON S. WOOD, THE CREATION OF THE AMERICAN REPUBLIC 1776–1787 69 (1969) (quoting Samuel Magaw, A Discourse Preached in Philadelphia (Oct. 8, 1775) ("[T]he practice of all the social virtues is the law of our nature, and the law of our nature is the law of God.").

183. James D. Gordon III, *The New Free Exercise Clause*, 26 CAP. U. L. REV. 65, 92 (1997); David E. Steinberg, *Rejecting the Case against the Free Exercise Exemption: A Critical Assessment*, 75 B.U. L. REV. 241 (1995); Michael W. McConnell, *The Origins and Historical Understanding of Free Exercise of Religion*, 103 HARV. L. REV. 1409, 1461–66 (1990); Douglas Laycock, *Formal, Substantive, and Disaggregated Neutrality toward Religion*, 39 DEPAUL L. REV. 993, 1002 (1990).

184. Olmstead v. United States, 277 U.S. 438,478 (1928) (Brandeis, J., dissenting) ("The makers of our Constitution . . . conferred, as against the Government, the right to be let alone – the most comprehensive of rights and the most valued by civilized men.").

185. STOUT, *supra* note 174, at 213.

186. POLITICAL SERMONS, *supra* note 170, at 914.

187. Thomas Paine, DISSERTATIONS ON GOVERNMENT, THE AFFAIRS OF THE BANK, AND PAPER MONEY 9 (1838).

188. WOOD, THE CREATION OF THE AMERICAN REPUBLIC, *supra* note 183, at 69, 61.

189. *Id.* at 60.

190. POLITICAL SERMONS, *supra* note 170, at 331–32.

191. Jonas Clarke, A Sermon 29 (Mass. election sermon 1781), *in* Hamburger, *Constitutional Right of Religious Exemption, supra* note 172, at 943 n. 112. *See also* WOOD, THE CREATION OF THE AMERICAN REPUBLIC, *supra* note 183, at 118 (referring to "common emphasis on the usefulness and goodness of devotion to the general welfare of the community"); AMERICAN STATE PAPERS 113 (Presbyterians stating that the "end of civil government is security to the temporal liberty and property of mankind . . . ").

192. Jonathan Edwards, *An Humble Attempt to Promote Explicit Agreement and Visible Union of God's People in Extraordinary* Prayer, Works, III, *reprinted in* A. Heimert, THE GREAT AWAKENING: DOCUMENTS ILLUSTRATING THE CRISIS AND ITS CONSEQUENCES 567 (1967). This view certainly did not die with the passing of the 18th century. *See, e.g.,* James W. Gordon, *Religion and the First Justice Harlan: A Case Study in Late Nineteenth-Century Presbyterian Constitutionalism,* 85 MARQ. L. REV. 317, 346, 369, 371 (2001) (discussing Justice Harlan's view of the role of the religious believer in aiming for the public good); SYDNEY AHLSTROM, A RELIGIOUS HISTORY OF THE AMERICAN PEOPLE 275–77 (1972), *cited in* Gordon, *supra,* at 366–67.

193. 7 THE WORKS OF JOHN WITHERSPOON 100 (1805).

194. POLITICAL SERMONS, *supra* note 170, at 334 (Isaac Backus 1773). The New York *Evening Post* echoed these views in 1747. *See* BAILYN, *supra* note 129, at 77 ("Liberty, that is, was the capacity to exercise 'natural rights' within limits set, not by the mere will or desire of men in power but by non-arbitrary law-law enacted by legislatures containing within them the proper balance of forces.").

195. POLITICAL SERMONS, *supra* note 170, at 1063 (Israel Evans 1791).

196. Moses Hemmenway, A Sermon 27, 30 (1784), *cited in* Hamburger, *Constitutional Right of Religious Exemption*, *supra* note 172, at 934 n. 84.

197. POLITICAL SERMONS, *supra* note 170, at 67 (Elisha Williams 1744); *id.* at 339 (Isaac Backus 1773) ("God always claimed it as his sole prerogative to determine by his own laws, what his worship shall be, who shall minister in it, and how they shall be supported, so it is evident that this prerogative has been, and still is, encroached upon in our land.").

198. POLITICAL SERMONS, *supra* note 170, at 1089.

199. THE WRITINGS OF THE LATE ELDER JOHN LELAND 228 (1845) (hereinafter LELAND WRITINGS). Thomas Jefferson made the same point in 1782, saying that "[t]he legitimate powers of government extend to such acts only as are injurious to others." THOMAS JEFFERSON, NOTES ON THE STATE OF VIRGINIA 152 (1964).

200. POLITICAL SERMONS, *supra* note 170, at 1089.

201. Caleb Blood, A Sermon (1792), *cited in* Hamburger, *Constitutional Right of Religious Exemption*, *supra* note 172, at 918 n. 15.

202. John Leland, *The Yankee Spy*, in LELAND WRITINGS, *supra* note 200, *cited in* Hamburger, *Constitutional Right of Religious Exemption*, *supra* note 172, at 942 n. 111.

203. HAMBURGER, SEPARATION OF CHURCH AND STATE, *supra* note 135, at 69 (*citing* William Balch, A Sermon (1749) "requiring Submission and Obedience to lawful Authority in the People, as well as Integrity and a public Spirit in Rulers"). Noah Webster extended the concept of subjugation to the law to clergy members as well. *Id.* at 88.

204. Samuel Stillman, *cited in* Hamburger, *Constitutional Right of Religious Exemption supra* note 172, at 942 n. 111. This reasoning appeared a century earlier in the works of Roger Williams, 3 THE COMPLETE WRITINGS OF ROGER WILLIAMS 127 (1963). These views also were explicitly embraced by the Supreme Court and especially Justice Harlan a century later. *See* Reynolds v. United States, 98 U.S. 145 (1878); Gordon, *supra* note 192, at 346.

205. ISAAC BACKUS, ISAAC BACKUS ON CHURCH, STATE, AND CALVINISM: PAMPHLETS, 1754–1789, app. 3, at 487 (W. McLoughlin, ed. 1968).

206. McConnell, *supra* note 184, at 1415 ("Constitutionally compelled exemptions were within the contemplation of the framers and ratifiers as a possible interpretation of the free exercise clause"); Michael W. McConnell, *The Problem of Singling out Religion*, 50 DEPAUL L. REV. 1 (2000); Michael W. McConnell, *Free Exercise Revisionism and the Smith Decision*, 57 U. CHI. L. REV. 1109 (1990); Douglas Laycock, *Towards a General Theory of the Religion Clauses: The Case of Church Labor Relations and the Right to Church Autonomy*, 81 COLUM. L. REV. 1373 (1981); *see also* Ira C. Lupu, *Reconstructing the Establishment Clause: The*

Case Against Discretionary Accommodation of Religion, 140 U. PA. L. REV. 555 (1991).

207. *See generally* Marci A. Hamilton, Symposium, *Religious Institutions, The No-Harm Doctrine, and the Public Good*, 2004 B.Y.U. L. REV. 1099 (2004); Frederick M. Gedicks, *An Unfirm Foundation: The Regrettable Indefensibility of Religious Exemptions*, 20 U. ARK. LITTLE ROCK L. J. 555, 574 (1998) ("[T]he historical moment for exemptions has come and gone. There no longer exist a plausible explanation of why religious believers – and only believers – are constitutionally entitled to be excused from complying with otherwise legitimate laws that burden practices."); William P. Marshall, *The Case against the Constitutionally Compelled Free Exercise Exemption*, 40 CASE W. RES. L. REV. 357 (1990); Hamburger, *A Constitutional Right of Religious Exemption, supra* note 172; Ellis West, *The Case against a Right to Religious-Based Exemptions*, 4 NOTRE DAME J. L. ETHICS & PUB. POL'Y 591, 624 (1989) (rejecting constitutionally compelled exemptions, but not legislative exemptions); *see also* Frederick Mark Gedicks, *Towards a Defensible Free Exercise Doctrine*, 68 GEO. WASH. L. REV. 925, 950–51 (2000) ("[I]n the long run, no effective defense is possible [for judicially mandated exemptions]. To the extent that a residuum of religious exemptions persists under state law,. . . I say enjoy them while they last.").

208. The Warren Court's distortion of the Free Exercise Clause from a principle of no harm to a virtually unfettered individual right was contrary to the intent of the First Amendment and fundamental common sense. *See, e.g.*, Sherbert v. Verner, 374 U.S. 398, 423 (1963) (Harlan, J., dissent) ("Those situations in which the Constitution may require special treatment on account of religion are, in my view, few and far between, and this view is amply supported by the course of constitutional litigation in this area").

209. *Boerne*, 521 U.S. at 539 (1997) (Scalia, J., concurring).

210. *Id.* (emphasis in original).

211. Queen v. Lane, 6 Mod. 128, 87 Eng. Rep. 884, 885 (Q. B. 1704).

212. *See* Marci A. Hamilton, *The "Licentiousness" in Religious Organizations and Why It Is Not Protected Under Religious Liberty Constitutional Provisions, supra* note 9, at 969–70 (2010), and notes accompanying text.

213. John Philip Reid, The Concept Of Liberty In The Age Of The American Revolution 35 (1988).

214. Bernard Bailyn, The Ideological Origins Of The American Revolution 76–77 (1992); *see also* David Jenkins, *The Sedition Act of 1798 and the Incorporation of Seditious Libel into First Amendment Jurisprudence*, 45 Am. J. Legal Hist. 154, 163–64 (2001).

215. *See* Zelman v. Simmons-Harris, 536 U.S. 369 (2002); Good News Club v. Milford, 533 U.S. 98 (2001).

10. The Path to the Public Good

1. 521 U.S. 507 (1997).

2. ARISTOTLE, ETHICA NICOMACHEA (W. D. Ross, trans.), *in* IX THE WORKS OF ARISTOTLE TRANSLATED INTO ENGLISH (W. D. Ross ed., 1925).

3. 406 U.S. 205 (1972).

4. *See generally* Marci A. Hamilton, *The Calvinist Paradox of Distrust and Hope at the Constitutional Convention, in* CHRISTIAN PERSPECTIVES ON LEGAL THOUGHT (Michael W. McConnell et al. eds., 2001) [hereinafter Hamilton, *Distrust and Hope*].

5. For example, the dual sovereignty of federalism was intended to divide power between the federal government and the states, with each checking the other. *See* THE FEDERALIST NO. 46 (James Madison) ("The federal and State governments are in fact but different agents and trustees of the people, constituted with different powers, and designed for different purposes."); *see id.* (noting that federal and state governments each possess a different "disposition and faculty" with which to "resist and frustrate the measures of the other"). Similarly, the three federal branches were assigned discrete powers and the power to check the other branches. *See* THE FEDERALIST NO. 47 (James Madison) ("[T]he preservation of liberty requires . . . that the three great departments of power should be separate and distinct."); THE FEDERALIST NO. 51 (James Madison) ("[T]he defect must be supplied, by so contriving the interior structure of the government, as that its several constituent parts may, by their mutual relations, be the means of keeping each other in their proper places.").

6. Articles of Confederation of 1781, art. II.

7. GORDON S. WOOD, THE CREATION OF THE AMERICAN REPUBLIC 1776–87, at 359 (1969) [hereinafter WOOD, THE CREATION].

8. *See* II THE RECORDS OF THE FEDERAL CONVENTION OF 1787, 288 (Max Farrand ed., 1966) [hereinafter II RECORDS] ("What led to the appointment of this convention? The corruption & mutability of the Legislative Councils of the States.") (Mercer); *id.* at 74 ("Experience in all the States had evidenced a powerful tendency in the Legislature to absorb all power into its vortex.") (Madison).

9. *See* Marci A. Hamilton, Symposium, *Direct Democracy and the Protestant Ethic*, 13 J. CONTEMP. LEGAL ISSUES 411, 418–22 (2004) [hereinafter Hamilton, *Direct Democracy*]; *see also* MARCI A. HAMILTON, WHY THE PEOPLE DO NOT RULE (Aug. 2004) (unpublished manuscript, on file with the author) [hereinafter HAMILTON, WHY THE PEOPLE DO NOT RULE].

10. *See* BERNARD BAILYN, THE IDEOLOGICAL ORIGINS OF THE AMERICAN REVOLUTION 57–60 (1967); WOOD, THE CREATION, *supra* note 7, at 135; *see also* Hamilton, *Direct Democracy*, *supra* note 9; *see generally* Hamilton, *Distrust and Hope*, *supra* note 4.

11. *See* M. N. S. SELLERS, THE SACRED FIRE OF LIBERTY: REPUBLICANISM, LIBERALISM AND THE LAW 39–40 (1998) [hereinafter SELLERS, SACRED FIRE] (discussing historical influences on the framing generation's choice of a republican form of representative government and concluding they chose it because "[t]his conception of liberty as subjection to equal laws made by common consent, for the general welfare, maintained the old republican connection between political rights and substantive freedom"); WOOD, THE CREATION, *supra* note 7, at 164 ("Only with the presence of the democracy in the Constitution [through

an elected legislature] could any government remain faithful to the public good."); HAMILTON, WHY THE PEOPLE DO NOT RULE, *supra* note 9 (discussing Calvin's influence on the Framers, and Calvin's notion that "[r]epresentatives were to be watched by the people and tethered to their common good, yet they bore the independent duty to make decisions serving the people on behalf of God").

12. *See* Donald S. Lutz, Symposium, *Religious Dimensions in the Development of American Constitutionalism*, 39 EMORY L.J. 21, 23–24 (1990).

13. *See generally* Hamilton, *Direct Democracy, supra* note 9; Hamilton, *Distrust and Hope, supra* note 4; *see also* HAMILTON, WHY THE PEOPLE DO NOT RULE, *supra* note 9.

14. U.S. CONST. amend. I.

15. U.S. CONST. amend. I ("Congress shall make no law respecting an establishment of religion, or prohibiting the free exercise thereof...."). *See generally* LEONARD W. LEVY, THE ESTABLISHMENT CLAUSE: RELIGION AND THE FIRST AMENDMENT (1983).

16. *See* James Madison, *Memorial and Remonstrance, in* 8 THE PAPERS OF JAMES MADISON 301–302 (Robert A. Rutland et al. eds., 1962).

17. BERNARD LEWIS, ISLAM AND THE WEST 186 (1993).

18. Jones v. Wolf, 443 U.S. 595, 602–03 (1979); *cf.* Emp't Div. v. Smith, 494 U.S. 872, 885 (1990).

19. Gillette v. United States, 401 U.S. 437, 461 (1971).

20. *See, e.g.,* Kathleen Brady, Symposium, *Religious Organizations and Free Exercise: The Surprising Lessons of Smith*, 2004 B.Y.U. L. REV. 1633 (2004); to a lesser extent, Ira C. Lupu & Robert W. Tuttle, Symposium, *Sexual Misconduct and Ecclesiastical Immunity*, 2004 B.Y.U. L. REV. 1789 (2004).

21. *See* Zelman v. Simmons-Harris, 536 U.S. 639 (2002); Good News Club v. Milford, 533 U.S. 98 (2001).

22. *Smith*, 494 U.S. at 890.

23. U.S. DRUG ENFORCEMENT ADMIN. & NAT'L GUARD, DRUGS OF ABUSE 34 (Carol Gibson ed., 1997).

24. *See* 42 U.S.C. § 1996a (2012); Ross E. Milloy, *Mirando City Journal; A Forbidding Landscape That's Eden for Peyote*, N.Y. TIMES, May 7, 2002, at A20. Peyote growers live in South Texas, and distribute to Native Americans across the country. *See* Edward F. Anderson, *The "Peyote Gardens" of South Texas: A Conservation Crisis?*, 67 CACTUS & SUCCULENT J. (1995), *available at* http://peyote.com/peyote/peyotegardens.html (last visited Mar. 2, 2014).

25. *See* National Prohibition Act of 1919, ch. 85, tit. II, § 3, 41 Stat. 305, 308–09 (1919).

26. Terrence A. Gerace, *The Toxic-Tobacco Law: "Appropriate Remedial Action,"* 20 J. PUB. HEALTH L. 394, 400 (1999).

27. The Military Selective Service Act provides: "Nothing contained in this title shall be construed to require any person to be subject to combatant training and service in the armed forces of the United States who, by reason of religious

training and belief, is conscientiously opposed to participation in war in any form." 50 U.S.C. Appx. § 456(j) (2012).

28. *See* Russell, *Development of Conscientious Objector Recognition in the United States*, 20 Geo. Wash. L. Rev. 409, 412–14 (1952) (citing colonial laws exempting Quakers from compulsory service).

29. *See, e.g.*, Welsh v. United States, 398 U.S. 333, 342–44 (1970).

30. Hanna v. Sec'y of the Army, 513 F.3d 4 (1st Cir. 2008).

31. 50 U.S.C. Appx. § 456(j) (2012).

32. II Records, *supra* note 8, at 287–88.

33. I have written in more detail about this in Hamilton, Why the People Do Not Rule, *supra* note 9; Hamilton, *Direct Democracy*, *supra* note 9; Marci A. Hamilton, *Discussion and Decisions: A Proposal to Replace the Myth of Self-Rule with an Attorneyship Model of Representation*, 69 N.Y.U. L. Rev. 477 (1994) (hereinafter Hamilton, *Discussion and Decisions*).

34. Mortimer Sellers, *Republicanism, Liberalism, and the Law*, 86 Ky. L.J. 1, 3 (1997).

35. *See* Stephan Thernstrom & Abigail Thernstrom, America in Black and White: One Nation, Indivisible 310–36 (1997).

36. 347 U.S. 483 (1954).

37. Geoffrey R. Stone et al., Constitutional Law 456 (4th ed. 2001).

38. *See* Morgan v. Hennigan, 379 F. Supp. 410 (D. Mass.), *aff'd*, 509 F.2d 580 (1st Cir. 1974), *cert. denied*, 421 U.S. 963 (1975).

39. *See* Keyes v. Sch. Dist. No. 1, 413 U.S. 189 (1973).

40. *See* Milliken v. Bradley, 418 U.S. 717 (1974) (reversing and remanding the Detroit desegregation plan implemented by District Court judge).

41. Katzenbach v. Morgan, 384 U.S. 641 (1966).

42. Loving v. Virginia, 388 U.S. 1 (1967) (holding that miscegenation statutes preventing marriages between persons solely on basis of racial classification violate equal protection and due process clauses of 14th Amendment).

43. Shelley v. Kraemer, 334 U.S. 1 (1948) (upholding restrictive covenants barring ownership or occupancy of property by Blacks).

44. Reitman v. Mulkey, 387 U.S. 369 (1967) (holding that provision of California's constitution prohibiting the state from denying property owners the right to decline to sell or rent to anyone at their discretion impermissibly involves the state in private racial discrimination).

45. *See New England Town Meeting*, New Rules, The Governance Sector, http://archive.is/RgpTO (last visited Feb. 14, 2014) (showing the rules and definitions for town meetings in Marshfield). *See generally* Frank M. Bryan, Real Democracy (2003).

46. *See* Hamilton, Why the People Do Not Rule, *supra* note 9.

47. *See* Mancur Olson, The Logic of Collective Action 144 (2d ed. 1971); *see also* Jeffrey M. Berry, The New Liberalism: The Rising Power of Citizen Groups 154 (1999) ("The dominant scholarly explanation of interest group mobilization – then and now – is Mancur Olson's selective incentive theory of collective action.").

48. *See* Peter Smith, *Protestants Are Close to Losing Majority Status*, LOUISVILLE COURIER-J., July 21, 2004, at 1A.

49. *See generally* HAMILTON, WHY THE PEOPLE DO NOT RULE, *supra* note 9.

50. *See* OLSON, *supra* note 47, at 144; *see also* BERRY, *supra* note 47, at 154.

51. *See generally* DIANA L. ECK, A NEW RELIGIOUS AMERICA (2001).

52. Maria Jow Parejo Guzman, *The Anomolous European Rights to Life and Death: Understanding the Struggle for Recognition of Religious Minority Rights by Examining the Cultural Identity of Spain and Other European Communities*, 35 TEXAS TECH. L. REV. 297, 308 (2004); *see also* Nathan A. Adams, IV, *A Human Rights Imperative: Extending Religious Liberty Beyond the Border*, 33 CORNELL INT'L L. REV. 1 (2000).

53. Church of Lukumi Babalu Aye v. City of Hialeah, 508 U.S. 520, 533 (1993).

54. *Id.*; *see also* Corp. of Presiding Bishop of the Church of Jesus Christ of Latter-day Saints v. Amos, 483 U.S. 327, 330 (1987) (upholding exemption from Title VII for the secular, non-profit activities of a religious organization).

55. For further elaboration of this concept, *see generally* Hamilton, *Direct Democracy*, *supra* note 9.

56. *Smith*, 494 U.S. at 878–79.

57. Press Release, The Pew Research Ctr., Religion and Politics: Contention and Consensus 42 (July 24, 2003), *available at* http://www.pewforum.org/files/2003/07/religion-politics.pdf (last visited Feb. 14, 2014) (answer to Question 17: "What is your religious preference – do you consider yourself Christian, Jewish, Muslim, other non-Christian such as Buddhist or Hindu, atheist, agnostic, something else, or don't you have a religious preference?" 82% of respondents in March 2002 identified themselves as Christian, 1% as Jewish, 1% as other non-Christian, 2% as an unlisted religion, 2% were agnostic, 1% were atheists. Only 10% said they didn't have a religious preference.).

58. Michael W. McConnell, *Free Exercise Revisionism and the Smith Decision*, 57 U. CHI. L. REV. 1109, 1142–43 (1990).

59. Hall v. Baptist Mem'l Health Care Corp., 215 F.3d 618 (6th Cir. 2000); *see also* George Mattar, *HGP Fires Gay Teacher Planning Wedding*, BUCKS CNTY. COURIER TIMES, Dec. 8, 2013, at A1; Lornet Turnbull, *Church Doctrine, Gay Marriage Colliding in Catholic Workplaces*, SEATTLE TIMES, Jan. 16, 2014, *available at* 2014 WLNR 1599627.

60. *See* Soc'y of Jesus of New England v. Boston Landmarks Comm'n, 564 N.E.2d 571 (Mass. 1990) (holding landmark commission approval of interior renovations of church violated the Massachusetts Constitution and not reaching the federal question); First Covenant Church v. Seattle, 840 P.2d 174, 184–85 (Wash. 1992) (holding an exemption from city's zoning ordinances that exempted structural changes for liturgical purposes was still unconstitutional because it requires the city to determine "what is liturgy and what is a valid religious purpose . . . foster[ing] exactly the kind of religious entanglement the constitution seeks to avoid").

61. *See, e.g.*, CAL. EDUC. CODE § 51938 (Deering 2013) ("A parent or guardian of a pupil has the right to excuse their child from all or part of comprehensive

sexual health education, HIV/AIDS prevention education, and assessments related to that education . . ."); R.I. GEN. LAWS § 16–22–17(c) (2012 . . . ."); IOWA CODE ANN. § 279.50 (West 2014) ("A pupil shall not be required to take instruction in human growth and development if the pupil's parent or guardian or files with the appropriate principal a written request that the pupil be excused from the instruction."); N.C. GEN. STAT. ANN. § 115C-81(e1)(7) (West 2013) ("Local boards of education shall adopt policies to provide opportunities either for parents and legal guardians to consent or for parents and legal guardians to withhold their consent to the students' participation in any or all of these [i. STD and pregnancy prevention, ii. Abstinence until marriage, iii. Comprehensive sexual education] programs."); R.I. GEN. LAWS § 16–22–17(c) (2013) ("A parent or legal guardian may exempt his or her child from the [HIV/AIDS education] program by written directive to the principal of the school."); S.C. CODE ANN. § 59–32–50 (2013) ("A public school principal, upon receipt of a statement signed by a student's parent or legal guardian stating that participation by the student in the health education program conflicts with the family's beliefs, shall exempt that student from any portion or all of the units on reproductive health, family life, and pregnancy prevention where any conflicts occur.").

62. Ford v. McGinnis, 352 F.3d 582, 598 n.17 (2d Cir. 2003) (in case of Muslim inmate denied religious meal, "we hold as a matter of law that the prison officials' conduct was not objectively reasonable"); see also Love v. Reed, 216 F.3d 682, 690 (8th Cir. 2000) (in case of inmate practicing "Hebrew religion" who wished to observe the Sabbath, prison's "failure to provide the requested accommodation . . . substantially burdens [inmate's] ability to freely exercise his religion."); Jackson v. Mann, 196 F.3d 316, 320 (2d Cir. 1999) (in case of Jewish inmate denied access to kosher meal program, the court noted that "prison officials must provide a prisoner a diet that is consistent with his religious scruples") (quoting Bass v. Coughlin, 976 F.2d 98, 99 (2d Cir. 1992) (per curiam)).

·63. Liberty Univ., Inc. v. Lew, 733 F.3d 72 (4th Cir. 2013).

64. 42 U.S.C. § 300a-7 (2012).

65. 26 U.S.C. § 501(c)(3) (2012).

66. STEPHEN L. CARTER, THE CULTURE OF DISBELIEF: HOW AMERICAN LAW AND POLITICS TRIVIALIZE RELIGIOUS DEVOTION (1993).

67. See MARTIN E. MARTY, RELIGION AND REPUBLIC 71–72 (1987) (describing advent of secularization in law and commenting that Supreme Court decisions in the 1960s and 1970s drained "the last trace of religious substance" from the law). See generally MARTIN E. MARTY, THE INFIDEL: FREE THOUGHT AND AMERICAN RELIGION (1961).

68. See generally Marci Hamilton, Protecting Religious Institutions Right to Political Speech, FINDLAW'S WRIT (Aug. 15 2002), http://writ.news.findlaw.com/hamilton/20020815.html. There have been a series of bills and one now pending in both Houses of Congress that would effect an repeal. To Restore the Free Speech and First Amendment Rights of Churches and Exempt Organizations by Repealing the 1954 Johnson Amendment, H.R. 127, 113th Cong. (2013–14).

69. Emp't Div. v. Smith, 494 U.S. 872 (1990).

70. 139 CONG. REC. S14350, 103d Cong., 1st Sess. (Oct. 26, 1993) (statement of Sen. Hatch).

71. McConnell, *supra* note 58, at 1152.

72. *See generally* Kent Greenawalt, *Religion and American Political Judgments*, 36 WAKE FOREST L. REV. 401 (2001).

73. U.S. RELIGION CENSUS 2010: SUMMARY FINDINGS 5 (May 1, 2012), *available at* http://www.rcms2010.org/press_release/ACP%2020120501.pdf.

74. It is estimated that as of January 2014, the total U.S. population is 317,601,653. U.S. CENSUS BUREAU, *Monthly Population Estimates for the United States: April 1, 2010 to December 1, 2014*, http://factfinder2.census.gov/faces/tableservices/jsf/pages/productview.xhtml?pid=PEP_2013_PEPMONTHN&prodType=table (last visited Feb. 7, 2014). The Census reported a total U.S. population of 308,745,538. U.S. CENSUS 2010, *Interactive Population Map*, http://www.census.gov/2010census/popmap/ (last visited Feb. 7, 2014).

75. McConnell, *supra* note 58, at 1150.

76. Model Rules of Prof'l Conduct and Code of Judicial Conduct Canon 3(B)(5) (1999).

77. 28 U.S.C. § 453 (2012).

78. *Id.* § 455(a).

79. That is in fact happening in the context of children's interests. Religious organizations have been successful in obtaining state and federal laws that exempt faith-healing parents from the force of the laws that protect children. *See* Rita Swan, Ph.D., Symposium, *Moral, Economic, and Social Issues in Children's Health Care: On Statutes Depriving a Class of Children of Rights to Medical Care: Can this Discrimination be Litigated?*, 2 QUINNIPIAC HEALTH L.J. 73, 79–80 (1988). Children's rights, however, have become internationally recognized and the arguments for giving such latitude to parents to harm their children, even if religiously motivated, have lost a significant degree of force. *See, e.g., Weld Approves Child Abuse Law*, BOSTON GLOBE, Dec. 29, 1993, at Metro-24 (reporting the passage of legislation that "repeals a statutory provision that states a child shall not be deemed neglected if treated with spiritual healing alone"); CAL. PEN. CODE § 11166(c)(2) (West 2014) (Duty to report statute excludes reporting information received during "penitential communication" but clarifies that "[n]othing in this subdivision shall be construed to modify or limit a clergy member's duty to report known or suspected child abuse or neglect when the clergy member is acting in some other capacity that would otherwise make the clergy member a mandated reporter.").

80. For overview of state mandatory reporting laws and exemptions as applied to the clergy generally, *see* CHILD WELFARE INFORMATION GATEWAY *Clergy as Mandatory Reporters of Child Abuse and Neglect: Summary of State Laws*, 4 (2010), *available at* http://www.childwelfare.gov/systemwide/laws_policies/statutes/clergymandated.pdf.

81. *Religious Exemptions From Health Care For Children*, CHILDREN'S HEALTH CARE IS A LEGAL DUTY, INC., http://childrenshealthcare.org/?page_id=24#Exemptions (last visited Feb. 11, 2014).

82. The investigation by Oregon's medical examiner showed that the deaths of at least 21 of the 78 children who died since 1955 probably could have been prevented with medical treatment. Mark Larabee & Peter D. Sleeth, *Followers Children Needed Medical Care, Experts Say*, CLEVELAND PLAIN DEALER, June 28, 1998, at 21A.

83. Mark Larabee, *Bill Aims to Lift All Oregon Religious Shields*, OREGONIAN, Jan. 22, 1999, at C6.

84. 2011 Or. Laws, Ch. 291 (H.B. 2721).

85. Emp't Div. v. Smith, 494 U.S. 872, 890 (1990).

86. Press Release, The Pew Research Ctr., Religion and Politics: Contention and Consensus, *supra* note 57.

87. *More See "Too Much" Religious Talk by Politicians*, PEW RESEARCH CTR., RELIGION & PUB. LIFE PROJECT, (Mar. 21, 2012), http://www.pewforum.org/2012/03/21/more-see-too-much-religious-talk-by-politicians/; *see also* Michelle Boorstein, *Religious Lobbying Groups Multiply on Capital Hill*, WASH. POST (Nov. 21, 2011), http://www.washingtonpost.com/local/religious-advocacy-grows-on-capitol-hill/2011/11/21/gIQA3AZVjN_story.html; Jonathan Easley, *In Reversal from 2010, Poll Finds Too Much "Religious Talk" by Politicians*, THE HILL (Mar. 21, 2012, 8:08 PM), http://thehill.com/blogs/ballot-box/presidential-races/217375-poll-too-much-religious-talk-by-politicians; *Lobbying for the Faithful*, PEW RESEARCH CTR., RELIGION & PUBLIC LIFE PROJECT (May 15, 2012), *available at* http://www.pewforum.org/2011/11/21/lobbying-for-the-faithful-exec/.

88. *See* Joe Coscarelli, *D.A. Won't Identify Orthodox Sex-Crime Suspects*, N.Y. MAG. (May 11, 2013, 4:17 PM), http://nymag.com/daily/intelligencer/2012/04/brooklyn-da-wont-identify-orthodox-sex-crime-suspects.html; Vivan Yee, *Thompson Defeats Hynes, Again, for Brooklyn District Attorney*, N.Y. TIMES, Nov. 6, 2013, at A10.

89. Kentucky actually passed such a law, over the Governor's veto. *See* Beth Musgrave & Jack Brammer, *Kentucky Legislature Overrides Governor's Veto of "Religious Freedom" Bill*, LEXINGTON HERALD-LEADER (Mar. 26, 2013), http://www.kentucky.com/2013/03/26/2575323/kentucky-house-votes-to-override.html. It was introduced in Texas as an amendment to the pre-existing TRFRA, but not passed. *See SJR 4: A Poor Solution in Search of a Problem*, TEX. FREEDOM NETWORK, http://www.tfn.org/site/DocServer/SJR4Final.pdf?docID=3861 (last visited Apr. 20, 2014); Legislative Watch: The 83rd Session of the Texas Legislature, TEX. FREEDOM NETWORK, http://www.tfn.org/site/PageServer?pagename=issues_legislative_watch_index (last visited Mar. 1, 2014); Laura Wright, *Campbell Faces Unexpected Opposition on Religious Liberties Bill*, TEXAS MONTHLY (Apr. 16, 2013, 1:45 PM), http://www.texasmonthly.com/story/campbell-faces-unexpected-opposition-religious-liberties-bill; *see also* Matthew Brown, *North Dakota Voters Soundly Defeat Religious Liberty Amendment*, DESERET MORNING NEWS (June 13, 2012, 4:09 PM), http://www.deseretnews.com/article/865557418/North-Dakota-voters-soundly-defeat-religious-liberty-amendment.html?pg=all (proposing language stating "Government may not *burden* a person's or religious organization's religious liberty.") (emphasis added); Christopher Cousins, *Maine House Deals*

Another Blow to Republican Senator's "Religious Freedom" Bill, BANGOR DAILY NEWS (Feb. 20, 2014), http://bangordailynews.com/2014/02/20/politics/maine-house-deals-another-blow-to-republican-senators-religious-freedom-bill/; Jo Ingles, *State Lawmakers Pull "Religious Freedom" Bill*, NPR NEWS (Ohio) (Feb. 27, 2014, 8:22 AM), http://wosu.org/2012/news/2014/02/27/state-lawmakers-pull-religious-freedom-bill; Paul Stanley, *Focus on the Family Withdraws Religious Freedom Measure in Colorado*, CHRISTIAN POST (May 5, 2012, 11:42 AM), http://www.christianpost.com/news/focus-on-the-family-withdraws-religious-freedom-measure-in-colorado-74422 (also including solely "burden" language).

90. *See* David Ferguson, *Idaho Republicans Kill Bill Designed to Protect Kids from 'Faith Healing' Deaths*, RAW STORY (Feb. 27, 2014, 1:28 PM), http://www.rawstory.com/rs/2014/02/27/idaho-republicans-kill-bill-dsigned-to-protect-kids-from-faith-healing-deaths.

91. In 1844, Karl Marx said, "Religion is the sigh of the oppressed creature, the heart of a heartless world, and the soul of soulless conditions. It is the opium of the people." KARL MARX, CRITIQUE OF HEGEL'S 'PHILOSOPHY OF RIGHT' 131 (Joseph O'Malley ed., Annette Jolin & Joseph O'Malley trans., 1970). Thomas Mann paraphrased Marx in 1930, saying, "Fanaticism turns into a means of salvation, enthusiasm into epileptic ecstacy, politics becomes an opiate for the masses, a proletarian eschatology; and reason veils her face." THOMAS MANN, An Appeal to Reason, *in* ORDER OF THE DAY, POLITICAL ESSAYS AND SPEECHES OF TWO DECADES 57 (Helen T. Lowe-Porter trans., 1942).

92. C.B. MACPHERSON, THE POLITICAL THEORY OF POSSESSIVE INDIVIDUALISM: HOBBES TO LOCKE 3 (1962).

93. *See generally* Symposium, *Foundations of Church Autonomy*, 2004 BYU. L REV. (2004).

94. FRIEDRICH NIETZSCHE, BEYOND GOOD AND EVIL 52 (Helen Zimmern trans., 1967) ("Granted, finally, that we succeeded in explaining our entire instinctive life as the development and ramification of one fundamental form of will – namely, the Will to Power, as *my* thesis puts it; granted that all organic functions could be traced back to this Will to Power, and that the solution of the problem of generation and nutrition – it is one problem – could also be found therein: one would thus have acquired the right to define *all* active force unequivocally as *Will to Power*. The world seen from within, the world defined and designated according to its 'intelligible character' – it would simply be 'Will to Power' and nothing else.") (emphasis in original).

Epilogue: Follow the Money

1. *See* 139 CONG. REC. H2356-03 (daily ed. May 11, 1993); *see also* Yang v. Sturner,750 F. Supp. 558 (D.R.I. 1990) (reversal of previous decision upholding religious objection to autopsy on Hmong individual).

2. *See* Christopher C. Lund, *Autopsies and Free Exercise Beliefs*, AMERICAN CIVIL LIBERTIES (Oct. 11, 2011, 3:42 PM), http://uscivilliberties.org/themes/3153-autopsies-and-freeexercise-beliefs.html.

3. *Id.*

4. *See* 146 Cong. Rec. E1562-01, 2000 WL 1369379 (daily ed. Sept. 22, 2000) (statement of Hon. Henry J. Hyde); Congregation Etz Chaim v. City of Los Angeles, 371 F.3d 1122 (9th Cir. 2004).

5. *Id.*

6. *Preventative Health Services for Women*, HealthCare.gov, https://www .healthcare.gov/what-are-my-preventive-care-benefits/#part=2 (last visited Mar. 2, 2014).

7. 25 U.S.C. § 5000A(d)(2)(A) (2012).

8. *See* 45 C.F.R. § 147.130(a)(1)(iv)(B).

9. "Coverage of Certain Preventive Services Under the Affordable Care Act," 78 Fed. Reg. 39870, 39875–90 (July 2, 2013); 29 C.F.R. § 2590.715-2713A(a); 45 C.F.R. § 147.131(b).

10. 45 C.F.R. 147.131(b)(4) ("The organization self-certifies, in a form and manner specified by the Secretary, that it satisfies the criteria in paragraphs (b)(1) through (3) of this section, and makes such self-certification available for examination upon request by the first day of the first plan year to which the accommodation in paragraph (c) of this section applies. The self-certification must be executed by a person authorized to make the certification on behalf of the organization, and must be maintained in a manner consistent with the record retention requirements under section 107 of the Employee Retirement Income Security Act of 1974.").

11. *See* University of Notre Dame v. Sebelius, No. 13-3853, 2014 WL 697134 (7th Cir., Feb. 21, 2014).

12. *Hobby Lobby Stores on the Forbes America's Largest Private Companies List*, Forbes, http://www.forbes.com/companies/hobby-lobby-stores/ (last visited Mar. 2, 2014).

13. *Our Company*, Hobby Lobby, http://www.hobbylobby.com/our_company/ (last visited Mar, 2, 2014).

14. 42 U.S.C. § 2000e-1 (2012).

15. EEOC v. Townley Eng'g & Mfg. Co., 859 F.2d 610, 618 (9th Cir. 1988). *See also* LeBoon v. Lancaster Jewish Community Center, 503 F.3d 217 (3d Cir. 2007), Hall v. Baptist Mem. Health Care Corp., 215 F.3d 618, 624-25 (6th Cir. 2000).

16. Brief of Corporate and Criminal Law Professors in Support of Petitioners, Sebelius v. Hobby Lobby Stores, Inc., 133 S.Ct. 641 (2012) (Nos. 13-354, 13-356), 2014 WL 333889, at *3, 7-8, 20-21.

17. *Id.* at *2-3.

18. *See, e.g.*, Smith v. Fair Employment & Housing Comm'n, 913 P.2d 909 (Cal. 1996); Intermountain Fair Housing Council v. Boise Rescue Mission Ministries, 655 F. Supp.2d 1150 (D. Idaho, 2009); Ungar v. N.Y. City Housing Auth., No. 06civi968, 2009 WL 125326 (S.D.N.Y, Jan. 14, 2009); Open Homes Fellowship, Inc. v. Orange Cnty, Fla., 325 F. Supp.2d 1349 (M.D. Fla. 2009).

19. 145 Cong. Rec. H5580-02, 1999 WL 498990 (July 15, 1999) (statement of Rep. Nadler).

20. 145 Cong. Rec. H5580-02, 1999 WL 498990 (July 15, 1999) (statement of Rep. Canady).

21. 146 CONG. REC. E1563-01, 2000 WL 1369378 (Sept. 22, 2000) (statement of Hon. Charles T. Canady).

22. 146 CONG. REC. H7190-02, 2000 WL 1079439 (July 27, 2000) (statement of Hon. Charles T. Canady).

23. 42 U.S.C. § 2000e (West).

24. *"Nones" on the Rise*, PEW RESEARCH (Oct. 9, 2012), http://www.pewforum
.org/2012/10/09/nones-on-the-rise/.

25. Elane Photography, LLC v. Willock, 309 P.3d 53 (N.M. 2013).

26. H.B. 2453, 2014 Leg, 33d Session (Kan. 2014), *available at* http://www
.kslegislature.org/li/b2013_14/measures/documents/hb2453_01_0000.pdf.

27. S.B. 1062, 51st Leg., 2d Reg. Sess. (Ariz. 2014), *available at* http://www.azleg
.gov/legtext/51leg/2r/bills/sb1062p.pdf.

28. 42 U.S.C. § 2000bb-1 (2012).

29. 42 U.S.C. § 2000cc-2(b) (2012) ("If a plaintiff produces prima facie evidence to support a claim alleging a violation of the Free Exercise Clause or a violation [of a provision of this Act enforcing that clause], the government shall bear the burden of persuasion on any element of the claim . . . ").

30. Michael W. McConnell, *Free Exercise Revisionism and the Smith Decision,* 57 U. CHI. L. REV. 1109, 1142–43 (1990).

31. *See supra* note 26.

32. *See supra* note 27.

33. The list includes the Dioceses of Portland, Tucson, Spokane, Davenport, San Diego, Fairbanks, Province of the Jesuits, Wilmington, Milwaukee, Gallup, Stockton, and Helena. *See Bankruptcy Protection in the Abuse Crisis,* BISHOPACCOUNTABILITY.ORG, http://www.bishop-accountability.org/bankruptcy
.htm (last visited Mar. 2, 2014).

INDEX

Made in the USA
San Bernardino, CA
02 April 2015